International Military Alliances
1648–2008

Correlates of War Series

The Correlates of War (COW) project has promoted the systematic study of war by utilizing rigorous scientific analysis to identify its causes and precursors, collecting data on conflicts between state, non-state, and intra-state actors since the end of the Napoleonic era. COW was founded under the leadership of University of Michigan political scientist J. David Singer in 1963 and is now recognized as the authoritative source for international war data.

International Military Alliances, 1648–2008
by Douglas M. Gibler

Resort to War, 1816–2007 (forthcoming in 2009)
by Meredith Reid Sarkees and Frank Wayman

Guide to Intrastate Wars: A Handbook on Civil Wars (forthcoming in 2010)
by Jeffery Dixon and Meredith Reid Sarkees

Handbook of International Rivalries (forthcoming in 2010)
by William Thompson

INTERNATIONAL MILITARY ALLIANCES 1648–2008

Douglas M. Gibler

CQ PRESS

A Division of SAGE
Washington, D.C.

CQ Press
2300 N Street, N.W., Suite 800
Washington, D.C. 20037

Phone: 202-729-1900; toll-free, 1-866-4CQ-PRESS (1-866-427-7737)

Web: www.cqpress.com

Cover design: Paula Goldstein
Cover photos: The Congress of Berlin by Anton von Werner 1892, oil on canvas. Bildarchiv Preussischer Klturbesitz/Art Resource, NY.
Composition: MacPS, LLC

⊚ The paper used in this publication meets the minimum requirements of the American National Standard for Information Sciences—Permanence of Paper for Printed Library Materials, ANSI Z39.48-1992.

Printed and bound in the United States of America

12   11   10   09   08   1   2   3   4   5

Library of Congress Cataloging in Publication Data

Gibler, Douglas M.
  International military alliances, 1648–2008 / Douglas M. Gibler.
     p. cm.
  Includes bibliographical references and index.
  ISBN 978-1-56802-824-8 (alk. paper)
  1. Alliances—History. 2. Treaties—Sources. 3. Military policy—
Sources. I. Title.

  KZ5900.G53 2009
  355'.03109—dc22
                                                        2008041959

Table of Contents

Guide to Alliances by Century

CHAPTER 2

18th Century: 2.1046–2.1119

CHAPTER 3

19th Century: 3.1120–3.1204

CHAPTER 4

20th Century: 4.1205–4.1449

Guide to Alliances by Region

Americas

Asia, the Middle East, and the Pacific

Europe

List of Maps

The maps below illustrate, with captions, the following: the international state system after the Peace of Westphalia; Europe in the 18th century following the wars of Spanish Succession; the world in the early 19th century, showing newly independent states in the New World; Europe prior to World War I; Europe following World War II; revised borders after the fall of the Soviet Union; and the global political map as of 2005.

CHAPTER FOUR: 20th Century

Map 5. 1911

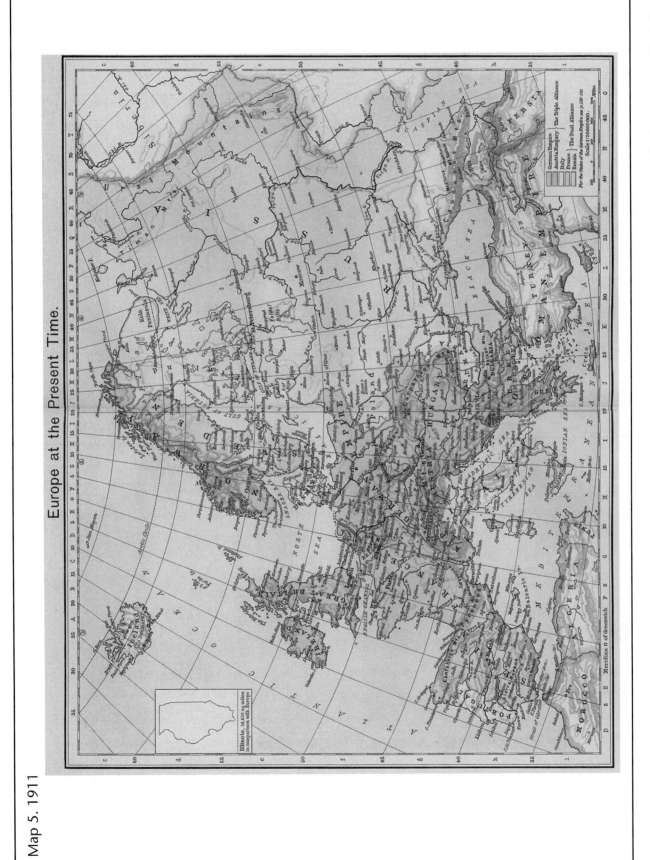

Europe at the Present Time.

Cooperation among the major states began to strain severely in 1911 as territorial issues in the Balkans and Africa became more difficult to manage. The Balkan Wars upset the precarious balance of interests and power in 1912, and the assassination of Archduke Ferdinand in Sarajevo, Bosnia, heralded the start of World War I in 1914.

Map 6. 1949

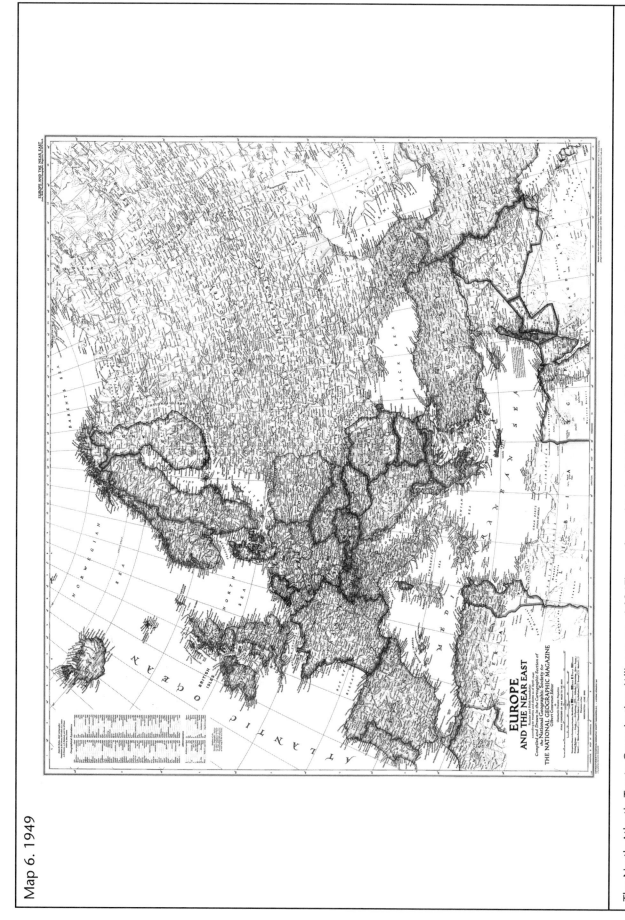

The North Atlantic Treaty Organization (Alliance no. 4.1347) was formed in April 1949 amid the backdrop of increasing tensions between the United States and the Soviet Union at the start of the cold war. Europe was divided between the two superpowers and soon, in May 1955, the North Atlantic Treaty was countered with the Warsaw Pact (Alliance no. 4.1360). The world of 1949 was dominated by these dueling influences of East and West and would remain so until the breakup of the Soviet Union in 1991.

Map 7. 1993

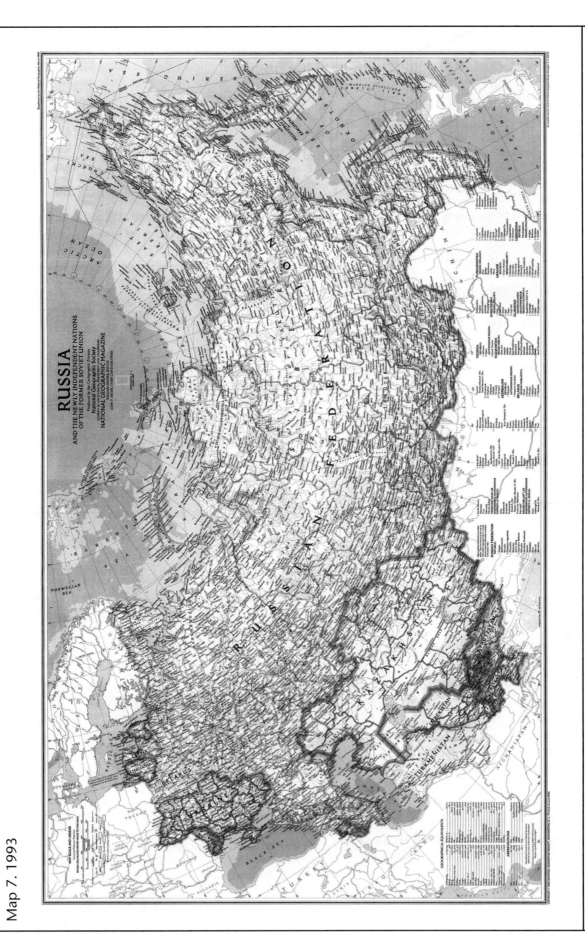

By 1993, Russia had given up its claims to the Baltic states and the many former Soviet territories in eastern Europe and across central Asia. Still dominant on the continent militarily, Russia was reeling from economic uncertainty and heavily dependent on aid from and cooperation with the West. It was in this context that the Russians began seeking greater security and economic ties with neighbors (Alliance no. 4.1436 and 4.1441) and key western states such as France (Alliance no. 4.1445) and Italy (Alliance no. 4.1437), while it also sought a non-aggression pact with its former NATO adversaries (Alliance no. 4.1438).

4.1205 Anglo-Japanese Alliance

Alliance Members: Japan and Great Britain
Signed On: January 30, 1902, in the city of London. In force until August 17, 1923.
Alliance Type: Defense Pact (Type I)

Source: *British and Foreign State Papers,* vol. 95, p. 83.

SUMMARY

As tensions rose between Russia and a rising Japan over domination of the Far East, especially Manchuria and Korea, Japan sought to match Russian dominance in Manchuria by securing an alliance with the United Kingdom. Each party promised to remain neutral in wars waged by the other party and to cooperate in protecting the independence of Manchuria and Korea, clearly aiming this alliance at limiting Russian expansion.

The alliance's intended goal of preserving stability proved optimistic, however, as the Russo-Japanese War forced the issue of Russian influence in the region to a violent resolution. The terms of the treaty formally ended with the British failure to renew it in 1923, although the alliance was effectively replaced by the four-power treaty on the Pacific in 1921, signed by Japan, Britain, France, and the United States.

ALLIANCE TEXT

The Governments of Great Britain and Japan actuated solely by a desire to maintain the status quo and general peace in the extreme East, being moreover specially interested in maintaining the independence and territorial integrity of the Empire of China and the Empire of Corea, and in securing equal opportunities in those countries for the commerce and industry of all nations, hereby agree as follows:

Article I. The High Contracting Parties having mutually recognized the independence of China and Corea, declare themselves to be entirely uninfluenced by any aggressive tendencies in either country. Having in view, however, their special interests, of which those of Great Britain relate principally to China, while Japan, in addition to the interests which she possesses in China, is interested in a peculiar degree, politically, as well as commercially and industrially, in Corea, the High Contracting Parties recognize that it will be admissible for either of them to take such measures as may be indispensable in order to safeguard those interests if threatened either by the aggressive action of any other Power, or by disturbances arising in China or Corea, and necessitating the intervention of either of the High Contracting Parties for the protection of the lives and properties of its subjects.

Article II. If either Great Britain or Japan, in the defence of their respective interests as above described, should become involved in war with another Power, the other High Contracting Party will maintain a strict neutrality, and use its efforts to prevent other Powers from joining in hostilities against its ally.

Article III. If in the above event any other Power or Powers should join in hostilities against that ally, the other High Contracting Party will come to its assistance and will conduct the war in common, and make peace in mutual agreement with it.

Article IV. The High Contracting Parties agree that neither of them will, without consulting the other, enter into separate arrangements with another Power to the prejudice of the interests above described.

Article V. Whenever, in opinion of either Great Britain or Japan, the above-mentioned interests are in jeopardy, the two Governments will communicate with one another fully and frankly.

Article VI. The present Agreement shall come into effect immediately after the date of its signature, and remain in force for five years from that date.

In case neither of the High Contracting Parties should have notified twelve months before the expiration of the said five years the intention of terminating it, it shall remain binding until the expiration of one year from the day on which either of the High Contracting Parties shall have denounced it. But if, when the date fixed for its expiration arrives, either ally is actually engaged in war, the alliance shall, ipso facto, continue until peace is concluded.

In faith whereof the Undersigned, duly authorized by their respective Governments, have signed this Agreement, and have affixed thereto their seals.

Done in duplicate at London, the 30th January, 1902.

(L.S.) (Signed) Lansdowne,
His Britannic Majesty's Principal Secretary of State for Foreign Affairs
(L.S.) (Signed) Hayashi,
Envoy Extraordinary and Minister Plenipotentiary of His Majesty the Emperor of Japan at the Court of St James.

4.1206 Exchange of letters declaring that no divergence subsists between the two countries as to their respective interests in the Mediterranean

Alliance Members: France and Italy
Signed On: November 1, 1902, in the city of Rome. In force until November 15, 1918, with the end of World War I.
Alliance Type: Neutrality Pact (Type II)

Source: *Key Treaties for the Great Powers, 1814–1914,* vol. 2, p. 735.

SUMMARY

The following exchange of letters, signed five months after the renewal of the Triple Alliance (see Alliance no. 3.1195), nullified most of Italy's pledges to Austria-Hungary and Germany in that alliance. The exchange of letters followed disputes in the Balkans and along the coasts and on the islands of the Adriatic and Aegean seas. In the exchange, Italy and France pledged neutrality in the event of an attack on the other.

The Triple Alliance continued to be renewed (in 1907 and in 1912), but Italy entered World War I in May 1915 in opposition to both Germany and Austria-Hungary. Exchanges of letters like this one are common instruments for acknowledging state intentions in the event of conflict.

Exchange of Notes

M. Prinetti, Minister of Foreign Affairs of Italy, to M. Barrère, Ambassador of the French Republic at Rome.

Rome, November 1, 1902

In continuation of the conversations which we have had concerning the reciprocal situation of Italy and of France in the Mediterranean basin, and concerning more especially the respective interests of the two countries in Tripolitania-Cyrenaica and in Morocco, it seemed to us opportune to define the engagements which result from the letters exchanged on this subject, between Your Excellency and Marquis Visconti-Venosta, on December 14 and 16, 1900, in this sense, that each of the two Powers can freely develop its sphere of influence in the abovementioned regions at the moment it deems it opportune, and without the action of one of them being necessarily subordinated to that of the other. It was explained on that occasion that the limit of French expansion in Northern Africa contemplated in the abovementioned letter of Your Excellency of December 14, 1900, was fully understood to be the frontier of Tripolitania indicated by the map attached to the Declaration of March 21, 1899, additional to the Franco-English Convention of June 14, 1898.

We noted that this interpretation left no divergence still existing between our Governments as to their respective interests in the Mediterranean.

Profiting by the occasion of these conferences, and in order to eliminate in a definitive manner any possible misunderstanding between our two countries, I do hot hesitate, in order to define their general relations, to make of my own accord to Your Excellency, in the name of the Government of His Majesty the King, the following declarations:

In case France should be the object of a direct or indirect aggression on the part of one or more Powers, Italy will maintain a strict neutrality.

The same shall hold good in case France, as the result of a direct provocation, should find herself compelled, in defence of her honor or of her security, to take the initiative of a declaration of war. In that eventuality, the Government of the Republic shall previously communicate its intention to the Royal Government, which will thus be enabled to determine whether there is really a case of direct provocation.

In order to remain faithful to the spirit of friendship which has inspired the present declarations, I am authorized further to confirm to you that on the part of Italy no protocol or military provision in the nature of an international contract which would be in disagreement with the present declarations exists or will be concluded by her.

I may add that—save as concerns the interpretation of the Mediterranean interests of the two Powers, which has a final

character—in conformity with the spirit of the correspondence exchanged between Your Excellency and Marquis Visconti-Venosta, on December 14 and 16, 1900, as the preceding declarations are in harmony with the present international engagements of Italy, the Royal Government understands that they shall retain their full validity so long as it has not notified the Government of the Republic that these engagements have been modified.

I should be obliged if Your Excellency would be kind enough to acknowledge receipt of the present communication, which must remain secret, and to take note thereof in the name of the Government of the Republic.

Prinetti.

M. Barrere, Ambassador of the French Republic at Rome, to M. Prinetti, Minister of Foreign Affairs of Italy.

Rome, November 1, 1902

By your letter of today's date, Your Excellency has been kind enough to recall to me that in the continuation of our conversations relative to the reciprocal situation of France and of Italy in the Mediterranean basin, and more especially to the respective interests of the two countries in Tripolitania-Cyrenaica and in Morocco, it seemed to us opportune to define the engagements which result from the letters exchanged on this subject between Marquis Visconti-Venosta and myself on December 14 and 16, 1900, in this sense, that each of the two Powers can freely develop its sphere of influence in the abovementioned regions at the moment it deems it opportune, and without the action of one of them being necessarily subordinated to that of the other.

It was explained on that occasion that the limit of French expansion in Northern Africa contemplated in my abovementioned letter of December 14, 1900, was fully understood to be the frontier of Tripolitania indicated by the map attached to the Declaration of March, 1899, additional to the English Convention of June 14, 1898.

This interpretation leaving, as we have noted, no divergence as to their respective interests in the Mediterranean still existing between our Governments, and with the purpose of eliminating in a definitive manner any possible misunderstanding between our two countries, you have been authorized by the Government of His Majesty to formulate of your own accord certain declarations intended to define the general relations of Italy towards France.

I have the honour to acknowledge receipt thereof to Your Excellency and to give you note of these declarations in the name of my Government.

I am authorized, in return, to formulate in the following manner the conditions under which France on her side intends, in the same friendly spirit, to order her general relations towards Italy.

In case Italy should be the object of a direct or indirect aggression on the part of one or more Powers, France will maintain a strict neutrality.

The same shall hold good in case Italy, as the result of a direct provocation, should find herself compelled, in defence of her honor or of her security, to take the initiative of a declaration of war. In that eventuality, the Royal Government shall previously communicate its eventuality, intention to the Government of the Republic, which will thus be enabled to determine whether there is really a case of direct provocation.

I am authorized equally to declare to you that on the part of France no protocol or military provision in the nature of an international contract which would be in disagreement with the present declarations exists or will be concluded by her.

It is fully understood finally that—save as concerns the interpretation of the Mediterranean interests of the two Powers, which has a final character—in conformity with the spirit of the correspondence exchanged between Marquis Visconti-Venosta and myself, on December 14 and 16, 1900, as the declarations which precede, and which must remain secret, are in harmony with the present international engagements of Italy, they shall retain their full validity so long as the Royal Government has not notified the Government of the Republic that these engagements have been modified.

Barrère.

4.1207 Treaty of Alliance between the Principality of Bulgaria and the Kingdom of Serbia

Alliance Members: Bulgaria and Serbia
Signed On: March 30, 1904, in the city of Belgrade (Serbia). In force until March 30, 1909, when the treaty was not renewed.
Alliance Type: Defense Pact (Type I)

Source: *Key Treaties for the Great Powers, 1814–1914*, vol. 2, p. 752–753.

SUMMARY

As Austria-Hungary made moves to annex Bosnia, Serbia and Bulgaria, locked in their own bid for independence from Turkey, signed an alliance in 1904 against the possibility of further Austrian expansion. Although the agreement did not last beyond March of 1909, its members would ally again on the Russian side in World War I after Austria's invasion of Serbia.

The *vilayets* mentioned in the treaty refer to Ottoman administrative units. As is evident from the treaty, policies in the *vilayets* of Adrianople, Salonika, Bitolya, and Kosovo all posed possible sources of friction between the two emerging states.

ALLIANCE TEXT

The government of H. R. H. Prince Ferdinand I of Bulgaria and the government of H. M. King Peter I of Serbia, guided by the principle of "The Balkans for the Balkan nations," and inspired by a desire to safeguard the peace and security of their peoples, to preserve the territorial *status quo* on the Balkan peninsula, and to improve the condition of their fellow-countrymen in the Ottoman Empire, agree on the following:

I. Convinced of the utility of the programme of reforms adopted at Mürzsteg for the vilayets of Salonica, Bitolya and Kossovo (Macedonia and Old Serbia), the two allied states hereby promise to promote jointly and by all peaceful means at their disposal the execution of these reforms in the said three vilayets, at the same time encouraging their introduction into the vilayet of Adrianople, thus safeguarding the lives, property and free development of their fellow-countrymen in these vilayets, on the basis of political and national equality in all respects.

II. Firmly resolved to apply all of their loyal efforts and goodwill for the preservation of peace on the Balkan peninsula, the two allied states hereby promise jointly to defend themselves with all the power and resources at their command, against any encroachment from whatever source, be it on the present territorial unity and independence of their respective states, or on the security and inviolability of the reigning dynasties.

III. Likewise the two allied states promise to oppose, with all the power and resources at their command, any hostile act or isolated occupation of the above-mentioned four vilayets, whatever nation may be responsible.

IV. In the circumstances foreseen in Articles II and III, the two allied states will conclude a special military convention, in which all possible eventualities and all their consequences will be provided for.

V. In the desire to prepare the ground for the full co-operation between the Slavs on the Balkan peninsula and to create favourable circumstances for an immediate agreement between the Kingdom of Serbia and the Principality of Montenegro, the two allied states hereby promise—whenever the question of Albania should arise—to support such a solution as would favour the interests of Montenegro.

VI. The two allied states hereby promise to discuss and decide jointly all questions which, by their nature and spirit, are within the sphere of this treaty.

VII. The two allied states hereby promise to submit to the final decision of His Imperial Majesty the Tsar of All Russians, all of those controversies which they are not able to decide among themselves. In case the Russian emperor declines to award a decision on such a controversial question, it will be placed in the hands of the Permanent Court of Arbitration at The Hague.

VIII. The present allied treaty remains secret. It may be communicated to a third party—in whole or in part—only after a preliminary agreement between the two allied governments.

After five years this treaty may be brought up for revision if the two allied states consider it desirable.

It becomes valid on the day of its ratification.

Concluded in Belgrade the thirtieth day of the month of March [O.S] the one thousand nine hundred and fourth year after the birth of Christ, the third day of Easter,

In the name of the Principality of Bulgaria:
(s) D. RIZOV.
(s) Colonel of the General Staff HESAPCHIEV.

In the name of the Kingdom of Serbia:
(s) GENERAL SAVA GRUIĆ
(s) NIKOLA PAŠIĆ

4.1208 Convention Respecting Morocco between France and Spain

Alliance Members: France and Spain
Signed On: October 3, 1904, in the city of Paris. In force until May 16, 1907, when Britain, France, and Spain signed a separate entente.
Alliance Type: Entente (Type III)

Source: *The American Journal of International Law,* vol. 34, no. 3, Supplement: Official Documents (July 1940), p. 127–131.
Additional Citations: *British and Foreign State Papers,* vol. 102, p. 402ff.

SUMMARY

As one of the last independent states in Africa, Morocco represented an important economic and political prize for the European great powers. After securing Italian and British compliance for its bid to dominate Morocco, France won Spanish support in 1904. The alliance's terms were simple, effectively seeking to preserve both Moroccan independence for the time being and the rights of France and Spain to shape its future to the exclusion of other parties.

Imperial Germany would spark the First Moroccan Crisis in 1905 in order to isolate France by proving the fragility of the British commitment. The plan failed, however, as both the British and the Russians supported France in negotiations. The Franco-Spanish alliance won the rights in 1906 to cooperate in the defense of Morocco as well as implement plans for the eventual partition of the country.

The alliance ended in 1907, however, after the Moroccan partition was effectively completed, but cooperation with the British and Russians would continue for some time beyond the negotiations surrounding the first crisis.

ALLIANCE TEXT

DECLARATION.

The Government of the French Republic and the Government of His Majesty the King of Spain, having reached accord over fixing the extent of the rights and the guarantee of interests which arise for France from her Algerian possessions, and for Spain from her possessions on the coast of Morocco, and, the Government of His Majesty the King of Spain having in consequence its adherence to the Franco-British Declaration Relating to Morocco and Egypt, communication of which had been made to it by the French Government, DECLARE that they remain firmly attached to the integrity of the Moroccan Empire under the sovereignty of the Sultan.

In testimony whereof, the undersigned, His Excellence the Minister of Foreign Affairs and His Excellency the Ambassador Extraordinary and Plenipotentiary of His Majesty the King of Spain to the President of the French Republic, duly authorised

to this effect, have drawn up the present Declaration to which they have apposed their seals.

Done in duplicate at Paris, 3rd October, 1904.

Signed
DELCASSÉ
F. de LÉON y CASTILLO.

CONVENTION.

The President of the French Republic and His Majesty the King of Spain, wishing to fix the extent of the rights and the guarantee of interests which arise for France from her Algerian possessions and for Spain from her possessions on the coast of Morocco, have decided to conclude a Convention and have nominated for this purpose as their Plenipotentiaries the following: The President of the French Republic, His Excellence M. Th. Delcassé, Deputy, Minister of Foreign Affairs of the French Republic, etc; His Majesty the King of Spain, His Excellence M. de Léon y Castillo, Marquis del Muni, his Ambassador Extraordinary and Plenipotentiary to the President of the French Republic etc.;

Who, after having had their plenary powers communicated to them, drawn up in due and proper form, have agreed upon the following articles:—

Art. I. Spain adheres under the terms of the present Convention to the Franco-British Declaration of 8th April, 1904 Relating to Morocco and Egypt.

Art. II. The region situated to the West and North of the line hereinafter determined constitutes the sphere of influence which arises for Spain from her possessions on the coast of Morocco.

In this zone the same right of action is reserved for Spain as is accorded to France by the second paragraph of Article II of the Declaration of 8th April, 1904 Relating to Morocco and Egypt.

However, taking into account of the existing difficulties and of the mutual interest there is in settling them, Spain declares that she will not exercise this right of action except after previous accord with France during the first period of application of the present Convention—a period which shall not exceed fifteen years from the signature of the Convention.

On its part, during the same period, France, desirous that the rights and interests accorded to Spain by the present should always be respected, will make known beforehand to the King's Government its action at the Court of the Sultan of Morocco in matters concerning the Spanish sphere of influence.

After this first period has expired and so long as the status quo endures, French action in relation to the Moroccan Government over matters concerning the sphere of influence reserved to Spain will not be taken except after previous accord with the Spanish Government.

During the first period the Government of the French Republic will do its best to secure that in two of the Customs ports of the region determined below the delegate of the Representative General of the Bondholders of the Moroccan loan of the 12th July, 1904 should be of Spanish nationality.

Starting from the point where the Moulouia enters the Mediterranean Sea, the abovementioned dividing line will run upstream along the Thalweg of this river as far as the line of the ridge of heights nearest to the left bank of the Wadi Defla. From this point, without under any circumstances being allowed to intersect the course of the Moulouia, the demarcation line shall proceed as directly as possible to the watershed separating the basins of the Moulouia and the Wadi Inaouen from that of the Wadi Kert. Then it will run on westwards along the watershed separating the basins of the Wadi Inaouen and the Wadi Sebou from those of the Wadi Kert and the Wadi Ouergha to reach the Jebel Moulai Bou Chta by the most northern ridge. Then it will head north remaining at a distance of at least twenty-five kilometres to the east of the road from Fez to Kear-el-Kebir by way of Ouezzan as far as the meeting place with the Wadi Loukkos or Wadi el Kous, the Thalweg of which it will descend for five kilometres downstream from the meeting of this river with the abovementioned road from Fear-el-Kebir by way of Ouezzan. From this point it will reach shore of the Atlantic Ocean as directly as possible above the lagoon of Ez Zerga.

This delimitation is in conformity with the delimitation marked out on the map attached to the present Convention designated No. 1.

Art. III. In the case where the political state of Morocco and the Sherifean Government would be able to remain in existence no longer, or if, through the weakness of this government and through its persistent inability to guarantee safety and public order, or for any other reason to establish mutual agreement, the maintenance of the status quo should become impossible, Spain would be able to act freely in the region delimited in the previous Article, which from now on constitutes her sphere of influence.

Art. IV. The Moroccan Government having, by Article VII of the treaty of 26th April, 1860, conceded to Spain a colony at Santa Cruz de mar Pequeña (Ifni), it is agreed that the territory of this colony shall not go beyond the course of the Wadi Tazeroualt from its source up to its confluence with the Wadi Mesa and the course of the Wadi Mesa from this confluence as far as the sea, in accordance with the map attached to the present Convention.

Art. V. To complete the delimitation laid down by Article I of the Convention of 27th June, 1900, it is agreed that the demarcation between the French and Spanish spheres of influence will begin from the intersection of the meridian 14° 20' West of Paris and the line of 26° of latitude North, which it will follow eastwards as far as the meeting point with meridian 11° West of Paris. It will go up this meridian as far as the place where it reaches the Wadi Draa, then along the Thalweg of the Wadi Draa until it meets meridian 10° West of Paris, finally keeping to meridian 10° West of Paris as far as the watershed between the basins of the Wadi Draa and the Wadi

Sous, and will follow the watershed between the basins of the Wadi Draa and the Wadi Sous in a westerly direction, afterwards going between coastal basins of the Wadi Messa and the Wadi Noun as far as the point nearest to the source of the Wadi Tazeroualt.

This delimitation is in conformity with the delimitation marked out on Map No 2 already cited and attached to the present Convention.

Art. VI. Articles IV and V will be applicable at the same time as Article II of the present Convention.

However, the Government of the French Republic allows that Spain can establish herself at any time within the area defined by Article IV, on the condition of being in agreement beforehand with the Sultan.

In the same way, the Government of the French Republic accords from now on to the Spanish Government full liberty of action in the region contained between 26° and 27° 40' North and meridian 11° West of Paris which are outside Moroccan territory.

Art. VII. Spain undertakes not to alienate or cede in any way whatsoever, even by way of temporary title, all or part of the territories designated in Articles II, IV and V of the present Convention.

Art. VIII. If, in the application of Articles II, IV, and V of the present Convention one of the two contracting parties has a military operation forced upon it, it shall notify the other of it at once. In no case will it call upon a foreign power for assistance.

Art. IX. The town of Tangiers shall retain the special character given it by the presence of the diplomatic corps and its municipal and sanitary institutions.

Art. X. As long as the existing political condition shall endure, public works enterprizes, railways, roads, canals leaving from a point in Morocco and leading into the region specified in Article II and vice versa, will be carried out by the companies which the French and Spanish shall be able to set up.

In the same way, it shall be permissible for the French and the Spanish in Morocco to join together for the exploitation of mines, quarries and economic enterprizes generally.

Art. XI. The Spanish schools and institutions acting existing in Morocco shall be respected. The circulation of Spanish money will be neither prevented nor hindered. Spaniards will continue to enjoy in Morocco the rights secured them by the Treaties, Conventions and usages in force, including the right of navigation and fishing in Moroccan waters and ports.

Art. XII. The French shall enjoy, in the regions designated in Articles II, IV, and V of the present Convention, the same rights recognised for the Spaniards in the remainder of Morocco by the preceding Article.

Art. XIII. In the case where the Moroccan Government should forbid the sale of arms and ammunition in its territory, the two contracting Powers undertake to introduce in their African possessions the measures necessary to prevent them being brought into Morocco as contraband.

Art. XIV. It is agreed that the zone defined in paragraph I of Article VII of the Franco-English Convention of 8th April, 1904 relating to Morocco and Egypt begins on the coast thirty kilometres south-east of Melilla.

Art. XV. In the case where the denunciation provided for under paragraph III of Article IV of the Franco-English relating to Morocco and Egypt were to have taken place, the French and Spanish Governments will act in concert for the establishment of an economic administration especially in keeping with their reciprocal interests.

Art. XVI. The present Convention will be published when the two governments shall judge, by mutual agreement, that it can be done without disadvantages.

In any case, it will be able to be published by one of the two governments at the expiration of its first period of application—a period defined by paragraph III of Article II.

In testimony whereof the respective Plenipotentiaries have signed the present Convention and have apposed to it their seals.

Done in duplicate at Paris, 3rd October, 1904.

(L.S.) (Signe) DELCASSÉ.
(L.S.) (Signe) F. de LÉON y CASTILLO.

4.1209 Joint Declaration of Austria-Hungary and Russia in Regard to the Maintenance of Neutrality by Either If the Other Is at War

Alliance Members: Austria-Hungary and Russia
Signed On: October 15, 1904, in the city of St. Petersburg. In force until October, 1908, when Austria-Hungary annexed Bosnia.
Alliance Type: Neutrality Pact (Type II)

Source: *Key Treaties for the Great Powers, 1814–1914,* vol. 2, p. 765–766.
Additional Citations: *Pribram,* vol. 1, p. 236.

SUMMARY

The slow death of the Ottoman Empire continued to pose problems for eastern European great powers by 1904, especially Austria-Hungary and Russia, both of which harbored designs on the Balkans. The neutrality pact signed in St. Petersburg affirmed each state's commitment to the status quo in the region and provided for neutrality in the case of either party engaging in hostilities with third parties—with the Balkans excluded. The treaty's terms were also to be kept secret.

By 1908, however, as the crisis between Austria-Hungary and Serbia heated up, the terms of the treaty were no longer useful, and it was allowed to come to an end.

ALLIANCE TEXT

The undersigned, duly authorized by their August Sovereigns, have met together today at the Imperial Ministry of Foreign Affairs to sign the following Declaration:

Austria-Hungary and Russia, united by identical views as to the conservative policy to be followed in the Balkan countries,

and much satisfied with the result obtained so far by their close collaboration, are firmly decided to persevere in this course. Happy to record once more this understanding, the Cabinets of Vienna and of St. Petersburg attach great importance to offering each other in due form a mark of friendship and reciprocal confidence.

It is with this purpose that the two Powers have come to an agreement to observe a loyal and absolute neutrality in case one of the two Parties signatory to this Declaration should find itself, alone and without provocation on its part, in a state of war with a third Power which sought to endanger its security or the status quo; the maintenance of which constitutes the basis of their understanding, as pacific as it is conservative.

The engagement between Austria-Hungary and Russia stipulated in the above naturally does not apply to the Balkan countries, whose destinies are obviously closely attached to the agreement established between the two neighboring Empires. The said engagement is understood to remain valid so long as these two great Powers shall pursue their policy of an understanding in the affairs of Turkey; it shall be kept secret, and cannot be communicated to any other Government, except after a previous understanding between the Cabinets of Vienna and of St. Petersburg.

Done in duplicate at St. Petersburg, October 2/15, 1904.

L. Aehrenthal.
Count Lamsdorff.

4.1210 Treaty of Björkö

Alliance Members: Germany and Russia
Signed On: July 24, 1905, in the Björkö Sound (Russia). In force until December 2, 1905, when Russia failed to include France in the treaty (in violation of Article IV).
Alliance Type: Defense Pact (Type I)

Source: *Readings in European International Relations since 1879,* p. 105.

SUMMARY

Russia's defeat in the Russo-Japanese War signaled to Germany an opportunity to offer assistance with the hopes of pulling the Russians out of their rapprochement with the British, and in 1905 the two signed a defensive pact aimed at doing just that. A final clause also committed the Russians to invite the French into the alliance, making clear its goal of driving a wedge between the British and the Russians.

The alliance was short-lived, surviving only from July to December, as British and Russian relations went on the mend before the First Moroccan Crisis, making the Triple Entente an increasingly viable counter to the Central Powers.

ALLIANCE TEXT

Their Imperial Majesties, the Emperor of All the Russias on the one side, and the German Emperor on the other, in order to insure the peace of Europe, have placed themselves in accord on

217

the following points of the herein treaty relative to a defensive alliance:

Art. I. If any European state attacks one of the two empires, the allied party engages to aid the other contracting party with all his military and naval forces.

Art. II. The high contracting parties engage not to conclude with any common enemy a separate peace.

Art. III. The present treaty will become effective from the moment of the conclusion of the peace between Russia and Japan and may be denounced with a year's previous notification.

Art. IV. When this treaty has become effective, Russia undertake the necessary steps to inform France of it and to propose to the latter to adhere to it as an ally.

[Signed] NICOLAS.
WILLIAM.
[Countersigned] Von Tschirschky.
Naval Minister, Birilev.
Count Benkendorf.

4.1211 Exchange of Notes between Great Britain and Spain Respecting the Maintenance of the Territorial Status Quo in the Mediterranean and in That Part of the Atlantic Ocean Which Washes the Shores of Europe and Africa

Alliance Members: Great Britain and Spain
Signed On: May 16, 1907, in the city of London. In force until April 26, 1915, when Britain and France promised status quo changes to Italy in exchange for Italy's entrance into World War I.
Alliance Type: Entente (Type III)

Source: *The American Journal of International Law,* vol. 1, no. 4, Supplement: Official Documents (October 1907), p. 425.

SUMMARY

Increasing fear of German expansion into the Balearic and Canary Islands led in 1907 to an agreement among the members of the Entente Cordiale—France, Great Britain, and Spain—regarding the protection of the status quo in that region. Signatories also agreed to cooperate in balancing what had become rapidly growing German naval strength.

The signing of the agreement signaled that German designs on dividing her potential balancers was hardly effective, as the understanding between these powers and, subsequently, Russia would survive up to the outbreak of the First World War. No longer did the status quo demand protection, and new understandings between the allies would lead to a new structure of agreements by war's outbreak in 1915.

EXCHANGE OF NOTES

The Minister for Foreign Affairs to the Spanish Ambassador.

FOREIGN OFFICE,

London, May 16, 1907.

YOUR EXCELLENCY: Animated by the desire to contribute in every possible way to the maintenance of peace, and convinced that the preservation of the territorial status quo and of the rights of Great Britain and Spain in the Mediterranean and in that part of the Atlantic Ocean which washes the shores of Europe and Africa must materially serve this end, and is, moreover, to the mutual advantage of the two nations bound to each other by the closest ties of ancient friendship and of community of interests;

The Government of His Britannic Majesty desire to lay before that of His Catholic Majesty the following declaration of policy, in the confident hope that it will not only still further strengthen the good understanding so happily existing between them, but will also promote the cause of peace.

The general policy of the Government of His Britannic Majesty in the regions above defined is directed to the maintenance of the territorial status quo, and in pursuance of this policy they are firmly resolved to preserve intact the rights of the British Crown over its insular and maritime possessions in those regions.

Should circumstances arise which, in the opinion of the Government of His Britannic Majesty, would alter, or tend to alter, the existing territorial status quo in the said regions, they will communicate with the Government of His Catholic Majesty, in order to afford them the opportunity to concert, if desired, by mutual agreement the course of action which the two powers shall adopt in common.

I have the honour to be, with the highest consideration,

Your Excellency's most obedient humble servant,

E. GREY.

4.1212 General Treaty of Peace and Amity Concluded at the Central American Peace Conference

Alliance Members: Costa Rica, Guatemala, Honduras, Nicaragua, and El Salvador
Signed On: December 20, 1907, in the city of Washington, D.C. In force until March 10, 1918.
Alliance Type: Neutrality Pact (Type II)

Source: *British Foreign and State Papers,* vol. 100, p. 835.

SUMMARY

Guatemala, Honduras, El Salvador, Nicaragua, and Costa Rica signed this general treaty of peace in 1907, creating in essence a broad neutrality pact aimed at enhancing cooperation in both economic and security matters. Intended to last ten years unless a majority of members should amend it, it did not survive beyond this original mandate.

Central to the terms of the treaty was the establishment of a Central American Court of Justice, but by 1918 most states were dissatisfied with the sovereignty they had yielded to the body. Nicaragua was the first to leave the court in 1918, signaling what would be the end of the alliance.

Alliance Text

The Governments of the Republics of Costa Rica, Guatemala, Honduras, Nicaragua, and Salvador, being desirous of establishing the foundations which fix the general relations of said countries, have seen fit to conclude a general Treaty of Peace and Amity which will attain said end, and for that purpose have named as Delegates:

Costa Rica: Their Excellencies Doctor Don Luis Anderson and Don Joaquin B. Calvo;

Guatemala: Their Excellencies Doctor Don Antonio Batres Jáuregui, Doctor Don Luis Toledo Herrarte, and Don Víctor Sánchez Ocaña.

Honduras: Their Excellencies Doctor Don Policarpo Bonilla, Doctor Don Angel Ugarte, and Don E. Constantino Fiallos;

Nicaragua: Their Excellencies Doctor Don José Madriz and Don Luis F. Corea; and

Salvador: Their Excellencies Doctor Done Salvador Gallegos, Doctor Don Salvador Rodríguez Gonzálex, and Doctor Don Federico Majía.

By virtue of the invitation sent in accordance with Article II of the protocol signed at Washington on September 17 1907, by the Plenipotentiary Representatives of the five Central American Republics, their excellencies, the Representative of the Government of the United Mexican States, Ambassador Don Enrique C. Creel, and the Representative of the Government of the United States of America, Mr William I. Buchanan, were present at all the deliberations.

The Delegates assembled in the Central American Peace Conference at Washington, after having communicated to one another their respective full powers, which they found to be in due form, have agreed to carry out the said purpose in the following manner:

Article I. The Republics of Central America consider as one of their first duties, in their mutual relations, the maintenance of peace; and they bind themselves always to observe the most complete harmony, and decide every difference or difficulty that may arise amongst them, of whatsoever nature it may be, by means of the Central American Court of Justice, created by the Convention which they have concluded for that purpose on this date.

Article II. Desiring to secure in the Republics of Central America the benefits which are derived from the maintenance of their institutions, and to contribute at the same time to strengthening their stability and the prestige with which they ought to be surrounded, it is declared that every disposition or measure which may tend to alter the constitutional organization in any of them is to be deemed a menace to the peace of said Republics.

Article III. Taking into account the central geographical position of Honduras and the facilities which owing to this circumstance have made its territory most often the theater of Central American conflicts, Honduras declares from now on its absolute neutrality in event of any conflict between the other Republics; and the latter, in their turn, provided such neutrality be observed, bind themselves to respect it and in no case to violate the Honduranean territory.

Article IV. Bearing in mind the advantages which must be gained from the creation of Central American institutions for the development of their most vital interests, besides the Pedagogical Institute and the International Central American Bureau which are to be established according to the Conventions concluded to that end by this Conference, the creation of a practical Agricultural School in the Republic of Salvador, one of Mines and Mechanics in that of Honduras, and another of Arts and Trades in that of Nicaragua, is especially recommended to the Governments.

Article V. In order to cultivate the relations between the States, the contracting Parties obligate themselves each to accredit to the others a permanent Legation.

Article VI. The citizens of one of the contracting Parties, residing in the territory of any of the others, shall enjoy the same civil rights as are enjoyed by nationals, and shall be considered as citizens in the country of their residence if they fulfil the conditions which the respective constituent laws provide. Those that are not naturalized shall be exempt from obligatory military service, either on sea or land, and from every forced loan or military requisition, and they shall not be obliged on any account to pay greater contributions or ordinary or extraordinary imposts than those which natives pay.

Article VII. The individuals who have acquired a professional degree in any of the contracting Republics, may, without special exaction, practice their professions, in accordance with the respective laws, in any one of the others, without other requirements than those of presenting the respective degree or diploma properly authenticated and of proving, in case of necessity, their personal identity and of obtaining a permit from the Executive Power where the law so requires.

In like manner shall validity attach to the scientific studies pursued in the universities, professional schools, and the schools of higher education of any one of the contracting countries, provided the documents which evidence such studies have been authenticated, and the identity of the person proved.

Article VIII. Citizens of the signatory countries who reside in the territory of the others shall enjoy the right of literary, artistic, or industrial property in the same manner and subject to the same requirements as natives.

Article IX. The merchant ships of the signatory countries shall be considered upon the sea, along the coasts, and in the ports of said countries as national vessels; they shall enjoy the same exemptions, immunities and concessions as the latter, and shall not pay other dues nor be subject to further taxes than those imposed upon and paid by the vessels of the country.

Article X. The Governments of the contracting Republics bind themselves to respect the inviolability of the right of asylum aboard the merchant vessels of whatsoever nationality anchored in their ports. Therefore, only persons accused of common crimes can be taken from them after due legal procedure and by order of the competent judge. Those prosecuted on account of political crimes or common crimes in connection with political ones, can only be taken therefrom in case they have embarked in a port of the State which claims them, during their stay in its jurisdictional waters, and after the requirements hereinbefore set forth in the case of common crimes have been fulfilled.

Article XI. The Diplomatic and Consular Agents of the contracting Republics in foreign cities, towns, and ports shall afford to the persons, vessels, and other property of the citizens of any one of them, the same protection as to the persons, ships, and other properties of their compatriots, without demanding for their services other or higher charges than those usually made with respect to their nationals.

Article XII. In the desire of promoting commerce between the contracting Republics, their respective Governments shall agree upon the establishment of national merchant marines engaged in coastwise commerce and the arrangements to be made with and the subsidies to be granted to steamship companies engaged in the trade between national and foreign ports.

Article XIII. There shall be a complete and regular exchange of every class of official publications between the contracting Parties.

Article XIV. Public instruments executed in one of the contracting Republics shall be valid in the others, provided they shall have been properly authenticated and in their execution the laws of the Republic whence they issue shall have been observed.

Article XV. The judicial authorities of the contracting Republics shall carry out the judicial commissions and warrants in civil, commercial, or criminal matters, with regard to citations, interrogatories, and other acts of procedure or judicial function.

Other judicial acts, in civil or commercial matters, arising out of a personal suit, shall have in the territory of any one of the contracting Parties equal force with those of the local tribunals and shall be executed in the same manner, provided always that they shall first have been declared executory by the Supreme Tribunal of the Republic wherein they are to be executed, which shall be done if they meet the essential requirements of their respective legislation and they shall be carried out in accordance with the laws enacted in each country for the execution of judgments.

Article XVI. Desiring to prevent one of the most frequent causes of disturbances in the Republics, the contracting Governments shall not permit the leaders or principal chiefs of political refugees, nor their agents, to reside in the departments bordering on the countries whose peace they might disturb.

Those who may have established their permanent residence in a frontier department may remain in the place of their residence under the immediate surveillance of the Government affording them an asylum, but from the moment when they become a menace to public order, they shall be included in the rule of the preceding paragraph.

Article XVII. Every person, no matter what his nationality, who, within the territory of one of the contracting Parties, shall initiate or foster revolutionary movements against any of the others, shall be immediately brought to the capital of the Republic, where he shall be submitted to trial according to law.

Article XVIII. With respect to the Bureau of Central American Republics which shall be established in Guatemala, and with respect to the Pedagogical Institute which is to be created in Costa Rica, the Conventions celebrated to that end shall be observed, and those that refer to Extradition, Communications, and Annual Conferences shall remain in full force for the unification of Central American interests.

Article XIX. The present Treaty shall remain in force for the term of ten years counted from the day of the exchange of ratifications. Nevertheless, if one year before the expiration of said term none of the contracting Parties shall have given special notice to the others concerning its intention to terminate it, it shall remain in force until one year after such notification shall have been made.

Article XX. The stipulation of the Treaties heretofore concluded among the contracting Countries, being comprised or suitably modified in this, it is declared that all stipulations remain void and revoked by the present, after final approval and exchange of ratifications.

Article XXI. The exchange of ratifications of the present Treaty, as well as that of the other Conventions of this date, shall be made by means of communications which are to be addressed by the Governments to that of Costa Rica, in order that the latter shall notify the other contracting States. The Government of Costa Rica shall also communicate its ratification if it affects it.

Signed at the city of Washington on the twentieth day of December, one thousand nine hundred and seven.

LUIS ANDERSON.
J.B. CALVO.
ANTONIO BATRES JÁUREGUI.
LUIS TOLEDO HERRARTE.
VICTOR SÁNCHEZ O.
POLICARPO BONILLA.
ANGEL UGARTE.
E. CONSTANTINO FIALLOS.
JOSÉ MADRIZ.
LUIS F COREA.
SALVADOR GALLEGOS.
SALVADOR RODRÍGUEZ G.
F. MEJÍA.

ADDITIONAL CONVENTION TO THE GENERAL TREATY.

The Governments of the Republics of Costa Rica, Guatemala, Honduras, Nicaragua, and Salvador have seen fit to conclude a

Convention additional to the General Treaty, and to that end have named as Delegates:

Costa Rica.—Their Excellencies Doctor Don Luis Anderson and Don Joaquín B. Calvo;

Guatemala.—Their Excellencies Doctor Don Antonia Batres Jáuregui, Doctor Don Luis Toledo Herrarte, and Don Victor Sánches Ocaña;

Honduras.—Their Excellencies Doctor Don Policarpo Bonilla, Doctor Don Angel Ugarte, and Don E. Constantino Fiallos;

Nicaragua.—Their Excellencies Doctors Don José Madriz and Don Luis F. Corea; and

Salvador.—Their Excellencies Doctor Don Salvador Gallegos, Doctor Don Salvador Rodrígues González, and Don Federico Mejía.

By virtue of the invitation sent in accordance with Article II of the protocol signed at Washington on September 17, 1907, by the Plenipotentiary Representatives of the five Central American Republics, their excellencies, the Representative of the Government of the United Mexican States, Ambassador Don Enrique C. Creel, and the Representative of the Government of the United States of America, Mr. William I. Buchanan, were present at all the deliberations.

The Delegates assembled in the Central American Peace Conference at Washington, after having communicated to one another their respective full powers, which they found to be in due form, have agreed to carry out the said purpose in the following manner:

Article I. The Governments of the High Contracting Parties shall not recognize any other Government which may come into power in any of the five Republics as a consequence of a *coup d'etat,* or of a revolution against the recognized Government, so long as the freely elected representatives of the people thereof have not constitutionally reorganized the country.

Article II. No Government of Central America shall in case of civil war intervene in favor of or against the Government of the country where the struggle takes place.

Article III. The Governments of Central America, in the first place, are recommended to endeavor to bring about, by the means at their command, a constitutional reform int eh sense of prohibiting the reelection of the President of a Republic, where such prohibition does not exist, secondly to adopt all measures necessary to effect a complete guarantee of the principle of alternation in power.

Signed at the city of Washington on the twentieth day of December, on thousand nine hundred and seven.

LUIS ANDERSON.
J.B. CALVO.
ANTONIO BATRES JÁUREGUI.
LUIS TOLEDO HERRARTE.
VICTOR SÁNCHEZ O.
POLICARPO BONILLA.
ANGEL UGARTE.
E. CONSTANTINO FIALLOS.

JOSÉ MADRIZ.
LUIS F COREA.
SALVADOR GALLEGOS.
SALVADOR RODRÍGUEZ G.
F. MEJÍA.

4.1213 Root-Takahira Exchange of Notes

Alliance Members: United States and Japan
Signed On: November 30, 1908, in the city of Washington, D.C. In force until July 4, 1910, the time of the signing of the Russo-Japanese convention concerning Manchuria.
Alliance Type: Entente (Type III)

Source: Tokutomi, Itchiro. 1922. *Japanese-American Relations.* Trans. Sukeshige Yanagiwara. New York: MacMillan Co., p. 167–168.

SUMMARY

This agreement between the U.S. secretary of state, Elihu Root, and the Japanese ambassador, Takahira Kogoro, affirmed the territorial status quo in Asia and confirmed a free and independent China (the U.S. Open Door Policy) and U.S. annexation of Hawaii and the Philippines. The agreement also implicitly guaranteed Japanese interests in Manchuria and the Korean peninsula.

The agreement served as a framework of understanding between two emerging major states in the Pacific. The United States had defeated Spain just ten years prior, and Japan had soundly defeated Russia in its 1904 war on the continent. The alliance did not last long, however, as the 1910 Russo-Japanese convention afforded Japan the power to effectively dominate Manchuria and Korea.

EXCHANGE OF NOTES

Note from the Japanese ambassador to the Secretary of State

JAPANESE EMBASSY,
Washington, Nov. 30, 1908
SIR:

The exchange of views between us, which has taken place at the several interviews which I have recently had the honor of holding with you, has shown that Japan and the United States, holding important outlying insular possessions in the region of the Pacific Ocean, the governments of the two countries are animated by a common aim, policy and intention in that region.

Believing that a frank avowal of that aim, policy and intention would not only tend to strengthen the relations of friendship and good neighborhood which have immemorially existed between Japan and the United States, but would materially contribute to the preservation of the general peace, the Imperial Government have authorized me to present to you an outline of their understanding of that common aim, policy and intention:

1. It is the wish of the two governments to encourage the free and peaceful development of their commerce on the Pacific Ocean.

2. The policy of both governments, uninfluenced by any aggressive tendencies, is directed to the maintenance of the existing *status quo* in the region above mentioned and to the defense of the principle of equal opportunity for commerce and industry in Japan.

3. They are accordingly firmly resolved reciprocally to respect the territorial possessions belonging to each other in said region.

4. They are also determined to preserve the common interests of all powers in China by supporting by all pacific means at their disposal the independence and integrity of China and the principles of equal opportunity for commerce and industry of all nations in that Empire.

5. Should any event occur threatening the *status quo* as above described or the principle of equal opportunity, as above defined, it remains for the two governments to communicate with each other, in order to arrive at an understanding as to what measures they may consider it useful to take.

If the foregoing outline accords with the view of the government of the United States, I shall be gratified to receive your confirmation.

I take, etc.

K. TAKAHIRA.

Note from the Secretary of State to the Japanese Ambassador

DEPARTMENT OF STATE,
Washington, NOV. 30, 1908.
EXCELLENCY:

I have the honor to acknowledge the receipt of your note today, setting forth the result of the exchange of views between us in our recent interviews, defining the understanding of the two governments in regard to their policy in the region of the Pacific Ocean.

It is a pleasure to inform you that this expression of mutual understanding is welcome to the government of the United States as appropriate to the happy relation of the two countries and the occasion for a concise, mutual affirmation of that accordant policy respecting the Far East which the two governments have so frequently declared in the past.

I am happy to be able to confirm to Your Excellency, on behalf of the United States, the declaration of the two governments embodied in the following words:

(Here follows a declaration identical to that given by Baron Takahira over the signature of Mr. Elihu Root.)

4.1214 Russo-Italian Accord Concluded at Racconigi

Alliance Members: Russia and Italy
Signed On: October 24, 1909, in the city of Racconigi (Italy). In force until November 8, 1917, when the Russian Revolution effectively abrogated all treaties of tsarist Russia.
Alliance Type: Entente (Type III)

Source: *Readings in European International Relations since 1879*, p. 152.

SUMMARY

European worries over the so-called Eastern Question would plague the great powers all the way through the run-up to World War I. In 1909 Italy and Russia signed a secret agreement (often referred to as the Racconigi Agreement) pledging the protection of the status quo in the Balkans as well as promising future support for potential changes to the status quo—namely, Russia's desire to win access to the Mediterranean by controlling the Bosporus and the Dardanelles and Italy's designs on Tripoli. Further terms of the treaty promised support for the new Yugoslavian state against attacks by the Young Turks as well as the total secrecy of the agreement.

The understanding survived until the Bolshevik Revolution. Russia's separate peace with Germany led to Russia's exit from the war in 1917.

DESCRIPTION OF TERMS

1. Russia and Italy agree to act together, in the maintenance of the status quo in the Balkan Peninsula.

2. In any eventuality which may occur in the Balkans, they agree to support the application of the principle of nationality by the development of the Balkan States to the exclusion of all foreign domination.

3. They agree to oppose by common action all activity opposed to these ends; by "common action" is meant diplomatic action, all action of a different sort being simply reserved for a future understanding.

4. If Russia and Italy should wish to contract for Eastern Europe new agreements with a third party besides those which already exist, each would do so only with the participation of the other.

5. Italy and Russia engage themselves to consider with good will, the former, Russian interests in the question of the Straits, the latter, Italian interests in Tripoli and Cyrenaica.

4.1215 Convention in Regard to Manchuria

Alliance Members: Russia and Japan
Signed On: July 4, 1910, in the city of St. Petersburg. In force until July 3, 1916, when it was succeeded by Alliance no. 4.1226.
Alliance Type: Entente (Type III)

Source: *Treaties and Agreements with and Concerning China, 1919–1929*, p. 803–804.
Additional Citations: *Imperial Russia: A Source Book, 1700–1917*, p. 434–436.

SUMMARY

Five years after the end of the Russo-Japanese War, Russia and Japan signed an agreement carving out spheres of influence in Manchuria and legitimizing Japanese occupation of Korea. The United States, hoping to win another agreement with Japan following the conclusion of the Gentlemen's Agreement of 1907, had been effectively left out of the security equation in the region, and the Japanese gained a foothold for what eventually became more than the simple occupation of Manchuria but the invasion of China at the outset of World War II.

The Russo-Japanese agreement lasted only until 1916, but the legitimacy it conferred on Japanese rights in northern China lasted until the end of the Second World War, when the United States and the Soviet Union competed to fill the void created by Japan's surrender.

ALLIANCE TEXT

The Imperial Government of Russia and the Imperial Government of Japan, sincerely attached to the principles established by the convention concluded between them July 17/30, 1907, and desiring to develop the results of that convention with a view to the consolidation of peace in the Far East, have agreed to complete the said arrangement by the following agreements:

Art. I.—For the purpose of facilitating the communications and developing the commerce of the nations, the two High Contracting Parties engage mutually to lend each other their friendly cooperation with a view to the improvement of their respective lines of railroad in Manchuria, and to the perfecting of the connecting service of the said railways, and to refrain from all competition unfavorable to the attainment of this result.

Art. II.—Each of the High Contracting Parties engages to maintain and to respect the *status quo* in Manchuria as it results from all the treaties, conventions or other arrangements hitherto concluded, either between Russia and Japan or between these two Powers and China. Copies of the aforesaid arrangements have been exchanged between Russia and Japan.

Art. III.—In case any event of such a nature as to menace the above-mentioned *status quo* should be brought about, the two High Contracting Parties will in each instance enter into communication with each other, for the purpose of agreeing upon the measures that they may judge it necessary to take for the maintenance of the said *status quo*.

In faith of which the undersigned, duly authorized by their respective Governments, have signed this convention and set their seals thereto.

Done at St. Petersburg, June 21 (July 4), 1910, corresponding to the 4th day of the 7th month of the forty-third year of Meiji.

(Signed) (L.S) ISWOLSKY
(Signed) (L.S.) MOTONO

4.1216 Treaty of Friendship and Alliance between the Kingdom of Bulgaria and the Kingdom of Serbia

Alliance Members: Bulgaria and Serbia
Signed On: February 29, 1912, in the city of Sofia (Bulgaria). In force until June 30, 1913, upon the outbreak of the Second Balkan War between Serbia and Bulgaria.
Alliance Type: Defense Pact (Type I)

Source: *The Aspirations of Bulgaria,* p. 96–101.

SUMMARY

As Austrian and Turkish competition for control of the Balkans intensified through the spring and summer of 1912, Bulgaria and Serbia, followed by Montenegro and Greece, signed a defensive alliance. Its terms included agreement to assist Bulgaria against a Romanian attack and Serbia against an Austrian one, although the alliance expanded to include the additional signatories as they joined during the summer.

The allies would fight together in the First Balkan War, set off by a Montenegrin attack on Ottoman positions, a subsequent Ottoman declaration of war, and activation of the terms of the Balkan League's alliance. Although the alliance held through the war, it was strained by a Serbian refusal to abide by an agreement to cede to Bulgaria land captured in Macedonia. Greece also resisted Bulgarian aims, and when Bulgarian forces attacked Serbian and Greek positions in Macedonia in June 1913, the alliance fell apart.

ALLIANCE TEXT

His Majesty, Ferdinand I, King of the Bulgars, and His Majesty Peter I, King of Serbia, animated by the conviction of the community of the interests and of the identity of the destinies of their countries and of both brother-nations, the Bulgarian and the Serbian, and determined to defend their interests solidly and with united forces and to safeguard their full progress, hereby agree as follows:

Article 1.—The Kingdom of Bulgaria and the Kingdom of Serbia guarantee each other their mutual independence and the inviolability of their respective territories, and for that object they engage, absolutely and without limit, to succour each other with their entire forces, in the case that one of them should be attacked by one or several foreign States.

Article 2.—Both contracting parties engage themselves to proceed to the help of the other with their entire forces should any Great Power whatever attempt to annex, or militarily occupy, even if only temporarily, any portion of Balkan territory which is now under the Turkish rule, if one of the contracting parties should consider that action as opposed to her vital interests and as a *casus belli*.

Article 3.—Both contracting parties engage themselves not to conclude peace otherwise than together and after a previous understanding between them.

Article 4.—With a view to the most complete and expeditious fulfilment of this Treaty, a Military Convention shall be concluded in which everything for which each contracting party shall have to prepare in the case of war shall be provided for, as well as everything which—with respect to military organisation, dislocation, mobilisation of the armies, and the mutual relations of the Supreme Commands—should be fixed in the time of peace in order to prepare for conditions of war and for the successful prosecution of the war. The Military Convention shall be considered as an integral part of this Treaty. The elaboration of the Military Convention must be commenced within twenty-five days after the signature of this Treaty, and for its elaboration a term of not longer than two months is allowed.

Article 5.—The Treaty and the Military Convention shall be considered as valid from the date of their signature until December 31st, 1920, inclusive. Their duration can be prolonged beyond that term, but only after a supplementary agreement shall have been concluded between the contracting parties. But should the contracting parties find themselves still in the state of war, or should the liquidation of results of such a war be uncompleted on the date fixed for the expiration of this Treaty and its annexed Military Convention, this Treaty and the Convention shall continue valid until the conclusion of peace and until the liquidation of the situation created by the war shall have been completed.

Article 6.—The Treaty shall be signed in two copies in both the Bulgarian and Serbian languages. It shall be signed by the Sovereigns and their Ministers of Foreign Affairs. Similarly the Military Convention shall be drawn up in two copies in the Serbian and Bulgarian languages and signed by the Sovereigns and their Ministers of Foreign Affairs and special military representatives endowed with full powers.

Article 7.—The Treaty and Convention may be announced or communicated to other States only after previous agreement between the contracting parties, and then together and at the same time.

Similarly, another State may be received into alliance only after a previous agreement.

Given at Sofia, February 29th, 1912

THE SECRET ANNEX TO THE TREATY OF FRIENDSHIP AND ALLIANCE BETWEEN THE KINGDOM OF BULGARIA AND THE KINGDOM OF SERBIA

Article 1.—In the case that internal disorder should break out in Turkey, of a nature calculated to endanger the national and State interests of the contracting parties, or of one of them, or in the case that, in consequence of the internal or external difficulties of Turkey, the question of maintaining the *status quo* in the Balkan Peninsula should be opened, the contracting party which first arrives at the conviction that armed action should, in consequence, be taken, must address itself to the other contracting party with a proposal to that effect which must be supported by reasons and a statement of motive. The other contracting party shall be obliged to enter at once into

exchange of ideas, and—if she does not agree with her Ally—to give an answer explaining her reasons for disagreement.

If an agreement for joint action should be made, Russia is to be informed thereof, and if she be not thereto opposed, action shall be commenced on the basis of the agreement concluded, being guided in everything by the sentiment of solidarity and community of interests. In the contrary event, if an agreement is not reached, the Allies will ask Russia for her opinion, which opinion, if and so far as Russia gives it, shall be binding on both parties.

If Russia does not wish to give an opinion, and if the contracting parties afterwards fail to reach an agreement, and if that party which favours an armed action should take such action against Turkey on her own responsibility, then the other party should be bound to maintain an attitude of friendly neutrality towards her Ally, and mobilise her army in the manner foreseen by the Military Convention, and to proceed with all her forces to the assistance of her Ally if some other State should help Turkey.

Article 2.—All the territory won by a joint action in the sense of Articles 1 and 2 of the Treaty and Art. 1 of this Convention, will become the joint possession (condominium) of both the Allies, and the liquidation shall be executed immediately and within a term of three months from the conclusion of peace, on the following basis:

Serbia recognises Bulgaria's right to the country lying to the east of Rodopes and the river Struma, and Bulgaria that of Serbia to the country to the north and to the west of the Shar mountain.

With respect to the territory lying between the Shar mountain and the Rodopes, the Archipelago and the lake of Ochrida, if both contracting parties arrive at the conclusion that it is impossible to organise it into an autonomous province out of consideration for the general interests of the Bulgarian and Serbian nations, or for whatever interior or exterior reasons, then that territory shall be treated in the following manner: Serbia engages herself not to demand anything across the line marked on the annexed map, and which starts from the point Golemi Vrh on the Turko-Bulgarian frontier (to the north of Kriva Palanka) and runs generally in a south-westerly direction to the lake of Ochrida, passing across the hill Kitka, between the villages Metechovo and Podrzikon, across the height of the village Nerava, by the watershed up to height 1,000, northwards of the village Bashchevo, between the villages Lyubenatz and Potrlitsa, across the hill Ostrich—the height 1,000 (the mountain Lissatz), the height 1,050, between the villages Drach and Opilo, across the village Tamishmanatz and Zivalyevo, the heights 1,050 and 1,000, across the village Kushalo, following the main watershed of the mountain Gradishte up to the hill Gorich, by the height 1,023, by the watershed between the villages Ivankovtse and Loguintsi and by the Voterski and Sopot to Vardar, crosses the Vardar and continues by the mountain top across the height 2,550 up to the mountains Perepole, following its watershed between the villages Krap and Barbaress up to the height 1,200, then between the villages Erkenovo and Drenovo up to the hill Tchesma (height 1,254) by the watershed of the mountains Baba and Krushka—Tepessi, between the villages Seltse and Tsarsko, up to the hill on the mountain Protiska eastwards of the village Belitsa, across Brezane, by the height 1,200 (Ilinska Planina), by its watershed across the heights 1,330 and 1,277, between the villages Livoishte and Goreltsi till the monastery Gubavatz on the lake of Ochrida: and Bulgaria likewise engages to accept that boundary, if His Majesty the Tsar of Russia—who will be requested to decide the question by arbitration—declares himself in favour of same. It is understood that both sides bind themselves to accept as the definite boundary that line which His Majesty the Russian Tsar shall decide, within the above-mentioned limits, as answering to the best interests of both contracting parties.

Article 3.—The two contracting parties will together communicate the stipulations of the Treaty, the Secret Annex, and the Military Convention, to the Imperial Russian Government, which will then be requested to retain a copy of them and to agree to the purpose for which they have been concluded, and H.M. the Tsar of Russia will be requested to be graciously pleased to accept and to approve the rôle which is thereby offered to him and to his Government.

Article 4.—Every dispute which might arise concerning the interpretation or execution of whatever stipulation of the Treaty, Secret Annex, and Military Convention, will be submitted to the definitive decision of Russia, as soon as one of the contracting parties declares that she considers it impossible to arrive at an understanding by direct negotiations.

Article 5.—No stipulation of this Secret Annex can be published or communicated to another State without a previous understanding between the contracting parties and without the consent of Russia.

Given in Sofia, February 29, 1912.

4.1217 Treaty of Alliance and Defense between Bulgaria and Greece (Balkan League)

Alliance Members: Bulgaria and Greece
Signed On: May 16, 1912, in the city of Sofia (Bulgaria). In force until June 30, 1913, when Bulgaria attacked Greece and Serbia, beginning the Second Balkan War.
Alliance Type: Defense Pact (Type I)

Source: *The American Journal of International Law,* vol. 8, no. 2, Supplement: Official Documents, April 1914, p. 81–83.
Additional Citations: *British and Foreign State Papers,* vol. 106, p. 908.

SUMMARY

Hoping to capitalize on the disintegration of the Ottoman Empire in the face of the Young Turk rebellion, Greece and Bulgaria signed a treaty establishing the Balkan League in 1912 with the purpose of preparing a campaign aimed at carving up the remnants of the empire. After the signing of a military convention in September, each state stationed troops on its border with Turkey and prepared for war. The Balkan League operated with Russian blessings, as it represented an obstacle to Austrian expansion into the region and a potentially useful balance against the Central Powers.

Hostilities began soon afterward, with Greece, Bulgaria, and Serbia declaring war on the Ottomans. By December, an armistice put an end to the fighting, although a Young Turk uprising in Adrianople forced Greece and Bulgaria back into the fray together by January of 1913. By May, however, Bulgaria had signed the Treaty of London to end the war and cement its domination of Macedonia. In response, in June Greece and Serbia signed a secret alliance that was aimed at frustrating Bulgarian aspirations, leading to outright hostilities among the members of the league and bringing it to its official end on June 30, with open warfare among the member states.

ALLIANCE TEXT

Considering that the two kingdoms firmly desire to keep peace in the Balkan Penninsula and that they can, by means of an effective treaty of alliance and defense, better respond to this need;

Considering, with the same object in mind, that the peaceful existence of different nationalities side by side in Turkey, on the basis of a real and *bona fide* political equality, and respect for the rights proceeding from treaties or otherwise granted to the Christian nationalities of the Empire constitute the conditions necessary for the stability of the state of affairs in the Orient;

Considering, finally, that the co-operation of the two kingdoms, in the manner indicated, is of a kind, in the very interest of their good relations with the Ottoman Empire, to facilitate and strengthen good understanding between Greek and Bulgar in Turkey;

The Government of His Majesty the King of the Bulgarians, and the Government of His Majesty the King of the Hellenes promise not to give this agreement, which is purely one of defense, an aggressive tendency in any way whatsoever, and having resolved to conclude an alliance of peace and of reciprocal protection in the terms here below indicated, have appointed as their plenipotentiaries [names of plenipotentiaries],

Who, after having exchanged their full powers, have agreed upon the following:

Article 1. If, contrary to the sincere desire of the high contracting parties and in spite of the attitude of their governments in avoiding all acts of aggression and all provocation toward the Ottoman Empire, either of the two states should be attacked by Turkey, either in its territory, or by a systematic infringement of the rights proceeding from treaties or from the fundamental principles of the law of nations, the two high contracting parties are bound to aid each other reciprocally with their entire armed forces, and consequently not to make peace except conjointly and in concert.

Article 2. The two high contracting parties mutually promise, on the one hand, to use their moral influence with their nationals in Turkey to contribute sincerely to the peaceful co-existence of the elements forming the population of the Empire, and, on the other hand, to give each other reciprocal aid and to act in concert, in taking any step with the Ottoman Government or with the great Powers, with a view of obtaining or insuring the enjoyment of rights proceeding from treaties or otherwise granted to Greek and Bulgarian nationals, the application of political equality, and constitutional guarantees.

Article 3. The present treaty shall remain in force for three years from the date on which it is signed and shall be tacitly renewed for one year, except in case of denunciation. Its denunciation must be made known at least six months before the expiration of the third year from the date on which it is signed.

Article 4. The present treaty shall be kept secret. It may not be communicated to a third Power, either in whole or in part, nor may it be divulged, in whole or in part, except with the consent of the two high contracting parties.

The present treaty shall be ratified as soon as possible. The ratifications shall be exchanged at Sofia (or at Athens).

In faith whereof, the respective plenipotentiaries have signed the present treaty and have thereto affixed their seals.

Done, in duplicate, at Sofia, on May 16, 1912.

I. E. GUECHOFF.
D. PANAS.

DECLARATION

Article 1 does not apply in case of war between Greece and Turkey as a result of the admission of Cretan deputies to the Greek Parliament against the will of the Ottoman Government. In such case, Bulgaria is bound only to observe friendly neutrality toward Greece; and, as the settlement of the crisis in the affairs of the Orient, resulting from the events of 1908 (likewise as to the Cretan question), is a matter of general interest and of a kind, without disturbing the equilibrium in the Balkan Peninsula, to strengthen the international situation there in the interest of peace, Bulgaria (independently of the engagements assumed by the present treaty) promises not to hinder in any way any action which may be taken by Greece aiming to settle this question.

I. E. GUECHOFF.
D. PANAS.

4.1218 Exchange of Letters between France and Great Britain Respecting Armed Assistance (Grey-Cambon Letters)

Alliance Members: France and Great Britain
Signed On: November 23, 1912, in the city of London. In force until November 11, 1918, with the armistice ending World War I.
Alliance Type: Entente (Type III)

Source: *The New York Times Current History,* p. 355.
Additional Citations: *Readings in Twentieth-Century European History,* p. 37–38.

SUMMARY

The potential emergence of Germany as the major power on the Continent, made obvious by its participation in the naval race with Britain as well as agreements with Austria and the Turks aimed at carving up the remains of the Ottoman Empire, alarmed Britain and France enough by 1912 that in a series of letters they established a defensive alliance against potential German expansion.

English naval strength could account for only so much resistance to German ascendancy, and French land forces were expected to be necessary for preventing the Germans from sitting across the Channel. German power had become such a threat that other allies would soon be sought in order to increase pressure on the Central Powers and force them into a two-front war. The signing of the alliance marked the failure of Chancellor Otto von Bismarck's long-standing policy of isolating France, although the alliance was not a deterrent sufficient for preventing the outbreak of war in the East and its quick spread to a western front.

Russia also participated as an ally, although Russia exited the war after the Bolshevik Revolution in 1917; other late signatories were Italy, Japan, and the United States. The alliance survived in some form through the signing of the armistice in 1918, when its terms became useless.

EXCHANGE OF NOTES

Foreign Office,
November 22, 1912.
My dear Ambassador:

From time to time in recent years the French and British naval and military experts have consulted together. It has always been understood that such consultation does not restrict the freedom of either government to decide at any future time whether or not to assist the other by armed force. We have agreed that consultation between experts is not, and ought not to be regarded as, an engagement that commits either government to action in a contingency that has not arisen and may never arise. The disposition, for instance, of the French and British fleets respectively at the present moment is not based upon an engagement to co-operate in war.

You have, however, pointed out that, if either government had grave reason to expect an unprovoked attack by a third Power, it might become essential to know whether it could in that event depend upon the armed assistance of the other.

I agree that, if either government had grave reason to expect an unprovoked attack by a third Power, or something that threatened the general peace, it should immediately discuss with the other whether both governments should act together to prevent aggression and to preserve peace, and, if so, what measures they would be prepared to take in common. If these measures involved action, the plans of the General Staffs would at once be taken into consideration, and the governments would then decide what effect should be given to them.
Yours, &c.,

E. GREY.

4.1219 Military Convention between Greece and Serbia

Alliance Members: Greece and Serbia
Signed On: May 19, 1913, in the city of Salonika (Greece). In force until November 11, 1918, with the armistice ending World War I.
Alliance Type: Defense Pact (Type I)

Source: *The American Journal of International Law,* vol. 12, no. 2, Supplement: Official Documents, April 1918, p. 86–139.
Additional Citations: *British and Foreign State Papers,* vol. 108, p. 689.

SUMMARY

This secret alliance was a response to the rising tensions among the Balkan states following the first Balkan War, which witnessed large territorial gains by Bulgaria, Greece, and Serbia from the slowly dying Ottoman Empire. Because they were not satisfied with the size of Macedonian territories ceded to Bulgaria, Bulgarian leaders petitioned Greece for a greater share of its territorial division. That request, plus the nearby presence of the large Bulgarian army, unsettled the Greek leadership, which sought assurances from Serbia. Note that the treaty stipulates carefully how the Serbian and Greek forces would position their armies in the event of conflict. The Balkan borders were newly formed, and legitimacy at this point often corresponded with how many troops each country had in any given region.

The allies fought together against Bulgaria within one year, following Bulgaria's separate attacks on Greek and Serbian forces that started the Second Balkan War. Greece also eventually (1917) entered World War I, backing the Allies, recapturing Serbia, and forcing Bulgaria to sue for peace.

ALLIANCE TEXT

His Majesty the King of the Hellenes and His Majesty the King of Serbia, considering that it is their duty to look after the security of their people and the tranquility of their kingdoms; considering furthermore, in their firm desire to preserve a durable peace in the Balkan Peninsula, that the most effective means to attain it is to be united by a close defensive alliance;

Have resolved to conclude an alliance of peace, of friendship, and of mutual protection, promising to each other never to give to their purely defensive agreement an offensive character, and for that purpose they have appointed as their plenipotentiaries:

His Majesty the King of the Hellenes; Mr. John Alexandropoulos, his Minister at Belgrade, Commander of the Royal Order of the Savior, Grand Commander of the Royal Order of Takovo; His Majesty the King of Serbia; Mr. Mathias Boschkovitch, his Minister at Athens, Grand Commander of the Royal Order of Saint Sava, Commander of the Royal Order of the Savior, who, after having exchanged their full powers found in good and due form, have today agreed as follows:

Article 1. The two high contracting parties covenant expressly the mutual guarantee of their possessions and bind themselves, in case, contrary to their hopes, one of the two kingdoms should be attacked without any provocation on its part, to afford to each other assistance with all their armed forces and not to conclude peace subsequently except jointly and together.

Article 2. At the division of the territories of European Turkey, which will be ceded to the Balkan States after the termination of the present war by the treaty of peace with the Ottoman Empire, the two high contracting parties bind themselves not to come to any separate understanding with Bulgaria, to afford each other constant assistance, and to proceed always together, upholding mutually their territorial claims and the boundary lines hereafter to be indicated.

Article 3. The two high contracting parties, considering that it is to the vital interest of their kingdoms that no other state should interpose between their respective possessions to the west of the Axios (Vardar) river, declare that they will mutually assist one another in order that Greece and Serbia may have a common boundary line. This boundary line, based on the principle of effective occupation, shall start from the highest summit of the mountain range of Kamna, delimiting the basin of the Upper Schkoumbi, it shall pass round the lake Achris (Ochrida), shall reach the western shore of the Prespa lake in the Kousko village and the eastern shore to the Lower Dupliani (Dolni Dupliani), shall run near Rahmanli, shall follow the line of separation of the waters between the Erigon (Tserna) river and Moglenica and shall reach the Axios (Vardar) river at a distance of nearly three kilometers to the south of Ghevgheli, according to the line drawn in detail in Annex I of the present treaty.

Article 4. The two high contracting parties agree that the Greco-Bulgarian and Serbo-Bulgarian boundary lines shall be established on the principle of actual possession and the equilibrium between the three states, as follows:

The eastern frontier of Serbia from Ghevgheli shall follow the course of the Axios (Vardar) river up to the confluence of Bojimia-Dere, shall ascend that river, and, passing by the altitudes 120, 350, 754, 895, 571, and the rivers Kriva, Lakavitza, Bregalnica and Zletovska shall proceed towards a point of the old Turkish-Bulgarian frontier on the Osogovska Planina, altitude 2225, according to the line drawn in detail in the Annex II of the present treaty.

The Greek frontier on the side of Bulgaria shall leave to Greece on the left shore of Axios (Vardar) the territories occupied by the Greek and Serbian troops opposite Ghevgheli and Davidovo as far as the mountain Beles and the Doïran lake; then, passing to the south of Kilkitch it shall run through the Strymon river by the north of the Orliako bridge and shall proceed through the Achinos (Tachinos) lake and the Angitis (Anghista) river to the sea, a little to the east of the Gulf of Eleutherai according to the line drawn in detail in the Annex III of the present treaty.

Article 5. Should a dissension arise with Bulgaria in regard to the frontiers as indicated above, and if every friendly settlement becomes impossible, the two high contracting parties reserve to themselves the right to propose by common agreement, to Bulgaria, that the dispute be submitted to the mediation or arbitration of the sovereigns of the Entente Powers or the chiefs of other states. In case Bulgaria shall refuse to accept this manner of peaceful settlement and assume a menacing attitude against either of the two kingdoms, or attempt to impose her claims by force, the two high contracting parties bind themselves solemnly to afford assistance to each other with all their armed forces and not to conclude peace subsequently except jointly and together.

Article 6. In order to prepare and to secure the means of military defense, a military convention shall be concluded with the least possible delay from the signature of the present treaty.

Article 7. His Majesty the King of the Hellenes covenants that his government shall grant all the necessary facilities and guarantees for a period of fifty years for the complete freedom of the export and import trade of Serbia through the port of Salonika and the railway lines from Salonika to Uskup and Monastir. This freedom shall be as large as possible, provided only it is compatible with the full and entire exercise of the Hellenic sovereignty.

A special convention shall be concluded between the two high contracting parties within one year from this day in order to regulate in detail the carrying out of this article.

Article 8. The two high contracting parties agree that upon the final settlement of all the questions resulting from the present war, the General Staffs of the two armies shall come to an understanding with the view of regulating in a parallel manner the increase of the military forces of each state.

Article 9. The two high contracting parties agree furthermore that, upon the final settlement of all the questions resulting from the present war, they will proceed by common agreement to the study of a plan of a custom convention, in order to draw closer the commercial and economic relations of the two countries.

Article 10. The present treaty shall be put in force after its signature. It can not be denounced before the expiration of ten years. The intention for the cessation of its force shall be notified by one of the two high contracting parties to the other six months in advance, in the absence of which the agreement shall continue to be binding upon the two states until the expiration of one year from the date of the denunciation.

Article 11. The present treaty shall be kept strictly secret. It can not be communicated to another Power either totally or partially, except with the consent of the two high contracting parties.

It shall be ratified as soon as possible. The ratifications shall be exchanged in Athens.

In faith whereof the respective plenipotentiaries have signed this treaty and affixed their seals.

Executed in Salonika, in duplicate, the nineteenth day of May in the year one thousand nine hundred and thirteen.

John Alexandropoulos.
M. Boschkovitch.

4.1220 Treaty of Alliance between Germany and Turkey

Alliance Members: Germany and Turkey
Signed On: August 2, 1914, in the city of Constantinople (Istanbul, Turkey). In force until October 30, 1918, when Turkey signed the armistice ending its involvement in World War I.
Alliance Type: Defense Pact (Type I)

Source: *Japanese-American Relations*, p. 167–168.

SUMMARY

This secret agreement provided Germany with a useful ally in the Mediterranean and established the Ottoman Empire as an ally to the Central Powers, resulting eventually in the Triple Alliance. The arrangement was formulated after both Great Britain and France refused to align with the Turkish Committee of Union and Progress (CUP). On the eve of World War I, Germany convinced Turkey to sign this treaty to ensure that Germany retained an ally in the war. The alliance deflected Russian forces from Germany to Turkey and enabled Germany and other Central Powers to fight their war on the Western Front.

The treaty mandated that Germany and Turkey observe strict neutrality in the conflict between Austria-Hungary and Serbia. Both states agreed to aid Austria-Hungary in the event that Russia intervened with military force. In case of war, Germany pledged that its military mission would work with Turkey in return for Turkey's assurance that the military mission would have a limited say over the conduct of its army. Germany also committed to protect the Ottoman Empire by force, if necessary.

The Turco-German alliance ended as a result of Turkey's defeat in World War I in the Middle East. Turkey signed an armistice on October 30, 1918.

ALLIANCE TEXT

1. The two contracting parties agree to observe strict neutrality in regard to the present conflict between Austria-Hungary and Serbia.

2. In case Russia should intervene with active military measures, and should thus bring about a casus foederis for Germany with relation to Austria-Hungary, this casus foederis would also come into existence for Turkey.

3. In case of war, Germany will leave her military mission at the disposal of Turkey. The latter, for her part, assures the said military mission an effective influence on the general conduct of the army, in accordance with the understanding arrived at directly between His Excellency the Minister of War and His Excellency the Chief of the Military Mission.

4. Germany obligates herself, if necessary by force of arms... [cipher group lacking] Ottoman territory in case it should be threatened.

5. This agreement which has been concluded for the purpose of protecting both Empires from international complications which may result from the present conflict goes into force as soon as it is signed by the above-mentioned plenipotentiaries, and shall remain valid, together with any similar mutual agreements, until December 31, 1918.

6. In case it shall not be denounced by one of the high contracting parties six months before the expiration of the term named above, this treaty shall remain in force for a further period of five years.

7. This present document shall be ratified by His Majesty the German Emperor, King of Prussia, and by His Majesty the Emperor of the Ottomans, and the ratifications shall be exchanged within a period of one month from the date of its signing.

8. The present treaty shall remain secret and can only be made public as a result of an agreement arrived at between the two high contracting parties. In testimony whereof, etc.

BARON v. WANGENHEIM
SAID HALIM

4.1221 Treaty of Alliance between the Ottoman Empire and Bulgaria

Alliance Members: Ottoman Empire and Bulgaria
Signed On: August 19, 1914, in the city of Sofia (Bulgaria). In force until September 30, 1918, when Bulgaria signed the armistice ending its involvement in World War I.
Alliance Type: Defense Pact (Type I)

Source: *British and Foreign State Papers,* vol. 152, p. 253.

SUMMARY

This treaty was an attempt to clarify the diplomatic positions of both the Ottoman Empire and Bulgaria immediately following several years of open warfare in the Balkans. The latest hostilities occurred just one year prior to the signing of the treaty, when the Ottomans and Romanians, witnessing the depletion of the Bulgarian forces at the hands of the Greeks and Serbs, entered Bulgarian-controlled territories and marched toward Sofia, the capital of Bulgaria. Only a quickly formed armistice stopped the Ottoman advance, and Bulgaria was forced to guarantee the Ottoman recapture of Adrianople and part of Thrace, both of which were key European territories for the mostly Asian empire.

With the outbreak of what would be World War I just days prior to the treaty, Bulgaria immediately declared a defensive neutrality, and as Bulgaria was uncertain of the intentions of its Balkan neighbors, this alliance guaranteed Ottoman aid in the event of attack. Nevertheless, Bulgaria eventually declared its support for the Central Powers with an alliance three weeks later.

DESCRIPTION OF TERMS

If one of the parties is attacked by one or more Balkan states, the other party, on the demand of its ally, will declare war and attack the aggressing state immediately with all its available forces. The two parties commit themselves not to take any action against one or more Balkan states without prior approval from their ally. The mobilization of the Bulgarian army will begin when its government judges appropriate, and Bulgaria will inform Turkey when it will start its military operations.

Should one of the parties find it necessary to declare war against a Balkan state without prior consent from its ally, the ally may adhere to benevolent neutrality if it does not want to cooperate militarily.

Bulgaria stipulates that the current treaty concerning its offensive military action based on an accord with Turkey cannot enter into force until Bulgaria obtains a sufficient guarantee of Romania. This could come in the form of a triple accord that includes Bulgaria, Turkey and Romania, or a special entente between Bulgaria and Romania promising neutrality.

The treaty will stay in force until the termination of the European War and the demobilization of the troops. However, it can continue in force for 5 years if not denounced by one of the parties within 3 months of the demobilization of Turkish and Bulgarian troops.

4.1222 Treaty of Alliance between Austria-Hungary and Bulgaria

Alliance Members: Austria-Hungary and Bulgaria
Signed On: September 6, 1914, in the city of Sofia (Bulgaria). In force until September 30, 1918, when Bulgaria signed the armistice ending its involvement in World War I.
Alliance Type: Defense Pact (Type I)

Source: *Consolidated Treaty Series,* vol. 220, 1914–1915, p. 290–291.

SUMMARY

Bulgaria began World War I with a declaration of strict neutrality. However, both Russia (a member of the Triple Entente) and Germany (a Central Power) began to vie for Bulgarian intervention owing to Bulgaria's strategic location, proximate to the Ottomans, Serbia, and Austria-Hungary. Hampered by fighting on the part of its smaller allies, the Triple Entente found it impossible to offer the same type of territorial gains promised by the Central Powers. Thus, by October of 1915, Bulgarian troops were fighting Serbia and making large initial gains, pushing the Serbs out of Macedonia. Romania declared its backing of the Triple Entente, but by December of 1916 a joint German-Bulgarian force had occupied Romania's capital, Bucharest.

The war effort eventually collapsed when Bulgaria met with stalemate on all its fronts. Both the failure to advance and the populist uprisings spreading from Russia contributed to popular unrest in Bulgaria. The defining moment for the Bulgarian government came with the territorial division of Romania at the hands of the Central Powers—Bulgaria could not secure the territorial war aims initially promised by its allies. The Bulgarian government collapsed in June of 1918, and a joint British-French force routed Bulgarian troops and entered Bulgaria, which led to an armistice by September.

DESCRIPTION OF TERMS

Austria-Hungary guarantees the political independence and the territorial integrity of Bulgaria against any attack during the lifetime of this treaty, so long as the attack is not provoked by the Bulgarian Government. If Austria-Hungary, without provocation on its part, has been attacked by another state bordering Bulgaria, the latter agrees to intervene with military force, provided that Austria-Hungary requests such aid.

This treaty is valid until December 31st, 1920. If the treaty is not canceled 6 months before termination, it will be extended by a year and for every year thereafter. The treaty is to be kept secret. This treaty will be ratified in 8 days in Sofia.

4.1223 Exchange of Notes between Romania and Russia Respecting the Increase of Romanian Territory

Alliance Members: Romania and Russia
Signed On: October 1, 1914, in the city of Petrograd (St. Petersburg, Russia). In force until August 17, 1916, when the alliance was replaced by a new agreement that also included Great Britain, France, and Italy.
Alliance Type: Defense Pact (Type I)

Source: *Consolidated Treaty Series,* vol. 220, p. 333.

SUMMARY

Negotiations between Romania and Russia ended with Russia's agreement to defend Romanian interests and recognize Romanian claims to Austro-Hungarian territories with a Romanian population and with Russia's assurances of support for these conditions during postwar negotiations with Britain and France. In return, Romania agreed to remain neutral in the war, including the blocking of all supplies sent from Germany to Turkey.

The alliance terms are important because they signal the cleaving of Romania from the Triple Alliance powers. Before the treaty, Romania was believed to be an unmovable ally of both Austria-Hungary and Germany. However, when the alliance among Bulgaria, Serbia, and Greece broke down over the distribution of Macedonia, Romanian leaders saw an opportunity to side with the Russian-backed forces of Serbia and Greece against the Austro-Hungarian–backed Bulgaria. Romania used this rift to secure additional territories in the Bulgarian-held Dobrudja. The Bucharest Treaty, which ended the Balkan War, gave Romania the territory it wanted, laid the foundation for the Russo-Romanian defense alliance, and fueled Romanian interests in additional territorial aggrandizement.

DESCRIPTION OF TERMS

The treaty commits Russia to resist any attack against the territorial status quo of Romania. The treaty also gives Romania the right to annex Austro-Hungarian territories that are currently inhabited by Romanians.

Romania will maintain benevolent neutrality towards Russia until it gains the Austro-Hungarian territories inhabited by Romanians.

4.1224 Agreement among France, Great Britain, Russia, and Italy providing for Italian naval and military co-operation with the Allied Powers and making certain territorial and other arrangements

Alliance Members: France, Great Britain, Russia, and Italy

Signed On: April 26, 1915, in the city of London. In force until November 11, 1918, upon the end of World War I. Note: Russia terminated its commitments on November 8, 1917, following the Bolshevik Revolution.
Alliance Type: Defense Pact (Type I)

Source: *British and Foreign State Papers,* vol. 112, p. 973.
Additional Citations: *Consolidated Treaty Series,* vol. 221, p. 57.

SUMMARY

The Treaty of London was negotiated secretly by the three major Allied Powers (France, Russia, Great Britain) and Italy. In exchange for postwar territorial promises to Italy and specific guarantees of Russian assistance against Austria on land and British and French naval assistance throughout the war, Italy committed its entire military to the Allied Powers. The negotiations were conducted in secret, and the Italians insisted that Serbia not be informed of the terms of the treaty. However, soon after the signing of the alliance (on August 4, 1915), the Allies sent Serbia an official note confirming the postwar territorial claims of Serbia and Montenegro.

Following the Bolshevik Revolution, Russia terminated all involvement with the treaty, and one of the Russian journals published the secret terms in their entirety. The territorial terms of the treaty proved costly for conciliation during the postwar peace process as much of the antebellum territorial divisions near Italy were significantly altered.

At the Paris Peace Conference, the Italians insisted that they would negotiate only with their wartime allies Serbia and Montenegro and not with defeated enemies included in the delegation of the new state of Serbs, Croats, and Slovenes. The Italians were particularly incensed when three members of the delegation were former Austro-Hungarian deputies, with one even a member of the wartime Austrian cabinet. Nevertheless, the Italians finally relented on some of their demands, primarily under the pressure of the then U.S. president, Woodrow Wilson; but the terms of the treaty, the negotiation process, and the secret territorial agreements caused much acrimony among the participants.

DESCRIPTION OF TERMS

The General Staffs of France, Great Britain, Italy, and Russia proclaim a military convention, effective immediately. This convention settles the minimum number of military forces to be employed by Russia against Austria-Hungary in order to prevent the latter from concentrating all its strength against Italy. This guarantees that Russia does not focus its entire efforts against Germany.

In exchange for this agreement, Italy will use its entire resources for the purpose of waging war jointly with France, Great Britain, and Russia against all their enemies.

The French and British Fleets shall assist Italy until the Austro-Hungarian fleet shall have been destroyed or until peace shall have been concluded. A naval convention shall be immediately concluded to this effect between France, Great Britain, and Italy.

Since the Italian territorial demands included the Yugo-Slavic lands under Austria-Hungary, the negotiations had to involve also the future borders of two co-belligerent Allied states, the Kingdoms of Serbia and Montenegro. However, the territorial promises to the latter were fairly precise only along the areas assigned to Italy. Thus, the Kingdom of Serbia was promised Split (Spalato, in Italian), the coast and islands south of Krka to Dubrovnik (Ragusa), and peninsula Peljesac (Sabbioncello). The Kingdom of Montenegro was assigned Dubrovnik and the coast south to the Albanian port San Giovanni di Medua. Also, but less precisely, Serbia was promised Bosnia-Herzegovina, Srem, Backa, Slavonia (this one against the Italian objections), and some unspecified areas of Albania (to be divided among Serbia, Montenegro, and Greece). The Italians insisted, and the Allies agreed, that the question of the Croatian coast between Zadar (Zara) and Istra (Istria) should be settled after the war.

4.1225 Military Convention among Germany, Austria-Hungary, and Bulgaria

Alliance Members: Germany, Austria-Hungary, and Bulgaria
Signed On: September 6, 1915, in the city of Pless (Austria). In force until September 30, 1918, when Bulgaria signed an armistice ending its involvement in World War I.
Alliance Type: Defense Pact (Type I)

Source: *Consolidated Treaty Series,* vol. 221, p. 135.

SUMMARY

Bulgaria had remained neutral at the start of World War I, primarily waiting to see which side would offer the greatest advantage. With the quick victories by Germany in Poland and the failed Allied attempt to open the Dardanelles, Bulgaria committed its support to Germany and Austria-Hungary and quickly mobilized its armed forces. Bulgarian leaders, believing that Bulgaria had been cheated out of territorial gains following the Balkan Wars of 1912 and 1913, immediately targeted neighboring Serbia as a potential acquisition. The tripartite force invaded Serbia October 7, 1915, and entered Belgrade two days later. Despite early successes in Serbia, Macedonia, Greece, and Romania, Bulgarian advances stalled, and internal dissension, poor supplies, and a demoralized fighting force led the Bulgarians to quit the war by September 1918.

DESCRIPTION OF TERMS

The three countries pledge to act in concert against Serbia. Germany and Austria-Hungary will march towards Serbian borders within 30 days, while Bulgarian forces will march within 35 days of the conclusion of this treaty. Germany and Austria-Hungary will each send at least 6 divisions of infantry, and Bulgaria will send 4 of its divisions.

Bulgaria commits itself to neutrality with Romania and Greece until the end of operations against Serbia, and longer if those countries do not mobilize, remain neutral, and do not occupy militarily Serbian territory.

The supreme German command commits itself, if the Bulgarian roads are open and Bulgaria desires the aid, to send a contingent of its troops to Bourgas and Varna and to send as many German submarines as possible. Bulgaria will house these troops, and their supplies will be provided by the German command.

The supreme German command will also use its influence towards the Turkish command so that the latter sends troops for the protection of Dedeagatch. In the case of a common action of Bulgarian and Turkish troops, the Turkish troops will be put under Bulgarian command.

4.1226 Agreement between Japan and Russia for the Maintenance of a Permanent Peace in the Far East

Alliance Members: Japan and Russia
Signed On: July 3, 1916, in the city of Petrograd (St. Petersburg, Russia). In force until November 8, 1917, following the Bolshevik Revolution and Russia's abrogation of all international treaties.
Alliance Type: Defense Pact (Type I)

Source: *British Foreign and State Papers,* vol. 110, p. 922.
Additional Citations: *Consolidated Treaty Series,* vol. 221, p. 367.

SUMMARY

This alliance was formed almost two years after the start of World War I, Japan's declaration of war against Germany, and the signing of a renewed defensive alliance between Japan and Britain. The public version of the treaty held that Russia and Japan would not attack the other and would seek counsel in order to safeguard and defend each nation's interests. A secret treaty was also signed that included provisions guaranteeing that China—which had been courted by Germany—would be kept free from political intervention by any third party with hostile designs toward Russia or Japan. This treaty assured continued Japanese naval support for the Entente powers; and because the Entente powers were consumed by events in Europe, the treaty also further strengthened Japanese hegemony in Manchuria and Inner Mongolia.

DESCRIPTION OF TERMS

Both the high contracting parties recognize that the vital interests of both countries require the safeguarding of China from political domination by any third power. Therefore the allies mutually obligate themselves to take any necessary measures in order to prevent such interventions.

If any state declares war against either ally, the other party must come to the aid of its alliance partner. Each of the contracting parties also agrees, in the event such a condition arises, not to conclude peace with the common enemy without the prior consent of its ally.

4.1227 Treaty of Alliance and Military Convention among France, Great Britain, Italy, Russia, and Romania

Alliance Members: France, Great Britain, Italy, Russia, and Romania
Signed On: August 17, 1916, in the city of Bucharest (Romania). In force until November 11, 1918, with the end of World War I. Note: Russia terminated its commitments on November 8, 1917, following

the Bolshevik Revolution.
Alliance Type: Defense Pact (Type I)

Source: *Martens,* vol. 10, p. 342.
Additional Citations: *Consolidated Treaty Series,* vol. 221, p. 412.

SUMMARY

Though an ally of Austria-Hungary, Romania refused to enter the war on the side of its ally, arguing that Austria-Hungary had started the conflict, and thus the defensive alliance was not applicable. Romania sat out the conflict for two years, demanding from the Allies a guarantee over the rights to Transylvania, which contained a large Romanian population but was controlled by Hungary. With this alliance, the Entente powers capitulated to Romania's demands so that their new alliance partner could aid Russia in the conflict. However, some historians suggest that the Entente powers had agreed not to honor this commitment after the end of the war.

Description of Terms

The allies guarantee Romania's territorial integrity. Romania will attack Austria-Hungary and stop trade with the enemy of the allies. The allies concede that Romania will annex territories from Austria-Hungary. The allies will not make peace individually. Romania will have the same rights as the other allies in the convention for peace. This treaty is secret. Russia will make vigorous attacks on its Austrian front to help the Romanian effort. The Russian fleet will protect the Romanian coast. The allies will send military matériel to Romania. Russia and Romania will remain in control of their troops. The money, prisoners, etc., that is obtained during the war will belong to the army that conquered it, in common combat it will be proportionally separated according to the number of soldiers involved in the conflict. The convention ends when the peace is signed.

4.1228 Convention of Alliance between the Kingdom of the Serbs, Croats, and Slovenes and the Czechoslovak Republic

Alliance Members: Serbia and Czechoslovak Republic
Signed On: August 14, 1920, in the city of Belgrade (Serbia). In force until July 1, 1930, when King Alexander assumed the throne of Serbia (Yugoslavia) and attempted an alignment with Mussolini's Italy.
Alliance Type: Defense Pact (Type I)

Source: *League of Nations Treaty Series,* vol. 6, p. 211.

SUMMARY

The main focus of the convention was to preclude a Hapsburg restoration and thereby eliminate the threat of an ambitious Hungary. Following the Polish-Soviet war, the Kingdom of the Serbs, Croats, and Slovenes and the Czechoslovak Republic opposed the growing Hungarian influence in the region. Hungary, maintaining its immense force, tried to forcefully separate Slovakia from the Czechoslovak Republic. France tried to counter Hungarian intentions by suggesting a Balkan alliance in which it would be a silent partner, but this defensive alliance provided more guarantees against an immediate threat.

The treaty assured mutual assistance from both parties in the event of attack by Hungary, and both states had to pledge to avoid all third-party arrangements outside the terms of the alliance. The agreement ended in 1931 when King Alexander came to rule the Kingdom of the Serbs, Croats, and Slovenes, created a monarchy, and renamed the new kingdom Yugoslavia. A repressive ruler, King Alexander attempted to align with Mussolini's Italy, thus breaking with the spirit of this treaty as Italy had previously aligned with Hungary.

Alliance Text

Firmly resolved to maintain the Peace obtained by so many sacrifices, and provided for by the Covenant of the League of Nations, as well as the situation created by the treaty concluded at Trianon on June 4, 1920, between the Allied and Associated Powers on the one hand, and Hungary on the other, the President of the Czechoslovak Republic and His Majesty the King of the Serbs, Croats and Slovenes have agreed to conclude a defensive Convention.

For this purpose, they have nominated as their Plenipotentiary Delegates:

For the President of the Czechoslovak Republic: M. Edouard Benes, the Minister for Foreign Affairs;

For His Majesty the King of the Serbs, Croats and Slovenes: M. Montchilo Nintchitch, Doctor of Law, Minister of Commerce and Industry, and acting Minister for Foreign Affairs.

Who, having exchanged their full powers and found them to be in good and due form, have agreed as follows:

Article I. In case of an unprovoked attack on the part of Hungary against one of the High Contracting Parties, the other Party agrees to assist in the defence of the Party attacked, in the manner laid down by the arrangement provided for in Article 2 of the present Convention.

Article 2. The competent Technical Authorities of the Czecho-Slovak Republic and the Kingdom of the Serbs, Croats and Slovenes shall decide, by mutual agreement, upon the provisions necessary for the execution of the present Convention.

Article 3. Neither of the High Contracting Parties shall conclude an alliance with a third Power without preliminary notice to the other.

Article 4. The present Convention shall be valid for two years from the date of the exchange of ratifications. On the expiration of this period, each of the Contracting Parties shall have the option of denouncing the present Convention. It shall, however, remain in force for six months after the date of denunciation.

Article 5. The present Convention shall be communicated to the League of Nations (Covenant of the League of Nations).

Article 6. The present Convention shall be ratified, and the ratifications shall be exchanged at Belgrade, as soon as possible.

In witness whereof, the Plenipotentiaries named have signed and have affixed their seals thereto.

Done at Belgrade, in duplicate, August 14 1920.

(Signed) Mom. NINTCHITCH.
(Signed) Dr EDOUARD BENES.

4.1229 Defensive Military Accord between France and Belgium in the Case of an Unprovoked German Attack

Alliance Members: France and Belgium
Signed On: September 7, 1920, in the city of Paris. In force until October 14, 1936, when Belgium denounced the alliance and reasserted its neutrality following German reoccupation of the Rhineland.
Alliance Type: Defense Pact (Type I)

Source: *Martens,* no. 10, p. 342.
Additional Citations: *Consolidated Treaty Series,* vol. 221, p. 412.

SUMMARY

France's postwar strategy revolved around several bilateral agreements aimed at containing any renewed German threat. This alliance with Belgium was an obvious part of that process, given the location of both countries relative to Germany and the location of much of the fighting during World War I.

The alliance was more problematic for Belgium because the Flemish population thought any broader association with France would increase the political power of the French-speaking Walloons. Regardless, the alliance withered as Hitler's Germany became a real threat to both countries. Belgium, not nearly capable of withstanding a direct German attack, renounced the alliance and attempted to pursue an ultimately unsuccessful policy of neutrality during World War II.

DESCRIPTION OF TERMS

In case of a threat or an aggression by Germany and a reinforcement of the French and Belgian troops stationed in the Rhineland becomes necessary, France will send nine divisions of infantry and Belgium will send two divisions of infantry.

If Germany generally arms, the two powers will mobilize their forces and France will provide fifty-five divisions while Belgium will provide twelve divisions. The French navy will send the necessary ships to protect the Belgian coast.

After the occupation of the Rhineland ends, French and Belgian headquarters will immediately begin the organization of a system of defense for their frontiers and the frontier of Luxembourg.

4.1230 Political Agreement between France and Poland

Alliance Members: France and Poland
Signed On: February 19, 1921, in the city of Paris. In force until September 27, 1939, upon the dissolution of Poland following the German and Russian invasions.
Alliance Type: Defense Pact (Type I)

Source: *League of Nations Treaty Series,* no. 449.
Additional Citations: *France and Her Eastern Allies 1919–1925,* p. 393.

SUMMARY

Both France and Poland had significant interests in pacifying Europe after the devastation of World War I. While the French economy prospered far beyond that of any other European state following the war, Poland was a fledgling state that had recently gained independence from Russian occupation. The main objective for Poland was to build a viable state, both politically and economically, free from Soviet interference. Poland found an ally in France, which sought to maintain its dominant status and replace the former French-Russian alliance.

In this agreement, France and Poland agree to consult each other on any foreign policy endeavors that concerned either party in accordance with the Covenant of the League of Nations. To restore international order and peace in Europe, the two parties pledged to develop economic relations under special agreements and commercial treaties, and if either state were to be attacked, the two governments were to take up arms to defend the territory and interests of the other. Each government also pledged to consult the other when taking part in additional agreements that would potentially affect their policies in central and eastern Europe.

The alliance began to deteriorate when Germany invaded Poland on September 1, 1939. France, with the help of Britain, issued Germany an ultimatum to leave Poland. World War II then began as Germany ignored this ultimatum. On September 17, 1939, the Soviet Union invaded Poland, and by September 27, Poland was effectively eliminated as a sovereign state.

ALLIANCE TEXT

The Polish Government and the French Government, both desirous of safeguarding, by the maintenance of the Treaties which both have signed or which may in future be recognised by both Parties, the peace of Europe, the security of their territories and their common political and economic interests, have agreed as follows:

(1) In order to co-ordinate their endeavours towards peace, the two Governments undertake to consult each other on all questions of foreign policy which concern both States, so far as those questions affect the settlement of international relations in the spirit of the Treaties and in accordance with the Covenant of the League of Nations.

(2) In view of the fact that economic restoration is the essential preliminary condition of the re-establishment of international order and peace in Europe, the two Governments shall come to an understanding in this regard, with a view to concerted action and mutual support.

They will endeavour to develop their economic relations, and for this purpose will conclude special agreements and a Commercial Treaty.

(3) If, notwithstanding the sincerely peaceful views and intentions of the two Contracting States, either or both of them should be attacked without giving provocation, the two Governments shall take concerted measures for the defence of their territory and the protection of their legitimate interests, within the limits specified in the preamble.

(4) The two Governments undertake to consult each other before concluding new agreements which will affect their policy in Central and Eastern Europe.

(5) The present Agreement shall not come into force until the commercial agreements now in course of negotiation have been signed.

Paris, February 19, 1921.
(Signed) A. BRIAND.
(Signed) E. SAPIEHA.

4.1231 Treaty of Friendship between Persia and the Russian Socialist Federal Soviet Republic

Alliance Members: Persia and the Soviet Union
Signed On: February 26, 1921, in the city of Moscow. In force until August 25, 1941, when the Soviets invaded northern Iran.
Alliance Type: Defense Pact (Type I)

Source: *League of Nations Treaty Series,* no. 268, vol. 9, p. 401.
Additional Citations: *Consolidated Treaty Series,* vol. 221, p. 412.

SUMMARY

This friendship treaty between the two countries set the territorial basis for the relationship between the Soviets and Iran. The treaty canceled all prior agreements and territorial arrangements and explicitly called on free navigation of the Caspian Sea, an important commercial source for both countries. The Soviets wanted the alliance to counter any interference from White Russian groups seeking to cause insurrection against the new Bolshevik government. The treaty terms included the right of intervention in Iran, should any insurgent groups attack Soviet territories or should any events threaten Soviet security. Iran, for its part, received debt forgiveness, a small segment of territory, and the promise of noninterference in Iranian affairs.

The alliance proved troublesome for future Iranian regimes. The terms of the alliance stated that the treaty would continue indefinitely without termination. Further, Soviet leaders often interpreted any British influence in Iran as counter to the security interests of the Soviet Union. The alliance finally ended with the simultaneous invasion of Iran by both Soviet and British forces in 1941.

ALLIANCE TEXT

The Persian Government of the one part, and the Russian Socialist Federal Soviet Republic of the other part, desiring to establish relations of friendship and fraternity between the two nations, have decided to engage in negotiations for this purpose, and have therefore appointed the following plenipotentiaries:—

For Persia: Ali Gholi Khan Mochaverol-Memalek, and for Russia: O. V. Tchitcherin and L. M. Karakhan,

who after the verification of their respective powers, have agreed as follows:

Article 1. In order to confirm its declarations regarding Russian policy towards the Persian nation, which formed the subject of correspondence on January 14, 1918, and June 26, 1919, the R. S. F. S. R. formally affirms once again that it definitely renounces the tyrannical policy carried out by the Colonising Governments of Russia which have been overthrown by the will of the workers and peasants of Russia.

Inspired by this principle, and desiring that the Persian people should be happy independent and should be able to dispose freely of its patrimony, the Russian Republic declares the whole body of treaties and conventions concluded with Persia by the Tsarist Government, which crushed the rights of the Persian people, to be null and void.

Article 2. The R. S. F. S. R. expresses its reprobation of the policy of the Tsarist Governments of Russia, which, on the pretext of ensuring the independence of the peoples of Asia, concluded, without the consent of the latter, treaties with European Powers, the sole object of which was to subjugate those peoples.

This criminal policy, which infringed upon the independence of the countries of Asia and which made the living nations of the East a prey to the cupidity and the tyranny of European robbers, is abandoned unconditionally by Federal Russia.

Federal Russia, therefore, in accordance with the principles laid down in Articles I and 4 of this Treaty, declares its refusal to participate in any action which might destroy or weaken Persian sovereignty. It regards as null and void the whole body of treaties and conventions concluded by the former Russian Government with third parties in respect of Persia or to the detriment of that country.

Article 3. The two Contracting Powers agree to accept and respect the Russo-Persian frontiers, as drawn by the Frontier Commission in 1881.

At the same time, in view of the repugnance which the Russian Federal Government feels to enjoying the fruit of the policy of usurpation of the Tsarist Government, it renounces all claim to the Achouradeh Islands and to the other islands on the Astrabad Littoral, and restores to Persia the village of Firouzeh and the adjacent land ceded to Russia in virtue of the Convention of May 28, 1893.

The Persian Government agrees for its part that the Russian Sarakhs, or " old" Sarakhs, and the land adjacent to the Sarakhs River, shall be retained by Russia.

The two High Contracting Parties shall have equal rights of usage over the Atrak River and the other frontier rivers and waterways. In order finally to solve the question of the waterways and all disputes concerning frontiers or territories, a Commission, composed of Russian and Persian representatives, shall be appointed.

Article 4. In consideration of the fact that each nation has the right to determine freely its political destiny, each of the two Contracting Parties formally expresses its desire to abstain from any intervention in the internal affairs of the other.

Article 5. The two High Contracting Parties undertake:

(I) To prohibit the formation or presence within their respective territories, of any organisations or groups of persons, irrespective of the name by which they are known, whose object is to engage in acts of hostility against Persia or Russia, or against the Allies of Russia.

They will likewise prohibit the formation of troops or armies within their respective territories with the aforementioned object.

(2) Not to allow a third Party or any organisation, whatever it be called, which is hostile to the other Contracting

Party, to import or to convey in transit across their countries material which can be used against the other Party.

(3) To prevent by all means in their power the presence within their territories or within the territories of their Allies of all armies or forces of a third Party in cases in which the presence of such forces would be regarded as a menace to the frontiers, interests or safety of the other Contracting Party.

Article 6. If a third Party should attempt to carry out a policy of usurpation by means of armed intervention in Persia, or if such Power should desire to use Persian territory as a base of operations against Russia, or if a Foreign Power should threaten the frontiers of Federal Russia or those of its Allies, and if the Persian Government should not be able to put a stop to such menace after having been once called upon to do so by Russia, Russia shall have the right to advance her troops into the Persian interior for the purpose of carrying out the military operations necessary for its defence. Russia undertakes, however, to withdraw her troops from Persian territory as soon as the danger has been removed.

Article 7. The considerations set forth in Article 6 have equal weight in the matter of the security of the Caspian Sea. The two High Contracting Parties therefore have agreed that Federal Russia shall have the right to require the Persian Government to send away foreign subjects, in the event of their taking advantage of their engagement in the Persian navy to undertake hostile action against Russia.

Article 8. Federal Russia finally renounces the economic policy pursued in the East by the Tsarist Government, which consisted in lending money to the Person Government, not with a view to the economic development of the country, but rather for purposes of political subjugation.

Federal Russia accordingly renounces its rights in respect of the loans granted to Persia by the Tsarist Governments. It regards the debts due to it as void, and will not require their repayment. Russia likewise renounces its claims to the resources of Persia which were specified as security for the loans in question.

Article 9. In view of the declaration by which it has repudiated the colonial and capitalist policy which occasioned so many misfortunes and was the cause of so much bloodshed, Federal Russia abandons the continuation of the economic undertakings of the Tsarist Government, the object of which was the economic subjugation of Persia. Federal Russia therefore cedes to the Persian Government the full ownership of all funds and of all real and other property, which the Russian Discount Bank possesses on Persian territory, and likewise transfers to it all the assets and liabilities of that Bank. The Persian Government nevertheless agrees that in the towns where it has been decided that the Russian Socialist Republic may establish Consulates, and where buildings exist belonging to the Discount Bank, one of these buildings, to be chosen by the Russian Government, shall be placed at the disposal of the Russian Consulate, free of charge.

Article 10. The Russian Federal Government, having abandoned the colonial policy, which consisted in the construction of roads and telegraph lines more in order to obtain military influence in other countries than for the purpose of developing their civilisations, and being desirous of providing the Persian people with those means of communication indispensable for the independence and development of any nation, and also in order to compensate the Persian people as far as possible for the losses incurred by the sojourn in its territory of the Tsarist armies, cedes free of charge to the Persian Government the following Russian installations:

(a) The high-roads from Enzeli to Teheran, and from Kazvin to Hamadan, and all land and installations in connection with these roads.

(b) The rail-road Djoulfa-Tauris-Sofian Urmiah, with all installations, rolling-stock and accessories.

(c) The landing-stages, warehouses, steamships, canals, and all means of transport of the lake of Urmiah.

(d) All telegraph and telephone lines established in Persia by the Tsarist Governments, with all moveable and immoveable installations and dependencies.

(e) The port of Enzeli and the warehouses, with the electrical installation, and other buildings.

Article 11. In view of the fact that the Treaty of Turkomantchai, concluded on February 10, 1828 (old style), between Persia and Russia, which forbids Persia, under the terms of Article 8, to-have vessels in the waters of the Caspian Sea, is abrogated in accordance with the principles set forth in Article 1 of the present Treaty, the two High Contracting Parties shall enjoy equal rights of free navigation on that Sea, under their own flags, as from the date of the signing of the present Treaty.

Article 12. The Russian Federal Government, having officially renounced all economic interests obtained by military preponderance, further declares that, apart from the concessions which form the subject of Articles 9 and 10, the other concessions obtained by force by the Tsarist Government and its subjects shall also be regarded as null and void.

In conformity with which the Russian Federal Government restores, as from the date of the signing of the present Treaty, to the Persian Government, as representing the Persian people, all the concessions in question, whether already being worked or not, together with all land taken over in virtue of those concessions.

Of the lands and properties situated in Persia and belonging to the former Tsarist Government, only the premises of the Russian Legation at Teheran and at Zerguendeh with all moveable and immoveable appurtenances, as well as all real and other property of the Consulates and Vice-Consulates, shall be retained by Russia. Russia abandons, however, her right to administer the village of Zerguendeh, which was assigned by the ex-Government of the Tsar.

Article 13. The Persian Government, for its part, promises not to cede to a third Power, or to its subjects, the concessions and property restored to Persia by virtue of the present Treaty, and to maintain those rights for the Persian nation.

Article 14. The Persian Government, recognising the importance of the Caspian fisheries for the food supply of Russia, promises to conclude with the Food Service of the Russian Socialist Federal Soviet Republic immediately upon the expiry of the legal period of these existing engagements, a contract relating to the fisheries, containing appropriate clauses. Furthermore, the Persian Government promises to examine, in agreement with the Government of the Russian Socialist Federal Soviet Republic, the means of at once conveying the produce of the fisheries to the Food Service of Soviet Russia pending the conclusion of the above contract.

Article 15. In accordance with the principle of liberty of conscience proclaimed by Soviet Russia, and with a desire to put an end, in Moslem countries, to religious propaganda, the real object of which was to exercise political influence over the masses and thus to satisfy the rapacity of the Tsarist Government, the Government of Soviet Russia declares that the religious settlements established in Persia by the former Tsarist Governments are abolished. Soviet Russia will take steps to prevent such missions from being sent to Persia in the future.

Soviet Russia cedes unconditionally to the nation represented by the Persian Government, the lands, property and buildings belonging to the Orthodox Mission situated at Urmia, together with the other similar establishments. The Persian Government shall use these properties for the construction of schools and other institutions intended for educational purposes.

Article 16. By virtue of the communication from Soviet Russia dated June 25, 1919, with reference to the abolition of consular jurisdictions, it is decided that Russian subjects in Persia and Persian subjects in Russia shall, as from the date of the present Treaty, be placed upon the same footing as the inhabitants of the towns in which they reside; they shall be subject to the laws of their country of residence, and shall submit their complaints to the local courts.

Article 17. Persian subjects in Russia and Russian subjects in Persia shall be exempt from military service and from all military taxation.

Article 18. Persian subjects in Russia and Russian subjects in Persia shall, as regards travel within the respective countries, enjoy the rights granted to the most favoured nations other than countries allied to them.

Article 19. Within a short period after the signature of the Present Treaty, the two High Contracting Parties shall resume commercial relations. The methods to be adopted for the organisation of the import and export of goods, methods of payment, and the customs duties to be levied by the Persian Government on goods originating in Russia, shall be determined, under a commercial convention, by a special commission consisting of representatives of the two High Contracting Parties.

Article 20. Each of the two High Contracting Parties grants to the other the right of transit for the transport of goods passing through Persia or Russia and consigned to a third country.

The dues exacted in such cases shall not be higher than those levied on the goods of the most favoured nations other than countries allied to the Russian Socialist Federal Soviet Republic.

Article 21. The two High Contracting Parties shall open telegraphic and postal relations between Russia and Persia within the shortest possible period after the signature of the present Treaty.

The conditions of these relations shall be fixed by a postal and telegraphic convention.

Article 22. In order to consolidate the good relations between the two neighbouring Powers and to facilitate the realisation of the friendly intentions of each country towards the other, each of the High Contracting Parties shall, immediately after the signature of the present Treaty, be represented in the capital of the other by a Plenipotentiary Representative, who shall enjoy the rights of extra-territoriality and other privileges to which diplomatic representatives are entitled by international law and usage and by the regulations and customs of the two countries.

Article 23. In order to develop their mutual relations, the two High Contracting Parties shall establish Consulates in places to be determined by common agreement.

The rights and duties of the Consuls shall be fixed by a specia greement to be concluded without delay after the signature of the present Treaty. This agreement shall conform to the provisions in force in the two countries with regard to consular establishments.

Article 24. This Treaty shall be ratified within a period of three months. The exchange of ratifications shall take place at Teheran as soon as possible.

Article 25. The present Treaty is drawn up in Russian and Persian. Both texts shall be regarded as originals and both shall be authentic.

Article 26. The present Treaty shall come into force immediately upon signature.

In faith whereof the undersigned have signed the present Treaty and have affixed their seals thereto.

Done at Moscow February 26, 1921.

(Signed) G. TCHITCHERIN.

L. KARAKHAN

MOCHAVEROL-MEMALEK.

ANNEX I.

TEHERAN, December 12, 1921.

SIR,

The Persian Government and the Mejlis have observed that Articles 5 and 6 of the Treaty concluded between our two countries are worded vaguely; the Mejlis moreover, desires that the retrocession of Russian concessions to the Persian Government should be made without reserve or condition, and, that Article 20 should be so worded as to allow the Persian Government full powers for the transit of imports and exports. Conversations have taken place with you on these questions, and you have given explanations with regard to Articles 5 and 6 and promises concerning Articles 13 and 20, to the effect that if the Treaty were passed by the Mejlis you would give all the assistance in your power to ensure that the two Articles in question should be revised on the lines desired by the Mejlis and the Persian Government. The Persian Government and the Mejlis are most desirous that friendly relations should be re-established between our two Governments, and that the Treaty, which is based upon the most amicable sentiments, should be concluded as soon as possible.

I have, therefore, the honour to request you to give in writing your explanations with regard to the interpretation of Articles 5 and 6, and to repeat the promises of support which you have already given as regards the revision of Articles 13 and 20, in order that the Persian Government may be enabled to secure the passing of the Treaty by the Mejlis.

I also wish to ask you to take the necessary steps to repair the error which has been made in Article 3, in which the word "commission" was written instead of "treaty", as the only treaty which was concluded in 1881 was a frontier delimitation treaty, and this is the treaty referred to in Article 3.

I have the honour to be, Sir, etc.

(Signed) MOCHAROS-SALTANEH.

ANNEX II.

TEHERAN, December 12, 1921.
YOUR EXCELLENCY,

In reply to your letter dated 20th day of Ghows, I have the honour to inform you that Articles 5 and 6 are intended to apply only to cases in which preparations have been made for a considerable armed attack upon Russia or the Soviet Republics allied to her, by the partisans of the regime which has been overthrown or by its supporters among those foreign Powers which are in a position to assist the enemies of the Workers' and Peasants' Republics and at the same time to possess themselves, by force or by underhand methods, of part of the Persian territory, thereby establishing a base of operations for any attacks—made either directly or through the counter-revolutionary forces—which they might meditate against Russia or the Soviet Republics allied to her. The Articles referred to are therefore in no sense intended to apply to verbal or written attacks directed against the Soviet Government by the various Persian groups, or even by any Russian émigrés in Persia, in so far as such attacks are generally tolerated as between neighbouring Powers animated by sentiments of mutual friendship.

With regard to Articles 13 and 20, and the small error to which you draw attention in Article 3 with reference to the Convention of 1881, I am in a position to state categorically, as I have always stated, that my Government, whose attitude towards the Persian nation is entirely friendly, has never sought to place any restriction upon the progress and prosperity f Persia. I myself fully share this attitude, and would be prepared,

should friendly relations be maintained between the two countries, to promote negotiations with a view to a total or partial revision of these Articles on the lines desired by the Persian Government, as far as the interests of Russia permit.

In view of the preceding statements, I trust that, as you promised me in your letter, your Government and the Mejlis will ratify the Treaty in question as soon as possible.

I have the honour to be, Your Excellency, etc.

(Signed) ROTSTEIN,
Diplomatic Representative of the Russian Socialist Federal Soviet Republic.

4.1232 Treaty of Alliance between Turkey and Afghanistan

Alliance Members: Turkey and Afghanistan
Signed On: March 1, 1921, in the city of Moscow. In force until December 31, 1947, as Afghan relations with the Soviet Union strengthened while Turkey grew closer to the United States.
Alliance Type: Defense Pact (Type I)

Source: *British Foreign and State Papers,* vol. 118, p. 10.

SUMMARY

The rationale behind this friendship treaty establishing relations between Afghanistan and Turkey was essentially twofold. Distrustful of continued British influence in both countries and in Asia more generally, the two countries affirmed their independence and pledged mutual support against an attack by any "imperialistic state." The treaty was signed in Moscow.

ALLIANCE TEXT

In the name of God, the Merciful, the Compassionate!

The Turkish and Afghan Governments, convinced that they are bound together by sincere ties of sympathy, are imbued with one desire and one sacred purpose, and each possess the same high moral and material interests, and that the happiness or misfortune of one State will redound to the happiness or misfortune of the other, and recognising that it is no longer possible that they should remain disconnected and isolated as in the past, and that certain historical duties necessarily devolve upon them at this moment, when is seen with infinite thankfulness that an era of awakening and deliverance of the Eastern world has begun;

These two brother States and nations, therefore, observing that as with the members of one body the troubles and afflictions of one of the parties must affect and pain the other, have resolved to transfer their age-long moral unity and natural alliance to the political sphere, to bring about a state of material and official alliance, and, in the name of the future welfare of the whole East, to conclude a Treaty of Alliance as a prelude to future welfare.

For this purpose Delegates have been nominated—

Youssouf Kemal Bey, Commissioner (Minister) of Economic Affairs; and

Dr. Reza Nour. Bey, Commissaire of Public Instruction, Members of the Government, on behalf of the Government of the Grand National Assembly of Turkey; and

His Highness General Muhammad Wali Khan, Ambassador Extraordinary, on behalf of Afghanistan;

Who, having communicated their full powers, found to be in due and proper order, have accepted the following Articles:—

Art. I. The Turkish nation, in possession of an independent existence for such time as God wills, considers it to be a sacred duty to recognise the independence, in the full significance of the term, of the Afghan nation, to which she is bound with ties of the utmost sincerity and conscientiousness.

II. The two High Contracting Parties recognise that all Eastern nations possess complete liberty and right of independence, and that each of these nations is free to administer itself by such form of administration as it may particularly desire, and they recognise the independence of the States of Bokhara and Khiva.

III. Turkey having for centuries given guidance to and rendered distinguished services to Islam, and holding in her hand the standard of the Caliphate, Afghanistan in this connection recognises the leadership of Turkey.

IV. Each of the High Contracting Parties will consider as directed against herself personally, and will oppose with all the means at her disposal, any attack made against the other by any Imperialistic State in pursuance of the policy of invasion and exploitation of the East.

V. Each of the Contracting Parties undertakes not to conclude any Treaty or Convention injurious to the interests of the other party or which would be in the interests of a third State with which the other is not on friendly terms, and to give prior notice to the other of the forthcoming conclusion of an Agreement with any nation whatsoever.

VI. With a view to the regularisation of commercial and economic relations and Consular affairs, the two Contracting Parties will conclude the necessary Conventions separately, and Ambassadors will from henceforth be sent by each to the capital of the other.

VII. Turkey agrees to help Afghanistan militarily and to send instructors and officers. These missions of teachers and officers will serve for a minimum period of five years, and on the expiration of that period, if Afghanistan so desires, a new mission of instructors will be sent. . . .

IX. This Treaty will be ratified with the least possible delay, and its clauses will be in force from that time.

X. This Treaty has been drawn up at Moscow in duplicate signed and exchanged by the Delegates of the two parties.

This Treaty has been signed on Tuesday, the 1st day of March, 1337 (1921), corresponding with the 21st day of Djumadi-ul-Akhir in the 1339th year of the Hijra.

YOUSSOUF KEMAL.
Dr. REXA NOUR.

MUHAMMAD WALI,
Ambassador Extraordinary.

4.1233 Convention for a Defensive Alliance between the Polish Republic and the Kingdom of Romania

Alliance Members: Poland and Romania
Signed On: March 3, 1921, in the city of Bucharest (Romania). In force until September 27, 1939, upon the dissolution of Poland following the German and Russian invasions.
Alliance Type: Defense Pact (Type I)

Source: *League of Nations Treaty Series,* no. 175, vol. 7, p. 79.

SUMMARY

Romania emerged from World War I as a new state with double the territory it had as part of the Ottoman Empire. Poland's borders were redrawn following the war, and both states searched for security against the potential threat of German expansion. This defensive alliance, then, provided one opportunity to guarantee a defense of the then territorial status quo for both parties.

The terms of the agreement specify that in the event of any aggression Poland and Romania would provide mutual assistance to the state attacked, including a declaration of war against the attacking state. Consultations and coordination through the alliance, as well as assurances against coordination with parties outside the alliance, acted as a consistent effort to counter any threats to the two territories.

The agreement lasted until Romania withheld military assistance to Poland during the German invasion that began World War II; the Nazi-Soviet occupation crushed Poland and ended this alliance by late September 1939.

ALLIANCE TEXT

Being firmly resolved to safeguard a peace which was gained at the price of so many sacrifices,

the Chief of the State of the Polish Republic and His Majesty the King of Roumania have agreed to conclude a Convention for a defensive alliance.

For this purpose they have named as their plenipotentiaries:

For the Chief of the State of the Polish Republic: Prince Eustache Sapieha, His Minister for Foreign Affairs; and

For His Majesty the King of Roumania: M. Take Jonesco, His Minister for Foreign Affairs,

Who, after exchanging their full powers, found in good and due form, agreed to the following articles:

Article 1. Poland and Roumania undertake to assist each other in the event of their being the object of an unprovoked attack on their present eastern frontiers.

Accordingly, if either State is the object of an unprovoked attack, the other shall consider itself in a state of war and shall render armed assistance.

Article 2. In order to co-ordinate their efforts to maintain peace, both Governments undertake to consult together on such questions of foreign policy as concern their relations with their eastern neighbours.

Article 3. A military Convention shall determine the manner in which either country shall render assistance to the other should the occasion arise.

This Convention shall be subject to the same conditions as the present Convention as regards duration and denunciation.

Article 4. If in spite of their efforts to maintain peace, the two States are compelled to enter on a defensive war under the terms of Article 1, each undertakes not to negotiate nor to conclude an armistice or a peace without the participation of the other State.

Article 5. The duration of the present Convention shall be five years from the date of its signature, but either Government shall be at liberty to denounce it after two years on giving the other State six months, notice.

Article 6. Neither of the High Contracting Parties shall be at liberty to conclude an alliance with a third Power without having previously obtained the assent of the other Party.

Alliances with a view to the maintenance of treaties already signed jointly by both Poland and Roumania are excepted from this provision.

Such alliances must, however, be notified.

The Polish Government hereby declares that it is acquainted with the agreements entered into by Roumania with other States with a view to upholding the Treaties of Trianon and Neuilly, which agreements may be transformed into treaties of alliance.

The Roumanian Government hereby declares that it is acquainted with the agreements entered into by Poland with the French Republic.

Article 7. The present Convention shall be communicated to the League of Nations in accordance with Treaty of Versailles.

Article 8. The present Convention shall be ratified and the ratifications exchanged at Bucarest as soon as possible.

In witness whereof the Plenipotentiaries have signed the present Convention and have thereto set their seal.

Done at Bucarest in duplicate this third day of March 1921.

(L.S.) *Take JONESCO.*
(L.S.) *E. SAPIEHA.*

4.1234 Convention of Alliance between the Kingdom of Romania and the Czechoslovak Republic

Alliance Members: Romania and Czechoslovakia
Signed On: April 23, 1921, in the city of Bucharest (Romania). In force until June 27, 1930, when the alliance ended with the signing of the Little Entente.
Alliance Type: Defense Pact (Type I)

Source: *League of Nations Treaty Series,* vol. 6, p. 217.

SUMMARY

This alliance was based on the three treaties that formed the Little Entente. The Little Entente comprised the treaties between Czechoslovakia and Yugoslavia (August 1920), Romania and Czechoslovakia (April 1921), and Romania and Yugoslavia (June 1921), and each of these bilateral agreements fostered both defensive and economic cooperation among the central European countries. The objective of this alliance between Romania and the Czechoslovak Republic was to contain possible Hungarian revisionism and the emerging Soviet threat in the region. Caught literally between two emerging powers, the smaller states had little choice but to coordinate and ally against the external threats.

In case of attack by Hungary, both states pledged defensive aid to the other. Neither party would sign an alliance with another state unless the third party was also a member of the Triple Entente, and the governments of both Romania and the Czechoslovak Republic would coordinate their foreign policies toward Hungary.

This alliance became part of the three-party defensive alliance of the Little Entente in June of 1930. Eventually, the agreements of the Little Entente succumbed to a third threat—the enormous economic and political pressure of Hitler's Germany.

ALLIANCE TEXT

Firmly resolved to maintain the peace obtained by so many sacrifices, and provided for by the Covenant of the League of Nations, as well as the situation created by the Treaty concluded at Trianon on June 4, 1920, between the Allied and Associated Powers on the one hand, and Hungary on the other,

the President of the Czechoslovak Republic and His Majesty the King of Roumania, have agreed to conclude a defensive Convention.

For this purpose they have nominated as their Plenipotentiary Delegates:

For the President of the Czechoslovak Republic: M. Ferdinand Veverka, Envoy Extraordinary and Minister Plenipotentiary of the CzechoSlovak Republic at Bucarest;

For His Majesty the King of Roumania: M.Take Jonesco, His State Minister for Foreign Affairs;

Who, having exchanged their full powers and found them to be in good and due form, have agreed as follows:

Article 1. In case of an unprovoked attack on the part of Hungary against one of the High Contracting Parties, the other party agrees to assist in the defence of the party attacked, in the manner laid down by the arrangement provided for in Article 2 of the present Convention.

Article 2. The competent Technical Authorities of the Czechoslovak Republic and Roumania shall decide by mutual agreement and in a Military Convention to be concluded, upon the provisions necessary for the execution of the present Convention.

Article 3. Neither of the High Contracting Parties shall conclude an alliance with a third Power without preliminary notice to the other.

Article 4. For the purpose of coordinating their efforts to maintain peace, the two Governments undertake to consult together on questions of foreign policy concerning their relations with Hungary.

Article 5. The present Convention shall be valid for two years from the date of the exchange of ratifications the expiration of this period, each of the Contracting Parties shall have the option of denouncing the present Convention. It shall, however, remain in force for six months after the date of denunciation.

Article 6. The present Convention shall be communicated to the League of Nations (Covenant of the League of Nations).

Article 7. The present Convention shall be ratified, and the ratifications shall be exchanged at Bucarest as soon as possible.

In witness whereof, the Plenipotentiaries named have signed the present Convention and have affixed their seals thereto.

Done at Bucarest in duplicate, April 23, 1921.

(L. S.) (Signed) Dr. Ferdinand VEVERKA.

(L. S.) (Signed) Take JONESCO.

4.1235 Convention of Defensive Alliance between Romania and the Kingdom of the Serbs, Croats, and Slovenes

Alliance Members: Yugoslavia and Romania
Signed On: June 7, 1921, in the city of Belgrade (Serbia). In force until August 30, 1940.
Alliance Type: Defense Pact (Type I)

Source: *League of Nations Treaty Series,* vol. 54, p. 259–265.

SUMMARY

This treaty had terms almost identical with the other alliances comprising the Little Entente, including common defense against an attack by Hungary and mutual cooperation in foreign policy. The Little Entente was effective at stopping the restoration of the Hapsburgs in Hungary. When Karl I of Austria returned from Switzerland to assume the monarchy in October of 1921, the states of the Little Entente mobilized and threatened military action. The Hungarians relented and arrested Karl I. The combination of several alliances encouraged cooperation among the Balkan states, and the various treaties were consolidated and, by 1933, reorganized into a general framework for cooperation. The alliance lasted until the early years of World War II, when Romania was forced to cede territory to Hungary.

ALLIANCE TEXT

Firmly resolved to maintain the peace obtained by so many sacrifices and the situation created by the Treaty concluded at Trianon on June 4, 1920, between the Allied and Associated Powers, on the one part, and Hungary, of the other part, and by the Treaty of Neuilly-sur-Seine, concluded on November 27, 1919, between the Allied and Associated Powers, of the one part, and Bulgaria, of the other part, His Majesty the King of Roumania and His Majesty the King of the Serbs, Croats and Slovenes have agreed to conclude a Defensive Convention:

For this purpose they have nominated as their plenipotentiary Delegates:

His Majesty the King of Roumania: M. Take Jonesco, His Minister for Foreign Affairs;

His Majesty the King of the Serbs, Croats and Slovenes:M. Nikolas Pachitch, President of His Council of Ministers, His Minister for Affairs;

Who, having communicated their full powers, found in good and due form, have agreed as follows:

Article 1. In case of an unprovoked attack on the part of Hungary or of Bulgaria or of both these Powers against one of the High Contracting Parties with the object of subverting the situation created by the Treaty of Peace concluded at Trianon, or by that concluded at Neuilly-sur-Seine, the other Party agrees to assist in the defense of the Party attacked in the manner laid down by the arrangement provided for in Article 2 of the present Convention.

Article 2. The competent technical authorities of Roumania and of the Kingdom of the Serbs, Croats and Slovenes shall by mutual agreement determine in a military Convention to be concluded as soon as possible, the provisions necessary for the execution of the present Convention.

Article 3. Neither of the High Contracting Parties shall conclude an alliance with a third Power without giving notice to the other.

Article 4. For the purpose of co-ordinating their efforts to maintain peace, the two Governments undertake to consult together on questions of foreign policy concerning their relations with Hungary and Bulgaria.

Article 5. The present Convention shall be valid for two years from the date of the exchange of ratifications. On the expiration of this period each of the Contracting Parties shall have the right to denounce the present Constitution. It shall, however, remain in force for six months after the date of denunciation.

Article 6. The present Convention shall be communicated to the League of Nations (Covenant of the League of Nations).

Article 7. The present Convention shall be ratified and the ratifications shall be exchanged as soon as possible.

In faith whereof the Plenipotentiaries named have signed the present Convention and have affixed their seals thereto.

Done at Belgrade, in duplicate, June 7, 1921.

(L.S.) (Signed) Take Jonesco.

(L.S.) (Signed) Nik. P. Pachitch.

4.1236 Treaty of Friendship and Security between Persia and Afghanistan

Alliance Members: Persia (Iran) and Afghanistan
Signed On: June 22, 1921, in the city of Kabul (Afghanistan). In force until July 8, 1937.
Alliance Type: Neutrality Pact (Type II)

Source: *League of Nations Treaty Series,* no. 853.

SUMMARY

This neutrality pact established formal relations between the two neighboring countries after Afghanistan's independence from British rule. The two countries agreed not to harbor insurgencies that would target the other government, pledged neutrality in the event of conflict, and vowed not to enter into alliances against the other state. Additional protocols signed the same day established a commission for resolving disputes and began the process toward greater collaboration on trade.

The alliance ended in 1937 when a regional neutrality pact was signed that also included Turkey and Iraq.

ALLIANCE TEXT

In the name of God, Clement, and All-Merciful;
There is no God but God, and Mohammad is the Prophet of God.
Seek all of ye your refuge in the bosom of God and do not go astray (*Koran*).

His Imperial Majesty the Shah of Persia and His Majesty the Emir of Afghanistan, being equally of opinion that the relations of Persia and Afghanistan, which spring from unity of religion and race, as well as from ties of neighbourliness, require consolidation by means of a Treaty, have appointed for this purpose as their Plenipotentiaries:

His Majesty the Shah of Persia: His Excellency Hadji Mirza Hassan Khan Mohtachem-Os-Saltaneh, His Minister for Foreign Affairs;

His Majesty the Emir of Afghanistan: His Excellency Sirdar Abdul Aziz Khan, His Envoy Extraordinary and Minister Plenipotentiary at Teheran.

The two Plenipotentiaries, having exchanged their full powers, have agreed on the following articles:

Article I. From this day forward, sincere friendship and a permanent and cordial understanding shall be established between Persia and Afghanistan and their respective nationals.

Article II. The Ambassadors, Ministers Plenipotentiary and Chargés d'Affaires of each of the High Contracting Parties at the Court of the other, shall enjoy all the rights and privileges established by international custom and usage.

Article III. The subjects of each of the High Contracting Parties, whether travelling or residing in the territory of the other, shall be respected by the authorities of that country and fully protected by the representatives of their own country.

Article IV. The subjects of one of the two High Contracting Parties shall, while in the territory of the other, either as travellers or as residents, be subject to the local jurisdiction of the latter country. Thus, all legal proceedings, law suits and disputes, as well as all penal or criminal proceedings which may be instituted against them, shall be heard in Persia before the Persian tribunals and in Afghanistan before the Afghan tribunals. In connection with the foregoing it shall be clearly understood that the diplomatic and consular officials of one of the two High Contracting Parties in the territory of the other shall in no case intervene in the legal actions of their nationals, whether they be civil or commercial suits or penal proceedings. The local tribunals of the country of residence or passage are alone competent finally to deal with such litigation.

Article V. The two High Contracting Parties reserve to themselves the power to appoint Consuls-General, Consuls, Vice-Consuls and Consular Agents to reside in the principal towns and commercial centres of the two countries.

The Consuls-General, Consuls, Vice-Consuls and Consular agents shall, before entering upon their duties, obtain, in the usual manner, the exequatur of the Government of the country in which those duties are to be performed.

Article VI. The nationals of one of the High Contracting Parties in the territory of the other shall be exempt from military service and from all obligations which are strictly personal to the nationals of that country.

Article VII. In case where a subject of one of the High Contracting Parties, after having committed a grave offence in his own country, takes refuge in the territory of the other, the representatives of the former are entitled to demand extradition through the diplomatic channel.

The Government of the latter country shall do all in its power to facilitate the extradition, but it is to be clearly understood that persons guilty of political offences may not be extradited.

Article VIII. In order to consolidate their relations of friendship and commerce, the two High Contracting Parties shall, with the least possible delay, draw up treaties and agreements respecting their commercial, Customs, postal and telegraphic relations; the said treaties and agreements shall, after signature and ratification, be put into execution.

Article IX. The relations of cordial understanding between Persia and Afghanistan shall not be affected in the event of one of the High Contracting Parties becoming involved in a war with a third Power. But in this case the other Party shall undertake, in accordance with the rules of neutrality, not to favour this third Power in any respect.

Article X. In order to emphasise the sincere friendship and mutual confidence existing between the Empire of Persia and the Kingdom of Afghanistan, the two Contracting Parties have decided, in conformity with international usage, to submit to arbitration all the difficulties arising between the two countries of which a solution cannot be arrived at by diplomatic negotiations.

Further, the High Contracting Parties undertake loyally to carry out the decisions of the arbitrators.

Article XI. The present Treaty shall be drawn up in duplicate in Persian.

Article XII. The Plenipotentiaries of the two High Contracting Parties undertake to exchange the ratifications of the present Treaty at Teheran or Kabul within three months from this date, or sooner if possible.

In faith whereof the Plenipotentiaries of the two High Contracting Parties have signed the present Treaty and have thereto affixed their seals.

Teheran, the 15 Chaval-ol-Moharram 1339 (1st Saratan 1330).

The Minister for Foreign Affairs,
(Signed) HASSAN MOHTACHEM-OS-SALTANEH.

(Signed) ABDUL AZIZ,
Minister of Afghanistan.

ADDITIONAL ARTICLES.

Article I. The stipulations of Article III, to the effect that, "the subjects of each of the High Contracting Parties, whether travelling or residing in the territory of the other, shall be respected by the authorities of that country and fully protected by the representatives of their own country", shall be understood to mean that the representatives of one of the two High Contracting Parties shall have the right, within the limits of the laws in force in the country of residence and on application to the local authorities, to obtain for their nationals certain facilities.

Article II. The tribes and nomads, such as Berberi and others, who emigrated in former times from Afghanistan to Persia, shall remain, as formerly, Persian subjects. The Berberi visiting Afghanistan shall not be permitted to enter Afghan territory without first obtaining a visa for their passports from the diplomatic and consular authorities of Afghanistan in Persia. The nomads living on the frontiers of the two countries who pass the winter in the territory of one of the two High Contracting Parties and the summer in that of the other, shall be considered as Persians during their sojourn in Persia and as Afghans during their sojourn in Afghanistan.

Persons who, before the establishment of the Afghan Legation at Teheran, emigrated from Afghanistan and established themselves in Persia, shall, as formerly, be considered Persian subjects.

Only merchants who have proceeded to Persia from Afghanistan in the course of their business and are in temporary residence shall be considered as Afghan subjects, on condition that documentary proof is forthcoming that the Persian authorities have not heretofore treated them as Persian subjects.

The 25 Djamad-el-Awal 1340 (14 Dalw 1300).

The Persian Minister for Foreign Affairs,
ASSADOLLAH MOCHAR-OS-SALTANEH

ABDUL-AZIZ, Khan,
The Afghan Minister at Teheran.

NASROLLAH EETELA-OL-MOLK.
The Persian Minister at Kabul.

MOHAMMAD WALI,
The Afghan Minister for Foreign Affairs.

Article III. It is likewise agreed that the nomad tribes who have emigrated from Persia to Afghanistan shall remain as formerly under Afghan sovereignty and shall have no right to enter Persian territory without first obtaining a visa from the Persian diplomatic or consular authorities, as laid down *mutatis nutandis* in additional Article II of the present Treaty, and as a measure of reciprocity for the treatment accorded to the nomads and tribes who, in former times, emigrated from Afghanistan to Persia. Persons who, before the establishment of the Persian Legation at Kabul, emigrated from Persia to Afghanistan shall, as formerly, be considered as Afghan subjects.

Only merchants who have proceeded to Afghanistan from Persia in the course of their business and are in temporary residence shall be considered as Persian subjects, on condition that documentary proof is forthcoming that the Afghan authorities have not, heretofore, treated them as Afghan subjects.

Djamad-el-Sani 1341 (Dalw 1301).

(Signed) MOHAMMAD WALI,
Afghan Minister for Foreign Affairs.

(Signed) ABDUL AZIZ, Khan,
Afghan Minister at Teheran.

(Signed) NASSROLLAH EETELA-OL-MOLK
Persian Minister at Kabul.

In the name of God, to Whom be given glory, We, creature and soldier of the Holy Cause of God, Ameer Amanollah, King of Afghanistan, ratify the present Treaty of friendship, consisting of 12 articles and 3 additional articles, which has been concluded by the official Representatives of the two High Powers on behalf and on that of His Majesty, Sultan Ahmed Shah Kadjar, Shahinshah of all Persia, at different dates, and We undertake to put it into execution in its entirety.

15 Sombeleh 1302 (25 Moharam 1342).

(Signed) AMIR AMANOLLAH KHAN.

4.1237 Treaty among the United States of America, the British Empire, France, and Japan

Alliance Members: United States, Great Britain, France, and Japan
Signed On: December 13, 1921, in the city of Washington, D.C. In force until September 18, 1931, when Japan unilaterally occupied Manchuria.
Alliance Type: Entente (Type III)

Source: *League of Nations Treaty Series,* vol. 25, p. 185.

SUMMARY

This entente was designed to provide a framework agreement for negotiations over possible disagreements in the Pacific. The bulk of the treaty establishes sovereign respect for the insular possessions and dominions of all states in the Pacific. Importantly, disagreements not settled by diplomacy were to be handled by a joint conference for reconciliation and adjudication. The terms that make this treaty an alliance are the commitments regarding actions following any regional threat to member states. In case of threat, the entente establishes that clear communication would facilitate a full understanding among alliance members, whether that understanding was arrived at jointly or separately. The key provision of the alliance declared the sovereignty and neutrality of China for all member states.

The arrangement lasted ten years and ended when Japan violated the neutrality of China in the summer of 1931. Japan, in the midst of an economic depression, turned to Manchuria as an attempt to spur growth and secure important natural resources for the Japanese economy. Despite repeated calls for intervention against Japan's unilateral actions, the invasion of Manchuria and subsequent creation of Manchuko were left condemned but unchecked by the League of Nations.

ALLIANCE TEXT

The United States of America, the British Empire, France and Japan,

With a view to the preservation of the general peace and the maintenance of their rights in relation to their insular possessions and insular dominions in the region of the Pacific Ocean,

Have determined to conclude a Treaty to this effect and have appointed as their Plenipotentiaries:

The President of the United States of America: Charles Evans Hughes, Henry Cabot Lodge, Oscar W. Underwood and Elihu Root, citizens of the United States;

His Majesty the King of the United Kingdom of Great Britain and Ireland and of the British Dominions beyond the Seas, Emperor of India: The Right Honourable Arthur James Balfour, O.M., M.P., Lord President of His Privy Council; The Right Honourable Baron Lee of Fareham, G.B.E., K.C.B., First Lord of His Admiralty; The Right Honourable Sir Auckland Campbell Geddes, K. (I.B. His Ambassador Extraordinary and Plenipotentiary to the United States of America;

And for the Dominion of Canada: The Right Honourable Robert Laird Borden, G.C.M.G., K.C.;

for the Commonwealth of Australia: The Honourable George Foster Pearce, Minister of Defence;

for the Dominion of New Zealand: Sir John William Salmond, K.C., Judge of the Supreme Court of New Zealand;

for the Union of South Africa: The Right Honourable Arthur James Balfour, O.M., M.P.;

for India: The Right Honourable Valingman Sankaranarayana Srinivasa Sastri, Member of the Indian Council of State;

The President of the French Republic: Mr. Rene Viviani, Deputy, Former President of the Council of Ministers; Mr. Albert Sarraut, Deputy, Minister of the Colonies; Mr. Jules J. Jusserand, Ambassador Extraordinary and Plenipotentiary to the United States of America, Grand Cross of the National Order of the Legion of Honour;

His Majesty the Emperor of Japan: Baron Tomosaburo Kato, Minister for the Navy, Junii, a member of the First Class of the Imperial Order of the Grand Cordon of the Rising Sun with the Paulownia Flower; Baron Kijuro Shidehara, His Ambassador Extraordinary and Plenipotentiary at Washington, Joshii, a member of the First Class of the Imperial Order of the Rising Sun; Prince Iyesato Tokugawa, Junii, a member of the First Class of the Imperial Order of the Rising Sun; Mr. Masanao Hanihara, Vice-Minister for Foreign Affairs, Jushii, a member of the Second Class of the Imperial Order of the Rising Sun;

Who, having communicated their Full Powers, found in good and due form, have agreed as follows:

I. The High Contracting Parties agree as between themselves to respect their rights in relation to their insular possessions and insular dominions in the region of the Pacific Ocean.

If there should develop between any of the High Contracting Parties a controversy arising out of any Pacific question and involving their said rights which is not satisfactorily settled by diplomacy and is likely to affect the harmonious accord now happily subsisting between them, they shall invite the other High Contracting Parties to a joint conference to which the whole subject will be referred for consideration and adjustment.

II. If the said rights are threatened by the aggressive action of any other Power, the High Contracting Parties shall communicate with one another fully and frankly in order to arrive at an understanding as to the most efficient measures to be taken, jointly or separately, to meet the exigencies of the particular situation.

III. This Treaty shall remain in force for ten years from the time it shall take effect, and after the expiration of said period it shall continue to be in force subject to the right of any of the High Contracting Parties to terminate it upon twelve months' notice.

IV. This Treaty shall be ratified as soon as possible in accordance with the constitutional methods of the High Contracting Parties and shall take effect on the deposit of ratifications, which shall take place at Washington, and thereupon the agreement between Great Britain and Japan, which was concluded at London on July 13, 1911, shall terminate. The Government of the United States will transmit to all the Signatory Powers a certified copy of the procès-verbal of the deposit of ratifications.

The present Treaty, in French and in English, shall remain deposited in the Archives of the Government of the United States, and duly certified copies thereof will be transmitted by that Government to each of the Signatory Powers.

In Faith Whereof the above named Plenipotentiaries have signed the present Treaty.

Done at the City of Washington, the thirteenth day of December, One Thousand Nine Hundred and Twenty-One.

CHARLES EVANS HUGHES
HENRY CABOT LODGE
OSCAR W. UNDERWOOD
ELIHU ROOT

ARTHUR JAMES BALFOUR

LEE OF FAREHAM

A. C. GEDDES

R. L. BORDEN

G. F. PEARCE

JOHN W. SALMOND

V. S. SRINIVASA SASTRI

RENE VIVIANI

A. SARRAUT

JUSSERAND

T. NATO

E. SHIDEHARA

TOKUGAEA IYESATO

M. HANIHARA

4.1238 Political Agreement between Austria and Czechoslovakia

Alliance Members: Austria and Czechoslovakia
Signed On: December 16, 1921, in the city of Prague (Czech Republic). In force until March 15, 1927, when the treaty was not renewed.
Alliance Type: Neutrality Pact (Type II)

Source: *League of Nations Treaty Series,* vol. 9, p. 249.

SUMMARY

Czechoslovakia, formed from the remnants of Austria-Hungary in 1918, affirmed friendly political relations and economic cooperation between the two countries. Austria had just won a plebiscite that wrested control of the Burgenland from Hungarian irregulars. For its part, Edvard Benes's Czech foreign ministry had allied itself with Yugoslavia and Romania in the Little Entente in the hope of allaying any threats should the Hapsburg dynasty be renewed in Hungary. Both countries pledged adherence to the peace treaties ending World War I and acknowledged the existing international border.

ALLIANCE TEXT

The Government of the Czechoslovak Republic on the one part and the Government of the Federal Republic of Austria on the other part, with a view to maintaining peace in Europe and to regulating their mutual political and economic relations, have arranged to conclude a political Agreement and have for this purpose appointed as their Plenipotentiaries:

The President of the Czechoslovak Republic: M. Edouard Benes, the President of the Council and Minister for Foreign Affairs;

The Federal President of the Republic of Austria: M. Jean Schober, Federal Chancellor and Director of the Federal Ministry for Foreign Affairs. who, having exchanged their full powers found in good and due form, have agreed upon the following provisions:

Article 1. Both States undertake to carry out in full all the provisions of the Treaty of Peace concluded with Austria at St.

Germain-en-Laye on September 10, 1919, and the Treaty of Peace concluded with Hungary at Trianon on June 4, 1920.

Article 2. The two States mutually guarantee their territories as fixed by the Treaties of Peace referred to in Article 1; and, with a view to maintaining peace and safeguarding the integrity of these territories, they undertake to afford each other mutual political and diplomatic support.

Article 3. Each State undertakes to remain neutral should the other be compelled to defend itself against attack.

Article 4. Both States undertake not to tolerate on their territories any political or military organisation directed against the integrity and security of the other contracting party. They agree to work together and afford each other mutual aid against any plans or attempts to restore the former regime, either as regards foreign and domestic policy, or in respect of the form of the State and of Government. The competent authorities of both States shall afford each other mutual assistance effectively combating secret intrigues having this object.

Article 5. The Czechoslovak Republic will communicate to the Federal Republic of Austria certain political and economic conventions which the Czechoslovak Republic has concluded with the Kingdom of the Serbs, Croats and Slovenes, the Kingdom of Roumania and the Republic of Poland. Similar conventions concluded by the Federal Republic of Austria shall be communicated to the Czechoslovak Republic.

Article 6. Both States undertake to enforce the observance of agreements concluded or to be concluded for the settlement of economic and financial questions, or of questions relating to minorities, and to arrive at an understanding as soon as possible with regard to any disputes which may not yet have been settled.

Article 7. Should disputes arise between the two States after the conclusion of the present agreement, the two Governments undertake to endeavour to settle them by amicable arrangement; they will if need be submit the dispute to the Permanent Court of International Justice or to an arbitrator or arbitrators chosen ad hoc.

Article 8. Each State undertakes not to conclude with any other State any agreement which would conflict with the Agreement now entered into by the two contracting parties. They further declare that the present Agreement is not in conflict with agreements previously concluded.

Article 9. The present Agreement is concluded for a period of five years dating from the day on which the instruments of ratification are exchanged; after a period of three years dating from the said date, each of the contracting parties is free to denounce the present Agreement, six months' notice being given.

Article 10. The present Agreement shall be ratified and the instruments of ratification shall be exchanged at Prague as soon as possible.

Article 11. The present Agreement shall be communicated to the League of Nations.

In witness whereof the two Plenipotentiaries have signed the present Agreement and affixed their seals thereto.

Done in duplicate at Prague on December 16, 1921.

(L. S.) Dr. EDOUARD BENES

(L. S.) SCHOBER.

4.1239 Defense Pact between Estonia and Latvia

Alliance Members: Estonia and Latvia
Signed On: November 1, 1923, in the city of Tallinn (Estonia). In force until June 15, 1940, when both allies lost their independence following the Soviet invasion.
Alliance Type: Defense Pact (Type I)

Source: *League of Nations Treaty Series*, vol. 23, p. 83.

SUMMARY

Soon after the conclusion of World War I, the newly independent countries that were once part of the Russian Empire (Poland, Finland, Estonia, Latvia, and Lithuania) began negotiations for a broad alliance to counter any possible Soviet influence. The plans collapsed, but Estonia and Latvia formed this alliance, which later (in 1934) proved to be the basis for a Baltic pact that also included Lithuania. In the alliance between Estonia and Latvia, both countries pledged economic and political cooperation in addition to the terms specifying mutual defense in case of attack.

ALLIANCE TEXT

The Republic of Esthonia and the Republic of Latvia, being firmly resolved to maintain the national sovereignty and independence which they have gained at the cost of heavy sacrifices, and to preserve their territorial integrity, have decided to conclude a treaty of defensive alliance.

For this purpose they have appointed as their plenipotentiaries:

Esthonia: M. Fr. Axel, Minister for Foreign Affairs;

Latvia: M. Z. A. Meierovics, Prime Minister and Minister for Foreign Affairs.

Who, having communicated their full powers, found in good and due form, have agreed upon the following provisions:

Article 1. The High Contracting Parties undertake to follow a wholly pacific policy, directed towards maintaining and strengthening the bonds of friendship and developing their economic relations with all nations, more especially with the Baltic States and neighbouring countries.

Article 2. The two Governments undertake to co-ordinate their efforts for peace by consulting each other on such questions of foreign policy as are important to both, and by affording each other political and diplomatic assistance in their international relations.

Article 3. The High Contracting Parties undertake to afford each other assistance should either of them suffer an unprovoked attack on its present frontiers.

Accordingly, should one of the High Contracting Parties suffer an unprovoked attack, the other shall consider itself in a state of war and shall furnish armed assistance.

Article 4. The competent technical authorities of the Esthonian Republic and of the Latvian Republic shall determine by common agreement the manner in which the two countries will assist each other, and shall establish the necessary provisions for the execution of Article 3 of the present Treaty.

Article 5. Should the High Contracting Parties, notwithstanding their efforts for peace, find themselves in a state of defensive war, as defined in Article 3, they undertake that neither will separately negotiate or conclude an armistice or peace.

Article 6. All disputed questions which may arise between the High Contracting Parties, and which cannot be settled by diplomatic means, shall be laid before the Court of International justice or submitted to international arbitration.

Article 7. Neither of the High Contracting Parties shall conclude an alliance with a third power without the consent of the other Party. Each undertakes to communicate to the other forthwith the text of any treaties which it may have concluded with any other State or States.

Article 8. The present Treaty shall remain in force for ten years from the date of the exchange of ratifications; thereafter either of the two Contracting Parties may denounce it on giving one year's notice to the other Party.

Article 9. The present Treaty shall be communicated to the League of Nations for registration and Publication.

Article 10. The present Treaty shall be ratified, and the instruments of ratification shall be exchanged at Riga as early as possible.

In faith whereof the plenipotentiaries have signed the present Treaty and have thereto affixed their seals.

Done in duplicate at Tallinn on November 1st, one thousand nine hundred and twenty-three.

(Signed) Fr. AKEL.

(Signed) Z. A. MEIEROVICS.

4.1240 Treaty of Alliance and Friendship between France and Czechoslovakia

Alliance Members: France and Czechoslovakia
Signed On: January 25, 1924, in the city of Paris. In force until September 30, 1938, when France accepted German annexation of Czech territory in the Munich Agreement.
Alliance Type: Entente (Type III)

Source: *League of Nations Treaty Series*, vol. 23, p. 165.

SUMMARY

Czechoslovakia had been aggressively pursuing a policy of alliance with neighboring states as a method of aiding the fledgling country while also stanching any possible reformulation of the Hapsburgs in Hungary. The French leadership encouraged this policy as a means by which they could exert at least some control over the region, stemming possible threats from not only the Hapsburgs but also Germany and the new Soviet Union. This entente, then, fit well with the foreign policies of both countries, and their mutual understanding lasted until France's attempt to appease Hitler's Germany during the Munich Conference in 1938.

ALLIANCE TEXT

The President of the French Republic and the President of the Czechoslovak Republic,

being earnestly desirous of upholding the principle of international agreements which was solemnly confirmed by the Covenant of the League of Nations,

being further desirous of guarding against any infraction of the peace, the maintenance of which is necessary for the political stability and economic restoration of Europe,

being resolved for this purpose to ensure respect for the international juridical and political situation created by the Treaties of which they were both signatories,

and having regard to the fact that, in order to attain this object, certain mutual guarantees are indispensable for security against possible aggression and for the protection of their common interests,

have appointed as their plenipotentiaries:

For the President of the French Repubic: M. Raymond Poincaré, President of the Council, Minister for Foreign Affairs;

For the President of the Czechoslovak Republic: M. Edvard Benes, Minister for Foreign Affairs,

who, after examining their full powers, which were found in good and due form, have agreed to the following provisions:

Article 1. The Governments of the French Republic and of the Czechoslovak Republic undertake to concert their action in all matters of foreign policy which may threaten their security or which may tend to subvert the situation created by the Treaties of Peace of which both parties are signatories.

Article 2. The High Contracting Parties shall agree together as to the measures to be adopted to safeguard their common interests in case the latter are threatened.

Article 3. The High Contracting Parties, being fully in agreement as to the importance, for the maintenance of the world's peace, of the political principles laid down in Article 88 of the Treaty of Peace of St. Germain-en-Laye of September 10, 1919, and in the Protocols of Geneva dated October 4, 1922, of which instruments they both are signatories, undertake to consult each other as to the measures to be taken in case there should be an danger of an infraction of these principles.

Article 4. The High Contracting Parties, having special regard to the declarations made by the Conference of Ambassadors on February 3, 1920, and April 1, 1921, on which their policy will continue to be based, and to the declaration made on November 10, 1921, by the Hungarian Government to the Allied diplomatic representatives, undertake to consult each other in case their interests are threatened by a failure to observe the principles laid down in the aforesaid declarations.

Article 5. The High Contracting Parties solemnly declare that they are in complete agreement as to the necessity, for the maintenance of peace, of taking common action in the event of

any attempt to restore the Hohenzollern dynasty in Germany, and they undertake to consult each other in such a contingency.

Article 6. In conformity with the principles laid down in the Covenant of the League of Nations, the High Contracting Parties agree that if in future any dispute should arise between them which cannot be settled by friendly agreement and through diplomatic channels, they will submit such dispute either to the Permanent Court of International Justice or to such other arbitrator or arbitrators as they may select.

Article 7. The High Contracting Parties undertake to communicate to each other all Agreements affecting their policy in Central Europe which they may have previously concluded, and to consult one another before concluding any further Agreements. They declare that, in this matter, nothing in the present Treaty is contrary to the above Agreements, and in particular to the Treaty of Alliance between France and Poland, or to the Conventions and Agreements concluded by Czechoslovakia with the Federal Republic of Austria, Roumania, the Kingdom of the Serbs, Croats and Slovenes, or to the Agreement effected by an exchange of notes on February 8, 1921, between the Italian Government and the Czechoslovak Government.

Article 8. The present Treaty shall be communicated to the League of Nations in conformity with Article 18 of the Covenant.

The present Treaty shall be ratified and the instruments of ratification shall be exchanged at Paris as soon as possible.

In faith whereof the respective plenipotentiaries, being duly empowered for this purpose, have signed the present Treaty and have thereto affixed their seals.

Done at Paris, in duplicate, on January 25, 1924.

(L.S.) (Signed) R. POINCARÉ.

(L.S.) (Signed) Dr. Edvard BENES.

4.1241 Pact of Friendship and Cordial Co-operation between the Kingdom of Italy and the Kingdom of the Serbs, Croats, and Slovenes (Treaty of Rome)

Alliance Members: Italy and Yugoslavia
Signed On: January 27, 1924, in the city of Rome. In force until February 22, 1929, when the treaty was not renewed.
Alliance Type: Neutrality Pact (Type II)

Source: *League of Nations Treaty Series,* vol. 24, p. 33.

SUMMARY

After World War I, the city of Fiume became a source of contention between Italy and Yugoslavia. The secret Treaty of London (1915) promised the city to Yugoslavia, but at the Paris Peace Conference Italy claimed the city on the premise that the majority of the population spoke Italian. While negotiations continued, in September of 1919, the poet Gabriele D'Annunzio, head of the Italian Free Corps, captured the city. With the Treaty of Rapallo in 1920, Italy and Yugoslavia agreed to establish Fiume as a free state. After the 1922 Fascist coup d'état overthrew the government in Fiume, Italian troops entered as occupiers. This Treaty of Rome provided a negotiated compromise between the two states and softened dissension somewhat by leaving Fiume in Italian hands while granting territories east of Fiume (Susak) to Yugoslavia.

ALLIANCE TEXT

The Government of His Majesty the King of Italy and the Government of His Majesty the King of the Serbs, Croats and Slovenes, being firmly resolved to secure peace and to safeguard the results obtained during the great war and sanctioned by the Treaties of Peace, have concurred in the conclusion of the present Convention as a natural consequence of the friendship between the two Kingdoms and of the respect of each for the rights of the other both on land and on sea, and have agreed upon the following Articles:

Article I. The two High Contracting Parties undertake to afford each other support and cordial cooperation in order to maintain the position established by the Treaties of Peace concluded at Trianon, Saint Germain and Neuilly, and to ensure respect and fulfilment of the obligations laid down in those Treaties.

Article 2. In the event of one of the High Contracting Parties suffering an unprovoked attack from any Power or Powers, the other Party undertakes to remain neutral throughout the conflict. Furthermore, in the event of the safety and the interests of one of the High Contracting Parties being threatened as the result of forcible incursions from without, the other Party undertakes to afford political and diplomatic support in the form of friendly co-operation for the purpose of assisting to remove the external cause of such threat.

Article 3. In the event of international complications, if the two High Contracting Parties are agreed that their common interests are or may be threatened, they undertake to consult one another as to the steps to be taken in common to protect those interests.

Article 4. The present Convention shall remain in force for five years, and may be denounced or renewed one year before its expiration.

Article 5. The present Treaty shall be ratified and the ratifications shall be exchanged at Rome. It shall come into force immediately upon the exchange of ratifications.

In faith whereof the respective Plenipotentiaries have signed it in duplicate and have thereto affixed their seals.

Done at Rome on January 27, 1924.

Benito MUSSOLINI.
Nik. P. PACHITCH.
M. NINTCHITCH.

4.1242 Pact of Cordial Collaboration between the Kingdom of Italy and the Czechoslovak Republic

Alliance Members: Italy and Czechoslovakia
Signed On: July 5, 1924, in the city of Rome. In force until August 21, 1929, when the treaty was not renewed.
Alliance Type: Entente (Type III)

Source: *League of Nations Treaty Series,* vol. 26, p. 23.

SUMMARY

In many ways this alliance was a response by Italy to France's moves to ally itself with the newly formed central European states. France encouraged the tightened unions found in the Little Entente (Czechoslovakia, Romania, and Yugoslavia) and also nearly allied itself with Hungary. Italy's response reinforced its role within the region, and this entente affirmed friendly relations with Czechoslovakia. The entente was not renewed after its expiry five years later, as Italian foreign policy began to take on a decidedly revisionist tone.

ALLIANCE TEXT

The Government of His Majesty the King of Italy and the Government of the Czechoslovak Republic:

being anxious to maintain peace and desirous of co-operating to ensure the stability and economic reconstruction of Europe;

and being firmly resolved to ensure the maintenance of the international legal and political situation established by the Treaties of Peace;

have agreed to conclude the present Pact of Cordial Collaboration, which is a natural consequence of the friendship existing between the two Contracting Parties and of the respect of each for the rights of the other,

and to this end have agreed upon the following provisions:

Article I. The High Contracting Parties will decide in concert upon the measures best designed to protect their common interests in the event of their being agreed as to the existence or possibility of a menace.

Article 2. The two High Contracting Parties undertake to afford mutual support and assistance in order to ensure the maintenance of the situation established by the Treaties of Peace concluded at St. Germain-en-Laye, Trianon and Neuilly, and the observance and fulfilment of the obligations specified in the said Treaties.

Article 3. The present Convention shall remain in force for five years and may be denounced or renewed one year before its expiration.

Article 4. The present Treaty shall be communicated to the League of Nations in accordance with Article 18 of the Covenant.

The present Treaty shall be ratified and the ratifications shall be exchanged at Rome. It shall come into force immediately upon the exchange of ratifications.

In faith whereof the respective Plenipotentiaries have signed this Treaty in duplicate and have thereto affixed their seals.

Done at Rome this 5th day of July, 1924.

(Signed) Benito MUSSOLINI,
Plenipotentiary of the Kingdom of Italy.
(Signed) Vlastimil KYBAL,
Plenipotentiary of the Czechoslovak Republic.

4.1243 Treaty of Mutual Guaranty among Germany, Belgium, France, Great Britain, and Italy

Alliance Members: Germany, Belgium, France, Great Britain, and Italy
Signed On: October 16, 1925, in the city of Locarno (Switzerland). In force until March 24, 1937, when Germany militarized the Rhineland.
Alliance Type: Defense Pact (Type I)

Source: *League of Nations Treaty Series,* vol. 54, p. 291.

SUMMARY

This alliance is part of the Locarno Pacts, a series of treaties designed to ensure the stability of German borders and, by extension, to maintain the peace in Europe. This particular alliance resulted from disputes over the Ruhr region, which had come under French and Belgian control following German refusal to pay war reparations after World War I. The main objectives of the alliance were to disarm and deter the possibility of a rising Germany. Under the treaty, the parties agreed to maintain Franco-German and German-Belgian borders as well as to faithfully observe the newly created borders of the Versailles Treaty. Dispute resolution mechanisms were articulated in the text of the treaty.

The alliance ended with remilitarization of the Rhineland and was followed quickly by the start of World War II.

ALLIANCE TEXT

The President of the German Reich, His Majesty the King of the Belgians, the President of the French Republic, His Majesty the King of the United Kingdom of Great Britain and Ireland and of the British Dominions beyond the seas, Emperor of India, His Majesty the King of Italy;

Anxious to satisfy the desire for security and protection which animates the peoples upon whom fell the scourge of the war of 1914–18;

Taking note of the abrogation of the treaties for the neutralization of Belgium, and conscious of the necessity of insuring peace in the area which has so frequently been the scene of European conflicts;

Animated also with the sincere desire of giving to all the signatory Powers concerned supplementary guaranties within the framework of the Covenant of the League of Nations and the treaties in force between them;

Have determined to conclude a treaty with these objects, and have appointed as their Plenipotentiaries:

The President of the German Empire: Dr. Hans Luther, Chancellor of the Empire; Dr. Gustav Stresemann, Minister for Foreign Affairs;

His Majesty the King of the Belgians: M. Emile Vandervelde, Minister for Foreign Affairs;

The President of the French Republic: M. Aristide Briand, Prime Minister and Minister for Foreign Affairs;

His Majesty the King of the United Kingdom of Great Britain and Ireland and of the British Dominions beyond the Seas, Emperor of India: The Right Honourable Stanley Baldwin, M.P., First Lord of the Treasury and Prime Minister; The Right Honourable Joseph Austen Chamberlain, M.P., Principal Secretary of State for Foreign Affairs;

His Majesty the King of Italy: The Honourable Vittorio Scialoja, Senator of the Kingdom;

Who, having communicated their full powers, found in good and due form have agreed as follows:

Article 1. The High Contracting Parties collectively and severally guarantee, in the manner provided in the following Articles, the maintenance of the territorial *status quo* resulting from the frontiers between Germany and Belgium and between Germany and France, and the inviolability of the said frontiers as fixed by or in pursuance of the Treaty of Peace signed at Versailles on June 28, 1919, and also the observance of the stipulations of Articles 42 and 43 of the said Treaty concerning the demilitarized zone.

Article. 2. Germany and Belgium, and also Germany and France, mutually undertake that they will in no case attack or invade each other or resort to war against each other. This stipulation shall not, however, apply in the case of:

(1) The exercise of the right of legitimate defense, that is to say, resistance to a violation of the undertaking contained in the previous paragraph or to a flagrant breach of Articles 42 or 43 of the said Treaty of Versailles, if such breach constitutes an unprovoked act of aggression and by reason of the assembly of armed forces in the demilitarized zone, immediate action is necessary;

(2) Action in pursuance of Article 16 of the Covenant of the League of Nations;

(3) Action as the result of a decision taken by the Assembly or by the Council of the League of Nations or in pursuance of Article l5, paragraph 7, of the Covenant of the League of Nations, provided that in this last event the action is directed against a State which was the first to attack.

Article 3. In view of the undertakings entered into in Article 2 of the present Treaty, Germany and Belgium, and Germany and France, undertake to settle by peaceful means and in the manner laid down herein all questions of every kind which may arise between them and which it may not be possible to settle by the normal methods of diplomacy:

Any question with regard to which the Parties are in conflict as to their respective rights shall be submitted to judicial decision, and the Parties undertake to comply with such decision.

All other questions shall be submitted to a conciliation commission. If the proposals of this commission are not accepted by the two Parties, the question shall be brought before the Council of the League of Nations, which will deal with it in accordance with Article 15 of the Covenant of the League.

The detailed arrangements for effecting such peaceful settlement are the subject of special agreements signed this day.

Article 4. (1) If one of the High Contracting Parties alleges that a violation of Article 2 of the present Treaty or a breach of Articles 42 or 43 of the Treaty of Versailles has been or is being committed, it shall bring the question at once before the Council of the League of Nations.

(2) As soon as the Council of the League of Nations is satisfied that such violation or breach has been committed, it will notify its finding without delay to the Powers signatory of the present Treaty, who severally agree that in such case they will each of them come immediately to the assistance of the Power against whom the act complained of is directed.

(3) In case of a flagrant violation of Article 2 of the present Treaty or of a flagrant breach of Articles 42 or 43 of the Treaty of Versailles by one of the High Contracting Parties, each of the other Contracting Parties hereby undertakes immediately to come to the help of the Party against whom such a violation or breach has been directed as soon as the said Power has been able to satisfy itself that this violation constitutes an unprovoked act of aggression and that by reason either of the crossing of the frontier or of the outbreak of hostilities or of the assembly of armed forces in the demilitarized zone immediate action is necessary. Nevertheless, the Council of the League of Nations, which will be seized of the question in accordance with the first paragraph of this Article, will issue its findings, and the High Contracting Parties undertake to act in accordance with the recommendations of the Council, provided that they are concurred in by all the Members other than the representatives of the Parties which have engaged in hostilities.

Article 5. The provisions of Article 3 of the present Treaty are placed under the guaranty of the High Contracting Parties as provided by the following stipulations:

If one of the Powers referred to in Article 3 refuses to submit a dispute to peaceful settlement or to comply with an arbitral or judicial decision and commits a violation of Article 2 of the present Treaty or a breach of Articles 42 or 43 of the Treaty of Versailles, the provisions of Article 4 of the present Treaty shall apply.

Where one of the Powers referred to in Article 3, without committing a violation of Article 2 of the present Treaty or a breach of Articles 42 or 43 of the Treaty of Versailles, refuses to submit a dispute to peaceful settlement or to comply with an arbitral or judicial decision, the other Party shall bring the matter before the Council of the League of Nations, and the Council shall propose what steps shall be taken; the High Contracting Parties shall comply with these proposals.

Article 6. The provisions of the present Treaty do not affect the rights and obligations of the High Contracting Parties under the Treaty of Versailles or under arrangements supplementary thereto, including the Agreements signed in London on August 30, 1924.

Article 7. The present treaty, which is designed to insure the maintenance of peace, and is in conformity with the Covenant of the League of Nations, shall not be interpreted as restricting the duty of the League to take whatever action may be deemed wise and effectual to safeguard the peace of the world.

Article 8. The present Treaty shall be registered at the League of Nations in accordance with the Covenant of the League. It shall remain in force until the Council, acting on a request of one or other of the High Contracting Parties notified to the other signatory Powers three months in advance, and voting at least by a two-thirds' majority, decides that the League of Nations ensures sufficient protection to the High Contracting Parties; the Treaty shall cease to have effect on the expiration of a period of one year from such decision.

Article 9. The present Treaty shall impose no obligation upon any of the British dominions, or upon India, unless the Government of such dominion, or of India, signifies its acceptance thereof.

Article 10. The present Treaty shall be ratified and the ratifications shall be deposited at Geneva in the archives of the League of Nations as soon as possible.

It shall enter into force as soon as all the ratifications have been deposited and Germany has become a Member of the League of Nations.

The present Treaty, done in a single copy, will be deposited in the archives of the League of Nations, and the Secretary-General will be requested to transmit certified copies to each of the High Contracting Parties.

In faith whereof the above-mentioned Plenipotentiaries have signed the present treaty.

Done at Locarno, October 16, 1925.

(L.S.) (Signed) HANS LUTHER.
(L.S.) (Signed) GUSTAV STRESEMANN.
(L.S.) (Signed) EMILE VANDERVELDE.
(L.S.) (Signed) ARISTIDE BRIAND.
(L.S.) (Signed) STANLEY BALDWIN.
(L.S.) (Signed) AUSTEN CHAMBERLAIN.
(L.S.) (Signed) VITTORIO SCIALOJA.

4.1244 Treaty of Locarno between France and Poland

Alliance Members: France and Poland
Signed On: October 16, 1925, in the city of Locarno (Switzerland). In force until September 27, 1939, upon the loss of Polish independence following invasions by Germany and the Soviet Union.
Alliance Type: Defense Pact (Type I)

Source: *League of Nations Treaty Series,* vol. 54, p. 355.

SUMMARY

This treaty served as reaffirmation of France's commitment to Poland in the case of renewed German expansionism. The Locarno agreements followed an exchange of letters among Britain, France, and Germany on the basis of Germany's request to reaffirm its commitment to the peaceful status quo. France used the opportunity of the conference to reaffirm its commitments to both Poland and Czechoslovakia.

The alliance ended with the dissolution of Poland following German and Soviet invasions in September of 1939. France's pledge of support did not materialize; instead, the Germans invaded France in the summer of 1940.

ALLIANCE TEXT

The President of the French Republic and the President of the Polish Republic;

Equally desirous to see Europe spared from war by a sincere observance of the undertakings arrived at this day with a view to the maintenance of general peace;

Have resolved to guarantee their benefits to each other reciprocally by a treaty concluded within the framework of the Covenant of the League of Nations and of the treaties existing between them;

And have, to this effect, nominated for their Plenipotentiaries:

The President of the French Republic: M. Aristide Briand, Minister for Foreign Affairs;

The President of the Polish Republic: Count Alexandre Skrzynski, Prime Minister, Minister for Foreign Affairs;

Who, after having exchanged their full powers, found in good and due form, have agreed on the following provisions:

Article I. In the event of Poland or France suffering from a failure to observe undertakings arrived at this day between them and Germany, with a view to the maintenance of general peace, France, and reciprocally Poland, acting in application of Article 16 of the Covenant of the League of Nations, undertake to lend each other immediate aid and assistance, if such a failure is accompanied by an unprovoked recourse to arms.

In the event of the Council of the League of Nations, when dealing with a question brought before it in accordance with the said undertakings, being unable to succeed making its report accepted by all its members other than the representatives of the Parties to the dispute, and in the event of Poland or France being attacked without provocation, France, or reciprocally Poland, acting in application of Article 15, paragraph 7, of the Covenant of the League of Nations, will immediately lend aid and assistance.

Article 2. Nothing in the present Treaty shall affect the rights and obligations of the High Contracting Parties as Members of the League of Nations, or shall be interpreted as restricting the duty of the League to take whatever action may be deemed wise and effectual to safeguard the peace of the world.

Article 3. The present Treaty shall be registered with the League of Nations in accordance with the Covenant.

Article 4. The present Treaty shall be ratified. The ratifications shall be deposited at Geneva with the League of Nations at the same time as the ratification of the Treaty concluded this day between Germany, Belgium, France, Great Britain and Italy, and the ratification of the Treaty concluded at same time between Germany and Poland.

It will come into force and remain in force under the same conditions as the said Treaties.

The present Treaty, done in a single copy will be deposited in the archives of the League of Nations, and the Secretary-General of the League will be requested to transmit certified copies to each of the High Contracting Parties.

In faith whereof the above-mentioned Plenipotentiaries have signed the present Treaty.

Done at Locarno, the sixteenth of October, nineteen hundred and twenty-five.

(L.S.) (Signed) ARISTIDE BRIAND.
(L.S.) (Signed) AL. SKRZYNSKY.

4.1245 Treaty of Mutual Guarantee between France and Czechoslovakia

Alliance Members: France and Czechoslovakia
Signed On: October 16, 1925, in the city of Locarno (Switzerland). In force until September 30, 1938, ending upon the French signature of the Munich Agreement.
Alliance Type: Defense Pact (Type I)

Source: *League of Nations Treaty Series,* vol. 54, p. 361.

SUMMARY

Also part of French efforts to secure eastern Europe, this alliance pledged a strong defensive commitment to the Czechoslovak government. The pact held until the French signed the Munich Pact, which permitted German occupation of the Czechoslovakian Sudetenland. With occupation of the strategic Sudeten Mountains, a full invasion of the rump of the state followed quickly with the start of the war. Neville Chamberlain, prime minister of Great Britain, convinced his weakened French counterpart, Edouard Daladier, to settle the dispute with Germany at the cost of Czechoslovakia, but this policy of appeasement did not contain Hitler's push for new territories.

ALLIANCE TEXT

The President of the French Republic and the President of the Czechoslovak Republic;

Equally desirous to see Europe spared from war by a sincere observance of the undertakings arrived at this day with a view to the maintenance of general peace;

Have resolved to guarantee their benefits to each other reciprocally by a treaty concluded within the framework of the Covenant of the League of Nations and of the treaties existing between them;

And have to this effect, nominated for their Plenipotentiaries:

The President of the French Republic: M. Aristide Briand, Minister for Foreign Affairs;

The President of the Czechoslovak Republic: M. Edouard

Beneš, Minister for Foreign Affairs;

Who, after having exchanged their full powers, found in good and due form, have agreed on the following provisions:

Article 1. In the event of Czechoslovakia or France suffering from a failure to observe the undertakings arrived at this day between them and Germany with a view to the maintenance of general peace, France, and reciprocally, Czechoslovakia, acting in application of Article 16 of the Covenant of League of Nations, undertake to lend each other immediate aid and assistance, if such a failure is accompanied by an unprovoked recourse to arms.

In the event of the Council of the League of Nations, when dealing with a question brought before it in accordance with the said undertakings, being unable to succeed in making its report accepted by all its members other than the representatives of the Parties to the dispute, and in the event of Czechoslovakia or France being attacked without provocation, France, or reciprocally Czechoslovakia, acting in application of Article 15, paragraph 7, of the Covenant of the League of Nations, will immediately lend aid and assistance.

Article 2. Nothing in the present treaty shall affect the rights and obligations of the High Contracting Parties as Members of the League of Nations, or shall be interpreted as restricting the duty of the League to take whatever action may be deemed wise and effectual to safeguard the peace of the world.

Article 3. The present Treaty shall be registered with the League of Nations, in accordance with the Covenant.

Article 4. The present Treaty shall be ratified. The ratifications shall be deposited at Geneva with the League of Nations at the same time as the ratification of the Treaty concluded this day between Germany, Belgium, France, Great Britain and Italy, and the ratification of the Treaty concluded at the same time between Germany and Czechoslovakia.

It will enter into force and remain in force under the same conditions as the said Treaties.

The present Treaty done in a single copy will be deposited in the archives of the League of Nations, and the Secretary-General of the League will be requested to transmit certified copies to each of the High Contracting Parties.

In faith whereof the above-mentioned Plenipotentiaries have signed the present Treaty. Done at Locarno, the sixteenth October, nineteen hundred and twenty-five.

(L.S.)(Signed) Aristide BRIAND.

(L.S.)(Signed) DR. Edouard BENEŠ.

4.1246 Treaty of Friendship and Neutrality between Turkey and the Union of Soviet Socialist Republics

Alliance Members: Italy and Czechoslovakia
Signed On: December 17, 1925, in the city of Paris. In force until September 1, 1939, when the Soviets denounced the treaty at the start of World War II.
Alliance Type: Neutrality Pact (Type II)

Source: *League of Nations Treaty Series,* vol. 157, p. 354.

SUMMARY

Soviet leaders anxiously entered the interwar period fearful that the major economic powers would shut the communist state out of international economic cooperation. Little concerned with the technical details of trade agreements, Soviet leaders thus actively sought guarantees of peace and political neutrality and the opportunity to conduct trade across borders. This agreement with the newly established Turkish Republic, a Soviet neighbor, provided for neutrality and, importantly, that neither party would engage in international agreements that ran counter to the interests of the other party.

The Soviets tried to force a redrawn border between the two countries in 1936, but the neutrality agreement lasted until the start of World War II. Turkey continued to remain neutral toward the Soviet Union during the war, but that foreign policy was more the result of Turkish worries over the intentions of its powerful northern neighbor, especially during the two years of cooperation between Germany and the Soviet Union. The Soviet Union formally ended the neutrality agreement and demanded Turkish-held territories in March of 1945.

ALLIANCE TEXT

The Government of the Union of Soviet Socialist Republics and the Government of the Turkish Republic, recognising that it is in the interest of the two Contracting Parties to define the exact conditions which would contribute to strengthen the permanent normal relations and sincere friendship which unite them, have appointed for that purpose M. Georges Tchitcherine, People's Commissar for Foreign Affairs of the Union of Soviet Socialist Republics, and M. Tevfik Rouchdi Bey, Minister for Foreign Affairs of Turkey, who have agreed on the following provisions:

Article 1. In the case of military action being taken against either Contracting Party by one or more other Powers, the other Contracting Party undertakes to maintain neutrality as towards the first Contracting Party.

Note: The expression "military action" shall not be held to include military manoeuvres, since they do not cause any prejudice to the other Party.

Article 2. Each Contracting Party undertakes to abstain from any aggression against the other; it likewise undertakes not to participate in any alliance or agreement of a political character with one or more other Powers directed against the other Contracting Party, or in any alliance or agreement with one or more other Powers directed against the military or naval security of the other Contracting Party. Furthermore, each of the two Contracting Parties undertakes not to participate in any hostile act by one or more other Powers directed against the other Contracting Party.

Article 3. The present Treaty shall come into force as soon as it is ratified and shall remain in force for three years. After that period the Treaty shall be regarded as extended automatically for a period of one year, unless one of the Contracting Parties notifies its desire to terminate the Treaty six months before its expiry.

Done at Paris on the 17th day of December, 1925.

(L. S.) (Signed) Georges TCHITCHERINE.
(L. S.) (Signed) Dr. T. RÜŞTÜ.

4.1247 Treaty of Friendship and Security between Persia and Turkey

Alliance Members: Persia (Iran) and Turkey
Signed On: April 22, 1926, in the city of Tehran (Iran). In force until July 15, 1937.
Alliance Type: Neutrality Pact (Type II)

Source: *League of Nations Treaty Series,* no. 2449

SUMMARY

In April 1926 Reza Khan had enough political power to proclaim himself shah of Iran. Reza Shah then immediately moved to secure his international borders. This treaty with Turkey, together with an additional pact with Afghanistan two years later (1928), affirmed Iran's border and provided some regional and internal security. Both countries had security concerns over the presence of a large Kurdish minority that spanned their border regions. Article VI of this treaty provided for cooperation to put an end to any "reprehensible activities" with which the Kurdish minorities might target the two governments. The alliance lasted until the formation of a larger non-aggression pact, the Saadabad Pact, formed with Turkey, Iraq, and Afghanistan in 1937.

Alliance Text

Preamble.

Persia, of the one part, and Turkey, of the other part, noting that the present time imposes the same needs and obligations on their respective nations,

And being firmly convinced that it is essential for the two States to strengthen the ties of friendship and fraternity existing between them,

Have resolved to lay down specific conditions for the cordial relations between them and with that object to conclude a Treaty of Friendship and Security.

For this purpose, they have agreed to choose Teheran as the seat of negotiations, and have appointed as their Plenipotentiaries:

His Imperial Majesty the Shah of Persia: His Highness Mirza Mohammad Ali Khan Foroughi, Prime Minister; His Excellency Mirza Davoud Khan Meftah, Acting Head of the Ministry of Foreign Affairs;

The President of the Turkish Republic: Memdouh Shevket Bey, Turkish Ambassador Extraordinary and Plenipotentiary in Persia;

Who, having communicated their full powers, found in good and due form, have agreed on the following provisions:

Article I. There shall be inviolable peace and sincere and perpetual friendship between the Empire of Persia and the Turkish Republic as well as between the citizens of both States.

Article II. Should military action be directed against either High Contracting Party by one or more third Powers, the other Contracting Party undertakes to observe neutrality towards the former.

Article III. Each of the two Contracting Parties undertakes not to engage in any aggression against the other and not to be a party to any alliance or political, economic, or financial agreement concluded by one or more third Powers and directed against the other Party or against the military and naval security of that Party's country.

Each of the two Contracting Parties further undertakes not to participate in any hostile action whatsoever directed by one or more third Powers against the other Party.

Article IV. Should one or more third Powers proceeding to acts of hostility and military operations against either High Contracting Party violate the neutrality of the other Party, with a view to using his territory for the passage of troops, arms or munitions of war, or for obtaining supplies of provisions, live stock or any other objects capable of being employed for warlike purposes, or for the passage of troops in retreat; or with a view to exciting and stirring up the populations of the neutral territory with the object of using them for their own purposes or with a view to carrying out military reconnaissances in the said territory, that Party shall be bound, in order to safeguard his neutrality, to oppose such actions by force of arms.

Article V. The two Contracting Parties undertake not to allow in their territory the formation or presence of organisations or groups of persons whose object is to disturb the peace and security of the other country or to change its government, or the presence of persons or groups of persons planning to attack the other country by propaganda or by any other means.

Article VI. To ensure the peace and security of the inhabitants of the frontier zones, the two Contracting Parties will take all necessary measures to put an end to any reprehensible activities which may be liable to affect the peace of the two countries and in which tribes in the territories adjoining the frontiers may engage.

These measures shall be taken by the respective Governments of the two Parties separately, or by common agreement if they consider it necessary.

Article VII. The High Contracting Parties have agreed that their Plenipotentiaries shall meet at Teheran within six months at most from the date of the signature of the present Treaty for the purpose of concluding commercial, consular, Customs and postal and telegraph conventions, and also establishment and extradition conventions.

Article VIII. The two Contracting Parties have agreed to determine the procedure to be followed with a view to settling any differences that may arise between them and that it may not have been possible to settle by the ordinary methods of diplomacy.

Article IX. It is agreed that, apart from the mutual undertakings entered into in the present Treaty, each of the High Contracting Parties retains full liberty of actions as regards his relations with third Powers.

Article X. The present Treaty has been drawn up in Persian,

Turkish and French. In case of divergence, the French text shall be authentic.

Article XI. The present Treaty shall be submitted as soon as possible for the approval of the National Assemblies of both States, and the ratifications thereof shall be exchanged at Teheran.

It shall enter into force as from the date of signature and shall remain valid for five years. Unless this Treaty is denounced by either High Contracting Party six months before the expiration of the said period of five years, it shall be considered as automatically renewed for one year more, denunciation becoming in all cases effective only after six months.

In faith whereof the respective Plenipotentiaries have signed the present Treaty and have thereto affixed their seals.

Done in duplicate at Teheran on the twenty-second day of April, one thousand nine hundred and twenty-six.

M. A. FOROUGHI.

MEMDOUH SHEVKET BEY.

D. MEFTAH.

4.1248 Treaty between Germany and the Union of Soviet Socialist Republics

Alliance Members: Germany and the Union of Soviet Socialist Republics
Signed On: April 24, 1926, in the city of Berlin. In force until September 1933, when Germany ended all military cooperation with the Soviet Union.
Alliance Type: Neutrality Pact (Type II)

Source: *British Foreign and State Papers,* vol. 125, p. 738.

SUMMARY

The Soviet leadership became increasingly fearful of economic and political isolation following Germany's participation in the Locarno agreements of 1925. Easing western tensions and the shift of German foreign policy away from isolation were not encouraging for the Soviets. This neutrality agreement, then, served as affirmation that cooperation between the two countries would continue in accord with the Treaty of Rapallo (1922).

The rise of Hitler and the National Socialists doomed Soviet-German military cooperation, and the neutrality agreement was effectively dead by September of 1933, when the Soviets responded to growing Nazi propaganda and German targeting of Russian citizens by closing several military training facilities. The German-Polish non-aggression pact in January of 1934 confirmed the foreign policy split.

ALLIANCE TEXT

The German Government and the Government of the Union of Soviet Socialist Republics, being desirous of doing all in their power to promote the maintenance of general peace,

And being convinced that the interests of the German people and of the peoples of the Union of Socialist Soviet Republics demand constant and trustful co-operation,

Have agreed to strengthen the friendly relations existing between them by means of a special Treaty and have for this purpose appointed as their Plenipotentiaries:

The German Government: Dr. Gustav Stresemann, Minister for Foreign Affairs;

The Government of the Union of Socialist Soviet Republics: M. Nikolaï Nicolaïwitsch Krestinski, Ambassador Extraordinary and Plenipotentiary of the Union of Socialist Soviet Republics;

Who, having communicated their full powers found in good and due form, have agreed upon the following provisions:

Article I. The relations between Germany and the Union of Socialist Soviet Republics shall continue to be based on the Treaty of Rapallo.

The German Government and the Government of the Union of Socialist Soviet Republics

shall remain in friendly touch in order to promote an understanding with regard to all political and economic questions jointly affecting their two countries.

Article 2. Should one of the Contracting Parties, despite its peaceful attitude, be attacked by one or more third Powers, the other Contracting Party shall observe neutrality for the whole duration of the conflict.

Article 3. If on the occasion of a conflict of the nature mentioned in Article 2, or at a time when neither of the Contracting Parties is engaged in warlike operations, a coalition is formed between third Powers with a view to the economic or financial boycott of either of the Contracting Parties, the other Contracting Party undertakes not to adhere to such coalition.

Article 4. The present Treaty shall be ratified and the instruments of ratification shall be exchanged at Berlin.

It shall enter into force on the date of the exchange of the instruments of ratification and shall remain in force for five years. The two Contracting Parties shall confer in good time before the expiration of this period with regard to the future development of their political relations.

In faith whereof the Plenipotentiaries have signed the present Treaty.

Done in duplicate at Berlin, April 24, 1926.

(Signed) STRESEMANN.

(Signed) KRESTINSKI.

4.1249 Treaty of Friendship between France and Romania

Alliance Members: France and Romania
Signed On: June 10, 1926, in the city of Paris. In force until June 22, 1940.
Alliance Type: Neutrality Pact (Type II)

Source: *League of Nations Treaty Series,* no. 1373.

SUMMARY

After the formation of the Little Entente in 1920 and 1921, this treaty was part of a series of treaties made by France to forge tighter security relations among the countries of eastern Europe. Together with similar treaties separately signed by France with Czechoslovakia and Yugoslavia, this neutrality pact with Romania was aimed at securing a common front against the rising influence of the Soviet Union. All the bilateral treaties were institutionalized by the reorganization of the Entente powers in 1933, and this particular alliance lasted until the fall of France in World War II.

ALLIANCE TEXT

The President of the French Republic and His Majesty the King of Roumania being equally desirous of maintaining in Europe that state of peace and political stability which is essential alike for social progress and for economic prosperity in France and Roumania, firmly attached to the principle of respect for international undertakings, as solemnly reaffirmed in the Covenant of the League of Nations, desirous within the framework of that Covenant of ensuring community of action in the event of any attempt to subvert the situation established by the Treaties of which they are signatories, and convinced that it is the duty of modem Governments to prevent any recurrence of war by providing for the pacific settlement of such disputes as may arise between them, have resolved to give one another fresh guarantees of peace, goodwill, and friendship, and have appointed as their Plenipotentiaries:

The President of the French Republic: M. Aristide Briand, Member of the Chamber of Deputies, President of the Council, Minister for Foreign Affairs;

His Majesty the King of Roumania: M. Constantin Diamandy, Envoy Extraordinary and Minister Plenipotentiary accredited to the President of the French Republic;

Who, having communicated their full powers, found in good and due form, have agreed as follows:

Article 1. France and Roumania mutually undertake that they will in no case attack or invade each other or resort to war against each other.

This stipulation shall not, however, apply in the case of:

(1) The exercise of the right of legitimate defense, that is to say, resistance to a violation of the undertaking contained in the first paragraph of the present Article;

(2) Action in pursuance of Article 16 of the Covenant of the League of Nations;

(3) Action as the result of a decision taken by the Assembly or Council of the League of Nations or in pursuance of Article 15, paragraph 7, of the Covenant of the League of Nations, provided that in this last event the action is directed against a State which was the first to attack.

Article 2. In view of the undertakings entered into in Article 1 of the present Treaty, France and Roumania undertake to settle by peaceful means and in the manner laid down herein all questions of every kind which may arise between them and which it may not be possible to settle by the normal methods of diplomacy. Any question with regard to which the Parties are in conflict as to their respective rights shall be submitted to judicial decision, and the Parties undertake to comply with such decision.

All other questions shall be submitted to a conciliation commission. If the proposals of this commission are not accepted by the two Parties, the question shall be brought before the Council of the League of Nations, which will deal with it in accordance with Article 15 of the Covenant of the League.

The detailed arrangements for effecting such peaceful settlement are the subject of a special Convention signed this day.

Article 3. The French and Roumanian Governments undertake, subject to any resolutions that may be passed by the Council or Assembly of the League of Nations, to consult each other in all matters which may threaten the external security of France or Roumania or which may tend to subvert the situation created by the Treaties of Peace of which both Parties are signatories.

Article 4. If, notwithstanding the sincerely peaceful intentions of the French and Roumanian Governments, France or Roumania should be attacked without giving provocation, the two Governments will immediately consult one another as to the action to be taken by each Party within the framework of the Covenant of the League of Nations, with a view to safeguarding their legitimate national interests and maintaining the order established by the treaties of which both Parties are signatories.

Article 5. The High Contracting Parties agree to concert their policy in the event of any modification or attempted modification of the political status of the countries of Europe and subject to such resolutions as may be passed in the matter by the Council or the Assembly of the League of Nations, to confer with one another concerning the attitude to be observed in such an event by each Party.

Article 6. The High Contracting Parties declare that nothing in the present Treaty shall be interpreted as contrary to the provisions of the existing treaties, signed by France or by Roumania, which concern the policy of those countries in Europe. They undertake to consult one another on questions of European policy with a view to co-ordinated action in the cause of peace, and for this purpose to inform one another in future of any treaties or agreements on this same subject which they may conclude with third Powers and they further undertake that such treaties or agreements shall always be consistent with the maintenance of peace.

Article 7. No provision in this Treaty shall be interpreted or applied in a manner prejudicial to the rights or obligations of the High Contracting Parties under the Covenant of the League of Nations.

Article 8. The present Treaty shall be communicated for registration to the League of Nations in conformity with Article 18 of the Covenant.

Article 9. The present Treaty shall be ratified and the instruments of ratification shall be exchanged at Paris as soon as possible.

It shall come into force on the exchange of ratifications and shall remain in force for ten years, or the expiry of which period it may be renewed, if due notice to this effect has been given at the end of the ninth year.

In faith whereof the respective Plenipotentiaries, duly authorised, have signed the present

Treaty and have affixed their seals thereto.

Done at Paris in duplicate, June 10, 1926.

{Signed} A. BRIAND.

{Signed} Const. DIAMANDY.

4.1250 Treaty of Friendship, Conciliation and Judicial Settlement between Spain and Italy

Alliance Members: Spain and Italy
Signed On: August 7, 1926, in the city of Madrid. In force until July 18, 1936.
Alliance Type: Neutrality Pact (Type II)

Source: *League of Nations Treaty Series,* no. 1558.

SUMMARY

The newly fascist governments of Italy and Spain seemed to have much in common, and close cooperation was expected, especially with a powerful France serving as a foil that would encourage close security ties. However, few treaties were actually signed between the two governments. An economic treaty provided both countries mutual most-favored trading status. This treaty followed, establishing neutrality and settlement terms, resulting in a much weaker commitment than either government had anticipated upon establishing relations in 1923. The agreement lasted for ten years, until Italy's intervention in the Spanish Civil War.

ALLIANCE TEXT

His Majesty the King of Italy, and His Majesty the King of Spain, being desirous of further strengthening the ties of friendship which already unite the two countries and of helping to maintain general peace, have decided to conclude a Treaty of friendship, conciliation and judicial settlement in regard to questions which may arise between the two countries.

They have therefore appointed as their Plenipotentiaries:

His Majesty the King of Italy: His Excellency the Marquis Paulucci Di' Calboli, His Ambassador Extraordinary and Plenipotentiary, accredited to His Most Catholic Majesty, Senator of the Kingdom;

His Majesty the King of Spain: His Excellency Don José De Yangüas Messia, His Minister for Foreign Affairs,

Who, having communicated their full powers found in good and due form, have agreed upon the following provisions:

Article I. The Contracting Parties undertake to submit to the procedure of conciliation all disputes of any nature whatever which may arise between them, and which it may not have been possible to settle within a reasonable time by diplomatic methods.

In the event of the procedure of conciliation proving unsuccessful, a judicial settlement shall be sought in accordance with Articles VII *et seq.* of the present Treaty.

Disputes for the solution of which a special procedure has been laid down in other conventions in force between the Contracting Parties shall, however, remain subject to such special procedure.

Article II. In the case of a dispute which, according to the law of one of the Parties, comes within the jurisdiction of the Courts, the defendant Party may oppose the submission of the dispute to a procedure of conciliation and ultimately to judicial settlement, so long as no final judgment has been pronounced by the Court in question. Should the complainant Party desire to contest the judgment, the conciliation procedure must be applied to the dispute within one year from the date on which the judgment was pronounced.

Article III. The Contracting Parties shall establish a Permanent Commission of Conciliation consisting of five members.

Each Party shall appoint one member of its own choosing, the other three being appointed by agreement between the Parties. The three latter members may not be nationals of the Contracting Parties or be domiciled in their territories or be employed in their service. The Contracting Parties shall by agreement appoint one of these three members as president.

So long as no proceedings have been begun, either Contracting Party may revoke the appointment of its Commissioner and nominate a successor; it may also withdraw its consent to the appointment of any of the three Commissioners appointed jointly. In this case the Commissioners whose mandates are terminated shall be replaced without delay.

The Commissioners shall be replaced in the same manner as they were appointed. For the actual duration of the procedure the jointly appointed Commissioners shall receive an allowance, to be fixed by agreement between the Contracting Parties and to be paid by them in equal shares. On the other hand, each Party shall fix and pay the allowance of the Commissioner appointed by itself.

The general expenses of the Commission shall be borne by the Contracting Parties in equal shares.

The Commission shall be constituted within six months after the exchange of the ratifications of the present Treaty. It shall meet in the place selected by its President.

If the appointment of the members to be nominated jointly is not made within six months as from the date of the exchange of ratifications, or, in the case of replacement, within three months after the vacancy occurs, these appointments shall be made in conformity with Article 45 of the Hague Convention of October 18, 1907, for the Pacific Settlement of International Disputes.

Article IV. Failing any special agreement to the contrary, the procedure of conciliation shall be governed by the rules laid down in the Hague Convention of October 18, 1907, for the Pacific Settlement of International Disputes.

Article V. A question may be submitted to the Commission of Conciliation by either of the Parties, who shall notify its request to the President of the Commission and to the other Party. The Commission, however, may offer its services, should its President and two of the Commissioners agree to such a course of action.

The Contracting Parties undertake to assist the Commission in its work, in every possible way and in every respect, and in particular to employ all the means they possess under their respective laws to invest it with the same powers as their Supreme Courts as regards the calling and hearing of witnesses and experts and the carrying out of investigations on the spot.

Article VI. It shall be the duty of the Conciliation Commission to consider the various questions submitted to it and to embody the results of its enquiry in a report, the object of which shall be to elucidate questions of fact and thus to facilitate the settlement of the dispute. In its report it shall state the controversial points in the case and shall then make such recommendations as might lead to an agreement between the Parties.

The Commission shall report within six months from the day on which the dispute is submitted to it unless the Contracting Parties decide to curtail or extend this period. The report shall be drawn up in triplicate, one copy being sent to each of the Parties and the third being filed in the archives of the Commission.

The Commission shall prescribe a period within which the Parties shall be required to take their decision as regards its recommendations, and also a period within which the Parties may, in case the procedure of conciliation should prove unsuccessful, submit the dispute to a judicial settlement. These periods may not, however, exceed six months in the case of the first period, and three months in the case of the second.

The Commission's report shall not be in the nature of a compulsory final award as regards either the statement of facts or the legal considerations.

Article VII. Should the Parties not accept the recommendations of the Commission of Conciliation, either of them may, within a period prescribed by the Commission, request that the dispute be submitted to the Permanent Court of International Justice. If, in the opinion of the Court, the case is not of a juridical nature, the Parties shall agree to its being settled *ex aequo et bono.*

Article VIII. Nevertheless, the Contracting Parties may decide to refer any dispute to a Court of Arbitration established in conformity with Articles 55 *et seq.* of the Convention of October 18, 1907, for the Pacific Settlement of International Disputes, or in conformity with any other agreement concluded between them.

Article IX. On the basis of the Statute and the Rules of the Permanent Court of International Justice, the Contracting Parties shall draw up a special agreement (*compromise*) specifying the subject of the dispute, the special jurisdiction conferred upon the Court and any other conditions agreed upon between the Parties.

The special agreement shall be constituted by an exchange of notes between the Governments of the Contracting Parties and all points contained therein shall be interpreted by the Court of Justice.

If the special agreement is not drawn up within three months from the day on which one of the Parties was requested to sub-mit the matter for judicial settlement, either Party may bring the question before the Court of Justice by a simple request.

Article X. If, in a judgment rendered in conformity with the present Treaty, it is found that a ruling of a Court of Law or any other authority of one of the Contracting Parties is wholly or partly at variance with international law, and should the constitutional law of that Party not allow, or only inadequately allow, the cancellation of this decision by administrative procedure, the Party prejudiced shall be granted equitable satisfaction in some other form.

Article XI. The judgment rendered by the Permanent Court of International justice shall be carried out by the Parties in good faith.

During the procedure of conciliation or the judicial procedure, the Contracting Parties shall undertake to abstain as far as possible from all measures which might prejudicially affect the acceptance of the proposals of the Commission of Conciliation or the execution of the judgment.

Article XII. Any disputes which may arise as to the interpretation or the execution of the present Treaty shall, in the absence of agreement to the contrary be submitted direct to the Permanent Court of International justice by a simple request.

Article XIII. Should one of the Contracting Parties, notwithstanding its peaceful attitude, be attacked by a third Power or third Powers, the other Contracting Party shall observe neutrality during the whole of the conflict.

Article XIV. The present Treaty shall be ratified as soon as possible and the instruments of ratification shall be exchanged at Madrid.

The Treaty shall remain in force for a period of ten years from the date of the exchange of ratifications. Unless denounced six months before the expiration of this period it shall remain in force for a further period of five years, and similarly thereafter. If a procedure of conciliation or a judicial procedure is pending at the time of the expiration of the present Treaty, it shall pursue its course in accordance with the provisions of the present Treaty or of any other Convention which the Contracting Parties may have agreed to substitute therefor.

Article XV. The present Treaty has been drawn up in two original copies, one in Spanish and one in Italian, both copies being authentic.

In faith whereof the Plenipotentiaries have signed the present Treaty.

Done at Madrid on August 7, 1926.

For Italy:

(L. S.) PAULUCCI DI' CALBOLI.

For Spain:

(L. S.) YANGÜAS MESSIA.

4.1251 Treaty of Neutrality and Non-Aggression between the Soviet Union and Afghanistan

Alliance Members: Soviet Union and Afghanistan
Signed On: August 31, 1926, in the city of Paghman (Afghanistan). In force until December 8, 1979.
Alliance Type: Neutrality Pact (Type II)

Source: *British Foreign and State Papers,* vol. 125, p. 3.

SUMMARY

This treaty marks the beginning of closer relations between Afghanistan and the Soviet Union. The agreement affirms neutrality in the case of international conflict and establishes that both countries would not support or establish subversive elements in the territories of their neighboring alliance partner. The agreement was followed one month later by a friendship treaty and soon thereafter by a trade agreement.

The closer ties between the two countries increased the suspicions of Afghanistan's southern neighbor, India, and this led the Afghan government to downplay the level of military cooperation between the signatories. The pact lasted until the Soviet invasion of Afghanistan in December 1979.

ALLIANCE TEXT

With a view to the consolidation of the friendly relations and the strengthening of amicable neighbourly connexions, happily existing between the USSR and the Sovereign State of Afghanistan on the basis of the treaty signed in Moscow 28 February 1921, which remains in force in all its parts irrespective of whether the present treaty remains in force or is annulled, the plenipotentiaries of the two high contracting parties:

The plenipotentiary representative of the USSR in Afghanistan M. Leonid Stark and His Excellency the Foreign Minister of the Sovereign State of Afghanistan M. Mahmud-Bek-Khan-Tarzi on 31 August 1925 [1926] in the city of Paghman, having exchanged their credentials, which were found to be in due form, have drawn up and signed the following articles, designed to strengthen friendly relations between the two States and to ensure lasting peace.

I. In the event of war or of military action between one of the contracting parties and a third or several other Powers, the other contracting party undertakes to observe neutrality in regard to the first.

II. Each of the contracting parties undertakes to refrain from any attack on the other, and on its own territories it will take no steps which might inflict political or military injury on the other contracting party. In particular, each of the contracting parties undertakes not to take part in any alliances or agreements of a military or political character with another or several third Powers which might be directed against the other contracting party, or in any boycott or blockade of a financial or economic character directed against the other contracting party. Furthermore, should the conduct of a third Power or of third Powers towards one of the contracting parties be of an inimical character, the other contracting party undertakes not only to refrain from supporting such conduct, but is bound on its own territory to oppose it and the hostile actions and designs arising therefrom.

III. The high contracting parties, mutually recognizing their state sovereignty, undertake to refrain from any armed or unarmed intervention in the internal affairs of the other contracting party and they will refrain completely from assisting or participating in any intervention by a third or several third Powers which might take steps against the other contracting party. The contracting parties will not permit and will prevent on their territory the organization and activity of groups and the activity of individuals prejudicial to the other contracting party or which are aimed at the overthrow of the political regime of the other contracting party, or which make attempts on its territorial integrity, or which assemble and recruit armed forces against the other contracting party. In like manner the two sides will not allow or give permission for the passage through their territory of armed forces, arms, stores of firearms, military equipment, or any kind of war material designed for use against the other contracting party.

IV. The contracting parties agree to enter within four months into negotiations for establishing the method of settling differences which may arise between them and which cannot be settled by the customary diplomatic means.

V. Each of the contracting parties retains complete freedom of action to take steps to establish any sort of relations and alliances with third Powers which lie outside the limits of the obligations, the terms of which are set forth in the present treaty.

VI. The present treaty enters into force from the moment of its ratification, which shall take place not more than three months after its signature, and shall remain in force for three years. After the expiration of that term the treaty shall be considered as automatically prolonged for successive periods of one year unless either of the contracting parties shall inform the other contracting party six months before the expiration of the treaty of its desire to discontinue it.

VII. The present treaty is drawn up in two copies, in the Russian and Persian languages, both texts being authentic.

Paghman, 31 August 1926

4.1252 Pact of Friendship and Cordial Collaboration between Italy and Romania

Alliance Members: Italy and Romania
Signed On: September 16, 1926, in the city of Rome. In force until July 18, 1932.
Alliance Type: Entente (Type III)

Source: *League of Nations Treaty Series,* no. 1560.

SUMMARY

This alliance was one of several made by both governments as they attempted to bring tighter security to the region. With this treaty, both parties pledged consultations should conflict begin in Europe. Although it was not mentioned in the treaty, Italy also made a significant loan to the Romanian government in exchange for rights to oil and some other concessions. According to the terms of the treaty, the entente was not renewed, and it expired in 1932.

ALLIANCE TEXT

His Majesty the King of Italy and His Majesty the King of Roumania, animated with the desire of strengthening still further the ties of friendship which exist between the two countries,

Desirous of ensuring general peace and the security of their peoples and of consolidating the political stability which is essential to the moral economic recovery of Europe,

Being resolved, with this object, to promote international legal and political order,

Desirous of giving to their peoples supplementary guarantees within the framework of the Covenant of the League of Nations, and

Guided by the principles laid down in the Treaty of Locarno,

Have agreed to conclude the present pact of friendship and cordial co-operation, which is a natural consequence of the friendship existing between their respective kingdoms and of their community of interests, and with this object have appointed as their Plenipotentiaries:

His Majesty the King of Italy: His Excellency the Chevalier Benito Mussolini, Head of the Government, Prime Minister and Secretary of State, Minister and Secretary of State for Foreign Affairs;

His Majesty the King of Roumania: His Excellency General Alexander Averescu, President of the Council of Ministers;

Who, having exchanged their full powers, found in good and due form, have agreed as follows:

Article 1. The High Contracting Parties undertake reciprocally to lend each other their mutual support and cordial co-operation for the maintenance of international order and to ensure respect for, and the execution of, the undertakings contained in the treaties to which they are signatories.

Article 2. In the event of international complications and if they are agreed that their common interests are or may be endangered, the High Contracting Parties undertake to confer with one another as to the joint measures to be taken to safeguard those interests.

Article 3. Should the security or interests of one of the High Contracting Parties be threatened as a result of violent incursions from without, the other Party undertakes by means of its friendly support to lend the said Party its political and diplomatic assistance, with a view to removing the external cause of such threats.

Article 4. The High Contracting Parties undertake to submit to a procedure of conciliation or arbitration questions in regard to which a difference of opinion exists between them, which it may not be possible to settle by the normal methods of diplomacy.

The rules for this procedure of pacific settlement shall form the subject of a special Convention, which shall be concluded at the earliest possible date.

Article 5. The present Treaty shall be concluded for a period of five years and may be denounced or renewed one year before its expiry.

Article 6. The present Treaty shall be ratified and the ratifications shall be exchanged at Rome. It shall come into force immediately after the exchange of ratifications.

In faith whereof, both Plenipotentiaries have signed the present Treaty in duplicate and have affixed their seals thereto.

Done at Rome, September the sixteenth, one thousand nine hundred and twenty-six.
For Italy:

(L. S.) Benito MUSSOLINI.
For Roumania:

(L. S.) General AVERESCU.

4.1253 Pact of Friendship and Cordial Cooperation between Poland and the Kingdom of the Serbs, Croats, and Slovenes

Alliance Members: Poland and Yugoslavia
Signed On: September 18, 1926, in the city of Geneva. In force until September 27, 1939.
Alliance Type: Entente (Type III)

Source: *League of Nations Treaty Series,* no. 1799.

SUMMARY

Following common practice for most of eastern and central Europe during this part of the interwar period, Poland and Yugoslavia sought closer security ties and greater economic cooperation. This entente provided for consultation between the countries in the case of conflict and also the establishment of an arbitration commission, should any disputes arise. The entente was also meant to initiate greater economic cooperation between the two states. The agreement lasted until the German invasion and defeat of Poland in 1939.

ALLIANCE TEXT

The President of the Polish Republic and His Majesty the King of the Serbs, Croats and Slovenes, being firmly resolved to safeguard peace, the maintenance of which is essential for political stability and the economic recovery of Europe, have agreed to conclude a Treaty of Friendship, which is a natural consequence of the friendly relations existing between the two countries. For this purpose they have appointed as their Plenipotentiaries:

The President of the Polish Republic: M. August Zaleski, Minister for Foreign Affairs;

His Majesty the King of the Serbs, Croats and Slovenes: M. Momtchilo Nintchitch, Doctor of Laws, Minister for Foreign Affairs,

Who, having communicated their full powers, found in good and due form, have agreed upon the following provisions:

Article 1. The continuance of the sincere friendship and permanent good understanding which happily already exist between the Polish Republic and the Kingdom of the Serbs, Croats and Slovenes is solemnly confirmed.

Article 2. In order to co-ordinate their efforts for peace, the two Governments undertake to consult together regarding questions of foreign policy which, in their opinion, affect both Contracting Parties.

Article 3. As regards other questions of foreign policy, the two Contracting Parties undertake, in the case of international difficulties, to proceed to an immediate exchange of views in the most friendly spirit.

Article 4. The High Contracting Parties undertake to conclude as soon as possible an Arbitration Convention applicable to any disputes which may in future arise between them and which it may not be possible to settle by friendly agreement through the diplomatic channel.

Article 5. The present Pact shall remain in force for a period of three years as from the date of signature, but either of the Contracting Parties shall be free to denounce it after two years, by giving the other Party six months' notice.

Article 6. The present Pact shall be communicated to the League of Nations in conformity with Article 18 of the Covenant.

Article 7. The present Pact shall be ratified and the instruments of ratification exchanged at Belgrade as soon as possible.

In faith whereof the Plenipotentiaries have signed the present Treaty and have thereto affixed their seals.

Done at Geneva, in duplicate, on September 18, 1926.

(L. S.) August ZALESKI.
(L. S.) M. NINTCHITCH.

4.1254 Non-Aggression Treaty between the Lithuanian Republic and the Soviet Union

Alliance Members: Soviet Union and Lithuania
Signed On: September 28, 1926, in the city of Moscow. In force until October 10, 1939.
Alliance Type: Non-Aggression Pact (Type II)

Source: *The American Journal of International Law,* vol. 27, no. 4, Supplement: Official Documents (October 1933), p. 184–188.

SUMMARY

This pact was one of many that the Soviet Union established with its neighbors in order to thwart any possibility of economic or political isolation by non-communist states. Completely overmatched in capabilities by the Soviet Union, the Lithuanian government was still able to secure a small diplomatic victory with this treaty, as the question of control over the city of Vilnius—a city in modern Lithuania, then near Soviet Russia and with a majority Polish population—was not pressed by the Soviets. Instead, this treaty called for non-aggression between the neighboring countries, which was a policy that lasted until a bilateral defense pact was signed in October 1939. The Soviets invaded and incorporated Lithuania into the Soviet Union in 1940.

ALLIANCE TEXT

The President of the Lithuanian Republic, of the one part, and the Central Executive Committee of the Union of Socialist Soviet Republics, of the other part, being convinced that the interests of the Lithuanian people and of the peoples of the Union of Soviet Socialist Republics demand constant co-operation based on mutual confidence, have agreed, in order to contribute to the best of their ability to the maintenance of universal peace, to conclude a treaty with a view to strengthening the friendly relations existing between them, and to this end have appointed as their Plenipotentiaries:

The President of the Lithuanian Republic: Mykolas Sleževičius, Prime Minister and Minister of Justice, Acting Minister for Foreign Affairs, of the Lithuanian Republic; and Jurjis Baltrušaitis, Envoy Extraordinary and Minister Plenipotentiary of the Lithuanian Republic accredited to the Union of Soviet Socialist Republics; and

The Central Executive Committee of the Union of Socialist Soviet Republics: Georges Tchitcherine, Member of the C. E. C. of the Union of Socialist Soviet Republics, People's Commissary for Foreign Affairs; and Serge Alexandrovsky, Plenipotentiary Representative of the Union of Socialist Soviet Republics in Lithuania;

who having met in Moscow and exchanged their full powers found in good and due form, have agreed upon the following provisions:

Article 1. The relations between the Union of Socialist Soviet Republics and the Lithuania Republic shall continue to be based on the Treaty of Peace between Lithuania and Russia, concluded at Moscow on July 12, 1920, all the provisions of which retain their force and inviolability.

Article 2. The Lithuanian Republic and the Union of Soviet Socialist Republics undertake to respect, in all circumstances each others sovereignty and territorial integrity and inviolability.

Article 3. Each of the two Contracting Parties undertakes to refrain from any act of aggression whatsoever against the other Party.

Should one of the Contracting Parties, despite its peaceful attitude, be attacked by one or several third Powers, the other Contracting Party undertakes not to support the said third Power or Powers against the Contracting Party attacked.

Article 4. If, on the occasion of a conflict of the type mentioned in Article 3, second paragraph, or at a time when neither of the Contracting Parties is engaged in warlike operations, a political agreement directed against one of the Contracting Parties is concluded between third Powers with a view to the economic or financial boycott of either of the Contracting Parties, the other Contracting Party undertakes not to adhere to such agreement or coalition.

Article 5. Should a dispute arise between them, the Contracting Parties undertake to appoint conciliation commissions, if it should not prove possible to settle the dispute by diplomatic means.

The composition of the conciliation commissions, their rights and the procedure they shall observe shall be settled in virtue of a separate agreement to be concluded between the two Parties.

Article 6. The present Treaty is subject to ratification, which must take place within six weeks of the day of its signature. The exchange of the instruments of ratification shall take place at Kovno. The present Treaty has been drawn up in Lithuanian and Russian.

As regards interpretation, both texts shall be considered as authentic.

Article 7. The present Treaty shall enter into force on the date of the exchange of the instruments of ratifications and shall remain in force for five years, except Articles 1 and 2, the duration of the validity of which is not limited.

The validity of the present Treaty shall be prolonged automatically, on each occasion for one year, until either of the Contracting Parties expresses, at least six months before the expiration of the Treaty, the desire to enter upon negotiations regarding the future form of political relations between the two States.

In faith whereof, the Plenipotentiaries have affixed to the present treaty their autograph signatures, and their seals.

The original has been done and signed in duplicate at Moscow the twenty-eighth day of September, One thousand nine hundred and twenty-six.

(L.S.) (Signed) Mykolas SLEŽEVIČIUS.
(Signed) JURJIS BALTRUŠAITIS.
(L.S.) (Signed) G. V. TCHITCHERINE.
(Signed) SERGE ALEXSANDROVSKY.

4.1255 Pact of Friendship and Security between Albania and Italy

Alliance Members: Albania and Italy
Signed On: November 27, 1926, in the city of Tirana (Albania). In force until November 22, 1927.
Alliance Type: Entente (Type III)

Source: *League of Nations Treaty Series,* no. 1402.

SUMMARY

Italy's leadership had long viewed Albania as strategically important for Italian security. Control of Albania's ports would give Italy control of the Adriatic Sea and also a beachhead from which to advance into the Balkans. After Benito Mussolini assumed power in Italy, Il Duce moved to secure an entente with his country's eastern neighbor. This entente quickly led to even closer security cooperation as both countries signed a defense pact one year later, effectively ending the terms of this entente.

ALLIANCE TEXT

Albania and Italy, with the object of strengthening the ties of mutual friendship and security, having regard to their geographical position, and in order to promote the consolidation of peace,

Actuated by the desire to maintain the political, legal, and territorial *status quo* of Albania, within the scope of the treaties to which they both are Signatories and by the Covenant of the League of Nations,

Have agreed to conclude the present Pact of Friendship and Security,

And have for that purpose appointed as their Plenipotentiaries:

His Excellency, the President of the Albanian Republic: H. E. Hyssen Bey Vrioni, Minister for Foreign Affairs of the Albanian Republic,

His Majesty the King of Italy: H. E. Pompeo Aloisi, Envoy Extraordinary and Minister Plenipotentiary of His Majesty in Albania;

Who, having examined their full powers, found to be in good and due form, have agreed on the following provisions:

Article 1. Albania and Italy recognise that any disturbance threatening the political, legal and territorial *status quo* of Albania is contrary to their common political interests.

Article 2. In order to safeguard the above-mentioned interests, the High Contracting Parties undertake to afford each other mutual support and cordial co-operation; they also undertake not to conclude with other Powers any political or military agreements prejudicial to the interests of the other Party, including those defined (*anche definiti*) in the present Pact.

Article 3. The High Contracting Parties undertake to submit to special conciliation and arbitration procedure any questions which may give rise to dispute between them, and which it may not have been possible to settle by ordinary diplomatic procedure. The details of this procedure of pacific settlement shall form the subject of a special Convention to be concluded as soon as possible.

Article 4. The present Pact shall remain in force for five years, and may be denounced or renewed one year before its expiration.

Article 5. The present Pact shall be ratified and subsequently registered with the League of Nations. The ratifications shall be exchanged at Rome.

Done at Tirana, November 27, 1926.

(Signé) H. VRIONI.
(Signé) Pompeo ALOISI

4.1256 Treaty of Guarantee and Neutrality between Persia and the Soviet Union

Alliance Members: Persia (Iran) and the Soviet Union
Signed On: October 1, 1927, in the city of Moscow. In force until August 25, 1941.
Alliance Type: Neutrality Pact (Type II)

Source: *British and Foreign State Papers,* vol. 126, p. 943.

SUMMARY

This neutrality pact provided for a comprehensive settlement of differences between these two neighboring countries. In 1921, Iran had allowed the Soviets to send troops and occupy Iranian territory should a security threat materialize. This treaty actually gave the Soviets even broader powers. The right of Soviet entry into Iranian territories remained intact, and the Iranians pledged never to enter into any alliance or alignment that targeted the Soviet state. Further, Iran pledged to never participate in any economic or political boycotts against the Soviets—an important concession given the length of the Iranian border with the Soviet Union.

The neutrality pact ended when Soviet and British forces occupied Iran and installed a new government during World War II.

ALLIANCE TEXT

His Imperial Majesty the Shah of Persia and the Central Executive Committee of the Union of Soviet Socialist Republics, recognising the desirability, in the interests of the two Contracting Parties, of defining the precise conditions for the consolidation of normal stable relations and of the sincere friendship which unites them, have appointed as their Plenipotentiaries:

His Imperial Majesty the Shah of Persia: M. Ali Goli Khan Ansari, Persian Minister for Foreign Affairs;

The Central Executive Committee of the Union of Soviet Socialist Republics: MM. George Tchitcherine, People's Commissary for Foreign Affairs of the Union of Soviet Socialist Republics, and Lev Karakhan, Deputy People's Commissary for Foreign Affairs of the Union of Soviet Socialist Republics;

Who, having exchanged their full powers, found in good and due form. have agreed upon the following provisions:

Article I. The mutual relations between Persia and the Union of Soviet Socialist Republics shall continue to be governed by the Treaty of February 26, 1921, of which all the articles and provisions shall remain in force, and which shall be applicable throughout the territory of the Union of Soviet Socialist Republics.

Article 2. Each of the High Contracting Parties undertakes to refrain from any aggression and from any hostile acts directed against the other Party, and not to introduce its military forces into the territory of the other Party.

Should either of the Contracting Parties become the victim of aggression on the part of one or more third Powers, the other Contracting Party agrees to observe neutrality throughout the duration of the conflict, while the Party which is the victim of the aggression shall not violate that neutrality, notwithstanding any strategical, tactical or political considerations or any advantages it might thereby obtain.

Article 3. Each of the Contracting Parties agrees to take no part, whether *de facto* or *de jure,* in political alliances or agreements directed against the safety of the territory or territorial waters of the other Contracting Party or against its integrity, independence or sovereignty.

Each of the Contracting Parties likewise agrees to take no part in any economic boycotts or blockades organised by third Powers against one of the Contracting Parties.

Article 4. In view of the obligations laid down in Articles 4 and 5 of the Treaty of February 26, 1921, each of the Contracting Parties, being determined to abstain from any intervention in the internal affairs of the other Party and from any propaganda or campaign against the Government of the other Party, shall strictly forbid its officials to commit such acts in the territory of the other Party.

Should the citizens of either of the Contracting Parties in the territory of the other Party engage in any propaganda or campaign prohibited by the authorities of this latter Party, the Government of that territory shall have the right to put a stop to the activities of such citizens and to impose the statutory penalties.

The two Parties likewise undertake, in virtue of the above-mentioned Articles, not to encourage or to allow in their respective territories the formation or activities of: (1) organisations or groups of any description whatever, whose object is to overthrow the Government of the other Contracting Party by means of violence, insurrection or outrage; (2) organisations or groups usurping the office of the Government of the other country or of part of its territory, also having as their object the subversion of the Government of the other Contracting Party by the above-mentioned means, a breach of its peace and security, or an infringement of its territorial integrity.

In accordance with the foregoing principles, the two Contracting Parties likewise undertake to prohibit military enrollment and the introduction into their territory of armed forces, arms, ammunition, and all other war material, intended for the organisations mentioned above.

Article 5. The two Contracting Parties undertake to settle by a pacific procedure appropriate to the circumstances all disputes of any description which may arise between them and which it has not been possible to settle through the ordinary diplomatic channels.

Article 6. Apart from the obligations undertaken by the two Contracting Parties in virtue of the present Treaty, the two Parties shall retain full freedom of action in their international relations.

Article 7. The present Treaty is concluded for a period of three years and shall be approved and ratified within the shortest possible time by the legislative organs of the two Parties, after which it shall come into force.

The exchange of the instruments of ratification shall take place at Teheran one month after ratification.

After the expiry of the original period of validity, the Treaty shall be regarded as automatically prolonged for successive periods of one year until one of the Contracting Parties notifies the other of its desire to denounce the Treaty. In that case the present Treaty shall remain in force for six months from the date of the notification of its denunciation by one of the Parties.

Article 8. The present Treaty is drawn up in the Persian, Russian, and French languages, in three authentic copies for each of the Contracting Parties.

For the purpose of interpretation, all three texts shall be regarded as authentic. In the case of any divergencies with regard to interpretation, the French text shall prevail.

In faith whereof the above-named Plenipotentiaries have signed the present Treaty and have thereto affixed their seals.

Done at Moscow, October 1, 1927.

(Signed) Ali Goli Khan ANSARI.
(Signed) George TCHITCHERINE.
(Signed) L. KARAKHAN.

4.1257 Treaty of Friendly Understanding between France and the Kingdom of the Serbs, Croats, and Slovenes

Alliance Members: France and Yugoslavia
Signed On: November 11, 1927, in the city of Paris. In force until June 22, 1940.
Alliance Type: Neutrality Pact (Type II)

Source: *League of Nations Treaty* no. 1592.

SUMMARY

This alliance was part of the network of alliances France was building in central Europe, strengthening the Little Entente powers of Yugoslavia, Czechoslovakia and Romania. The broad goal was creating a cordon sanitaire, or safe zone, between Germany and the Soviet Union. This alliance, like the other French alliances in the region, provided for close cooperation and neutrality in the event of international crisis. The alliance lasted until France was occupied by Hitler's Germany during World War II.

ALLIANCE TEXT

The President of the French Republic and His Majesty the King of the Serbs, Croats and Slovenes, being equally desirous of maintaining in Europe that state of peace and political stability, which is essential for the social advancement and economic prosperity both of France and of the Serb-Croat-Slovene Kingdom;

Being firmly attached to the principle of respect for international undertakings, a principle which has been solemnly confirmed by the Covenant of the League of Nations;

Being desirous, within the framework of the aforesaid Covenant of ensuring, in advance, the adoption of a common attitude in the event of the order established by the treaties which they have signed being endangered;

And being convinced that it is the duty of modern Governments to prevent a return to war by providing for the pacific settlement of any disputes which may arise between them;

Have resolved, for this purpose, to give each other renewed pledges of peace, understanding and friendship, and have appointed as their Plenipotentiaries the following:

The President of the French Republic; M. Aristide Briand, Deputy, Minister for Foreign Affairs;

His Majesty the King of the Serbs, Croats and Slovenes; Dr. V. Marinkovitch, Minister for Foreign Affairs;

Who, having exchanged their full powers, found in good and due form, have agreed upon the following provisions:

Article I. France and the Kingdom of the Serbs, Croats and Slovenes reciprocally undertake to refrain from all attacks or invasions directed against one another and in no circumstances to resort to war against one another.

Nevertheless, this stipulation shall not apply:

(1) To the exercise of the right of legitimate defence, that is to say, the right of resisting a violation of the undertaking given in paragraph 1 of the present Article;

(2) To action undertaken in application of Article 16 of the Covenant of the League of Nations;

(3) To action undertaken in virtue of a decision by the Assembly or Council of the League of Nations, or in application of paragraph 7 of Article 15 of the Covenant of the League of Nations, provided that, in the latter case, such action is directed against a State which was the first to attack.

Article II. Taking into consideration their respective obligations under Article I of the present Treaty, France and the Kingdom of the Serbs, Croats and Slovenes undertake to settle by pacific means and in the following manner all questions whatever which may divide them and which it may not have been possible to settle by the normal methods of diplomacy; all questions regarding which the Parties may be in dispute as to their respective rights shall be submitted to judges, with whose decisions the Parties undertake to comply; all other questions shall be submitted to a Conciliation Commission, and if the arrangement proposed by that Commission is not accepted by both Parties, the question shall be brought before the Council of the League of Nations, which shall decide in accordance with Article 15 of the League Covenant.

The procedure in regard to these methods of pacific settlement is laid down in special conventions which have been signed on this day.

Article III. The Government of the French Republic and the Royal Government of the Serb-Croat-Slovene Kingdom undertake to give joint consideration, subject to any resolutions adopted by the Council or Assembly of the League of Nations, to questions which are of such a nature as to endanger the external security of France or the Serb-Croat-Slovene State, or to impair the order established by treaties which they have both signed.

Article IV. If, in spite of the sincerely pacific intentions of the

French and Serb-Croat-Slovene Governments, either France or the Kingdom of the Serbs, Croats and Slovenes should be attacked without provocation, the two Governments shall, without delay confer with one another as to the measures which each shall take, within the framework of the Covenant of the League of Nations, in order to safeguard their legitimate national interests and to uphold the order established by the treaties of which they are both signatories.

Article V. The High Contracting Parties agree to take counsel together in the event of any modification, or attempted modification, of the political status of European countries and, subject to any resolutions which may be adopted in such case by the Council or Assembly of the League of Nations, to come to an understanding as to the attitude which they should respectively observe in such an eventuality.

Article VI. The High Contracting Parties declare that nothing in this Treaty is to be interpreted as contradicting the stipulations of the treaties at present in force which have been signed by France or the Kingdom of the Serbs, Croats and Slovenes, and which concern their policy in Europe. They undertake to exchange views on questions affecting European policy in order to co-ordinate their efforts in the cause of peace, and for this purpose to communicate to each other henceforward any treaties or agreements which they may conclude with third Powers on the same subject. Such treaties or agreements shall invariably be directed to aims which are compatible with the maintenance of peace.

Article VII. Nothing in the present Treaty may be interpreted or applied in such a way as to prejudice the rights and obligations of the High Contracting Parties under the Covenant of the League of Nations.

Article VIII. The present Treaty shall be communicated for registration to the League of Nations in conformity with Article 18 of the Covenant.

Article IX. The present Treaty shall be ratified and the instruments of ratification shall be exchanged in Paris as soon as possible.

It shall enter into force immediately upon the exchange of ratifications and shall remain in force for five years, after which it may be renewed in virtue of previous notice, which must have been duly given at the end of the fourth year, and for a period to be determined.

In faith whereof, the respective Plenipotentiaries duly authorised for this purpose, have signed the present Treaty and have thereto affixed their seals.

Done in Paris in duplicate, November 11, 1927.

(L. S.) (Signed) A. BRIAND.
(L. S.) (Signed) Dr. V. MARINKOVITCH.

4.1258 Treaty of Defensive Alliance between Italy and Albania

Alliance Members: Italy and Albania
Signed On: November 22, 1927, in the city of Tirana (Albania). In force until April 7, 1939.
Alliance Type: Defense Pact (Type I)

Source: *League of Nations Treaty Series,* no. 1616.

SUMMARY

What began as an entente in 1926 moved to the level of a tighter security relationship one year later as Benito Mussolini's Italy signed this defense pact with Albania. Italy subsidized the Albanians with low-cost loans and trained the Albanian military. In exchange, Albania gave Italy the right to exploit many of its natural resources.

The defense pact soured in 1931 as Albania tried to distance itself from Italian foreign policy. Albania even signed trade agreements with Greece and Yugoslavia in 1934, prompting Mussolini to send a fleet of ships to the Albanian coast as a show of force. Ultimately, the defense pact ended with the Italian invasion of Albania in 1939.

ALLIANCE TEXT

Italy and Albania, being desirous of solemnly re-affirming and strengthening the solidarity which happily exists between the two States, and of devoting all their efforts to the removal of any causes which might disturb the peace between them, and between them and other States,

Recognising the benefits of close co-operation between the two States,

And once more confirming the fact that the interests and the security of each are bound up with those of the other,

Have decided to conclude a defensive alliance by this Treaty, with the sole object of stabilising the natural relations which happily exist between the two States and thus ensuring a policy of peaceful development,

and have accordingly appointed as their Plenipotentiaries:

His Majesty the King of Italy: His Excellency M. Ugo Sola, Knight of the Order of Sts. Maurice and Lazarus, Knight Grand Commander of the Order of Skanderbeg, etc., etc., His Envoy Extraordinary and Minister Plenipotentiary in Albania;

His Excellency the President of the Albanian Republic: His Excellency Ilias Bey Vrioni, Knight Grand Commander of the Orders of Skanderbeg and of the Crown of Italy, etc., etc., His Minister for Foreign Affairs;

Who, having communicated their full powers, found in good and due form, have agreed as follows:

Article I. All previous Treaties concluded between the two High Contracting Parties since the admission of Albania to the League of Nations shall be exactly and faithfully observed within the limits laid down in the text of the same, so that there shall be sincere and perfect friendship between the two peoples and between the two Governments, and that each shall assist the other, it being understood that each of the High Contracting Parties shall uphold the interests and advantages of the other with the same zeal as it displays in upholding its own.

Article 2. Between Italy, of the one part, and Albania, of the other part, there shall be for twenty years an unalterable defensive alliance, which may be denounced during the eighteenth or nineteenth year of its duration. Should no such denunciation take place, the alliance shall be understood to be renewed by tacit consent for a like period. The two High Contracting Parties shall employ all their diligence and all the means at their command to ensure the security of their respective countries, and to defend and safeguard each other against any attack from without.

Article 3. As a result of the undertakings given in the foregoing Articles, the two High Contracting Parties shall act in concert to maintain peace and tranquillity, and, should one of them be threatened with war which it has not provoked, the other Party shall employ the most effectual means at its command, not only to prevent hostilities, but also to secure just satisfaction for the threatened Party.

Article 4. Should every means of conciliation have been exhausted without avail, each of the High Contracting Parties undertakes to throw in its lot with the other, and to place at the disposal of its ally all military, financial, and other resources which may be of assistance in terminating the conflict, should such assistance be called for by the threatened Party.

Article 5. In any case covered by Article 4, the two High Contracting Parties undertake not to conclude or enter into negotiations for a peace, armistice, or truce except by common consent.

Article 6. The present Treaty has been signed in four original copies, two in Italian and two in Albanian, both texts being authentic.

Article 7. The present Treaty shall be ratified, and shall thereafter be registered with the League of Nations. The ratifications shall be exchanged at Rome.

Done at Tirana, this twenty-second day of November, one thousand nine hundred and twenty-seven (1927).

Ugo SOLA.
Ilias VRIONI.

4.1259 Pact of Non-Aggression and Arbitration between the Hellenic Republic and the Kingdom of Romania

Alliance Members: Greece and Romania
Signed On: March 21, 1928, in the city of Geneva. In force until February 9, 1934.
Alliance Type: Neutrality Pact (Type II)

Source: *League of Nations Treaty Series*, no. 2508.

SUMMARY

This treaty established the terms of relations between Greece and Romania. Note that most of the clauses of the treaty were concerned with how disputes were to be handled between the countries, including the establishment of a commission for arbitration and the relation of that commission to the League of Nations. Only the first article contains a provision constituting a military alliance as both countries "undertake not to attack each other or invade each other's territories and in no case to resort to war against each other." The alliance was reorganized in 1934 within a broader pact that also included Turkey and Yugoslavia.

ALLIANCE TEXT

The President of the Hellenic Republic and His Majesty the King of Roumania,

Being desirous of maintaining the order of affairs established by the Treaties and of pursuing in all circumstances a policy of peace and concord,

Considering that the faithful observance of methods of pacific procedure renders possible the settlement of all international disputes without a resort to force ever being necessary,

Being of opinion that it is their duty to contribute, for their part, towards establishing this principle in practice,

Taking into account the relations of cordial friendship and mutual confidence and the community of interests and ideals of peace which have always existed between their countries,

Have decided for this purpose to conclude a Pact of non-aggression and arbitration and have appointed as their Plenipotentiaries:

The President of the Hellenic Republic: M. André Michalacopoulos, Minister for Foreign Affairs;

His Majesty the King of Roumania: M. Nicolas Titulesco, Minister for Foreign Affairs;

Who, having communicated their full powers, found in good and due form, have agreed on the following provisions:

Article 1. The High Contracting Parties mutually undertake not to attack each other or invade each other's territories and in no case to resort to war against each other.

Nevertheless, these stipulations shall not apply in the case of:
(1) The exercise of the right of self-defence;
(2) Action in pursuance of Article 16 of the Covenant of the League of Nations;
(3) Action by reason of a decision taken by the Assembly or by the Council of the League of Nations or in pursuance of Article 13, paragraph 7, of the Covenant of the League of Nations, provided that in this last case the action is directed against a State which was the first to attack.

Article 2. Should either High Contracting Party consider that an infraction of the preceding Article has taken place or is taking place, it shall immediately bring the question before the Council of the League of Nations.

Article 3. The High Contracting Parties undertake to settle by means of conciliation or judicial procedure or arbitration, in the manner provided for hereinafter, all questions whatsoever on which they may differ and which it has not been possible to settle by the normal methods of diplomacy.

This undertaking shall not, however, apply to:

(1) Disputes connected with events prior to the present Pact;

(2) Disputes concerning claims made by private persons against one of the High Contracting Parties, which will be finally decided by the competent national courts of one or other of the High Contracting Parties;

(3) Disputes concerning questions which, by international law, are solely within the jurisdiction of States, such as municipal law;

(4) Disputes relating to the territorial status of the High Contracting Parties or affecting their vital interests.

Article 4. Disputes for the settlement of which a special procedure is laid down in other conventions in force between the High Contracting Parties shall be settled in conformity with the provisions of those conventions.

Article 5. Disputes coming under Article 3 which are of a purely legal nature shall be submitted for decision to the Permanent Court of International Justice unless the Parties agree, in the manner hereinafter provided, to have recourse to an arbitral tribunal. If there is a difference of opinion as to whether a dispute is of a purely legal nature, the question shall be submitted, at the request of one or other of the Parties, to the Council of the League of Nations for consideration in virtue of Article II, paragraph 2, of the Covenant of the League of Nations.

The Parties undertake to comply with the unanimous recommendation of the Council of the League of Nations.

Article 6. If the Parties agree to submit the dispute to an arbitral tribunal, they shall draw up a special agreement. If they do not agree simply to follow the procedure laid down in the Hague Convention of October 18, 1907, for the Pacific Settlement of International Disputes, the Parties shall specify in this special agreement, in addition to the arbitrators selected and the subject of the dispute, the details of the procedure and the substantive rules to be applied by the arbitrators.

Article 7. If the Parties agree to submit the dispute to an arbitral tribunal but fail to agree concerning the special agreement referred to in the preceding Article or fail to appoint arbitrators, either Party shall be at liberty, after giving three months' notice, to bring the dispute by an application direct before the Permanent Court of International Justice.

Article 8. The judgment of the Permanent Court of International Justice or the award of the Arbitral Tribunal shall be executed in good faith by the Parties.

Any difficulties to which the interpretation or execution of the judgments of the Permanent Court of International Justice or the arbitral awards given under the conditions mentioned above may give rise shall be decided by the Permanent Court of International Justice, to which such difficulties shall be submitted on the request of one or other of the Parties.

Article 9. Previous to any arbitration proceedings or proceedings before the Permanent Court of International Justice under the conditions mentioned above, the dispute may, by agreement between the Parties, be submitted to the conciliation procedure provided for in the present Pact.

In the event of failure of conciliation the dispute may, after the expiration of the period laid down in Article 21, be submitted to the Permanent Court of International Justice or the Arbitral Tribunal, according to circumstances, under the conditions laid down in the preceding Articles.

Article 10. All disputes coming under Article 3 which are not of a purely legal nature and are therefore not capable of being submitted to arbitration as provided for in Articles 5 to 9 above, shall be obligatorily submitted to the procedure of conciliation provided for in the following provisions.

Article 11. On a request to that effect being made by one of the Contracting Parties to the other Party, a permanent Conciliation Commission shall be constituted within a period of three months.

Article 12. The permanent Conciliation Commission shall be composed of three members. The High Contracting Parties shall each nominate one commissioner chosen from among their respective nationals.

They shall jointly designate the President, who must not be a national of the High Contracting Parties or be habitually resident in the territories or be in the service of the Parties. If the President is not appointed within the period laid down in the preceding Article, or, in the case of replacement, within three months from the date on which the vacancy occurs, he shall be appointed, in the absence of agreement between the Parties and on the request of one of them, the President of the Swiss Confederation if the latter agrees thereto.

The commissioners shall be appointed for three years. They shall be re-eligible. They shall continue in office until they are replaced and, in any case, until the expiration of their mandate.

As long as proceedings have not been opened, each of the High Contracting Parties shall be entitled to recall the commissioner appointed by it and to appoint a successor. It shall also have the right to withdraw its consent to the appointment of the President.

Vacancies occurring as a result of the expiration of a term of office, recall, death, resignation or any other cause shall be filled within the shortest possible time in the manner fixed for the appointments.

Article 13. Disputes shall be brought before the Conciliation Commission by means of an application addressed to the President the by two Parties acting in agreement, or, in default thereof, by one or other of the Parties. The application, after stating the subject of the dispute, shall contain the invitation to the Commission to take all necessary measures with a view to arriving at an amicable solution.

If the application emanates from only one of the Parties, the other Party shall without delay be notified by it.

Article 14. Within fifteen days from the date on which a dispute has been brought by one of the Parties before the Conciliation Commission, either Party may remplace its commissioner, for the examination of the particular dispute, by a person possessing special competence in the matter.

The Party making use of this right shall immediately notify the other Party; the latter shall in such case be entitled to take similar action within fifteen days from the date on which the notification reaches it.

Article 15. In the absence of agreement to the contrary between the Parties, the Conciliation Commission shall meet at the place selected by its President.

Article 16. The task of the Conciliation Commission shall be to elucidate the questions in dispute, to collect with that object all necessary information and to endeavour to bring the Parties to an agreement.

It shall, after the case has been examined, draw up a report containing proposals for the settlement of the dispute.

Article 17. The procedure before the Conciliation Commission must provide for both Parties being heard.

The Commission shall lay down its own procedure, regard being had, in the absence of unanimous decisions to the contrary, to the provisions of Chapter III of the Hague Convention of October 18, 1907, for the Pacific Settlement of International Disputes.

Article 18. The deliberations of the Conciliation Commission shall be held in private, unless the Commission decides otherwise in agreement with the Parties.

Article 19. The Parties shall have the right to appoint to the Commission agents, counsel and experts, who shall also act as intermediaries between them and the Commission, and to request that any person whose evidence appears to them desirable shall be heard.

The Commission for its part shall be entitled to request oral explanations from the agents, counsel and experts of both Parties, as well as from all persons it may think desirable to summon with the consent of their Governments.

Article 20. The Parties undertake to facilitate the work of the Conciliation Commission and, in particular, to supply it to the greatest possible extent with all relevant documents and information, as well as to use all the means at their disposal under their laws to enable it to proceed to the summoning and hearing of witnesses or experts.

Article 21. The Conciliation Commission shall submit its report within four months from the date on which the dispute was brought before it, unless the Parties agree to extend this period.

A copy of the report shall be delivered to each of the Parties. The report shall not be in the nature of an arbitral award, as regards either the statement of the facts or the legal considerations.

Article 22. The Conciliation Commission shall fix the period within which the Parties must decide as to the proposals for settlement contained in its report. This period must not exceed three months.

Article 23. During the proceedings of the Commission, each of the Commissioners shall receive emoluments the amount of which shall be fixed by agreement between the Parties, each of which shall contribute an equal share.

The general expenses arising out of the working of the Commission shall be divided in the same manner.

Article 24. If one of the Parties does not accept the proposals of the Conciliation Commission or does not take a decision within the period laid down in the Commissions report, the question shall, at the request of either Party, be brought before the Council of the League of Nations, which shall decide in accordance with Article 15 of the Covenant of the League.

This provision shall not apply in the case provided for in Article 9.

Article 25. The present Pact, which is in conformity with the Covenant of the League of Nations, may not be interpreted as restricting the duty of the League to take, at any time and notwithstanding any proceedings of conciliation and arbitration, whatever action may be deemed wise and effectual to safeguard the peace of the world.

Article 26. The present Pact shall be ratified and the instruments of ratification shall be exchanged as soon as possible.

The Pact shall come into force as soon as the ratifications have been exchanged. It is concluded for a period of ten years from the date of its coming into force.

If it has not been denounced six months before the expiration of this period, it shall be deemed to be renewed for a further period of five years, and similarly thereafter.

If conciliation proceedings or arbitral or judicial proceedings are pending on the expiration of the present Pact, they shall, unless the Parties otherwise agree, be continued in accordance with the provisions of the present Pact.

Done at Geneva in duplicate on the twenty-first day of March, one thousand nine hundred and twenty-eight.

(Signed) M. TITULESCO.

(Signed) A. MICHALAKOPOULOS.

4.1260 Treaty of Neutrality, Conciliation, and Judicial Settlement between the Kingdom of Italy and the Turkish Republic

Alliance Members: Italy and Turkey
Signed On: May 30, 1928, in the city of Rome. In force until November 18, 1935.
Alliance Type: Neutrality Pact (Type II)

Source: *League of Nations Treaty Series,* no. 2172.

SUMMARY

This neutrality and non-aggression pact was signed with Italy during a formal visit by Turkish leaders to Rome. The treaty provided for the peaceful resolution of disputes between the contracting parties and allowed for renewal after five years. However, the agreement effectively died after renewal when Turkey participated in sanctions against Italy following the invasion of Ethiopia by Mussolini's forces in October of 1935.

ALLIANCE TEXT

His Majesty the King of Italy and the President of the Turkish Republic, being desirous of firmly establishing the ties of friendship between the two countries and of contributing to the maintenance of general peace, have decided to conclude a Treaty of Neutrality, Conciliation and Judicial Settlement, and have for this purpose appointed as their Plenipotentiaries:

His Majesty the King of Italy: His Excellency Benito Mussolini, Head of the Government, Prime Minister, Secretary of State, Minister Secretary of State for Foreign Affairs;

The President of the Turkish Republic: His Excellency Suad Bey, Ambassador Extraordinary and Plenipotentiary of the Turkish Republic accredited to His Majesty the King of Italy;

Who, having communicated their full powers, found in good and due form, have agreed upon the following provisions:

Article 1. Each of the High Contracting Parties undertakes not to enter into any agreement of a political or economic nature or into any combination directed against the other.

Article 2. Should one of the High Contracting Parties, notwithstanding its peaceful attitude, be attacked by a third Power or third Powers, the other Party shall observe neutrality during the whole of the conflict.

Article 3. The High Contracting Parties undertake to submit to a procedure of conciliation all disputes of any nature whatever which may arise between them, and which it may not halve been possible to settle by the normal methods of diplomacy. In the event of the procedure of conciliation proving unsuccessful, a judicial settlement shall be sought. The Protocol hereto annexed lays down the procedure for conciliation and judicial settlement.

The present Article shall not apply to questions which, in virtue of treaties in force between the two High Contracting Parties, come within the jurisdiction of either of them. Furthermore, it shall not apply to questions which, according to international law, relate to the right of sovereignty.

Each of the High Contracting Parties shall, by a written declaration, specify unilaterally whether any question comes under the right of sovereignty.

No question may be submitted to the procedure of conciliation or to arbitration in accordance with the clauses of the annexed Protocol unless it has been previously recognised to be of a nature conforming to the provisions of the present Article.

The arbitral award shall be rendered according to the principles of international law.

Article 4. Any disputes which may arise as to the interpretation or the execution of the present Treaty shall be submitted direct to the Permanent Court of International Justice at The Hague by a simple request.

Article 5. The present Treaty shall be ratified as soon as possible and shall enter into force immediately after the exchange of the ratifications, which shall take place at Rome.

It shall remain in force for five years as from the date of the exchange of the instruments of ratification. Unless denounced six months before the expiration of this period, it shall remain in force for a further period of five years.

Done at Rome, on the thirtieth day of May, one thousand nine hundred and twenty-eight, in two copies, both of which shall be authentic and one of which shall be transmitted to each of the signatory States.

In faith whereof the above-named Plenipotentiaries have signed the present Treaty and have thereto affixed their seals.

(L. S.) Benito MUSSOLINI.
(L. S.) SUAD.

4.1261 Treaty of Friendship between Abyssinia and Italy

Alliance Members: Abyssinia (Ethiopia) and Italy
Signed On: August 2, 1928, in the city of Addis Ababa (Ethiopia). In force until October 3, 1935.
Alliance Type: Non-Aggression Pact (Type II)

Source: *British and Foreign State Papers,* vol. 129, p. 1.

SUMMARY

Italy had begun expansion into Africa in the late nineteenth century at the behest of the British, who wanted to counter French influence in North Africa. In 1899, the British transferred Eritrea to the Italians. After coming to power in Italy, Mussolini wanted to use the Italian colonial presence as a base for dominating Ethiopia and the Horn of Africa, and this agreement between the two countries established initial relations between the new Italian government and Ethiopia. By 1934, after an incident at the village of Wal-wal on the border of Italian Somaliland and Ethiopia became a full-blown crisis involving the League of Nations, Britain and France tried to temper the growing tensions along the border. But by October of 1935, Mussolini invaded Ethiopia, which effectively ended this neutrality pact.

ALLIANCE TEXT

His Majesty King Victor Emmanuel III of Italy and Her Majesty the Empress Zauditu of Abyssinia;

Desiring that the friendship between their two States should be on a more solid and durable basis, and that the economic relations between the two countries should continue to extend;

Commendatore Giuliano Cora, Minister Plenipotentiary of the Kingdom of Italy, on behalf of His Majesty King Victor Emmanuel III and of his successors, and His Imperial Highness Tafari Maconnen, Heir to the Throne and Regent of the Ethiopian Empire, in the name of the Empress Zauditu, in his own name and in that of their successors, have agreed as follows:—

Art. 1. There shall be continual peace and perpetual friendship between the Kingdom of Italy and the Ethiopian Empire.

2. The two Governments reciprocally undertake not to take, under any pretext, any action which may prejudice or damage the independence of the other, and to safeguard the interests of their respective countries.

3. The two Governments undertake to develop and promote the commerce existing between the two countries.

4. Italian citizens, subjects and protected persons on their establishment in Abyssinia, and Abyssinians on their establishment in Italy and its colonies, shall be obliged in respect of their commerce and work, the necessities of life and subsistence, and all that concerns the exercise of their professions, commerce and work, to observe and respect the laws of the State in which they reside.

It is understood that the provisions of article 7 of the treaty between the Ethiopian Empire and the French Republic concluded on the 10th January, 1908, shall continue to apply to Italian citizens, subjects and protected persons in Abyssinia so long as the said treaty remains in force.

5. The two Governments undertake to submit to a procedure of conciliation or of arbitration the questions which may arise between them, and which they may not be able to decide by the normal process of diplomacy, without having recourse to force of arms. Notes shall be exchanged by agreement between the two Governments relative to the method of selecting the arbitrators.

6. The present treaty, which shall be registered with the League of Nations, shall be ratified, and the exchange of ratifications shall take place at Addis Ababa as soon as possible.

7. The present treaty shall have a duration of 20 years dating from the exchange of ratifications. On the termination of that period it shall be renewable from year to year.

Done in duplicate, both texts being identical, in the official Italian and Amharic languages. One of the copies shall remain in the possession of the Italian Government and the other in that of the Abyssinian Government.

Addis Ababa, August 2, 1928,—Year VI—(The 6th day of Hamlé of the year 1901 of Grace).

(L. S.) *GIULTANO CORA.*

(L. S.) *TAFARI MACONNEN, Heir to the Throne of Ethiopia.*

4.1262 Treaty of Friendship, Conciliation, and Judicial Settlement between Greece and Italy

Alliance Members: Italy and Greece
Signed On: September 23, 1928, in the city of Rome. In force until November 18, 1935.
Alliance Type: Neutrality Pact (Type II)

Source: *League of Nations Treaty,* no. 2510.

SUMMARY

At the time this treaty was signed, relations between Greece and Italy had been strained for some time because Italy had backed Turkish nationalists during the Greco-Turkish War (1919–1922). Mussolini's new fascist government used the killing of one of its generals at the border of Greece and Albania as a pretext to demand reparations from Greece, and Italy followed this demand with a bombing and occupation of the Greek island of Corfu.

Bilateral relations normalized to some extent, though, with the signing of this friendship treaty, four months after Italy signed a similar pact with Greece's rival, Turkey. As with the Italo-Turkish treaty, this pact calls for non-aggression and neutrality in the event of conflict and provides mechanisms for dispute resolution. The pact itself lasted until Greece joined Turkey and other nations in sanctions against Italy following its invasion of Ethiopia.

ALLIANCE TEXT

The President of the Hellenic Republic and His Majesty the King of Italy, having regard to the ties of sincere friendship and mutual confidence which happily unite the two countries and desiring by a solemn act to affirm their desire for political and economic cooperation with a view to contributing towards the work of general peace,

Being equally desirous of maintaining the state of peace and political stability in accordance with the principles laid down in the Covenant of the League of Nations,

Considering that the faithful observance of the methods of pacific procedure renders it possible to settle disputes without resort to force, and,

Deeming it to be their duty to contribute towards the establishment in practice of these principles,

Have decided for this purpose to conclude a Pact of Friendship, Conciliation and Judicial Settlement, and have appointed as their Plenipotentiaries:

The President of the Hellenic Republic: His Excellency M. Eleftherios Veniselos, President of the Council of Ministers;

His Majesty the King of Italy: His Excellency Cav. Benito Mussolini, Head of the Government, Prime Minister Secretary of State, Minister Secretary of State for Foreign Affairs;

Who, having communicated their full powers, found in good and due form, have agreed on the following provisions:

Article 1. The two High Contracting Parties reciprocally undertake to lend each other mutual support and to cooperate cordially for the purpose of maintaining the order established by the Treaties of Peace of which they are both signatories, and of ensuring that the obligations laid down in the said treaties are respected and fulfilled.

Article 2. Should a Power or Powers make unprovoked attack on either High Contracting Party, the other Party undertakes to observe neutrality throughout the conflict.

Article 3. Should the security and interests of either High Contracting Party be threatened by violent incursions from without, the other Party undertakes to lend it its political and diplomatic support with a view to removing the cause of these threats.

Article 4. In the event of international complications the two High Contracting Parties undertake, if they agree that their joint interests are or may be threatened, to consult together as to the measures to be adopted to safeguard these interests.

Article 5. Greece and Italy undertake to submit to the procedure of conciliation provided for in Articles 8 to 19 below all questions on which they may differ and which it has not been possible to settle by the normal methods of diplomacy.

In the event of the procedure of conciliation being resorted to without success, a judicial settlement shall be sought in accordance with Articles 20 and following of the present Treaty.

Article 6. Disputes for the settlement of which a special procedure is laid down in other conventions in force between the Parties to the dispute shall be settled in conformity with the provisions of those conventions.

Article 7. 1. In the case of a dispute the occasion of which, according to the municipal law of one of the Parties, falls within the competence of the judicial or administrative authorities, the Party in question may object to the dispute being submitted for settlement by the different proceedings laid down in the present Convention until a decision with final effect has been pronounced, within a reasonable time, by the competent authority.

2. In this case, the Party which desires to resort to the procedures laid down in the present Convention must notify the other Party of its intention within one year from the date of the aforementioned decision.

Article 8. A permanent Conciliation Commission shall be constituted within six months from the date the exchange of ratifications of the present Treaty.

This Commission shall be composed of three members. The High Contracting Parties shall each nominate one commissioner, chosen from among their respective nationals.

They shall jointly designate the President, who must not be a national of the High Contracting Parties nor be habitually resident in the territories or be in the service of the Parties. If, in the absence of agreement, the President is not appointed within the period laid down in the preceding paragraph or, in the event of replacement, within three months of the date on which the vacancy occurs, he shall be designated in the following manner:

Each of the two High Contracting Parties shall put forward two candidates taken from the list of the members of the Hague Permanent Court who have not been designated by the Parties and are not nationals of either of them. It shall be determined by lot which of the candidates thus put forward shall be President.

The commissioners shall be appointed for three years. They shall be reeligible. They shall continue to exercise their functions until their replacement and in any case until the expiration of their mandate.

As long as the proceedings have not been opened, either High Contracting Party shall have the right to recall the commissioner appointed by it and designate a successor. It shall also have the right to withdraw its consent to the appointment of the president.

Vacancies occurring as a result of the expiration of a mandate, recall, death, resignation or any other cause shall be filled within the shortest possible time in the manner laid down for the appointments.

Article 9. Disputes shall be brought before the Conciliation Commission by means of an application addressed to the President by the two Parties acting in agreement, or, in default

thereof, by one or other of the Parties. The application, after stating the subject of the dispute shall contain an invitation to the Commission to take all necessary measures with a view to arriving at an amicable solution.

If the application emanates from only one of the Parties, that Party shall at the same time notify the other Party.

Article 10. Within fifteen days from the date on which a dispute has been brought by one of the Parties before the Conciliation Commission, either Party may replace its own commissioner, for the examination of the particular dispute, by a person possessing special competence in the matter.

The Party making use of this right shall immediately notify the other Party; the latter shall in such case be entitled to take samilar action within fifteen days from the date on which the notification reaches it.

Article 11. In the absence of agreement to the contrary between the Parties, the Conciliation Commission shall meet at the place selected by its President.

Article 12. The task of the Conciliation Commission shall be to elucidate the questions in dispute, to collect with that object all necessary information and to endeavour to bring the Parties to an agreement.

It shall, after the case has been examined, draw up a report containing proposals for the settlement of the dispute.

Article 13. The procedure before the Conciliation Commission must provide for both Parties being heard.

The Commission shall lay down its own procedure, regard being had, in the absence of unanimous decisions to the contrary, to the provisions of Part III of the Hague Convention of October 18, 1907, for the Pacific Settlement of International Disputes.

Article 14. The deliberations of the Conciliation Commission shall be held in private unless the Commission in agreement with the Parties, decides otherwise.

Article 15. The Parties shall have the right to appoint to the Commission agents, counsel and experts, who shall also act as intermediaries between them and the Commission, and they may request that all persons whose evidence appears to them desirable shall be heard.

The Commission for its part shall be entitled to request oral explanations from the agents, counsel and experts of both Parties as well as from all persons it may think desirable to summon with the consent of their Governments.

Article 16. The Parties undertake to facilitate the work of the Conciliation Commission and in particular, to supply it to the greatest possible extent with all relevant documents and information, as well as to use all means at their disposal in accordance with their law to allow it to proceed to the summoning and hearing of witnesses or experts.

Article 17. The Conciliation Commission shall submit its report within four months from the date on which the dispute is submitted to it, unless the Parties agree to extend this period.

A copy of the report shall be sent to each of the Parties. The report shall not have the character of an arbitral award, either as regards the statement of the facts or as regards the legal considerations.

Article 18. The Conciliation Commission shall fix the period within which the Parties must decide with regard to the proposals for settlement contained in its report. This period may not exceed three months.

Article 19. During the actual period of the proceedings, each of the commissioners shall receive emoluments the amount of which shall be fixed by agreement between the Parties, each of which shall contribute an equal share.

The general expenses arising out of the working of the Commission shall be divided in the same manner.

Article 20. If one of the Parties does not accept the proposals of the Conciliation Commission or does not take a decision within the the period laid down in its report, either Party may request that the dispute be submitted to the Permanent Court of International Justice.

The Parties agree that if, in the opinion of the Court of Justice, the dispute is not of a legal nature it shall be decided *ex aequo et bono.*

Article 21. The High Contracting Parties shall draw up, for each particular case, a special agreement clearly determining the subject of the dispute, the particular competence which may devolve upon the Permanent Court of International Justice, and also any other conditions agreed upon between them.

The special agreement shall be established by an exchange of notes between the Governments of the Contracting Parties.

It shall on all points be interpreted by the Court of Justice.

If the special agreement has not been drawn up within three months from the date on which one of the Parties has been informed of a request for the purposes of judicial settlement, either Party may submit the matter to the Court of Justice by a simple application.

Article 22. If the Permanent Court of International justice should find that a decision of a court of law or other authority of one of the Contracting Parties is wholly or in part contrary to international law, and if the constitutional law of that Party does not permit or only partially permits the consequences of the decision in question to be annulled by administrative action, the injured Party shall be granted other equitable satisfaction.

Article 23. The judgment given by the Permanent Court of International justice shall be carried out in good faith by the Parties.

Any difficulties to which the interpretation of the judgment may give rise shall be settled by the Court of Justice, which may be informed for this purpose by either Party by a simple application.

Article 24. During the conciliation or judicial proceedings, the Contracting Parties shall abstain from any measure which might prejudicially affect the acceptance of the proposals of the Conciliation Commission or the execution of the judgment of the Permanent Court of International Justice.

Article 25. If conciliation or judicial proceedings are pending on the expiration of the present Treaty, they shall be pursued in accordance with the provisions of the present Treaty or any other convention which the Contracting Parties may have agreed to substitute therefor.

Article 26. The present Treaty, the interpretation or application of which may not affect the rights and obligations of the High Contracting Parties in virtue of the Covenant of the League of Nations, shall be communicated to the League of Nations for registration, in accordance with Article 18 of the Covenant.

Article 27. Any disputes which may arise with regard either to the interpretation or the execution of the present Treaty shall be submitted direct to the Permanent Court of International justice at The Hague by a simple application.

Article 28. This Treaty shall be ratified as soon as possible and shall come into force immediately after the exchange of ratifications, which shall take place at Rome. It shall be concluded for a period of five years from the date of the exchange of the instruments of ratification. If it is not denounced six months before the expiration of this period, it shall remain in force for a further period of five years.

In faith whereof the above-named Plenipotentiaries have signed the present Treaty and have affixed their seals thereto.

Done at Rome in duplicate on the twenty-third day of September, one thousand nine hundred and twenty-eight.

(L. S.) E. K. VÉSISÉLOS.
(L. S.) B. MUSSOLINI.

4.1263 Treaty of Neutrality, Conciliation, and Arbitration between Hungary and Turkey

Alliance Members: Hungary and Turkey
Signed On: January 5, 1929, in the city of Budapest (Hungary). In force until January 20, 1945.
Alliance Type: Neutrality Pact (Type II)

Source: *League of Nations Treaty Series,* no. 2300.

SUMMARY

This treaty established a non-aggression and neutrality agreement between the two countries. The terms are quite similar to the pact signed between Turkey and Bulgaria two months later, but this treaty addresses the dispute conciliation and arbitration procedures in a separate protocol not included here. The alliance lasted until Hungary's surrender at the end of World War II.

ALLIANCE TEXT

His Most Serene Highness the Regent of the Kingdom of Hungary and the President of the Turkish Republic, desirous of strengthening the bonds of friendship which exist between the two countries and of contributing towards the maintenance of world peace, have decided to conclude a Treaty of Neutrality, Conciliation and Arbitration and, for this purpose, have appointed as their Plenipotentiaries:

His Most Serene Highness the Regent of the Kingdom of Hungary: M. Louis Walko, Royal Hungarian Minister for Foreign Affairs;

The President of the Turkish Republic: M. Behidj Bey, Turkish Envoy Extraordinary and Minister Plenipotentiary in Hungary;

Who, having exchanged their full powers, found in good and due form, have agreed to the following provisions:

Article I. Each of the High Contracting Parties undertakes not to enter into any political or economic agreement or any alliance directed against the other High Contracting Party.

Article 2. Should one of the High Contracting Parties, despite his pacific attitude, be attacked by one or more third Powers, the other Party shall observe neutrality throughout the dispute.

Article 3. The High Contracting Parties undertake to submit to conciliation procedure and, if necessary, to arbitration procedure disputes of any kind which may arise between them and which it has not been found possible to settle, within a reasonable time, through diplomatic channels.

This provision shall not apply to disputes arising out of facts prior to the present Treaty or belonging to the past.

Disputes for the settlement of which a special procedure is laid down in other Conventions in force between the High Contracting Parties shall be settled in conformity with the provisions of those Conventions.

Article 4. Failing a settlement by conciliation, either of the High Contracting Parties may request that the matter in dispute be submitted to arbitration, provided that the question at issue be of a legal character.

Article 5. The formalities for conciliation and arbitration procedure shall form the subject of a Protocol of Procedure, to be annexed to the present Treaty.

Article 6. The present Treaty shall not apply to questions relating, under international law, to sovereign rights.

Each of the High Contracting Parties shall state unilaterally, by a declaration in writing, whether the question comes within its rights of sovereignty.

Article 7. Disputes that may arise concerning the interpretation or execution of the present Treaty shall, unless otherwise agreed, be submitted directly to arbitration.

Article 8. The present Treaty shall be ratified and shall come into force on the day of the exchange of ratifications, which shall take place at Angora as soon as possible.

The Treaty shall be concluded for a period of five years, dating from its entry into force. If it has not been denounced at least one year before the expiry of that period, it shall remain in force for further successive periods of five years.

In faith whereof the Plenipotentiaries have signed the present Treaty.

Done at Budapest, January 5, 1929.

(L. S.) (Signed) Louis WALKO.

(L. S.) (Signed) BEHIC.

4.1264 Treaty of Neutrality, Conciliation, Judicial Settlement and Arbitration Between Bulgaria and Turkey

Alliance Members: Bulgaria and Turkey
Signed On: March 6, 1929, in the city of Angora (Ankara, Turkey). In force until December 3, 1939.
Alliance Type: Neutrality Pact (Type II)

Source: *League of Nations Treaty Series,* no. 2668.

SUMMARY

As with the Turkish-Hungarian treaty signed in January of the same year, this treaty sets the terms for dispute resolution and guarantees non-aggression and neutrality in the event of conflict with a third party. The treaty was renewed only once (in 1933) and expired, as per the terms of the treaty, in 1939.

ALLIANCE TEXT

Bulgaria, of the one part and Turkey, of the other part, being desirous of strengthening the traditional ties existing between the Kingdom of Bulgaria and the Turkish Republic and of settling by means of conciliation, judicial settlement and arbitration any disputes which may arise between the two countries, have resolved to conclude a treaty for this purpose and have appointed as their Plenipotentiaries:

His Majesty the King of the Bulgarians: His Excellency M. Theodore C. Pavloff, Bulgarian Envoy Extraordinary and Minister Plenipotentiary at Angora; and

The President of the Turkish Republic: His Excellency Dr. Tevfik Rüstü Bey, Turkish Minister for Foreign Affairs and Deputy for Smyrna;

Who, having communicated their full powers, found in good and due form, have agreed upon the following provisions:

Article I. The High Contracting Parties undertake not to enter upon any political or economic agreement which is in opposition with Article I of the Treaty of Friendship concluded between Bulgaria and Turkey on October 18, 1925.

Article 2. If one of the Contracting Parties is, in spite of its pacific attitude, attacked by one or more other Powers, the other Party shall observe neutrality for the whole duration of the conflict.

Article 3. Disputes of every kind which may arise between the High Contracting Parties and which it has not been possible to settle by diplomacy shall be submitted, under the conditions laid down in the present Treaty, to conciliation, judicial settlement or arbitration.

Article 4. The provisions of Article 3 shall not apply to questions which, in virtue of Treaties in force between the High Contracting Parties, come within the competence of one of them.

They shall not apply to questions relating to sovereign rights.

Each of the High Contracting Parties shall have the right to determine, by means of a written statement, whether a question relates to sovereign rights or not.

Nevertheless, in the event of the other Party disputing the fact that the questions relates to sovereignty, it may have recourse to arbitration in order to establish whether the question relates to sovereign rights or not.

Article 5. I. In the case of a dispute the occasion of which, according to the municipal law of one of the Parties, falls within the competence of the judicial authorities, the Party in question may object to the matter in dispute being submitted for settlement by the different methods laid down in the present Treaty, until a decision with final effect has been pronounced, within a reasonable time, by the competent authority.

2. In such a case, the Party which desires to resort to the procedures laid down in the present Treaty must notify the other Party of its intention within a period of one year from the date of the afore-mentioned decision.

Article 6. All disputes with regard to which the Parties are in conflict as to their respective rights and which it may not have been possible to settle amicably by diplomacy or by conciliation shall be submitted for decision to the Permanent Court of International Justice, unless the Parties have agreed to have recourse to an arbitral tribunal by means of a special agreement and in the conditions enumerated hereunder.

The judicial or arbitral award shall be given in accordance with the principles of international law.

Article 7. If the Parties agree to submit the disputes mentioned in the preceding Article to an arbitral tribunal, they shall draw up a special agreement in which they shall specify the subject of the disputes, the arbitrators selected and the procedure to be followed.

In the absence of sufficient particulars in the special agreement, the provisions of the Hague Convention of October 18, 1907, for the Pacific Settlement of International Disputes shall apply, with full force of law.

Article 8. If the Parties fail to agree concerning the special agreement referred to in the preceding Article, or fail to appoint arbitrators, either Party shall be at liberty, after giving three month's notice, to bring the dispute, by an application, direct before the Permanent Court of International Justice.

Article 9. If in a judicial sentence or arbitral award it is declared that a judgment or a measure enjoined by a court of law or other authority of one of the Parties to the dispute is wholly or in part contrary to international law, and if the constitutional law of that party does not permit or only partially permits the consequences of the judgment or measure in question to be annulled, the Parties agree that the judicial sentence or arbitral award shall award the injured Party equitable satisfaction.

Article 10. I. Subject to the provisions of Article 4, in the case of the disputes mentioned in Article 3, the High Contracting Parties undertake prior to any procedure before the Permanent Court of International Justice or any arbitral procedure, to have recourse to the conciliation procedure provided for in the present Treaty.

2. In the event of recourse to, and failure of, conciliation, and after the expiration of one month from the termination of the proceedings of the Conciliation Commission, the dispute shall be submitted to the Permanent Court of International Justice or the arbitral tribunal mentioned in Article 7.

Article 11. The disputes referred to in the preceding Article shall be submitted to a special permanent conciliation commission constituted by the Parties.

Article 12. On a request being sent by one of the Contracting Parties to the other Party, a permanent conciliation commission shall be constituted within a period of six months.

Article 13. Conciliation procedure shall be entrusted to a conciliation commission composed of three members, to be appointed as follows: the High Contracting Parties shall each nominate one commissioner from among their respective nationals and shall jointly appoint the President of the Commission from among the nationals of third Powers. The Commissioners shall be appointed for three years. They shall be re-eligible. The commissioner appointed jointly may be replaced during the course of his term of office by agreement between the Parties. Either Party may, however, at any time replace the commissioner whom it has itself appointed. Even if replaced, the commissioners shall continue to exercise their functions until the termination of the work in hand.

Vacancies which may occur as a result of death, resignation or any other cause shall be filled within the shortest possible time in the manner fixed for appointments.

Article 14. If, when a dispute arises, no permanent conciliation commission appointed by the Parties is in existence, a special commission shall be constituted for the examination of the dispute in accordance with the conditions of appointment laid down in the preceding Article, unless the Parties decide otherwise.

Article 15. If, within a period of three months from the date on which one of the High Contracting Parties has notified the other of its intention of resorting to conciliation procedure, the nomination of the commissioner of the other Party or the joint designation by the High Contracting Parties of the President of the Commission has not been effected, the President of the Swiss Confederation shall be requested to make the necessary appointments.

Article 16. I. Disputes shall be brought before the Conciliation Commission by means of an application addressed to the President by the two Parties, acting in agreement, or, in default thereof, by one or other of the Parties.

2. The application, after giving a summary account of the subject of the dispute, shall contain an invitation to the Commission to take all necessary measures with a view to arriving at an amicable solution.

3. If the application emanates from only one oft he Parties, notification thereof shall be given without delay by that Party to the other Party.

Article 17. I. Within fifteen days from the date on which a dispute has been brought by one of the Parties before a permanent conciliation commission, either Party may replace its own commissioner, for the examination of the particular dispute, by a person possessing special competence in the matter.

2. The Party making use of this right shall immediately notify the other Party; the latter shall in such a case be entitled to take similar action within fifteen days from the date on which it has received notification.

Article 18. In the absence of agreement to the contrary between the Parties, the Conciliation Commission shall meet at the place selected by the President.

Article 19. The work of the Conciliation Commission shall not be conducted in public unless a decision to that effect is taken by the Commission with the consent of the Parties.

Article 20. I. In the absence of agreement to the contrary, the conciliation commission shall lay down its own procedure which in any case must provide for both Parties being heard. In regard to enquiries, the Commission, unless it decides unanimously to the contrary, shall act in accordance with the provisions of Part III of the Hague Convention of October 18, 1907 for the Pacific Settlement of International Disputes.

2. The Parties shall be represented before the Conciliation Commission by agents, whose duty it shall be to act as intermediaries between them and the Commission. They may, moreover, be assisted by counsel and experts appointed by them for that purpose and may request that all persons whose evidence appears to them desirable shall be heard.

3. The Commission, for its part, shall be entitled to request oral explanations from the agents, counsel and experts of both Parties, as well as from all persons it may think desirable to summon with the consent of their Governments.

Article 21. In the absence of agreement to the contrary between the Parties, the decisions of the Conciliation Commission shall be taken by a majority vote, and the commission may only take decisions on the substance of the dispute if all its members are present. Nevertheless, the High Contracting Parties must when duly notified of the meetings of the Commission, be represented by their commissioner, or, should he be prevented from attending, by a substitute appointed subject to the conditions laid down in Article 17.

Article 22. The Parties undertake to facilitate the work of the Conciliation Commission and particularly to supply it to the greatest possible extent with all relevant documents and information, as well as to use the means at their disposal to enable it to proceed in their territory and in accordance with their law, to the summoning and hearing of witnesses or experts, and to carry out enquiries on the spot.

Article 23. I. During the proceedings of the Commission, each of the Commissioners shall receive emoluments the amount of which shall be fixed by agreement between the Parties, each of which shall contribute an equal share.

2. The general expenses arising out of the working of the Commission shall be divided in the same manner.

Article 24. I. The task of the Conciliation Commission shall be to elucidate the questions in dispute, to collect with that object all necessary information by means of enquiry or otherwise, and to endeavour to bring the Parties to an agreement. It may, after the case has been examined, inform the Parties of the terms of settlement which seem suitable to it, and lay down the period within which they are to make their decision.

2. At the close of the proceedings, the Commission shall draw up a report stating, as the case may be, either that the Parties have come to an agreement and, if need be, the terms of the agreement, or that it has been impossible to effect a settlement. No mention shall be made in the report as to whether the Commission's decisions were taken unanimously or not.

3. The proceedings of the Commission must, unless the Parties otherwise agree, be terminated within six months from the date on which the Commission shall have been given cognisance of the dispute.

Article 25. The Commission's report shall be communicated without delay to the Parties. The Partie shall decide whether it shall be published.

Article 26. I. If the Parties have not reached an agreement within a month from the termination of the proceedings of the Conciliation Commission, either of them may ask that the dispute be submitted to the Permanent Court of International Justice, which shall deal with the case in accordance with the principles of international law.

2. If in the opinion of the Court, the dispute is not of a legal nature, the Parties agree that the Court may decide *ex aequo et bono* in so far as there is no rule of international law applicable to the dispute.

Article 27. I. The Parties undertake to abstain from all measures likely to react prejudicially on the execution of the judicial or arbitral decision or upon the arrangements proposed by the Conciliation Commission, and in general to abstain from any action which might aggravate or extend the dispute.

2. If the dispute is brought before the Conciliation Commission, the latter may recommend to the Parties the adoption of such provisional measures as it considers suitable.

Article 28. Disputes relating to the interpretation or application of the present Treaty shall be submitted to the Permanent Court of International Justice.

Article 29. I. The present Treaty shall be ratified and the ratifications shall be exchanged at Sofia.

2. The Treaty shall be concluded for a period of five years as from the date of the exchange of ratifications.

3. Unless it is denounced at least six months before the expiration of these periods, it shall remain in force for further successive periods of five years.

4. Notwithstanding denunciation by one of the Contracting Parties, all proceedings pending at the expiration of the current period of the Treaty shall be duly completed.

In faith whereof, the above-mentioned Plenipotentiaries have signed the present Treaty.

Done in duplicate at Angora, March the sixth one thousand nine hundred an twenty-nine.

(Signed) Th. PAVLOFF.

(Signed) Dr. T. RÜSTÜ.

4.1265 Pact of Friendship, Conciliation, and Judicial Settlement between Greece and the Kingdom of the Serbs, Croats, and Slovenes

Alliance Members: Greece and Yugoslavia
Signed On: March 27, 1929, in the city of Belgrade (Serbia). In force until April 20, 1941.
Alliance Type: Neutrality Pact (Type II)

Source: *League of Nations Treaty Series,* no. 2250.

SUMMARY

The Greeks and Serbs moved to resolve the controversy over the free trade zone in early March of 1929. By March 17, the Serbs had been granted many more privileges than prior agreements had allowed, and that spirit of cooperation carried over to this broader security pact signed ten days later. As with most friendship treaties of the period, the treaty calls for non-aggression, neutrality, and the peaceful settlement of bilateral disputes. In this case, the terms for dispute settlement were quite extensive.

The friendship treaty lasted until Yugoslavia lost its independence to Germany during World War II.

ALLIANCE TEXT

The President of the Hellenic Republic and His Majesty the King of the Serbs, Croats and Slovenes,

Having regard to the ties of sincere friendship and mutual confidence which happily unite the two countries and desiring by a solemn act to affirm their desire to cooperate with a view to contributing towards the work of general peace.

Being equally desirous of maintaining the state of peace and political stability in accordance with the principles laid down in the Covenant of the League of Nations,

Considering that the faithful observance of the methods for the pacific settlement of international disputes renders it possible, without resort to force, to settle all questions on which States may differ,

Have decided for this purpose to conclude a Pact of Friendship, Conciliation and Judicial Settlement and have appointed as their Plenipotentiaries:

> The President of the Hellenic Republic: M. Alexandre Carapanos, Minister for Foreign Affairs;
>
> His Majesty the King of the Serbs, Croats and Slovenes: Dr. Kosta Koumanoudi, Minister for Foreign Affairs *ad interim;*

Who, having communicated their full powers, found in good and due form, have agreed on the following provisions:

Article I. The two High Contracting Parties reciprocally undertake to lend each other mutual support and to cooperate cordially for the purpose of maintaining the order established by the Treaties of Peace of which they are both signatories, and of ensuring that the obligations laid down in the said Treaties are respected and fulfilled.

In the event of international complications, the two High Contracting Parties undertake that, if they agree that their joint interests are or may be threatened, they will confer as to the measures to be taken in common for safeguarding these interests.

Article 2. The High Contracting Parties reciprocally undertake in no case to resort to war against each other.

This stipulation shall not, however, apply in the case of:
(I) The exercise of the right of self defence, that is to say, resistance to an infraction of the undertaking contained in the first paragraph;
(2) Action in pursuance of Article 26 of the Covenant of the League of Nations;
(3) Action by reason of a decision taken by the Assembly or by the Council of the League of Nations in pursuance of Article 15, paragraph 7, of the Covenant of the League of Nations, provided that in this last event the action is directed against a State which was the first to attack.

Article 3. The High Contracting Parties undertake to settle by pacific methods, in the manner provided or in the present Pact, all questions whatsoever on which they may differ and which it has not been possible to settle by the normal methods of diplomacy.

Article 4. This undertaking shall not apply to:
(I) Disputes arising prior to the conclusion of the present Pact;
(2) Disputes concerning questions which by international law are solely within the jurisdiction of States;
(3) Disputes concerning the territorial status of the Parties. If a difference should arise between the Parties as to whether a dispute comes under one of the three above-mentioned exceptions, this preliminary question shall, without prejudice to the substance of the dispute and upon the request of either Party; be submitted to the Permanent Court of International Justice for arbitration.

Article 5. Disputes for the settlement of which a special procedure is laid down in other conventions shall be settled in conformity with the provisions of those conventions.

Article 6. The present Pact shall not affect the agreements in force by which conciliation procedure is established between the High Contracting Parties or by which they have assumed obligations to resort to arbitration or judicial settlement for the purpose of settling the dispute. If, however, these agreements provide only for a procedure of conciliation, then after such procedure has been followed without result, the provisions of the present Agreement concerning judicial settlement or arbitration shall be applied.

Article 7. I. In the case of a dispute the occasion of which, according to the municipal law of one of the Parties, falls within the competence of the judicial or administrative authorities, the Party in question may object to the dispute being submitted for settlement by the different methods laid down in the present Pact until a decision with final effect has been pronounced, within a reasonable time, by the competent authority.

2. In such a case, the Party which desires to resort to the procedures laid down in the present Pact must notify the other Party of its intention within a period of one year from the date of the aforementioned decision.

Article 8. All disputes with regard to which the Parties are in conflict as to their respective rights shall be submitted for decision to the Permanent Court of International justice unless the Parties agree, in the manner hereinafter provided, to have resort to a tribunal.

It is understood that the disputes referred to above include in particular those mentioned in Article 36 of the Statute of the Permanent Court of International Justice.

Article 9. If the Parties agree to submit the disputes mentioned in the preceding Article to an arbitral tribunal, they shall draw up a special agreement in which they shall specify the subject of the dispute, the arbitrators selected, and the procedure to be followed. In the absence of sufficient indications or particulars in the special agreement, the provisions of the Hague Convention of October 18, 1907, for the Pacific Settlement of International Disputes shall apply so far as is necessary. If nothing is laid down in the special agreement as to the rules regarding the substance of the dispute to be followed by the arbitrators, the tribunal shall apply the substantive rules enumerated in Article 38 of the Statute of the Permanent Court of International Justice.

Article 10. If the Parties fail to agree concerning the special agreement referred to in the preceding Article or fail to appoint arbitrators, either Party shall be at liberty, after giving three months' notice, to bring the dispute by an application direct before the Permanent Court of International Justice.

Article 11.   I. In the case of disputes mentioned in Article 8, before any procedure before the Permanent Court of International Justice or any arbitral procedure, the Parties may agree to have recourse to the conciliation procedure provided for in the present Pact.

2. In the event of recourse to and failure of conciliation, neither Party may bring the dispute before the Permanent Court of International Justice or call for the constitution of the Arbitral Tribunal referred to in Article 9 before the expiration of one month from the termination of the proceedings of the Conciliation Commission.

Article 12. All disputes between the Parties other than the disputes mentioned in Article 8 shall be submitted obligatorily to a procedure of conciliation.

Article 13. The disputes referred to in the preceding Article shall be submitted to a permanent or special Conciliation Commission constituted by the Parties.

Article 14. On a request to that effect made by one of the Contracting Parties to the other Party, a Permanent Conciliation Commission shall be constituted within a period of six months.

Article 15. Unless the Parties agree otherwise, the Conciliation Commission shall be constituted as follows:

I. The Commission shall be composed of five members. The Parties shall each nominate one commissioner, who may be chosen from among their respective nationals. The other three commissioners shall be appointed by agreement from among the nationals of third Powers. These three commissioners must be of different nationalities and must not be habitually resident in the territories or be in the service of the Parties. The Parties shall appoint the President of the Commission from among them.

(2) The Commissioners shall be appointed for three years. They shall be re-eligible. The commissioners jointly appointed may be replaced during their period of office by agreement between the Parties. Either Party may, however, at any time replace the commissioner whom it has appointed. Even if replaced, the commissioners shall continue to exercise their functions until the termination of the work in hand.

(3) Vacancies occurring as a result of death, resignation or any other cause shall be filled within the shortest possible time in the manner fixed for the appointments.

Article 16. If, when a dispute arises, no Permanent Conciliation Commission appointed by the Parties is in existence, a special commission shall be constituted for the examination of the dispute within a period of three months from the date on which a request to that effect is made by one of the Parties to the other Party. The appointments shall be made in the manner laid down in the preceding Article unless the Parties decide otherwise.

Article 17.   I. If the appointment of the commissioners to be designated jointly is not made within the periods provided for in Articles 14 and 16, the making of the necessary appointments shall be entrusted to a third Power chosen by agreement between the Parties or, on request of the Parties, to the President of the Council of the League of Nations.

2. If no agreement is reached on either of these procedures, each Party shall designate a different Power and the appointments shall be made in concert by the Powers thus chosen.

3. If, within a period of three months, these two Powers have been unable to reach an agreement, each of them shall submit a number of candidates equal to the number of members to be appointed. It shall then be decided by lot which of the candidates thus designated shall be appointed.

Article 18.   I. Disputes shall be brought before the Conciliation Commission by means of an application addressed to the President by the two Parties acting in agreement, or, in default thereof, by one or other of the Parties.

2. The application, after giving a summary account of the subject of the dispute, shall contain the invitation to the Commission to take all necessary measures with a view to arriving at an amicable solution.

3. If the application emanates from only one of the Parties, the other Party shall without delay be notified by it.

Article 19.   I. Within fifteen days from the date on which a dispute has been brought by one of the Parties before a Permanent Conciliation Commission, either Party may replace its own commissioner, for the examination of the particular dispute, by a person possessing special competence in the matter.

2. The Party making use of this right shall immediately notify the other Party; the latter shall in such case be entitled to take similar action within fifteen days from the date on which the notification reaches it.

Article 20.   I. In the absence of agreement to the contrary between the Parties, the Conciliation Commission shall meet at the seat of the League of Nations or at some other place selected by its President.

2. The Commission may in all circumstances request the Secretary-General of the League of Nations to afford it his assistance.

Article 21. The work of the Conciliation Commission shall not be conducted in public, unless a decision to that effect is taken by the Commission with the consent of the Parties.

Article 22.   I. In the absence of agreement to the contrary between the Parties, the Conciliation Commission shall lay down its own procedure, which in any case must provide for both Parties being heard. In regard to enquiries, the Commission, unless it decides unanimously to the contrary, shall act in accordance with the provisions of Part II of the Hague Convention of October 18, 1907, for the Pacific Settlement of International Disputes.

2. The Parties shall be represented before the Conciliation Commission by agents whose duty shall be to act as intermediaries between them and the Commission; they may, moreover, be assisted by counsel and experts appointed by them for that purpose and may request that all persons whose evidence appears to them desirable shall be heard.

3. The Commission, for its part, shall be entitled to request oral explanations from the agents, counsel and experts of both Parties as well as from all persons it may think desirable to summon with the consent of their Governments.

Article 23. In the absence of agreement to the contrary between the Parties, the decisions of the Conciliation Commission shall be taken by a majority vote and the Commission may only take decisions on the substance of the dispute if all its members are present.

Article 24. The Parties undertake to facilitate the work of the Conciliation Commission and in particular to supply it to the greatest possible extent with all relevant documents and information, as well as to use the means at their disposal to allow it to proceed in their territory, and in accordance with their law, to the summoning and hearing of witnesses or experts and to visit the localities in question.

Article 25.   I. During the proceedings of the Commission, each of the commissioners shall receive emoluments the amount of which shall be fixed by agreement between the Parties, each of which shall contribute an equal share.

2. The general expenses arising out of the working of the Commission shall be divided in the same manner.

Article 26.   I. The task of the Conciliation Commission shall be to elucidate the questions in dispute, to collect with that object all necessary information by means of enquiry or otherwise, and to endeavour to bring the Parties to an agreement. It may, after the case has been examined, inform the Parties of the terms of settlement which seem suitable to it, and lay down a period within which they are to make their decision.

2. At the close of its proceedings, the Commission shall draw up a *procès-verbal* stating, as the case may be, either that the Parties have come to an agreement, and, if need arises, the terms of the agreement, or that it has been impossible to effect a settlement. No mention shall be made in the *procès-verbal* of whether the Commission's decisions were taken unanimously or by a majority vote.

3. The proceedings of the Commission must, unless the Parties otherwise agree, be terminated within six months from the date on which the Commission shall have been given cognisance of the dispute.

Article 27. The Commission's *procès-verbal* shall be communicated without delay to the Parties. The Parties shall decide whether it shall be published.

Article 28. Should the Parties not have reached an agreement within a month from the termination of the proceedings of the Conciliation Commission, the question may, if the Parties agree thereto, be brought before an Arbitral Tribunal. (This provision shall not apply in the case provided for in Articles 8 and 11).

In such case the Arbitral Tribunal shall, unless the Parties otherwise agree, be constituted as follows:

Article 29.   (a) The Arbitral Tribunal shall consist of five members. The Parties shall each nominate one member, who may be chosen from among their respective nationals. The other two arbitrators and the Chairman shall be chosen by common agreement from among the nationals of third Powers. They must be of different nationalities and must not be habitually resident in the territories or be in the service of the Parties.

(b)   I. If the appointment of the members of the Arbitral Tribunal is not made within a period of three months from the date on which one of the Parties requested the other Party to constitute an arbitral tribunal, a third Power, chosen by agreement between the Parties, shall be requested to make the necessary appointments.

2. If no agreement is reached on this point, each Party shall designate a different Power, and the appointments shall be made in concert by the Powers thus chosen.

3. If, within a period of three months, the Powers so chosen have been unable to reach an agreement, the necessary appointments shall be made by the President of the Permanent Court of International Justice. If the latter is prevented from acting or is a national of one of the Parties, the appointments shall be made by the Vice-President. If the latter is prevented from acting or is a national of one of the Parties, the appointments shall be made by the oldest Member of the Court who is not a national of either Party.

(c) Vacancies which may occur as a result of death, resignation or any other cause shall be filled within the shortest possible time in the manner fixed for the appointments.

(d) If the two High Contracting Parties agree to bring the dispute before an arbitral tribunal, they shall at the same time draw up a special agreement determining the subject of the dispute and the procedure to be followed.

In the absence of sufficient indications or particulars in the special agreement regarding the points indicated in the previous paragraph, the provisions of the Hague Convention of October 18, 1907, for the Pacific Settlement of International Disputes shall apply so far as is necessary.

If nothing is laid down in the special agreement, the Tribunal shall apply the rules in regard to the substance of the dispute indicated in Article 38 of the Statute of the Permanent Court of International Justice. In so far as there exist no such rules applicable to the dispute, the Tribunal shall decide *ex oequo et bono.*

Article 30. If on the expiration of the month following the termination of the proceedings of the Conciliation Commission, the Parties have not agreed, in accordance with Article 28 above, to submit the dispute to an Arbitral Tribunal, the dispute shall be dealt with under Article 15 of the Covenant of the League of Nations.

Article 31. I. In all cases where a dispute forms the object of arbitration or judicial proceedings and in particular, if the question on which the Parties differ arises out of acts already committed or on the point of being committed, the Permanent Court of International justice, acting in accordance with Article 41 of its Statute, or the Arbitral Tribunal, shall lay down, within the shortest possible time, the provisional measures to be adopted. The Parties shall be bound to accept such measures.

2. If the dispute is brought before a Conciliation Commission, the latter may recommend to the Parties the adoption of such provisional measures as it considers suitable.

3. The Parties undertake to abstain from all measures likely to react prejudicially upon the execution of the judicial decision or arbitral award, or upon the arrangements proposed by the Conciliation Commission and, in general, to abstain from any act whatsoever which might aggravate or extend the dispute.

Article 32. If, in a judicial sentence or arbitral award, it is declared that a decision taken or a measure enjoined by a court of law, or other authority of one of the Parties to the dispute is wholly or in part contrary to international law, and if the constitutional law of that Party does not permit or only partially permits the consequence of the decision or measure in question to be annulled, the Parties agree that the judicial sentence or arbitral award shall grant the injured Party equitable satisfaction.

Article 33. The present Pact shall be applicable as between the High Contracting Parties even though a third Power has an interest in the dispute.

Article 34. Disputes relating to the interpretation or application of the present Pact, including those concerning the classification of disputes and the scope of the reservations, shall be submitted to the Permanent Court of International Justice.

Article 35. The present Pact, the interpretation or application of which may not in any way affect the rights and obligations of the High Contracting Parties in virtue of the Covenant of the League of Nations and in virtue of the provisions of treaties previously concluded by the High Contracting Parties and communicated to the League of Nations for registration in accordance with Article 18 of the Covenant, shall be communicated to the League of Nations for registration in accordance with that Article.

Article 36. The present Pact shall be ratified as soon as possible and shall come into force immediately after the exchange of ratifications, which shall take place at Athens. It shall be concluded for a period of 5 (five) years, dating from the exchange of the instruments of ratification. If it is not denounced six months before the expiration of this period, it shall remain in force for a further period of five years.

In faith whereof the Plenipotentiaries have signed the present Pact.

Done at Belgrade on the twenty-seventh day of March, one thousand nine hundred and twenty-nine.

A. CARAPANOS.
Dr. KOUMANOUDI.

4.1266 Treaty of Neutrality, Conciliation, and Arbitration between France and Turkey

Alliance Members: France and Turkey
Signed On: February 3, 1930, in the city of Paris. In force until June 22, 1940.
Alliance Type: Neutrality Pact (Type II)

Source: *British and Foreign State Papers,* vol. 132, p. 777.

SUMMARY

This non-aggression and neutrality agreement was signed by Turkish ambassador Fethi Bey and French ambassador Aristide Briand. Unremarkable in most respects, the treaty was mostly an attempt by France to maintain friendly relations with Turkey, a northern neighbor to its mandate in Syria. Once again, as with most treaties during these years between the world wars, the method of dispute resolution was well defined and institutionalized by both the treaty and additional protocols. The alliance lasted until France's surrender to Germany during World War II.

DESCRIPTION OF TERMS

Both countries commit to neutrality should either be attacked by a third party. If a problem were to occur that could not be resolved through normal diplomatic actions, the two parties would submit their dispute to the Permanent Court of Justice. The countries also agreed to establish a permanent commission to resolve their disputes before seeking decisions from the Permanent Court.

The treaty was to remain in force for a period of five years. Unless one of the parties denounced the agreement within six months of its termination, the treaty would be automatically renewed every year.

4.1267 Treaty of Preferential Alliance: The United Kingdom and Iraq

Alliance Members: United Kingdom and Iraq
Signed On: June 30, 1930, in the city of Baghdad (Iraq). In force until April 4, 1955, when it was replaced by a new alliance.
Alliance Type: Defense Pact (Type I)

Source: *British Foreign and State Papers*, vol. 132, p. 280.

SUMMARY

Following the defeat of the Ottoman Empire in World War I, the allied powers divided the territories into separate mandates. This Anglo-Iraq alliance gave Iraq a path toward independence two years later. In the one-sided treaty, Britain gained commercial and military rights, including the unlimited ability to move British troops in and out of the country, an ability that would be maintained even after Iraqi independence. The strategic location of Iraq and the discovery of oil in 1927 fueled continuing British interests in the country.

ALLIANCE TEXT

His Majesty the King of Great Britain, Ireland and the British dominions beyond the Seas, Emperor of India, and His Majesty the King of Iraq,

Whereas they desire to consolidate the friendship and to maintain and perpetuate the relations of good understanding between their respective countries; and

Whereas His Britannic Majesty undertook in the treaty of alliance signed at Bagdad on the 13th day of January, 1926, of the Christian era, corresponding to the 28th day of Jamadi-al-Ukhra, 1344, Hijrah, that he would take into active considerations at successive intervals of 4 years the question whether it was possible for him to press for admission of Iraq into the League of Nations; and

Whereas His Majesty's Government in the United Kingdom of Great Britain and Northern Ireland informed the Iraq Government without qualification or proviso on the 14th day of September 1929, that they were prepared to support the candidature of Iraq for admission to the League of Nations in the year 1932 and announced to the Council of the League on the 4th day of November, 1929, that this was their intention; and

Whereas the mandatory responsibilities accepted by His Britannic Majesty in respect of Iraq will automatically terminate upon the admission of Iraq to the League of Nations; and

Whereas His Britannic Majesty and His Majesty the King of Iraq consider that the relations which will subsist between them as independent Sovereigns should be defined by the conclusion of a treaty of alliance and amity;

Have agreed to conclude a new treaty for this purpose on terms of complete freedom, equality and independence which will become operative upon the entry of Iraq into the League of Nations, and have appointed as their plenipotentiaries:

[Here follow the names.]

Art. 1. There shall be perpetual peace and friendship between His Britannic Majesty and His Majesty the King of Iraq.

There shall be established between the high contracting parties a close alliance in consecration of their friendship, their cordial understanding and their good relations, and there shall be full and frank consultation between them in all matters of foreign policy which may affect their common interests.

Each of the high contracting pparties undertakes not to adopt in foreign countries an attitude which is inconsistent with the alliance or might create difficulties for the other party thereto.

2. Each high contracting party will be represented at the court of the other high contracting party by a diplomatic representative duly accredited.

3. Should any dispute between Iraq and a third State produce a situation which involves the risk of a rupture with that State, the high contracting parties will concert together with a view to the settlement of the said dispute by peaceful means in accordance with the provisions of the Covenant of the League of Nations and of any other international obligations which may be applicable to the case.

4. Should, notwithstanding the provisions of article 3 above, either of the high contracting parties become engaged in war, the other high contracting party will, subject always to the provisions of article 9 below, immediately come to his aid in the capacity of an ally. In the event of an imminent menace of war the high contracting parties will immediately concert together the necessary measures of defence. The aid of His Majesty the King of Iraq in the event of war or the imminent menace of war will consist in furnishing to His Britannic Majesty on Iraq territory all facilities and assistance in his power including the use of railways, rivers, ports, aerodromes and means of communication.

5. It is understood between the high contracting parties that responsibility for the maintenance of internal order in Iraq and, subject to the provisions of article 4 above, for the defence of Iraq from external aggression rests with His Majesty the King of Iraq. Nevertheless His Majesty the King of Iraq recognises that the permanent maintenance and protection in all circumstances of the essential communications of His Britannic Majesty is in the common interest of the high contracting parties. For this purpose and in order to facilitate the discharge of the obligations of His Britannic Majesty under article 4 above His Majesty the King of Iraq undertakes to grant to His Britannic Majesty for the duration of the alliance sites for air bases to be selected by His Britannic Majesty at or in the vicinity of Basra and for an air base to be selected by His Britannic Majesty to the west of the Euphrates. His Majesty the King of Iraq further authorises His Britannic Majesty to maintain forces upon Iraq territory at the above localities in accordance with the provisions of the annexure of this treaty on the understanding that the presence of those forces shall not constitute in any manner an occupation and will in no way prejudice the sovereign rights of Iraq.

6. The annexure hereto shall be regarded as an integral part of the present treaty.

7. This treaty shall replace the treaties of alliance signed at Bagdad on the 10th day of October, 1922, of the Christian era, corresponding to the 19th day of Safar, 1341,, Hijrah, and on the 13th day of January, 1926,, of the Christian era, corresponding to the 28th day of Jamadi-al-Ukhra,1344, Hijrah, and the subsidiary agreements thereto, which shall cease to have effect upon the entry into force of this treaty. It shall be executed in duplicate, in the English and Arabic languages, of which the former shall be regarded as the authoritative version.

8. The high contracting parties recognise that, upon the entry into force of this treaty, all responsibilities devolving under the treaties and agreements referred to in article 7 hereof upon His Britannic Majesty in respect of Iraq will, in so far as His Britannic Majesty is concerned, then automatically and completely come to an end, and that such responsibilities, in so far as they continue at all, will devolve upon His Majesty the King of Iraq alone.

It is also recognised that all responsibilities devolving upon His Britannic Majesty in respect of Iraq under any other international instrument, in so far as they continue at all, should similarly devolve upon His Majesty the King of Iraq alone, and the high contracting parties shall immediately take such steps as may be necessary to secure the transference to His Majesty the King of Iraq of these responsibilities.

9. Nothing in the present Treaty is intended to or shall in any way prejudice the rights and obligations which devolve, or may devolve, upon either of the High Contracting Parties under the Covenant of the League of Nations or the Treaty for the Renunciation of War signed at Paris on the twenty-seventh day of August, One thousand nine hundred and twenty-eight.

10. Should any difference arise relative to the application or the interpretation of this treaty and should the high contracting parties fail to settle such difference by direct negotiation, then it shall be dealt with in accordance with the provisions of the Covenant of the League of Nations.

11. This treaty shall be ratified and ratifications shall be exchanged as soon as possible. Thereafter it shall come into force as soon as Iraq has been admitted to membership of the League of Nations.

The present treaty shall remain in force for a period of 25 years from the date of its coming into force. At any time after 20 years from the date of the coming into force of this treaty, the high contracting parties will, at the request of either of them, conclude a new treaty which shall provide for the continued maintenance and protection in all circumstances of the essential communications of His Britannic Majesty. In case of disagreement in this matter the difference will be submitted to the Council of the League of Nations.

In faith whereof the respective plenipotentiaries have signed the present treaty and have affixed thereto their seals.

Done at Bagdad, in duplicate, this 30th day of June 1930, of the Christian era, corresponding to the 4th day of Safar, 1349, Hijrah.

(L.S.) F.H. HUMPHRYS.
(L.S.) NOURY SAID.

ANNEXURE

1. The strength of the forces maintained in Iraq by His Britannic Majesty in accordance with the terms of article 5 of this treaty shall be determined by His Britannic Majesty from time to time after consultation with His Majesty the King of Iraq.

His Britannic Majesty shall maintain forces at Hinaidi for a period of 5 years after the entry into force of this treaty in order to enable His Majesty the King of Iraq to organise the necessary forces to replace them. By the expiration of that period the said forces of His Britannic Majesty shall have been withdrawn from Hinaidi. It shall be also open to His Britannic Majesty to maintain forces at Mosul for a maximum period of 5years from the entry into force of this treaty. Thereafter it shall be open to His Britannic Majesty to station his forces in the localities mentioned in article 5 of this treaty, and His Majesty the King of Iraq will grant to His Britannic Majesty for the duration of the alliance leases of the necessary sites for the accommodation of the forces of His Britannic Majesty in those localities.

2. Subject to any modifications which the two high contracting parties may agree to introduce in the future, the immunities and privileges in jurisdictional and fiscal matters, including freedom from taxation, enjoyed by the British forces in Iraq will continue to extend to the forces referred to in clause 1 above and to such of His Britannic Majesty's forces of all arms as may be in Iraq in pursuance of the present treaty and its annexure or otherwise by agreement between the high contracting parties, and the existing provisions of any local legislation affecting the armed forces of His Britannic Majesty in Iraq shall also continue. The Iraq Government will take the necessary steps to ensure that the altered conditions will not render the position of the British forces as regards immunities and privileges in any way less favourable than that enjoyed by them at the date of the entry into force of this treaty.

3. His Majesty the King of Iraq agrees to provide all possible facilities for the movement, training and maintenance of the forces referred to in clause 1 above and to accord to those forces the same facilities for the use of wireless telegraphy as those enjoyed by them at the date of the entry into force of the present treaty.

4. His Majesty the King of Iraq undertakes to provide at the request and at the expense of His Britannic Majesty and upon such conditions as may be agreed between the high contracting parties special guards from his own forces for the protection of such air bases as may, in accordance with the provisions of this treaty, be occupied by the forces of His Britannic Majesty, and to secure the enactment of such legislation as may be necessary for the fulfilment of the conditions referred to above.

5. His Britannic Majesty undertakes to grant whenever they may be required by His Majesty the King of Iraq all possible

facilities in the following matters, the cost of which will be met by His Majesty the King of Iraq:—

(1). Naval, military and aeronautical instruction of Iraqi officers in the United Kingdom.

(2). The provision of arms, ammunition, equipment, ships and aeroplanes of the latest available pattern for the forces of His Majesty the King of Iraq.

(3). The provision of British naval, military and air force officers to serve in an advisory capacity with the forces of His Majesty the King of Iraq.

6. In view of the desirability of identity in training and methods between the Iraq and British armies, His Majesty the King of Iraq undertakes that, should he deem it necessary to have recourse to foreign military instructors, these shall be chosen from amongst British subjects.

He further undertakes that any personnel of his forces that may be sent abroad for military training will be sent to military schools, colleges and training centres in the territories of His Britannic Majesty, provided that this shall not prevent him from sending to any other country such personnel as cannot be received in the said institutions and training centres.

He further undertakes that the armament and essential equipment of his forces shall not differ in type from those of the forces of His Britannic Majesty.

7. His Majesty the King of Iraq agrees to afford, when requested to do so by His Britannic Majesty, all possible facilities for the movement of the forces of His Britannic Majesty of all arms in transit across Iraq and for the transport and storage of all supplies and equipment that may be required by these forces during their passage across Iraq. These facilities shall cover the use of the roads, railways, waterways, ports and aerodromes of Iraq, and His Britannic Majesty's ships shall have general permission to visit the Shatt-al-Arab on the understanding that His Majesty the King of Iraq is given prior notification of visits to Iraq ports.

F.H.H.
N.S.

4.1268 Treaty of Friendship, Neutrality, Conciliation, and Arbitration between Greece and Turkey

Alliance Members: Greece and Turkey
Signed On: October 30, 1930, in the city of Ankara (Turkey). In force until April 27, 1941.
Alliance Type II: Neutrality Pact

Source: *League of Nations Treaty Series,* no. 2841.

SUMMARY

This treaty sets, in quite some detail, the processes for dispute resolution between Greece and Turkey. Articles 1 and 2 contain the neutrality provisions of the agreement, which renders this a military alliance.

The Greek-Turkish relationship at this time was built on the Treaty of Lausanne (1923), which fixed the terms by which the post–World War I peace would be established with Turkey. For Greece, the principal concern of the relationship was the status of the significant Greek population in Istanbul at the time. Although there was a compulsory exchange of minority populations across the border, the Greeks of Istanbul and the Muslims of Thrace were exempted from the exchanges and given due citizenship. This treaty, along with a similar arbitration pact signed in July of 1930 (but absent the neutrality clause), reaffirmed the peace agreements signed at Lausanne and before.

ALLIANCE TEXT

The President of the Hellenic Republic and the President of the Turkish Republic, anxious to pursue on all occasions a policy of friendship and wishing to affirm their desire to promote the work of world peace and to settle in accordance with the highest principles of Public International Law any disputes that may arise between Greece and Turkey, have resolved to give effect to their common purpose in a Treaty and have appointed as their Plenipotentiaries:

The President of the Hellenic Republic: His Excellency M. Elefterios K. Venizelos, President of the Council of Ministers; His Excellency M. André Michalakopoulos, Vice-President of the Council of Ministers, Minister for Foreign Affairs;

The President of the Turkish Republic: His Excellency Ismet Pasha, President of the Council of Ministers, Deputy for Malatya; His Excellency Dr. Tevfik Rustu Bey, Minister for Foreign Affairs, Deputy for Izmir;

Who, having exchanged their full powers, found in good and due form, have agreed on the following provisions:

Article I. Each of the High Contracting Parties undertakes not to enter into any political or economic agreement or any alliance directed against the other Party.

Article 2. Should one of the High Contracting Parties, despite its pacific attitude, be the object of an aggression by one or more Powers, the other Party undertakes to observe neutrality throughout the dispute.

Article 3. The High Contracting Parties undertake to submit to the procedure of conciliation provided for in Articles 7 to 19 hereinafter any questions on which they may disagree and which it may not be possible to settle by the normal methods of diplomacy. Should the procedure of conciliation prove unsuccessful, a judicial settlement shall be sought in conformity with Articles 20 to 23 of the present Treaty, unless the Parties agree to have recourse to an arbitral tribunal established in conformity with Articles 55 *et seq.* of the Convention of October 18, 1907, for the Pacific Settlement of International Disputes or to any other agreement existing between them.

Article 4. The provisions of the foregoing Article shall not apply to questions which, in virtue of Treaties in force between the High Contracting Parties, come within the jurisdiction of either Party, or to questions relating to the right of sovereignty. Each of the Parties shall have the right to decide, by means of a declaration in writing, whether a question concerns the right of sovereignty, and if the point is contested, the other Party shall be entitled to have recourse to arbitration or to apply to the Permanent Court of International Justice with a view to deciding the previous question.

The provisions of the foregoing Article shall not apply to disputes arising from facts prior to the present Treaty and belonging to the past.

Article 5. Disputes for the settlement of which a special procedure is provided for by other Conventions in force between the disputing Parties may be settled in conformity with the provisions of such Conventions.

Article 6. In the case of a dispute which, according to the domestic legislation of one of the Parties, comes within the jurisdiction of the judicial or administrative authorities, such Party may oppose the submission of the dispute to the various procedures provided for by the present Treaty until a final decision has been given, within a reasonable time, by the competent authority.

In such a case the Party wishing to have recourse to the procedures provided for by the present Treaty shall be required to notify the other Party of its intention within a period of one year from the date of the above-mentioned decision.

Article 7. On the presentation of a request from one Contracting Party to the other, a Permanent Conciliation Commission shall be established within six months following the exchange of the ratifications of the present Treaty.

In the absence of any agreement to the contrary between the Parties, the Conciliation

Commission shall be established in the following manner:

I. The Commission shall consist of five members. The Parties shall each nominate one member, chosen from among their respective nationals. The remaining three Commissioners shall be chosen by joint agreement from among the nationals of third Powers. Such persons must be of different nationalities and must not be habitually domiciled in the territory of the Parties or employed in their service. The Parties shall appoint the President of the Commission from among them, and, in the event of disagreement, the President shall be chosen by lot from among the said three Commissionners.

2. The Commissioners shall be appointed for three years and shall be re-eligible. The Commissioners appointed jointly may be replaced during the their term of office by consent of the Parties. So long as the procedure has not begun, each of the Parties shall be entitled to effect the replacement of its nominee.

3. Vacancies arising as the result of death or resignation or any other impediment shall be filled as soon as possible in accordance with the method established for nominations.

Article 8. Should a dispute arise before the Parties have nominated a Permanent Conciliation Commission, a Special Conciliation Commission shall be established to investigate the dispute within a period of three months from the date on which

the request is addressed by one Party to the other. Nominations shall be made in conformity with the provisions of the foregoing Article unless otherwise decided by the Parties.

Article 9. If the Commissioners to be appointed jointly have not been nominated within the time-limits laid down in Articles 7 and 8, the task of making the necessary appointments shall be entrusted to a third Power chosen by common consent of the Parties and should agreement not be reached in the matter, each Party shall designate a different Power and the appointments shall be made jointly by the Powers thus chosen. Lastly, if within a period of three months these two Powers have not been able to agree, each of them shall present as many candidates as there are members to be appointed. Lots shall be drawn to decide which of the candidates thus presented shall be appointed.

Article 10. The dispute shall be brought before the Conciliation Commission by means of a request addressed to the President by both Parties acting in agreement, or, failing agreement, by one or other of the Parties.

The request shall indicate briefly the subject of the dispute and shall invite the Commission to take the necessary measures with a view to arriving at an amicable settlement.

If a request is submitted by only one of the Parties, notification thereof shall be made without delay to the other.

Article 11. Within fifteen days from the date on which one of the Parties shall have brought a dispute before the Conciliation Commission, either Party may replace its nominee for the investigation of such dispute by a person possessing special competence in the matter. The Party making use of this right shall immediately notify the other Party, and in that case the latter shall be entitled to take similar action within a period of fifteen days from the date when the notification reaches it.

Article 12. The Conciliation Commission shall meet, unless otherwise agreed between the Parties, at a place selected by its President.

Article 13. It shall be the duty of the Conciliation Commission to elucidate the questions in dispute, with that object to collect all relevant information, and to endeavour to effect a settlement between the Parties.

After examination of the case it shall draw up a report containing proposals for the settlement of the dispute.

Article 14. The Conciliation Commission shall establish its own procedure, which shall provide in all cases for both Parties being heard, regard being had, except in the case of a unanimous decision to the contrary, to the provisions of Chapter III of the Hague Convention of October 18, 1907 for the Pacific Settlement of International Disputes.

Article 15. The work of the Conciliation Commission shall not be conducted in public unless, subject to the consent of the Parties, the Commission itself so decides.

Article 16. The Parties shall be represented before the Conciliation Commission by agents, who shall act as intermediaries between them and the Commission; they may, moreover, be assisted by counsel and experts appointed by them for that purpose, and may request that any persons whose evidence they consider desirable shall be heard.

The Commission, for its part, shall have the right to request oral explanations from the agents, counsel and experts of both Parties and from such persons as it may think fit to summon, subject to their Government's consent.

Article 17. The Parties undertake to facilitate the work of the Conciliation Commission, in particular to supply it, to the best of their ability, with all relevant documents and information, and to use the means at their disposal to enable it, in their territory and in accordance with their laws, to summon and hear witnesses or experts and to carry out enquiries on the spot.

Article 18. The Conciliation Commission shall present its report within four months from the date on which it has been informed of the dispute, unless the Parties agree to extend this period.

A copy of the report shall be sent to each of the Parties.

The report shall not be in the nature of an arbitral award, as regards either the statement of facts or the legal considerations or findings.

Article 19. The Conciliation Commission shall fix the time-limit within which the Parties shall have to take a decision with regard to the proposals for a settlement contained in its report. Such time-limit shall not exceed three months.

Article 20. For the actual duration of the procedure each of the joint nominees shall receive an allowance, the amount of which shall be fixed by the Parties and which shall be paid by the latter in equal shares. On the other hand, each Party shall fix and bear the cost of the allowance of its own nominee.

The general expenses entailed by the work of the Commission shall be shared equally by both Parties.

Article 21. If the Commission's recommendations are not accepted by both Parties, each Party shall have the right to submit the dispute to the Permanent Court of International Justice within the time-limit fixed by the Commission's report.

Should the Court be of opinion that the dispute is not of a juridical nature, the Parties shall agree to settle it *ex aequo et bono*, if no rule of international law can be applied to it.

Article 22. In each particular case the Contracting Parties shall draw up a special agreement specifying clearly the subject of the dispute, the particular competence which might devolve on the Permanent Court of International Justice, and any other conditions fixed between themselves.

The special agreement shall be drawn up by an exchange of notes between the Governments of the Contracting Parties and shall be interpreted in all points by the Permanent Court. If the text of the special agreement has not been drawn up within three months from the date on which one of the Parties has been notified of a request for judicial settlement, either Party may bring the question before the Permanent Court by a simple application.

Article 23. Should the Permanent Court of International Justice find that a decision of a court of law or other authority of one of the Contracting Parties is wholly or partly at variance with international law, and should the constitutional law of that Party not allow, or only inadequately allow the cancellation of the effects of such decision, the Parties agree that equitable satisfaction shall be given to the injured Party by the judgment of the Court.

Article 24. The judgment given by the Permanent Court of International Justice shall be carried out in good faith by the Parties.

Any difficulties that may arise with regard to its interpretation shall be decided by the Permanent Court, to which the matter may be referred by either of the Parties by means of a simple application.

Article 25. During the procedure of conciliation or the judicial procedure, the Contracting Parties shall refrain from any measures that might prejudicially affect the acceptance of the Conciliation Commission's proposals or the execution of the judgment of the Permanent Court of International Justice.

Article 26. If at the date of the expiry of the present Treaty conciliation procedure or judicial procedure is pending, it shall follow its course in conformity with the provisions of the present Treaty or of any other Convention that the Parties may have agreed to substitute therefor.

Article 27. Any disputes that may arise as to the interpretation or the execution of the present Treaty, including such as relate to the character of the disputes, shall be submitted direct to the Permanent Court of International Justice by simple application.

Article 28. The present Treaty shall be ratified at the earliest possible date and shall come into force immediately after the exchange of ratifications. It is concluded for a period of five years as from the date of its coming into force. If it is not denounced six months before the expiry of that period, it shall be deemed to be renewed for a second period of five years, and similarly thereafter.

In faith whereof the above-mentioned Plenipotentiaries have signed the present Treaty.

Done at Ankara, October 30, 1930.

(Signed) E. K. VENIZELOS.
(Signed) A. MICHALAKOPOULOS.

(Signed) ISMET.
(Signed) T. RUSTU.

4.1269 Treaty of Non-Aggression and Pacific Settlement of Disputes between the Soviet Union and Finland

Alliance Members: Soviet Union and Finland
Signed On: January 21, 1932, in the city of Helsinki (Finland). In force until November 30, 1939.
Alliance Type: Neutrality Pact (Type II)

Source: *League of Nations Treaty Series*, no. 3613.

SUMMARY

This non-aggression and neutrality pact is similar to all the other agreements negotiated by the Soviet Union with its neighbors during this period, except for one important clause. Japan, a country that tsarist Russia had previously fought, launched an attack on Manchuria in September of 1931. This incident led the Soviets to include the second clause of Article 2, which allows either party to denounce the treaty without notice, should either alliance member "resort to aggression against a third Party." The new clause appeared in all Soviet-negotiated neutrality pacts until the infamous Hitler-Stalin Pact of 1939.

The terms of the treaty ended with the Soviet invasion of Finland, after the Finns' refusal to sign a new agreement that was much more favorable to Soviet interests.

ALLIANCE TEXT

The Central Executive Committee of the Union of Soviet Socialist Republics, of the one part, and

The President of the Republic of Finland, of the other part,

Actuated by the desire to contribute to the maintenance of general peace;

Being convinced that the conclusion of the undertakings mentioned below and the pacific settlement of any dispute whatsoever between Union of Socialist Soviet Republics and Republic of Finland is in the interests of both High Contracting Parties and will contribute towards the development of friendly and neighbourly relations between the two counties;

Declaring that none of the international obligations which they have hitherto assumed debars the pacific development of their mutual relations or is incompatible with the present Treaty;

Being desirous of confirming and completing the General Pact of August 27, 1928, for the Renunciation of War;

Have resolved to conclude the present Treaty and have for that purpose appointed:

The Central Executive Committee of the Socialist Soviet Republics: Monsieur Jean Maisky, Envoy Extraordinary and Minister Plenipotentiary; and

The President of the Republic of Finland: Baron A. S. Yrjö-Koskinen, Minister for Foreign Affairs;

Who, having exchanged their full powers, found in good and due form, have agreed upon the following provisions:

Article 1. 1. The High Contracting Parties mutually guarantee the inviolability of the existing frontiers between the Union of Socialist Soviet Republics and the Republic of Finland, as fixed by the Treaty of Peace concluded at Dorpat on October 14th, 1920, which shall remain the firm foundation of their relations, and reciprocally undertake to refrain from any act of aggression directed against each other.

2. Any act of violence attacking the integrity and inviolability of the territory or the political independence of the other High Contracting Party shall be regarded as an act of aggression, even if it is committed without declaration of war and avoids warlike manifestations.

Protocol to Article 1.

In conformity with the provisions of Article 4 of the present Treaty, the Agreement of June 1, 1922, regarding measures ensuring the inviolability of the frontiers shall not be affected by the provisions of the present Treaty and shall continue to remain fully in force.

Article 2. 1. Should either High Contracting Party be the object of aggression on the part of one or more third Powers, the other High Contracting Party undertakes to maintain neutrality throughout the duration of the conflict.

2. Should either High Contracting Party resort to aggression against a third Party, the other High Contracting Party may denounce the present Treaty without notice.

Article 3. Each of the High Contracting Parties undertakes not to become a party of any treaty, agreement or convention which is openly hostile to the other Party or contrary, whether formally or in substance, to the present Treaty.

Article 4. The obligations mentioned in the preceding Articles of the present Treaty may in no case affect or modify the international rights or obligations of the High Contracting Parties under agreements concluded or undertakings assumed before the coming into force of the present Treaty, in so far as such agreements contain no elements of aggression within the meaning of the present Treaty.

Article 5. The High Contracting Parties declare that they will always endeavour to settle in a spirit of justice any disputes of whatever nature or origin which may arise between them, and will resort exclusively to pacific means of settling such disputes. For this purpose, the High Contracting Parties undertake to submit any disputes which may arise between them after the signature of the present Treaty, and which it may not have been possible to settle through diplomatic proceedings within a reasonable time, to a procedure of conciliation before a joint conciliation commission whose powers, composition and working shall be fixed by a special supplementary Convention, which shall form an integral part of the present Treaty and which the High Contracting Parties undertake to conclude as soon as possible and in any event before the present Treaty is ratified. Conciliation procedure shall also be applied in the event of any dispute as to application or interpretation of a Convention concluded between the High Contracting Parties, and particularly the question whether the mutual undertaking as to non-aggression has or has not been violated.

Article 6. The present Treaty shall be ratified and the instruments of ratification shall be exchanged at Moscow.

Article 7. The present Treaty shall enter into force on the exchange of the instruments of ratification.

Article 8. The present Treaty is concluded for three years. If it is not denounced by either of the High Contracting Parties after previous notice of not less than six months before the expiry of that period, it shall be deemed automatically renewed for a further period of two years.

Article 9. The present Treaty is drawn up in duplicate in French, in the town of Helsingfors, the 21st of January, 1932.

In faith whereof the Plenipotentiaries have signed the present Treaty and have thereto affixed their seals.

(L.S.) (Signed) *J. MAISKY.*

(L.S.) (Signed) *A. S. YRJÖ-KOSKINEN.*

4.1270 Treaty of Non-Aggression between Latvia and the Union of Soviet Socialist Republics

Alliance Members: Soviet Union and Latvia
Signed On: February 5, 1932, in the city of Riga (Latvia). In force until October 5, 1939.
Alliance Type: Non-Aggression Pact (Type II)

Source: *League of Nations Treaty Series,* no. 3408.

SUMMARY

This non-aggression pact between the Soviets and Latvia, its neighbor on the Baltic Sea, carried the pledge that both parties would refrain from acts of aggression against the other party. Further, both allies pledged not to participate in any violent actions directed against the territorial inviolability of the other party (Article 1) or any military or political treaties directed against the other party (Article 2).

The treaty lasted until 1939, when it was replaced by a new alliance. The Soviet invasion and occupation of Latvia effectively ended the alliance in June of 1940.

ALLIANCE TEXT

The President of the Latvian Republic and the Central Executive Committee of the Union of Soviet Socialist Republics;

Having in view the Peace Treaty concluded on August 11th, 1920, between Latvia and the Russian Socialist Federative Soviet Republic, the effect of which extends to the entire territory of the Union of Soviet Socialist Republics, and all the provisions of which invariably and permanently the firm foundation of the relations between the High Contracting Parties;

Being convinced that it is in the interests of both High Contracting Parties to adopt certain provisions which may contribute to the development and consolidation of friendly relations between the two States;

Being firmly resolved to respect mutually and unreservedly each other's sovereignty, political independence, territorial integrity and inviolability;

Being guided by the desire to contribute to the consolidation of world peace;

Declaring that none of the obligations so far assumed by either of the Parties hinders the peaceful development of their mutual relations or is incompatible with the present Treaty;

Being desirous of confirming and supplementing in their relations the General Pact on the Renunciation of War of August 27th,1928, which continues to retain its effect as in the pas between the High Contracting Parties, independently of the duration or the normal expiry of the present Treaty or its possible denunciation before the date provided for;

Have decided to conclude the present Treaty, and have for that purpose appointed as their Plenipotentiaries;

The President of the Latvian Republic: M. Margers Skuje-nieks, Prime Minister, acting Minister for Foreign Affairs;

The Central Executive Committee of the Union of Soviet Socialist Republics: M. Boris Spiridonovich Stomoniakov, Member of the Council of the People's Commissariat for Foreign Affairs, and Alexis Ivanovitch Sviderski, Plenipotentiary Representative of the Union of Soviet Socialist Republics;

Who, having communicated their full powers, found in good and due form, have agreed as follows:

Article I. Each of the High Contracting Parties undertakes to refrain from any act of aggression directed against the other, and also from any acts of violence directed against the territorial integrity and inviolability or the political independence of the other Contracting Party, regardless of whether such an aggression or such acts are committed separately or together with other Powers, with or without a declaration of war.

Article 2. Each of the High Contracting Parties undertakes not to be a party to any military or political treaties, conventions or agreements directed against the independence, territorial integrity or political security of the other Party, or to any treaties, conventions, or agreements aiming at an economic or financial boycot of either of the Contracting Parties.

Article 3. The obligations provided for in the present Treaty may not in any way limit or change the international rights and obligations devolving on the High Contracting Parties from treaties concluded by them before the coming into force of the present Treaty and duly published in the official publications of each Party, in so far as these treaties do not include any elements of aggression within the meaning of the present Treaty.

Article 4. In view of the obligations assumed in the present Treaty, the High Contracting Parties undertake to submit all disputes, whatever their kind or origin, which may arise between them after the signature of the present Treaty and which cannot be settled within a reasonable period by ordinary diplomatic procedure, to a procedure of conciliation in a joint conciliation commission of which the composition, powers, and procedure are to be fixed by a special Convention which the two Parties undertake to conclude as early as possible, and which shall come into force at the same time as the present Treaty.

Article 5. The present Treaty is drawn up in duplicate in the Latvian and Russian languages, both texts being equally authentic. It shall be ratified and the instruments of ratification shall be exchanged between the High Contracting Parties in Moscow.

Article 6. The present Treaty shall come into force at the moment of the exchange of the instruments of ratification and shall remain in force for three years. Each of the High Contracting Parties shall be entitled to denounce the Treaty by giving notice six months before the expiry of this period, or without giving notice if the other Contracting Party commits an aggression upon any third State. If the Treaty is not denounced by either of the High Contracting Parties, its period of validity shall be automatically prolonged for two years; in the same manner, the Treaty shall be deemed to be prolonged on each occasion for a further period of two years, if it is not denounced by either of the Contracting Parties in the manner provided in the present Article.

In witness whereof the above-named Plenipotentiaries have signed the present Treaty and thereto affixed their seals.

Done at Riga, in duplicate, in the Latvian and Russian languages, February 5th 1932.

Margers SKUJENIEKS.
B. STOMONIAKOV.
A. SVIDERSKI.

4.1271 Treaty of Non-Aggression between Estonia and the Union of Soviet Socialist Republics

Alliance Members: Soviet Union and Estonia
Signed On: May 4, 1932, in the city of Moscow. In force until September 29, 1939.
Alliance Type: Non-Aggression Pact (Type II)

Source: *League of Nations Treaty Series*, no. 3020.

SUMMARY

Continuing its policy of calming smaller neighbors and establishing security ties across its borders, the Soviet Union signed this non-aggression pact with Estonia. Like the other Baltic States, Estonia had fought for its independence in the aftermath of World War I against a Red Army that was intent on keeping Estonia part of the new Soviet system. Winning its independence in 1920, Estonia reaffirmed its relationship with the new Soviet Union several times, including this non-aggression pact and the defense treaty that replaced it in 1939. Ultimately, the Soviet Union ended the alliance with its invasion and occupation in June of 1940.

ALLIANCE TEXT

The President of the Estonian Republic, of the one part, and the Central Executive Committee of the Union of Soviet Socialist Republics, of the other part,

Being convinced that it is in the interests of the two High Contracting Parties to lay down definite conditions contributing to strengthen the friendly relations existing between them,

Animated by the desire to contribute in that manner to the maintenance of universal peace,

Considering that the Peace Treaty of February 2, 1920, constitutes, now as heretofore, the unshakable foundation of their mutual relations and obligations,

Declaring that not one of the international obligations assumed by either of the High Contracting Parties is incompatible with the peaceful development of their mutual relations or in contradiction with the present Treaty,

Being desirous of supplementing and defining, so far as concerns their mutual relations, the Pact for the Renunciation of War signed at Paris on August 27, 1928,

Have decided to conclude the present Treaty, and to this end have appointed as their Plenipotentiaries:

The President of the Estonian Republic: M. Julius Seljamaa, Envoy Extraordinary and Minister Plenipotentiary to the Union of Soviet Socialist Republics;

The Central Executive Committee of the Union of Soviet Socialist Republics: M. Maxim Maximovitch Litvinov, People's Commissary for Foreign Affairs, Member of the Central Executive Committee of the Union of Soviet Socialist Republics,

Who, having communicated their full powers, found in good and proper form, have agreed upon the following provisions:

Article 1. Each of the High Contracting Parties guarantees to the other Party the inviolability of the existing frontiers between them, as defined by the Peace Treaty signed on February 2, 1920, and undertake to refrain from any act of aggression or any violent measures directed against the integrity and inviolability of the territory or against the political independence of the other Contracting Party, whether such acts of aggression or such violent measures are undertaken separately or in conjunction with other Powers, with or without a declaration of war.

Article 2. Each of the High Contracting Parties undertakes not to take part in political agreements manifestly directed in an aggressive sense against the other Party, nor in coalitions of the same nature having as their object to subject the other Party to economic or financial boycott.

Article 3. The obligations mentioned in the preceding Articles of the present Treaty shall in no case affect or modify the rights and international obligations devolving on the High Contracting Parties from treaties concluded or obligations assumed prior to the entry into force of the present Treaty, so far as the said rights and obligations contain no elements of aggression within the meaning of the present Treaty.

Article 4. Taking into consideration the obligations assumed in virtue of the present Treaty, the High Contracting Parties undertake to submit all disputes, whatever their nature or origin, which may arise between them subsequent to the coming into force of the present Treaty, and which it may not have been possible to settle within a reasonable time through the ordinary diplomatic channel, to a procedure of conciliation in a mixed Conciliation Commission, whose composition, powers, and procedure shall be fixed by a separate Convention, which the two Parties undertake to conclude within the shortest possible time, and which shall come into force simultaneously with the present Treaty.

Article 5. The present Treaty is drawn up in duplicate Estonian and Russian, both texts being authentic. It shall be ratified within the shortest possible time, and the instruments of ratification shall be exchanged between the High Contracting Parties in Tallinn within forty-five days from the date of the ratification of the present Treaty by Estonia and the Union of Soviet Socialist Republics.

Article 6. The present Treaty shall come into force on the day of the exchange of the instruments of ratification, and shall remain in force for three years from that date.

Either of the High Contracting Parties shall have the right to denounce the Treaty by notifying the other Party of its intension six months before the expiry of the said period, or without giving such notice in the event of an act of aggression being committed by the other High Contracting Party against any third Power whatsoever.

If the Treaty is not denounced by one or other of the High Contracting Parties, its validity shall be tacitly prolonged for a period of two years; similarly, the Treaty shall be deemed to be prolonged on each subsequent occasion for a further period of two years provided it has not been denounced by one or other of the High Contracting Parties, according to the procedure laid down in the present Article.

In faith whereof the above-mentioned Plenipotentiaries have signed the present Treaty and have thereto affixed their seals.

Done at Moscow, in duplicate, May 4, 1932.

(L.S.) *Jul. SELJAMAA.*
(L.S.) *M. LITVINOV*

4.1272 Pact of Non-Aggression between Poland and the Union of Soviet Socialist Republics

Alliance Members: Soviet Union and Poland
Signed On: July 25, 1932, in the city of Moscow. In force until September 17, 1939.
Alliance Type: Non-Aggression Pact (Type II)

Source: *League of Nations Treaty Series,* no. 3124.

SUMMARY

Following the war between the Poles and the Bolsheviks (1919–1921), Poland tried to maintain a balanced policy between Germany and Soviet Russia while it also relied on a strong commitment from France. Polish leaders started negotiations with the Soviets in early 1926 over a non-aggression pact that would confirm the Polish territorial gains during the war, but negotiations quickly ceased and were only resumed five years later. Negotiations with Germany over a similar pact were not started until after this pact had been finalized.

The Soviets sent Poland a communiqué in 1938 that stated this pact would be broken if Poland participated in the occupation of Czechoslovakia following the Munich Conference. Nevertheless, even after Poland found modest territorial gains along its southern border, the Soviets did not break the treaty and even publicly reaffirmed its provisions in November of 1938. Ultimately, however, the pact was broken when Soviet troops entered and occupied half of Poland in September of 1939.

ALLIANCE TEXT

The President of the Polish Republic, of the one part, and the Central Executive Committee of the Union of Soviet Socialist Republics, of the other part,

Desirous of maintaining the present state of peace between their countries, and convinced that the maintenance of peace between them constitutes an important factor in the work of preserving universal peace;

Considering that the Treaty of Peace of March 18, 1921, constitutes, now as in the past, the basis of their reciprocal relations and undertakings;

Convinced that the peaceful settlement of international disputes and the exclusion of all that might be contrary to the normal condition of relations between States are the surest means of arriving at the goal desired;

Declaring that none of the obligations hitherto assumed by either of the Parties stands in the way of the peaceful development of their mutual relations or is incompatible with the present Pact;

Have decided to conclude the present Pact with the object of amplifying and completing the Pact for the renunciation of war signed at Paris on August 27, 1928, and put into force by the Protocol signed at Moscow on February 9, 1929, and for that purpose have designated as their Plenipotentiaries:

The President of the Polish Republic: Stanislaw Patek, Envoy Extraordinary and Minister Plenipotentiary of the Polish Republic at Moscow;

The Central Executive Committee of the Union of Soviet Socialist Republics: Nicolai Krestinski, Member of the Central Executive Committee of the Union of Soviet Socialist Republics, replacing the People's Commissar for Foreign Affairs,

Who, after exchanging their full powers, found in good and due form, have agreed on the following provisions:

Article I. The two Contracting Parties, recording the fact that they have renounced war as an instrument of national policy in their mutual relations, reciprocally undertake to refrain from taking any aggressive action against or invading the territory of the other Party, either alone or in conjunction with other Powers.

Any act of violence attacking the integrity and inviolability of the territory of the political independence of the other Contracting Party shall be regarded contrary to the undertakings contained in the present Article, even if such acts are committed without declaration of war and avoid all warlike manifestations as far as possible.

Article 2. Should one of the Contracting Parties be attacked by a third State or by a group of other States, the other Contracting Party undertakes not to give aid or assistance, either directly or indirectly, to the aggressor State during the whole period of the conflict.

Should one of the Contracting Parties commits an act of aggression against a third State the other Contracting Party shall have the right to denounce the present Pact without notice.

Article 3. Each of the Contracting Parties undertakes not to be a party to any agreement openly hostile to the other Party from the point of view of aggression.

Article 4. The undertakings provided for in Articles I and 2 of the present Pact shall in no case limit or modify the international rights and obligations of each Contracting Party under agreements concluded by it before the coming into force of the present Pact, so far as the said agreements contain no aggressive elements.

Article 5. The two Contracting Parties, desirous of settling and solving, exclusively by peaceful means, any disputes and differences, of whatever nature or origin, which may arise between them, undertake to submit questions at issue, which it has not been possible to settle within a reasonable period by diplomacy, to a procedure of conciliation, in accordance with the provisions of the Convention for the application of the procedure of conciliation, which constitutes an integral part of the present Pact and shall be signed separately and ratified as soon as possible simultaneously with the Pact of Non-Aggression.

Article 6. The present Pact shall be ratified as soon as possible, and the instruments of ratification shall be exchanged at Warsaw within thirty days following the ratification by Poland and the Union of Soviet Socialist Republics, after which the Pact shall come into force immediately.

Article 7. The Pact is concluded for three years. If it is not denounced by one of the Contracting Parties, after previous notice of not less than six months before the expiry of that period, it shall be automatically renewed for a further period of two years.

Article 8. The present Pact is drawn up in Polish and Russian, both texts being authentic.

In faith whereof the above-named Plenipotentiaries have signed the present Pact and have thereto affixed their seals.

Done at Moscow, in two copies, July 25, 1932.

(—) *St. PATEK.*

(—) *N. KRESTINSKI.*

4.1273 Pact of Non-Aggression between France and the Union of Soviet Socialist Republics

Alliance Members: Soviet Union and France
Signed On: November 29, 1932, in the city of Paris. In force until May 2, 1935.
Alliance Type: Non-Aggression Pact (Type II)

Source: *League of Nations Treaty Series,* no. 3615.

SUMMARY

France and Poland were staunch allies during the period between the world wars; thus, after the Soviet Union committed to the Soviet-Polish non-aggression pact, this similar agreement with France led to little change in foreign policy for the Soviets. These two non-aggression agreements effectively marked the end of the intense period of German-Soviet cooperation between 1930 and 1932, as rumors of a German rapprochement with the French provided the impetus for the Soviets to seek guarantees from both Poland and France. The coordination with France ultimately led to a Franco-Soviet trade agreement

in 1934 and a joint defense pact signed on May 2, 1935. The latter treaty replaced this agreement (see Alliance no. 4.1283).

ALLIANCE TEXT

The Central Executive Committee of the U. S. S. R. and the President of the French Republic, animated by the desire to consolidate peace, convinced that the improvement and development of relations between the two countries is in the interests of both high contracting parties, true to previously undertaken international obligations, none of which, according to the declaration of both sides, interferes with the peaceful development of their mutual relations nor contradicts the present treaty, desiring to confirm and define more accurately in their relations the general Pact for the Renunciation of War of August 27, 1928, have decided to conclude a treaty for this purpose and have appointed their plenipotentiaries, to wit:

The Central Executive Committee of the U. S. S. R.—Valerian Dovgalevsky, Envoy Extraordinary and Plenipotentiary of the U. S. S. R., accredited to the President of the French Republic, and

The President of the French Republic—M. Herriot, President of the Council of Ministers and Minister of Foreign Affairs,

Who, upon exchange of their full powers, found in good and proper form,

agreed upon the following provisions:

Article I. Each of the high contracting parties binds itself before the other in no case, either separately or jointly with one or several other Powers, to have recourse either to war against the other, or to any kind of attack by land, sea or air; and each further undertakes to respect the inviolability of territories under the sovereignty of the other or in relation to which the other has undertaken representation in foreign affairs and administrative control.

Article II. If one of the high contracting parties should be the object of attack from one or several third Powers, then the other high contracting party binds itself to give, during the course of the conflict, neither direct nor indirect aid and support to the aggressor or aggressors.

If one of the high contracting parties attacks a third Power, then the other high contracting party is entitled to denounce the present treaty without previous notice.

Article III. The obligations set forth in Articles I and II can by no means restrict or modify the rights and obligations resulting to each of the high contracting parties from agreements concluded prior to the entry into effect of the present treaty, and furthermore both of the parties hereby declare that they are bound by no obligations to participate in aggression undertaken by a third state.

Article IV. Each of the high contracting parties undertakes, during the period the present treaty is in force, to participate in no international agreements which would have the practical consequence of prohibiting purchases to be made of the other party, or the sale of goods, or the granting of credits to the

287

other, and to take no measures which would result in excluding the other party from any kind of participation in its foreign trade.

Article V. Each of the high contracting parties undertakes to respect in all relations the sovereignty or dominion of the other party over all its territories as defined in Article I of the present treaty, in no way to interfere in its internal affairs, and in particular, to refrain from any action inclining toward incitement or encouragement of any kind of agitation, propaganda or attempts at intervention which would have the aim of violating the territorial integrity of the other party or of changing by force the political or social structure of all or part of its territory.

Each of the high contracting parties binds itself in particular not to form, nor support, nor subsidize, nor permit on its territory either any military organizations whose purpose is armed struggle against the other party, nor organizations taking upon themselves the rôle of government or of representatives of all or part of the territory of the other.

Article VI. The high contracting parties, having already recognized in the General Pact for the Renunciation of War of August 27,1928, that the regulation and settlement of all disputes and conflicts, whatever their nature or origin, which might arise between them should always be sought by peaceful means only, confirm this statement, and in order to make it effective, attach a Convention on Conciliation Procedure to the present treaty.

Article VII. The present treaty, of which both Russian and French texts will have identical force, will be ratified and ratification instruments exchanged in Moscow.

It will enter into force beginning with the aforesaid exchange of instruments and will remain in force until the expiration of a period of one year from the day when one of the high contracting parties informs the other of its intention to denounce it. Announcement of such intention may not, however, take place before the expiration of a two-year period counted from the day of the entry into effect of the present treaty.

Done in Paris, in two copies, November 29, 1932.

DOVGALEVSKY.

HERRIOT.

4.1274 Pact of Friendship, Non-Aggression, and Neutrality between Italy and the USSR

Alliance Members: Soviet Union and Italy
Signed On: September 2, 1933, in the city of Rome. In force until June 22, 1941.
Alliance Type: Neutrality Pact (Type II)

Source: *League of Nations Treaty Series,* no. 3418.

SUMMARY

This treaty was one of the final collective security agreements penned by the Soviets during the interwar period. Relations with Mussolini's Italy had been strong, and this pact reinforced those bilateral ties. After

signing the pact, Foreign Minister Maxim Litvinov of the Soviet Union visited Rome and concluded a trade agreement. The Italians were also instrumental in opening ties between the Soviets and Hungary. Although the Soviets thought these agreements isolated Germany, the Italo-German alignment that formed the backbone of the coalition of Axis powers was stronger, and this agreement ended in June of 1941 when Italy backed Nazi forces and attacked Soviet Russia.

ALLIANCE TEXT

His Majesty the King of Italy and the Central Executive Committee of the Union of Soviet Socialist Republics,

Animated by a desire to contribute by all means in their power to the maintenance of general peace,

Having regard to the continuity of the friendly relations which unite the two countries,

Being resolved to continue to follow their policy of the most complete abstention from interference in the internal affairs of their respective countries,

Have agreed to consolidate the relations existing between Italy and the Union of Soviet Socialist Republics by the conclusion of the present Treaty and have for that purpose appointed their Plenipotentiaries:

His Majesty the King of Italy: His Excellency Benito Mussolini, Head of the Government, Prime Minister Secretary of State, Minister Secretary of State for Foreign Affairs;

The Central Executive Committee of the Union of Soviet Socialist Republics: M. Vladimir Potemkine, Ambassador of the Union of Soviet Socialist Republics in Rome;

Who, having exchanged their full powers, found in good and due form, have agreed upon the following provisions:

Article 1. Each of the High Contracting Parties undertakes with regard to the other, whether alone or jointly with one or more third Powers, either to war or to any aggression by land, sea, or air against that other Party, and to respect the inviolability of the territories placed under that Party's sovereignty.

Article 2. Should either High Contracting Party by the object of aggression on the part of one or more third Powers, the other High Contracting Party undertakes to maintain neutrality throughout the duration of the conflict.

Should either High Contracting Party resort to aggression against any Power, the other High Contracting Party may denounce the present Treaty without notice.

Article 3. Each of the High Contracting Parties undertakes, for the duration of the present Treaty, not to become a party to any international agreement of which the effect in practice would be to prevent the purchase of goods from or the sale of goods or granting of credits to the other Party, and not to take any measure which would result in the exclusion of the other Party from any participation in its foreign trade.

Article 4. Each of the High Contracting Parties undertakes not to become a party to any agreement of a political or economic character or any combination directed against either Party.

Article 5. The undertakings set forth in the preceding Articles shall not in any way limit or modify the rights and obligations of either High Contracting Party resulting from agreements concluded by that Party prior to the entry into force of the present Treaty, and each Party declares by the present Article that it is not bound by any agreement under which it is obliged to participate in an aggression undertaken by a third State.

Article 6. The High Contracting Parties undertake to submit to a procedure of conciliation any questions which may arise between them and which it may not have been possible to settle through the ordinary diplomatic channel.

Article 7. The present Treaty, of which the Italian and Russian texts shall both be authentic, shall be ratified, and the ratifications exchanged at Moscow. It shall enter into effect as from the date of the exchange of ratifications, and shall remain in force for the period of one year as from the date on which either High Contracting Party shall have notified the other of its intention to denounce it.

Such a denunciation may, however, not be given before the expiration of a period of five years from the date of the entry into force of the present Treaty.

In faith whereof the Plenipotentiaries have signed the present Pact and have thereto affixed their seals.

Done in two copies, one in Italian and the other in Russian, at Rome, September 2nd, 1933.

(L.S.) B. MUSSOLINI.

(L.S.) V. POTEMKINE.

4.1275 Treaty of Friendship, Non-Aggression, Arbitration, and Conciliation between Roumania and Turkey

Alliance Members: Romania and Turkey
Signed On: October 17, 1933, in the city of Ankara (Turkey). In force until February 9, 1934.
Alliance Type: Non-Aggression Pact (Type II)

Source: *League of Nations Treaty Series*, no. 3814.

SUMMARY

This agreement and the agreement between Turkey and Yugoslavia (see Alliance no. 4.1276) aimed to encourage cooperation among the Balkan states. After the agreement was signed in Ankara, both countries hoped that Turkey would be able to persuade Bulgaria to join a similar pact. However, the Bulgarian-Turkish pact never materialized. Instead, this agreement between Romania and Turkey was replaced by a multilateral defense pact that included Greece and Yugoslavia, creating a four-nation alliance with the goal of preserving the Balkan territorial status quo.

ALLIANCE TEXT

His Majesty the King of Roumania and the President of the Turkish Republic,

Being equally solicitous for the maintenance of general peace,

Convinced that Roumania and Turkey should co-operate in a spirit of mutual confidence in preparing for the pacific settlement of any disputes that may arise between them,

Mindful that both States are signatories to the Pact of Paris of August 27th, 1928, for the renunciation of war and the Conventions of July 3rd and 4th, 1933, defining aggression,

And desirous, in the common interest of both countries, of strengthening the bonds of friendship between them, which constitute a pledge to them for the future,

Have decided to conclude with one another the present Treaty of Friendship, Non-Aggression, Arbitration and Conciliation,

And for this purpose have appointed as their Plenipotentiaries:

His Majesty the King of Roumania: His Excellency Monsieur Nicolas Titulesco, Minister for Foreign Affairs of Roumania;

The President of the Turkish Republic: His Excellency Doctor Tevfik Rüştü Bey, Minister for Foreign Affairs of Turkey, Deputy of Izmir;

Who, having exchanged their full powers, found in good and due form, have agreed upon the following provisions:

Article 1. There shall be inviolable peace and sincere and perpetual friendship between the Kingdom of Roumania and the Turkish Republic and their people.

Article 2. Faithful to their undertakings that neither, as against the other, shall resort to war as an instrument of national policy, or to acts of aggression as defined by the Conventions of July 3rd and 4th, 1933, and accordingly to refrain from participation in any act of aggression committed by a third party, the two High Contracting Parties further undertake to condemn any act of aggression or participation in any act of aggression whatsoever attempted by third parties, or any aggressive agreement against either country.

Article 3. The High Contracting Parties undertake to settle by conciliation, judicial settlement or arbitration, in the manner hereinafter provided, all disputes arising out of situations or events prior to the entry into force of the present Treaty, with regard to which the Parties are in conflict as to their respective rights and which it has not been possible to settle by the ordinary diplomatic methods within a reasonable period.

In so far as the application of the present Agreement is concerned, the two High Contracting Parties maintain the reservations which they made on acceding to the Optional Clause of Article 36 of the Statute of the Permanent Court of International Justice. It is also understood that the above-mentioned undertaking does not extend to:

(1) Disputes relating to the claims of private individuals against either High Contracting Party which will be definitively settled by the competent national Courts of either High Contracting Party;

(2) Disputes relating to questions which, according to international law, come within the exclusive jurisdiction of the States, such as municipal law or concern the exercise of sovereign rights;

(3) Disputes concerning the territorial status of the Parties.

Article 4. Disputes for the settlement of which a special procedure is laid down in other conventions in force between the High Contracting Parties shall be settled in conformity with the provisions of those conventions.

Article 5. If the Parties agree to submit the dispute to an arbitral tribunal, they shall draw up a special agreement.

Should they not agree to rely solely on the Hague Convention of October 18th, 1907, for the pacific settlement of international disputes, this special agreement should determine not only the choice of arbitrators and the subject of the dispute but the procedure to be followed and the rules regarding the substance of the dispute to be applied by the arbitrators.

Article 6. If the Parties agree to submit the dispute to an arbitral tribunal and fail to agree concerning the special agreement referred to in the preceding Article or fail to appoint arbitrators, either Party shall be at liberty, after giving three months' notice, to bring the dispute by an application direct before the Permanent Court of International Justice.

Article 7. The decision of the Permanent Court of International justice or the award of the arbitral tribunal shall be executed by the Parties in good faith.

Any difficulties that may arise out of the interpretation or execution of the decisions of the Permanent Court of International justice or arbitral awards given in the above conditions shall be settled by the Permanent Court of International Justice, to which they may be referred at the request of either Party.

Article 8. Pending any arbitral procedure or procedure before the Permanent Court of International Justice in the above conditions, the dispute may by common agreement between the Parties be submitted to the conciliation procedure laid down in the present Agreement.

In the event of the failure of conciliation the dispute may be referred, after the expiration of the time-limit laid down in Article 21, to the Permanent Court of International Justice or to the arbitral tribunal, as the case may be, under the conditions laid down in the preceding Articles.

Article 9. On a request to that effect being made by one of the Contracting Parties to the other, a Permanent Conciliation Commission shall be constituted within a period of three months.

Article 10. The Permanent Conciliation Commission shall be composed of three members. The High Contracting Parties shall each nominate a commissioner chosen from among their respective nationals.

They shall appoint the President by common agreement. He shall not be a national of the

High Contracting Parties, nor be habitually resident in their territories, nor be employed in their service. If the appointment of the President is not made within the period provided for in the preceding Article, or in the case of a vacancy within three months from the date on which the vacancy occurs, he shall be appointed, in the absence of an agreement between the Parties, and at the request of either Party, by the Head of State of a

Power to be designated by common agreement, subject to the consent of the said Head of State.

The commissioners shall be appointed for three years. They shall be re-eligible. They shall continue to exercise their functions until they are replaced and in any event until the expiration of their mandate.

Until the proceedings are opened, each High Contracting Party may recall the commissioner appointed by it and appoint a successor. It may also withdraw its approval of the appointment of the President.

Vacancies which may occur as a result of the expiration of a mandate, recall, death, resignation or any other cause, shall be filled within the shortest possible time in the manner fixed for nominations.

Article 11. Disputes shall be brought before the Conciliation Commission by means of an application addressed to the President by the two Parties acting in agreement, or, in default thereof, by one or other of the Parties. The application, after giving an account of the subject of the dispute, shall contain the invitation to the Commission to take all necessary measures with a view to arriving at an amicable solution.

If the application emanates from only one of the Parties, the other Party shall be notified by it at the same time.

Article 12. Within fifteen days from the date on which a dispute has been brought by one of the Parties before the Conciliation Commission, either Party may replace its own commissioner, for the examination of the particular dispute, by a person possessing special competence in the matter.

The Party making use of this right shall immediately notify the other Party; the latter shall in such case be entitled to take similar action within fifteen days from the date on which it received the notification.

Article 13. In the absence of agreement to the contrary between the Parties, the Conciliation Commission shall meet at a place selected by its President.

Article 14. The task of the Conciliation Commission shall be to elucidate the questions in dispute, to collect with that object all necessary information, and to endeavour to bring the Parties to an agreement.

After the case has been examined, it shall draw up a report formulating proposals for the settlement of the dispute.

Article 15. The procedure of the Conciliation Commission shall provide for the hearing of both Parties.

The Commission shall lay down its own procedure, taking account, in the absence of unanimous agreement to the contrary, of the provisions of Part III of the Hague Convention of October 18th, 1907, for the Pacific Settlement of International Disputes.

Article 16. The Commission's proceedings shall be conducted in camera, unless, in agreement with the Parties, it decides otherwise.

Article 17. The Parties shall be entitled to be represented before the Commission by agents, counsel and experts who shall, at the same time, act as intermediaries between them and the Commission, and shall request that all persons whose evidence appears to them desirable shall be heard.

The Commission, for its part, shall be entitled to request oral explanations from the agents, counsel and experts of both Parties, as well as from all persons it may think desirable to summon with the consent of their Governments.

Article 18. The Parties undertake to facilitate the work of the Conciliation Commission and particularly to supply it to the greatest possible extent with all relevant documents and information, as well as to use all the means at their disposal, in accordance with their law, to allow it to proceed to the summoning and hearing of witnesses or experts.

Article 19. The Conciliation Commission shall present its report within four months of the day on which the dispute was brought before it, unless the Parties agree to prolong this period.

A copy of the report shall be handed to each Party. The report shall not have the character of an arbitral award, either as regards the statement of facts or as regards the legal arguments.

Article 20. The Conciliation Commission shall prescribe the period within which the Parties must give their decision as to the proposals for a settlement contained in its report. This period shall not exceed three months.

Article 21. During the proceedings of the Commission, each of the commissioners shall receive emoluments the amount of which shall be fixed by agreement between the Parties, each of which shall contribute an equal share.

The general expenses arising out of the working of the Commission shall be divided in the same manner.

Article 22. The present Treaty shall be ratified and the instruments of ratification shall be exchanged as soon as possible.

The Treaty shall come into force on the date of the exchange of ratifications.

It shall be concluded for a period of ten years from the date on which it comes into force.

Unless denounced six months before the expiration of this period, it shall be deemed to be renewed for a further period of five years and similarly thereafter.

If conciliation, arbitral or judicial proceedings are pending at the time of the expiration of the present Treaty, such proceedings shall be continued in conformity with the provisions of the present Treaty, unless the Parties agree otherwise.

Done at Ankara, in duplicate, this seventeenth day of October, one thousand nine hundred and thirty-three.

(L. S.) (Signed) N. TITULESCO.
(L. S.) (Signed) Dr. T. RÜŞTÜ.

4.1276 Treaty of Friendship, Non-Aggression, Arbitration, and Conciliation between the Turkish Republic and the Kingdom of Yugoslavia

Alliance Members: Yugoslavia and Turkey
Signed On: November 27, 1933, in the city of Ankara (Turkey). In force until February 9, 1934.
Alliance Type: Non-Aggression Pact (Type II)

Source: *League of Nations Treaty Series,* no. 3715.

SUMMARY

Territorial issues had plagued the Balkans for more than a century prior to the signing of the Turkish cooperation treaties of 1933, as the region had witnessed the slow disintegration of the Ottoman Empire, two Balkan Wars, and a world war that began on Serbian soil. The kings of the various Balkan nations accordingly sought security through these non-aggression pacts, hoping that the cooperation would lead to increased ties, trade, and a general pacification of the region. This agreement mirrors the cooperation agreement signed by Turkey and Romania in October 1933, as both treaties provide ample details for the methods by which disputes would be resolved. This agreement was ultimately successful in encouraging cooperation between these signatories, as Yugoslavia and Turkey joined Greece and Romania in a regional defense pact less than three months later.

ALLIANCE TEXT

His Majesty the King of Yugoslavia and the President of the Turkish Republic,

Equally solicitous for the maintenance of general peace;

Convinced that Yugoslavia and Turkey should collaborate to that end in a spirit of mutual confidence by preparing for the pacific settlement of any disputes that may arise between them;

Mindful of the fact that the two States are signatories of the Pact of Paris of August 27th, 1928, relating to the renunciation of war;

Desirous, in the common interests of both countries, of strengthening the friendly bonds between them which constitute a promise for the future;

Have decided to conclude with one another a Treaty of friendship, non-aggression, judicial settlement, arbitration and conciliation and have with this object appointed as their Plenipotentiaries:

His Majesty the King of Yugoslavia: His Excellency Monsieur Bogoljub Jevtitch, Minister for Foreign Affairs;

The President of the Turkish Republic: His Excellency Dr. Tevfik Rüştü Bey, Minister for Foreign Affairs;

Who, having communicated their full powers, found in good and due form, have agreed on the following provisions:

Article 1. The High Contracting Parties undertake that they will in no case seek the settlement of disputes or conflicts, of whatever nature they may be, which may arise between the Kingdom of Yugoslavia and the Turkish Republic and which it may not have been possible to settle within a reasonable time by ordinary diplomatic procedures, otherwise than by pacific means and in accordance with the methods provided for in the present Treaty.

The High Contracting Parties pledge themselves not to resort to war as an instrument of national policy in their relations with one another and to condemn all aggression and any share in any form of aggression by third parties or any aggressive agreement directed against one or other of the two countries.

CHAPTER I.

Article 2. The Yugoslav Government and the Turkish Government agree that, failing a friendly settlement by the normal methods of diplomacy and failing any other agreement, they will submit for judgment either to the Permanent Court of International Justice or to an arbitral tribunal as provided hereunder, disputes between the Parties in regard to a right and in particular any suit having as its object:

(1) The interpretation of a treaty;

(2) Any question of international law;

(3) The existence of any fact which, if established, would constitute a breach of an international obligation;

(4) The extent or nature of the reparation to be made for such breach.

Disputes for the solution of which a special procedure is provided by other Conventions in force between the High Contracting Parties shall be settled in conformity with the provisions of those Conventions.

Article 3. This undertaking shall not apply:

(1) To disputes arising out of facts existing prior to the present Treaty;

(2) To disputes concerning questions which, in the opinion of one of the Parties, are, according to the principles of international law, exclusively within its sovereignty or, according to the Treaties in force between the Parties, within its exclusive jurisdiction. Nevertheless, the other Party may, if it is of a different opinion, ask for a previous decision by the Permanent Court of International justice as to whether a dispute is within the jurisdiction of one only of the Parties;

(3) To disputes relating to the territorial status of the Parties.

Article 4. In the case of a dispute the occasion of which, according to the municipal law of one of the Parties, falls within the competence of the Courts of such Party, the matter in dispute shall not be submitted to the procedure laid down in the present Treaty until a judgment with final effect has been pronounced, within a reasonable time, by the competent national judicial authority.

Similarly, in the case of a dispute which is within the jurisdiction of the administrative authorities, the matter in dispute shall not be submitted to the various procedures laid down in the present Treaty until a final decision has been given, within a reasonable time, by the competent authority.

If either Party in such a case wishes to have recourse to the procedure laid down in the present Treaty, it shall notify the other Party of its intention within a period of one year after the aforesaid decision.

Article 5. (a) The Arbitral Tribunal mentioned in Article 2 shall consist of five members. The Parties shall each nominate one member, who may be chosen from among their respective nationals. The other two arbitrators and the Chairman shall be chosen by common agreement from among the nationals of third Powers. They must be of different nationalities and must not be habitually resident in the territories or be in the service of the Parties.

(b) 1. If the appointment of the members of the Arbitral Tribunal is not made within a period of three months from the date on which one of the Parties requested the other Party to constitute an arbitral tribunal, a third Power, chosen by agreement between the Parties, shall be requested to make the necessary appointments.

2. If no agreement is reached on this point, each Party shall designate a different Power, and the necessary appointments shall be made by the President of the Permanent Court of International Justice. If the latter is prevented from acting or is a national of one of the Parties, the appointments shall be made by the Vice-President. If the latter is prevented from acting or is a national of one of the Parties, the appointments shall be made by the oldest member of the Court who is not a national of either Party.

(c) Vacancies which may occur as a result of death, resignation or any other cause shall be filled within the shortest possible time in the manner fixed for the appointments.

(d) If the two High Contracting Parties agree to bring the dispute before an arbitral tribunal, they shall at the same time draw up a special agreement determining the subject of the dispute and the procedure to be followed.

In the absence of sufficient indication or particulars in the special agreement, regarding the points indicated in the previous paragraph, the provisions of the Hague Convention of October 18th, 1907, for the Pacific Settlement of International Disputes shall apply so far as is necessary.

If nothing is laid down in the special agreement, the Tribunal shall apply the rules in regard to the substance of the dispute indicated in Article 38 of the Statute of the Permanent Court of International Justice.

Article 6. Before any resort is made to procedure before the Permanent Court of International justice or to arbitral procedure, the dispute may, by agreement between the Parties, be submitted, with a view to amicable settlement, to the Permanent Conciliation Commission constituted in accordance with the present Treaty.

Article 7. If, in a judicial sentence or arbitral award, it is declared that a decision taken or a measure enjoined by a court of law or other authority of one of the Parties to the dispute is wholly or in part contrary to international law, and if the constitutional law of that Party only partially permits the consequences of the decision or measure in question to be annulled, the Parties agree that the judicial sentence or arbitral award shall grant the injured Party equitable satisfaction.

CHAPTER II.

Article 8. All questions on which the High Contracting Parties shall differ without being able to reach an amicable solution by means of the normal methods of diplomacy and the settlement of which cannot be attained by means of a judicial decision, as provided in Article 2 of the present Treaty, and for the settlement of which no procedure has been laid down by any treaty or convention in force between the Parties shall be submitted to the Permanent Conciliation Commission, whose duty it shall be to propose to the Parties an acceptable solution and in any case to present a report to them.

Failing agreement between the Parties concerning the request to be submitted to the Commission, either of them shall have the right, after giving the other Party one month's notice, to submit the question direct to the said Commission.

Article 9. The Permanent Conciliation Commission mentioned in the present Treaty shall be composed of five members, who shall be appointed as follows, that is to say: the High Contracting Parties shall each nominate a commissioner chosen from among their respective nationals and shall appoint, by common agreement, the three other commissioners from among the nationals of third Powers; these three commissioners must be of different nationalities, and the High Contracting Parties shall appoint the President of the Commission from among them.

The commissioners shall be appointed for three years. They shall be re-eligible. The commissioners appointed jointly may be replaced during their term of office by agreement between the Parties. Further, each Party may at any time replace the commissioner appointed by it. Notwithstanding their replacement, the appointments of the commissioners shall continue until the termination of the work in hand.

Vacancies which may occur as a result of death, resignation, replacement or any temporary cause shall be filled within the shortest possible time and, in any case, within three months in the manner fixed for the nominations.

Article 10. The Permanent Conciliation Commission shall be constituted within six months from the exchange of ratifications of the present Treaty.

If the nomination of the members to be appointed by common agreement should not have taken place within the said period, or, in the case of the filling of a vacancy, within three months from the time when the seat falls vacant, the President of the Swiss Confederation shall, in the absence of other agreement, be requested to make the necessary appointments.

Article 11. The Permanent Conciliation Commission shall be informed by means of a request addressed to the President under the conditions provided, according to the case, by Articles 6 and 8.

The request, after having given a summary account of the subject of the dispute, shall contain an invitation to the Commission to take all necessary measures with a view to arriving at an amicable settlement.

If the request emanates from only one of the Parties, notification thereof shall be made without delay to the other Party.

Article 12. Within fifteen days from the date when either of the High Contracting Parties shall have brought a dispute before the Permanent Conciliation Commission, either Party may, for the examination of the particular dispute, replace its commissioner by a person possessing special competence in the matter.

The Party making use of this right shall immediately inform the other Party; the latter shall, in that case, be entitled to take similar action within fifteen days from the date on which it receives notification.

Article 13. The task of the Permanent Conciliation Commission shall be to elucidate questions in dispute, to collect with that object all necessary information by means of enquiry or otherwise, and to endeavour to bring the Parties to an agreement. It may, after the case has been examined, inform the Parties of the terms of settlement which seem suitable to it and, if necessary, lay down a period within which they are to make their decision.

At the close of its proceedings the Commission shall draw up a report stating the result, and a copy of that report shall be delivered to each of the Parties.

The Parties shall in no case be bound by considerations of fact or law or by other considerations referred to by the Commission.

The proceedings of the Commission must, unless the Parties otherwise agree, be terminated within six months from the day on which the Commission shall have been notified of the dispute.

Article 14. Failing any special provision to the contrary, the Permanent Conciliation Commission shall lay down its own procedure, which in any case must provide for both Parties being heard. In regard to enquiries, the Commission, unless it decides unanimously to the contrary, shall act in accordance with the provisions of Chapter III (International Commissions of Enquiry) of the Hague Convention of October 18th, 1907, for the Pacific Settlement of International Disputes.

Article 15. The Permanent Conciliation Commission shall meet, in the absence of agreement by the Parties to the contrary, at a place selected by the President. If, in the course of the procedure, the nature of the case necessitates changing the seat thus chosen, the Commission shall take a decision accordingly.

Article 16. The proceedings of the Permanent Conciliation Commission shall not be public, except when a decision to that effect has been taken by the Commission with the consent of the Parties.

The High Contracting Parties pledge themselves not to publish the result of the Commission's proceedings without first consulting one another.

Article 17. The Parties shall be represented before the Permanent Conciliation Commission by agents whose duty it shall be to act as intermediaries between them and the Commission; they may, moreover, be assisted by counsel and experts appointed by them for that purpose, and may request that all persons whose evidence appears to them useful should be heard.

The Commission, on its side, shall be entitled to request oral explanations from the agents, counsel and experts of the two Parties, as well as from all persons it may think useful to summon with the consent of their Governments.

Article 18. Unless otherwise provided in the present Treaty, the decisions of the Permanent Conciliation Commission shall be taken by a majority vote.

The Commission shall only be entitled to take decisions relating to the substance of a dispute if all its members have been duly convened and if at least all the members chosen jointly are present.

Article 19. The High Contracting Parties undertake to facilitate the labours of the Permanent Conciliation Commission and particularly to ensure it the assistance of their competent authorities, to supply it to the greatest possible extent with all relevant documents and information and to take the measures necessary to permit the Commission to proceed in their territory to the summoning and hearing of witnesses or experts and to visit the localities in question.

Article 20. During the labours of the Permanent Conciliation Commission each commissioner shall receive emoluments, the amount of which shall be fixed by agreement between the High Contracting Parties, each of which shall contribute an equal share.

GENERAL PROVISIONS

Article 21. In any case in which the dispute forms the subject of arbitral or judicial procedure and particularly if the question on which the Parties differ arises out of acts already committed or on the point of being committed, the Permanent Court of International justice, acting in accordance with Article 41 of its Statute, or, according to the case, the Arbitral Tribunal, shall lay down within the shortest possible time the provisional measures to be adopted; the Permanent Conciliation Commission may, if necessary, act in the same way after agreement between the Parties.

Each of the High Contracting Parties undertakes to abstain from all measures likely to have a repercussion prejudicial to the execution of the decision or to the arrangements proposed by the Permanent Conciliation Commission, and, in general, to abstain from any sort of action whatsoever that may aggravate or extend the dispute.

Article 22. The present Treaty shall remain applicable as between the High Contracting Parties, even when other Powers are also interested in the dispute.

Article 23. In the event of any dispute arising between the High Contracting Parties as to the interpretation of the present Treaty, such dispute shall be submitted to the Permanent Court of International Justice, in accordance with the procedure laid down in Article 2 of the present Treaty.

Article 24. The present Treaty shall be ratified. The ratifications shall be exchanged at Ankara as soon as possible.

Article 25. The present Treaty shall come into force immediately upon the exchange of ratifications and shall remain in force for five years dating from its entry into force. Unless denounced six months before the expiration of that period, it shall be regarded as renewed by tacit consent for a fresh period of five years and similarly thereafter.

If, at the time of the expiration of the present Treaty, any proceedings are pending in virtue of this Treaty before the Permanent Conciliation Commission, the Permanent Court of International Justice or the Arbitral Tribunal, such proceedings shall pursue their course until their completion.

In faith whereof the Plenipotentiaries have signed the present Treaty.

Done at Belgrade, in duplicate, the 27th day of November, one thousand nine hundred and thirty-three.

(L. S.) B. D. JEVTIĆ, m.p.
(L. S.) Tevfik RÜŞTÜ Bey, m.p.

4.1277 Polish-German Declaration

Alliance Members: Poland and Germany
Signed On: January 26, 1934, in the city of Berlin. In force until April 28, 1939.
Alliance Type: Non-Aggression Pact (Type II)

Source: *Documentary Background of World War II 1931–1941*, p. 999.

SUMMARY

This treaty signified the normalization of relations between Poland and Germany following a series of border disputes after World War I until the late 1920s. The treaty effectively recognizes Poland's changed borders and ended several small trade disputes. Józef Piłsudski's Poland used the Franco-Polish alliance to leverage this agreement from Hitler's Germany. Knowing that France's Maginot Line—a series of fortifications along France's eastern border with Germany—privileged a defensive war should conflict with Germany begin, Piłsudski wanted assurances that France's fortifications would not turn a rearmed Germany toward Poland. Caught geographically between two rising powers, Germany and the Soviet Union, Poland eventually lost its independence in 1939 at the start of World War II. This treaty ended when Germany denounced the agreement less than five months before the launch of the German blitzkrieg attack.

ALLIANCE TEXT

The German Government and the Polish Government consider that the time has come to introduce a new phase in the political relations between Germany and Poland by a direct understanding between State and State. They have, therefore, decided to lay down the principles for the future development of these relations in the present declaration.

The two Governments base their action on the fact that the maintenance and guarantee of a lasting peace between their countries is an essential pre-requisite for the general peace of Europe.

They have therefore decided to base their mutual relations on the principles laid down in the Pact of Paris of the 17th August, 1928, and propose to define more exactly the application of these principles in so far as the relations between Germany and Poland are concerned.

Each of the two Governments, therefore, lays it down that the international obligations undertaken by it towards a third party do not hinder the peaceful development of their mutual relations, do not conflict with the present declaration, and are not affected by this declaration. They establish, moreover, that this declaration does not extend to those questions which under international law are to be regarded exclusively as the internal concern of either of the two States.

Both Governments announce their intention to settle directly all questions of whatever sort which concern their mutual relations.

Should any disputes arise between them and agreement thereon not be reached by direct negotiation, they will, in each particular case, on the basis of mutual agreement, seek a solution by other peaceful means, without prejudice to the possibility of applying, if necessary, those methods of procedure in which provision is made for such cases in other agreements in force between them. In no circumstances, however, will they proceed to the application of force for the purpose of reaching a decision in such disputes.

The guarantee of peace created by these principles will facilitate the great task of both Governments of finding a solution for problems of political, economic and social kinds, based on a just and fair adjustment of the interests of both parties.

Both Governments are convinced that the relations between their countries will in this manner develop fruitfully, and will lead to the establishment of a neighbourly relationship which will contribute to the well-being not only of both their countries, but of the other peoples of Europe as well.

The present declaration shall be ratified, and the instruments of ratification shall be exchanged in Warsaw as soon as possible.

The declaration is valid for a period of ten years, reckoned from the day of the exchange of the instruments of ratification.

If the declaration is not denounced by one of the two Governments six months before the expiration of this period, it will continue in force, but can then be denounced by either Government at any time on notice of six months being given. Made in duplicate in the German and Polish languages.

Berlin, January 26, 1934.

For the German Government:
FREIHERR VON NEURATH.
For the Polish Government:
JOZEF LIPSKI.

4.1278 Balkan Pact of Alliance

Alliance Members: Yugoslavia, Greece, Romania, and Turkey
Signed On: February 9, 1934, in the city of Athens. In force until October 28, 1940.
Alliance Type: Defense Pact (Type II)

Source: *League of Nations Treaty Series,* vol. 153, p. 155.

SUMMARY

This Balkan Entente combined several bilateral treaty commitments into one multilateral defense pact that guaranteed the territorial status quo in the Balkans. Any state attempting to alter the status quo in the region would be considered an aggressor by the alliance signatories. Notably absent from the pact was Bulgaria, which still harbored territorial ambitions regarding Macedonia and western Thrace. Combined with Turkey's support for the League of Nations and the movement of its foreign policy in line with Western powers such as France and Britain, the pact signified Turkish rapprochement with Europe and a commitment to peace in the Balkans.

The defense pact lasted for just over six years; it ended when Italy invaded Greece through Albania. Greece's allies failed to provide aid, effectively disbanding the alliance.

ALLIANCE TEXT

The President of the Hellenic Republic, His Majesty the King of Roumania, the President of the Turkish Republic, and His Majesty the King of Yugoslavia, being desirous of contributing to the consolidation of peace in the Balkans;

Animated by the spirit of understanding and conciliation which inspired the drawing-up of the Briand-Kellogg Pact and the decisions of the Assembly of the League of Nations in relation thereto;

Firmly resolved to ensure the observance of the contractual obligations already in existence and the maintenance of the territorial situation in the Balkans as at present established;

Have resolved to conclude a "Pact of Balkan Entente"

And to that end have designated their respective Plenipotentiaries, to wit:

The President of the Hellenic Republic: His Excellency Monsieur Demetre Maximos, Minister for Foreign Affairs;

His Majesty the King of Roumania: His Excellency Monsieur Nicolas Titulescu, Minister for Foreign Affairs;

The President of the Turkish Republic: His Excellency Monsieur Tevfik Rüstü Bey, Minister for Foreign Affairs;

His Majesty the King of Yugoslavia: His Excellency Monsieur Bogolioub Jevtitch, Minister for Foreign Affairs,

Who, having exchanged their full powers, found in good and due form, have agreed upon the following provisions:

Article 1. Greece, Roumania, Turkey and Yugoslavia mutually guarantee the security of each and all of their Balkan frontiers.

Article 2. The High Contracting Parties undertake to concert together in regard to the measures to be taken in contingencies liable to affect their interests as defined by the present Agreement. They undertake not to embark upon any political action in relation to any other Balkan country not a signatory of the present Agreement without previous mutual consultation, nor to incur any political obligation to any other Balkan country without the consent of the other Contracting Parties.

Article 3. The present Agreement shall come into force on the date of its signature by all the Contracting Parties, and shall be ratified as rapidly as possible. It shall be open to any Balkan country whose accession thereto is favourably regarded by the Contracting Parties, and such accession shall take effect as soon as the other signatory countries have notified their agreement.

In faith whereof the said Plenipotentiaries have signed the present Pact.

Done at Athens, this ninth day of February, nineteen hundred and thirty-four, in four copies, one of which has been delivered to each of the High Contracting Parties.

D. MAXIMOS.
Dr. T. RÜSTÜ.
N. TITULESCU.
B. JEVTITCH.

PROTOCOL-ANNEX.

In proceeding to sign the Pact of Balkan Entente, the four Ministers for Foreign Affairs of Greece, Roumania, Yugoslavia, and Turkey have seen fit to define as follows the nature of the undertakings assumed by their respective countries, and to stipulate explicitly that the said definitions form an integral part of the Pact.

1. Any country committing one of the acts of aggression to which Article 2 of the London Conventions of July 3rd and 4th, 1933, relates shall be treated as an aggressor.

2. The Pact of Balkan Entente is not directed against any Power. Its object is to guarantee the security of the several Balkan frontiers against any aggression on the part of any Balkan State.

3. Nevertheless, if one of the High Contracting Parties is the victim of aggression on the part of any other non-Balkan Power, and a Balkan State associates itself with such aggression, whether at the time or subsequently, the Pact of Balkan Entente shall be applicable in its entirety in relation to such Balkan State.

4. The High Contracting Parties undertake to conclude appropriate Conventions for the furtherance of the objects pursued by the Pact of Balkan Entente. The negotiation of such Conventions shall begin within six months.

5. As the Pact of Balkan Entente does not conflict with previous undertakings, all previous undertakings and all Conventions based on previous Treaties shall be applicable in their entirety, the said undertakings and the said Treaties having all been published.

6. The words "Firmly resolved to ensure the observance of the contractual obligations already in existence", in the Preamble to the Pact, shall cover the observance by the High

Contracting Parties of existing Treaties between Balkan States, to which one or more of the High Contracting Parties is a signatory party.

7. The Pact of Balkan Entente is a defensive instrument; accordingly, the obligations on the High Contracting Parties which arise out of the said Pact shall cease to exist in relation to a High Contracting Party becoming an aggressor against any other country within the meaning of Article 2 of the London Conventions.

8. The maintenance of the territorial situation in the Balkans as at present established is binding definitively on the High Contracting Parties. The duration of the obligations under the Pact shall be fixed by the High Contracting Parties in the course of the two years following the signature of the Pact, or afterwards. During the two years in question the Pact cannot be denounced. The duration of the Pact shall be fixed at not less than five years, and may be longer. If, two years after the signature of the same, no duration has been fixed, the Pact of Balkan Entente shall *ipso facto* remain in force for five years from the expiry of the two years after the signature thereof. On the expiry of the said five years, or of the period on which the High Contracting Parties have agreed for its duration, the Pact of Balkan Entente shall be renewed automatically by tacit agreement for the period for which, it was previously in force, failing denunciation by any one of the High Contracting Parties one year before the date of its expiry; provided always that no denunciation or notice of denunciation shall be admissible, whether in the first period of the Pact's validity (namely, seven or more than seven years) or in any subsequent period fixed automatically by tacit agreement, before the year preceding the date on which the Pact expires.

9. The High Contracting Parties shall inform each other as soon as the Pact of Balkan

Entente is ratified in accordance with their respective laws.

Athens, this ninth day of February, nineteen hundred and thirty-four.

(S.) D. MAXIMOS.
(S.) N. TITULESCU.
(S.) Dr. T. RÜSTÜ.
(S.) B. JEVTIĊ.

4.1279 Protocol No. 1 among Austria, Hungary, and Italy

Alliance Members: Austria, Hungary, and Italy
Signed On: March 17, 1934, in the city of Rome. In force until March 13, 1938, when Austria lost its independence after the German *Anschluss*.
Alliance Type: Entente (Type III)

Source: *League of Nations Treaty Series,* vol. 154, p. 285.

SUMMARY

Fearing the rise of German hegemony in Central Europe, the leaders of Hungary (G. Gömbös), Austria (E. Dollfuss), and Italy (B. Mussolini) convened in Rome on March 17, 1934, to discuss what became known as the Roman Protocols. National Socialist political movements were gaining momentum inside Austria. Mussolini preferred a small, independent Austria on its northern border to the possibility of a powerful and expansionist Germany, especially following the Italian annexation of German-speaking Tyrol in 1919.

The pact began to decline with the expansion of influential National Socialist forces following the assassination of Chancellor Dollfuss. On March 12, 1938, the new government of Austria, formed by National Socialist Arthur Seyss-Inquart, watched as the German *Wehrmacht* crossed the border into Austria and declared annexation over Austrian frontiers.

ALLIANCE TEXT

The Federal Chancellor of the Republic of Austria, the Head of the Government of His Majesty the King of Italy, the President of the Royal Council of Ministers of Hungary,

Being anxious to contribute to the maintenance of peace and to the economic reconstruction of Europe on the basis of respect for the independence and rights of every State,

Being convinced that co-operation in this direction between the three Governments is likely to create a genuine basis for wider co-operation with other States,

Undertake, with a view to achieving the above-mentioned purposes:

> To confer together on all problems which particularly concern them, and on problems of a general character, with a view to pursuing, in the spirit of the existing treaties of friendship between Italy and Austria, Italy and Hungary and Austria and Hungary, which are based on a recognition of the existence of numerous common interests, a concordant policy directed towards the promotion of effective co-operation between the States of Europe and particularly between Italy, Austria and Hungary.
>
> To this end, the three Governments shall proceed to hold joint consultations whenever at least one of them deems it desirable.

The present Protocol is drawn up in three copies, in German, Italian and Hungarian. In the case of any difference of opinion, the Italian text shall be taken as authentic.

In faith whereof the undersigned have signed the present Protocol.

ROME, March 17th, 1934.

DOLLFUSS, m.p.
MUSSOLINI, m.p.
GÖMBÖS, m.p.

4.1280 Treaty of Taif

Alliance Members: Saudi Arabia and the Yemen Arab Republic
Signed On: May 20, 1934, in the city of Taif (Saudi Arabia). In force until November 6, 1962, when Saudi Arabia backed royalists during Yemen's civil war.
Alliance Type: Non-Aggression Pact (Type II)

Source: *British Foreign and State Papers,* vol. 137, p. 670.

SUMMARY

This non-aggression pact formed as a means to end the border conflicts between the former British protectorates of Saudi Arabia and Yemen. The treaty affirmed border definitions for both states and established methods for conciliation should any disputes erupt. Recognition of both kingdoms was also affirmed. Both pledged to refrain from alignments with any third parties that may harm the other country's interests, and in the case of political instability in either ally, the ally must refrain from aiding any insurrections or other causes of instability.

The treaty effectively ended when civil war broke out between Yemen royalists and republicans. Egypt supplied support to the new republican government and Saudi Arabia supported the royalists.

ALLIANCE TEXT

In the Name of God the Merciful, the Compassionate. His Honourable Majesty the Imam Abdul Aziz Abdurrahman-al-Feysal al-Saud, King of the Saudi Arabian Kingdom on the one part, and His Honourable Majesty the Imam Yahya-bin-Muhammad Hamiduddin, King of the Yemen, on the other part.

Being desirous of ending the state of war unfortunately existing between them and their Governments and peoples;

And of uniting the Islamic Arab nation and raising its condition and maintaining its prestige and independence,

And in view of the necessity of establishing firm treaty relations between them

and their Governments and countries on a basis of mutual advantage and reciprocal interests;

And wishing to fix the frontiers between their countries and to establish relations of good neighbourship and ties of Islamic friendship between them and to strengthen the foundations of peace and tranquillity between their peoples and countries; And being desirous that there should be a united front against sudden mishaps and a solid structure to preserve the safety of the Arabian peninsula:

Have resolved to conclude a treaty of Islamic friendship and Arab brotherhood between them and for that purpose have nominated the following representatives plenipotentiaries on their behalf.

[Here follow the names.]

Their Majesties the two Kings have accorded to their above-mentioned representatives full powers and absolute authority; and their above-mentioned representatives, having perused each other's credentials and found them in proper form, have, in the name of their Kings, agreed upon the following articles:

Article 1: The state of war existing between the Kingdom of the Yemen and the Kingdom of Saudi Arabia shall be terminated as from the moment of signature of this treaty, and there shall forthwith be established between Their Majesties the Kings and their countries and peoples a state of perpetual peace, firm friendship and everlasting Islamic Arab brotherhood, inviolable in part or whole. The two high contracting parties undertake to settle in a spirit of affection and friendship all disputes and differences which may arise between them, and to ensure that a spirit of Islamic Arab brotherhood shall dominate their relations in all states and conditions. They call God to witness the goodness of their intentions and their true desire for concord and agreement, both secretly and openly, and they pray the Almighty to grant them and their successors and heirs and Governments success in the continuance of this proper attitude, which is pleasing to the Creator and honourable to their race and religion.

Article 2: Each of the two high contracting parties recognises the full and absolute independence of the Kingdom of the other party and his sovereignty over it. His Majesty the Imam Abdul Aziz-bin Abdurrahman-al-Feysal-al-Saud, King of the Saudi Arabian Kingdom, acknowledges to His Majesty the Imam Yahya and his lawful descendants the full and absolute independence of the Kingdom of the Yemen and his sovereignty over it, and His Majesty the Imam Yahya-bin-Muhammad Hamiduddin, King of the Yemen, acknowledges to His Majesty the Imam Abdul Aziz and his lawful descendants the full and absolute independence of the Saudi Arabian Kingdom and his sovereignty over it. Each of them gives up any right he claimed over the any part or parts of the country of the other party beyond the frontiers fixed and defined in the text of this treaty. His Majesty the Imam King Abdul Aziz abandons by this treaty any right of protection or occupation, or any other right, which he claimed in the country which, according to this treaty, belongs to the Yemen and which was (formerly) in the possession of the Idrisis and others. His Majesty the Imam Yahya similarly abandons by this treaty any right he claimed in the name of Yemeni unity or otherwise, in the country (formerly) in the possession of the Idrisis or the Al-Aidh, or in Najran, or in the Yam country, which according to this treaty belongs to the Saudi Arabian Kingdom.

Article 3: The two high contracting parties agree to conduct their relations and communications in such a manner as will secure the interests of both parties and will cause no harm to either of them, provided that neither of the high contracting parties shall concede to the other party less than he concedes to a third party. Neither of the two parties shall be bound to concede to the other party more than he receives in return.

Article 4: The frontier line which divides the countries of the two high contracting parties is explained in sufficient detail hereunder. This line is considered as a fixed dividing boundary between the territories subject to each.

The frontier line between the two Kingdoms begins at a point half way between Midi and Al Muim on the coast of the Red Sea, and (runs) up to the mountains of the Tihama in an easterly direction. It then turns northwards until it ends on the north-west boundary between the Beni Jama'a and (the tribes) adjacent to them on the north and west. It then bends east until it ends at a point between the limits of the Naqa'a and Wa'ar, which belong to the Waila tribe, and the limits of the Yam. It then bends until it reaches the pass of Marwan and Aqaba Rifada. It then bends eastwards until it ends, on the east, on the edge of the boundary between those of the Hamdan-bin-Zaid, Waila, etc, who are outside Yam, and Yarm. Everything which runs on the right-hand side of the above-mentioned line, which runs from the point mentioned on the sea shore up to the end of the borders on all sides of the mountains mentioned, shall belong to Yemen, and everything to the left of the above-mentioned line shall belong to the Saudi Arabian Kingdom. On the Yemen side are Medi, Haradh, part of the Harth tribe, Mir, the Dhahir Mountains, Shada, Dhay'a, part of the Abadil, all the country and the mountains of Razih, Manbah, with Arwa-al-Amshaykk, all the country and the mountains of Beni Jama'a, Sahar-ash-Sham, Yabad and its neighbourhood, the Maraisagha area of the Sahar-ash-Sham, the whole of Sahar, Naqa'a, Wa'ar, the whole of Waila, and also Far with Aqabat Nahuqa, the whole of Hamdan-bin-Zaid, which is outside Yamand Wad'a Dhahran. These mentioned, and their territories within their known limits, and all between the said directions and their vicinities, the names of which are not mentioned and which were actually subject to or under the control of the Yemeni Kingdom before the year 1352, are on the Yemeni side and belong to the Yemen. On the left-hand side are Muim, Wa'lan , most of the Harth, the Khuba,the Jabri, most of the Abadil, all Faifa, Beni Malik, Beni Haris, the Al Talid, Qahtan, Dhahran, Wadi'a, all the Wadi'a Dhahran, together with the pass of Marwan, and Aqaba Rifada, and the area lying beyond on the east and north of Yam and Najran, Hadhim, Zur Wada, all the Waila in Najran, and all below the Aqaba Nuhuqa, up to the edges of Najran and Yam on the east, all these, and their territories within known limits, and all between the named directions and their vicinities which have not been mentioned by name, and which were actually subject to or under the control of the Saudi Arabian Kingdom before the year 1352, are on the left-hand side of the said line and belong to the Saudi Arabian Kingdom. Everything mentioned regarding Yam, Najran, Hadan, Zur Wad'a, and all the Waila in Najran, is in accordance with the decision (tahkim) of His Majesty the Imam Yahya to His Majesty King Abdul Aziz as regards Yam, and the judgement (hukm) of His Majesty King Abdul Aziz that all of it should belong to the Saudi Arabian Kingdom; and while the Hadan and Zur Wad'a and the Waila in Najran belong to Waila, and, except in so far as has been mentioned, do not come within the Saudi Arabian Kingdom, this shall not prevent them or their brothers of Waila from enjoying mutual relations and intercourse and the usual and customary co-operation. This line then extends from the end of the above-mentioned limits between the edges of the Saudi Arabian tribes and of those of the Hamdam-bin-Zaid, and all the Yemeni tribes who are outside Yam. All the borders and the Yemeni territories up to the end of the Yemeni frontier in all directions belong to the Yemeni Kingdom; and all the borders and territories up to the end of their boundaries, in all directions, belong to the Saudi Arabian Kingdom. All points mentioned in this article, whether north, south, east or west, are to be considered in accordance with the general trend of the frontier line in the directions indicated; often obstacles cause it to bend into the country of one or other Kingdom. As regards the determination and fixing of the said line, the separating out of the tribes and the settlement of their diras in the best manner, these shall be effected by a committee formed of an equal number of persons from the two parties, in a friendly and brotherly way and without prejudice, according to tribal usage and custom.

Article 5: In view of the desire of both high contracting parties for the continuance of peace and tranquillity, and for the non-existence of anything which might disturb the thoughts of these two countries, they may mutually undertake not to construct any fortified building within a distance of 5 kilometres on either side of the frontier, anywhere along the frontier line.

Article 6: The two high contracting parties undertake immediately to withdraw their troops from the country which, by virtue of this treaty, becomes the property of the other party, and to safeguard the inhabitants and troops.

Article 7: The two high contracting parties undertake to prevent their people from committing any harmful or hostile act against the people of the other Kingdom, in any district or any route; to prevent raiding between the Bedouin on both sides; to return all property which is established by legal investigation, after the ratification of this treaty, as having been taken; to give compensation for all damage, according as may be legally necessary, where crimes of murder or wounding have been committed; and severely to punish anyone proved to have committed any hostile act. This article shall continue operative until another agreement shall have been drawn up between the two parties as to the manner of investigating and estimating damage and loss.

Article 8: The two high contracting parties mutually undertake to refrain from resorting to force in all difficulties between them, and to do their utmost to settle any disputes which may arise between them, whether caused by this treaty or the interpretation of all or any of its articles or resulting from any other cause, by friendly representations; in the event of inability to agree by this means, each of the two parties undertakes to resort to arbitration, of which the conditions, the manner of demand, and the conduct are explained in the appendix attached to this treaty. This appendix shall have the force and authority of this treaty, and shall be considered an integral part of it.

Article 9: The two high contracting parties undertake, by all moral and material means at their command, to prevent the use of their territory as a base and centre for any hostile action or enterprise, or preparations therefor, against the country of the other party. They also undertake to take the following measures immediately on receipt of a written demand from the Government of the other party:

a) If the person endeavouring to foment insurrection is a subject of the Government which receives the application to take measures, he should, after the matter has been legally investigated and established, receive a deterrent punishment which will put an end to his actions and prevent their recurrence.

b) If the person endeavouring to foment insurrection is a subject of the Government making the demand over to the Government making the demand. The Government asked to surrender him shall have no right to excuse itself from carrying out this demand, but shall be bound to take adequate steps to prevent the flight of the person asked for, and in the event of the person asked for being able to run away, the Government from whose territory he has fled should undertake not to allow him to return, and if he does so, to arrest him and hand him over to his Government.

c) If the person endeavouring to foment insurrection is a subject of a third Government, the Government to which the demand is made and which finds the person in its territories shall, immediately and directly after the receipt of the demand of the other Government, take steps to expel him from its country, and to consider him as undesirable and to prevent him from returning.

Article 10: The two high contracting parties agree not to receive anyone who has fled the jurisdiction of his Government, regardless of circumstances, and are bound to return any fugitives who cross the border to their own Government.

Article 11: The two high contracting parties undertake to prevent their Amirs, Amils and officials from interfering in any way with subjects of the other party, and to prevent any disturbance or misunderstandings arising from such actions.

Article 12: Each of the two high contracting parties recognises that the people of all areas accruing to the other party by virtue of this treaty are subjects of that party. Each of them undertakes not to accept as his subjects any person who is subject to another party except with the consent of party.

Article 13: Each of the two high contracting parties undertakes to announce a full and complete amnesty for all crimes and hostile acts which may have been committed by any person who is a subject of the other party. Similarly, each of the two high contracting parties undertake to issue a full, general and complete amnesty to those of his subjects who have taken refuge or joined with the other party in any manner.

Article 14: Each of the two high contracting parties undertakes to return the property of those it pardons, in accordance with the laws of the country. They similarly undertake not to retain any goods or chattels belonging to subjects of the other party.

Article 15: Each of the two high contracting parties undertakes not to intermeddle with a third party of any kind in any matter which may injure the interests of the other party in any way.

Article 16: The two high contracting parties, who are bound by Islamic brotherhood and Arab origin, announce that their two nations are one nation, that they do not wish evil to anyone, and that they will do their best to promote the interests of their nation, intending no hostility to anyone.

Article 17: In the event of any external aggression on the country of one of the two high contracting parties, the other party shall be bound to carry out the following undertakings:

a) To adopt complete neutrality secretly and openly.

b) To co-operate mentally and morally as far as possible.

c) To undertake negotiations with the other party to discover the best way of guaranteeing the safety of that party.

Article 18: In the event of insurrection or hostilities taking place within the country of one of the high contracting parties, both of them mutually undertake as follows:

a) To take all necessary effective measures to prevent aggressors or rebels from making use of their territories.

b) To prevent fugitives from taking refuge in their countries, and to expel them if they do enter.

c) To prevent his subjects from joining the rebels and to refrain from encouraging or supplying them.

d) To prevent assistance, supplies, arms and ammunition reaching the enemy or rebels.

Article 19: The two high contracting parties announce their desire to improve and increase communications and trade between the two countries, and to reach a customs agreement.

Article 20: Each of the two high contracting parties declares his readiness to authorise his representatives and delegates abroad, if such there be, to represent the other party, whenever the other party desires this, in any matter or at any time. It is understood that whenever representatives of both parties are together in one place they shall collaborate to unify their policy to promote the interests of their two countries, which are one nation. It is understood that this article does not restrict the freedom of either side in any manner whatsoever in any of its rights. Similarly, it cannot be interpreted as limiting the freedom of either of them or of compelling either to adopt this course.

Article 21: The contents of the agreement signed on 5 Shaban, 1350, shall in any case be cancelled as from the date of ratification of this treaty.

Article 22: This treaty shall be ratified and confirmed by Their Majesties the two Kings in the shortest possible time. It shall come into force as from the date of the exchange of the instruments of ratification, except as regards what has been laid down in Article 1, relative to the ending of the state of war immediately after signature. It shall continue for 20 complete lunar years. It may be renewed or modified during the six months preceding its expiry. If not renewed or modified by that date, it shall remain in force until 6 months after such time as one party has given notice to the other party of his desire to modify it.

Article 23: This treaty shall be called the "Treaty of Taif". It has been drawn up in two copies in the noble Arabic language, each of the two high contracting parties having one copy.

SUMMARY OF ARBITRATION COVENANT

Each of the two high contracting parties agree to refer to arbitration in the case of dispute within one month of receiving such a demand for arbitration from the other party. The arbitration committee shall be composed of equal numbers selected by each party, and decisions will be made on the basis of a majority vote. Decisions of the arbitration committee shall be immediately binding and the costs of arbitration will be shared.

4.1281 Treaty of Understanding and Collaboration among Estonia, Latvia, and Lithuania

Alliance Members: Estonia, Latvia, and Lithuania
Signed On: September 12, 1934, in the city of Geneva. In force until June 15, 1940, when all three states lost their independence following the Soviet invasion.
Alliance Type: Entente (Type III)

Source: *League of Nations Treaty Series*, vol. 154, p. 95–99.
Additional Citations: *The American Journal of International Law*, vol. 30, no. 4, Supplement: Official Documents (October 1936), p. 174–177.

SUMMARY

Despite attempts by Bolshevik forces after World War I to reclaim these former Russian territories in the Baltic area, these three states formed independent governments with Allied and German support. Attempts at forming a Baltic union were rendered impossible, however, because of border disputes between Poland and Lithuania. The three states began to develop three independent foreign policies until the rise of Adolf Hitler in Germany and the warming of German-Polish relations in 1933. The political reality of a Baltic pact soon began to form. The 1923 Estonia-Latvia treaty on cooperation was renewed with an invitation to Lithuania, and the three nations entered into this pact in September 1934.

This pact focused exclusively on political cooperation and diplomacy. At Lithuania's request, the proposal of military cooperation was noticeably absent. The agreement had a special exception clause whereby neutrality was required of Estonia and Latvia regarding the border disputes between Poland and Lithuania, which was considered to be a major obstacle for Baltic integration westward.

The hostile overtures of the great powers in the late 1930s began to shake the foundation of Baltic cooperation. The lack of genuine cooperation and collaboration on military issues left the allies ill prepared for a Soviet invasion. Furthermore, the agreement hindered further expansion of the alliance to either Germany or Poland as it required approval of all "contracting members." The agreement thus turned out to be a victory for the Soviet Union because of the treaty's self-limiting ability to expand, the failure to address the border dispute between Poland and Lithuania jointly, and the failure to change the Lithuanian government's commitment to Lithuanian-Soviet relations that "is of greater importance than any other agreement." The end of 1941 saw the three former Russian territories absorbed into the Soviet Union's empire.

ALLIANCE TEXT

The President of the Republic of Latvia, the President of the Republic of Lithuania, and the President of the Republic of Estonia,

Having decided to develop co-operation between the three countries and to promote a closer understanding between the Baltic States,

Being firmly determined to play their part in maintaining and guaranteeing peace and to co-ordinate their foreign policy in the spirit of the principles of the Covenant of the League of Nations,

Have resolved to conclude a treaty and have appointed for that purpose their Plenipotentiaries for that purpose:

The President of the Republic of Lithuania: His Excellency Monsieur Stasys Lozoraitis, Minister for Foreign Affairs;

The President of the Republic of Estonia: His Excellency Monsieur Julius Seljamaa, Minister for Foreign Affairs;

The President of the Republic of Latvia: Monsieur Vilhelms Munters, Secretary-General of the Ministry of Foreign Affairs;

Who, having communicated their full powers, found in good and due form, have agreed as follows:

Article 1. In order to co-ordinate their efforts in the cause of peace, the three Governments undertake to confer together on questions of foreign policy which are of common importance and to afford one another mutual political and diplomatic assistance in their international relations.

Article 2. For the purpose set forth in Article 1, the High Contracting Parties hereby decide to institute periodic conferences of the Ministers for Foreign Affairs of the three countries, to take place at regular intervals, at least twice a year, in the territory of each of the three States in turn. At the request of one of the High Contracting Parties and by joint agreement, extraordinary conferences may be held in the territory of one of the three States or elsewhere.

Each Conference shall be presided over by the Minister for Foreign Affairs of the State in whose territory it takes place; if, however, a Conference meets outside the territory of the three States, its President shall be the Minister for Foreign Affairs of the country in whose territory the previous conference was held.

The President in office shall be responsible for the execution of the decisions taken by the Conference over which he has presided, and, when necessary, shall be instructed to provide for the application of such decisions in the field of international relations.

The periodical Conferences of the Ministers for Foreign Affairs of Estonia and Latvia provided for in Articles 1and 2 of the Treaty between Latvia and Estonia for the organization of the Alliance, signed at Riga on February 17th, 1934, shall be replaced by the above-mentioned Conferences for the duration of the present treaty.

Article 3. The High Contracting Parties recognize the existence of the specific problems which might make a concerted attitude with regard to them difficult. They agree that such problems constitute an exception to the undertakings laid down in Article 1 of the present Treaty.

Article 4. The High Contracting Parties shall endeavor to settle amicably and in a spirit of justice and equity any questions in respect of which their interests may clash and also to do so in the shortest possible time. They agree to negotiate with each other such agreements as may appear suitable for attaining this end.

Article 5. The three Governments shall give instructions to their diplomatic and consular representatives abroad and to their delegates to international conferences to establish appropriate contacts.

Article 6. The High Contracting Parties undertake to communicate to one another forthwith the text of the treaties concluded between one of them and one or more other States.

Article 7. The present Treaty is open for accession by other States, such accession to take place only if all the High Contracting Parties consent thereto.

Article 8. The present Treaty shall be ratified; it shall come into force upon the deposit of ratifications which shall take place at Riga. The Government of Latvia shall transmit to each of the two other High Contracting Parties a certified true copy of the procès-verbal of deposit of ratifications.

Article 9. The present Treaty shall be in force for ten years. Should the treaty not be denounced by one of the High Contracting Parties one year before the expiry of that period, it shall be extended by tacit consent and shall cease to have effect one year after its denunciation by one of the High Contracting Parties.

In faith whereof the above-mentioned Plenipotentiaries have signed the present Treaty and have affixed their seals thereto.

Done at Geneva, in triplicate, this 12th day of September, 1934.

St. LOZORAITIS.
J. SELJAMAA.
V. MUNTERS.

DECLARATION

Upon signing the Treaty of this day's date, the Plenipotentiaries of Lithuania, Estonia, and Latvia hereby declare that their respective Governments will foster the growth and general diffusion in their respective countries of the spirit of mutual understanding and friendship among the three nations and they bind themselves to take or to promote all suitable measures and efforts to that end.

Done at Geneva, in triplicate, this 12th day of September, 1934.

St. LOZORAITIS.
J. SELJAMAA.
V. MUNTERS.

4.1282 Franco-Italian Declaration

Alliance Members: France and Italy
Signed On: January 7, 1935, in the city of Rome. In force until October 11, 1935, when France joined in the sanctions against Italy in response to Italy's invasion of Ethiopia.
Alliance Type: Entente (Type III)

Source: *Documents Diplomatiques Francais 1932–1939*, Series II, vol. 1, p. 603.

SUMMARY

The French and Italian governments sought a common method of limiting Germany's possible expansionism and arrived at these Rome Accords, signed in January 1935. Bettering ties, symbolized in part by the pact itself, were seen by many world leaders as giving Italy freer rein to indulge in African territorial gains. However, Italy's invasion of Ethiopia in October 1935 led to the disintegration of the short-lived pact.

DESCRIPTION OF TERMS

The minister of foreign affairs of France and the chief of the Italian government, considering that the conventions had solved their problems and all the issues concerning the application of the article 13 of the accord of London of April 26, 1915; considering that issues in the future will be solved diplomatically, declare that the two countries want to develop their traditional friendship and maintain general peace.

In order to maintain the independence and integrity of Austria, Italy and France agree that when Austrian independence and integrity are threatened, they will consult with respect to the measures to be taken.

Should Germany want to unilaterally free itself from previous treaties in order to be able to rearm, the two governments, animated by the desire to produce a common accord, agree to consult on the proper attitude to adopt.

4.1283 Defense Pact between France and the Union of Soviet Socialist States

Alliance Members: France and the Union of Soviet Socialist Republics
Signed On: May 2, 1935, in the city of Paris. In force until September 3, 1939, when France entered the war against Germany, then an ally of the Soviet Union.
Alliance Type: Defense Pact (Type I)

Source: *The American Journal of International Law*, vol. 30, no. 4, Supplement: Official Documents (October 1936), p. 177–180.

SUMMARY

During the years following World War I, the Russians viewed Germany as a natural ally as both nations were excluded from the League of Nations. This changed, however, with the rise in Germany of Adolf Hitler, whom Stalin eventually viewed as a threat to peace in Europe and to his industrialization plan at home. By 1935, Stalin wanted an alternative to the Treaty of Rapallo, which linked Germany and the Soviet Union via military cooperation.

Despite this alliance, mutual mistrust grew between France and the Soviets. Both leaderships had a common enemy in Germany, but the Soviets began to doubt France's willingness to thwart Hitler's growing power, especially as Germany began to arm in violation of the Treaty of Versailles. The pact collapsed when the Soviet Union exercised its options in the secret clauses of the Russo-German Non-Aggression Pact of 1939 and occupied one-third of Poland as France quickly entered the war against Germany.

ALLIANCE TEXT

The Central Executive Committee of the Union of Soviet Socialist Republics and The President of the French Republic,

Being desirous of strengthening peace in Europe and of guaranteeing its benefits to their respective countries by securing a fuller and stricter application of the provisions of the Covenant of the League of Nations which are designed to maintain the national security, territorial integrity and political independence of States;

Determined to devote their efforts to the preparation and conclusion of a European agreement for that purpose, and in the meantime to promote, as far as lies in their power, the effective application of the provisions of the Covenant of the League of Nations;

Have resolved to conclude a Treaty to this end and have appointed as their Plenipotentiaries:

The Central Executive Committee of the Union of Soviet Socialist Republics: Monsieur Vladimir Potemkine, Member of the Central Executive Committee, Ambassador Extraordinary and Plenipotentiary of the Union of Soviet Socialist Republics accredited to the President of the French Republic;

The President of the French Republic: Monsieur Pierre Laval, Senator, Minister for Foreign Affairs;

Who, having exchanged their full powers, found in good and due form, have agreed upon the following provisions:

Article 1. In the event of France or the Union of Soviet Socialist Republics being threatened with or in danger of aggression on the part of a European State, the Union of Soviet Socialist Republics and reciprocally France undertake to proceed to an immediate consultation as regards the measures to be taken for the observance of the provisions of Article 10 of the Covenant of the League of Nations.

Article 2. Should, in the circumstances specified in Article 15, paragraph 7, of the Covenant of the League of Nations, France or the Union of Soviet Socialist Republics be the object, notwithstanding the sincerely peaceful intentions of both countries, of an unprovoked aggression on the part of a European State, the Union of Soviet Socialist Republics and reciprocally France shall immediately come to each other's aid and assistance.

Article 3. In consideration of the fact that under article 16 of the Covenant of the League of Nations any member of the League which resorts to war in disregard of its covenants under Articles 12, 13 or 15 of the Covenant is *ipso facto* deemed to have committed an act of war against all the other Members of the League, France and reciprocally the Union of Soviet Socialist Republics undertake, in the event of one of them being the object, in these conditions and notwithstanding the sincerely peaceful intentions of both countries, of an unprovoked aggression on the part of a European State, immediately to come to each other's aid and assistance in application of article 16 of the Covenant.

The same obligation is assumed in the event of France or the Union of Soviet Socialist Republics being the object of an aggression on the part of a European State in the circumstances specified in Article 17, paragraphs 1 and 3, of the Covenant of the League of Nations.

Article 4. The undertakings stipulated above being in consonant with the obligations of the High Contracting Parties as Members of the League of Nations, nothing in the present Treaty shall be interpreted as restricting the duty of the latter to take any action that may be deemed wise and effectual to safeguard the peace of the world or as restricting the obligations resulting for the High Contracting Parties by the Covenant of the League of Nations.

Article 5. The present Treaty, both the French and Russian texts whereof shall be equally authentic, shall be ratified and the instruments of ratification shall be exchanged at Moscow as soon as possible. It shall be registered with the Secretariat of the League of Nations.

It shall take effect as soon as the ratifications have been exchanged, and shall remain in force for five years. If it is not denounced by either of the High Contracting Parties giving notice thereof at least one year before the expiry of that period, it shall remain in force indefinitely, each of the High Contracting Parties being at liberty to terminate it at a year's notice by a declaration to that effect.

In faith whereof the Plenipotentiaries have signed the present Treaty and have thereto affixed their seals.

Done at Paris, in duplicate, this 2nd day of May, 1935.

(L.S.) (Signed) V. POTEMKINE.

(L.S.) (Signed) Pierre LAVAL.

Protocol of Signature.

Upon proceeding to the signature of the Franco-Soviet Treaty of Mutual Assistance of to-day's date, the Plenipotentiaries have signed the following protocol, which shall be included in the exchange of ratifications of the Treaty:

I. It is agreed that the effect of Article 3 is to oblige each Contracting Party immediately to come to the assistance of the other by immediately complying with the recommendations of the Council of the League of Nations as soon as they have been issued in virtue of Article 16 of the Covenant. It is further agreed that the two contracting parties will act in concert to ensure that the Council shall issue the said recommendations with all the speed required by the circumstances of the case, and that, should the Council nevertheless, for whatever reason, issue no recommendation or fail to reach a unanimous decision, effect shall non the less be given to the obligation to render assistance. It is also agreed that the undertakings to render assistance mentioned in the present Treaty refer only to the case of an aggression committed against either of the Contracting Party's own territory.

II. It being the common intention of the two Governments in no way to contradict, by the present Treaty, undertakings previously assumed towards third States by France and by the Union of Soviet Socialist Republics in virtue of published treaties, it is agreed that effect shall not be given to the provisions of the said Treaty in a manner which, being incompatible with treaty obligations assumed by one of the Contracting Parties, would expose the latter to sanctions of an international character.

III. The two Governments, deeming it desirable that a regional agreement should be concluded aiming at organising security between Contracting States, and which might moreover embody or be accompanied by pledges of mutual assistance, recognise their right to become parties by mutual consent, should occasion arise, to similar agreements in any form, direct or indirect, that may seem appropriate, the obligations under these various agreements to take the place of those assumed under the present Treaty.

IV. The two Governments place on record the fact that the negotiations which have resulted in the signature of the present Treaty were originally undertaken with a view to supplementing a Security Agreement embracing the countries of North-Eastern Europe, namely, the Union of Soviet Socialist Republics, Germany, Czechoslovakia, Poland and the Baltic States which are neighbors of the Union of Soviet Socialist Republics; in addition to that Agreement, there was to have been concluded a Treaty of Assistance between the Union of the Soviet Socialist Republics, France and Germany, by which each of these three States was to have undertaken to come to the assistance of any one of them which might be the object of aggression on the part of any other of those three States. Although circumstances have not hitherto permitted of the conclusion of those Agreements, which the two parties continue to regard as desirable, it is none the less the case that the undertakings stipulated in the Franco-Soviet Treaty of Assistance are to be understood as intended to apply only within the limits contemplated in the three-party Agreement previously planned. Independently of the obligations assumed under the present Treaty, it is further recalled that, in accordance with the Franco-Soviet Pact of Non-Aggression signed on November 29th, 1932, and moreover, without affecting the universal character of the undertakings assumed in that Pact, in the event of either Party becoming the object of aggression by one or more third European Powers not referred to in the above-mentioned three-party Agreement, the other Contracting Party is bound to abstain, during the period of the conflict, from giving any aid or assistance, either direct or indirect, to the aggressor or aggressors, each Party declaring further that it is not bound by any Assistance Agreement which would be contrary to this undertaking.

Done at Paris, this 2nd day of May, 1935.

(Signed) V. POTEMKINE.
(Signed) PIERRE LAVAL.

4.1284 Treaty of Mutual Assistance between the Czechoslovak Republic and the Union of Soviet Socialist Republics

Alliance Members: Czechoslovakia and the Union of Soviet Socialist Republics
Signed On: May 16, 1935, in the city of Prague (Czech Republic). In force until December 10, 1989, when Czechoslovakia's communist government collapsed.
Alliance Type: Defense Pact (Type I)

Source: *The American Journal of International Law,* vol. 30, no. 4, Supplement: Official Documents (October 1936) p. 177–180.

SUMMARY

Similar to the Soviet agreement with France, this alliance was a means by which the Soviets could check the growing power of an expansionist Germany. Alliances such as this one, together with the French accord, provided alternatives to the military cooperation the Soviets had previously had with Germany under the Treaty of Rapallo.

The Munich Agreement gave major portions of Czech territory to Germany and led to the effective domination of Czechoslovakia by Germany. Despite the inaction of the Soviets during this crisis, this alliance was extended following World War II. The pact lasted until 1989, when the Soviet satellite states began to topple and the network of alliances that held them together dissolved. The alliance officially ended with the collapse of the communist government in Czechoslovakia in December of 1989.

ALLIANCE TEXT

The President of the Czechoslovak Republic and the Central Executive Committee of the Union of Soviet Socialist Republics,

Being desirous of strengthening peace in Europe and of guaranteeing its benefits to their respective countries by securing a fuller and stricter application of those provisions of the Covenant of the League of Nations which are designed to maintain the national security, territorial integrity and political independence of States,

Determined to devote their efforts to the preparation and conclusion of a European agreement for that purpose, and in the meantime to promote, as far as lies in their power, the effective application of the provisions of the Covenant of the League of Nations,

Have resolved to conclude a Treaty to this end and have appointed as their Plenipotentiaries:

The President of the Czechoslovak Republic; Monsieur Edouard Beneš, Minister for Foreign Affairs;

The Central Executive Committee of the Union of Soviet

Socialist Republics: Monsieur Serge Alexandrovsky, Envoy Extraordinary and Minister Plenipotentiary of the Union of Soviet Socialist Republics;

Who, having exchanged their full powers, found in good and due form, have agreed upon the following provisions:

Article I. In the event of the Czechoslovak Republic or the Union of Soviet Socialist Republics being threatened with or in danger of aggression on the part of any European State, the Union of Soviet Socialist Republics and reciprocally the Czechoslovak Republic undertake mutually to proceed to an immediate consultation as regards the measures to be taken for the observance of the provisions of Article 10 of the Covenant of the League of Nations.

Article 2. Should, in the circumstances specified in Article 15, paragraph 7, of the Covenant of the League of Nations, the Czechoslovak Republic or the Union of Soviet Socialist Republics be the object, notwithstanding the sincerely peaceful intentions of both countries, of an unprovoked aggression on the part of a European State, the Union of Soviet Socialist Republics and reciprocally the Czechoslovak Republic shall immediately come to each other's aid and assistance.

Article 3. In consideration of the fact that under Article 16 of the Covenant of the League of Nations any Member of the League which resorts to war in disregard of its covenants under Articles 12, 13 or 15 of the Covenant is *ipso facto* deemed to have committed an act of war against all Members of the League, the Czechoslovak Republic and reciprocally the Union of Soviet Socialist Republics undertake, in the event of one of them being the object, in these conditions and notwithstanding the sincerely peaceful intentions of both countries, of an unprovoked aggression on the part of a European State, immediately to come to each other's aid and assistance in application of Article 16 of the Covenant.

The same obligation is assumed in the event of the Czechoslovak Republic or the Union of Soviet Socialist Republics being the object of an aggression on the part of a European State in the circumstances specified in Article 17, paragraphs I and 3, of the Covenant of the League of Nations.

Article 4. Without prejudice to the preceding provisions of the present Treaty, it is stipulated that should either of the High Contracting Parties become the object of an aggression on the part of one or more third Powers in conditions not giving ground for aid or assistance within the meaning of the present Treaty, the other High Contracting Party undertakes not to lend, for the duration of the conflict, aid or assistance, either directly or indirectly, to the aggressor or aggressors. Each High Contracting Party further declares that it is not bound by any other agreement for assistance which is incompatible with the present undertaking.

Article 5. The undertakings stipulated above being consonant with the obligations of the High Contracting Parties as Members of the League of Nations, nothing in the present Treaty shall be interpreted as restricting the duty of the latter to take any action that may be deemed wise and effectual to safeguard the peace of the world or as restricting the obligations resulting for the High Contracting Parties from the Covenant of the League of Nations.

Article 6. The present Treaty, both the Czechoslovak and the Russian texts whereof shall be equally authentic, shall be ratified and the instruments of ratification shall be exchanged at Moscow as soon as possible. It shall be registered with the Secretariat of the League of Nations.

It shall take effect as soon as the ratifications have been exchanged and shall remain in force for five years. If it is not denounced by either of the High Contracting Parties giving notice thereof at least one year before the expiry of that period, it shall remain in force indefinitely, each of the High Contracting Parties being at liberty to terminate it at a year's notice by a declaration to that effect.

In faith whereof the Plenipotentiaries have signed the present Treaty and have thereto affixed their seals.

Done at Prague, in duplicate, this 16th day of May, one thousand nine hundred and thirty-five.

(L. S.) (Signed) Dr. Edouard BENEŠ.
(L. S.) (Signed) S. ALEXANDROVSKY.

PROTOCOL OF SIGNATURE.

Upon proceeding to the signature of the Treaty of Mutual Assistance between the Czechoslovak Republic and the Union of Soviet Socialist Republics of to-day's date, the Plenipotentiaries have signed the following Protocol, which shall be included in the exchange of ratifications of the Treaty.

I. It is agreed that the effect of Article 3 is to oblige each Contracting Party immediately to come to the assistance of the other by immediately complying with the recommendations of the Council of the League of Nations as soon as they have been issued in virtue of Article 16 of the Covenant. It is further agreed that the two Contracting Parties will act in concert to ensure that the Council shall issue the said recommendations with all the speed required by the circumstances and that, should the Council nevertheless, for whatever reason, issue no recommendation or fail to reach a unanimous decision, effect shall none the less be given to the obligation to render assistance. It is also agreed that the undertakings to render assistance mentioned in the present Treaty refer only to the case of an aggression committed against either Contracting Party's own territory.

II. The two Governments declare that the undertakings laid down in Articles I, 2 and 3 of the present Treaty, concluded with a view to promoting the establishment in Eastern Europe of a regional system of security, inaugurated by the Franco-Soviet Treaty of May 2nd, 1935, will be restricted within the same limits as were laid down in paragraph 4 of the Protocol of Signature of the said Treaty. At the same time, the two Governments recognise that the undertakings to render mutual assistance will operate between them only in so far as the conditions laid down in the present Treaty may be fulfilled and in so far as assistance may be rendered by France to the Party victim of the aggression.

III. The two Governments, deeming it desirable that a regional agreement should be concluded aiming at organising security between Contracting States, and which might moreover embody or be accompanied by pledges of mutual assistance, recognise their right to become parties by mutual consent, should occasion arise, to similar agreements in any form, direct or indirect, that may seem appropriate, the obligations under these various agreements to take the place of those resulting from the present Treaty.

Done at Prague, this 16th day of May, 1935.

(Signed) Dr. Edouard BENEŠ.
(Signed) S. ALEXANDROVSKY.

4.1285 Soviet Pact of Mutual Assistance with the Mongolian People's Republic

Alliance Members: Union of Soviet Socialist Republics and Mongolia
Signed On: March 12, 1936, in the city of Ulan Bator (Mongolia). In force until December 25, 1991.
Alliance Type: Defense Pact (Type I)

Source: *British and Foreign State Papers,* vol. 140, p. 666.
Additional Citations: *United Nations Treaty,* no. 744.

SUMMARY

Soviet interest in Mongolia rose dramatically after the Soviet defeat by the Japanese at the beginning of the twentieth century. The large territory of Mongolia served well as a buffer against both Japanese and Chinese expansion toward Soviet territory. In 1934, as the Japanese began to advance through Manchuria toward Mongolia, an assistance agreement was reached between Mongolia and the Soviets. The Soviets then sent Red Army troops into the country in early 1935, and by March of 1936 this defense pact was signed.

With the help of the Soviets, Mongolia immediately started a rapid militarization program. The government also modernized the infrastructure by building roads, railways, and communication lines, all with the help of Soviet aid. By the start of World War II, almost 10 percent of the population was serving in the military. A five-month war with the Japanese in 1939 proved decisive for the combined Mongolian-Soviet forces, and a truce was signed in September of that year. While the border between Manchuria and Mongolia remained militarized, the Japanese turned their military toward China and never invaded Mongolia again.

The alliance ultimately lasted for fifty-five years and ended upon the dissolution of the Soviet Union.

ALLIANCE TEXT

The Governments of the USSR and the Mongolian People's Republic, proceeding from the unchanging friendship that has existed between their countries since the liberation in 1921 of the territory of the Mongolian People's Republic, thanks to the support of the Red Army, from the White Guard detachments and the military forces with which the latter were connected and which had penetrated into Soviet territory,

And guided by the desire to maintain the peace of the Far East and to promote the further consolidation of the existing friendly relations between their countries,

have decided to formulate in the present protocol the gentlemen's agreement existing between them since 27 November 1934. This provides for mutual assistance in all possible ways to avert and forestall the danger of military attacks and to help and maintain each other in case of an attack by any third country on the USSR or the Mongolian People's Republic.

For these purposes, the present protocol has been signed.

Article I. In case of the threat of an attack on the territory of the USSR or the Mongolian People's Republic by a third country, the Governments of the USSR and the Mongolian People's Republic undertake to consult each other immediately regarding the situation and to adopt all measures that may be necessary for the protection and safety of their territories.

Article II. The Governments of the USSR and the Mongolian People's Republic are obliged, in case of a military attack against either party, to help one another with all means, including military assistance.

Article III. The Governments of the USSR and the Mongolian People's Republic are in full understanding that troops of either country that shall be sent by mutual agreement into the territory of the other, in accordance with Articles I and II of this protocol, shall immediately be withdrawn from that territory as soon as the period of emergency is over, as occurred in 1925, when Soviet troops were withdrawn from the territory of the Mongolian People's Republic.

Article IV. The present protocol is drawn up in two copies, in the Russian and Mongolian languages. The two texts are equally valid. The protocol enters into force from the moment of signature and shall be valid for ten years thereafter.

Signed at Ulan Bator, 12 March 1936.

TAIROV, Plenipotentiary Envoy of the USSR in the Mongolian People's Republic

AMOR, President of the Little Hural

GENDUN, Chairman of the Council of Ministers and Foreign Minister of the Mongolian People's Republic

---

4.1286 Treaty of Arab Brotherhood and Alliance between the Kingdom of Saudi Arabia and Iraq

Alliance Members: Saudi Arabia, Iraq, and Yemen Arab Republic (joined April 29, 1937)
Signed On: April 2, 1936, in the city of Baghdad (Iraq). In force until April 2, 1956.
Alliance Type: Entente (Type III)

Source: *British and Foreign State Papers*, vol. 140, p. 620.

SUMMARY

Saudi control of Arabian territory neared its present size by the early 1930s. Surrounded by water and British-controlled territories, the Saudis sought assurances from their neighbors that their sovereignty would be respected. This entente ostensibly resolved the lingering border disputes with Iraq. Yemen joined the alliance the following year, three years after the Saudis defeated Yemeni forces in a short war to put down a cross-border insurgency supported by the Yemeni imam. The entente lasted until 1956, when the treaty was left to expire.

ALLIANCE TEXT

In the name of God the Merciful the Compassionate.

His Majesty the King of 'Iraq and His Majesty the King of Saudi Arabia,

In view of the ties of the Islamic faith and of racial unity which unite them; desirous of safeguarding the integrity of their territories; and having regard to the necessity which they feel for mutual co-operation and understanding in regard to matters affecting the interests of their Kingdoms;

Have agreed to conclude a Treaty of Arab Brotherhood and Alliance, and

For this purpose have appointed as their Plenipotentiaries:

His Majesty the King of 'Iraq: His Excellency Nouri Pasha El Said, Minister for Foreign Affairs of the Kingdom of 'Iraq, Order of the Rafidain First Class Military;

His Majesty the King of Saudi Arabia: His Excellency Shaikh Yusuf Yassin, Private Secretary to His Majesty and Director of the Political Section of the Royal Diwan;

Who, having reciprocally communicated their full powers found in due form, have entered into an Alliance and have concluded the following Treaty:

Article 1.   (a) Each of the High Contracting Parties reciprocally undertakes not to enter with any third party into any understanding or agreement over any matter whatever of a nature prejudicial to the interests of the other High Contracting Party or to his country or its interests, or of a nature calculated to expose to danger or harm the safety or interests of his country.

(b) The two High Contracting Parties shall consult together when necessary with a view to furthering the objects set forth in the Preamble to this Treaty.

Article 2. The High Contracting Parties undertake to settle any disputes arising between them by means of friendly negotiations and, in the event of the settlement of any such dispute by the said method proving difficult, to resort to the methods to be laid down in a Protocol to be annexed to this Treaty and to be agreed to as soon as possible after the exchange of ratifications of this Treaty.

Article 3. Should any dispute between either High Contracting Party and a third State produce a situation involving a threat of war, in that case the High Contracting Parties shall jointly endeavour to settle such dispute by peaceful means in accordance with such international undertakings as may be applicable to the case.

Article 4. (a) In the event of an act of aggression being committed against either High Contracting Party by a third State notwithstanding efforts exerted in accordance with the provisions of Article 3 above, and similarly in the event of the occurrence of a sudden act of aggression which does not leave time for the application of the provisions of Article 3 referred to above, the High Contracting Parties shall consult together regarding the measures which shall be taken with the object of concerting their efforts in a useful manner to repel the said aggression.

(b) The following shall be deemed acts of aggression:

(1) The declaration of war.

(2) The seizure by an armed force of a third State of territory belonging to either High Contracting Party, even without a declaration of war.

(3) An attack on the territory, vessels or aircraft of either High Contracting Party by the land, naval or air forces of a third State, even without a declaration of war.

(4) Direct or indirect support or assistance to the aggressor.

(c) The following shall not be deemed acts of aggression:

(1) The exercise of the right of legitimate defence, *i.e.* resisting any act of aggression as defined above.

(2) Action taken in enforcement of Article 16 of the Covenant of the League of Nations.

(3) Action taken in pursuance of a decision emanating from the League of Nations or the Council of the League of Nations or in enforcement of Clause 7 of Article 15 of the Covenant of the League of Nations, provided that in the last case action is directed against the State which was the first to attack.

(4) Assistance by a third State to another State attacked or whose territory is invaded by one of the High Contracting Parties contrary to the provisions of the Treaty for the Renunciation of War, signed at Paris on the 27th August, 1928, to which both High Contracting Parties have adhered.

Article 5. In the event of the outbreak of disturbances or disorders in the territory of one of the High Contracting Parties each of them undertakes reciprocally as follows:

(1) To take all possible measures:

(a) To make it impossible for the insurgents to utilise his territory against the interests of the other High Contracting Party, and

(b) To prevent his subjects from taking part in the disturbances or disorders or from helping or encouraging the insurgents, and

(c) To prevent any kind of help being given to the insurgents either directly from his own territory or otherwise.

(2) In the event of insurgents from the territory of one of the High Contracting Parties taking refuge in the territory of the other High Contracting Party, the latter shall immediately disarm them and remove them to an area from which it shall be impossible for them to do any harm to the country of the other High Contracting Party until such time as the two High Contracting Parties shall have reached a decision regarding their future.

(3) If circumstances should necessitate the adoption of joint measures to suppress disturbances or disorders the two High Contracting Parties shall consult with each other concerning the policy of co-operation which shall be followed for this purpose.

Article 6. Having regard to the Islamic brotherhood and Arab unity which unite the Kingdom of the Yaman to the High Contracting Parties they shall both endeavour to secure the accession of the Government of the Yaman to this Treaty. Any other independent Arab State shall on request be permitted to accede to this Treaty.

Article 7. The two High Contracting Parties will co-operate with a view to unifying the Islamic and Arab culture and the military systems of their two countries by means of the exchange of educational and military missions to study the systems followed in their respective countries and as far as possible to co-ordinate these systems and to seek to obtain reciprocal benefit from their respective educational and military institutions and the training and instruction which is available in them. The number of persons to compose each mission shall be determined by discussion between the High Contracting Parties from time to time.

Article 8. The Diplomatic and Consular Representatives of either High Contracting Party may if requested undertake the representation of the interests of the other High Contracting Party in foreign countries where such other Party has no representatives; provided that this shall not in any way affect the freedom of such other Party to appoint separate representatives of his own should he so desire.

Article 9. It is agreed by the High Contracting Parties that there is nothing in the present Treaty to prejudice the rights and undertakings of the Government of 'Iraq under the Covenant of the League of Nations and the Treaty of Alliance concluded between 'Iraq and Great Britain on 30th June, 1930. The High Contracting Parties further agree to carry out the provisions of Article 17 of the Covenant of the League of Nations, and to observe the principles of the Treaty for the Renunciation of War, signed at Paris on the 27th August, 1928, to which both High Contracting Parties have adhered.

Article 10. If one of the High Contracting Parties commits an act of aggression against another State, the other High Contracting Party may denounce this Treaty without previous warning. This denunciation shall not affect the friendship which links their two countries and shall not affect the Treaties and Conventions mentioned in Article II of this Treaty.

Article 11. All provisions of the following treaties concluded between the two Kingdoms which do not conflict with the provisions of the present Treaty shall remain in force until they are amended or cancelled by other treaties:

I. Treaty of Mohammerah dated 7 Ramadhan 1340 of the Hijra corresponding to 5 May 1922 of the Christian era.

2. Uqair Protocol No. 1 dated 12 Rabi-al-Thani 1341 of

the Hijra corresponding to 2 December 1922 of the Christian era.

3. Uqair Protocol No. 2 dated 12 Rabi-al-Thani 1341 of the Hijra corresponding to 2 December 1922 of the Christian era.

4. Bahra Agreement dated 14 Rabi-al-Thani 1344 of the Hijra corresponding to 1 November 1925 of the Christian era.

5. Treaty of Friendship and Bon Voisinage and the Protocol of Arbitration dated 20 The-Al-Qada 1349 of the Hijra corresponding to 7 April 1931 of the Christian era.

6. Extradition Treaty dated 21 The-Al-Qada 1349 of the Hijra corresponding to 8 April 1931 of the Christian era.

Article 12. The High Contracting Parties undertake within one year from the date of coming into force of the present Treaty to start negotiations for the conclusion of agreements on the following subjects:

1. Residence, Passports and Laissez-Passer.
2. Economic, Financial and Customs Affairs.
3. Organisation of means of communication.

Article 13. This Treaty shall come into force from the date of the exchange of ratifications.

Article 14. The present Treaty shall remain in force for a period of ten years from the date of its coming into force and it shall be deemed to have been renewed for a further period of ten years, unless notice of desire to terminate it shall have been given by either High Contracting Party to the other one year prior to the date of expiry of its period.

Done at Bagdad on the tenth day of Muharram-Al-Haram in the year one thousand three hundred and fifty-five of the Hijra corresponding to the second day of April in the year one thousand nine hundred and thirty-six of the Christian era.

(Signed) Nouri EL SAID.
(Signed) Yusuf YASSIN.

4.1287 Treaty of Alliance between His Majesty, in Respect of the United Kingdom, and His Majesty the King of Egypt

Alliance Members: United Kingdom and Egypt
Signed On: August 26, 1936, in the city of London. In force until October 24, 1951.
Alliance Type: Defense Pact (Type I)

Source: *The American Journal of International Law,* vol. 31, no. 2, Supplement: Official Documents (April 1937), p. 77–90.

SUMMARY

Negotiations over the end of British occupation of Egypt began as early as 1929, but several issues kept the two parties from reaching a final deal. For Egypt, the Sudan held special importance given that state's ability to control the Nile River, the lifeline for Cairo and Egypt more generally. Of course, the Sudan also held strategic importance for Britain given the territory's proximity to the Red Sea, the Suez Canal, and British territories in East Africa. Only the Italian invasion of Ethiopia changed the bargaining positions of both sides. Egypt was now threatened by the rise of Italian influence and the large influx of British troops along the Suez. British leaders wanted, and were given, unrestricted access to Egyptian airspace, harboring rights at Alexandria, and basing rights for British troops along the Suez. The disposition of the Sudan was essentially ignored.

The alliance was signed on August 26, 1936, and Egypt became a recognized member of the United Nations on May 26, 1937. The defense pact lasted until 1951, when Egypt abrogated the treaty.

ALLIANCE TEXT

His Majesty The King of Great Britain, Ireland and the British Dominions beyond the Seas, Emperor of India, and His Majesty the King of Egypt;

Being anxious to consolidate the friendship and the relations of good understanding between them and to co-operate in the execution of their inter-national obligations in preserving the peace of the world;

And considering that these objects will best be achieved by the conclusion of a treaty of friendship and alliance, which in their common interest will provide for effective co-operation in preserving peace and ensuring the defence of their respective territories, and shall govern their mutual relations in the future;

Have agreed to conclude a treaty for this purpose, and have appointed as their plenipotentiaries:

His Majesty The King of Great Britain, Ireland and the British Dominions beyond the Seas, Emperor of India (hereinafter referred to as His Majesty The King and Emperor): For Great Britain and Northern Ireland: The Rt. Hon. Anthony Eden, M.C., M.P., His Principal Secretary of State for Foreign Affairs. The Rt. Hon. James Ramsay MacDonald, M.P., Lord President of the Council. The Rt. Hon. Sir John Simon, G.C.S.I., K.C.V.O., O.B.E., K.C., M.P., His Principal Secretary of State for the Home Department. The Rt. Hon. Viscount Halifax, K.G., G.C.S.I., G.C.I.E., Lord Privy Seal. Sir Miles Wedderburn Lampson, K.C.M.G., C.B., M.V.O., His High Commissioner for Egypt and the Sudan.

His Majesty The King of Egypt: Moustapha El Nahas Pacha, President of the Council of Ministers. Dr. Ahmed Maher, President of the Chamber of Deputies. Mohamed Mahmoud Pacha, former President of the Council of Ministers. Ismail Sedky Pacha, former President of the Council of Ministers. Abdel Fattah Yéhia Pacha, former President of the Council of Ministers. Wacyf Boutros Ghali Pacha, Minister of Foreign Affairs. Osman Moharram Pacha, Minister of Public Works. Makram Ebeid Pacha, Minister of Finance. Mahmoud Fahmy El-Nokrachi Pacha, Minister of Communications. Ahmed Hamdi Seif El Nasr Pacha, Minister of Agriculture. Aly El Chamsi Pacha, former Minister. Mohamed Helmi Issa Pacha, former Minister. Hafez Afifi Pacha, former Minister.

Who, having communicated their full powers, found in good and due form, have agreed as follows:

Article 1. The military occupation of Egypt by the forces of His Majesty The King and Emperor is terminated.

Article 2. His Majesty The King and Emperor will henceforth be represented at the Court of His Majesty the King of Egypt and His Majesty the King of Egypt will be represented at the Court of St. James's by Ambassadors duly accredited.

Article 3. Egypt intends to apply for membership to the League of Nations. His Majesty's Government in the United Kingdom, recognizing Egypt as a sovereign independent State, will support any request for admission which the Egyptian Government may present in the conditions prescribed by Article 1 of the Covenant.

Article 4. An alliance is established between the high contracting parties with a view to consolidating their friendship, their cordial understanding and their good relations.

Article 5. Each of the high contracting parties undertakes not to adopt in relation to foreign countries an attitude which is inconsistent with the alliance, nor to conclude political treaties inconsistent with the provisions of the present treaty.

Article 6. Should any dispute with a third State produce a situation which involves a risk of a rupture with that State, the high contracting parties will consult each other with a view to the settlement of the said dispute by peaceful means, in accordance with the provisions of the Covenant of the League of Nations and of any other international obligations which may be applicable to the case.

Article 7. Should, notwithstanding the provisions of Article 6 above, either of the high contracting parties become engaged in war, the other high contracting party will, subject always to the provisions of Article 10 below, immediately come to his aid in the capacity of an ally.

The aid of His Majesty the King of Egypt in the event of war, imminent menace of war or apprehended international emergency will consist in furnishing to His Majesty The King and Emperor on Egyptian territory, in accordance with the Egyptian system of administration and legislation, all the facilities and assistance in his power, including the use of his ports, aerodromes and means of communication. It will accordingly be for the Egyptian Government to take all the administrative and legislative measures, including the establishment of martial law and an effective censorship, necessary to render these facilities and assistance effective.

Article 8. In view of the fact that the Suez Canal, whilst being an integral part of Egypt, is a universal means of communication as also an essential means of communication between the different parts of the British Empire, His Majesty the King of Egypt, until such time as the high contracting parties agree that the Egyptian Army is in a position to ensure by its own resources the liberty and entire security of navigation of the Canal, authorizes His Majesty The King and Emperor to station forces in Egyptian territory in the vicinity of the Canal, in the zone specified in the annex to this article, with a view to ensuring in co-operation with the Egyptian forces the defence of the Canal. The detailed arrangements for the carrying into effect of this article are contained in the annex hereto. The presence of these forces shall not constitute in any manner an occupation and will in no way prejudice the sovereign rights of Egypt.

It is understood that at the end of the period of twenty years specified in Article 16 the question whether the presence of British forces is no longer necessary owing to the fact that the Egyptian Army is in a position to ensure by its own resources the liberty and entire security of navigation of the Canal may, if the high contracting parties do not agree thereon, be submitted to the Council of the League of Nations for decision in accordance with the provisions of the Covenant in force at the time of signature of the present treaty or to such other person or body of persons for decision in accordance with such other procedure as the high contracting parties may agree.

Annex to Article 8

1. Without prejudice to the provisions of Article 7, the numbers of the forces of His Majesty The King and Emperor to be maintained in the vicinity of the Canal shall not exceed, of the land forces, 10,000, and of the air forces, 400 pilots, together with the necessary ancillary personnel for administrative and technical duties. These numbers do not include civilian personnel, *e.g.*, clerks, artisans and laborers.

2. The British forces to be maintained in the vicinity of the Canal will be distributed (a) as regards the land forces, in Moascar and the Geneifa area on the south-west side of the Great Bitter Lake, and (b) as regards the air forces, within 5 miles of the Port Said-Suez rail- way from Kantara in the north, to the junction of the railway Suez-Cairo and Suez-Ismailia in the south, together with an extension along the Ismailia-Cairo railway to include the Royal Air Force Station at Abu Sueir and its satellite landing grounds; together with areas suitable for air firing and bombing ranges, which may have to be placed east of the Canal.

3. In the localities specified above there shall be provided for the British land and air forces of the numbers specified in paragraph 1 above, including 4,000 civilian personnel (but less 2,000 of the land forces, 700 of the air forces and 450 civilian personnel (for whom accommodation already exists), the necessary lands and durable barrack and technical accommodation, including an emergency water supply. The lands, accommodation and water supply shall be suitable according to modern standards. In addition, amenities such as are reason-able, having regard to the character of these localities, will be provided by the planting of trees and the provision of gardens, playing fields, &c., for the troops, and a site for the erection of a convalescent camp on the Mediterranean coast.

4. The Egyptian Government will make available the lands and construct the accommodation, water supplies, amenities and convalescent camp, referred to in the preceding paragraph as being necessary over and above the accommodation already existing in these localities, at its own expense, but His Majesty's

Government in the United Kingdom will contribute (1) the actual sum spent by the Egyptian Government before 1914 on the construction of new barracks as alternative accommodation to the Kasr-el-Nil Barracks in Cairo, and (2) the cost of one-fourth of the barrack and technical accommodation for the land forces. The first of these sums shall be paid at the time specified in paragraph 8 below for the withdrawal of the British forces from Cairo and the second at the time for the withdrawal of the British forces from Alexandria under paragraph 18 below. The Egyptian Government may charge a fair rental for the residential accommodation provided for the civilian personnel. The amount of the rent will be agreed between His Majesty's Government in the United Kingdom and the Egyptian Government.

5. The two Governments will each appoint, immediately the present treaty comes into force, two or more persons who shall together form a committee to whom all questions relating to the execution of these works from the time of their commencement to the time of their completion shall be entrusted. Proposals for, or outlines of, plans and specifications put forward by the representatives of His Majesty's Government in the United Kingdom will be accepted, provided they are reasonable and do not fall outside the scope of the obligations of the Egyptian Government under paragraph 4. The plans and specifications of each of the works TO be undertaken by the Egyptian Government shall be approved by the representatives of both Governments on this committee before the work is begun. Any member of this committee, as well as the commanders of the British forces or their representatives, shall have the right to examine the works at all stages of their construction, and the United Kingdom members of the committee may make suggestions as regards the manner in which the work is carried out. The United Kingdom members shall also have the right to make at any time, while the work is in progress, proposals for modifications or alterations in the plans and specifications. Effect shall be given to suggestions and proposals by the United Kingdom members, subject to the condition that they are reasonable and do not fall outside the scope of the obligations of the Egyptian Government under paragraph 4. In the case of machinery and other stores, where standardization of type is important, it is agreed that stores of the standard type in general use by the British forces will be obtained and installed. It is, of course, understood that His Majesty's Government in the United Kingdom may, when the barracks and accommodation are being used by the British forces, make at their own expense improvements or alterations thereto and construct new buildings in the areas specified in paragraph 2 above.

6. In pursuance of their programme for the development of road and railway communications in Egypt, and in order to bring the means of communications in Egypt up to modern strategic requirements, the Egyptian Government will construct and maintain the following roads, bridges and railways:

(A)—*Roads*

(i) Ismailia-Alexandria, via Tel-el-Kebir, Zagnzig, Zifta, Tanta, Kafr-el-Zayat, Damanhour.

(ii) Ismailia-Cairo, via Tel-el-Kebir and thence continuing along the Sweet Water Canal to Heliopolis.

(iii) Port Said-Ismailia-Suez.

(iv) A link between the south end of the Great Bitter Lake and the Cairo-Suez road about 15 miles west of Suez.

In order to bring them up to the general standard of good-class roads for general traffic, these roads will be 20 feet wide, have bye-passes round villages, &c., and be made of such material as to be permanently utilizable for military purposes, and will be constructed in the above order of importance. They will comply with the technical specifications set out below which are the ordinary specifications for a good-class road for general traffic.

Bridges and roads shall be capable of carrying a double line of continuous columns of either heavy four-wheeled mechanical transport, six-wheeled mechanical transport or medium tanks. With regard to four-wheeled vehicles, the distance between the front axle of one vehicle and the rear axle of the vehicle next ahead shall be calculated at 20 feet, the load on each rear axle to be 14 tons, on each front axle to be 6 tons and the distance between axles 18 feet. With regard to six-wheeled vehicles, the distance between the front axle of one vehicle and the rear axle of that next ahead shall be calculated to be 20 feet, between rear axle and middle axle to be 4 feet and between middle axle and front axle 13 feet; the load on each rear and middle axle to be 8.1 tons and on each front axle to be 4 tons. Tanks shall be calculated for as weighing 19.25 tons, to be 25 feet over all in length and to have a distance of 3 feet between the front of one tank and the rear of the next ahead; the load of 19.25 tons to be carried by tracks which have a bearing of 13 feet upon the road or bridge.

(B)—*Railways*

(i) Railway facilities in the Canal Zone will be increased and improved to meet the needs of the increased garrison in the zone and to provide facilities for rapid entrainment of personnel, guns, vehicles and stores according to the requirements of a modern army. His Majesty's Government in the United Kingdom are hereby authorized to make at their own expense such subsequent additions and modifications to these railway facilities as the future requirements of the British forces may demand. Where such additions or modifications affect railway lines used for general traffic, the permission of the Egyptian Government must be obtained.

(ii) The line between Zagazig and Tanta will be doubled.

(iii) The Alexandria-Merea Matruh line will be improved and made permanent.

7. In addition to the roads specified in paragraph 6 (A) above, and for the same purposes, the Egyptian Government will construct and maintain the following roads:

(i) Cairo south along the Nile to Kena and Kus;

(ii) Kus to Kosseir;

(iii) Kena to Hurghada.

These roads and the bridges thereon will be constructed to satisfy the same standards as those specified in paragraph 6 above.

It may not be possible for the construction of the roads referred to in this paragraph to be undertaken at the same time as the roads referred to in paragraph 6, but they will be constructed as soon as possible.

8. When, to the satisfaction of both the high contracting parties, the accommodation referred to in paragraph 4 is ready (accommodation for the forces retained temporarily at Alexandria in accordance with paragraph 18 below not being included) and the works referred to in paragraph 6 above (other than the railways referred to in (ii) and (iii) of part (B) of that paragraph) have been completed, then the British forces in parts of Egypt other than the areas in the Canal Zone specified in paragraph 2 above and except for those maintained temporarily at Alexandria, will withdraw and the lands, barracks, aircraft landing grounds, seaplane anchorages and accommodation occupied by them will be vacated and, save in so far as they may belong to private persons, be handed over to the Egyptian Government.

9. Any difference of opinion between the two Governments relating to the execution of paragraphs 3, 4, 5, 6, 7 and 8 above will be submitted to the decision of an arbitral board, composed of three members, the two Governments nominating each a member and the third being nominated by the two Governments in common agreement. The decision of the board shall be final.

10. In order to ensure the proper training of British troops, it is agreed that the area defined below will be available for the training of British forces: (a) and (b)at all times of the year, and (c) during February and March for annual manoeuvres:

(a) West of the Canal: From Kantara in the north to the Suez-Cairo railway (inclusive) in the south and as far as longitude 31 degrees 30 minutes east, exclusive of all cultivation;

(b) East of the Canal as required;

(c) A continuation of (a) as far south as latitude 29 degrees 52 minutes north, thence south-east to the junction of latitude 29 degrees 30 minutes north and longitude 31 degrees 44 minutes east and from that point eastwards along latitude 29 degrees 30 minutes north.

The areas of the localities referred to above are included in the map (scale 1: 500,000) which is annexed to the present treaty.

11. Unless the two Governments agree to the contrary, the Egyptian Government will prohibit the passage of aircraft over the territories situated on either side of the Suez Canal and within 20 kilometres of it, except for the purpose of passage from east to west or *vice versa* by means of a corridor 10 kilometres wide at Kantara. This prohibition will not, however, apply to the forces of the high contracting parties or to genuinely Egyptian air organizations or to air organizations genuinely belonging to any part of the British Common-wealth of Nations operating under the authority of the Egyptian Government.

12. The Egyptian Government will provide when necessary reasonable means of communication and access to and from the localities where the British forces are situated and will also accord facilities at Port Said and Suez for the landing and storage of material and supplies for the British forces, including the maintenance of a small detachment of the British forces in these ports to handle and guard this material and these supplies in transit.

13. In view of the fact that the speed and range of modern aircraft necessitate the use of wide areas for the efficient training of air forces, the Egyptian Government will accord permission to the British air forces to fly wherever they consider it necessary for the purpose of training. Reciprocal treatment will be accorded to Egyptian air forces in British territories.

14. In view of the fact that the safety of flying is dependent upon provision of a large number of places where aircraft can alight, the Egyptian Government will secure the maintenance and constant availability of adequate landing grounds and seaplane anchorages in Egyptian territory and waters. The Egyptian Government will accede to any request from the British air forces for such additional landing grounds and seaplane anchorages as experience may show to be necessary to make the number adequate for allied requirements.

15. The Egyptian Government will accord permission for the British air forces to use the said landing grounds and seaplane anchorages, and in the case of certain of them to send stocks of fuel and stores thereto, to be kept in sheds to be erected thereon for this purpose, and in case of urgency to undertake such work as may be necessary for the safety of aircraft.

16. The Egyptian Government will give all necessary facilities for the passage of the personnel of the British forces, aircraft and stores to and from the said landing grounds and seaplane anchorages. Similar facilities will be afforded to the personnel, aircraft and stores of the Egyptian forces at the air bases of the British forces.

17. The British military authorities shall be at liberty to request permission from the Egyptian Government to send parties of officers in civilian clothes to the Western Desert to study the ground and draw up tactical schemes. This permission shall not be unreason- ably withheld.

18. His Majesty the King of Egypt authorizes His Majesty The King and Emperor to maintain units of his forces at or near Alexandria for a period not exceeding eight years from the date of the coming into force of the present treaty, this being the approximate period considered necessary by the two high contracting parties—

(a) For the final completion of the barrack accommodation in the Canal zone;

(b) For the improvement of the roads—

(i) Cairo-Suez;

(ii) Cairo-Alexandria via Giza and the desert;

(iii) Alexandria-Mersa Matruh;

so as to bring them up to the standard specified in part (A) of paragraph 6;

(c) The improvement of the railway facilities between Ismailia and Alexandria, and Alexandria and Mersa Matruh referred to in (ii) and (iii), of part (B) of paragraph 6.

The Egyptian Government will complete the work specified in (a), (b) and (c) above before the expiry of the period of eight years aforesaid. The roads and railway facilities mentioned above will, of course, be maintained by the Egyptian Government.

19. The British forces in or near Cairo shall, until the time for withdrawal under paragraph 8 above, and the British forces in or near Alexandria until the expiry of the time specified in paragraph 18 above, continue to enjoy the same facilities as at present.

Article 9. The immunities and privileges in jurisdictional and fiscal matters to be enjoyed by the forces of His Majesty The King and Emperor who are in Egypt in accordance with the provisions of the present treaty will be determined in a separate convention to be concluded between the Egyptian Government and His Majesty's Government in the United Kingdom.

Article 10. Nothing in the present treaty is intended to or shall in any way prejudice the rights and obligations which devolve, or may devolve, upon either of the high contracting parties under the Covenant of the League of Nations or the Treaty for the Renunciation of War signed at Paris on the 27th August, 1928.

Article 11. 1. While reserving liberty to conclude new conventions in future, modifying the agreements of the 19th January and the 10th July, 1899, the high contracting parties agree that the administration of the Sudan shall continue to be that resulting from the said agreements. The Governor-General shall continue to exercise on the joint behalf of the high contracting parties the powers conferred upon him by the said agreements.

The high contracting parties agree that the primary aim of their administration in the Sudan must be the welfare of the Sudanese.

Nothing in this article prejudices the question of sovereignty over the Sudan.

2. Appointments and promotions of officials in the Sudan will in consequence remain vested in the Governor-General, who, in making new appointments to posts for which qualified Sudanese are not available, will select suitable candidates of British and Egyptian nationality.

3. In addition to Sudanese troops, both British and Egyptian troops shall be placed at the disposal of the Governor-General for the defence of the Sudan.

4. Egyptian immigration into the Sudan shall be unrestricted except for reasons of public order and health.

5. There shall be no discrimination in the Sudan between British subjects and Egyptian nationals in matters of commerce, immigration or the possession of property.

6. The high contracting parties are agreed on the provisions set out in the annex to this article as regards the method by which international conventions are to be made applicable to the Sudan.

Annex to Article 11

1. Unless and until the high contracting parties agree to the contrary in application of paragraph 1 of this article, the general principle for the future shall be that international conventions shall only become applicable to the Sudan by the joint action of the Governments of the United Kingdom and of Egypt, and that such joint action shall similarly also be required if it is desired to terminate the participation of the Sudan in an international convention which already applies to this territory.

2. Conventions to which it will be desired that the Sudan should be a party will generally be conventions of a technical or humanitarian character. Such conventions almost in- variably contain a provision for subsequent accession, and in such cases this method of making the convention applicable to the Sudan will be adopted. Accession will be effected by a joint instrument, signed on behalf of Egypt and the United Kingdom respectively by two persons duly authorized for the purpose. The method of depositing the instruments of accession will be the subject of agreement in each case between the two Governments. In the event of its being desired to apply to the Sudan a convention which does not contain an accession clause, the method by which this should be effected will be the subject of consultation and agreement between the two Governments.

3. If the Sudan is already a party to a convention, and it is desired to terminate the participation of the Sudan therein, the necessary notice of termination will be given jointly by the United Kingdom and by Egypt.

4. It is understood that the participation of the Sudan in a convention and the termination of such participation can only be effected by joint action specifically taken in respect of the Sudan, and does not follow merely from the fact that the United Kingdom and Egypt are both parties to a convention or have both denounced a convention.

5. At international conferences where such conventions are negotiated, the Egyptian and the United Kingdom delegates would naturally keep in touch with a view to any action which they may agree to be desirable in the interests of the Sudan.

Article 12. His Majesty The King and Emperor recognizes that the responsibility for the lives and property of foreigners in Egypt devolves exclusively upon the Egyptian Government, who will ensure the fulfilment of their obligations in this respect.

Article 13. His Majesty The King and Emperor recognizes that the capitulatory régime now existing in Egypt is no longer in accordance with the spirit of the times and with the present state of Egypt.

His Majesty the King of Egypt desires the abolition of this régime without delay.

Both high contracting parties are agreed upon the arrangements with regard to this matter as set forth in the annex to this article.

Annex to Article 13

1. It is the object of the arrangements set out in this annex:
    (i) To bring about speedily the abolition of the Capitulations in Egypt with the disappearance of the existing restrictions on Egyptian sovereignty in the matter of the application of Egyptian legislation (including financial legislation) to foreigners as its necessary consequence;
    (ii) To institute a transitional régime for a reasonable and not unduly prolonged period to be fixed, during which the Mixed Tribunals will remain and will, in addition to their present judicial jurisdiction, exercise the jurisdiction at present vested in the Consular Courts.

At the end of this transitional period the Egyptian Government will be free to dispense with the Mixed Tribunals.

2. As a first step, the Egyptian Government will approach the Capitulatory Powers as soon as possible with a view to (a) the removal of all restrictions on the application of Egyptian legislation to foreigners, and (b) the institution of a transitional régime for the Mixed Tribunals as provided in paragraph 1 (ii) above.

3. His Majesty's Government in the United Kingdom, as the Government of a Capitulatory Power and as an ally of Egypt, are in no way opposed to the arrangements referred to in the preceding paragraph and will collaborate actively with the Egyptian Government in giving effect to them by using their influence with the Powers exercising capitulatory rights in Egypt.

4. It is understood that in the event of its being found impossible to bring into effect the arrangements referred to in paragraph 2, the Egyptian Government retains its full rights unimpaired with regard to the capitulatory regime, including the Mixed Tribunals.

5. It is understood that paragraph 2 (a) involves not merely that the assent of the Capitulatory Powers will be no longer necessary for the application of any Egyptian legislation to their nationals, but also that the present legislative functions of the Mixed Tribunals as regards the application of Egyptian legislation to foreigners will terminate. It would follow from this that the Mixed Tribunals in their judicial capacity would no longer have to pronounce upon the validity of the application to foreigners of an Egyptian law or decree which has been applied to foreigners by the Egyptian Parliament or Government, as the case may be.

6. His Majesty the King of Egypt hereby declares that no Egyptian legislation made applicable to foreigners will be inconsistent with the principles generally adopted in modern legislation or, with particular relation to legislation of a fiscal nature, discriminate against foreigners, including foreign corporate bodies.

7. In view of the fact that it is the practice in most countries to apply to foreigners the law of their nationality in matters of "statut personnel," consideration will be given to the desirability of excepting from the transfer of jurisdiction, at any rate in the first place, matters relating to "statut personnel" affecting nationals of those Capitulatory Powers who wish that their consular authorities should continue to exercise such jurisdiction.

8. The transitional régime for the Mixed Tribunals and the transfer to them of the jurisdiction at present exercised by the Consular Courts (which régime and transfer will, of course, be subject to the provisions of the special convention referred to in Article 9) will necessitate the revision of existing laws relating to the organization and jurisdiction of the Mixed Tribunals, including the preparation and promulgation of a new Code of Criminal Procedure. It is understood that this revision will include amongst other matters:
    (i) The definition of the word "foreigner" for the purpose of the future jurisdiction of the Mixed Tribunals;
    (ii) The increase of the personnel of the Mixed Tribunals and the Mixed Parquet, which will be necessitated by the proposed extension of their jurisdiction;
    (iii) The procedure in the case of pardons or remissions of sentences imposed on foreigners and also in connection with the execution of capital sentences passed on foreigners.

Article 14. The present treaty abrogates any existing agreements or other instruments whose continued existence is inconsistent with its provisions. Should either high contracting party so request, a list of the agreements and instruments thus abrogated shall be drawn up in agreement between them within six months of the coming into force of the present treaty.

Article 15. The high contracting parties agree that any difference on the subject of the application or interpretation of the provisions of the present treaty which they are unable to settle by direct negotiation shall be dealt with in accordance with the provisions of the Covenant of the League of Nations.

Article 16. At any time after the expiration of a period of twenty years from the coming into force of the treaty, the high contracting parties will, at the request of either of them, enter into negotiations with a view to such revision of its terms by agreement between them as may be appropriate in the circumstances as they then exist. In case of the high contracting parties being unable to agree upon the terms of the revised treaty, the difference will be submitted to the Council of the League of Nations for decision in accordance with the provisions of the Covenant in force at the time of signature of the present treaty or to such other person or body of persons for decision in accordance with such procedure as the high contracting parties may agree. It is agreed that any revision of this treaty will provide for the continuation of the alliance between the high contracting parties in accordance with the principles contained in Articles 4, 5, 6 and 7. Nevertheless, with the consent of both high contracting parties, negotiations may be entered into at any time after the expiration of a period of ten years after the coming into force of the treaty, with a view to such revision as aforesaid.

Article 17. The present treaty is subject to ratification. Ratifications shall be exchanged in Cairo as soon as possible. The treaty shall come into force on the date of the exchange of ratifications, and shall thereupon be registered with the Secretary-General of the League of Nations.

In witness whereof the above-named plenipotentiaries have signed the present treaty and affixed thereto their seals.

Done at London in duplicate this 26th day of August, 1936.

(L.S.) ANTHONY EDEN
(L.S.) J. RAMSAY MACDONALD
(L.S.) JOHN SIMON
(L.S.) HALIFAX
(L.S.) MILES W. LAMPSON
(L.S.) MOUSTAPHA EL-NAHAS
(L.S.) AHMAD MAHER
(L.S.) M. MAHMOUD
(L.S.) I. SEDKI
(L.S.) A. YEHIA
(L.S.) WACYF BOUTROS GHALI
(L.S.) O.MOHARRAM
(L.S.) MAKRAN EBEID
(L.S.) MAHMOUD FAHMY EL-NOKRACHY
(L.S.) A. HAMDY SEIF EL NASR
(L.S.) ALY EL CHAMSI
(L.S.) M. H. ISSA
(L.S.) HAFEZ AFIFI

AGREED MINUTE

THE United Kingdom and Egyptian Delegations desire at the moment of signature to record in a minute certain points of interpretation of the provisions of the Treaty of Alliance upon which they are agreed.

These points are as follows:

(i) It is of course understood that the facilities provided for in Article 7 to be furnished to His Majesty The King and Emperor include the sending of British forces or reinforcements in the eventualities specified in that article.

(ii) With reference to Article 7, it is understood that as a result of the provisions of Article 6, there will have been mutual consultation between the two Governments in the case of a risk of a rupture. In the case of an apprehended international emergency, the same principle of mutual consultation applies.

(iii) The "means of communication" referred to in the second sentence of Article 7 include telecommunications (cables, telegraphs, telephones and wireless).

(iv) Amongst the military, administrative and legislative measures referred to in the third sentence of Article 7 are included measures under which the Egyptian Government, in the exercise of their powers as regards radio-electric communications, will take into account the requirements of the W/T stations of the British forces in Egypt, and will continue to co-operate with the British authorities to prevent any mutual interference between British and Egyptian W/T stations, and measures providing for the effective control of all means of communications referred to in that article.

(v) The words "Geneifa area" in paragraph 2 (a) of the annex to Article 8 mean: along the shore of the Great Bitter Lake from a point 3 kilometres north of Geneifa Station to a point 3 kilometres south-east of Fayid Station to a depth of 3 kilometres from the shore of the lake.

(vi) With reference to paragraph 2 (b) of the annex to Article 8, it is understood that the exact sites in the area therein referred to where the air forces will be located will be defined as soon as possible.

The Royal Air Force Depot at present situated at Aboukir will also be transferred to this area not later than the date of the withdrawal of the British forces from Cairo under paragraph 8.

(vii) With reference to paragraph 3 of the annex to Article 8, it is understood (a) that British barrack accommodation includes married quarters for officers and for a proportion of the other ranks, (b) that though the site of the convalescent camp cannot be definitely fixed at the moment, El Arish might possibly prove suitable, and (c) that the Egyptian Government, in pursuance of the policy which it has already taken in hand for the benefit of the inhabitants of those areas, will take all reasonable sanitary measures for the combating of malaria in the areas adjacent to those where the British forces are situated.

(viii) With reference to paragraph 6 of the annex to Article 8, it is understood that, with regard to road No. (iii), the Egyptian Government will, unless they are able to make arrangements with the Suez Canal Company for the use of this road by the British and Egyptian forces and for the improvement of those sections which are not already up to this standard so as to satisfy the conditions laid down in paragraph 6, construct an entirely new road connecting these places.

(ix) With reference to paragraph 12 of the annex to Article 8, it is understood that the number of the detachment referred to shall be limited to the minimum strictly necessary to handle and guard this material.

(x) With reference to paragraph 13 of the annex to Article 8, it is understood that flying will take place for training purposes mostly over desert areas, and that populated areas will only be flown over where necessity so demands.

(xi) With reference to paragraph 2 of the Egyptian note relating to military matters, it is of course understood that the cost of the Military Mission will be defrayed by the Egyptian Government, and that the words "proper training" in this paragraph include training in British military colleges and academies.

(xii) Paragraph 2 of the Egyptian note relating to military matters only applies to persons who are already at the time members of the Egyptian armed forces.

(xiii) The word "equipment" in paragraph 3 of the Egyptian note relating to military matters, means all such stores as it is desirable for forces acting together to have as a common pattern. It does not include articles of clothing or articles of local production.

(xiv) With reference to paragraph 1 of Article 11, it is agreed that the Governor-General shall furnish to His Majesty's Government in the United Kingdom and the Egyptian Government an annual report on the administration of the Sudan. Sudan legislation will be notified directly to the President of the Egyptian Council of Ministers.

(xv) With reference to paragraph 2 of Article 11, it is understood that, while the appointment of Egyptian nationals to official posts in the Sudan must necessarily be governed by the number of suitable vacancies, the time of their occurrence and the qualifications of the candidates forthcoming, the provisions of this paragraph will take effect forthwith on the coming into force of the treaty. The promotion and advancement of members of the Sudan Service shall be irrespective of nationality up to any rank by selection in accordance with individual merits.

It is also understood that these provisions will not prevent the Governor-General occasionally appointing to special posts persons of another nationality when no qualified British subjects, Egyptian nationals or Sudanese are available.

(xvi) With reference to paragraph 3 of Article 11, it is understood that, as the Egyptian Government are willing to send troops to the Sudan, the Governor-General will give immediate consideration to the question of the number of Egyptian troops required for service in the Sudan, the precise places where they will be stationed and the accommodation necessary for them, and that the Egyptian Government will send forthwith, on the coming into force of the treaty, an Egyptian military officer of high rank whom the Governor-General can consult with regard to these matters.

(xvii) With reference to Article 11, as it has been arranged between the Egyptian Government and His Majesty's Government in the United Kingdom that the question of the indebtedness of the Sudan to Egypt and other financial questions affecting the Sudan shall be discussed between the Egyptian Ministry of Finance and the Treasury of the United Kingdom, and as such discussions have already commenced, it has been considered unnecessary to insert in the treaty any provision in regard to this question.

(xviii) With regard to paragraph 6 of the annex to Article 13, it is understood that questions relating to this declaration are not subjects for the appreciation of any courts in Egypt.

Signed in duplicate at London this 26th day of August, 1936.

ANTHONY EDEN,

His Majesty's Principal Secretary of State for Foreign Affairs

MOUSTAPHA EL-NAHAS,
President of the Egyptian Council of Ministers

4.1288 German-Japanese Agreement and Supplementary Protocol, Agreement Guarding against the Communistic International (Anti-Comintern Pact)

Alliance Members: Germany, Japan, Italy (November 6, 1937), Hungary (February 24, 1939), and Spain (April 7, 1939)
Signed On: November 25, 1936, in the city of Berlin. In force until August 23, 1939.
Alliance Type: Entente (Type III)

Source: *Documentary Background of World War II, 1931–1941,* p. 988–991.

SUMMARY

This agreement signaled to the world the open association between Japan and Germany. Directed against the Communist International, the alliance directly targeted the Soviet Union and provided the first indication of military coordination among fascist states prior to World War II. Italy quickly joined the pact, and Hungary and Spain joined just prior to the start of hostilities that began World War II.

The agreement was rendered void in 1939 when Germany agreed to a non-aggression pact with the Communist Soviet Union.

ALLIANCE TEXT

The Imperial Government of Japan and the Government of Germany,

In cognizance of the fact that the object of the Communistic International (the so-called Komintern) is the disintegration of, and the commission of violence against, existing States by the exercise of all means at its command,

Believing that the toleration of interference by the Communistic International in the internal affairs of nations not only endangers their internal peace and social welfare, but threatens the general peace of the world,

Desiring to co-operate for defense against communistic disintegration, have agreed as follows.

Article I. The High Contracting States agree that they will mutually keep each other informed concerning the activities of the Communistic International, will confer upon the necessary measure of defense, and will carry out such measures in close co-operation.

Article II. The High Contracting States will jointly invite third States whose internal peace is menaced by the disintegrating work of the Communistic International, to adopt defensive measures in the spirit of the present Agreement or to participate in the present Agreement.

Article III. The Japanese and German texts are each valid as the original text of this Agreement. The Agreement shall come into force on the day of its signature and shall remain in force for the term of five years. The High Contracting States will, in a reasonable time before the expiration of the said term, come to an understanding upon the further manner of their co-operation.

In witness whereof the undersigned, duly authorized by their respective Governments, have affixed hereto their seals and signatures.

Done in duplicate at Berlin, November 25th, 11th year of Showa, corresponding to November 25th, 1936.

Viscount Kintomo Mushakoji,
Imperial Japanese Ambassador Extraordinary and Plenipotentiary
Joachim von Ribbentrop,
German Ambassador Extraordinary and Plenipotentiary

Supplementary Protocol to the Agreement Guarding against the Communistic International

On the occasion of the signature this day of the Agreement guarding against the Communistic International the undersigned plenipotentiaries have agreed as follows:

a. The competent authorities of both High Contracting States will closely co-operate in the exchange of reports on the activities of the Communistic International and on measures of information and defense against the Communistic International.

b. The competent authorities of both High Contracting States will, within the framework of the existing law, take stringent measures against those who at home or abroad work on direct or indirect duty of the Communistic International or assist its disintegrating activities.

c. To facilitate the co-operation of the competent authorities of the two High Contracting States as set out in (a) above, a standing committee shall be established. By this committee the further measures to be adopted in order to counter the disintegrating activities of thé Communistic International shall be considered and conferred upon.

Done at Berlin, November 25th, 11th year of Showa, corresponding to November 25th, 1936.

Viscount Kintomo Mushakoji, Imperial Japanese Ambassador Extraordinary and Plenipotentiary Joachim von Ribbentrop, German Ambassador Extraordinary and Plenipotentiary

4.1289 Convention for the Maintenance, Preservation, and Reestablishment of Peace

Alliance Members: Brazil, Chile, Colombia, Costa Rica, Cuba, Dominican Republic, Ecuador, El Salvador, Guatemala, Haiti, Honduras, Mexico, Nicaragua, Panama, Paraguay, United States, Venezuela
Signed On: December 23, 1936, in the city of Buenos Aires. In force until March 23, 1945.
Alliance Type: Entente (Type III)

Source: *The American Journal of International Law,* vol. 31, no. 2, Supplement: Official Documents. (April 1937), p. 53–57.

SUMMARY

This agreement to peacefully resolve disputes was signed at the 1936 Inter-American Conference for the Maintenance of Peace. President Franklin Delano Roosevelt of the United States had begun the Good Neighbor policy toward Central and South American states in which the United States pledged nonintervention in the internal affairs of its southern neighbors. The United States adhered to this policy as it withdrew its forces from Haiti, the Dominican Republic, and Nicaragua, and the United States refused to act during political turmoil in Cuba and Panama or following moves by several dictators to extend their terms in office.

The agreement was replaced by a defense pact (the Act of Chapultepec) in 1945.

ALLIANCE TEXT

The Governments represented at the Inter-American Conference for the Maintenance of Peace,

Considering:

That according to the statement of Franklin D. Roosevelt, President of the United States, to whose lofty ideals the meeting of this Conference is due, the measures to be adopted by it "would advance the cause of world peace, inasmuch as the agreements which might be reached would supplement and reinforce the efforts of the League of Nations and of all other existing or future peace agencies in seeking to prevent war";

That every war or threat of war affects directly or indirectly all civilized peoples and endangers the great principles of liberty and justice which constitute the American ideal and the standard of American international policy;

That the Treaty of Paris of 1928 (Kellogg-Briand Pact) has been accepted by almost all the civilized states, whether or not members of other peace organizations, and that the Treaty of Non-Aggression and Conciliation of 1933 (Saavedra Lamas Pact signed at Rio de Janeiro) has the approval of the twenty-one American Republics represented in this Conference,

Have resolved to give contractual form to these purposes by concluding the present convention, to which end they have appointed the plenipotentiaries hereafter mentioned:

Argentina: Carlos Saavedra Lamas, Roberto M. Ortiz, Miguel Angel Cárcano, José María Cantillo, Felipe A. Espil, Leopoldo Melo, Isidoro Ruiz Moreno, Daniel Antokoletz, Carlos Brebbia, César Díaz Cisneros.

Paraguay: Miguel Angel Soler, J. Isidro Ramírez.

Honduras: Antonio Bermúdez M., Julián López Pineda.

Costa Rica: Manuel F. Jiménez, Carlos Brenes.

Venezuela: Caracciolo Parra Pérez, Gustavo Herrera, Alberto Zerega Fombona.

Peru: Carlos Concha, Alberto Ulloa, Felipe Barreda Laos, Diómedes Arias Schreiber.

El Salvador: Manuel Castro Ramírez, Maximiliano Patricio Brannon.

Mexico: Francisco Castillo Nájera, Alfonso Reyes, Ramón Beteta, Juan Manuel Alvarez del Castillo.

Brazil: José Carlos de Macedo Soares, Oswaldo Aranha,

José de Paula Rodrigues Alves, Helio Lobo, Hildebrando Pompeu Pinto Accioly, Edmundo da Luz Pinto, Roberto Carneiro de Mendonça, Rosalina Coelho Lisboa de Miller, María Luiza Bittencourt.

Uruguay: José Espalter, Pedro Manini Ríos, Eugenio Martínez Thedy, Juan Antonio Buero, Felipe Ferreiro, Andrés F. Puyol, Abalcázar García, José G. Antuñna, Julio César Cerdeiras Alonso, Gervasio Posadas Belgrano.

Guatemala: Carlos Salazar, José A. Medrano, Alfonso Carrillo.

Nicaragua: Luis Manuel Debayle, José María Moncada, Modesto Valle.

Dominican Republic: Max Henríque Ureña, Tulio M. Cestero, Enrique Jiménez.

Colombia: Jorge Soto del Corral, Miguel López Pumarejo, Roberto Urdaneta Arbeláez, Alberto Lleras Camargo, José Ignacio Díaz Granados.

Panama: Harmodio Arias M., Julio Fábrega, Eduardo Chiari.

United States of America: Cordell Hull, Sumner Welles, Alexander W. Weddell, Adolf A. Berle, Jr., Alexander F. Whitney, Charles G. Fenwick, Michael Francis Doyle, Elise F. Musser.

Chile: Miguel Cruchaga Tocornal, Luis Barros Borgoño, Félix Nieto del Río, Ricardo Montaner Bello.

Ecuador: Humberto Albornoz, Antonio Pons, José Gabriel Navarro, Francisco Guarderas, Eduardo Salazar Gómez.

Bolivia: Enrique Finot, David Alvéstegui, Eduardo Diez de Medina, Alberto Ostria Gutiérrez, Carlos Romero, Alberto Cortadellas, Javier Paz Campero.

Haiti: Horacio Pauleus Sannon, Camille J. León, Elie Lescot, Edmé Manigat, Pierre Eugene de Lespinasse, Clément Magloire.

Cuba: José Manuel Cortina, Ramón Zaydin, Carlos Márquez Sterling, Rafael Santos Jiménez, César Salaya, Calixto Whitmarsh, José Manuel Carbonell.

Who, after having deposited their full powers, found to be in good and due form, have agreed as follows:

Article I.—In the event that the peace of the American Republics is menaced, and in order to coördinate efforts to prevent war, any of the Governments of the American Republics signatory to the Treaty of Paris of 1928 or to the Treaty of Non-Aggression and Conciliation of 1933, or to both, whether or not a member of other peace organizations, shall consult with the other Governments of the American Republics, which, in such event, shall consult together for the purpose of finding and adopting methods of peaceful coöperation.

Article II.—In the event of war, or a virtual state of war between American States, the Governments of the American Republics represented at this Conference shall undertake without delay the necessary mutual consultations, in order to exchange views and to seek, within the obligations resulting from the pacts above mentioned and from the standards of international morality, a method of peaceful collaboration; and, in the event of an international war outside America which might menace the peace of the American Republics, such

consultation shall also take place to determine the proper time and manner in which the signatory States, if they so desire, may eventually coöperate in some action tending to preserve the peace of the American Continent.

Article III.—It is agreed that any question regarding the interpretation of the present convention, which it has not been possible to settle through diplomatic channels, shall be submitted to the procedure of conciliation provided by existing agreements, or to arbitration or to judicial settlement.

Article IV.—The present convention shall be ratified by the high contracting parties in conformity with their respective constitutional procedures. The original convention shall be deposited in the Ministry of Foreign Affairs of the Argentine Republic which shall communicate the ratifications to the other signatories. The convention shall come into effect between the high contracting parties in the order in which they have deposited their ratifications.

Article V.—The present convention shall remain in effect indefinitely but may be denounced by means of one year's notice, after the expiration of which period the convention shall cease in its effects as regards the party which denounces it but shall remain in effect for the remaining signatory States. Denunciations shall be addressed to the Government of the Argentine Republic, which shall transmit them to the other contracting States.

In witness whereof, the above mentioned plenipotentiaries sign the present convention in English, Spanish, Portuguese and French and hereunto affix their respective seals, at the City of Buenos Aires, capital of the Argentine Republic, on the twenty-third day of the month of December, nineteen hundred and thirty-six.

Reservation of Paraguay: "With the express and definite reservation in respect to its peculiar international position as regards the League of Nations."

Argentina: Carlos Saavedra Lamas, Roberto M. Ortiz, Miguel Angel Cárcano, José María Cantillo, Felipe A. Espil, Leopoldo Melo, Isidoro Ruiz Moreno, Daniel Antokoletz, Carlos Brebbia, César Díaz Cisneros.
Paraguay: Miguel Angel Soler, J. Isidro Ramírez.
Honduras: Antonio Bermúdez M., Julián López Pineda.
Costa Rica: Manuel F. Jiménez, Carlos Brenes.
Venezuela: Caracciolo Parra Pérez, Gustavo Herrera, Alberto Zerega Fombona.
Peru: Carlos Concha, Alberto Ulloa, Felipe Barreda Laos, Diómedes Arias Schreiber.
El Salvador: Manuel Castro Ramírez, Maximiliano Patricio Brannon.
Mexico: Francisco Castillo Nájera, Alfonso Reyes, Ramón Beteta, Juan Manuel Alvarez del Castillo.
Brazil: José Carlos de Macedo Soares, Oswaldo Aranha, José de Paula Rodrigues Alves, Helio Lobo,

Hildebrando Pompeu Pinto Accioly, Edmundo da Luz Pinto, Roberto Carneiro de Mendonça, Rosalina Coelho Lisboa de Miller, María Luiza Bittencourt.
Uruguay: José Espalter, Pedro Manini Ríos, Eugenio Martínez Thedy, Juan Antonio Buero, Felipe Ferreiro, Andrés F. Puyol, Abalcázar García, José G. Antuña, Julio César Cerdeiras Alonso, Gervasio Posadas Belgrano.
Guatemala: Carlos Salazar, José A. Medrano, Alfonso Carrillo.
Nicaragua: Luis Manuel Debayle, José María Moncada, Modesto Valle.
Dominican Republic: Max Henríque Ureña, Tulio M. Cestero, Enrique Jiménez.
Colombia: Jorge Soto del Corral, Miguel López Pumarejo, Roberto Urdaneta Arbeláez, Alberto Lleras Camargo, José Ignacio Díaz Granados.
Panama: Harmodio Arias M., Julio Fábrega, Eduardo Chiari.
United States of America: Cordell Hull, Sumner Welles, Alexander W. Weddell, Adolf A. Berle, Jr., Alexander F. Whitney, Charles G. Fenwick, Michael Francis Doyle, Elise F. Musser.
Chile: Miguel Cruchaga Tocornal, Luis Barros Borgoño, Félix Nieto del Río, Ricardo Montaner Bello.
Ecuador: Humberto Albornoz, Antonio Pons, José Gabriel Navarro, Francisco Guarderas, Eduardo Salazar Gómez.
Bolivia: Enrique Finot, David Alvéstegui, Eduardo Diez de Medina, Alberto Ostria Gutiérrez, Carlos Romero, Alberto Cortadellas, Javier Paz Campero.
Haiti: Horacio Pauleus Sannon, Camille J. León, Elie Lescot, Edmé Manigat, Pierre Eugene de Lespinasse, Clément Magloire.
Cuba: José Manuel Cortina, Ramón Zaydin, Carlos Márquez Sterling, Rafael Santos Jiménez, César Salaya, Calixto Whitmarsh, José Manuel Carbonell.

ADDITIONAL PROTOCOL RELATIVE TO NON-INTERVENTION

The Governments represented at the Inter-American Conference for the Maintenance of Peace,

Desiring to assure the benefits of peace in their mutual relations and in their relations with all the nations of the earth, and to abolish the practice of intervention; and

Taking into account that the Convention on Rights and Duties of States, signed at the Seventh International Conference of American States, December 26,1933, solemnly affirmed the fundamental principle that "no State has the right to intervene in the internal or external affairs of another",

Have resolved to reaffirm this principle through the negotiation of the following Additional Protocol, and to that end they have appointed the plenipotentiaries hereafter mentioned:

[Here follow the names of the plenipotentiaries as in convention above.]

Who, after having deposited their full powers, found to be in good and due form, have agreed as follows:

Article 1.—The high contracting parties declare inadmissible the intervention of any one of them, directly or indirectly, and for whatever reason, in the internal or external affairs of any other of the parties.

The violation of the provisions of this article shall give rise to mutual consultation, with the object of exchanging views and seeking methods of peaceful adjustment.

Article 2.—It is agreed that every question concerning the interpretation of the present Additional Protocol, which it has not been possible to settle through diplomatic channels, shall be submitted to the procedure of conciliation provided for in the agreements in force, or to arbitration, or to judicial settlement.

Article 3.—The present Additional Protocol shall be ratified by the high contracting parties in conformity with their respective constitutional procedures. The original instrument and the instruments of ratification shall be deposited in the Ministry of Foreign Affairs of the Argentine Republic which shall communicate the ratifications to the other signatories. The Additional Protocol shall come into effect between the high contracting parties in the order in which they shall have deposited their ratifications.

Article 4.—The present Additional Protocol shall remain in effect indefinitely but may be denounced by means of one year's notice after the expiration of which period the protocol shall cease in its effects as regards the party which denounces it but shall remain in effect for the remaining signatory States. Denunciations shall be addressed to the Government of the Argentine Republic which shall notify them to the other contracting States.

In witness whereof, the above mentioned plenipotentiaries sign the present Additional Protocol in English, Spanish, Portuguese and French and hereunto affix their respective seals, at the City of Buenos Aires, capital of the Argentine Republic, on the twenty-third day of the month of December, nineteen hundred and thirty-six.

[Here follow signatures as in convention above.]

4.1290 Italo-Yugoslav Agreement of March 25, 1937

Alliance Members: Italy and Yugoslavia
Signed On: March 25, 1937, in the city of Belgrade (Serbia). In force until April 20, 1941, when Yugoslavia lost its independence to Germany.
Alliance Type: Neutrality Pact (Type II)

Source: *British Foreign and State Papers,* vol. 141, p. 1119.

SUMMARY

This no-attack agreement represented for Yugoslavia a turn away from the Little Entente of the central states. By allying with Italy, the Yugoslav government hoped to avoid the dangers of Italian and German expansionism. The signing of the Hitler-Stalin Pact in 1939, the occupation of Bessarabia (Romania) by the Soviets soon after, and the granting of Transylvania by Italy and Germany to Hungary made it clear that the policy of Axis appeasement would soon fail.

Yugoslav leaders were summoned to Berchtesgaden, Hitler's retreat, where they were told by the Germans that if the Yugoslav leadership joined the Tripartite Pact the Germans would confine themselves to Yugoslav roads and railways when they attacked Greece or any other neighbor. The alternative would be a march of German forces through the countryside. Prince Paul, the Yugoslav leader, relented and signed the Tripartite Pact on March 25, 1941. When pro-French and anti-German Serbian populations in Yugoslavia heard the news, they organized a violent demonstration in Belgrade. With the help of British agents, the Yugoslavs deposed Prince Paul and replaced him with Prince Peter, the son of former King Alexander. Upon taking the throne, Peter redirected Yugoslav foreign policy away from the Axis powers by signing a friendship treaty with the Soviet Union on April 5, 1941. Despite these efforts, Germany and Yugoslavia's neighbors quickly invaded and overthrew the new government.

ALLIANCE TEXT

The Royal Regents in the name of H.M. the King of Yugoslavia and H.M. the King of Italy, Emperor of Ethiopia, convinced that it is in the interests of their two countries as well as that of general peace to strengthen the bonds of sincere and lasting friendship, and being desirous of providing a new basis for this and of inaugurating a new era in the political and economic relations between the two States;

Persuaded that the maintenance and consolidation of a durable peace between their countries is also an important condition for the peace of Europe;

Have decided to conclude an agreement and to this purpose have designated as their respective plenipotentiaries:

The Royal Regents in the name of H.M. the King of Yugoslavia: H.E. Dr. Milan Stoyadinović, President of the Council of Ministers, Minister for Foreign Affairs;

H.M. the King of Italy, Emperor of Ethiopia: H.E. Count Galeazzo Ciano of Cortellazzo, Minister for Foreign Affairs;

Who, after having exchanged their full powers, found in good and due form, have agreed upon the following provisions:

Article 1.–The High Contracting Parties undertake to respect their common frontiers on land, as well as the maritime frontiers of the two States in the Adriatic, and in the event of either of them being the object of an unprovoked aggression by one or more Powers, the other Party undertakes to abstain from any action calculated to benefit the aggressor.

Article 2.–In case of international complications, and if the two countries are agreed that their common interests are or may be threatened, they undertake to concert together regarding the measures to be taken to safeguard them.

Article 3.–The two High Contracting Parties reaffirm their will not to resort to war in their mutual relations as an instrument of their national policy and to resolve by pacific means all differences and conflicts which may arise between them.

Article 4.–The High Contracting Parties undertake not to tolerate in their respective territories or aid in any way activities directed against the territorial integrity or existing order of the other Contracting Party, or of a nature calculated to prejudice the friendly relations between the two countries.

Article 5.–In order to give a new impulse to their commercial relations, in harmony with the amicable relations established between their two countries, the High Contracting Parties agree to intensify and expand the present exchange of goods and services and to investigate the possibilities of closer economic collaboration. Special agreements to this end will be concluded with a minimum of delay.

Article 6.–The High Contracting Parties agree that nothing in this agreement should be considered as contrary to the existing international obligations of the two countries, these obligations being public.

Article 7.–The present agreement is concluded for a term of five years. If it is not denounced six months before the lapse of this time it will be tacitly prolonged year by year.

Article 8.–The present agreement will be ratified. It will enter into force with the exchange of ratifications. This will take place at Belgrade as soon as possible.

In faith whereof, the said Plenipotentiaries have signed the present Agreement.

Done at Belgrade, the twenty-fifth day of March, 1937, in two copies, of which one has been handed to each of the High Contracting Parties.

4.1291 Treaty of Non-Aggression among the Kingdom of Afghanistan, the Kingdom of Iraq, the Empire of Iran, and the Republic of Turkey

Alliance Members: Afghanistan, Iraq, Iran, and Turkey
Signed On: July 8, 1937, in the city of Tehran (Iran). In force until February 15, 1955.
Alliance Type: Non-Aggression Pact (Type II)

Source: *League of Nations Treaty Series,* vol. 190, p. 23.

SUMMARY

This alliance was signed four days after a border agreement between Iraq and Iran settled some outstanding disputes between the two countries after the emergence of Iraq in the international system. Both countries relented on some of their territorial demands in order to ink the regional non-aggression agreement. For Iran, Iraq, and Turkey, this alliance promised noninterference in the sovereignty of allied states, including the withdrawal of support for any opposition groups within their territories. For Afghanistan, the treaty brought regional recognition. Iran and Iraq also signed a trade agreement soon after this alliance; thus, this period probably represented the highest point for relations between the two countries.

The alliance ended when the parties signed the Baghdad Pact in 1955, from which Afghanistan abstained.

ALLIANCE TEXT

PREAMBLE

His Imperial Majesty the Shahinshah of Iran, His Majesty the King of Afghanistan, His Majesty the King of Iraq, The President of the Republic of Turkey;

Being desirous of contributing by every means in their power to the maintenance of friendly and harmonious relations between them;

Actuated by the common purpose of ensuring peace and security in the Near East by means of additional guarantees within the framework of the Covenant of the League of Nations, and of thus contributing to general peace; and

Deeply conscious of their obligations under the Treaty for Renunciation of War, signed at Paris on August 27th, 1928, and of the other treaties to which they are parties, all of which are in harmony with the Covenant of the League of Nations and the Treaty for Renunciation of War:

Have decided to conclude the present Treaty and have for that purpose appointed:

His Imperial Majesty the Shahinshah of Iran: His Excellency Monsieur Enayatollah Samiy, Minister for Foreign Affairs of Iran;

His Majesty the King of Afghanistan: His Excellency Monsieur Faiz Mohammad Khan, Minister for Foreign Affairs of Afghanistan;

His Majesty the King of Iraq: His Excellency Dr. Nadji-Al-Asil, Minister for Foreign Affairs of Iraq;

The President of the Republic of Turkey: His Excellency Dr. Tevfik Rustu Aras, Minister for Foreign Affairs of Turkey;

Who, having exchanged their full powers, found in good and due form, have agreed upon the following provisions:

Article I. The High Contracting Parties undertake to pursue a policy of complete abstention from any interference in each other's internal affairs.

Article 2. The High Contracting Parties expressly undertake to respect the inviolability of their common frontiers.

Article 3. The High Contracting Parties agree to consult together in all international disputes affecting their common interests.

Article 4. Each of the High Contracting Parties undertakes in no event to resort, whether singly or jointly with one or more third Powers, to any act of aggression directed against any other of the Contracting Parties.

The following shall be deemed to be acts of aggression:
1. Declaration of war;
2. Invasion by the armed forces of one State, with or without a declaration of war, of the territory of another State;
3. An attack by the land, naval or air forces of one State, with or without a declaration of war, on the territory, vessels or aircraft of another State;
4. Directly or indirectly aiding or assisting an aggressor.

The following shall not constitute acts of aggression:
1. The exercise of the right of legitimate self-defence, that is to say, resistance to an act of aggression as defined above;
2. Action under Article 16 of the Covenant of the League of Nations;
3. Action in pursuance of a decision of the Assembly or Council of the League of Nations, or under Article 15, paragraph 7, of the Covenant of the League of Nations, provided always that in the latter case such action is directed against the State which was the first to attack;
4. Action to assist a State subjected to attack, invasion or recourse to war by another of the High Contracting Parties, in violation of the Treaty for Renunciation of War signed in Paris on August 27th, 1928.

Article 5. Should one of the High Contracting Parties consider that a breach of Article 4 of the present Treaty has been or is about to be committed, he shall at once bring the matter before the Council of the League of Nations.

The foregoing provision shall not affect the right of such High Contracting Party to take any steps which, in the circumstances, he may deem necessary.

Article 6. Should one of the High Contracting Parties commit an aggression against a third Power, any other High Contracting Party may denounce the present Treaty, without notice, as towards the aggressor.

Article 7. Each of the High Contracting Parties undertakes to prevent, within his respective frontiers, the formation or activities of armed bands, associations or organisations to subvert the established institutions, or disturb the order or security of any part, whether situated on the frontier or elsewhere, of the territory of another Party, or to change the constitutional system of such other Party.

Article 8. The High Contracting Parties, having already recognised, in the General Treaty for Renunciation of War of August 27th, 1928, that the settlement or solution of all disputes or conflicts, whatever their nature or origin, which may arise among them, shall never be sought by other than pacific means, reaffirm that principle and undertake to rely upon such modes of procedure as have been or shall be established between the High Contracting Parties in that respect.

Article 9. No Articles of the present Treaty shall be considered as in any way diminishing the obligations assumed by each of the High Contracting Parties under the Covenant of the League of Nations.

Article 10. The present Treaty, drawn up in the French language and signed in quadruplicate, one copy having, as they severally recognise, been delivered to each of the High Contracting Parties, is concluded for a period of five years.

On the expiry of that period, and failing its denunciation, with six months' notice, by one of the High Contracting Parties, the Treaty shall be deemed to be renewed for successive periods of five years, until its denunciation with six months' notice by one or more of the High Contracting Parties. On its denunciation as towards one of the Parties, the Treaty shall nevertheless remain in force as between the others.

The present Treaty shall be ratified by each of the High Contracting Parties in accordance with its Constitution, and registered at the League of Nations by the Secretary-General, who shall be requested to bring it to the knowledge of the other Members of the League.

The instruments of ratification shall be deposited by each of the High Contracting Parties with the Iranian Government.

On the deposit of instruments of ratification by two of the High Contracting Parties, the present Treaty shall at once come into force as between those two Parties. It shall come into force as regards the third and fourth Parties respectively on the deposit of their instruments of ratification.

On the deposit of each instrument of ratification, the Government of Iran shall immediately notify all the signatories of the present Treaty.

Done at the Palace of Saad-Abad (Teheran), on the eighth day of July, one thousand nine hundred and thirty-seven.

Enayatollah SAMIY, Minister for Foreign Affairs of Iran.

FAIZ MOHAMMAD Khan, Minister for Foreign Affairs of Afghanistan.

Dr. NADJI-AL-ASIL, Minister for Foreign Affairs of Iraq.

Dr. Tevfik RUSTU ARAS, Minister for Foreign Affairs of Turkey.

4.1292 Treaty of Non-Aggression between the Republic of China and the Union of Soviet Socialist Republics

Alliance Members: China and the Union of Soviet Socialist Republics
Signed On: August 21, 1937, in the city of Nanking (China). In force until April 13, 1941, when the Soviets signed a neutrality agreement with Japan.
Alliance Type: Neutrality Pact (Type II)

Source: *League of Nations Treaty Series,* vol. 181, p. 102.

SUMMARY

In the late 1930s, the Soviet Union was attempting to adapt its foreign policy to deal with the growing Japanese and German threats on both flanks. By the terms of this treaty, Stalin agreed to provide arms to Chiang Kai-shek, the leader of nationalist forces in China. The Soviet goal for the treaty was to tie down the Japanese in a prolonged war of occupation in China so that Siberia would remain safe from Japanese attack. The policy worked to some extent, as Japanese forces committed in strength to the occupation. The Soviets reversed policy by 1941, however, and signed a neutrality agreement with the Japanese on April 13, 1941. The Soviets then denounced their earlier agreement with the Chinese nationalists.

ALLIANCE TEXT

The National Government of the Republic of China and the Government of the Union of Soviet Socialist Republics, animated by the desire to contribute to the maintenance of general peace, to consolidate the amicable relations now existing between them on a firm and lasting basis, and to confirm in a more precise manner the obligations mutually undertaken under the Treaty for the Renunciation of War signed in Paris on August 27th, 1928, have resolved to conclude the present Treaty and have for this purpose appointed as their Plenipotentiaries, that is to say:

His Excellency the President of the National Government of the Republic of China: Dr. Wang Chung-Hui, Minister for Foreign Affairs;

The Central Executive Committee of the Union of Soviet Socialist Republics: Mr. Dimitri Bogomoloff, Ambassador Extraordinary and Plenipotentiary to the Republic of China;

Who, having communicated their full powers, found in good and due form, have agreed upon the following Articles:

Article 1. The two High Contracting Parties solemnly reaffirm that they condemn recourse to war for the solution of international controversies, and that they renounce it as an instrument of national policy in their relations with each other, and, in pursuance of this pledge, they undertake to refrain from any aggression against each other either individually or jointly with one or more other Powers.

Article 2. In the event that either of the High Contracting Parties should be subjected to aggression on the part of one or more third Powers, the other High Contracting Party obligates itself not to render assistance of any kind, either directly or indirectly, to such third Power or Powers at any time during the entire conflict, and also to refrain from taking any action or entering into any agreement which may be used by the aggressor or aggressors to the disadvantage of the Party subjected to aggression.

Article 3. The provisions of the present Treaty shall not be so interpreted as to affect or modify the rights and obligations arising in respect of the High Contracting Parties, out of bilateral or multilateral treaties or agreements of which both High Contracting Parties are signatories and which were concluded prior to the entering into force of the present Treaty.

Article 4. The present Treaty is drawn up in duplicate in English. It comes into force on the day of signature by the above-mentioned Plenipotentiaries and shall remain in force for a period of five years. Either of the High Contracting Parties may notify the other, six months before the expiration of the period, of its desire to terminate the Treaty. In case both Parties fail to do so in time, the Treaty shall be considered as being automatically extended for a period of two years after the expiration of the first period. Should neither of the High Contracting Parties notify the other, six months before the expiration of the two-year period of its desire to terminate the Treaty, it shall continue in force for another period of two years, and so on successively.

In witness whereof the respective Plenipotentiaries have signed the present Treaty and have affixed thereunto their seals.

Done at Nanking, the twenty-first day of August, 1937.

(Signed) Wang CHUNG-HUI.

(Signed) D. BOGOMOLOFF.

4.1293 Nyon Arrangement among the United Kingdom of Great Britain and Northern Ireland, Bulgaria, Egypt, France, Greece, Romania, Turkey, the Soviet Union, and Yugoslavia

Alliance Members: United Kingdom, Bulgaria, Egypt, France, Greece, Romania, Turkey, the Union of Soviet Socialist Republics, and Yugoslavia

Signed On: September 14, 1937, in the city of Nyon (Switzerland). In force until March 28, 1939.

Alliance Type: Defense Pact (Type I)

Source: *League of Nations Treaty Series,* vol. 181, p. 137.

SUMMARY

This agreement was made at the Nyon Conference in order to deal with the large number of attacks on merchant vessels in the Mediterranean during the Spanish Civil War. The parties agreed to protect Spanish merchant vessels and also pledged that any attacks on merchant ships would be countered. Article IV divides among the signatories the responsibilities for patrolling and defending waterways. The alliance lasted until the end of the Spanish Civil War.

ALLIANCE TEXT

Whereas arising out of the Spanish conflict attacks have been repeatedly committed in the Mediterranean by submarines against merchant ships not belonging to either of the conflicting Spanish parties; and

Whereas these attacks are violations of the rules of international law referred to in Part IV of the Treaty of London of April 22nd, 1930, with regard to the sinking of merchant ships and constitute acts contrary to the most elementary dictates of humanity, which should be justly treated as acts of piracy; and

Whereas without in any way admitting the right of either party to the conflict in Spain to exercise belligerent rights or to interfere with merchant ships on the high seas even if the laws of warfare at sea are observed and without prejudice to the right of any Participating Power to take such action as may be proper to protect its merchant shipping from any kind of interference

on the high seas or to the possibility of further collective measures being agreed upon subsequently, it is necessary in the first place to agree upon certain special collective measures against piratical acts by submarines:

In view thereof the undersigned, being authorised to this effect by their respective Governments, have met in conference at Nyon between the 9th and the 14th September 1937, and have agreed upon the following provisions which shall enter immediately into force:

I. The Participating Powers will instruct their naval forces to take the action indicated in paragraphs II and III below with a view to the protection of all merchant ships not belonging to either of the conflicting Spanish parties.

II. Any submarine which attacks such a ship in a manner contrary to the rules of international law referred to in the International Treaty for the Limitation and Reduction of Naval Armaments signed in London on April 22nd, 1930, and confirmed in the Protocol signed in London on November 6th, 1936, shall be counter-attacked and, if possible, destroyed.

III. The instruction mentioned in the preceding paragraph shall extend to any submarine encountered in the vicinity of a position where a ship not belonging to either of the conflicting Spanish parties has recently been attacked in violation of the rules referred to in the preceding paragraph in circumstances which give valid grounds for the belief that the submarine was guilty of the attack.

IV. In order to facilitate the putting into force of the above-arrangements in a practical manner, the Participating Powers have agreed upon the following arrangements:

I. In the western Mediterranean and in the Malta Channel, with the exception of the Tyrrhenean Sea, which may form the subject of special arrangements, the British and French fleets will operate both on the high seas and in the territorial waters of the Participating Powers, in accordance with the division of the area agreed upon between the two Governments.

2. In the eastern Mediterranean,

(a) Each of the Participating Powers will operate in its own territorial waters;

(b) On the high seas, with the exception of the Adriatic Sea, the British and French fleets will operate up to the entrance to the Dardanelles, in those areas where there is reason to apprehend danger to shipping in accordance with the division of the area agreed upon between the two Governments. The other Participating Governments possessing a sea border on the Mediterranean undertake, within the limit of their resources, to furnish these fleets any assistance that may be asked for; in particular, they will permit them to take action in their territorial waters and to use such of their ports as they shall indicate.

3. It is further understood that the limits of the zones referred to in subparagraphs I and 2 above, and their allocation shall be subject at any time to revision by the

Participating Powers in order to take account of any change in the situation.

V. The Participating Powers agree that, in order to simplify the operation of the above-mentioned measures, they will for their part restrict the use of their submarines in the Mediterranean in the following manner:

(a) Except as stated in (b) and (c) below, no submarine will be sent to sea within the Mediterranean.

(b) Submarines may proceed on passage after notification to the other Participating Powers, provided that they proceed on the surface and are accompanied by a surface ship.

(c) Each Participating Power reserves for purposes of exercises certain areas defined in Annex I hereto in which its submarines are exempt from the restrictions mentioned in (a) or (b).

The Participating Powers further undertake not to allow the presence in their respective territorial waters of any foreign submarines except in case of urgent distress, or where the conditions prescribed in sub-paragraph (b) above are fulfilled.

VI. The Participating Powers also agree that, in order to simplify the problem involved in carrying out the measures above described, they may severally advise their merchant shipping to follow certain main routes in the Mediterranean agreed upon between them and defined in Annex II hereto.

VII. Nothing in the present agreement restricts the right of any Participating Power to send its surface vessels to any part of the Mediterranean.

VIII. Nothing in the present agreement in any way prejudices existing international engagements which have been registered with the Secretariat of the League of Nations.

IX. If any of the Participating Powers notifies its intention of withdrawing from

the present Arrangement, the notification will take effect after the expiry of thirty days and any of the other Participating Powers may withdraw on the same date if it communicates its intention to this effect before that date.

Done at Nyon, this fourteenth day of September nineteen hundred and thirty-seven, in a single copy., in the English and French languages, both texts being equally authentic, and which will be deposited in the archives of the Secretariat of the League of Nations.

United Kingdom of Great Britain and Northern Ireland: Anthony EDEN.
Bulgaria: G. KIOSSÉIVANOFF.
N. MOMTCHILOFF.
Egypt: Wacyf BOUTROS-GHALL.
H. AFIFI.
France: Yvon DELBOS.
Greece: N. MAVROUDIS.
N. POLITIS.
S. POLYCHRONIADIS.

Rumania: Victor ANTONESCO.
Turkey: Dr. R. ARAS.
Union of Soviet Socialist Republics: Maxime LITVI-NOFF.
Yugoslavia: Bojidar POURITCH.

4.1294 Treaty of Non-Aggression between the Balkan Entente and Bulgaria

Alliance Members: Yugoslavia, Greece, Romania, Turkey, and Bulgaria
Signed On: July 31, 1938, in the city of Thessalonica (Greece). In force until September 8, 1940, when Romania was forced by Germany to cede contested territory to Bulgaria.
Alliance Type: Non-Aggression Pact (Type II)

Source: *League of Nations Treaty Series,* vol. 196, p. 372.

SUMMARY

In 1919, as part of the peace of World War I, Bulgaria was forced to sign the Treaty of Neuilly. This treaty required that Bulgaria give up contested land near Rumania called Dobruja, stop conscription, decrease the number of its armaments, and pay reparations to the victors. The 1923 Treaty of Lausanne reinforced these sanctions on Bulgaria.

As the Italian and German foreign policies turned more expansionist, the states of central Europe sought Bulgaria as a potential ally, and on July 31, 1938, the five nations of the Balkan Entente signed an agreement renouncing the military sanctions that had been imposed on Bulgaria. This renouncement received the immediate approval of Great Britain, France, and Italy. In addition to a non-aggression pact among all parties, Greece signed a commercial accord with Bulgaria while Yugoslavia agreed to reduce the level of armaments stationed at its border with Bulgaria.

Despite the 1938 agreement, relations among the Balkan countries never normalized. The Dobruja territory continued to be a stumbling block for relations between Romania and Bulgaria. By September of 1940, relations between the two countries plummeted, and Germany forced Romania to sign a treaty giving Dobruja to Bulgaria. The new treaty violated the spirit, if not the letter, of the 1938 agreement, and in 1939 Bulgaria sided with Germany in the war.

ALLIANCE TEXT

Whereas Bulgaria is an adherent of the policy of consolidation of peace in the Balkans, and is desirous of maintaining relations of good neighbourhood and full and frank collaboration with the Balkan States, and

Whereas the States of the Balkan Entente are animated by the same pacific spirit in relation to Bulgaria and the same desire of co-operation,

Now therefore the undersigned:

His Excellency Monsieur Georges Kiosséivanov, President of the Council of Ministers, Bulgarian Minister for Foreign Affairs and Public Worship, of the one part, and

His Excellency Monsieur Jean Metaxas, President of the Council of Ministers, Greek Minister for Foreign Affairs, acting in his capacity as President in Office of the Permanent Council of the Balkan Entente, in the name of all the Members of the Balkan Entente, of the other part,

Hereby declare, on behalf of the States which they represent, that the said States undertake to abstain in their relations with one another from any resort to force, in accordance with the agreements to which they have severally subscribed in respect of non-aggression, and are agreed to waive the application in so far as they are concerned of the provisions contained in Part IV (Military, Naval and Air clauses) of the Treaty of Neuilly, as also of the provisions contained in the Convention respecting the Thracian Frontier, signed at Lausanne, July 24th, 1923.

Done at Thessalonica, in duplicate, this 31st day of July, 1938.

G. KIOSSÉIVANOV.
J. METAXAS.

4.1295 Franco-German Declaration of 1938

Alliance Members: France and Germany
Signed On: December 6, 1938, in the city of Paris. In force until September 3, 1939.
Alliance Type: Entente (Type III)

Source: *British and Foreign State Papers,* vol. 142, p. 573.

SUMMARY

This agreement, signed three months after the Munich Agreement signed by France, Great Britain, and Germany essentially gave Hitler's Germany permission to invade the Czechoslovak Sudetenland, was intended to ensure good-neighborly relations between France and Germany. It also carried with it an implicit guarantee of French control over Alsace and Lorraine, a disputed region on the border with Germany. In exchange for the recognition of French sovereignty in that region, Hitler sought from France a free hand in eastern Europe for greater expansion. However, the German general staff, along with Italy's general staff, was simultaneously planning the eventual attack on France as negotiations for this entente were taking place. This treaty lasted only nine months and ended when France and Britain declared war on Germany following the German invasion of Poland.

ALLIANCE TEXT

M. Georges Bonnet, Minister for Foreign Affairs of the French Republic and M. Joachim Von Ribbentrop, Minister for Foreign Affairs of the German Reich,

Acting in the name and by order of their respective Governments, have agreed on the following points at their meeting in Paris on December 6, 1938:

(1) The French Government and the German Government fully share the conviction that pacific and neighbourly relations between France and Germany constitute one of the essential elements of the consolidation of the situation in Europe and of the preservation of general peace. Consequently both Governments will endeavour with all their might to assure the development of the relations between their countries in this direction.

(2) Both Governments agree that no question of a territorial nature remains in suspense between their countries and solemnly recognize as permanent the frontier between their countries as it is actually drawn.

(3) Both Governments are resolved, without prejudice to their special relations with third Powers, to remain in contact on all questions of importance to both their countries and to have recourse to mutual consultation in case any complications arising out of these questions should threaten to lead to international difficulties.

In witness whereof the Representatives of the two Government have signed the present Declaration, which comes into force immediately.

Executed in duplicate in the French and German languages at Paris, on December 6, 1938.

Signed: Georges Bonnet,
Joachim Von Ribbentrop.

4.1296 Treaty of Friendship and Non-Aggression between Portugal and Spain

Alliance Members: Portugal and Spain
Signed On: March 17, 1939, in the city of Lisbon. In force until November 22, 1977.
Alliance Type: Neutrality Pact (Type II)

Source: *British and Foreign State Papers,* vol. 143, p. 673.

SUMMARY

Portugal provided logistical and some monetary support to General Francisco Franco's Nationalists during the Spanish Civil War. Along with the Axis powers, the Portuguese feared the establishment of a communist state on the peninsula, and Franco's strong commitment to Catholicism only strengthened the attraction of Portugal's leaders to the Nationalist cause.

The alliance was signed within days of Franco's final victory in the war. The treaty assured both parties that policies of non-aggression would be pursued across the border, with neither country aiding third parties in any way. The treaty was amended in July 1940 to include provisions for consultation in the case of crisis, and the entire alliance lasted until 1977, when it was replaced by a new treaty of friendship and cooperation.

ALLIANCE TEXT

Antonio Oscar de Fragoso Carmona, President of the Portuguese Republic, and Francisco Franco Bahamonde, Head of the Spanish State and Commander-in-Chief of the Spanish armies;

Desiring to place on record the solemn and sincere friendship between Portugal and Spain which is based on community of feeling and on the interests that arise from geographical and historical facts;

Desirous also of surrounding with all possible guarantees the maintenance of the good relations which exist between the two countries;

Being convinced that everything which contributes to the maintenance and assurance of peace between Portugal and Spain is an important factor in the peace of Europe;

Having established that no obligations hitherto assumed by either of the contracting parties with regard to third powers in any way opposed to the development and strengthening of their reciprocal relations or conflict with the provisions and articles of this treaty which does not affect them;

Have decided to conclude the following treaty of Friendship and Non-aggression and for this purpose have nominated as their plenipotentiaries:—

[Here follow the names]

Art. 1. The two contracting parties undertake to observe absolute respect of the frontiers and territories of the other party and not to commit any act of aggression or invasion against the other party.

Any act of violence against the integrity and inviolability of the territory of either party even if it is not preceded by a declaration of war, will be held as contrary to the provisions of this article.

2. The high contracting parties undertake not to render air or assistance to any aggressor or aggressors who may attack the other party, and in particular they will not permit any act of aggression or attack to be directed against the territories of the other party from within their territory, by land or by sea or by air.

3. Each contracting party undertakes not to enter into any pact or alliance directed against the other party or having as its purpose aggression against the territory of the other party.

4. Any pact or treaty of alliance which may in future be concluded between one of the contracting parties and a third power will respect the undertakings set out in this treaty.

5. This treaty will remain in force for 10 years and will be considered as automatically extended subject to denunciation by either party on 6 months' notice.

6. This treaty will be ratified and will come into force on the date of exchange of ratifications which will be carried out as soon as possible.

Done in duplicate in Lisbon on March 17, 1939, with two texts, Portuguese and Spanish, which will be of equal validity.

(L.S.) *ANTÓNIO De OLIVEIRA SALAZAR.*
(L.S.) *NICOLÁS FRANCO BAHAMONDE*

4.1297 Agreement of Mutual Assistance between the United Kingdom and Poland

Alliance Members: United Kingdom and Poland
Signed On: April 6, 1939, in the city of London. In force until September 27, 1939.
Alliance Type: Defense Pact (Type I)

Source: *Documentary Background of World War II, 1931–1941*, p. 1025. Additional Citations: *The Major International Treaties 1914–1945*, p. 189.

SUMMARY

The agreements made at Munich in September of 1938 were being ignored by Hitler, and by April 1939 it was clear to the Poles that German expansion would soon turn eastward toward the Polish countryside. The Polish leadership asked Britain to affirm its verbal guarantees of assistance to the Poles, and on April 6, the Polish government accepted this communiqué that committed Britain to aid the Poles in case of attack by a third party.

Even before this agreement, though, Hitler's Germany had already started plans on the eventual attack of Poland that commenced on September 1, 1939. This mutual assistance agreement ended when Poland lost its independence to Germany on September 27.

ALLIANCE TEXT

THE Government of the United Kingdom of Great Britain and Northern Ireland and the Polish Government:

Desiring to place on a permanent basis the collaboration between their respective countries resulting from the assurances of mutual assistance of a defensive character which they have already exchanged:

Have resolved to conclude an Agreement for that purpose and have appointed as their Plenipotentiaries:

The Government of the United Kingdom of Great Britain and Northern Ireland: The Rt. Hon. Viscount Halifax, K.G., G.C.S.I., G.C.I.E., Principal Secretary of State for Foreign Affairs;

The Polish Government: His Excellency Count Edward Raczynski, Ambassador Extraordinary and Plenipotentiary of the Polish Republic in London;

Who, having exchanged their Full Powers, found in good and due form, have agreed following provisions:—

Article 1. Should one of the Contracting Parties become engaged in hostilities with a European Power in consequence of aggression by the latter against that Contracting Party, the other Contracting Party will at once give the Contracting Party engaged in hostilities all the support and assistance in its power.

Article 2. (1) The provisions of Article 1 will also apply in the event of any action by a European Power which clearly threatened, directly or indirectly, the independence of one of the Contracting Parties, and was of such a nature that the Party in question considered it vital to resist it with its armed forces.

(2) Should one of the Contracting Parties become engaged in hostilities with a European Power in consequence of action by that Power which threatened the independence or neutrality of another European State in such a way as to constitute a clear menace to the security of that Contracting Party, the provisions of Article I will apply, without prejudice, however, to the rights of the other European State concerned.

Article 3. Should a European Power attempt to undermine the independence of one of the Contracting Parties by processes of economic penetration or in any other way, the Contracting Parties will support each other in resistance to such attempts. Should the European Power concerned thereupon embark on hostilities against one of the Contracting Parties, the provisions of Article I will apply.

Article 4. The methods of applying the undertakings of mutual assistance provided for by the present Agreement are established between the competent naval, military and air authorities of the Contracting Parties.

Article 5. Without prejudice to the foregoing undertakings of the Contracting Parties to give each other mutual support and assistance immediately on the outbreak of hostilities, they will exchange complete and speedy information concerning any development which might threaten their independence and, in particular, concerning any development which threatened to call the said undertakings into operation.

Article 6. (1) The Contracting Parties will communicate to each other the terms of any undertakings of assistance against aggression which they have already given or may in future give to other States.

(2) Should either of the Contracting Parties intend to give such an undertaking after the coming into force of the present Agreement, the other Contracting Party shall, in order to ensure the proper functioning of the Agreement, be informed thereof.

(3) Any new undertaking which the Contracting Parties may enter into in future shall neither limit their obligations under the present Agreement nor indirectly create new obligations between the Contracting Party not participating in these undertakings and the third State concerned.

Article 7. Should the Contracting Parties be engaged in hostilities in consequence of the application of the present Agreement, they will not conclude an armistice or treaty of peace except by mutual agreement.

Article 8. (1) The present Agreement shall remain in force for a period of five years.

(2) Unless denounced six months before the expiry of this period it shall continue in force, each Contracting Party having thereafter the right to denounce it at any time by giving six months' notice to that effect.

(3) The present Agreement shall come into force on signature.

In faith whereof the above-named Plenipotentiaries have signed the present Agreement and have affixed thereto their seals.

Done in English in duplicate, at London, the 15th August, 1939. A Polish text shall subsequently be agreed upon between the Contracting Parties and both texts will then be authentic.

(L.S.) HALIFAX.
(L.S.) EDWARD RACZYNSKI.

4.1298 Italo-German Alliance (The Pact of Steel)

Alliance Members: Italy and Germany
Signed On: May 22, 1939, in the city of Berlin. In force until September 2, 1943.
Alliance Type: Defense Pact (Type I)

Source: *British and Foreign State Papers,* vol. 143, p. 499.

SUMMARY

The Pact of Steel committed both Italy and Germany to a common foreign policy regarding peace and war. Some within the Italian leadership had reservations about the signing of the alliance. The Italian foreign minister and son-in-law of Benito Mussolini, Count Ciano, provided the Italian signature for the alliance but also thought the agreement was potentially damaging to the Italians, who had expended much money and matériel during the Spanish Civil War. Mussolini, however, wanted the prestige of signing an agreement with the most powerful country on the continent. The pact lasted until Italy's surrender during World War II.

ALLIANCE TEXT

The German Reich Chancellor and His Majesty the King of Italy and Albania, Emperor of Ethiopia, consider that the time has come to confirm through a solemn pact the close relation of friendship and affinity which exists between National Socialist Germany and Fascist Italy.

Since a secure bridge for mutual help and assistance has been established through the common boundary between Germany and Italy, fixed for all time, the two Governments acknowledge anew the principles and aims of the policy previously agreed upon by them, and which has shown itself successful in furthering the interests of the two countries as well as in ensuring the peace of Europe.

Firmly bound together through the inner unity of their ideologies and the comprehensive solidarity of their interests, the German and the Italian people are determined also in future to stand side by side and to strive with united effort for the securing of their *Lebensraum* [living space] and the maintenance of peace. In this way, prescribed for them by history, Germany and Italy wish, in a world of unrest and disintegration, to carry out the assignment of making safe the foundations of European culture. In order to establish these principles in treaty form, they have named as plenipotentiaries, the German Reich Chancellor, the Minister of Foreign Affairs, von Ribbentrop, His Majesty the King of Italy and Albania, Emperor of Ethiopia, the Minister of Foreign Affairs, Count Galeazzo Ciano, who, after the exchange of proper credentials, have agreed upon the following terms:

Article I. The Contracting Parties will remain in permanent contact with each other, in order to come to an understanding of all common interests or the European situation as a whole.

Article II. In the event that the common interests of the Contracting Parties be jeopardized through international happenings of any kind, they will immediately enter into consultation regarding the necessary measures to preserve these interests. Should the security or other vital interests of one of the Contracting Parties be threatened from outside, the other Contracting Party will afford the threatened Party its full political and diplomatic support in order to remove this threat.

Article III. If it should happen, against the wishes and hopes of the Contracting Parties, that one of them becomes involved in military complications with another Power or other Powers, the other Contracting Party will immediately step to its side as an ally and will support it with all its military might on land, at sea, and in the air.

Article IV. In order to ensure, in any given case, the rapid implementation of the alliance obligations of Article III, the Governments of the two Contracting Parties will further intensify their cooperation in the military sphere and the sphere of war economy. Similarly the two Governments will keep each other regularly informed of other measures necessary for the practical implementation of this pact. The two Governments will create standing commissions, under the direction of the Foreign Ministers, for the purposes indicated in paragraphs 1 and 2.

Article V. The Contracting Parties already at this point bind themselves, in the event of a jointly waged war, to conclude any armistice or peace only in full agreement with each other.

Article VI. The two Contracting Parties are aware of the importance of their joint relations to the Powers which are friendly to them. They are determined to maintain these relations in future and to promote the adequate development of the common interests which bind them to these Powers.

Article VII. This pact comes into force immediately upon its signing. The two Contracting Parties are agreed upon fixing the first period of its validity at ten years. In good time before the elapse of this period they will come to an agreement regarding the extension of the validity of the pact.

SECRET SUPPLEMENTARY PROTOCOL

On signing the friendship and alliance pact, agreement has been established by both parties on the following points:

1. The two Foreign Ministers will as quickly as possible come to an agreement on the organization, the seat, and the methods of work on the pact of the commissions on military questions and questions of war economy as stipulated in Article IV of the pact.

2. For the execution of Article IV, par. 2, the two Foreign Ministers will as quickly as possible arrange the necessary measures, guaranteeing a constant cooperation, conforming to the spirit and aims of the pact, in matters of the press, the news service and the propaganda. For this purpose in particular, each of the two Foreign Ministers will assign to the embassy of his country in the respective capital one or several especially well-experienced specialists, for constant discussion in direct close cooperation with the resp. Ministry of Foreign Affairs, of the suitable steps to be taken in matters of the press, the news service and the propaganda for the promotion of the policy of the Axis, and as a countermeasure against the policy of the enemy powers.

Berlin 22 May 1939 in the XVII year of the Fascist Era.

4.1299 Treaty of Non-Aggression between the German Reich and the Kingdom of Denmark

Alliance Members: Germany and Denmark
Signed On: May 31, 1939, in the city of Berlin. In force until April 9, 1940, when Germany invaded Denmark.
Alliance Type: Non-Aggression Pact (Type II)

Source: *League of Nations Treaty Series,* vol. 197, p. 40.

SUMMARY

In May of 1939, Hitler offered non-aggression pacts to several neighboring countries in hopes of easing their tensions with regard to German expansionism. Unlike other Scandinavian countries, Denmark accepted this agreement with Germany, and, following the outbreak of war in 1939, Denmark retained its neutrality. Seven months later, on April 9, 1940, encountering little resistance, German forces overran Norway and took control of Denmark.

ALLIANCE TREATY

His Majesty the King of Denmark and Iceland and the Chancellor of the German Reich,

Being firmly resolved to maintain peace between Denmark and Germany in all circumstances, have agreed to confirm this resolve by means of a Treaty and have appointed as their Plenipotentiaries:

His Majesty the King of Denmark and Iceland: M. Herluf Zahle, Chamberlain, Envoy Extraordinary and Minister Plenipotentiary in Berlin;

The Chancellor of the German Reich: M. Joachim von Ribbentrop, Minister for Foreign Affairs of the Reich;

Who, having exchanged their full powers, found in good and due form, have agreed on the following provisions:

Article I. The Kingdom of Denmark and the German Reich shall in no case resort to war or to any other use of force one against the other.

Should action of the kind referred to in paragraph I be taken by a third Power against one of the Contracting Parties, the other Contracting Party shall not support such action in any way.

Article 2. The present Treaty shall be ratified and the instruments of ratification shall be exchanged as soon as possible in Berlin.

The Treaty shall come into force on the exchange of the instruments of ratification and shall remain in force for a period of ten years from that date. Should the Treaty not be denounced by one of the Contracting Parties at least one year before the expiry of that period, its validity shall be extended for a fresh period of ten years. The same shall apply to subsequent periods.

In witness whereof the Plenipotentiaries of both Parties have signed the present Treaty.

Done in original duplicate, in Danish and German.

Berlin, May 31st, 1939.

Herluf ZAHLE.

Joachim v. RIBBENTROP.

4.1300 Treaty of Non-Aggression between the German Reich and the Republic of Estonia

Alliance Members: Germany and Estonia
Signed On: June 7, 1939, in the city of Berlin. In force until June 16, 1940.
Alliance Type: Non-Aggression Pact (Type II)

Source: *League of Nations Treaty Series,* vol. 198, p. 52.

SUMMARY

Estonia also availed itself of Hitler's offer for a pact of non-aggression. Almost identical in form to the pact with Denmark, the non-aggression treaty lasted until the Soviet invasion of Estonia in June of 1940. Germany never attacked Estonia, but the Hitler-Stalin Pact signed in August did contain secret provisions that allowed Soviet conquest of the Baltic States.

ALLIANCE TEXT

The President of the Republic of Estonia and The Chancellor of the German Reich,

Being firmly resolved to maintain peace between Estonia and Germany in all circumstances.

Have agreed to confirm this resolve by means of a Treaty and have appointed as their Plenipotentiaries:

The President of the Republic of Estonia: M. Karl Selter, Minister for Foreign Affairs;

The Chancellor of the German Reich: M. Joachim von Ribbentrop, Minister for Foreign Affairs of the Reich;

Who, having exchanged their full powers, found in good and due form, have agreed on the following provisions:

Article I. The Republic of Estonia and the German Reich shall in no case resort to war or to any other use of force one against the other.

Should action of the kind referred to in paragraph I be taken by a third Power against one of the Contracting Parties, the other Contracting Party shall not support such action in any way.

Article 2. The present Treaty shall be ratified and the instruments of ratification shall be exchanged as soon as possible in Berlin.

The Treaty shall come into force on the exchange of the instruments of ratification and shall remain in force for a period of ten years from that date. Should the Treaty not be denounced by one of the Contracting Parties at least one year before the expiry of that period its validity shall be extended for a fresh period of ten years. The same shall apply to subsequent periods.

Nevertheless, the Treaty shall not remain in force longer than the corresponding Treaty signed this day between Germany and Latvia. Should the Treaty lapse on these grounds before the expiry of the period specified in paragraph 2, the Estonian Government and the German Government shall, at the request of either Party, at once enter into negotiations for the renewal of the Treaty.

In witness whereof the Plenipotentiaries of both Parties have signed the present Treaty.

Done in original duplicate, at Berlin, in Estonian and German, this 7th day of June, 1939.

K. SELTER.

J. RIBBENTROP.

PROTOCOL OF SIGNATURE

On the signature, this day, of the Treaty between Estonia and Germany, the agreement existing between the two Parties on the following points has been put on record:

The Contracting Party which is not participating in the conflict shall not be deemed to be giving support, within the meaning of paragraph 2 of Article I of the Treaty, if the attitude of that Party is in harmony with the general rules of neutrality. Therefore, the fact of a normal exchange of goods and transit of goods continuing between the Contracting Party not involved in the conflict and the third Power shall not be regarded as constituting illicit support.

Berlin, June 7th, 1939.

K. SELTER.

J. RIBBENTROP.

4.1301 Treaty of Non-Aggression between the German Reich and the Republic of Latvia

Alliance Members: Germany and Latvia
Signed On: June 7, 1939, in the city of Berlin. In force until June 16, 1940, when Latvia lost its independence following the Soviet invasion.
Alliance Type: Non-Aggression Pact (Type II)

Source: *League of Nations Treaty Series,* vol. 198, p. 108.

SUMMARY

Signed on the same day as Estonia's non-aggression pact with Germany, the Latvian agreement was also almost identical in form to the agreements with Estonia and Denmark. This non-aggression treaty also lasted until the Soviet invasion in June of 1940, an act sanctioned under the secret terms of the Hitler-Stalin Pact signed in August of 1939.

ALLIANCE TEXT

The President of the Republic of Latvia and The Chancellor of the German Reich,

Being firmly resolved to maintain peace between Latvia and Germany in all circumstances.

Have agreed to confirm this resolve by means of a Treaty and have appointed as their Plenipotentiaries:

The President of the Republic of Latvia: M. Vilhelms Munters, Minister for Foreign Affairs;

The Chancellor of the German Reich: M. Joachim von Ribbentrop, Minister for Foreign Affairs of the Reich;

Who, having exchanged their full powers, found in good and

due form, have agreed on the following provisions:

Article I. The Republic of Latvia and the German Reich shall in no case resort to war or to any other use of force one against the other.

Should any action of the kind referred to in paragraph I be taken by a third Power against one of the Contracting Parties, the other Contracting Party shall not support such action in any way.

Article 2. The present Treaty shall be ratified and the instruments of ratification shall be exchanged as soon as possible in Berlin.

The Treaty shall come into force on the exchange of the instruments of ratification and shall remain in force for a period of ten years from that date. Should the Treaty not be denounced by one of the Contracting Parties at least one year before the expiry of that period, its validity shall be extended for a fresh period of ten years. The same shall apply to subsequent periods.

Nevertheless, the Treaty shall not remain in force longer than the corresponding Treaty signed this day between Germany and Estonia. Should the Treaty lapse on these grounds before the expiry of the period specified in paragraph 2, the Latvian Government and the German Government shall, at the request of either Party, at once enter into negotiations for the renewal of the Treaty.

In witness whereof the Plenipotentiaries of both Parties have signed the present Treaty.

Done in original duplicate at Berlin, in Latvian and German, this 7th day of June, 1939.

V. MUNTERS.

J. RIBBENTROP.

PROTOCOL OF SIGNATURE.

On the signature, this day, of the Treaty between Latvia and Germany, the agreement existing between the two Parties on the following points has been put on record:

The Contracting Party which is not participating in the conflict shall not be deemed to be giving support within the meaning of paragraph 2 of Article I of the Treaty if the attitude of that Party is in harmony with the general rules of neutrality. Therefore, the fact of a normal exchange of goods and transit of goods continuing between the Contracting Party not involved in the conflict and the third Power shall not be regarded as constituting illicit support.

Berlin, June 7th, 1939.

V. MUNTERS.

J. RIBBENTROP.

4.1302 Franco-Turkish Declaration of Mutual Assistance

Alliance Members: France and Turkey
Signed On: June 23, 1939, in the city of Paris. In force until October 19, 1939.
Alliance Type: Defense Pact (Type I)

Source: *British and Foreign State Papers,* vol. 143, p. 476.

SUMMARY

On June 21, 1939, France ceded the Republic of Hatay to Turkey in exchange for Turkish assistance in the Anglo-French bloc of nations. On June 29, the Hatay parliament voted itself out of existence and approved the transfer of territory to Turkey. This agreement, signed two days after the cession of Hatay, promised Turkish aid against aggression in the eastern Mediterranean. Both countries also pledged cooperation on security for the Balkans. The pact lasted until it was replaced by a new agreement in October 1939.

DESCRIPTION OF TERMS

France and Turkey declared that they would cooperate and provide each other all possible aid and assistance in the case of conflict in the Mediterranean (Article 3). Both parties recognized the necessity of establishing security in the Balkans and would consult as soon as possible regarding methods for arriving at that goal (Article 6).

4.1303 Treaty of Non-Aggression between Germany and the Union of Soviet Socialist Republics

Alliance Members: Germany and the Union of Soviet Socialist Republics
Signed On: August 23, 1939, in the city of Moscow. In force until June 22, 1941.
Alliance Type: Non-Aggression Pact (Type II)

Source: *The Major International Treaties: 1914–1945,* p. 195.

SUMMARY

Negotiations between the British and French and the Soviet Union, begun in earnest by April of 1939, stalled later that year amid mutual suspicions. The Western alliance had accepted most of the Soviet terms for participation, including greater Soviet influence in the foreign policies of its neighboring states. During the final negotiations for signing an alliance, between August 12 and August 17, the Soviets raised the question of Polish territory for the first time. Poland was refusing to allow Soviet bases on its territory, even after increasing pressure from the Western alliance, and this was also part of the new Soviet request. While negotiations with France and Britain stalled, the Soviets, who had already been negotiating the provisions of an agreement with the Germans, signed this non-aggression pact in the early hours of August 23. The world war began one week later.

The secret provisions of this non-aggression pact included the division of Poland and the Soviet occupation of the Baltic states to the north and Bessarabia to the south. The agreement lasted until Hitler's Germany attacked the Soviet Union.

ALLIANCE TEXT

The Government of the German Reich and the Government of the Union of Soviet Socialist Republics

Desirous of strengthening the cause of peace between Germany and the U.S.S.R., and proceeding from the fundamental provisions of the Neutrality Agreement concluded in April, 1926 between Germany and the U.S.S.R., have reached the following Agreement:

Article I. Both High Contracting Parties obligate themselves to desist from any act of violence, any aggressive action, and any attack on each other, either individually or jointly with other Powers.

Article II. Should one of the High Contracting Parties become the object of belligerent action by a third power, the other High Contracting Party shall in no manner lend its support to this third Power.

Article III. The Governments of the two High Contracting Parties shall in the future maintain continual contact with one another for the purpose of consultation in order to exchange information on problems affecting their common interests.

Article IV. Neither of the two High Contracting Parties shall participate in any grouping of powers whatsoever that is directly or indirectly aimed at the other party.

Article V. Should disputes or conflicts arise between the High Contracting Parties over problems of one kind or another, both parties shall settle these disputes or conflicts exclusively through friendly exchange of opinion or, if necessary, through the establishment of arbitration commissions.

Article VI. The present Treaty is concluded for a period of ten years, with the proviso that, in so far as one of the High Contracting Parties does not advance it one year prior to the expiration of this period, the validity of this Treaty shall automatically be extended for another five years.

Article VII. The present Treaty shall be ratified within the shortest possible time. The ratifications shall be exchanged in Berlin. The agreement shall enter into force as soon as it is signed.

Done in duplicate, in the German and Russian languages.

Moscow, August 23, 1939.

For the Government of the German Reich

V. RIBBENTROP

With full power of the Government of the U.S.S.R.

V. MOLOTOV

SECRET ADDITIONAL PROTOCOL

On the occasion of the signature of the Non-Aggression Pact between the German Reich and the Union of Socialist Soviet Republics the undersigned plenipotentiaries of each of the two parties discussed in strictly confidential conversations the question of the boundary of their respective spheres of influence in Eastern Europe. These conversations led to the following conclusions:

Article I. In the event of a territorial and political rearrangement in the areas belonging to the Baltic States (Finland, Estonia, Latvia, Lithuania), the northern boundary of Lithuania shall represent the boundary of the spheres of influence of Germany and the U.S.S.R. In this connection the interest of Lithuania in the Vilna area is recognized by each party.

Article II. In the event of a territorial and political rearrangement of the areas belonging to the Polish state the spheres of influence of Germany and the U.S.S.R. shall be bounded approximately by the line of the rivers Narew, Vistula and San.

The question of whether the interests of both parties make desirable the maintenance of an independent Polish State and how such a state should be bounded can only be definitely determined in the course of further political developments.

In any event both Governments will resolve this question by means of a friendly agreement.

Article III. With regard to Southeastern Europe attention is called by the Soviet side to its interest in Bessarabia. The German side declares its complete political disinterest in these areas.

This protocol shall be treated by both parties as strictly secret.

Moscow, August 23, 1939.

For the Government of the German Reich

V. RIBBENTROP

Plenipotentiary of the Government of the U.S.S.R.

V. MOLOTOV

4.1304 Pact of Mutual Assistance between the Republic of Estonia and the Union of Soviet Socialist Republics

Alliance Members: Estonia and the Union of Soviet Socialist Republics
Signed On: September 28, 1939, in the city of Moscow. In force until June 16, 1940.
Alliance Type: Defense Pact (Type I)

Source: *League of Nations Treaty Series,* vol. 198, p. 227.

SUMMARY

Germany and the Soviet Union had effectively divided Poland by the end of September 1939. By September 24, Soviet warships arrived off the coast of Estonia, and Soviet bombers had begun threatening patrols over Tallinn, the Estonian capital. The Soviets demanded basing rights and port access in exchange for mutual guarantees of protection, and because of the threat posed by the Soviets the Estonians relented on September 28. The agreement ended upon the invasion and occupation of Estonia by the Soviet Union nine months later.

ALLIANCE TEXT

The President of the Republic of Estonia, of the one part, and the Presidium of the Supreme Council of the Union of Soviet Socialist Republics, of the other part;

Desirous of developing the friendly relations established by the Treaty of Peace of February 2nd, 1920, based on the recognition of independent political existence and non-intervention by either Contracting Party in the internal affairs of the other Contracting Party;

Recognising that the Peace Treaty of February 2nd, 1920, and the Treaty of Non-Aggression and Peaceful Settlement of Disputes of May 4th, 1932, are and remain the solid foundation of their reciprocal relations and obligations;

Convinced that it is in the interest of both Contracting Parties to determine the exact conditions for the consolidation of their mutual security;

Have deemed it necessary to conclude between themselves the Pact of Mutual Assistance hereunder, and have for that purpose appointed as their Plenipotentiaries:

The President of the Republic of Estonia: M. Karl Selter, Minister for Foreign Affairs;

The Presidium of the Supreme Council of the Union of Soviet Socialist Republics: M. V. M. Molotoff, President of the Council of People's Commissaries and People's Commissary for Foreign Affairs;

Who have agreed as follows:

Article I. The two Contracting Parties undertake to render each other assistance of every kind, including military assistance, in the event of direct aggression or threat of aggression on the part of a European Great Power against the maritime frontiers of the Contracting Parties in the Baltic Sea, or against their land frontiers across the territory of the Republic of Latvia, and also against the bases provided for in Article III.

Article II. The Union of Soviet Socialist Republics undertakes to assist the Estonian army on advantageous terms, with armaments or other war material.

Article III. The Republic of Estonia grants the Union of Soviet Socialist Republics the right to have naval bases on the Estonian islands of Saare Maa and Hiiu Maa and in the town of Paldiski, together with a number of aerodromes for air forces, on lease at reasonable rates. The exact sites of the bases and aerodromes in question shall be assigned, and the limits thereof defined, by common accord.

With a view to the defence of the naval bases and aerodromes in question, the Union of Soviet Socialist Republics shall be entitled at its own expense to maintain strictly limited numbers of Soviet land and air armed forces, up to a maximum to be determined by special agreement, within the areas allotted for the said bases and aerodromes.

Article IV. The two Contracting Parties undertake not to conclude alliances or to take part in coalitions directed against either of the Contracting Parties.

Article V. The enforcement of the present Pact may in no way

impair the sovereign rights of the Contracting Parties or, more especially, their economic system or political structure.

The areas allotted for the bases and aerodromes (article III) shall remain territory of the Republic of Estonia.

Article VI. The present Pact shall enter into force on the date of the exchange of the instruments of ratification. The exchange of the instruments of ratification shall take place at Tallinn within six days from the date of signature of the present Pact.

The period of validity of the present Pact shall be ten years, provided always that, if neither of the Contracting Parties deem it necessary to denounce it one year before the expiry, of that period, its validity shall be automatically renewed for a further period of five years.

Article VII. The present Pact is drawn up in duplicate originals in the Estonian and Russian languages at Moscow, this 28th day of September, 1939.

September 28th, 1939.

K. SELTER.

V. MOLOTOFF.

4.1305 Pact of Mutual Assistance between the Republic of Latvia and the Union of Soviet Socialist Republics

Alliance Members: Latvia and the Union of Soviet Socialist Republics
Signed On: October 5, 1939, in the city of Moscow. In force until June 16, 1940.
Alliance Type: Defense Pact (Type I)

Source: *League of Nations Treaty Series*, vol. 198, p. 385.

SUMMARY

Defense pacts with the USSR were forced upon the Baltic states following the division of Poland by Germany and the Soviets. As Stalin told Vilhelm Munters, the Latvian foreign minister who signed this pact, the Germans had accepted Soviet control of the Baltic states, allowing the Soviets to occupy these countries at will. Given this threat and the Soviet willingness to pledge "mutual assistance," Latvia relented and signed the defense pact that was supposed to last at least ten years. The Soviet Union abrogated the agreement by occupying Latvia in 1940.

ALLIANCE TEXT

The Presidium of the Supreme Council of the Union of Soviet Socialist Republics, of the one part, and the President of the Republic of Latvia, of the other part,

With the object of developing the friendly relations established by the Treaty of Peace of August 11th, 1920, founded upon recognition of the independent political existence and non-interference in the internal affairs of the other Party;

Recognising that the Treaty of Peace of August 11th, 1920, and the Treaty of NonAggression and Peaceful Settlement of Disputes of February 5th, 1932, continue to constitute the firm foundation of their mutual relations and obligations;

Convinced that it is in the interests of both Contracting Parties that the exact conditions under which their mutual security is assured should be determined;

Have deemed it necessary to conclude between themselves the Pact of Mutual Assistance hereunder, and have for that purpose appointed as their Plenipotentiaries:

The Presidium of the Supreme Council of the Union of Soviet Socialist Republics: M. V. M. Molotoff, President of the Council of People's Commissaries and People's Commissary for Foreign Affairs;

The President of the Republic of Latvia: M. Vilhelm Munters, Minister for Foreign Affairs;

Who, having communicated to each other their full powers, found in good and due form, have agreed upon the following provisions:

Article I. The two Contracting Parties undertake to render each other assistance of every kind, including military assistance, in the event of a direct aggression or threat of aggression by any great European Power against the maritime frontiers of the Contracting Parties in the Baltic Sea or against their land frontiers across the territory of the Estonian or Lithuanian Republics, and also against the bases provided for in Article III.

Article II. The Union of Soviet Socialist Republics undertakes to assist the Latvian army, on advantageous terms, with armaments and other war material.

Article III. The Latvian Republic, with a view to ensuring the security of the Union of Soviet Socialist Republics and consolidating its own independence, grants to the Union of Soviet Socialist Republics the right to have in the towns of Liepaja (Libau) and Ventspils (Windau) naval bases and a number of aerodromes for an air force, these to be leased at a reasonable rent. The exact sites of the bases and aerodromes shall be assigned and their boundaries determined by special agreement.

With a view to the defence of the Strait of Irbes, the Union of Soviet Socialist Republics is granted the right, on the same conditions, to construct a base for coastal artillery on the littoral between Ventspils and Pitrags.

With a view to the defence of the naval bases, the aerodromes and the coastal artillery base, the Union of Soviet Socialist Republics shall have the right to maintain at its own expense, in the areas allotted for the bases and aerodromes, a strictly limited quantity of Soviet armed land and air forces, the maximum number of which shall be determined by a special agreement.

Article IV. The two Contracting Parties undertake not to conclude alliances or to take part in coalitions directed against either of the Contracting Parties.

Article V. The enforcement of the present Pact may in no way impair the sovereign rights of the Contracting Parties, more especially with regard to their political structure, economic and social systems, and military measures.

The areas allotted for the bases and aerodromes (Article III) shall remain Latvian territory.

Article VI. The present Pact shall enter into force on the date of the exchange of the instruments of ratification. The exchange of instruments shall take place at Riga within six days from the date of signature of the present Pact.

The period of validity of the present Pact shall be ten years, provided always that, if neither of the Contracting Parties finds it necessary to denounce the present Pact one year before the expiry of that period, the Pact shall automatically continue to have effect for the ten years following.

In faith whereof the above-named Plenipotentiaries have signed the present Pact and have thereto affixed their seals.

Done at Moscow in duplicate originals, in the Russian and Latvian languages, this 5th day of October, 1939.

V. MOLOTOFF.
V. MUNTERS.

4.1306 Treaty of the Transfer of Vilna to Lithuania and on Soviet-Lithuanian Mutual Assistance

Alliance Members: Lithuania and the Union of Soviet Socialist Republics
Signed On: October 10, 1939, in the city of Moscow. In force until June 14, 1940.
Alliance Type: Defense Pact (Type I)

Source: *United States State Department Documents,* 1948: Documents and State Papers, vol. 3, p. 386.

SUMMARY

This treaty mirrored the Soviet agreements made with both Estonia and Latvia, save for the transfer of territory to Lithuania. In exchange for declaring Vilna a Lithuanian territory, a right also guaranteed by the Soviets in the 1920 peace treaty between the two countries, Lithuania agreed to the pledge of mutual assistance in case of conflict. Given the threat posed by the Soviets in October of 1939, Lithuania had few policy alternatives.

Soviet forces were permitted by the Lithuanian government to occupy key Lithuanian cities on July 15, 1940. The request for control of urban centers was made in the form of an ultimatum. Immediately after accepting the proposal, Lithuanian prime minister Antanas Merkys resigned, and a government more favorable to the Soviets was formed. Two days later, a new socialist premier was appointed, and on August 25, 1940, Lithuania adopted the Soviet constitution and officially became a Soviet socialist republic.

ALLIANCE TEXT

The Presidium of the Supreme Soviet of the USSR on the one side, and the President of the Lithuanian Republic on the other,

For the purpose of developing the friendly relations established by the peace treaty of 12 July 1920, based on the recognition of independent State existence and of non-intervention in the internal affairs of the other party;

Recognizing that the peace treaty of 12 July 1920, and the pact on non-aggression and the peaceful settlement of conflicts of 28 September 1926, continue to provide a firm basis for their mutual relations and undertakings;

Convinced that it is in the interests of both contracting parties to define the exact conditions of ensuring mutual security and to make a just settlement of the question to which State the city of Vilna and the Vilna region (unlawfully wrested from Lithuania by Poland) belong;

Have found it necessary to conclude the following treaty on the transfer of the city of Vilna and the Vilna region to the Lithuanian Republic and on mutual assistance between the Soviet Union and Lithuania, and have appointed for this purpose as their plenipotentiaries;

The Presidium of the Supreme Soviet of the USSR: V. M. Molotov, Chairman of the Council of People's Commissars and People's Commissar for Foreign Affairs;

The President of the Lithuanian Republic: Jouzas Urbsys, Minister for Foreign Affairs;

Who, having presented their credentials, which were found to be drawn up in due form and proper order, agreed on the following:

Article I. For the purpose of consolidating the friendship between the USSR and Lithuania, the city of Vilna and the Vilna region are transferred by the Soviet Union to the Lithuanian Republic and included in the territory of the Lithuanian State, the frontier between the USSR and the Lithuanian Republic being established in accordance with the map appended hereto, which frontier shall be specified in more detail in a supplementary protocol.

Article II. The Soviet Union and the Lithuanian Republic undertake to render each other every assistance, including military assistance, should Lithuania be attacked or in danger of attack, or should the Soviet Union be attacked or in danger of attack through Lithuanian territory by any European Power.

Article III. The Soviet Union undertakes to render the Lithuanian army assistance in armaments and other military equipment on favourable terms.

Article IV. The Soviet Union and the Lithuanian Republic undertake jointly to protect the State frontiers of Lithuania, for which purpose the Soviet Union is granted the right to maintain at its own expense, at points in the Lithuanian Republic to be established by mutual agreement, Soviet land and air armed forces of strictly limited strength. The exact locations of these troops and the boundaries within which they may be quartered, their strength at each particular point, and also all other questions of an economic, administrative, or jurisdictional character, and other questions arising in connexion with the presence of Soviet armed forces on Lithuanian territory under the present treaty, shall be regulated by special agreements.

The sites and buildings necessary for this purpose shall be allotted by the Lithuanian Government on lease at a reasonable price.

Article V. In the event of the danger of an attack on Lithuania or on the USSR through Lithuanian territory, the two contracting parties shall immediately discuss the resulting

situation and take all measures found necessary by mutual agreement to secure the inviolability of the territories of the contracting parties.

Article VI. The two contracting parties undertake not to conclude any alliance or to participate in any coalition directed against either of the contracting parties.

Article VII. The coming into force of the present treaty shall not affect in any way the sovereign rights of the contracting parties, in particular their State organization, economic and social system, military measures, and the principle of non-intervention in internal affairs generally. The locations of the Soviet land and air armed forces (article III of the present treaty) remain in all circumstances a component part of the territory of the Lithuanian Republic.

Article VIII. The provisions of the present treaty concerned with undertakings for mutual assistance between the USSR and the Lithuanian Republic (articles II to VII) shall remain in force for fifteen years, and, unless one of the contracting parties finds it necessary to denounce the provisions of this treaty established for a specified term one year prior to the expiration of that term, they shall automatically continue in force for the next ten years.

Article IX. The present treaty comes into force upon exchange of instruments of ratification. Exchange of these instruments shall take place in Kaunas within six days from the day of signature of this treaty.

The present treaty is made in two originals, in the Russian and Lithuanian languages, at Moscow, 10 October 1939.

V. MOLOTOV
Jouzas URBSYS

4.1307 Treaty of Mutual Assistance among Great Britain and Northern Ireland, France, and Turkey

Alliance Members: Great Britain, France, and Turkey
Signed On: October 19, 1939, in the city of Ankara (Turkey). In force until June 22, 1940 (for France) and September 2, 1945 (for Britain and Turkey).
Alliance Type: Defense Pact (Type I)

Source: *British and Foreign State Papers,* vol. 151, p. 213.

SUMMARY

This mutual assistance agreement was arranged in such a way that Turkey would intervene in the war only if its interests were directly threatened, and in that case, France and Britain would be obliged to aid their alliance partner. At the request of the Turks, action against the Soviet Union was excluded from the treaty, and monetary loans were given by France and Britain to help militarize Turkey and resolve its debt.

As the war progressed, Italy invaded Greece and Albania while Germany conquered several Balkan states. Germany had conquered France by June of 1940, and by 1941 Turkey was isolated from its

British ally and was ultimately forced to sign a non-aggression pact with Germany on June 18, 1941, to avoid the increasing German threat near its border. The terms of the non-aggression pact of 1941 specifically excluded this agreement, which meant that British obligations remained. Had this agreement not been excluded, the 1941 pact could have been construed as a declaration of war against the Western allies. Turkish participation in World War II thus never materialized, but this mutual assistance agreement remained in force until the end of the war.

ALLIANCE TEXT

The President of the French Republic, His Majesty the King of Great Britain, Ireland and the British Dominions Beyond the Seas, Emperor of India (in respect of the United Kingdom of Great Britain and Northern Ireland), and The President of the Turkish Republic:

Desiring to conclude a treaty of a reciprocal character in the interests of their national security, and to provide for mutual assistance in resistance to aggression,

Have appointed as their Plenipotentiaries, namely:

The President of the French Republic: M. Renée Massigli, Ambassador Extraordinary and Plenipotentiary, Commander of the Legion of Honour;

His Majesty the King of Great Britain, Ireland and the British Dominions Beyond the Seas, (for the United Kingdom of Great Britain and Northern Ireland): Sir Hughe Montgomery Knatchbull-Hugessen, K.C.M.G., Ambassador Extraordinary and Plenipotentiary;

The President of the Turkish Republic: Dr. Refik Saydam, President of the Council, Minister for Foreign Affairs *ad interim*, Deputy for Istanbul;

Who, having communicated their full powers, found in good and due form, have agreed as follows:

Article 1. In the event of Turkey being involved in hostilities with a European Power in consequence of aggression by that Power against Turkey, France and the United Kingdom will co-operate effectively with Turkey and will lend her all aid and assistance in their power.

Article 2. (1) In the event of an act of aggression by a European Power leading to war in the Mediterranean area in which France and the United Kingdom are involved, Turkey will collaborate effectively with France and the United Kingdom and will lend them all aid and assistance in her power.

(2) In the event of an act of aggression by a European Power leading to war in the Mediterranean area in which Turkey is involved, France and the United Kingdom will collaborate effectively with Turkey and will lend her all aid and assistance in their power.

Article 3. So long as the guarantees given by France and the United Kingdom to Greece and Roumania by their respective Declarations of the 13th April, 1939, remain in force, Turkey will co-operate effectively with France and the United Kingdom and will lend them all aid and assistance in her power, in the event of France and the United Kingdom being engaged in hostilities in virtue of either of the said guarantees.

Article 4. In the event of France and the United Kingdom being involved in hostilities with a European Power in consequence of aggression committed by that Power against either of those States without the provisions of Articles 2 or 3 being applicable, the High Contracting Parties will immediately consult together.

It is nevertheless agreed that in such an eventuality Turkey will observe at least a benevolent neutrality towards France and the United Kingdom.

Article 5. Without prejudice to the provisions of Article 3 above, in the event of either:

(1) Aggression by a European Power against another European State which the Government of one of the High Contracting Parties had, with the approval of that State, undertaken to assist in maintaining its independence or neutrality against such aggression, or

(2) Aggression by a European Power which, while directed against another European State, constituted, in the opinion of the Government of one of the High Contracting Parties, a menace to its own security,

the High Contracting Parties will immediately consult together with a view to such common action as might be considered effective.

Article 6. The present Treaty is not directed against any country, but is designed to assure France, the United Kingdom and Turkey of mutual aid and assistance in resistance to aggression should the necessity arise.

Article 7. The provisions of the present Treaty are equally binding as bilateral obligations between Turkey and each of the two other High Contracting Parties.

Article 8. If the High Contracting Parties are engaged in hostilities in consequence of the operation of the present Treaty, they will not conclude an armistice or peace except by common agreement.

Article 9. The present Treaty shall be ratified and the instruments of ratification shall be deposited simultaneously at Angora as soon as possible. It shall enter into force on the date of this deposit.

The present Treaty is concluded for a period of fifteen years. If none of the High Contracting Parties has notified the two others of its intention to terminate it six months before the expiration of the said period, the Treaty will be renewed by tacit consent for a further period of five years, and so on.

In witness whereof the undersigned have signed the present Treaty and have thereto affixed their seals.

Done at Angora, in triplicate, the 19th October, 1939.

(L. S.) R. MASSIGLI.

(L. S.) H. M. KNATCHBULL-HUGESSEN.

(L. S.) Dr. R. SAYDAM.

4.1308 Treaty of Non-Aggression, Conciliation, Arbitration and Judicial Settlement between Colombia and Venezuela

Alliance Members: Colombia and Venezuela
Signed On: December 17, 1939, in the city of Bogota (Colombia). In force as of date of publication of this volume.
Alliance Type: Entente (Type III)

Source: *British and Foreign State Papers*, vol. 143, p. 142.

SUMMARY

This treaty outlines rules for territorial cooperation to ensure greater Latin American integration. Part of the treaty stipulates that in the event of a dispute, both nations would appoint a member to a commission designated to resolve the dispute. The commission would, in turn, elect a fifth member. Together, this commission would work jointly to resolve territorial disputes between the two nations.

The treaty continues to remain in force. In 1989, Colombia and Venezuela called upon this treaty to help settle a dispute in the Gulf of Venezuela. The negotiations lapsed in 1990 but were restarted in 2001 when the dispute once again became more active. At present, despite the use of the arbitration commission, border conflicts continue to occur between the two countries. In March 2008, Venezuela dispatched troops to its border with Colombia following Colombia's cross-border raid of narco-guerrilla bases within Ecuador.

ALLIANCE TEXT

The President of the Republic of Colombia and the President of the United States of Venezuela, sincerely desirous of expressing in solemn form the peaceful sentiments inspiring their respective peoples, and of manifesting their desire to renounce all recourse to armed force as an instrument of policy between the two nations, have resolved to conclude a treaty for the pacific settlement of disputes which may arise between them, and to this end have appointed as their Plenipotentiaries:

The President of the Republic of Colombia: Mr. Luis López de Mesa, Minister for Foreign Affairs; and

The President of the United States of Venezuela: Mr. José Santiago Rodríguez,

Ambassador Extraordinary and Plenipotentiary in Colombia,

Who, having exchanged their full powers, found in good and due form, have

agreed on the following provisions:

Article I. The two High Contracting Parties undertake in no case to resort to war or to commit any act of aggression one against the other.

Article II. The two High Contracting Parties undertake, in accordance with the terms of this Treaty, to submit to the procedures for pacific settlement established therein all disputes, whatever their nature or cause, which may arise between them and which it may not have been possible to settle peaceably through the ordinary diplomatic channels, with the sole exception of those which appertain to the vital interests, independence or territorial integrity of the Contracting States.

Disputes for which a special settlement procedure may have been provided for by agreements in force between the Parties shall be resolved in accordance with the provisions of those agreements.

Article III. If one of the Contracting Parties alleges that the dispute between the two is connected with a matter which by its nature and in accordance with international law lies exclusively within the competence and the jurisdiction of the said Party, and if the opposing Party does not admit the allegation, the matter shall be decided by the permanent Court of International Justice. If the Court declares that the claim is well-founded, the dispute shall be declared concluded. Otherwise the Court itself shall decide on the substance of the dispute and shall indicate the procedure for pacific settlement to be employed in accordance with this Treaty.

Article IV. All questions concerning which the two High Contracting Parties have not been able to reach friendly agreement through the ordinary diplomatic channels shall be submitted to the Permanent Conciliation Commission.

Article V. The High Contracting Parties shall establish a Permanent Conciliation Commission composed of five members.

Each of the Parties shall designate two members, only one of whom shall be a national of the State which nominates him. The fifth member shall be the President and shall be nominated by agreement between the Contracting Parties. The fifth member shall not be a national of any State already represented on the Commission

Article VI. The Permanent Conciliation Commission shall be established and ready to function within six months following the date of the exchange of the instruments of ratification of this Treaty.

Unless otherwise agreed between the Contracting Parties, the Commission shall be appointed for three years and similarly thereafter, unless during the last three months of each period the Parties decide to change the composition of the Commission or to renew it entirely.

Any vacancies occurring on the Commission shall be filled immediately.

Article VII. Unless otherwise agreed between the Parties, the Commission shall meet at the place designated by its President.

Article VIII. The Commission may be convened by either of the Contracting Parties, which to this end shall make application to the President.

Article IX. Unless otherwise stipulated between the High Contracting Parties, the Commission shall freely establish its rules of procedure, which in any case must provide for both Parties to be heard. In the absence of unanimity, the procedure established in part III of The Hague Convention of 18 October 1907 for the Pacific Settlement of International Disputes' shall be followed. The decisions of the Commission shall be taken by majority vote of its members, all of whom must be present.

The Parties shall be represented before the Commission by agents, who shall also act as intermediaries between them and the Commission.

Article X. The High Contracting Parties undertake to facilitate the work of the Permanent Conciliation Commission and particularly to supply it to the greatest possible extent with all relevant documents and information, as well as to use the means at their disposal to allow it to proceed in their territory and in accordance with their law to summon and hear witnesses or experts and conduct other proceedings.

Article XI. During the proceedings of the Commission, each of the Commissioners shall receive emoluments the amount of which shall be fixed by agreement between the Contracting Parties.

Each of the two Governments shall pay its own expenses and contribute an equal share to the common expenses of the Commission, including the emoluments provided for in the first paragraph of this article.

Article XII. The task of the Permanent Conciliation Commission shall be to examine the questions in dispute, to collect to this end all necessary information by means of inquiry or otherwise and to endeavour to bring the Parties to an agreement.

It may, after the case has been examined, inform the Parties of the terms of settlement which seem to it suitable and shall in all cases propose a solution to the dispute. The report of the Commission shall not be binding on the Parties with regard to either *de facto* or *de jure* considerations.

Article XIII. The recommendations of the Permanent Conciliation Commission shall be submitted within one year from the date on which it opened its proceedings. The High Contracting Parties may extend this period by mutual agreement.

Article XIV. When the recommendations of the Commission have been submitted to the Parties, they shall have six months to negotiate a settlement on the basis of the solution proposed. If no agreement is reached after six months, the dispute shall be submitted for judicial or arbitral decision, according to the provisions of articles XV *et seq* of this Treaty.

Article XV. Subject to the reservation established in article II, all disputes shall be submitted for a decision, based on law, by the Permanent Court of International Justice or of an arbitral tribunal constituted according to the provisions of this Treaty, if they have not been previously settled by the conciliation procedure and if they arise from:

(a) The existence, interpretation and application of an international treaty concluded between the Parties;

(b) Any point of international law;

(c) The existence of any fact which, if verified, would constitute the breach of an international agreement;

(d) The nature and extent of the reparation due for such a breach.

If there is disagreement between the two Contracting Parties as to whether or not the dispute can be classified under one of the above categories, the Permanent Court of International Justice shall take a decision concerning this preliminary question. The Contracting Parties undertake to accept the opinion of the Court and to proceed accordingly.

If the dispute arises from causes other than those listed in paragraphs (a), (b), (c) and (d) of this article, the Contracting Parties may submit the matter to the Arbitral Tribunal established in this Treaty and authorize it to decide *ex aequo et bono* if no rule of law is applicable.

Article XVI. In cases where recourse is had to settlement by arbitration, each of the Contracting Parties shall nominate an arbitrator, who shall not be a national of the Party appointing him, and shall endeavour to reach agreement with the other Party regarding the nomination of a third arbitrator, who shall not be of the same nationality as either of the other two. This third arbitrator shall be the President of the Tribunal thus constituted.

If there is disagreement with regard to the nomination of the third arbitrator, both Contracting Parties shall request the Permanent Court of International Justice to nominate the President of the Tribunal.

The decisions of the Arbitral Tribunal shall be taken by majority vote and shall be binding on the Parties.

Article XVII. In each individual case which may have to be submitted to the Permanent Court of International Justice or the Arbitral Tribunal, the Contracting Parties shall conclude a special agreement by an exchange of notes, which shall set forth clearly the matter in dispute, the powers conferred on the Court or the Arbitral Tribunal, the periods of time allowed and other conditions agreed upon between them.

If the Parties fail to agree concerning the terms of the special agreement, either Party shall have the right, subject to one month's notice, to submit the matter by means of a simple request directly to the Permanent Court of International Justice.

If the Court finds that the matter is not within its competence according to article XV, it shall so inform the Parties, which may constitute the Arbitral Tribunal in accordance with the provisions of article XV.

Article XVIII. Questions which have already been the subject of a definitive settlement between the Contracting Parties shall not be reopened before the Permanent Court of International Justice or submitted to the Arbitral Tribunal, unless the dispute arises from the interpretation or execution of the settlement.

Article XIX. In the case of a dispute the object of which, according to the internal legislation of one of the Contracting Parties, falls within the competence of its national courts, the question shall not be submitted for settlement by the methods laid down in this Treaty, unless denial of justice is alleged in a decision with final effect by the competent judicial authority.

Article XX. If, in the judgement of the Permanent Court of International Justice or the award of the Arbitral Tribunal, it is declared that a decision made by any authority of one of the Contracting Parties is, wholly or partly, contrary to international treaty law in force between the Parties and if the constitutional law of that Party permits, or only partly permits, the consequences of such decision to be annulled by administrative channels, the Parties agree that the judgement of the Court or the award of the Tribunal shall grant the injured Party equitable satisfaction.

Article XXI. The two Parties undertake to refrain, during the course of any proceedings opened under this Treaty, from any measures likely to aggravate the dispute, and to carry out the provisional measures which, in the case of disputes arising from acts already committed or in the course of being committed, the Permanent Court of International Justice, the Arbitral Tribunal or the Conciliation Commission, according to the circumstances, consider advisable.

Article XXII. The Party causing a dispute by acts which by their nature are to be resolved by the methods for pacific settlement established in this Treaty shall, as soon as the dispute is submitted to one of the procedures provided therein, terminate the effects of such acts and restore the *status quo.*

Article XXIII. Save as otherwise provided in the terms of the special agreement provided for in article XVII of this Treaty, each Contracting Party may request the Arbitral Tribunal which handed down the award to review it. However, such a request may be made only if some fact is brought to light which might have had a decisive effect on the award and which, at the time when the proceedings were closed, was not known to the Tribunal itself or to the Party making the request.

If, for any reason, one or more members of the Tribunal which handed down the award are prevented from taking part in the review, the vacancy or vacancies shall be filled in the manner fixed for the nominations.

The time limit within which a request for review must be submitted shall be prescribed in the arbitral award, unless this is already laid down in the special agreement.

Article XXIV. Unless otherwise agreed by the High Contracting Parties, disputes relating to the interpretation or execution of this Treaty shall be submitted to the Permanent Court of International Justice or to the Arbitral Tribunal, on the application of either Party.

Article XXV. As soon as the legal formalities in each of the Contracting States have been completed, this Treaty shall be ratified and the ratifications shall be exchanged in the city of Caracas as soon as possible.

It shall remain in force for a period of ten years from the date of exchange of ratifications. If it is not denounced six months before the expiry of this period, it shall be renewed by tacit agreement for a further period of ten years and similarly thereafter.

In any event, proceedings pending at the expiry of the current period of the Treaty shall be duly completed.

In Witness Whereof the above-named Plenipotentiaries have signed this Treaty in two copies and have thereto affixed their special seals, at Bogotá, on 17 December 1939.

LUIS LÓPEZ DE MESA
JOSÉ SANTIAGO RODRÍGUEZ

4.1309 Treaty of Peace between the USSR and Finland

Alliance Members: Union of Soviet Socialist Republics and Finland
Signed On: March 12, 1940, in the city of Moscow. In force until June 25, 1941.
Alliance Type: Non-Aggression Pact (Type II)

Source: *British and Foreign State Papers,* vol. 144, p. 383.
Additional Citations: *The American Journal of International Law,* vol. 34, no. 3, Supplement: Official Documents. (July 1940), p. 127–131.

SUMMARY

The Winter War began when the Soviets attacked the Finns on November 30, 1939, just three months after the German invasion of Poland. The Soviets intended to conquer all of Finland but tempered their demands after meeting stiff resistance. The Finns, greatly outnumbered, fought stalling battles in the hopes that the League of Nations or Britain, France, or Sweden would provide defensive aid. On March 6, 1940, a Finnish delegation went to Moscow to negotiate a peace treaty, and during the negotiations the Soviets were able to break through several Finnish lines of defense. Thus, the eventual treaty, signed on March 12, ceded more than 10 percent of Finnish territory to the Soviets. Those Finns residing in the ceded territory were forced to evacuate westward.

The peace treaty included the non-aggression provision in Article 3, but the relatively harsh peace terms inspired great antipathy among the Finnish population. On June 25, 1941, Finland joined Germany in its attack on the Soviet Union.

ALLIANCE TEXT

The Presidium of the Supreme Soviet of the Union of Soviet Socialist Republics on the one hand and the President of the Finnish Republic on the other hand, motivated by the desire to cease the military operations which have arisen between the two countries and to create enduring peaceful mutual relations, and being convinced that the interests of the two contracting parties correspond to the determination of the exact conditions for guaranteeing mutual security including the guarantee of the security of the cities of Leningrad and Murmansk as well as the Murmansk railway, have deemed it necessary to conclude a peace treaty for these purposes and have appointed as their plenipotentiary representatives—

The Presidium of the Supreme Soviet of the Union of Soviet Socialist Republics: Vyacheslav Mikhailovich Molotov, President of the Soviet of People's Commissars of the Union of Soviet Socialist Republics and People's Commissar for Foreign Affairs; Andrei Aleksandrovich Zhdanov, member of the Presidium of the Supreme Soviet of the Union of Soviet Socialist Republics; Aleksandr Mikhailovich Vasilevski, Brigade Commander;

The President of the Finnish Republic: Risto Ryti, the Prime Minister of the Cabinet of the Finnish Republic; Yukho Kusti Paasikivi, Minister; Karl Rudolf Valden, General; Vyaine Voionmaa, Professor.

The said plenipotentiary representatives, after reciprocal presentation of their plenipotentiary documents which were acknowledged to have been drawn up in the appropriate form and in complete order, have agreed with regard to the following:

Article 1. Military operations between the Union of Soviet Socialist Republics and Finland shall cease immediately in accordance with the procedure provided in the protocol attached to the present treaty.

Article 2. The national boundary between the Union of Soviet Socialist Republics and the Finnish Republic shall be established along a new line in accordance with which the entire Karelian isthmus with the city of Viborg (Viipuri) and Viborg bay with its islands; the western and northern shores of Lake Ladoga with the cities of Kexholm, Sortavala, and Suojärvi; a number of islands in the Gulf of Finland; territory to the east of Merkjärvi with the city of Kuolajärvi; and part of the Rybachi and Sredny peninsulas—in accordance with the map attached to the present treaty—shall be included within the territory of the Union of Soviet Socialist Republics.

A more detailed delineation of the boundary line shall be established by a mixed commission of representatives of the contracting parties, and such a commission must be appointed within ten days from the date of signature of the present treaty.

Article 3. The two contracting parties undertake to refrain mutually from any attack upon each other, and not to conclude any alliance or participate in coalitions directed against one of the contracting parties.

Article 4. The Finnish Republic agrees to rent to the Soviet Union for a period of thirty years, with the annual payment of eight million Finmarks by the Soviet Union, Hango peninsula and its surrounding waters within a radius of five miles to the south and east and of three miles to the west and north of the peninsula, as well as a number of islands adjacent to the peninsula—in accordance with the attached map—for the establishment of a naval base there capable of defending the entrance to the Gulf of Finland from aggression, and the Soviet Union shall be granted the right to maintain the requisite number of land and air armed forces there at its own expense for the purpose of defending the naval base.

Within ten days from the moment that the present treaty shall enter into effect, the Finnish Government shall withdraw all of its troops from Hango peninsula, and Hango peninsula with the adjacent islands shall be transferred to the administration of the Union of Soviet Socialist Republics, in accordance with the present article of the treaty.

Article 5. The Union of Soviet Socialist Republics undertakes to withdraw its troops from Petsamo province, which the Soviet state voluntarily ceded to Finland according to the Peace Treaty of 1920.

Finland undertakes—as was provided in the Treaty of 1920—not to maintain warships and other armed ships in the waters along the Finnish coast of the Arctic Ocean, with the exception of armed ships of less than one hundred tons displacement, of which Finland shall have the right to maintain an unlimited number, as well as to maintain not more than fifteen warships and other armed ships the tonnage of which may not exceed four hundred tons each.

Finland undertakes—as was provided by the same treaty—not to maintain submarines and armed aircraft in the said waters.

Likewise Finland undertakes—as was provided by the same treaty—not to construct naval ports, bases for a naval fleet or naval repair shops on this coast on a larger scale than is required for the above-mentioned ships and their armaments.

Article 6. The Soviet Union and its citizens—as was provided by the Treaty of 1920—shall be granted the right of unrestricted transit through Petsamo province to Norway and return, and the Soviet Union shall be granted the right to establish a consulate in Petsamo province.

Freight, which is transported through Petsamo province from the Union of Soviet Socialist Republics to Norway, as well as freight which is transported from Norway to the Union of Soviet Socialist Republics through the same province, shall not be subject to inspection and control, with the exception of that control which is necessary for regulation of transit communication, and shall be exempt from customs duties, transit, and other fees.

The above-mentioned control of freight in transit shall be permitted only in the manner observed in such cases by the established practices of international communication.

Citizens of the Union of Soviet Socialist Republics traveling to Norway or returning from Norway to the Union of Soviet Socialist Republics through Petsamo province, shall have the right of unrestricted travel on the basis of passports issued by the appropriate Soviet organs.

Upon observation of the general regulations in effect, Soviet unarmed aircraft shall have the right to aërial communication between the Union of Soviet Socialist Republics and Norway across Petsamo province.

Article 7. The Finnish Government shall grant to the Soviet Union the right of transit for freight between the Union of Soviet Socialist Republics and Sweden, and for the purpose of the development of this transit along the shortest railway route the Union of Soviet Socialist Republics and Finland consider it necessary for each party to construct, if possible during 1940, on its own territory a railway uniting the city of Kandalaksa with the city of Kemijarvi.

Article 8. Upon the entry of the present treaty into force, trade relations between the contracting parties shall be restored and for this purpose the contracting parties shall enter into negotiations for conclusion of a trade agreement.

Article 9. The present peace treaty shall enter into effect immediately upon its signature and shall be subject to subsequent ratification.

The exchange of instruments of ratification shall take place within ten days in the city of Moscow.

The present treaty is drawn up in two originals, each of which are in the Russian, Finnish, and Swedish languages, in the city of Moscow on March 12, 1940.

V. Molotov

A. Zhdanov

A. Vasilevski

Risto Ryti

Yu. Paasikivi

R. Valden

Vyaine Voionmaa

PROTOCOL TO THE PEACE TREATY OF MARCH 12, 1940

The contracting parties shall establish the following order of cessation of military operations and of removal of troops across the state boundary established by the treaty:

1. Both sides shall cease military operations at 12 o'clock, Leningrad time, on March 13, 1940.

2. Beginning at the time fixed for the cessation of military operations a neutral zone one kilometre wide shall be established between the positions of the advance detachments, and under this arrangement a military unit of one side which is on the territory of the other side, according to the new state boundary, shall be removed to the distance of one kilometre during the course of the first day.

3. The removal of troops across the new state boundary and the advance of troops of the other side up to the boundary shall begin at 10 o'clock on March 15, 1940, along the entire length of the boundary from the Finnish gulf to Lieksa and at 10 o'clock on March 16 north of Lieksa. The removal shall be effected by daily marches of not less than seven kilometres in twenty-four hours, and the advance of troops of the other side shall proceed on the basis of a reckoning whereby there shall be a space of not less than seven kilometres between the rear units of the retreating troops and the advance units of the troops of the other side, moving up to the new boundary.

4. The terms of removal on separate sectors of the state boundary shall be established, in accordance with paragraph 3, as follows:

a) in the sector from the sources of the river Tuntsajoki to Kuolajärvi, to Takala, and to the eastern shore of Lake Juokomojärvi, the removal of troops of both sides shall be completed by 20 o'clock on March 20, 1940;

b) in the sector to the south of Kuhmonieni in the region of Latva, the removal of troops shall be completed by 20 o'clock on March 22, 1940;

c) in the sector from Lopgavaara to Värtsilä to the station Matkaselkä, the removal of troops of both sides shall be completed by 20 o'clock on March 26, 1940;

d) in the sector from the station Matkaselkä to Koitsanlahti, the removal of troops shall be completed by 20 o'clock on March 22, 1940;

e) in the sector from Koitsanlahti to the station Enso, the removal of troops shall be completed by 20 o'clock on March 25, 1940;

f) in the sector from the station Enso to the island Bate, the removal of troops shall be completed by 20 o'clock on March 19, 1940.

5. The evacuation of the troops of the Red Army from the region of Petsamo shall be completed by April 10, 1940.

6. In the removal of troops across the state frontier, the military authorities of both sides shall be obliged to take the necessary measures in the towns and localities transferred to the other side for their preservation, and to take suitable measures to ensure that the towns, villages, military and economic structures (bridges, dams, airdromes, arsenals, warehouses, railroad junctions, manufacturing enterprises, telegraph, electric stations) shall be safe-guarded against damage and destruction.

7. All questions which may arise from the transfer from one side to the other of regions, points, towns, and other objects indicated in point six of the present protocol, shall be decided by representatives of both sides on the spot, for which purpose special delegates shall be designated by the military authorities on each basic line of movement of both armies.

8. The exchange of military prisoners shall be conducted in as short a time as possible after the cessation of military operations, on the basis of a special agreement.

V. Molotov

A. Zhdanov

A. Vasilevski

Risto Ryti

Yu. Paasikivi

R. Valden

Vyaine Voionmaa

4.1310 Treaty of Non-Aggression between His Majesty in Respect of the United Kingdom and the King of Thailand

Alliance Members: Thailand and United Kingdom
Signed On: June 12, 1940, in the city of Bangkok (Thailand). In force until December 1, 1940.
Alliance Type: Neutrality Pact (Type II)

Source: *League of Nations Treaty Series,* vol. 203, p. 422.

SUMMARY

Thailand signed three separate non-aggression and neutrality agreements with France, Britain, and Japan on June 12, 1940. The pact with France, however, was never ratified by the Thais. Instead, the Thai leadership sought to take advantage of French losses to Germany with territorial gains in French-held Laos and Cambodia. This agreement with Britain lasted less than six months because the Thai attack on French Indochina effectively abrogated the commitments to Britain, which was then a close ally of the French.

ALLIANCE TEXT

His Majesty the King of Great Britain, Ireland, and the British Dominions Beyond the Seas, Emperor of India (hereinafter referred to as His Majesty the King and Emperor), and His Majesty the King of Thailand, animated by the desire to ensure peace and convinced that it is in the interests of the two High Contracting Parties to improve and develop the relations between the two countries;

Bearing in mind the international engagements which they have previously undertaken, and which they declare do not constitute an obstacle to the pacific development of their mutual relations and are not in contradiction with the present Treaty;

Desiring to confirm and, as regards their mutual relations, to give effect to the General Pact for the Renunciation of War of the 27th August, 1928:

Have resolved to conclude a Treaty to this end and have designated as their Plenipotentiaries:

His Majesty the King of Great Britain, Ireland and the British Dominions Beyond the Seas, Emperor of India: For the United Kingdom of Great Britain and Northern Ireland: Sir Josiah Crosby, K.B.E., C.I.E., His Majesty's Envoy Extraordinary and Minister Plenipotentiary at Bangkok;

His Majesty the King of Thailand: Major-General Luang Pibulasonggram, His Majesty's President of the Council of Ministers and Minister of Foreign Affairs;

Who, after having communicated to each other their full powers, found in good and due form, have agreed as follows:

Article 1. Each High Contracting Party undertakes not to resort in any case either to war or to any act of violence or of aggression against the other, either alone, or in concert with one, or more than one, third Power, and to respect the territorial integrity of the other High Contracting Party.

Article 2. If one of the High Contracting Parties is the object of an act of war or of aggression on the part of one, or more than one, third Power, the other High Contracting Party undertakes not to give, either directly or indirectly, aid or assistance to the aggressor or aggressors for the duration of the present Treaty.

If one of the High Contracting Parties commits an act of war or of aggression against a third Power, the other High Contracting Party shall have the right to terminate the present Treaty immediately without notice.

Article 3. The engagements set out in Articles I and 2 shall not in any way limit or modify the rights and obligations of either of the High Contracting Parties as a result of agreements concluded by him before the entry into force of the present Treaty, and each High Contracting Party hereby declares that he is not bound by any agreement which carries with it an obligation to participate in an act of war or of aggression committed by a third Power against the other Party.

Article 4. Nothing in the present Treaty shall be held to affect in any way the rights and obligations of the High Contracting Parties under the Covenant of the League of Nations.

Article 5. Each High Contracting Party undertakes to respect in every way the sovereignty or authority of the other High Contracting Party over his territories; he shall not intervene in any way in the internal affairs of such territories and shall abstain from any action calculated to give rise to or assist any agitation, propaganda or attempted intervention aimed against the integrity of any such territory or which has for its purpose the changing by force of the form of government of any such territory.

Article 6. The present Treaty, of which the English and Thai texts are equally valid, shall be ratified and the ratifications shall be exchanged at Bangkok as soon as possible. It shall come into force on the date of the exchange of ratifications and shall remain in force for one year from the day on which either of the High Contracting Parties notifies the other of his intention to terminate the Treaty. This notification shall not in any case be made before the expiration of a period of five years after the date on which the present Treaty enters into force.

In Witness whereof the above-named Plenipotentiaries have signed the present Treaty have affixed thereto their seals.

Done in duplicate at Bangkok this 12th day of the third month in the two thousand four hundred and eighty-third year of the Buddhist Era, corresponding to the 12th day of June in the nineteen hundred and fortieth year of the Christian Era.

(L.S.) J. CROSBY.   *(L.S.) PIBULASONGGRAM.*
Certified true copy:
Delegate of Thailand.
[Signature illegible.]

4.1311 Treaty between Thailand and Japan Concerning the Continuance of Friendly Relations and the Mutual Respect of Each Other's Territorial Integrity

Alliance Members: Thailand and Japan
Signed On: June 12, 1940, in the city of Tokyo. In force until December 21, 1941.
Alliance Type: Neutrality Pact (Type II)

Source: *League of Nations Treaty Series,* vol. 204, p. 132.

SUMMARY

This is one of three non-aggression agreements signed between Thailand and foreign powers on June 12, essentially signaling that Thailand would not participate in the global war. Japan, however, wanted entry into Southeast Asia and seemed willing to grant Thailand as many concessions as necessary to bring the Thais closer to its sphere of influence. Thailand failed to ratify the treaty with France as German victories in western Europe encouraged Thai ambitions for territorial gains in Laos and Cambodia, both French Indo-Chinese territories. The French forces fought hard and forced Japanese intervention to cease hostilities, and the Franco-Thai peace treaty was signed in Tokyo on May 9, 1941. In December of 1941, this non-aggression agreement was replaced by a defense pact between the two countries.

ALLIANCE TEXT

His Majesty the King of Thailand and His Majesty the Emperor of Japan,

Being equally animated by the earnest desire of reaffirming and further strengthening the traditional bonds of friendship between Thailand and Japan, and

Being convinced that the peace and the stability of East Asia is the common concern of the two States,

Have resolved to conclude a treaty, and for that purpose have named as their Plenipotentiaries, that is to say:

His Majesty the King of Thailand: Phya Sri Sena, Knight Grand Cross of the Most Noble Order of the Crown of Thailand, His Majesty's Envoy Extraordinary and Minister Plenipotentiary at the Court of His Majesty the Emperor of Japan;

His Majesty the Emperor of Japan: Hachiro Arita, Zyosanmi, Grand Cordon of the Imperial Order of the Rising Sun, His Imperial Majesty's Minister for Foreign Affairs;

Who, after having communicated to each other their respective full powers, found to be in good and due form, have agreed upon the following articles:

Article I. The High Contracting Parties shall mutually respect each other's territorial integrity and hereby reaffirm the constant peace and the perpetual friendship existing between them.

Article 2. The High Contracting Parties shall mutually maintain friendly contact in order to exchange information, and to consult one another, on any question of common interest that may arise.

Article 3. In the event of one of the High Contracting Parties suffering an attack from any third Power or Powers, the other Party undertakes not to give aid or assistance to the said Power or Powers against the Party attacked.

Article 4. The present Treaty shall be ratified and the ratifications thereof shall be exchanged at Bangkok, as soon as possible.

Article 5. The present Treaty shall come into effect on the date of the exchange of ratifications and shall remain in force for five years from that date.

In case neither of the High Contracting Parties shall have given notice to the other six months before the expiration of the said period of five years of its intention to terminate the Treaty, it shall continue operative until the expiration of one year from the date on which either Party shall have given such notice.

In witness whereof the respective Plenipotentiaries have signed the present Treaty and have hereunto affixed their seals.

Done in duplicate, at Tōkyō, this twelfth day of the third month in the two thousand four hundred and eighty-third year of the Buddhist Era, corresponding to the twelfth day of the sixth month in the fifteenth year of Syōwa, and the twelfth day of June in the nineteen hundred and fortieth year of the Christian Era.

(L. S.) Phya Sri SENA.

(L. S.) Hachiro ARITA.

Certified true copy:

Delegate of Thailand.

(Signature illegible.)

4.1312 Three-Power Pact among Germany, Italy, and Japan (Tripartite Pact)

Alliance Members: Germany, Italy, Japan, Hungary (November 20, 1940), Romania (November 23, 1940), and Bulgaria (March 1, 1941)

Signed On: September 27, 1940, in the city of Berlin. In force until December 11, 1941.

Alliance Type: Defense Pact (Type I)

Source: *League of Nations Treaty Series,* vol. 204, p. 386.

SUMMARY

This agreement formed the basis for the Axis alliance during World War II. The agreement recognized spheres of influence within Europe and Asia and committed all signatories to cooperation against any eventual attack by a third party. Article Three, in many respects, served as a warning to the United States to remain neutral in both the European and Asian theaters of conflict.

The defense pact replaced the Anti-Comintern Pact and the earlier Japanese-German agreement on cooperation. The commitments made in this treaty were renegotiated for joint prosecution of the war after the United States entered the war against Japan in December 1941.

ALLIANCE TEXT

The governments of Germany, Italy and Japan, considering it as a condition precedent of any lasting peace that all nations of the world be given each its own proper place, have decided to stand by and co-operate with one another in regard to their efforts in greater East Asia and regions of Europe respectively wherein it is their prime purpose to establish and maintain a new order of things calculated to promote the mutual prosperity and welfare of the peoples concerned.

Furthermore, it is the desire of the three governments to extend co-operation to such nations in other spheres of the world as may be inclined to put forth endeavours along lines similar to their own, in order that their ultimate aspirations for world peace may thus be realized.

Accordingly, the governments of Germany, Italy and Japan have agreed as follows:

Article One. Japan recognizes and respects the leadership of Germany and Italy in establishment of a new order in Europe.

Article Two. Germany and Italy recognize and respect the leadership of Japan in the establishment of a new order in greater East Asia.

Article Three. Germany, Italy and Japan agree to co-operate in their efforts on aforesaid lines. They further undertake to assist one another with all political, economic and military means when one of the three contracting powers is attacked by a power at present not involved in the European war or in the Chinese-Japanese conflict.

Article Four. With the view to implementing the present pact, joint technical commissions, members which are to be appointed by the respective governments of Germany, Italy and Japan will meet without delay.

Article Five. Germany, Italy and Japan affirm that the aforesaid terms do not in any way affect the political status which exists at present as between each of the three contracting powers and Soviet Russia.

Article Six. The present pact shall come into effect immediately upon signature and shall remain in force 10 years from the date of its coming into force. At the proper time before expiration of said term, the high contracting parties shall at the request of any of them enter into negotiations for its renewal.

In faith whereof, the undersigned duly authorized by their respective governments have signed this pact and have affixed hereto their signatures.

Done in triplicate at Berlin, the 27th day of September, 1940, in the 19th year of the fascist era, corresponding to the 27th day of the ninth month of the 15th year of Showa (the reign of Emperor Hirohito).

4.1313 Treaty of Friendship and Non-Aggression with Yugoslavia

Alliance Members: Union of Soviet Socialist Republics and Yugoslavia
Signed On: April 5, 1941, in the city of Moscow. In force until April 20, 1941.
Alliance Type: Neutrality Pact (Type II)

Source: *British and Foreign State Papers,* vol. 144, p. 878–879.

SUMMARY

This agreement was signed one day before Hitler's attack on Yugoslavia. Germany invaded on April 6, 1941, and the various regions of Yugoslavia surrendered eleven days later, on April 17, in Belgrade. The alliance ended when Yugoslavia was disbanded into several puppet states controlled by the Germans. The Soviets liberated Yugoslavia from German forces in 1945. The pro-Communist partisan movement, led by Josip Broz Tito, came to power as the more influential opposition force during German occupation and subsequently modeled its new constitution after its Soviet counterpart.

ALLIANCE TEXT

The Presidium of the Supreme Soviet of the USSR and His Majesty the King of Yugoslavia, inspired by the friendship existing between their two countries, and convinced that the maintenance of peace is in their common interest, have decided to conclude a treaty of friendship and non-aggression, and for this purpose have appointed as their plenipotentiaries:

The Presidium of the Supreme Soviet of the USSR: V.M. Molotov, Chairman of the Council of People's Commissars and Commissar for Foreign Affairs;

His Majesty the King of Yugoslavia: M. Gavrilovich, Ambassador Extraordinary and Plenipotentiary Minister of Yugoslavia; B. Simich, and Colonel D. Savich

who, having exchanged their credentials, which were found to be in due form and proper order, agreed on the following

provisions:

1. The two contracting parties mutually undertake to refrain from any attack on one another and to respect the independence, sovereign rights, and territorial integrity of the USSR and Yugoslavia.

2. Should either of the contracting parties be subjected to attack from a third State, the other contracting party undertakes to observe a policy of friendship toward it.

3. The present treaty is concluded for a term of five years.

If, one year before the expiration of that term, neither of the contracting parties gives notice of its desire to denounce the present treaty, it shall automatically continue in force for the subsequent five years.

4. The present treaty enters into force upon its signature. The treaty is to be ratified as quickly as possible. The instruments of ratification shall be exchanged in Belgrade.

5. The treaty is drawn up in two copies, each in the Russian and Serbo-Croat languages; the two texts have equal force.

Moscow, 5 April 1941

4.1314 Pact of Neutrality between the Union of Soviet Socialist Republics and Japan

Alliance Members: Union of Soviet Socialist Republics and Japan
Signed On: April 13, 1941, in the city of Moscow. In force until April 5, 1945.
Alliance Type: Neutrality Pact (Type II)

Source: *British and Foreign State Papers,* vol. 144, p. 839.

SUMMARY

This neutrality pact was signed two years after the border war between Japan and the Soviet Union. The agreement led to additional agreements that affirmed Japanese control of Manchukuo and Soviet control over Mongolia. Japan considered renouncing the agreement after signing the Tripartite Pact with Germany and Italy and after Germany's attack on the Soviet Union. However, Japan instead pursued a policy of territorial conquest in Southeast Asia. The Soviets renounced the agreement in April 1945 and attacked Japan in August 1945.

ALLIANCE TEXT

The Presidium of the Supreme Soviet of the Union of Soviet Socialist Republics and His Majesty the Emperor of Japan, guided by a desire to strengthen peaceful and friendly relations between the two countries, have decided to conclude a pact on neutrality, for which purpose they have appointed as their Representatives:

the Presidium of the Supreme Soviet of the Union of Soviet Socialist Republics—Vyacheslav Mikhailovich Molotov, Chairman of the Council of People's Commissars and People's Commissar of Foreign Affairs of the Union of Soviet Socialist Republics;

His Majesty the Emperor of Japan—Yosuke Matsuoka, Minister of Foreign Affairs, Jusanmin, Cavalier of the Order of the Sacred Treasure of the First Class, and Yoshitsugu Tatekawa, Ambassador Extraordinary and Plenipotentiary to the Union of Soviet Socialist Republics, Lieutenant General, Jusanmin, Cavalier of the Order of the Rising Sun of the First Class and the Order of the Golden Kite of the Fourth Class,

who, after an exchange of their credentials, which were found in due and proper form, have agreed on the following:

Article One. Both Contracting Parties undertake to maintain peaceful and friendly relations between them and mutually respect the territorial integrity and inviolability of the other Contracting Party.

Article Two. Should one of the Contracting Parties become the object of hostilities on the part of one or several third powers, the other Contracting Party will observe neutrality throughout the duration of the conflict.

Article Three. The present Pact comes into force from the day of its ratification by both Contracting Parties and remains valid for five years. In case neither of the Contracting Parties denounces the Pact one year before the expiration of the term, it will be considered automatically prolonged for the next five years.

Article Four. The present Pact is subject to ratification as soon as possible. The instruments of ratification shall be exchanged in Tokyo, also as soon as possible.

In confirmation whereof the above-named Representatives have signed the present Pact in two copies, drawn up in the Russian and Japanese languages, and affixed thereto their seals.

Done in Moscow on April 13, 1941, which corresponds to the 13th day of the fourth month of the 16th year of Showa.

V. Molotov,
Yosuke Matsuoka,
Yoshitsugu Tatekawa

4.1315 Treaty of Friendship between Germany and Turkey

Alliance Members: Germany and Turkey
Signed On: June 18, 1941, in the city of Ankara (Turkey). In force until May 8, 1945.
Alliance Type: Non-Aggression Pact (Type II)

Source: *British and Foreign State Papers,* vol. 144, p. 816–817.

SUMMARY

Germany had been pressuring Ankara for Turkey's entry in the war as a German ally. In exchange for additional territories in Thrace and a guarantee of Turkish security, the Germans sought permission to pass through Turkish lands in order to attack the British and French territories of the Middle East. Because of their successful invasions and occupations of most of the Balkan states, Germany and Italy represented immediate threats to the integrity of Turkey. Further, as Turkey was isolated from its Western allies who were themselves involved on several fronts, Turkey expected little aid against an attack. The Turks realized, however, that granting permission to the Germans to pass

through their territory could be considered an act of aggression against their allies, the British and French. Thus, Turkey acquiesced to this non-aggression pact but did not grant permission to the Nazis to pass through its territory. The pact lasted until Germany was divided at the end of the war.

ALLIANCE TEXT

The German Government and the Turkish Republic, inspired by a desire to place relations between the two countries on a basis of mutual confidence and sincere friendship, agreed without prejudice to present obligations of both countries to conclude a treaty.

For this purpose the German Reich Chancellor appointed Ambassador Franz von Papen and the President of the Turkish Republic appointed Foreign Minister Shukru Saracoglu as plenipotentiaries, who, on the basis of full powers accorded them, have agreed on the following declaration:

Article I. Germany and Turkey bind themselves mutually to respect the integrity and inviolability of their territories and will take no measure that is aimed directly or indirectly against the other contracting party.

Article II. Germany and Turkey bind themselves in the future to communicate with each other in friendly manner on all questions affecting their common interests in order to bring about understanding on the treatment of such questions.

Article III. The foregoing treaty will be ratified by articles of ratification, which shall be exchanged forthwith in Berlin. The treaty enters into force on the day of signature and is effective from then onward for a period of ten years.

The parties concluding the treaty will agree at the proper time regarding the question of extending the treaty.

Drawn up in duplicate in the original, in the German and Turkish languages, in Ankara on June 18, 1941.

4.1316 Agreement between the United Kingdom and the Union of Soviet Socialist Republics

Alliance Members: United Kingdom and the Union of Soviet Socialist Republics
Signed On: July 12, 1941, in the city of Moscow. In force until May 26, 1955.
Alliance Type: Defense Pact (Type I)

Source: *League of Nations Treaty Series,* vol. 204, p. 278.

SUMMARY

On June 22, 1941, Hitler's Germany attacked its ally, the Soviet Union. British prime minister Winston Churchill immediately proclaimed his country's support for the Soviets and pledged any assistance necessary to help the Soviets fight against the fascist states. On July 12, this simple assistance agreement was signed in Moscow. Upon gaining its Soviet ally, Britain no longer stood alone against Hitler's Germany.

The initial mutual assistance agreement listed below was greatly expanded on May 22 of the following year, and the British began supplying Soviet forces through Persia. The overall Anglo-Soviet alliance lasted until May 26, 1955, when the Soviets protested British ratification of the Paris Treaty of October 23, 1954, which called for the remilitarization of West Germany.

ALLIANCE TEXT

His Majesty's Government in the United Kingdom and the Government of the Union of Soviet Socialistic Republics have concluded the present Agreement and declare as follows:—

(1) The two Governments mutually undertake to render each other assistance and support of all kinds in the present war against Hitlerite Germany.

(2) They further undertake that during this war they will neither negotiate nor conclude an armistice or treaty of peace except by mutual agreement.

The present Agreement has been concluded in duplicate in the English and Russian languages.

Both texts have equal force.

Moscow, the twelfth of July, nineteen hundred and forty-one.

By authority of His Majesty's Government in the United Kingdom:

R. STAFFORD CRIPPS

His Majesty's Ambassador Extraordinary and Plenipotentiary in the Union of Soviet Socialistic Republics.

By authority of the Government of the Union of Soviet Socialistic Republics:

V. MOLOTOV,

The Deputy President of the Council of People's Commissars and People's Commissar for Foreign Affairs of the Union of Soviet Socialistic Republics.

4.1317 Pact between Japan and Siam Establishing a Military Alliance and Providing for Joint Action as Regards Peace

Alliance Members: Japan and Thailand
Signed On: December 21, 1941, in the city of Bangkok (Thailand). In force until September 2, 1945.
Alliance Type: Defense Pact (Type I)

Source: *British and Foreign State Papers,* vol. 144, p. 838.

SUMMARY

The Japanese launched an invasion of Thailand on December 8, 1941, only hours after the Japanese attack on the United States at Pearl Harbor. The Thai leadership quickly ordered the cessation of all resistance, and the following alliance was signed with the Japanese less than two weeks after the start of the invasion. Thailand then declared war on both Great Britain and the United States.

Japan equipped the Thai military with its aircraft and other armaments, which the Thai eventually used in an invasion of Burma in 1942. This alliance lasted until the end of World War II.

ALLIANCE TEXT

The Government of His Thai Majesty and that of His Imperial Japanese Majesty firmly believing that the establishment of the New Order in East Asia is the only way to bring prosperity in this sphere and the conditions indispensable to restore and reinforce the peace of the world, and with the clear intention to obviate evil influences and other obstacles have concluded the following articles:

1. An alliance is to be established between Japan and Thailand on the basis that each will respect the independence and sovereignty of the other.

2. In case where either Japan or Thailand is engaged in an armed conflict with an outside country or countries Thailand or Japan will take side with the party to this Pact immediately and will accord all assistance politically, economically and militarily.

3. Details relative to the execution of article 2 will be determined by common agreement between the competent authorities of both Japan and Thailand.

4. In case Japan and Thailand are engaged in a common war Japan and Thailand agree that each party will not conclude an armistice or any peace treaty without the complete agreement of both parties.

5. The present Pact will come into force on the date of signature. It will be in force for a period of ten years. Both parties will consult each other on the subject of renewing the said Pact before its expiration.

Signed in duplicate by

H. E. Field-Marshal Plaek Pibulasonggram, the Thai Premier, and Minister of Foreign Affairs, and H. E. Mr. Teiji Tsubokami, the Japanese Ambassador at Bangkok.

4.1318 Tripartite Treaty of Alliance among Iran, the United Kingdom, and the Union of Soviet Socialist Republics

Alliance Members: Iran, United Kingdom, and the Union of Soviet Socialist Republics
Signed On: January 29, 1942, in the city of London. In force until March 2, 1946.
Alliance Type: Defense Pact (Type I)

Source: *The American Journal of International Law,* vol. 36, no. 3, Supplement: Official Documents (July 1942), p. 175–179.

SUMMARY

By August 1941, both the Soviets and Britain had entered Iran in order to establish a supply line for aid to Soviet troops fighting against Germany. The use of foreign troops in Iran proved unsettling, however, for both the Americans and Iran's neighbors, especially in light of previous Russian and British imperial designs on Iran. Thus, this treaty was signed to guarantee the integrity of Iran and confirm that troops would be withdrawn immediately following the end of the war. The treaty lasted until its expiry on March 2, 1946.

ALLIANCE TEXT

His Majesty The King of Great Britain, Ireland and the British Dominions beyond the Seas, Emperor of India, and the Union of Soviet Socialist Republics, on the one hand, and His Imperial Majesty The Shahinshah of Iran, on the other;

Having in view the principles of the Atlantic Charter jointly agreed upon and announced to the world by the President of the United States of America and the Prime Minister of the United Kingdom on the 14th August, 1941, and endorsed by the Government of the Union of Soviet Socialist Republics on the 24th September, 1941, with which His Imperial Majesty the Shahinshah declares his complete agreement and from which he wishes to benefit on an equal basis with other nations of the world; and

Being anxious to strengthen the bonds of friendship and mutual understanding between them; and

Considering that these objects will best be achieved by the conclusion of a Treaty of Alliance;

Have agreed to conclude a treaty for this purpose and have appointed as their plenipotentiaries;

His Majesty The King of Great Britain, Ireland and the British Dominions beyond the seas, Emperor of India, For the United Kingdom of Great Britain and Northern Ireland, His Excellency Sir Reader William Bullard, K.C.M.G., C.I.E., His Majesty's Envoy Extraordinary and Minister Plenipotentiary in Iran.

The Union of Soviet Socialist Republics, His Excellency M. Andre Andreewich Smirnov, Ambassador Extraordinary and Minister Plenipotentiary of the Union of Soviet Socialist Republics in Iran.

His Imperial Majesty The Shahinshah of Iran, His Excellency M. Ali Soheily, Minister for Foreign Affairs.

Who, having communicated their full powers, found in good and due form, have agreed as follows:

Article 1. His Majesty The King of Great Britain, Ireland and the British Dominions beyond the Seas, Emperor of India, and the Union of Soviet Socialist Republics (hereinafter referred to as the Allied Powers) jointly and severally undertake to respect the territorial integrity, sovereignty and political independence of Iran.

Article 2. An alliance is established between the Allied Powers on the one hand and His Imperial Majesty The Shahinshah of Iran on the other.

Article 3. (i) The Allied Powers jointly and severally undertake to defend Iran by all means at their command from all aggression on the part of Germany or any other Power.

(ii) His Imperial Majesty The Shahinshah undertakes—

(a) to co-operate with the Allied Powers with all the means at his command and in every way possible, in order that they may be able to fulfil the above undertaking. The assistance of the Iranian forces shall, however, be limited to the maintenance of internal security on Iranian territory;

(b) to secure to the Allied Powers, for the passage of troops or supplies from one Allied Power to the other or for other similar purposes, the unrestricted right to use, maintain, guard and, in case of military necessity, control in any way that they may require all means of communication throughout Iran, including railways, roads, rivers, aerodromes, ports, pipelines and telephone, telegraph and wireless installations;

(c) to furnish all possible assistance and facilities in obtaining material and recruiting labour for the purpose of the maintenance and improvement of the means of communication referred to in paragraph (b);

(d) to establish and maintain, in collaboration with the Allied Powers, such measures of censorship control as they may require for all the means of communication referred to in paragraph (b).

(iii) It is clearly understood that in the application of paragraph (ii) (b) (c) and (d) of the present article the Allied Powers will give full consideration to the essential needs of Iran.

Article 4. (i) The Allied Powers may maintain in Iranian territory, land, sea and air forces in such number as they consider necessary. The location of such forces shall be decided in agreement with the Iranian Government so long as the strategic situation allows. All questions concerning the relations between the forces of the Allied Powers and the Iranian authorities shall be settled so far as possible in co-operation with the Iranian authorities in such a way as to safeguard the security of the said forces. It is understood that the presence of these forces on Iranian territory does not constitute a military occupation and will disturb as little as possible the administration and the security forces of Iran, the economic life of the country, the normal movements of the population and the application of Iranian laws and regulations.

(ii) A separate agreement or agreements shall be concluded as soon as possible after the entry into force of the present Treaty regarding any financial obligations to be borne by the Allied Powers under the provisions of the present article and of paragraphs (ii) (b), (c) and (d) of Article 3 above in such matters as local purchases, the hiring of buildings and plant, the employment of labour, transport charges, &c. A special agreement shall be concluded between the Allied Governments and the Iranian Government defining the conditions for any transfers to the Iranian Government after the war of buildings and other improvements effected by the Allied Powers on Iranian territory. These agreements shall also settle the immunities to be enjoyed by the forces of the Allied Powers in Iran.

Article 5. The forces of the Allied Powers shall be withdrawn from Iranian territory not later than six months after all hostilities between the Allied Powers and Germany and her associates have been suspended by the conclusion of an armistice or armistices, or on the conclusion of peace between them, whichever date is the earlier. The expression "associates" of Germany means all other Powers which have engaged or may in the future engage in hostilities against either of the Allied Powers.

Article 6. (i) The Allied Powers undertake in their relations with foreign countries not to adopt an attitude which is prejudicial to the territorial integrity, sovereignty, or political independence of Iran, nor to conclude treaties inconsistent with the provisions of the present Treaty. They undertake to consult the Government of His Imperial Majesty The Shahinshah in all matters affecting the direct interests of Iran.

(ii) His Imperial Majesty The Shahinshah undertakes not to adopt in his relations with foreign countries an attitude which is inconsistent with the alliance, nor to conclude treaties inconsistent with the provisions of the present Treaty.

Article 7. The Allied Powers jointly undertake to use their best endeavours to safeguard the economic existence of the Iranian people against the privations and difficulties arising as a result of the present war. On the entry into force of the present Treaty, discussions shall be opened between the Government of Iran and the Governments of the Allied Powers as to the best possible methods of carrying out the above undertaking.

Article 8. The provisions of the present Treaty are equally binding as bilateral obligations between His Imperial Majesty The Shahinshah and each of the two other High Contracting Parties.

Article 9. The present Treaty shall come into force on signature and shall remain in force until the date fixed for the withdrawal of the forces of the Allied Powers from Iranian territory in accordance with Article 5.

In Witness Whereof, the above-named plenipotentiaries have signed the present Treaty and have affixed thereto their seals.

Done at Tehran in triplicate in English, Russian and Persian, all being equally authentic, on the 29th day of January, 1942.

[L.S.] R. W. BULLARD
[L.S.] A. A. SMIRNOV
[L.S.] ALI SOHEILY

EXCHANGE OF NOTES

ANNEX 1

Identic Notes addressed to the Iranian Minister for Foreign Affairs by His Majesty's Minister and the Soviet Ambassador

With reference to Article 6, paragraph (i), of the Treaty of Alliance signed to-day, I have the honour, on behalf of His Majesty's Government in the United Kingdom/the Government of the Union of Soviet Socialist Republics, to assure Your Excellency that my Government interpret the provisions of this clause as being applicable to any peace conference or conferences held at the conclusion of the present war, or other general international conferences. Consequently they consider themselves bound not to approve anything at any such conference which is prejudicial to the territorial integrity, sovereignty or political independence of Iran, and not to discuss at any such conference anything affecting the

direct interests of Iran without consultation with the Government of Iran.

His Majesty's Government/the Government of the Union of Soviet Socialist Republics will further do their best to secure that Iran will be represented on a footing of equality in any peace negotiations directly affecting her interests.

ANNEX 2

Identic Notes addressed to His Majesty's Minister and the Soviet Ambassador by the Iranian Minister for Foreign Affairs

With reference to Article 6, paragraph (ii), of the Treaty of Alliance signed this day, I have the honour, on behalf of the Iranian Government, to assure Your Excellency that the Iranian Government would consider it contrary to their obligations under this clause to maintain diplomatic relations with any State which is in diplomatic relations with neither of the Allied Powers.

ANNEX 3

Identic Notes addressed to the Iranian Minister for Foreign Affairs by His Majesty's Minister and the Soviet Ambassador

I have the honour, on behalf of His Majesty's Government in the United Kingdom/the Government of the Union of Soviet Socialist Republics, to convey to your Excellency the following assurances:—

(1) With reference to Article 3 (ii) (a) of the Treaty of Alliance which has been signed to-day, the Allied Powers will not require of Iran the participation of her armed forces in any war or military operations against any Foreign Power or Powers.

(2) With reference to Article 4 (ii), it is understood that there is no provision in the Treaty which requires that the Iranian Government shall bear the cost of any works which the Allied Powers carry out for their own military ends and which are not necessary for the needs of Iran.

(3) It is understood that Annex 1 will remain in force even if the Treaty ceases to be valid, in accordance with the provisions of Article 9, before peace has been concluded.

4.1319 Australia-New Zealand Agreement

Alliance Members: Australia and New Zealand
Signed On: January 21, 1944, in the city of Canberra (Australia). In force until September 1, 1951.
Alliance Type: Defense Pact (Type I)

Source: *1944 Australian Treaty Series*, p. 2.

SUMMARY

This agreement was in many ways the culmination of growing bilateral cooperation before and during the prosecution of the war in the Pacific. Australia and New Zealand, both British Commonwealth countries, hoped to counter the influence of Britain and the United

States in defining the terms of regional cooperation and security. The announcement of the pact caused concern in Washington, as the United States wanted to wait until the establishment of a general international system before developing any regional security systems. Britain similarly criticized the agreement because it was formed outside the Commonwealth conference system. In the end, the alliance encouraged bilateral cooperation but never gave Australia and New Zealand complete autonomy over South Pacific regional security. Instead, the alliance lasted until it was replaced by the Australia–New Zealand–United States Alliance (ANZUS) in 1951.

ALLIANCE TEXT

His Majesty's Government in the Commonwealth of Australia and His Majesty's Government in the Dominion of New Zealand (hereinafter referred to as "the two Governments") represented as follows

The Government of the Commonwealth of Australia by— the Right Honourable John Curtin, Prime Minister of Australia and Minister for Defence, the Honourable Francis Michael Forde, Minister for the Army, the Honourable Joseph Benedict Chifley, Treasurer and Minister for Post-War Reconstruction, the Right Honourable Herbert Vere Evatt, KC, LLD, Attorney-General and Minister for External Affairs, the Honourable John Albert Beasley, Minister for Supply and Shipping, the Honourable Norman John Oswald Makin, Minister for the Navy and Minister for Munitions, the Honourable Arthur Samuel Drakeford, Minister for Air and Minister for Civil Aviation, the Honourable John Johnstone Dedman, Minister for War Organisation of Industry, the Honourable Edward John Ward, Minister for Transport and Minister for External Territories, and the Honourable Thomas George de Largie D'Alton, High Commissioner for Australia in New Zealand, and

The Government of the Dominion of New Zealand by— the Right Honourable Peter Fraser, Prime Minister of New Zealand, Minister of External Affairs and Minister of Island Territories, the Honourable Frederick Jones, Minister of Defence and Minister in Charge of Civil Aviation, the Honourable Patrick Charles Webb, Postmaster-General and Minister of Labour, and Carl August Berendsen, Esq., CMG, High Commissioner for New Zealand in Australia:

Having met in Conference at Canberra from 17 to 21 January 1944, and desiring to maintain and strengthen the close and cordial relations between the two Governments do hereby enter into this Agreement.

Definition of Objectives of Australian-New Zealand Cooperation

1. The two Governments agree that, as a preliminary, provision shall be made for fuller exchange of information regarding both the views of each Government and the facts in the possession of either bearing on matters of common interest.

2. The two Governments give mutual assurances that, on matters which appear to be of common concern, each Government will, so far as possible, be made acquainted with the mind of the other before views are expressed elsewhere by either.

3. In furtherance of the above provisions with respect to exchange of views and information, the two Governments agree that there shall be the maximum degree of unity in the presentation, elsewhere, of the views of the two countries.

4. The two Governments agree to adopt an expeditious and continuous means of consultation by which each party will obtain directly the opinions of the other.

5. The two Governments agree to act together in matters of common concern in the South-West and South Pacific areas.

6. So far as compatible with the existence of separate military commands, the two Governments agree to co-ordinate their efforts for the purpose of prosecuting the war to a successful conclusion.

Armistice and Subsequent Arrangements

7. The two Governments declare that they have vital interests in all preparations for any armistice ending the present hostilities or any part thereof and also in arrangements subsequent to any such armistice, and agree that their interests should be protected by representation at the highest level on all armistice planning and executive bodies.

8. The two Governments are in agreement that the final peace settlement should be made in respect of all our enemies after hostilities with all of them are concluded.

9. Subject to the last two preceding clauses, the two Governments will seek agreement with each other on the terms of any armistice to be concluded.

10. The two Governments declare that they should actively participate in any armistice Commission to be set up.

11. His Majesty's Government in the Commonwealth of Australia shall set up in Australia, and His Majesty's Government in the Dominion of New Zealand shall set up in New Zealand, armistice and post-hostilities planning committees, and shall arrange for the work of those committees to be coordinated in order to give effect to the views of the respective Governments.

12. The two Governments will collaborate generally with regard to the location of machinery set up under international organisations, such as the United Nations Relief and Rehabilitation Administration, and, in particular, with regard to the location of the Far Eastern Committee of that Administration.

Security and Defence

13. The two Governments agree that, within the framework of a general system of world security, a regional zone of defence comprising the South-West and South Pacific areas shall be established and that this zone should be based on Australia and New Zealand, stretching through the arc of islands north and north-east of Australia, to Western Samoa and the Cook Islands.

14. The two Governments regard it as a matter of cardinal importance that they should both be associated, not only in the membership, but also in the planning and establishment, of the general international organization referred to in the Moscow

Declaration of October 1943, which organisation is based on the principle of the sovereign equality of all peace-loving states and open to membership by all such states, large or small, for the maintenance of international peace and security.

15. Pending the re-establishment of law and order and the inauguration of a system of general security, the two Governments hereby declare their vital interest in the action on behalf of the community of nations contemplated in Article 5 of the Moscow Declaration of October 1943. For that purpose it is agreed that it would be proper for Australia and New Zealand to assume full responsibility for policing or sharing in policing such areas in the South-West and South Pacific as may from time to time be agreed upon.

16. The two Governments accept as a recognized principle of international practice that the construction and use, in time of war by any power of naval, military, or air installations, in any territory under the sovereignty or control of another power, does not, in itself, afford any basis for territorial claims or rights of sovereignty or control after the conclusion of hostilities.

Civil Aviation

17. The two Governments agree that the regulation of all air transport services should be subject to the terms of a convention which will supersede the Convention relating to the Regulation of Aerial Navigation.

18. The two Governments declare that the air services using the international air trunk routes should be operated by an international air transport authority.

19. The two Governments support the principles that

(a) Full control of the international air trunk routes and the ownership of all aircraft and ancillary equipment should be vested in the international air transport authority; and

(b) The international air trunk routes should themselves be specified in the international agreement referred to in the next succeeding clause.

20. The two Governments agree that the creation of the international air transport authority should be effected by an international agreement.

21. Within the framework of the system set up under any such international agreement the two Governments support

(a) The right of each country to conduct all air transport services within its own national jurisdiction, including its own contiguous territories, subject only to agreed international requirements regarding safety, facilities, landing and transit rights for international services and exchange of mails,

(b) The right of Australia and New Zealand to utilise to the fullest extent their productive capacity in respect of aircraft and raw materials for the production of aircraft, and

(c) The right of Australia and New Zealand to use a fair proportion of their own personnel, agencies and materials in operating and maintaining international air trunk routes.

22. In the event of failure to obtain a satisfactory international agreement to establish and govern the use of international air trunk routes, the two Governments will support a system of air trunk routes controlled and operated by Governments of the British Commonwealth of Nations under government ownership.

23. The two Governments will act jointly in support of the above-mentioned principles with respect to civil aviation, and each will inform the other of its existing interests and commitments, as a basis of advancing the policy herein agreed upon.

Dependencies and Territories

24. Following the procedure adopted at the Conference which has just concluded, the two Governments will regularly exchange information and views in regard to all developments in or affecting the islands of the Pacific.

25. The two Governments take note of the intention of the Australian Government to resume administration at the earliest possible moment of those parts of its territories which have not yet been re-occupied.

26. The two Governments declare that the interim administration and ultimate disposal of enemy territories in the Pacific are of vital importance to Australia and New Zealand, and that any such disposal should be effected only with their agreement and as part of a general Pacific settlement.

27. The two Governments declare that no change in the sovereignty or system of control of any of the islands of the Pacific should be effected except as a result of an agreement to which they are parties or in the terms of which they have both concurred.

Welfare and Advancement of Native Peoples of the Pacific

28. The two Governments declare that, in applying the principles of the Atlantic Charter to the Pacific, the doctrine of "trusteeship" (already applicable in the case of the mandated territories of which the two Governments are mandatory powers) is applicable in broad principle to all colonial territories in the Pacific and elsewhere, and that the main purpose of the trust is the welfare of the native peoples and their social, economic and political development.

29. The two Governments agree that the future of the various territories of the Pacific and the welfare of their inhabitants cannot be successfully promoted without a greater measure of collaboration between the numerous authorities concerned in their control, and that such collaboration is particularly desirable in regard to health services and communications, matters of native education, anthropological investigation, assistance in native production, and material development generally.

30. The two Governments agree to promote the establishment, at the earliest possible date, of a regional organization with advisory powers, which could be called the South Seas Regional Commission, and on which, in addition to representatives of Australia and New Zealand, there might be accredited representatives of the Governments of the United Kingdom and the United States of America, and of the French Committee of National Liberation.

31. The two Governments agree that it shall be the function of such South Seas Regional Commission as may be established to secure a common policy on social, economic and political development directed towards the advancement and well-being of the native peoples themselves, and that in particular the Commission shall

(a) Recommend arrangements for the participation of natives in administration in increasing measure with a view to promoting the ultimate attainment of self-government in the form most suited to the circumstances of the native peoples concerned,

(b) Recommend arrangements for material development including production, finance, communications, and marketing,

(c) Recommend arrangements for coordination of health and medical services and education,

(d) Recommend arrangements for maintenance and improvement of standards of native welfare in regard to labour conditions and social services,

(e) Recommend arrangements for collaboration in economic, social, medical and anthropological research, and

(f) Make and publish periodical reviews of progress towards the development of self-governing institutions in the islands of the Pacific and in the improvement of standards of living, conditions of work, education, health and general welfare.

Migration

32. In the peace settlement or other negotiations the two Governments will accord one another full support in maintaining the accepted principle that every government has the right to control immigration and emigration in regard to all territories within its jurisdiction.

33. The two Governments will collaborate, exchange full information, and render full assistance to one another in all matters concerning migration to their respective territories.

International Conference Relating to the South-West and South Pacific

34. The two Governments agree that, as soon as practicable, there should be a frank exchange of views on the problems of security, post-war development, and native welfare between properly accredited representatives of the Governments with existing territorial interests in the South-West Pacific area or in the South Pacific area, or in both, namely, in addition to the two Governments, His Majesty's Government in the United Kingdom, the Government of the United States of America, the Government of the Netherlands, the French Committee of National Liberation and the Government of Portugal, and His Majesty's Government in the Commonwealth of Australia should take the necessary steps to call a conference of the governments concerned.

Permanent Machinery for Collaboration and Cooperation Between Australia and New Zealand

35. The two Governments agree that
(a) Their co-operation for defence should be developed by
(i) Continuous consultation in all defence matters of mutual interest,
(ii) The organization, equipment, training and exercising of the armed forces under a common doctrine,
(iii) Joint planning,
(iv) Interchange of staff, and
(v) The coordination of policy for the production of munitions, aircraft and supply items and for shipping, to ensure the greatest possible degree of mutual aid consistent with the maintenance of the policy of self-sufficiency in local production;
(b) Collaboration in external policy on all matters affecting the peace, welfare and good government of the Pacific should be secured through the exchange of information and frequent ministerial consultation;
(c) The development of commerce between Australia and New Zealand and their industrial development should be pursued by consultation and in agreed cases by joint planning;
(d) There should be cooperation in achieving full employment in Australia and New Zealand and the highest standards of social security both within their borders and throughout the islands of the Pacific and other territories for which they may jointly or severally be wholly or partly responsible, and
(e) There should be cooperation in encouraging missionary work and all other activities directed towards the improvement of the welfare of the native peoples in the islands and territories of the Pacific.

36. The two Governments declare their desire to have the adherence to the objectives set out in the last preceding clause of any other Government having or controlling territories in the Pacific.

37. The two Governments agree that the methods to be used for carrying out the provisions of clause 35 of this Agreement and of other provisions of this Agreement shall be consultation, exchange of information, and, where applicable, joint planning. They further agree that such methods shall include
(a) Conferences of Ministers of State to be held alternately in Canberra and Wellington, it being the aim of the two Governments that these conferences be held at least twice a year,
(b) Conferences of departmental officers and technical experts,
(c) Meetings of standing inter-Governmental committees on such subjects as are agreed to by the two Governments,
(d) The fullest use of the status and functions of the High Commissioner of the Commonwealth of Australia in New Zealand and of the High Commissioner of the

Dominion of New Zealand in Australia,

(e) Regular exchange of information,

(f) Exchange of officers, and

(g) The development of institutions in either country serving the common purposes of both.

Permanent Secretariat

38. In order to ensure continuous collaboration on the lines set out in this agreement and to facilitate the carrying-out of the duties and functions involved, the two Governments agree that a permanent secretariat shall be established in Australia and New Zealand.

39. The secretariat shall be known as the "Australian-New Zealand Affairs Secretariat", and shall consist of a secretariat of the like name to be set up in Australia and a secretariat of the like name to be set up in New Zealand, each under the control of the Ministry of External Affairs in the country concerned.

40. The functions of the Secretariat shall be

(a) To take the initiative in ensuring that effect is given to the provisions of this agreement,

(b) To make arrangements as the occasion arises for the holding of conferences or meetings,

(c) To carry out the directions of those conferences in regard to further consultation, exchange of information, or the examination of particular questions,

(d) To coordinate all forms of collaboration between the two Governments,

(e) To raise for joint discussion and action such other matters as may seem from day to day to require attention by the two Governments, and

(f) Generally to provide for more frequent and regular exchanges of information and views, those exchanges between the two Governments to take place normally through the respective High Commissioners.

41. His Majesty's Government in the Commonwealth of Australia and His Majesty's Government in the Dominion of New Zealand each shall nominate an officer or officers from the staff of their respective High Commissioners to act in closest collaboration with the Secretariat in which they shall be accorded full access to all relevant sources of information.

42. In each country the Minister of State for External Affairs and the Resident High Commissioner shall have joint responsibility for the effective functioning of the Secretariat.

Ratification and Title of Agreement

43. This agreement is subject to ratification by the respective Governments and shall come into force as soon as both Governments have ratified the agreement and have notified each other accordingly. It is intended that such notification will take place as soon as possible after the signing of this agreement.

44. This Agreement shall be known as the "Australian-New Zealand Agreement 1944."

Dated this twenty-first day of January, One thousand nine hundred and forty-four.

Signed on behalf of his signed on behalf of his Majesty's Government in the Majesty's Government in the Commonwealth of Australia: Dominion of New Zealand:

[Signed:]

JOHN CURTIN PETER FRASER

F M FORDE F JONES

J B CHIFLEY P C WEBB

H V EVATT C A BERENDSEN

JOHN A BEASLEY

NORMAN J C MAKIN

ARTHUR S DRAKEFORD

JOHN J DEDMAN

ED J WARD

TOM D'ALTON

4.1320 Treaty of Alliance and Mutual Assistance between the U.S.S.R. and France

Alliance Members: France and the Union of Soviet Socialist Republics
Signed On: December 10, 1944, in the city of Moscow. In force until May 7, 1955.
Alliance Type: Defense Pact (Type I)

Source: *British and Foreign State Papers,* vol. 149, p. 632.

SUMMARY

In this agreement France and the Soviet Union pledged to eliminate any possible future threat from Germany after the war and to cooperate together should a resurgent Germany attack either alliance partner. The treaty reinforces the Anglo-Soviet defense pact signed in 1941, as the Western allies hoped that overlapping alliances would improve regional security structures. The defense pact lasted until May 27, 1955, when the Soviets protested the Paris Treaty of October 23, 1954, which called for the remilitarization of West Germany.

ALLIANCE TEXT

The Presidium of the Supreme Soviet of the Union of Soviet Socialist Republics and the Provisional Government of the French Republic, determined to prosecute jointly and to the end the war against Germany, convinced that once victory is achieved, the reestablishment of peace on a stable basis and its prolonged maintenance in the future will be conditioned upon the existence of close collaboration between them and with all the United Nations; having resolved to collaborate in the cause of the creation of an international system of security for the effective maintenance of general peace and for insuring the harmonious development of relations between nations; desirous of confirming the mutual obligations resulting from the exchange of letters of September 20, 1941, concerning joint actions in the war against Germany; convinced that the conclusion of an alliance between the U.S.S.R. and France corresponds to the sentiments and interests of both peoples, the demands of war, and the requirements of peace and economic reconstruction in full conformity with the aims which the United Nations have set themselves, have decided to conclude a Treaty to this effect and appointed as their plenipotentiaries:

The Presidium of the Supreme Soviet of the Union of Soviet Socialist Republics—Vyacheslav Mikhailovich Molotov, People's Commissar of Foreign Affairs of the U.S.S.R.;

The Provisional Government of the French Republic—Georges Bidault, Minister of Foreign Affairs;

Who after exchange of their credentials, found in due form, agreed upon the following:

Article I. Each of the high contracting parties shall continue the struggle on the side of the other party and on the side of the United Nations until final victory over Germany. Each of the high contracting parties undertakes to render the other party aid and assistance in this struggle with all the means at its disposal.

Article II. The high contracting parties shall not agree to enter into separate negotiations with Germany or to conclude without mutual consent any armistice or peace treaty either with the Hitler government or with any other government or authority set up in Germany for the purpose of the continuation or support of the policy of German aggression.

Article III. The high contracting parties undertake also, after the termination of the present war with Germany, to take jointly all necessary measures for the elimination of any new threat coming from Germany, and to obstruct such actions as would make possible any new attempt at aggression on her part.

Article IV. In the event either of the high contracting parties finds itself involved in military operations against Germany, whether as a result of aggression committed by the latter or as a result of the operation of the above Article III, the other party shall at once render it every aid and assistance within its power.

Article V. The high contracting parties undertake not to conclude any alliance and not to take part in any coalition directed against either of the high contracting parties.

Article VI. The high contracting parties agree to render each other every possible economic assistance after the war, with a view to facilitating and accelerating reconstruction of both countries, and in order to contribute to the cause of world prosperity.

Article VII. The present treaty does not in any way affect obligations undertaken previously by the high contracting parties in regard to third states in virtue of published treaties.

Article VIII. The present treaty, whose Russian and French texts are equally valid, shall be ratified and ratification instruments shall be exchanged in Paris as early as possible. It comes into force from the moment of the exchange of ratification instruments and shall be valid for 20 years. If the treaty is not denounced by either of the high contracting parties at least one year before the expiration of this term, it shall remain valid for an unlimited time; each of the contracting parties will be able to terminate its operation by giving notice to that effect one year in advance.

In confirmation of which, the above plenipotentiaries signed the present treaty and affixed their seals to it.

Done in Moscow in two copies, December 10, 1944.

On the authorization of the Presidium of the Supreme Soviet of the U.S.S.R.

MOLOTOV

On the authorization of the Provisional Government of the French Republic.

BIDAULT

4.1321 Act of Chapultepec

Alliance Members: United States, Cuba, Haiti, Dominican Republic, Mexico, Guatemala, Honduras, Nicaragua, Costa Rica, Panama, Colombia, Venezuela, Ecuador, Peru, Brazil, Bolivia, Paraguay, Chile, Uruguay, and Argentina
Signed On: March 6, 1945, in the city of Mexico City. In force until August 14, 1945.
Alliance Type: Defense Pact (Type I)

Source: *1945 United States Department of State Bulletin,* p. 339.

SUMMARY

The Act of Chapultepec declared the incompatibility of communism with the Inter-American peace system and served as a preliminary treaty of collective self-defense during the final stages of World War II. Comprising three parts, the agreement declared unanimity in collective self-defense; recommended a large collective defense treaty be signed following the war; and confirmed that the agreement concerned regional affairs only. The agreement expired with the end of World War II, but the Chapultepec Conference formed the basis for the agreement that became the Rio Pact of 1947.

ALLIANCE TEXT

WHEREAS:

The peoples of the Americas, animated by a profound love of justice, remain sincerely devoted to the principles of international law;

It is their desire that such principles, notwithstanding the present difficult circumstances, prevail with even greater force in future international relations;

The inter-American conferences have repeatedly proclaimed certain fundamental principles, but these must be reaffirmed at a time when the juridical bases of the community of nations are being re-established;

The new situation in the world makes more imperative than ever the union and solidarity of the American peoples, for the defense of their rights and the maintenance of international peace;

The American states have been incorporating in their international law, since 1890, by means of conventions, resolutions and declarations, the following principles:

a) The proscription of territorial conquest and the non-recognition of all acquisitions made by force (First International Conference of American States, 1890);

b) The condemnation of intervention by one State in the

internal or external affairs of another (Seventh International Conference of American; States, 1933, and Inter-American Conference for the Maintenance of Peace, 1936);

c) The recognition that every war or threat of war affects directly or indirectly all civilized peoples, and endangers the great principles of liberty and justice which constitute the American ideal and the standard of American international policy (Inter-American Conference for the Maintenance of Peace, 1936);

d) The system of mutual consultation in order to find means of peaceful cooperation in the event of war or threat of war between American countries (Inter-American Conference for the Maintenance of Peace, 1936);

e) The recognition that every act susceptible of disturbing the peace of America affects each and every one of the American nations and justifies the initiation of the procedure of consultation (Inter-American Conference for: the Maintenance of Peace, 1936);

f) The adoption of conciliation, unrestricted arbitration, or the application of international justice, in the solution of any difference or dispute between American nations, whatever its nature or origin (Inter-American Conference for the Maintenance of Peace, 1936);

g) The recognition that respect for the personality, sovereignty and independence of each American State constitutes the essence of international order sustained by continental solidarity, which historically has been expressed and sustained by declarations and treaties in force (Eighth International Conference of American States, 1938);

h) The affirmation that respect for and the faithful observance of treaties constitute the indispensable rule for the development of peaceful relations between States, and that treaties can only be revised by agreement of the contracting parties (Declaration of American Principles, Eighth International Conference of American States, 1938);

i) The proclamation that, in case the peace, security or territorial integrity of any American republic is threatened by acts of any nature that may impair them, they proclaim their common concern and their determination to make effective their solidarity, coordinating their respective sovereign wills by means of the procedure of consultation, using the measures which in each case the circumstances may make advisable (Declaration of Lima, Eighth International Conference of American States, 1938);

j) The declaration that any attempt on the part of a non-American state against the integrity or inviolability of the territory, the sovereignty or the political independence of an American State shall be considered as an act of aggression against all the American States (Declaration XV of the Second Meeting of the Ministers of Foreign Affairs, Habana, 1940);

The furtherance of these principles, which the American States have constantly practiced in order to assure peace and solidarity among the nations of the Continent, constitutes an effective means of contributing to the general system of world security and of facilitating its establishment;

The security and solidarity of the Continent are affected to the same extent by an act of aggression against any of the American States by a non-American State, as by an act of aggression of an American State against one or more American States;

Part I

The Governments Represented at the Inter-American Conference on Problems of War and Peace
Declare:

1. That all sovereign States are juridically equal among themselves.

2. That every State has the right to the respect of its individuality and independence, on the part of the other members of the international community.

3. That every attack of a State against the integrity or the inviolability of the territory, or against the sovereignty or political independence of an American State, shall, conformably to Part III hereof, be considered as an act of aggression against the other States which sign this Act. In any case invasion by armed forces of one State into the territory of another trespassing boundaries established by treaty and demarcated in accordance therewith shall constitute an act of aggression.

4. That in case acts of aggression occur or there are reasons to believe that an aggression is being prepared by any other State against the integrity or inviolability of the territory, or against the sovereignty or political independence of an American State, the States signatory to this Act will consult among themselves in order to agree upon the measures it may be advisable to take.

5. That during the war, and until the treaty recommended in Part II hereof is concluded, the signatories of this Act recognize that such threats and acts of aggression, as indicated in paragraphs 3 and 4 above, constitute an interference with the war effort of the United Nations, calling for such procedures, within the scope of their constitutional powers of a general nature and for war, as may be found necessary, including: recall of chiefs of diplomatic missions; breaking of diplomatic relations; breaking of consular relations; breaking of postal, telegraphic, telephonic, radio-telephonic relations; interruption of economic, commercial and financial relations; use of armed force to prevent or repel aggression.

6. That the principles and procedure contained in this Declaration shall become effective immediately, inasmuch as any act of aggression or threat of aggression during the present state of war interferes with the war effort of the United Nations to obtain victory. Henceforth, and to the end that the principles and procedures herein stipulated shall conform with the constitutional processes of each Republic, the respective Governments shall take the necessary steps to perfect this instrument in order that it shall be in force at all times.

Part II

The Inter-American Conference on Problems of War and Peace Recommends:

That for the purpose of meeting threats or acts of aggression against any American Republic following the establishment of peace, the Governments of the American Republics consider the conclusion, in accordance with their constitutional processes, of a treaty establishing procedures whereby such threats or acts may be met by the use, by all or some of the signatories of said treaty, of any one or more of the following measures: recall of chiefs of diplomatic missions; breaking of diplomatic relations; breaking of consular relations; breaking of postal, telegraphic, telephonic, radio-telephonic relations; interruption of economic, commercial and financial relations; use of armed force to prevent or repel aggression.

Part III

The above Declaration and Recommendation constitute a regional arrangement for dealing with such matters relating to the maintenance of international peace and security as are appropriate for regional action in this Hemisphere. The said arrangement, and the pertinent activities and procedures, shall be consistent with the purposes and principles of the general international organization, when established.

This agreement shall be known as the "Act of Chapultepec."

4.1322 League of Arab States (Arab League)

Alliance Members: Egypt, Iraq, Jordan, Lebanon, Saudi Arabia, Syria, Yemen (May 5, 1945); Libya (March 28, 1953); Sudan (January 19, 1956); Morocco and Tunisia (October 1, 1958); Kuwait (July 20, 1961); Algeria (August 16, 1962); the United Arab Emirates [UAE] (June 12, 1972); Bahrain and Qatar (September 11, 1971); Oman (September 29, 1971); Mauritania (November 26, 1973); Somalia (February 14, 1974); Palestine (September 9, 1976); Djibouti (April 9, 1977); Comoros (November 20, 1993); Eritrea (observer since 2003); Venezuela (observer since 2006); India (observer since 2007)
Signed On: March 22, 1945, in the city of Cairo. In force as of date of publication of this volume.
Alliance Type: Entente (Type III)

Source: League of Arab States, http://arableagueonline.org/.

SUMMARY

Formed initially by Egypt, Iraq, Jordan, Lebanon, Saudi Arabia, and Syria, the League of Arab States was created to encourage cooperation among Arab states and to protect the sovereignty and territorial integrity of member states. The organization created by the league has served as a forum for the airing of disputes among members and has provided the necessary foundation for the creation of several additional treaties encouraging cooperation and integration. In this way, the activities of the league are similar to organizations such as the Council of Europe, the African Union, and the Organization of American States. Sixteen additional countries have joined the League since its inception.

ALLIANCE TEXT

His Excellency the President of the Syrian Republic, His Royal Highness the Emir of Transjordan, His Majesty the King of Iraq, His Majesty the King of Saudi-Arabia, His Excellency the President of the Lebanese Republic, His Majesty the King of Egypt, His Majesty the King of Yemen,

With a view to strengthen the close relations and numerous ties which bind the Arab States,

And out of concern for the cementing and reinforcing of these bonds on the basis of respect for the independence and sovereignty of these States,

And in order to direct their efforts toward the goal of the welfare of all the Arab States, their common weal, the guarantee of their future and the realization of their aspirations,

And in response to Arab public opinion in all the Arab countries,

Have agreed to conclude a pact to this effect and have delegated as their plenipotentiaries those whose names are given below:—

The President of the Syrian Republic Has Delegated for Syria:—H.E. Faris al Khury, President of the Council of Ministers. H.E. Jamil Mardam Bey, Minister of Foreign Affairs.

H.R.H. the Emir of Transjordan has Delegated for Transjordan:—H.E. Samir al Rifai Pasha, President of the Council of Ministers. H.E. Said al Mufti Pasha, Minister of the Interior. Sulaiman al Nabulsi Bey, Secretary of the Council of Ministers.

H.M. the King of Iraq has Delegated for Iraq:—H.E. Arshad al Umary, Minister of Foreign Affairs. H.E. Aly Jawdat al Ayyubi, Minister Plenipotentiary of Iraq in Washington. H.E. Tahsin al Askari, Minister Plenipotentiary of Iraq in Cairo.

H.M. the King of Saudi-Arabia has Delegated for Saudi-Arabia:—H.E. Sheikh Yusuf Yasin, Assistant Minister of Foreign Affairs. H.E. Khair al din al Zirikly, Counsellor of the Saudi Arabian Legation in Cairo.

The President of the Lebanese Republic has Delegated for Lebanon:—H.E. Abd Alhamid Karami, President of the Council of Ministers. H.E. Yusuf Salem, Minister Plenipotentiary of Lebanon in Cairo.

H.M. the King of Egypt has Delegated for Egypt:—H.E. Mahmoud Fahmy el Nokrachi Pasha, President of the Council of Ministers. H.E. Abd el Hamid Badawi Pasha, Minister of Foreign Affairs. H.E. Mohamed Hussein Heikal Pasha, President of the Senate. H.E. Makram Ebeid Pasha, Minister of finance. H.E. Mohamed Hafez Ramadan Pasha, Minister of Justice. H.E. Abd Al Razzak Ahmad Al Saniiury Bey, Minister of Education. H.E. Abd Al Rahman Azzam Bey, Minister Plenipotentiary in the Ministry of Foreign Affairs.

H.M. the King of Yemen has Delegated for Yemen:—

Who, after the exchange of the credentials granting them full authority, which were found valid and in proper form, have agreed upon the following:

Article 1.–The league of Arab State shall be composed of the independent Arab states that have signed this Pact.

Every independent Arab State shall have the right to adhere to the League. Should it desire to adhere, it shall present an application to this effect which shall be filed with the permanent General Secretariat and submitted to the Council at its first meeting following the presentation of the application.

Article 2.–The purpose of the League is to draw closer the relations between member States and co-ordinate their political activities with the aim of realizing a close collaboration between them, to safeguard their independence and sovereignty, and to consider in a general way the affairs and interests of the Arab countries:

It also has among its purposes a close co-operation of the member States with due regard to the structure of each of these States and the conditions prevailing therein, in the following matters:—

(a) Economic and financial matters, including trade, customs, currency, agriculture and industry.

(b) Communications, including railways, roads, aviation, navigation, and posts and telegraphs.

(c) Cultural matters.

(d) Matters connected with nationality, passports, visas, execution of judgments and extradition.

(e) Social welfare matters.

(f) Health matters.

Article 3.–The league shall have a Council composed of the representatives of the member States. Each state shall have a single vote, regardless of the number of its representatives.

The Council shall be entrusted with the function of realizing the purpose of the League and of supervising the execution of the agreements concluded between the member States on matters referred to in the preceding article or on other matters.

It shall also have the function of determining the means whereby the league will collaborate with the international organization which may be created in the future to guarantee peace and security and organize economic and social relations.

Article 4.–A special Committee shall be formed for each of the categories enumerated in Article 2, on which the members States shall be represented. These committees shall be entrusted with establishing the basis and scope of co-operation in the form of draft agreements which shall be submitted to the Council for its consideration preparatory to their being submitted to the States referred to.

Delegates representing the other Arab countries may participate in these committees as members. The Council shall determine the circumstances in which the participation of these representatives shall be allowed as well as the basis of the representation.

Article 5.–The recourse to force for the settlement of disputes between two or more member States shall not be allowed. Should there arise among them a dispute which does not involve the independence of a State, its sovereignty or its territorial integrity, and should the two contending parties apply to the Council for the settlement of this dispute, the decision of the Council shall then be effective and obligatory.

In such case, the States among whom the dispute has arisen shall not participate in the deliberations and decisions of the Council.

The Council shall mediate in a dispute which may lead to war between two member States or between a member State and another State in order to conciliate them.

The decisions relating to arbitration and mediation shall be taken by a majority vote.

Article 6.–In case of aggression or threat of aggression by a State against a member State, the attacked or threatened with attack may request an immediate meeting of the Council.

The Council shall determine the necessary measures to repel this aggression. Its decision shall be taken unanimously. If the aggression is committed by a member State the vote of that State will not be counted in determining unanimity.

If the aggression is committed in such a way as to render the Government of the State attacked unable to communicate with the Council, the representative of that State in the Council may request the Council to convene for the purpose set forth in the preceding paragraph. If the representative is unable to communicate with the Council, it shall be the right of any member State to request a meeting of the Council.

Article 7.–The decisions of the Council taken by a unanimous vote shall be binding upon all member States of the League; those that are reached by a majority vote shall bind only those accept them.

In both cases the decisions of the Council shall be executed in each State in accordance with the fundamental structure of that State.

Article 8.–Every member State of the League shall respect the form of government obtaining in the other States of the League, and shall recognize the form of government obtaining as one of the rights of those States, and shall pledge itself not to take any action tending to change that form.

Article 9.–The States of the Arab League that are desirous of establishing among themselves closer collaboration and stronger bonds than those provided for in the present Pact, may conclude among themselves whatever agreements they wish for this purpose.

The treaties and agreements already concluded or that may be concluded in the future between a member State and any other State, shall not be binding on the other members.

Article 10.–The permanent seat of the League of Arab States shall be Cairo. The Council of the League may meet at any other place it designates.

Article 11.–The Council of the League shall meet in ordinary session twice a year, during the months of March and October. It shall meet in extraordinary session at the request of two member States whenever the need arises.

Article 12.–The League shall have a permanent General Secretariat, composed of a Secretary-General, Assistant Secretaries and an adequate number of officials.

The Secretary-General shall be appointed by the Council upon the vote of two-thirds of the States of the League. The

Assistant Secretaries and the principal officials shall be appointed by the Secretary-General with the approval of the Council.

The Council of the League shall establish an internal organization for the General Secretariat as well as the conditions of service of the officials.

The Secretary-General shall have the rank of Ambassador; and the Assistant Secretaries the rank of Ministers Plenipotentiary.

The first Secretary-General of the League is designated in an annex to the present Pact.

Article 13.–The Secretary-General shall prepare the draft of the budget of the League and shall submit it for approval to the Council before the beginning of each fiscal year.

The Council shall determine the share of each of the States of the League in the expenses. It shall be allowed to revise the share if necessary.

Article 14.–The members of the Council of the League, the members of its Committees and such of its officials as shall be designated in the internal organization, shall enjoy, in the exercise of their duties, diplomatic privileges and immunities.

The premises occupied by the institutions of the League shall be inviolable.

Article 15.–The Council shall meet the first time at the invitation of the Head of the Egyptian Government. Later meeting shall be convoked by the Secretary General.

In each ordinary session the representatives of the States of the League shall assume the chairmanship of the Council in rotation.

Article 16.–Except for the cases provided for in the present Pact, a majority shall suffice for decisions by the Council effective in the following matters:—

(a) Matters concerning the officials.
(b) The approval of the budget of the League.
(c) The internal organization of the Council, the Committees and the General Secretariat.
(d) The termination of the sessions.

Article 17.–The member States of the League shall file with the General Secretariat copies of all treaties and agreements which they have concluded or will conclude with any other State, whether a member of the League or otherwise.

Article 18.–If one of the member States intends to withdraw from the League, the Council shall be informed of its intention one year before the withdrawal takes effect.

The Council of the League may consider any State that is not fulfilling the obligations resulting from this Pact as excluded from the League, by a decision taken by unanimous vote of all the States except the State referred to.

Article 19.–The present Pact may be amended with the approval of two-thirds of the members of the League in particular for the purpose of strengthening the ties between them, of creating an Arab Court of Justice, and of regulating the relations of the League with the international organizations that may be created in the future guarantee security and peace.

No decision shall be taken as regards an amendment except in the session following that in which it is proposed.

Any State that does not approve an amendment may withdraw from the League when the amendment becomes effective, without being bound by the provisions of the preceding article.

Article 20.–The present Pact and its annexes shall be ratified in accordance with the fundamental form of government in each of the contracting States.

The instruments of ratification shall be filed with the General Secretariat and the present Pact shall become binding on the States that ratify in fifteen days after the Secretary-General receives instruments of ratification from four States.

The present Pact has been drawn up in the Arabic Language in Cairo and dated 8 Rabi al'Thani 1364 (March 22, 1945), in a single text which shall be deposited with the General Secretariat.

A certified copy shall be sent to each of the States of the League.

4.1323 Treaty of Friendship, Mutual Aid, and Postwar Cooperation between the Soviet Union and Yugoslavia

Alliance Members: Union of Soviet Socialist Republics and Yugoslavia
Signed On: April 11, 1945, in the city of Moscow. In force until June 28, 1948.
Alliance Type: Defense Pact (Type I)

Source: *Russia and the Communist Countries: Documents, 1946–71*, p. 70–72.

SUMMARY

This agreement was one of several treaties of friendship and alliance that the Soviets signed at the end of World War II. After Belgrade's liberation by Soviet forces when the Soviets forced out the Germans, this agreement was a natural outgrowth of the cooperative relationship between Joseph Stalin and Yugoslavia's Josip Broz Tito. That relationship soured, however, when Tito declared Yugoslavia's neutrality during the cold war and began pursuing a policy of isolation in 1948. The move toward nonalignment not only ended this alliance but also increased the threat of Soviet intervention. Tense relations persisted until Nikita Khrushchev reconciled with Tito in 1956.

ALLIANCE TEXT

The Presidium of the Supreme Soviet of the Union of Soviet Socialist Republics and the Regency Council of Yugoslavia,

Resolved to bring the war against the German aggressors to its final conclusion; desirous still further to consolidate the friendship existing between the peoples of the Soviet Union and Yugoslavia, which together are fighting against the common enemy—Hitlerite Germany; desirous to ensure close cooperation between the peoples of the two countries and all United Nations during the war and in peacetime, and to make their contribution to the post-war organization of security and peace; convinced that the consolidation of friendship between the Soviet Union and Yugoslavia corresponds to the vital interests of the two peoples, and best serves the further economic development of the two countries, have . . . agreed on the following:

Article 1. Each of the Contracting Parties will continue the struggle in cooperation with one another and with all the United Nations against Germany until final victory. The two Contracting Parties pledge themselves to render each other military and other assistance and support of every kind.

Article 2. If one of the Contracting Parties should in the post-war period be drawn into military operations against Germany, which would have resumed her aggressive policy, or against any other State which would have joined Germany either directly or in any other form in a war of this nature, the other Contracting Party shall immediately render military or any other support with all the means available.

Article 3. The two Contracting Parties state that they will participate, in the spirit of closest cooperation, in all international activities designed to ensure peace and security of peoples, and will make their contribution for attaining these lofty purposes.

The Contracting Parties state that the application of the present Treaty will be in accordance with international principles in the acceptance of which they have participated.

Article 4. Each of the Contracting Parties undertakes not to conclude any alliance and not to take part in any coalition directed against the other party.

Article 5. The two Contracting Parties state that after the termination of the present war they will act in a spirit of friendship and cooperation for the purpose of further developing and consolidating the economic and cultural ties between the peoples of the two countries.

Article 6. The present Treaty comes into force immediately it is signed and is subject to ratification in the shortest possible time. The exchange of ratification documents will be effected in Belgrade as early as possible.

The present Treaty will remain in force for a period of twenty years. If one of the Contracting Parties at the end of this twenty years period does not, one year before the expiration of this term, announce its desire to renounce the Treaty, it will remain in force for the following five years, and so on each time until one of the Contracting Parties gives written notice of its desire to terminate the efficacy of the Treaty one year before the termination of the current five-year period.

4.1324 Treaty of Friendship, Mutual Assistance, and Postwar Collaboration between the Soviet Union and Polish Republic

Alliance Members: Union of Soviet Socialist Republics and Poland
Signed On: April 21, 1945, in the city of Moscow. In force until April 7, 1989.

Alliance Type: Defense Pact (Type I)

Source: *United Nations Treaty*, no. 70.

SUMMARY

This alliance was signed in the final days of World War II as Polish troops were fighting alongside the Soviet Red Army in order to push Germany out of Poland. The alliance was formed with the Polish Communists rather than the Polish government in exile in Britain, and this became a minor issue during the postwar period. Key leaders of the exiled government returned to form a unified government, mostly to prevent complete domination of the government by Soviet occupation forces. Their goal was not realized, however, and Communist Party control of Poland lasted until the final days of the Soviet Union. This alliance, amended several times during the cold war, was considered dead when the Communist Poles relinquished power following an accord with Poland's Solidarity leader, Lech Walesa.

ALLIANCE TEXT

The President of the National Council of the People's Republic of Poland and the Presidium of the Supreme Soviet of the Union of Soviet Socialist Republics,

Being inflexibly resolved jointly to carry on the war against the German aggressor until complete and final victory is achieved;

Desiring, at this critical turning-point in the history of Soviet-Polish relations, to consolidate the friendly, allied co-operation established between Poland and the USSR during the common struggle against German imperialism;

Being persuaded that the further strengthening of good-neighbourly and friendly relations between Poland and the adjacent Soviet Union is in accordance with the vital interests of the Polish and Soviet peoples;

Being convinced that the maintenance of friendship and close co-operation between the Polish and Soviet peoples will further the successful economic development of both countries, both during and after the war;

Being anxious to give all possible support after the war to the cause of international peace and security;

Have resolved for this purpose to conclude the present Treaty and have appointed as their Plenipotentiaries:

The President of the National Council of the People's Republic of Poland: Edward Osóbka-Morawski, Prime Minister and Minister of Foreign Affairs of the Republic of Poland;

The Presidium of the Supreme Soviet of the Union of Soviet Socialist Republics: Joseph Vissarionovich Stalin, Chairman of the Council of People's Commissars of the USSR,

Who, after having exchanged their full powers, found in good and due form, have agreed on the following provisions:

Article 1. The High Contracting Parties will continue, jointly with all the United Nations, the fight against Germany until final victory. In this fight the High Contracting Parties agree to render each other military and other assistance by all the means in their power.

Article 2. Believing that it is necessary, in the interests of the security and prosperity of the Polish and Soviet peoples, to maintain and strengthen a firm and lasting friendship both during and after the war, the High Contracting Parties will strengthen friendly co-operation between both countries in accordance with the principles of mutual respect for their independence and sovereignty and also of non-intervention in the internal affairs of the other State.

Article 3. The High Contracting Parties agree to take, on the conclusion also of the present war with Germany, all joint action within their power to obviate any threat of further aggression by Germany or any other Power which might be associated with Germany either directly or in any other way.

To this end the High Contracting Parties will, in a spirit of sincerest co-operation, participate in all international action for ensuring international peace and security and will fully contribute to the realization of these lofty aims.

In carrying out the present Treaty, the High Contracting Parties will act conformably to the international principles, in the adoption of which both Contracting Parties participated.

Article 4. Should either of the High Contracting Parties during the post-war period be involved in hostilities with a Germany, which had renewed her policy of aggression, or with any other State which had joined Germany in such a war either directly or in any other way, the other High Contracting Party shall without delay extend to the Contracting Party involved in hostilities military and other assistance and support with all the means at its disposal.

Article 5. The High Contracting Parties agree not to conclude without each other's consent any armistice or peace treaty either with the Hitlerite Government or with any other authority in Germany violating or likely to violate the independence, territorial integrity or security of either High Contracting Party.

Article 6. The High Contracting Parties respectively agree not to enter into any alliance or take part in any coalition directed against the other High Contracting Party.

Article 7. The High Contracting Parties will continue, on the termination of the present war, also to co-operate in a spirit of friendship with a view to the further development and strengthening of the economic and cultural ties between the two countries, and to assist one another in restoring the national economies of both countries.

Article 8. The present Treaty shall come into force immediately upon signature and shall be subject to ratification in the shortest possible time. The instruments of ratification will be exchanged in Moscow as soon as possible.

The present Treaty shall remain in force for twenty years from the date of signature. If neither of the High Contracting Parties gives notice twelve months before the expiration of the twenty-year period that it wishes to denounce the Treaty, it shall remain in force for a further five years until such time as either High Contracting Party gives notice in writing twelve months before the expiration of the current five-year period of its intention to denounce the Treaty.

In Faith Whereof the Plenipotentiaries have signed the present Treaty and attached their seals thereto.

Done in Moscow on 21 April 1945 in two copies, each in the Polish and Russian languages, both texts being equally authentic.

By authorization of the President of the National Council of the People's Republic of Poland:

[L.S.] E. Osóbka-MORAWSKI

By authorization of the Presidium of the Supreme Soviet of the USSR:

[L.S.] J. STALIN

4.1325 Sino-Soviet Treaty of Friendship and Alliance

Alliance Members: Union of Soviet Socialist Republics and China
Signed On: August 14, 1945, in the city of Moscow. In force until February 14, 1950.
Alliance Type: Defense Pact (Type I)

Source: *United Nations Treaty,* no. 68.

SUMMARY

The Soviets negotiated this treaty with China's Chiang Kai-shek, even though Chiang was in the midst of a civil war with the Communist, Mao Zedong. Stalin had urged Mao to join forces with Chiang against the Japanese during the war, and this advice continued after the war, as Stalin suggested negotiation with Chiang rather than continued fighting. After the war, however, Mao ignored Stalin's advice, finally pushed Chiang's forces out of mainland China, and proclaimed the People's Republic of China in October of 1949. This defense pact was then replaced with a new treaty, negotiated between Communist China and the Soviet Union in February 1950.

ALLIANCE TEXT

The President of the National Government of the Republic of China and the Praesidium of the Supreme Soviet of the Union of Soviet Socialist Republics,

Being desirous of strengthening the friendly relations which have always prevailed between the Republic of China and the Soviet Union, by means of an alliance and by good neighbourly post-war collaboration;

Determined to assist each other in the struggle against aggression on the part of the enemies of the United Nations in this World War and to collaborate in the common war against Japan until that country's unconditional surrender;

Expressing their unswerving resolve to collaborate in maintaining peace and security for the benefit of the peoples of both countries and of all peace-loving nations;

Who, having communicated to each other their full powers, found in good and due form, have agreed as follows:

Article 1. The High Contracting Parties undertake jointly with the other United Nations to prosecute the war against Japan until final victory is achieved. The High Contracting Parties mutually undertake to afford one another all necessary military and other assistance and support in this war.

Article 2. The High Contracting Parties undertake not to enter into separate negotiations with Japan or conclude, except by mutual consent, any armistice or peace treaty either with the present Japanese Government or any other Government or authority set up in Japan that does not clearly renounce all aggressive intentions.

Article 3. On the conclusion of the war against Japan, the High Contracting Parties undertake to carry out jointly all the measures in their power to render impossible a repetition of aggression and violation of the peace by Japan.

Should either of the High Contracting Parties become involved in hostilities with Japan in consequence of an attack by the latter against that Party, the other High Contracting Party will at once render to the High Contracting Party so involved in hostility all the military and other support and assistance in its power.

This Article shall remain in force until such time as, at the request of both High Contracting Parties, responsibility for the prevention of further aggression by Japan is placed upon the "United Nations" Organization.

Article 4. Each High Contracting Party undertakes not to conclude any alliance and not to take part in any coalition directed against the other Contracting Party.

Article 5. The High Contracting Parties, having regard to the interests of the security and economic development of each of them, agree to work together in close and friendly collaboration after the re-establishment of peace and to act in accordance with the principles of mutual respect for each other's sovereignty and territorial integrity and non-intervention in each other's internal affairs.

Article 6. The High Contracting Parties agree to afford one another all possible economic assistance in the post-war period in order to facilitate and expedite the rehabilitation of both countries and to make their contribution to the prosperity of the world.

Article 7. Nothing in this Treaty should be interpreted in such a way as to prejudice the rights and duties of the High Contracting Parties as Members of the Organization of the "United Nations".

Article 8. The present Treaty is subject to ratification in the shortest possible time. The instruments of ratification shall be exchanged in Chungking as soon as possible.

The Treaty comes into force immediately upon ratification, and shall remain in force for thirty years. Should neither of the High Contracting Parties make, one year before the date of the Treaty's expiry, a statement of its desire to denounce it, the Treaty will remain in force for an unlimited period, provided that each High Contracting Party may invalidate it by announcing its intention to do so to the other Contracting Party one year in advance.

In Witness Whereof, the respective Plenipotentiaries have signed this Treaty and have affixed thereto their seals.

Done in Moscow, the 14 August 1945 and the 14th day of the month of August in the year 34 of the Chinese Republic, in two copies, each copy in both Chinese and Russian, both texts being of equal validity.

By authority of the President of the National Government of the Chinese Republic

WANG SHIH-CHIEH

By Authority of the Praesidium of the Supreme Soviet of the USSR

V. MOLOTOV

EXCHANGE OF NOTES

No. 1. Note from the Peoples' Commissar for Foreign Affairs of the Union of Soviet Socialist Republics to Mr. Wang, Minister of Foreign Affairs of the National Government of the Chinese Republic

Moscow, 14 August 1945

Sir,

In connexion with the signing on this date of the Treaty of Friendship and Alliance between China and the Union of Soviet Socialist Republics, I have the honour to place on record that the following provisions are understood by both Contracting Parties as follows:

(1) In accordance with the spirit of the above-mentioned Treaty and to implement its general idea and its purposes, the Soviet Government agrees to render China moral support and assist her with military supplies and other material resources, it being understood that this support and assistance will go exclusively to the National Government as the Central Government of China.

(2) During the negotiations on the ports of Dairen and Port Arthur and on the joint operation of the Chinese Changchun Railway, the Soviet Government regarded the Three Eastern Provinces as part of China and again affirmed its respect for the complete sovereignty of China over the Three Eastern Provinces and recognition of their territorial and administrative integrity.

(3) With regard to recent events in Sinkiang, the Soviet Government confirms that, as stated in Article 5 of the Treaty of Friendship and Alliance, it has no intention of interfering in the internal affairs of China.

Should you confirm your agreement with this understanding of the above-mentioned points, the present Note and your answer to it will form part of the above-mentioned Treaty of Friendship and Alliance.

I have the honour to be, etc.

(Signed) V. Molotov

Mr. Wang Shih-Chieh
Minister of Foreign Affairs of the Chinese Republic
Moscow

No. 2. Note from Mr. Wang Shih-Chieh, Minister of Foreign Affairs of the National Government of the Republic of China, in answer to Mr. Molotov, Peoples' Commissar for Foreign Affairs of the Union of Soviet Socialist Republics

14 August of the 34th year
of the Republic of China,
corresponding to 14 August 1945
Sir,

I have the honour to acknowledge receipt of your Note of today's date reading as follows:

[See Note No. I]

I have the honour to confirm the correctness of the above understanding.

I have the honour to be, etc.

(Signed) WANG SHIH-CHIEH

Mr. Molotov
Peoples' Commissar for Foreign Affairs
of the Union of Soviet Socialist Republics
Moscow

No. 3. Note from Mr. Wang Shih-Chieh, Minister of Foreign Affairs of the National Government of the Republic of China, to Mr. Molotov, Peoples' Commissar for Foreign Affairs of the Union of Soviet Socialist Republics

14 August of the 34th year
of the Republic of China,
corresponding to 14 August 1945
Sir,

In view of the frequently manifested desire for independence of the people of Outer Mongolia, the Chinese Government states that, after the defeat of Japan, if this desire is confirmed by a plebiscite of the people of Outer Mongolia, the Chinese Government will recognize the independence of Outer Mongolia within her existing frontiers.

The above statement will have binding force after the ratification of the Treaty of Friendship and Alliance signed by the Chinese Republic and the Union of Soviet Socialist Republics on 14 August 1945.

I have the honour to be, etc.

(Signed) WANG SHIH-CHIEH

Mr. Molotov
Peoples' Commissar for Foreign Affairs
of the Union of Soviet Socialist Republics
Moscow

4.1326 Treaty of Friendship and Mutual Assistance between the Republic of Poland and the Federative People's Republic of Yugoslavia

Alliance Members: Poland and Yugoslavia
Signed On: March 18, 1946, in the city of Warsaw. In force until June 28, 1948.
Alliance Type: Defense Pact (Type I)

Source: *United Nations Treaty*, no. 13.

SUMMARY

This alliance was the first among eastern European states following World War II and effectively served as a method for establishing diplomatic recognition of both respective governments. The treaty itself assures that neither party will take part in an alliance against the other. In addition, if one of the signed parties were to become involved in hostile actions with Germany or any other country, the other signatory would give military assistance and support.

Marshall Tito hailed the alliance as an important diplomatic tool and guide for other states in the region, but the alliance itself lasted only three years. Poland followed the Soviet lead and renounced all ties with Yugoslavia in 1948 after Stalin's split with Tito.

ALLIANCE TEXT

The President of the National Council of the Republic of Poland on the one part, and the Presidium of the National Skuptshina of the Federative People's Republic of Yugoslavia on the other part,

Drawing conclusions from the experiences of the last war, which as the result of aggression by Germany and her allies wrought enormous destruction both in Poland and in Yugoslavia,

Desirous of tightening the bonds of secular friendship between the brother Slav nations of both countries, bonds which have been particularly strengthened and consolidated in the course of the joint struggle waged for liberty, independence and democracy against Germany and her allies in the last war,

Believing that the strengthening and deepening of the friendship between Poland and Yugoslavia corresponds to the most vital interest of both countries and will most effectively serve the cause of the cultural and economic development of Poland and Yugoslavia,

Being desirous of consolidating the peace and security of Poland and Yugoslavia as well as world peace and security,

Have resolved to conclude a Treaty of Friendship and Mutual Assistance and for this purpose have appointed as their plenipotentiaries:

The President of the National Council of the Republic of Poland: Edward Osobka-Morawski, Prime Minister of the Government of National Unity of the Republic of Poland, and

The Presidium of the National Skuptshina of the Federative People's Republic of Yugoslavia: Joseph Broz-Tito, Marshal of Yugoslavia and Prime Minister of the Government of the Federative People's Republic of Yugoslavia,

Who, after having exchanged their full powers, found in good and due form, have agreed on the following provisions:

Article I. Each of the High Contracting Parties undertakes not to enter into any alliance or participate in any action directed against the other High Contracting Party.

Article II. In the event of the peace and security of either country being threatened as well as in the more important matters affecting the interests of both countries the High Contracting Parties undertake to consult one another on their course of action.

Article III. Should either of the High Contracting Parties, as a result of aggression, become involved in hostilities against Germany, or against a country which was an ally of Germany in the last war, or against any other country, which either directly or in any other way whatsoever had allied itself with Germany, or with her allies in such aggression, the other High Contracting Party shall afford such Party immediate military and other assistance and support by all means at its disposal.

Article IV. The present Treaty shall not in any way prejudice the engagements entered into by both High Contracting Parties with third countries.

The High Contracting Parties shall execute the present Treaty in conformity with the Charter of the United Nations and shall support any steps taken to eliminate centres of aggression, as well as to consolidate peace and security throughout the world.

Article V. The present Treaty shall come into force on the date of signature and shall be binding for twenty years.

Unless notice of intention to terminate the Treaty is given by one of the High Contracting Parties at least one year before the expiration of the period agreed upon, it shall be considered as having been renewed for a further period of five years and similarly thereafter.

The Treaty is subject to ratification. The exchange of instruments of ratification shall take place at Belgrade at the earliest possible date.

In faith whereof the above mentioned Plenipotentiaries have signed this Treaty and have thereto affixed their seals.

Done at Warsaw in two copies, each in the Polish and Serbo-Croat languages, both of which are authentic, this 18th day of March, 1946.

By authority of the President of the National Council of the Republic of Poland

(Signed) Edward OSOBKA-MORAWSKI

By authority of the Presidium of the National Skuptshina of the Federative Peoples Republic of Yugoslavia

(Signed) Joseph BROZ-TITO

4.1327 Treaty of Alliance between His Majesty in Respect of the United Kingdom and His Highness the Amir of Transjordan

Alliance Members: United Kingdom and Jordan
Signed On: March 22, 1946, in the city of London. In force until October 29, 1956.
Alliance Type: Defense Pact (Type I)

Source: *United Nations Treaty,* no. 74

SUMMARY

This treaty affirms the existence of Transjordan, which was created by Great Britain in 1921 out of its mandate following the Versailles Treaty ending World War I. Amir Abdallah ibn Hussein served as semiautonomous ruler of Transjordan, and Abdallah had always remained an ally of Britain, even sending troops to assist Britain during World War II. The purpose of the treaty was to maintain the close ties between the countries, including the stationing of British troops near the Suez Canal, as it added legitimacy to Transjordan as an autonomous state in the international system. The treaty was also part of a series of agreements made on the partition of Palestine and the establishment of Israel, and the British later secretly endorsed the taking over of the Arab part of Palestine by Abdallah.

Prior to signing, the amir of Transjordan stated that the British plan for Transjordan's independence was a defeat for the Zionist plot to take over his country. After the Arab-Israeli war in 1948–1949, a British lieutenant general was dismissed as the British-subsidized Arab Legion commander because of his failure to prepare for an Israeli attack against Jordan. The tensions created by this war, along with the growing strength of Western support for Israel, led Egypt, Syria, and Jordan to sign a defense pact on October 25, 1956. Three days later, the French consulate in Jordan was attacked, and this pact effectively ended with Jordanian renunciation of the alliance ties on October 29. Formal termination came on March 14, 1957.

ALLIANCE TEXT

His Majesty The King of Great Britain, Ireland and the British Dominions beyond the seas, Emperor of India, and His Highness The Amir of Trans-Jordan;

Considering that the Government of the United Kingdom of Great Britain and Northern Ireland have formally declared in the General Assembly of the United Nations Organisation that they intend to recognise the status of Trans-Jordan as a sovereign independent State; and

Desiring to define the relations which will subsist between them in future as independent Sovereigns on the terms of complete freedom, equality and independence, and to consolidate and perpetuate the relations of friendship and good understanding which have hitherto subsisted between them,

Have decided to conclude a treaty of friendship and alliance for this purpose and have appointed as their plenipotentiaries:—

His Majesty The King of Great Britain, Ireland and the British Dominions

beyond the seas, Emperor of India (hereinafter referred to

as His Majesty The King); For the United Kingdom of Great Britain and Northern Ireland; The Right Honourable Ernest Bevin, M.P., His Majesty's Principal Secretary of State for Foreign Affairs; Arthur Creech Jones, M.P., Parliamentary Under-Secretary of State for the Colonies;

His Highness The Amir of Trans-Jordan; His Excellency Ibrahim Pasha Hashim, Order of the Nahda, Murassa'a, Order of the Istiglal, First Class, C.B.E., Prime Minister of Trans-Jordan and Minister of Defence;

Who, having communicated their full powers, found in good and due form, have agreed as follows:—

Article 1. His Majesty The King recognises Trans-Jordan as a fully independent State and His Highness The Amir as the sovereign thereof.

There shall be perpetual peace and friendship between His Majesty The King and His Highness The Amir of Trans-Jordan.

There shall be established between the High Contracting Parties a close alliance in consecration of their friendship, their cordial understanding and their good relations and there shall be a full and frank consultation between them in all matters of foreign policy which may affect their common interests.

Each of the High Contracting Parties undertakes not to adopt in foreign countries an attitude which is inconsistent with the alliance or might create difficulties for the other party thereto.

Article 2. Each High Contracting Party will be represented at the Court of the other High Contracting Party by a diplomatic representative duly accredited.

Article 3. It is understood between the High Contracting Parties that responsibility for the maintenance of internal order in Trans-Jordan and, subject to the provisions of Article 5 below, for the defence of Trans-Jordan from external aggression rests with His Highness The Amir of Trans-Jordan.

Article 4. Should a dispute arise with a third State, the continuance of which is likely to endanger the maintenance of international peace and security, the High Contracting Parties will, first of all, concert together to seek a solution by peaceful means as provided in Article 33 of the Charter of the United Nations.

Article 5. Should either High Contracting Party, notwithstanding the provisions of Article 4 of the present Treaty, become involved in hostilities, as a result of armed attack by a third party, the other High Contracting Party will, subject always to the provisions of Article 12 of the present Treaty, immediately come to his aid as a measure of collective self-defence. In the event of an imminent menace of hostilities the High Contracting Parties will immediately concert together the necessary measures of defence.

Article 6. In order to facilitate the discharge of the mutual obligations under Article 5 above, the High Contracting Parties have agreed to the provisions set forth in the Annex to the present Treaty.

Article 7. His Majesty The King will make every endeavour to obtain for His Highness's Government the services of any experts or officials with technical qualifications of whom Trans-Jordan may stand in need.

Article 8. 1. All obligations and responsibilities devolving on His Majesty The King in respect of Trans-Jordan in respect of any international instrument which is not legally terminated should devolve on His Highness The Amir of Trans-Jordan alone, and the High Contracting Parties will immediately take such steps as may be necessary to secure the transfer of His Highness The Amir of these responsibilities.

2. Any general international treaty, convention or agreement which has been made applicable to Trans-Jordan by His Majesty The King (or by his Government in the United Kingdom) as mandatory shall continue to be observed by His Highness The Amir until His Highness The Amir (or his Government) becomes a separate contracting party thereto or the instrument in question is legally terminated in respect of Trans-Jordan.

Article 9. 1. The High Contracting Parties will open negotiations for a Commercial and Establishment Agreement as soon as practicable.

2. Until the conclusion of the Agreement referred to in paragraph 1, or until the expiry of two years from the date of signature of the present Treaty, whichever is the earlier, each High Contracting Party will maintain in relation to the nationals and commerce of the other the régime applying at the date of signature of the Treaty; provided that neither High Contracting Party will extend to the nationals or commerce of the other treatment less favourable in any respect than that which he accords to the nationals and commerce of the most favoured foreign country.

3. The provisions of the second paragraph of this Article apply to the colonies, overseas territories and protectorates of His Majesty The King and the territories administered by His Majesty's Government in the United Kingdom under mandate or trusteeship.

4. The High Contracting Parties agree that the provisions of the second paragraph of this Article with regard to the grant of the treatment of the most favoured foreign country shall not extend to—

(1) Any special customs privileges which at the date of signature of this Treaty His Highness The Amir accords to goods produced or manufactured in any territory which in 1914 was wholly included in Asiatic Turkey or Arabia provided that such privileges are not accorded to any other foreign country, or

(2) customs privileges granted by one of the High Contracting Parties to a third country in virtue of a Customs Union which has already been or may hereafter be concluded.

Article 10. It is agreed by the High Contracting Parties that commercial concessions granted in respect of Trans-Jordan territory prior to the signature of this Treaty shall continue to be valid for the periods specified in their texts.

Article 11. On the coming into force of the present Treaty the Agreement between His Majesty The King and His Highness The Amir dated the 20th February, 1928, and subsequently revised by further Agreements dated the 2nd June, 1934, and the 19th July, 1941, shall cease to have effect.

Article 12. Nothing in the present Treaty is intended to or shall in any way prejudice the rights and obligations which devolve, or may devolve, upon either of the High Contracting Parties under the Charter of the United Nations or, save as may result from the provisions of Articles 8 and 11, under any other international agreements, conventions or treaties.

Article 13. Should any difference arise relative to the application or the interpretation of the present Treaty, and should the High Contracting Parties fail to settle such difference by direct negotiation, the difference shall be referred to the International Court of Justice unless the parties agree to another mode of settlement.

Article 14. The present Treaty shall be ratified and shall come into force upon the exchange of instruments of ratification, which shall take place as soon as possible.

The present Treaty shall remain in force for a period of twenty-five years from the date of its coming into force, and thereafter it shall remain in force until the expiry of one year after a notice of termination has been given by one High Contracting Party to the other through the diplomatic channel.

In Witness Whereof the above-named plenipotentiaries have signed the present Treaty and affixed thereto their seals.

Done in duplicate in London, this twenty-second day of March, 1946, in the English and Arabic languages, both texts being equally authentic.

(L.S.) Ernest BEVIN
(L.S.) A. CREECH JONES
(L.S.) Ibrahim HASHIM

ANNEX

Article 1. His Majesty The King may station armed forces in Trans-Jordan in places where they are stationed at the date of signature of the present Treaty, and in such other places as may be agreed upon, and His Highness The Amir will provide all, the facilities necessary for their accommodation and maintenance and the storage of their ammunition and supplies, including the lease of any land required. Any private rights on such land will, if necessary, be expropriated.

Article 2. His Highness The Amir of Trans-Jordan will grant facilities at all times for the movement and training of the armed forces of His Majesty The King, and for the transport of the supplies of fuel, ordnance, ammunition and other materials required by these forces, by air, road, railway, water-way and pipe-line and through the ports of Trans-Jordan.

Article 3. The armed forces of His Majesty The King will have the right to use their own systems of signal communication, including wireless.

Article 4. His Highness The Amir of Trans-Jordan will safeguard, maintain and develop as necessary in consultation with the Government of the United Kingdom the ports and lines of communication in and across Trans-Jordan, required for the free movement and maintenance of His Majesty's armed forces, and will call upon His Majesty's assistance as may be required for this purpose.

Article 5. His Majesty The King will reimburse to His Highness The Amir all expenditure to which His Highness's Government is put in connection with the provision of the facilities mentioned in Articles 1, 2 and 4 of this Annex and will repair or pay compensation for any damage, arising from actions by members of His Majesty's armed forces other than damage caused in military operations undertaken in accordance with Article 5 of this Treaty as a result of an attack on Trans-Jordan.

Article 6. Pending the conclusion of an agreement between the High Contracting Parties defining in detail the jurisdictional and fiscal immunities of members of the forces of His Majesty The King in Trans-Jordan, they will continue to enjoy the immunities which are accorded to them at present.

Article 7. No demand will be made for the payment by His Majesty The King of any Trans-Jordan taxation in respect of immovable property leased or owned by His Majesty or in respect of his movable property, including customs duty on goods imported or exported by or on behalf of His Majesty.

Article 8. His Majesty The King will afford financial assistance to His Highness The Amir in meeting the cost of the military units of the Amir's forces which are required to ensure the purposes of Article 5 of the Treaty. The strength of such units will be agreed upon annually by the High Contracting Parties, and His Highness The Amir will enable His Majesty's representative in Trans-Jordan to ascertain that the funds in question are expended for the purpose for which they are issued.

Article 9. In view of the desirability of identity in training and methods between the Trans-Jordan and British armies:—

(1) His Majesty The King will provide any British officers whose services are required to ensure the efficiency of the military units of the Amir's forces.

(2) His Majesty The King will (a) afford all possible facilities to His Highness The Amir of Trans-Jordan for the military and aeronautical instruction of Trans-Jordan officers at schools of instruction maintained for His Majesty's forces, and (b) provide arms, ammunition, equipment and aircraft and other material for the forces of His Highness The Amir of Trans-Jordan.

(3) His Highness The Amir will (a) meet the cost of instruction and equipment referred to in paragraph (2), (b) ensure that the armament and essential equipment of his forces shall not differ in type from those of the forces of His Majesty The King, (c) send any personnel of his forces, that may be sent abroad for training, to military schools, colleges and training centres maintained for His Majesty's forces.

Article 10. At the request of either of them the High Contracting Parties will consult together at any time to consider whether it is desirable to introduce by agreement any amendments to the provisions of this Annex designed to give fuller effect to its purposes.

E. B.

A. C. J.

I. H.

4.1328 Treaty of Friendship, Mutual Aid, and Peaceful Co-operation between the Federative People's Republic of Yugoslavia and the Czechoslovak Republic

Alliance Members: Yugoslavia and Czechoslovakia
Signed On: May 9, 1946, in the city of Belgrade (Serbia). In force until June 28, 1948.
Alliance Type: Defense Pact (Type I)

Source: *United Nations Treaty,* no. 14.

SUMMARY

This is the second of a set of five alliances by which Marshall Tito tried to bilaterally encourage foreign policy cooperation between Yugoslavia and its neighbors. Reminiscent of the policies of the Little Entente that included Serbia and its neighbors, Tito hoped closer ties could prevent future German aggression and also promote trade and greater state independence within eastern Europe. This drive for independence and regionalism quickly led to Tito's split from the Soviets and from Stalin, who demanded recognition as the supreme authority on communism.

ALLIANCE TEXT

The Presidium of the People's Assembly of the Federative People's Republic of Yugoslavia and the President of the Czechoslovak Republic,

Being desirous of solemnly confirming the ties of sincere friendship which from time immemorial have united the brother Slav peoples of Czechoslovakia and Yugoslavia and which in this victorious war were confirmed anew in their common struggle against the same enemy and the same dangers,

Bearing in mind the vital interest of both countries in mutual defence in the event of Germany renewing its policy of aggression against their freedom, political independence and territorial integrity,

Being convinced that mutual defence against such dangers is in the interest of the maintenance of international peace and security, which is also the aim of the Charter of the United Nations, to which both countries have subscribed,

Being resolved to strengthen and deepen still further the spiritual and economic ties already created by the mutual endeavours of both countries,

have decided to conclude a treaty and have for this purpose appointed as their plenipotentiaries:

The Presidium of the People's Assembly of the Federative People's Republic of Yugoslavia; the Head of the Government of the Federative People's Republic of Yugoslavia, Marshal of Yugoslavia, M. Josip Broza-Tito.

The President of the Czechoslovak Republic; the Head of the Government, M. Zdeněk Fierlinger,

who, after having exchanged their full powers, found in good and proper form, have agreed on the following:

Article I. The High Contracting Parties have agreed that it will be to the interest of both countries and their peoples to join together in a policy of tried and lasting friendship, which they will reinforce by close co-operation between both countries.

Article II. The High Contracting Parties agree to take all joint action within their power to frustrate any new threat and to prevent a renewed attack by Germany or any other Power which might be associated with it directly or in any other way.

To this end the High Contracting Parties shall in a spirit of the sincerest co-operation participate in all international action for the maintenance of international peace and security and shall fully contribute to the realization of this aim.

In carrying out this treaty the High Contracting Parties shall respect their obligations as Members of the United Nations.

Article III. Should either of the High Contracting Parties be involved in hostilities with Germany, which had renewed her policy of aggression, or with any other Power which had joined Germany for the purpose of aggressive action, the other High Contracting Party shall without delay extend to it military and other aid with all the means at its disposal.

Article IV. The High Contracting Parties agree that neither of them shall enter into an alliance or take part in a coalition directed against the other High Contracting Party.

Article V. The High Contracting Parties shall, jointly and each in its own particular sphere, strengthen the economic, spiritual and other ties between the two countries on the basis of the treaties and agreements concluded for this purpose.

Article VI. This Treaty shall come into force immediately upon signature and shall be ratified in the shortest possible time. The ratifications shall be exchanged in Prague as soon as possible.

This Treaty shall remain in force for twenty years from the date of signature. If, however, neither of the High Contracting Parties gives notice twelve months before the expiration of the period of twenty years that it wishes the validity of this Treaty to cease, its validity shall in such case be prolonged for a further five years until such time as either High Contracting Party gives notice in writing twelve months before the expiration of the current five-year period of its intention to terminate its validity.

In faith whereof the plenipotentiaries have signed the present Treaty and attached their seals thereto.

Done in duplicate in Czech and Serbo-Croat. Both texts are equally authentic.

Done in Belgrade the 9th day of May, 1946.

By authorization the of the President of the People's Assembly of the Federative People's Republic of Yugoslavia

J. B. TITO, m.p.

By authorization of the Presidium of Czechoslovak Republic

Zd. FIERLINGER, m.p.

4.1329 Treaty of Friendship and Mutual Assistance between the Federative People's Republic of Yugoslavia and the People's Republic of Albania

Alliance Members: Yugoslavia and Albania
Signed On: July 9, 1946, in the city of Tirana (Albania). In force until June 28, 1948.
Alliance Type: Defense Pact (Type I)

Source: *United Nations Treaty*, no. 15.

SUMMARY

This alliance is very similar to the alliance treaties signed by Yugoslavia with Poland (on March 18, 1946, Alliance no. 4.1326) and Czechoslovakia (on May 9, 1946, Alliance no. 4.1328) and follows Marshall Tito's foreign policy of actively connecting Yugoslavia to its neighbors in the region. The treaty assured mutual assistance in the event of attack by a third party and compelled both states not to form alliances targeting the other state. As with the other Yugoslav alliances, though, this treaty ended following Stalin's break with Tito. Albania chose a continued relationship with Stalin rather than join its neighbor in breaking from the Soviet sphere of influence.

ALLIANCE TEXT

The people of the Federative People's Republic of Yugoslavia and the People's Republic of Albania have had in the course of their history with the same enemies, who threatened their independence and endeavoured to seize and subjugate the whole or parts of their territory. This was shown particularly clearly, recently when Fascist Germany and Italy attacked and occupied both countries with a view to dismembering them and permanently appropriating them.

The people of Yugoslavia and Albania, true to their fighting tradition, rose in defense of their independence and freedom, and after an unyielding resistance, shoulder to shoulder, for four years, succeeded in safeguarding their independence and freedom.

Being desirous of strengthening still further the ties sealed with blood in the days that were fateful for the peoples of both countries, and of solemnly confirming their lasting friendship and their desire for cultural and economic co-operation, and being desirous of confirming their determination to unite also in the future in joint defense of the freedom, independence and integrity of their countries in case they are attacked by a third power aiming at subjugating them or seizing some parts of their territory.

Being convinced that joint defence serves of an interest, not only of both countries, but also of peace in the Balkans and in the world, and in complete conformity with the aspirations of the United Nations for the maintenance of peace,

The Presidium of the National Assembly of the Federative People's Republic of Yugoslavia and the Presidium of the National Assembly of the People's Republic of Albania have decided to conclude a treaty and have appointed their Plenipotentiaries to that effect as follows:

The Presidium of the National Assembly of the Federative People's Republic of Yugoslavia, Mr. Stanoje Simic, Minister for Foreign Affairs,

The Presidium of the National Assembly of the People's Republic of Albania, General Enver Hodja, President of the Government, Minister for National Defence, and Minister for Foreign Affairs,

Who, having exchanged their full powers, found in good and due form, have agreed on the following:

Article I. Both High Contracting Parties have agreed, in the interest of the people of both countries to further improve in every way the existing friendly relations by close co-operation between the two countries.

Article II. The High Contracting Parties will take jointly all measures necessary to ensure the independence and integrity of both countries, in order to prevent the future recurrence of attacks, similar to those made by the Germany of Hitler and the Fascist Italy of Mussolini.

To that effect, both High Contracting Parties will collaborate as closely as possible in all international actions undertaken for the maintenance of peace and security among nations. In fulfilling the obligations arising out of this Treaty, the High Contracting Parties will be guided by the principles laid down by the United Nations.

Article III. Should one of the High Contracting Parties be attacked by whomsoever with a view to threatening its independence, subjugating it or seizing certain parts of its territory, the other High Contracting Party will immediately extend to it military and all other assistance with all the means at its disposal.

Article IV. The High Contracting Parties undertake that neither of them will enter into an alliance or take part in a coalition directed against the other High Contracting Party.

Article V. The High Contracting Parties themselves will settle all questions of mutual interest, on the basis of the most sincere friendship.

Economic, cultural and other bonds between the two countries will be established by special agreements.

Article VI. The present Treaty shall come into force immediately upon signature and shall be ratified as soon as possible.

The instruments of ratification shall be exchanged at Belgrade.

This Treaty shall remain in force for twenty years from the date of signature. Unless it is denounced by either of the High Contracting Parties twelve months before the expiry of the twentieth year, it shall be extended for five years, and similarly thereafter until one of the High Contracting Parties notifies its intention to denounce the Treaty, twelve months before the expiry of the current five-year period.

In faith whereof the Plenipotentiaries have signed the present Treaty and thereto affixed their seals.

The Treaty is drawn up in duplicate in the Serbo-Croatian and Albanian languages, both texts being equally authentic.

Done at Tirana, 9 July 1946.

By authority of the Presidium of the National Assembly of the Federative People's Republic of Yugoslavia

(Signed) (L.S.) Stanoje SIMIC

By authority of the Presidium of the National Assembly of the People's Republic of Albania

(Signed) (L.S.) Enver HODJA

4.1330 Treaty of Alliance and Mutual Assistance between His Majesty in Respect of the United Kingdom of Great Britain and Northern Ireland and the President of the French Republic

Alliance Members: United Kingdom and France
Signed On: March 4, 1947, in the city of Dunkirk (France). In force until March 17, 1948.
Alliance Type: Defense Pact (Type I)

Source: *United Nations Treaty*, no. 132.

SUMMARY

After World War II, the British foreign secretary began the implementation of bilateral defense pacts with European states as a means of countering Soviet power and any possible resurgence of Germany. Soon after the signing of this treaty, the Belgian prime minister encouraged both France and Britain to consider expanding the agreement to include additional members. By January of 1948, Britain had responded with a proposal for a multilateral pact that added Belgium, Luxembourg, and the Netherlands. Negotiations were quick, especially after a communist coup in Czechoslovakia convinced Western leaders that the Soviets were trying to increase their influence over Europe. Thus, by March 17, 1948, an expansive western European defense pact replaced this bilateral treaty.

ALLIANCE TEXT

His Majesty The King of Great Britain, Ireland and the British Dominions beyond the Seas, Emperor of India, and the President of the French Republic,

Desiring to confirm in a Treaty of Alliance the cordial friendship and close association of interests between the United Kingdom and France;

Convinced that the conclusion of such a Treaty will facilitate the settlement in a spirit of mutual understanding of all questions arising between the two countries;

Resolved to co-operate closely with one another as well as with the other United Nations in preserving peace and resisting aggression, in accordance with the Charter of the United Nations and in particular with Articles 49, 51, 52, 53 and 107 thereof;

Determined to collaborate in measures of mutual assistance in the event of any renewal of German aggression, while considering most desirable the conclusion of a treaty between all the Powers having responsibility for action in relation to Germany with the object of preventing Germany from becoming again a menace to peace;

Having regard to the Treaties of Alliance and Mutual Assistance which they have respectively concluded with the Union of Soviet Socialist Republics;

Intending to strengthen the economic relations between the two countries to their mutual advantage and in the interests of general prosperity;

Have decided to conclude a Treaty with these objects and have appointed as their Plenipotentiaries:—

His Majesty The King of Great Britain, Ireland and the British Dominions beyond the Seas, Emperor of India: For the United Kingdom of Great Britain and Northern Ireland, The Right Honourable Ernest Bevin, M.P., His Majesty's Principal Secretary of State for Foreign Affairs, and The Right Honourable Alfred Duff Cooper, His Majesty's Ambassador Extraordinary and Plenipotentiary at Paris;

The President of the French Republic: For the French Republic, His Excellency Monsieur Georges Bidault, Minister for Foreign Affairs, and His Excellency Monsieur Renée Massigli, Ambassador Extraordinary and Plenipotentiary of the French Republic in London;

who, having communicated their Full Powers, found in good and due form, have agreed as follows:—

Article I. Without prejudice to any arrangements that may be made, under any Treaty concluded between all the Powers having responsibility for action in relation to Germany under Article 107 of the Charter of the United Nations, for the purpose of preventing any infringements by Germany of her obligations with regard to disarmament and de-militarisation and generally of ensuring that Germany shall not again become a menace to peace, the High Contracting Parties will, in the event of any threat to the security of either of them arising from the adoption by Germany of a policy of aggression or from action by Germany designed to facilitate such a policy, take, after consulting with each other and where appropriate with the other Powers having responsibility for action in relation to Germany, such agreed action (which so long as the said Article 107 remains operative shall be action under that Article) as is best calculated to put an end to this threat.

Article II. Should either of the High Contracting Parties become again involved in hostilities with Germany, either in consequence of an armed attack, within the meaning of Article 51 of the Charter of the United Nations, by Germany against that Party, or as a result of agreed action taken against Germany under Article I of this Treaty, or as a result of enforcement action taken against Germany by the United Nations Security Council, the other High Contracting Party will at once give the High Contracting Party so involved in hostilities all the military and other support and assistance in his power.

Article III. In the event of either High Contracting Party being prejudiced by the failure of Germany to fulfil any obligation of an economic character imposed on her as a result of the Instrument of Surrender or arising out of any subsequent settlement, the High Contracting Parties will consult with each other and where appropriate with the other Powers having responsibility for action in relation to Germany, with a view to taking agreed action to deal with the situation.

Article IV. Bearing in mind the interests of the other members of the United Nations, the High Contracting Parties will by constant consultation on matters affecting their economic relations with each other take all possible steps to promote the prosperity and economic security of both countries and thus enable each of them to contribute more effectively to the economic and social objectives of the United Nations.

Article V. (1) Nothing in the present Treaty should be interpreted as derogating in any way from the obligations devolving upon the High Contracting Parties from the provisions of the Charter of the United Nations or from any special agreements concluded in virtue of Article 43 of the Charter.

(2) Neither of the High Contracting Parties will conclude any alliance or take part in any coalition directed against the other High Contracting Party; nor will they enter into any obligation inconsistent with the provisions of the present Treaty.

Article VI. (1) The present Treaty is subject to ratification and the instruments of ratification will be exchanged in London as soon as possible.

(2) It will come into force immediately on the exchange of the instruments of ratification and will remain in force for a period of fifty years.

(3) Unless either of the High Contracting Parties gives to the other notice in writing to terminate it at least one year before the expiration of this period, it will remain in force without any specified time limit, subject to the right of either of the High Contracting Parties to terminate it by giving to the other in writing a year's notice of his intention to do so.

In Witness Whereof the above-mentioned Plenipotentiaries have signed the present Treaty and affixed thereto their seals.

Done in Dunkirk the fourth day of March, 1947, in duplicate in English and French, both texts being equally authentic.

[L.S.] Ernest BEVIN
[L.S.] DUFF COOPER
[L.S.] BIDAULT
[L.S.] R. MASSIGLI

4.1331 Treaty of Friendship and Mutual Aid between the Republic of Poland and the Czechoslovak Republic

Alliance Members: Poland and Czechoslovakia
Signed On: March 10, 1947, in the city of Warsaw. In force until August 7, 1989.
Alliance Type: Defense Pact (Type I)

Source: *United Nations Treaty,* no. 365.

SUMMARY

This treaty preceded the six-nation Council for Economic Mutual Assistance (CEMA), formalizing the "Molotov Plan," which was created as an eastern European alternative to the Marshall Plan. The alliance stipulated that both states would carry out joint measures to obviate any further threat by Germany and would offer military assistance if the other were attacked. Both parties also pledged not to take part in any alliances that targeted the other state.

A communist coup d'état occurred in Czechoslovakia in February of 1948, within one year of the signing this alliance. President Eduard Benes of Czechoslovakia was forced to accept Premier Klement Gottwald's terms that Communists be put in charge of all positions except the foreign ministry. Jan Masaryk remained foreign minister, but even in this case, all of Masaryk's aides were Communist Party members. Masaryk died just one month later. Most speculated that the foreign minister had been murdered and that his alleged suicide was a cover-up.

The alliance was revised at least once, in 1967, and lasted through the 1968 invasion of Czechoslovakia by Warsaw Pact forces. The alliance finally ended after more than forty years with the removal of communist governments in both states in 1989.

ALLIANCE TEXT

The President of the Republic of Poland and the President of the Czechoslovak Republic,

Being desirous of ensuring the peaceful development of both their Slav countries which, bordering directly upon Germany, have throughout their history been the object of German aggression which has repeatedly threatened their very existence,

Drawing appropriate conclusions from the experiences of the last war, which confronted both countries with deadly perils,

Realizing the vital interests of both countries in joint defence in the event of a renewal by Germany of her policy of aggression against their freedom, independence and territorial integrity,

Being convinced that joint defence against such a danger is in the interests of the maintenance of world peace and international security, the principal purpose of the United Nations, to which both States belong,

Recognizing that friendship and close co-operation between the Republic of Poland and the Czechoslovak Republic correspond with the most vital interests of both States and contribute to their cultural and economic development,

Have resolved to conclude a treaty of friendship and mutual aid and for this purpose have appointed as their plenipotentiaries:

The President of the Republic of Poland: Mr. Józef Cyrankiewicz, President of the Council of Ministers, and Mr. Zygmunt Modzelewski, Minister of Foreign Affairs;

The President of the Czechoslovak Republic: Mr. Kiement Gottwald, President of the Council of Ministers, and Mr. Jan Masaryk, Minister of Foreign Affairs,

Who, having exchanged their full powers, found in good and due form, have agreed on the following provisions:

Article 1. The High Contracting Parties undertake to establish their mutual relations on a basis of firm friendship, to develop and strengthen them together with economic and cultural co-operation.

Article 2. The High Contracting Parties undertake to carry out in mutual agreement all measures within their power to obviate any threat of further aggression by Germany or any other State associated with Germany for that purpose either directly or in any other way.

To this end, the High Contracting Parties will participate to the fullest extent in any international action aimed at ensuring international peace and security and will contribute fully to the realization of this aim.

In carrying out the present treaty, the High Contracting Parties will observe the obligations incumbent upon them as Members of the United Nations.

Article 3. Should either of the High Contracting Parties become involved in hostilities with Germany in consequence of her renewing her policy of aggression, or with any other State associated with Germany in such a policy, the other High Contracting Party shall without delay give the Party concerned military and all other assistance by every means at its disposal.

Article 4. Each of the High Contracting Parties undertakes not to enter into any alliance or take part in any coalition directed against the other High Contracting Party.

Article 5. The present treaty shall remain in force for twenty years from the date of its entry into force. If neither High Contracting Party denounces the treaty twelve months before the expiry of the aforementioned twenty-year period, it shall remain in force for a further period of five years and thus for subsequent five-year periods, until such time as either High Contracting Party denounces it twelve months before the expiry of the current five-year period.

The present treaty, whereof the additional protocol constitutes an integral part, shall be ratified in the shortest possible time and the instruments of ratification shall be exchanged at Prague as soon as possible.

The treaty shall come into force on the date of signature.

Article 6. The present treaty is drawn up in the Polish and Czech languages, both texts being equally authentic.

In Faith Whereof the plenipotentiaries have signed the present treaty and have affixed thereto their seals.

Done in duplicate, at Warsaw, on 10 March 1947.

For the President of the Republic of Poland:

[L.S.] (Signed) Józef CYRANKIEWICZ
(Signed) Zygmunt MODZELEWSKI

For the President of the Czechoslovak Republic:

[L.S.] (Signed) GOTTWALD
(Signed) Jan MASARYK

ADDITIONAL PROTOCOL TO THE TREATY OF FRIENDSHIP AND MUTUAL AID BETWEEN THE REPUBLIC OF POLAND AND THE CZECHOSLOVAK REPUBLIC

The High Contracting Parties

Being convinced that their firm friendship calls for the settlement of all the questions outstanding between their two States, also agree:

To settle all territorial questions at present outstanding between the two States on a basis of mutual agreement not later than two years from the date of the signature of the treaty of friendship and mutual aid;

In view of the need for the earliest possible economic and cultural rehabilitation of both countries, to conclude agreements for this purpose as soon as possible;

The exchange of the instruments of ratification took place at Prague on 4 July 1947.

To guarantee to roles in Czechoslovakia and to Czechs and Slovaks in Poland, within the limits of law and on the basis of reciprocity, the possibility of national, political, cultural and economic development (schools, societies and co-operatives, on the basis of the unity of co-operative organizations in Poland and in Czechoslovakia).

Done at Warsaw, on 10 March 1947.

(Signed) Józef CYRANKIEWICZ
(Signed) Zygmunt MODZELEWSKI
(Signed) GOTTWALD
(Signed) Jan MASARYK

4.1332 Treaty of Brotherhood and Alliance between the Kingdom of Iraq and the Hashemite Kingdom of Transjordan

Alliance Members: Iraq and Jordan
Signed On: April 14, 1947, in the city of Baghdad (Iraq). In force until July 15, 1958
Alliance Type: Entente (Type III)

Source: *United Nations Treaty,* no. 345.

SUMMARY

Iraq had been fighting in Palestine as part of the collective Arab effort to regain Palestinian territory lost owing to the post–World War II settlements establishing Israel. As part of this agreement, Iraq ended its involvement in the war without signing a cease-fire agreement with Israel, and Iraq ceded the territory under its control to Jordan.

The treaty further stipulated that both parties would not take part in alliances that targeted the other, would resolve disputes in a friendly manner, and would consult in the case of conflict. The neighboring states also pledged to suppress disturbances, disorders, and insurgents within their territories.

The two states united as the Arab Federal State of Jordan and Iraq on February 12, 1958, to counter the newly established United Arab Republic of Egypt and Syria. Although both King Hussein of Jordan and King Faisal of Iraq still possessed their thrones, King Faisal received a larger division of power from the combined rule. On July 14, 1958, an Iraqi brigadier general, Abdel Karim Kassem, led a revolution of so-called Free Officers that established a quick and bloody takeover and killed King Faisal, Crown Prince Abdel Ilah, and Foreign Minister Nuri al-Said. The old government was then officially replaced on the following day by Kassem, who immediately dissolved the Arab federation between Jordan and Iraq. Jordan's King Hussein responded by denouncing the coup leaders and this alliance.

ALLIANCE TEXT

In the name of God the Merciful, the Compassionate

His Majesty the King of Iraq and His Majesty the King of Transjordan,

In view of the ties of brotherhood and racial unity which unite them; desirous of safeguarding the integrity of their territories; and having regard to the necessity which they feel for closer mutual co-operation and full understanding in regard to matters affecting the interest of their kingdoms; and in execution of the provisions of Article 9 of the Pact of the League of Arab States;

Have agreed to conclude a Treaty of Brotherhood and Alliance, and for this purpose have appointed as their Plenipotentiaries:

His Majesty the King of Iraq: His Excellency Dr. Mohammed Fadhil Jamali, Minister for Foreign Affairs.

His Majesty the King of the Hashemite Kingdom of Transjordan: His Excellency Samir Pasha Al-Rifa'i, Prime Minister and Minister for Foreign Affairs.

Who having reciprocally communicated their full powers found in due form, have entered into an Alliance and have concluded the following Treaty:—

Article 1. There shall prevail relations of permanent brotherhood and alliance between the Kingdom of Iraq and the Hashemite Kingdom of Transjordan. The two High Contracting Parties shall consult together when necessary with a view to furthering the objects set forth in the Preamble to this Treaty.

Article 2. Each of the High Contracting Parties reciprocally undertakes not to enter with any third party into any understanding or agreement over any matter whatever of a nature prejudicial to the interests of the other High Contracting Party or to his country or its interests, or of a nature calculated to expose to danger or harm the safety or interests of his country.

Article 3. The High Contracting Parties undertake to settle any disputes arising between them by means of friendly negotiations.

Article 4. Should any dispute between either High Contracting Party and a third State produce a situation involving a threat of war, in that case the High Contracting Parties shall jointly endeavour to settle such dispute by peaceful means in accordance with such international understandings as may be applicable to the case.

Article 5. (a) In the event of an act of aggression being committed against either High Contracting Party by a third State notwithstanding efforts exerted in accordance with the provisions of Article 4 above; and similarly in the event of the occurrence of a sudden act of aggression which does not leave time for the application of the provisions of Article 4 referred to above, the High Contracting Parties shall consult together regarding the measures which shall be taken with the object of concerting their efforts in a manner to repel the said aggression.

(b) The following shall be deemed acts of aggression:
(1) The declaration of war.
(2) The seizure by an armed force of a third State, of territory belonging to either High Contracting Party even without a declaration of war.
(3) An attack on the territory, land, naval or air forces of either High Contracting Party by the land, naval or air forces of a third State, even without a declaration of war.
(4) Direct or indirect support or assistance to the aggressor.
(c) The following shall not be deemed acts of aggression:
(1) The exercise of the right of legitimate defence, i.e., resisting any act of aggression as defined above.
(2) Actions taken to implement the provisions of the Charter of the United Nations.

Article 6. In the event of the outbreak of disturbances or disorders in the territory of one of the High Contracting Parties each of them undertakes reciprocally as follows:—
(a) To take all possible measures or actions:
(1) To make it impossible for the insurgents to utilise his territory against the interests of the other High Contracting Party; and
(2) To prevent his subjects from taking part in the disturbances or disorders or from helping or encouraging the insurgents; and
(3) To prevent any kind of help being given to the insurgents either directly from his own territory or otherwise.
(b) In the event of insurgents from the territory of one of the High Contracting Parties taking refuge in the territory of the other High Contracting Party, the latter shall disarm them and hand them over to the other Party.
(c) If circumstances should necessitate the adoption of joint measures or actions to suppress disturbances or disorders, the two High Contracting Parties shall consult with each other concerning the policy of co-operation which shall be followed for this purpose.

Article 7. The two High Contracting Parties will co-operate with a view to unifying the military systems of their two countries by means of the exchange of military missions to study the systems followed in their respective countries and to seek to obtain reciprocal benefit from their respective military institutions and the training and instruction which is available in them.

Article 8. The Diplomatic and Consular Representatives of either High Contracting Party may if requested undertake the representation of the interests of the other High Contracting Party in foreign countries where such other Party has no representatives, provided that this shall not in any way affect the freedom of such other Party to appoint separate representatives of his own should he so desire.

Article 9. There shall be appointed permanent special commissions with executive powers comprising representatives of the two countries. It shall be their duty to achieve actual co-operation between the two High Contracting Parties in all matters stipulated in Article 2 of the Pact of the League of Arab States and also to carry out the requirements of Articles 5, 6, and 7 of the present Treaty.

Article 10. There is nothing in the present Treaty to prejudice the rights and duties arising from Treaties to which either High Contracting Party may be bound with any other State.

Article 11. This Treaty shall come into force from the date of the exchange of ratifications.

Article 12. The present Treaty shall remain in force for a period of ten years from the date of its coming into force and it shall be deemed to have been renewed for further periods of five years each, unless notice of desire to terminate it shall have been given by either High Contracting Party to the other one year prior to the date of expiry of its period. Each of the High Contracting Parties may, upon the expiry of the first period or any subsequent period of the periods of renewal, ask for reconsideration and revision of this Treaty with a view to augmenting the co-operation and strengthening the alliance to an extent greater than is provided for therein.

In Witness Whereof the above-mentioned plenipotentiaries have signed the present Treaty and have affixed thereto their seals.

Made at Baghdad in duplicate, in Arabic, on the 22nd day of Jamadi al Awal, 1366, corresponding to the 14th day of April, 1947.

(Signed) MOHAMMED FADHIL JAMALI
(Signed) SAMIR AL-RIFA'I

4.1333 Inter-American Treaty of Reciprocal Assistance

Alliance Members: United States, Argentina, Haiti, Bolivia, Honduras, Brazil, Mexico, Chile, Colombia, Panama, Costa Rica, Paraguay, Dominican Republic, Uruguay, Venezuela, El Salvador, Guatemala, Cuba (until January 22, 1962), Nicaragua (entered October 15, 1948), Ecuador (entered November 10, 1949), Trinidad and Tobago (entered April 6, 1967), and Bahamas (entered November 8, 1982).
Signed On: September 2, 1947, in the city of Rio de Janeiro. In force as of date of publication of this volume.
Alliance Type: Defense Pact (Type I)

Source: Organization of American States, Inter-American Treaty of Reciprocal Assistance, www.oas.org/juridico/english/Treaties/b-29.html.

SUMMARY

Following the conclusion of the Second World War, the nations of the Western hemisphere agreed to meet in Rio de Janeiro to adopt a system of collective security. The goal of the meeting was to ensure that the type intercontinental conflict that had occurred in Europe and Asia could not occur in the Americas. On September 2, 1947, numerous nations from the Western hemisphere signed the Inter-American Treaty of Reciprocal Assistance (also known as the Rio Treaty). This treaty acted as a precursor to the adoption of the Organization of American States Charter, which was adopted a year later in Bogota,

Colombia. On April 30, 1948, twenty-one nations of the Americas adopted the charter of the OAS. Cuba has remained a member but has been excluded from participation since 1962.

The OAS is broken down into a series of councils and committees. The main body is the General Assembly, which meets once a year and brings together all the foreign ministers of the Americas. The Permanent Council meets regularly in Washington, D.C., at the OAS headquarters. The Inter-American Council for Integral Development is a council devoted entirely to promotion of economic development. There also exists a series of subcommissions under the auspices of the OAS: Inter-American Children's Institute, Pan American Institute of Geography and History, Inter-American Commission of Women, Inter-American Institute for Cooperation on Agriculture, Inter-American Indian Institute, and Pan American Health Organization.

The initial goals of the OAS were to strengthen democracy across the continent, encourage free trade, strengthen education, and promote security. Since its inception, the organization has expanded its goals. At the most recent Summit of the Americas, the nations of the hemisphere agreed to support new mandates, including strengthening human rights, curbing illegal drugs, creating a Free Trade Area of the Americas, and promoting a greater civil participation in government.

ALLIANCE TEXT

In the name of their Peoples, the Governments represented at the Inter-American Conference for the Maintenance of Continental Peace and Security, desirous of consolidating and strengthening their relations of friendship and good neighborliness, and

Considering:

That Resolution VIII of the Inter-American Conference on Problems of War and Peace, which met in Mexico City, recommended the conclusion of a treaty to prevent and repel threats and acts of aggression against any of the countries of America;

That the High Contracting Parties reiterate their will to remain united in an inter-American system consistent with the purposes and principles of the United Nations, and reaffirm the existence of the agreement which they have concluded concerning those matters relating to the maintenance of international peace and security which are appropriate for regional action;

That the High Contracting Parties reaffirm their adherence to the principles of inter-American solidarity and cooperation, and especially to those set forth in the preamble and declarations of the Act of Chapultepec, all of which should be understood to be accepted as standards of their mutual relations and as the juridical basis of the Inter-American System;

That the American States propose, in order to improve the procedures for the pacific settlement of their controversies, to conclude the treaty concerning the "Inter-American Peace System" envisaged in Resolutions IX and XXXIX of the Inter-American Conference on Problems of War and Peace,

That the obligation of mutual assistance and common defense of the American Republics is essentially related to their democratic ideals and to their will to cooperate permanently in the fulfillment of the principles and purposes of a policy of peace;

That the American regional community affirms as a manifest truth that juridical organization is a necessary prerequisite of security and peace, and that peace is founded on justice and moral order and, consequently, on the international recognition and protection of human rights and freedoms, on the indispensable well-being of the people, and on the effectiveness of democracy for the international realization of justice and security,

Have resolved, in conformity with the objectives stated above, to conclude the following Treaty, in order to assure peace, through adequate means, to provide for effective reciprocal assistance to meet armed attacks against any American State, and in order to deal with threats of aggression against any of them:

Article 1. The High Contracting Parties formally condemn war and undertake in their international relations not to resort to the threat or the use of force in any manner inconsistent with the provisions of the Charter of the United Nations or of this Treaty.

Article 2. As a consequence of the principle set forth in the preceding Article, the High Contracting Parties undertake to submit every controversy which may arise between them to methods of peaceful settlement and to endeavor to settle any such controversy among themselves by means of the procedures in force in the Inter-American System before referring it to the General Assembly or the Security Council of the United Nations.

Article 3. 1. The High Contracting Parties agree that an armed attack by any State against an American State shall be considered as an attack against all the American States and, consequently, each one of the said Contracting Parties undertakes to assist in meeting the attack in the exercise of the inherent right of individual or collective self-defense recognized by Article 51 of the Charter of the United Nations.

2. On the request of the State or States directly attacked and until the decision of the Organ of Consultation of the Inter-American System, each one of the Contracting Parties may determine the immediate measures which it may individually take in fulfillment of the obligation contained in the preceding paragraph and in accordance with the principle of continental solidarity. The Organ of Consultation shall meet without delay for the purpose of examining those measures and agreeing upon the measures of a collective character that should be taken.

3. The provisions of this Article shall be applied in case of any armed attack which takes place within the region described in Article 4 or within the territory of an American State. When the attack takes place outside of the said areas, the provisions of Article 6 shall be applied.

4. Measures of self-defense provided for under this Article may be taken until the Security Council of the United Nations has taken the measures necessary to maintain international peace and security.

Article 4. The region to which this Treaty refers is bounded as follows: beginning at the North Pole; thence due south to a point 74 degrees north latitude, 10 degrees west longitude;

thence by a rhumb line to a point 47 degrees 30 minutes north latitude, 50 degrees west longitude; thence by a rhumb line to a point 35 degrees north latitude, 60 degrees west longitude; thence due south to a point in 20 degrees north latitude; thence by a rhumb line to a point 5 degrees north latitude, 24 degrees west longitude; thence due south to the South Pole; thence due north to a point 30 degrees south latitude, 90 degrees west longitude; thence by a rhumb line to a point on the Equator at 97 degrees west longitude; thence by a rhumb line to a point 15 degrees north latitude, 120 degrees west longitude; thence by a rhumb line to a point 50 degrees north latitude, 170 degrees east longitude; thence due north to a point in 54 degrees north latitude; thence by a rhumb line to a point 65 degrees 30 minutes north latitude, 168 degrees 58 minutes 5 seconds west longitude: thence due north to the North Pole.

Article 5. The High Contracting Parties shall immediately send to the Security Council of the United Nations, in conformity with Articles 51 and 54 of the Charter of the United Nations, complete information concerning the activities undertaken or in contemplation in the exercise of the right of self-defense or for the purpose of maintaining inter-American peace and security.

Article 6. If the inviolability or the integrity of the territory or the sovereignty or political independence of any American State should be affected by an aggression which is not an armed attack or by an extra-continental or intra-continental conflict, or by any other fact or situation might endanger the peace of America, the Organ of Consultation shall meet immediately in order to agree on the measures which must be taken in case of aggression to assist the victim of the aggression or, in any case, the measures which should be taken for the common defense and for the maintenance of the peace and security of the Continent.

Article 7. In the case of a conflict between two or more American States, without prejudice to the right of self-defense in conformity with Article 51 of the Charter of the United Nations, the High Contracting Parties, meeting in consultation shall call upon the contending States to suspend hostilities and restore matters to the status quo ante bellum, and shall take in addition all other necessary measures to reestablish or maintain inter-American peace and security and for the solution of the conflict by peaceful means. The rejection of the pacifying action will be considered in the determination of the aggressor and in the application of the measures which the consultative meeting may agree upon.

Article 8. For the purposes of this Treaty, the measures on which the Organ of Consultation may agree will comprise one or more of the following: recall of chiefs of diplomatic missions; breaking of diplomatic relations; breaking of consular relations; partial or complete interruption of economic relations or of rail, sea, air, postal, telegraphic, telephonic, and radiotelephonic or radiotelegraphic communications; and use of armed force.

Article 9. In addition to other acts which the Organ of Consultation may characterize as aggression, the following shall be considered as such:

a. Unprovoked armed attack by a State against the territory, the people, or the land, sea or air forces of another State;

b. Invasion, by the armed forces of a State, of the territory of an American State, through the trespassing of boundaries demarcated in accordance with a treaty, judicial decision, or arbitral award, or, in the absence of frontiers thus demarcated, invasion affecting a region which is under the effective jurisdiction of another State.

Article 10. None of the provisions of this Treaty shall be construed as impairing the rights and obligations of the High Contracting Parties under the Charter of the United Nations.

Article 11. The consultations to which this Treaty refers shall be carried out by means of the Meetings of Ministers of Foreign Affairs of the American Republics which have ratified the Treaty, or in the manner or by the organ which in the future may be agreed upon.

Article 12. The Governing Board of the Pan American Union may act provisionally as an organ of consultation until the meeting of the Organ of Consultation referred to in the preceding Article takes place.

Article 13. The consultations shall be initiated at the request addressed to the Governing Board of the Pan American Union by any of the Signatory States which has ratified the Treaty.

Article 14. In the voting referred to in this Treaty only the representatives of the Signatory States which have ratified the Treaty may take part.

Article 15. The Governing Board of the Pan American Union shall act in all matters concerning this treaty as an organ of liaison among the Signatory States which have ratified this Treaty between these States and the United Nations.

Article 16. The decisions of the Governing Board of the Pan American Union referred to in Articles 13 and 15 above shall be taken by an absolute majority of the Members entitled to vote.

Article 17. The Organ of Consultation shall take its decisions by a vote of two-thirds of the Signatory States which have ratified the Treaty.

Article 18. In the case of a situation or dispute between American States, the parties directly interested shall be excluded from the voting referred to in two preceding Articles.

Article 19. To constitute a quorum in all the meetings referred to in the previous Articles, it shall be necessary that the number of States represented shall be at least equal to the number of votes necessary for the taking of the decision.

Article 20. Decisions which require the application of the measures specified in Article 8 shall be binding upon all the Signatory States which have ratified this Treaty, with the sole exception that no State shall be required to use armed force without its consent.

Article 21. The measures agreed upon by the Organ of Consultation shall be executed through the procedures and agencies now existing or those which may in the future be established.

Article 22. This Treaty shall come into effect between the States which ratify it as soon as the ratifications of two-thirds of the Signatory States have been deposited.

Article 23. This Treaty is open for signature by the American States at the city of Rio de Janeiro, and shall be ratified by the Signatory States as soon as possible in accordance with their respective constitutional processes. The ratifications shall be deposited with the Pan American Union, which shall notify the Signatory States of each deposit. Such notification shall be considered as an exchange of ratifications.

Article 24. The present Treaty shall be registered with the Secretariat of the United Nations through the Pan American Union, when two-thirds of the Signatory States have deposited their ratifications.

Article 25. This Treaty shall remain in force indefinitely, but may be denounced by any High Contracting Party by a notification in writing to the Pan American Union, which shall inform all the other High Contracting Parties of each notification of denunciation received. After the expiration of two years from the date of the receipt by the Pan American Union of a notification of denunciation by any High Contracting Party, the present Treaty shall cease to be in force and with respect to such State, but shall remain in full force and effect with respect to all the other high Contracting Parties.

Article 26. The principles and fundamental provisions of this Treaty shall be incorporated in the Organic Pact of the Inter-American System.

In witness whereof, the undersigned Plenipotentiaries, having deposited their full powers found to be in due and proper form, sign this Treaty on behalf of their respective Governments, on the dates appearing opposite their signatures.

Done in the city of Rio de Janeiro, in four texts respectively in the English, French, Portuguese and Spanish languages, on the second of September nineteen hundred forty-seven.

4.1334 Treaty of Friendship, Co-operation, and Mutual Assistance between Yugoslavia and Hungary

Alliance Members: Yugoslavia and Hungary
Signed On: December 8, 1947, in the city of Budapest (Hungary). In force until June 28, 1948.
Alliance Type: Defense Pact (Type I)

Source: *U.S. State Department 1948, Documents and State Papers,* series 1, vol. 4, p. 242–243.

SUMMARY

As with the many other Yugoslav alliances signed by Marshall Tito in the years immediately after World War II, this treaty established friendly relations with a neighbor state and sought guarantees against renewed revisionism by Germany. Although the treaty called for close political, economic, and cultural cooperation, the agreement ended quickly as Eastern Bloc countries broke from Tito following Yugoslavia's pursuit of greater independence from Soviet Russia.

ALLIANCE TEXT

Convinced that intimate friendly ties and close collaboration correspond to the real interests of the peoples of the Federal People's Republic of Yugoslavia and the people of Hungary, who see in them a guaranty of their liberty and independence, their unlimited development and growth, as well as securing and consolidating peace in this part of Europe;

Having in view the vital interest of both countries in mutual defense and bearing in mind experience gained in the last World War, when Germany attacked a number of European nations and menaced their liberty, political independence and territorial integrity, firmly determined to fight jointly against every aggression aimed against their peoples and to resist with joint forces both all attempts to renew German imperialism as well as its possible allies or other aggressors, in whatever form;

Wishing to strengthen their existing friendly relations and to affirm, in a solemn manner, their unshakeable will jointly to defend in the future their liberty, independence and integrity and to establish their mutual relations in the spirit of friendship and collaboration in the interest of consolidating peace and international collaboration;

The Praesidium of the National Assembly of the Federal People's Republic of Yugoslavia and the President of the Hungarian Republic have decided to conclude a Treaty of Friendship, Collaboration and Mutual Assistance and for that purpose have appointed their Plenipotentiaries, namely:

The Praesidium of the National Assembly of the Federal People's Republic of Yugoslavia: Marshal Josip-Broz-Tito, Prime Minister of the Federal People's Republic of Yugoslavia, and

The President of the Hungarian Republic: Mr. Layos Dinnyes, Prime Minister of the Hungarian Republic,

Who, having exchanged their credentials, which were found to be correct, have agreed upon the following articles:

Article 1. The High Contracting Parties agree in the interests of their countries and peoples, to unite in a policy of lasting friendship which they will strengthen by close mutual collaboration.

Article 2. The High Contracting Parties shall confer on all those important international questions which concern the interests of both countries or peace and international collaboration, and will act by common consent in conformity with the spirit of the United Nations Charter, and shall execute in agreement all necessary measures in order to ensure their security, independence and integrity.

Article 3. In case Germany or any third state should attack one of the High Contracting Parties with the aim of threatening its independence, enslaving it or taking its territories, the other High Contracting Parties shall lend to it without delay military and every other assistance by all means at its disposal.

Article 4. The High Contracting Parties pledge themselves not to conclude any alliances or participate in any action directed against the other High Contracting Party.

Article 5. The parties shall mutually strengthen, by appropriate treaties and agreements within their sphere of competence, the economic, cultural and other relations between their countries.

Article 6. This Treaty does not affect in any respect the obligations assumed by the Federal People's Republic of Yugoslavia and the Republic of Hungary towards third states. The High Contracting Parties shall implement this Treaty in the spirit of the United Nations Charter and shall support every initiative aimed at removing the hot-beds of aggression and safeguarding peace and security in the world.

Article 7. The present Treaty becomes operative by the exchange of ratification documents in Belgrade, and remains valid for a period of twenty years after the date of signature. If at the end of this twenty-year period neither of the High Contracting Parties expresses a wish, one year prior to the date of expiration, to terminate this Treaty, it remains in force for a further period of five years, and after this time, until one of the High Contracting Parties terminates it in writing one year prior to the lapse of the five year term.

In witness whereof the Plenipotentiaries have signed the present agreement and placed their signatures hereunder.

Done at Budapest, this December 8, 1947, in duplicate, in Serbo-Croatian and Hungarian languages, both texts having equal validity.

4.1335 Treaty of Friendship, Peaceful Cooperation, and Mutual Aid between the Federal People's Republic of Yugoslavia and the Kingdom of Romania

Alliance Members: Yugoslavia and Romania
Signed On: December 19, 1947, in the city of Bucharest (Romania). In force until June 28, 1948.
Alliance Type: Defense Pact (Type I)

Source: *United Nations Treaty*, no. 1571.

SUMMARY

This treaty was the last alliance formed by Marshall Tito with Yugoslavia's neighbors prior to his break with the Soviet Union. As with the other alliances, both parties pledged cooperation and mutual aid in the case of attack and that neither party would engage in an alliance targeting the other state. Tito's foreign policy of regional cooperation came to an abrupt halt when Stalin sought to enforce Soviet supremacy in communist ideology. Romania officially renounced this pact in September of 1949.

ALLIANCE TEXT

Convinced that ties of sincere friendship and close co-operation in all fields will serve the real interests of the people of the Federal People's Republic of Yugoslavia and the Romanian people, safeguard their freedom, independence, development and prosperity, and strengthen and consolidate peace in the Balkans;

Bearing in mind the vital interest of both countries in mutual defence and the experience of the last world war, when Germany attacked several peoples of Europe and threatened their freedom, independence and territorial integrity;

Being firmly resolved to fight jointly against any aggression directed against their peoples, and to resist with their combined forces any new attempt at imperialist expansion by Germany or by its satellites of any kind,

Desiring to strengthen the bonds of friendship existing between them, and solemnly affirming their unwavering determination jointly in future to defend their freedom, independence and territorial integrity and to conduct their reciprocal relations in a spirit of friendship and co-operation with the aim of strengthening international peace and co-operation;

The Presidium of the National Skupshtina of the Federal People's Republic of Yugoslavia and His Majesty the King of Romania have resolved to conclude an agreement of friendship, co-operation and mutual aid and for this purpose have appointed as their plenipotentiaries:

The Presidium of the National Skupshtina of the Federal People's Republic of Yugoslavia: Marshal Joseph Broz-Tito, Prime Minister of the Government of the Federal People's Republic of Yugoslavia, and

His Majesty the King of Romania: Dr. Petru Groza, President of the Government of Romania,

Who, having exchanged their full powers found in good and due form, have agreed on the following provisions:

Article 1. The High Contracting Parties, in the interests of both countries and their peoples, agree to reaffirm their unwavering determination to join together in firm and lasting friendship and close co-operation between the two countries.

Article 2. The High Contracting Parties will consult together on all important international problems affecting the interests of their two countries or international peace and co-operation, will proceed jointly in accordance with the United Nations Charter, and will take jointly all measures necessary to ensure their security, independence and territorial integrity.

Article 3. If one of the High Contracting Parties becomes involved in hostilities with Germany because that country has again adopted a policy of aggression, or if it is attacked by any other country or countries with intent to threaten its independence, invade it or seize its territory, the other High Contracting Party shall afford it, by all available means, immediate military and other assistance and support.

Article 4. Each High Contracting Party undertakes not to enter into any alliance or to participate in any action directed against the other.

Article 5. The High Contracting Parties will take the most fitting measures to consolidate and amplify the economic, cultural and other ties between the two countries by treaties and agreements concluded for that purpose.

Article 6. This Treaty shall in no way prejudice engagements entered into by the Federal People's Republic of Yugoslavia and the Kingdom of Romania with other countries.

The High Contracting Parties will execute this Treaty in conformity with the United Nations Charter, and shall support any steps taken to eliminate centres of aggression or to promote peace and security throughout the world.

Article 7. This Treaty shall come into force on the date of signature and shall be subject to ratification. Instruments of ratification shall be exchanged at Belgrade.

This Treaty shall remain in force for twenty years from the date of signature. Unless a High Contracting Party, at least one year before the expiry of the twenty-year period, gives notice of intention to terminate the Treaty, it shall remain in force for a further period of five years and thereafter for successive similar periods until a High Contracting Party shall denounce it twelve months before the expiry of the current five-year period.

Done at Bucharest on 19 December 1947, in two copies in Serbo-Croat and Romanian, both texts being equally authentic.

In Faith Whereof the Plenipotentiaries have signed this Treaty and have affixed thereto their seals.

(Signed) Dr. Petru GROZA
(Signed) J. B. TITO

4.1336 Treaty of Friendship, Co-operation, and Mutual Assistance between the Hungarian Republic and the Romanian People's Republic

Alliance Members: Hungary and Romania
Signed On: January 24, 1948, in the city of Budapest (Hungary). In force until May 8, 1989.
Alliance Type: Defense Pact (Type I)

Source: *United Nations Treaty,* no. 6920.

SUMMARY

This alliance between neighbors was an effort to establish friendly relations and increased trade as well as solidify ties among communist states in the Soviet sphere of influence. The treaty committed the two parties to the establishment of a lasting policy of friendship and cooperation, consultation with each other on important international problems, extension of immediate military assistance to each other if faced with German aggression, and assurance of not entering into any alliance aimed against the other party. Both countries signed similar agreements with the Soviet Union within one month of signing this treaty. The alliance between Hungary and Romania lasted until the dissolution of the communist leadership in Hungary in 1989.

ALLIANCE TEXT

Convinced that the strengthening of friendly relations and the development of close co-operation are of the greatest importance in safeguarding the interests of the Hungarian and Romanian peoples and in ensuring their freedom, independence and development and serve at the same time to guarantee peace in the Danube Basin and the Balkans,

Bearing in mind the experience of the Second World War, when Germany taking advantage of the chauvinistic and

373

expansionistic ambitions of the reactionary and fascist ruling groups of both countries, destroyed the independence of Hungary and Romania and used the two countries as bases for its policy of conquest, involving them in war against the Union of Soviet Socialist Republics,

Being firmly resolved to resist with their combined forces any attempt to revive German imperialism and all those who support it and to act together in defending their freedom, independence and territorial integrity against any attack,

Desiring, with a view to consolidating peace in the Danube Basin and the Balkans and promoting international co-operation and peace, to strengthen the good relations existing between them and to conduct their future relations in a spirit of friendship and fraternal co-operation,

The President of the Hungarian Republic and the Provisional Presidium of the Romanian People's Republic have resolved to conclude a treaty of friendship, co-operation and mutual assistance and for that purpose have appointed as their plenipotentiaries:

Lajos Dinnyés, Chairman of the Council of Ministers of the Hungarian Republic, and

Dr. Petru Groza, Chairman of the Council of Ministers of the Romanian People's Republic, who, having exchanged their full powers, found in good and due form, have agreed as follows:

Article 1. The High Contracting Parties agree, in the interests of their countries and peoples, to affirm their determination to join forces in establishing a lasting policy of friendship by developing and consolidating co-operation between the two countries.

Article 2. The High Contracting Parties shall consult together on all important international problems affecting the interests of the two countries or of peace and international co-operation, shall act jointly in the spirit of the Charter of the United Nations, and shall by agreement take all measures required for the maintenance of their security, independence and territorial integrity.

Article 3. If Germany or any other State attacks one of the High Contracting Parties with intent to threaten its independence or territorial integrity or to subjugate it, the other High Contracting Party shall immediately extend military and all other assistance to it by every available means.

Article 4. Each High Contracting Party undertakes not to enter into any alliance or participate in any action directed against the other.

Article 5. The High Contracting Parties shall take the necessary measures to develop and strengthen the economic, cultural and other ties between the two countries and shall conclude treaties and agreements for that purpose.

Article 6. This Treaty shall in no way affect engagements already entered into by the Hungarian Republic or the Romanian People's Republic with other States. The High Contracting Parties shall implement this Treaty in the spirit of the Charter of the United Nations and shall support and promote any action

to eliminate centres of aggression and to safeguard peace and security in the world.

Article 7. This Treaty shall enter into force upon the exchange of the instruments of ratification, which shall take place at Bucharest, and shall remain in force for a period of twenty years from the date of its entry into force. If neither of the High Contracting Parties gives notice, one year before the expiry of the Treaty, of its desire to terminate the latter, the Treaty shall remain in force for a further period of five years and similarly thereafter until such time as one of the High Contracting Parties gives notice in writing, one year before the expiry of the current five-year period, of its intention to terminate the Treaty.

In Witness Whereof the plenipotentiaries have signed this Treaty and have thereto affixed their seals.

Done in duplicate in the Hungarian and Romanian languages, both texts being authentic.

Budapest, 24 January 1948.

For the Hungarian Republic:

DINNYÉS LAJOS
Chairman of the Council of Ministers

For the Romanian People's Republic:

Petru GROZA
Chairman of the Council of Ministers

4.1337 Treaty of Friendship, Co-operation, and Mutual Assistance between the Union of Soviet Socialist Republics and the Romanian People's Republic

Alliance Members: Union of Soviet Socialist Republics and Romania
Signed On: February 4, 1948, in the city of Moscow. In force until December 12, 1989.
Alliance Type: Defense Pact (Type I)

Source: *United Nations Treaty,* no. 745.

SUMMARY

This treaty continued a policy of cooperation between the Soviets and their eastern European neighbors that was initially begun with the Soviet alliance with Czechoslovakia during World War II. The intent of these treaties was to provide for common assistance in the event of renewed aggression by Germany, but, more broadly, the defense pacts served to reinforce ties between the Soviets and European countries within their sphere of influence. This alliance, and the similar alliance with Hungary signed two weeks later, also confirmed Soviet leadership over communist authority in southeastern Europe, which was under direct ideological attack following Tito's call for regionalism and limited independence. Leaders in both Romania and Hungary quickly renounced Tito following Yugoslavia's expulsion from the Cominform.

This alliance was replaced in 1970 by a similar treaty, and the alliance relationship lasted until Romanian president Ceausescu was overthrown.

ALLIANCE TEXT

The Presidium of the Supreme Soviet of the Union of Soviet Socialist Republics and the Presidium of the Romanian People's Republic,

Desiring to consolidate friendly relations between the Soviet Union and Romania,

Being anxious to maintain close co-operation with one another in the interests of strengthening universal peace and security, in conformity with the purposes and principles of the United Nations,

Being persuaded that the maintenance of friendship and good-neighbourly relations between the Soviet Union and Romania is in accordance with the vital interests of the peoples of both States and will best serve to promote their economic development,

Have resolved for this purpose to conclude the present Treaty and to appoint as their plenipotentiaries:

The Presidium of the Supreme Soviet of the Union of Soviet Socialist

Republics: Vyacheslav Mihailovich Molotov, Vice-President of the Council of Ministers and Minister of Foreign Affairs of the USSR;

The Presidium of the Romanian People's Republic: Petru Groza, President of the Council of Ministers of the Romanian People's Republic,

Who, having exchanged their full powers, found in good and due form, have agreed on the following provisions:

Article 1. The High Contracting Parties agree to take all joint action in their power to obviate any threat of renewed aggression by Germany or any other Power which might be associated with Germany either directly or in any other way.

The High Contracting Parties declare that they intend to participate, in the sincerest fashion, in all international action for ensuring the peace and security of peoples and will fully contribute to the realization of these lofty aims.

Article 2. Should either of the High Contracting Parties be involved in hostilities with a Germany which might seek to renew its policy of aggression, or with any other State which might have been associated with Germany in a policy of aggression either directly or in any other way, the other High Contracting Party shall immediately extend to the Contracting Party involved in hostilities military and other assistance with all the means at its disposal.

The present Treaty will be implemented in conformity with the principles of the United Nations Charter.

Article 3. The High Contracting Parties respectively agree not to enter into any alliance or take part in any coalition or in any action or measures directed against the other High Contracting Party.

Article 4. The High Contracting Parties will consult together on all important international questions involving the interests of both countries.

Article 5. The High Contracting Parties declare that they will act in a spirit of friendship and co-operation for the further development and strengthening of the economic and cultural ties between the two States, in accordance with the principles of mutual respect for their independence and sovereignty and of noninterference in the internal affairs of the other State.

Article 6. The present Treaty will remain in force for twenty years from the date of signature. If neither of the High Contracting Parties gives notice one year before the expiration of the said twenty-year period that it wishes to denounce the Treaty, it will remain in force for a further five years until such time as either High Contracting Party gives notice in writing one year before the expiration of the current five-year period of its intention to terminate the Treaty.

The present Treaty shall come into force immediately upon signature and shall be subject to ratification in the shortest possible time. The instruments of ratification will be exchanged at Bucharest at an early date.

In Faith Whereof the plenipotentiaries have signed the present Treaty and attached their seals thereto.

Done at Moscow on 4 February 1948, in two copies, each in the Russian and Romanian languages, both texts being equally authentic.

By authorization of the Presidium of the Supreme Soviet of the USSR:

(Signed) V. MOLOTOV
[SEAL]

By authorization of the Presidium of the Romanian People's Republic:

(Signed) Petru GROZA
[SEAL]

4.1338 Treaty of Friendship, Co-operation, and Mutual Assistance between the Union of Soviet Socialist Republics and the Republic of Hungary

Alliance Members: Union of Soviet Socialist Republics and Hungary
Signed On: February 18, 1948, in the city of Moscow. In force until October 7, 1989.
Alliance Type: Defense Pact (Type I)

Source: *United Nations Treaty*, no. 743.

SUMMARY

Similar in form and function to the Soviet alliance signed with Romania fourteen days earlier, this treaty called for concerted aid in the event of renewed German aggression. Both treaties served as a basis for establishing the terms for cooperation in the Warsaw Pact of 1955. This treaty was replaced by a similar alliance in 1967, and the Soviet-Hungarian defense pact lasted until October of 1989, when the Hungarian Communist Party renounced Marxism and embraced democratic socialism.

ALLIANCE TEXT

The Presidium of the Supreme Soviet of the Union of Soviet Socialist Republics and the President of the Republic of Hungary,

With a view to the further development of friendly relations between the USSR and Hungary,

Being convinced that the strengthening of good-neighbourly relations, cooperation and friendship between the peoples of the Soviet Union and Hungary is in accordance with their vital interests and will best serve to promote the economic development of both States,

Being inflexibly resolved to co-operate in the interest of strengthening universal peace and security in accordance with the purposes and principles of the United Nations,

Have decided for this purpose to conclude the present Treaty and to appoint as their plenipotentiaries:

The Presidium of the Supreme Soviet of the Union of Soviet Socialist

Republics: Vyacheslav Milhailovich Molotov, Vice-President of the Council of Ministers and Minister of Foreign Affairs of the USSR;

The President of the Republic of Hungary: Lajos Dinnyés, President of the Council of Ministers of the Republic of Hungary,

Who, having exchanged their full powers, found in good and due form, have agreed on the following provisions:

Article 1. The High Contracting Parties agree to take all joint action in their power to obviate any threat of renewed aggression by Germany or any other Power which might be associated with Germany, either directly or in any other way.

The High Contracting Parties confirm their intention to participate, in the sincerest fashion, in all international action for ensuring the peace and security of peoples and will fully contribute to the realization of these lofty aims.

Article 2. Should either of the High Contracting Parties be involved in hostilities with Germany or with any State associated with Germany in acts of aggression in Europe which States might seek to renew their policy of aggression, or with any other State which might be associated with Germany directly or in any other way in a policy of aggression, the other High Contracting Party shall immediately extend to the Contracting Party involved in hostilities military and other assistance with all the means at its disposal.

The present Treaty will be implemented in conformity with the principles of the United Nations Charter.

Article 3. The High Contracting Parties respectively agree not to enter into alliance or take part in any coalition or in any action or measures directed against the other High Contracting Party.

Article 4. The High Contracting Parties will consult together on all important international questions involving the interests of both countries.

Article 5. The High Contracting Parties affirm their resolve to act in a spirit of cooperation and friendship for the further development and strengthening of the economic and cultural ties between the USSR and Hungary; they will act in accordance with the principles of mutual respect for their independence and national sovereignty and of non-interference in the internal affairs of the other State.

Article 6. The present Treaty will remain in force for twenty years from the date of its coming into force. If neither of the High Contracting Parties gives notice one year before the expiration of the said twenty-year period that it wishes to denounce the Treaty, it will remain in force for a further five years, until such time as either High Contracting Party gives notice in writing one year before the expiration of the current five-year period of its intention to terminate the Treaty.

The present Treaty shall be subject to ratification in the shortest possible time and shall come into force on the date of the exchange of the instruments of ratification, which will take place at Budapest at an early date.

In Faith Whereof the plenipotentiaries have signed the present Treaty and attached their seals thereto.

Done at Moscow on 18 February 1948, in two copies, each in the Russian and Hungarian languages, both texts being equally authentic.

By authorization of the Presidium of the Supreme Soviet of the USSR:

(Signed) V. MOLOTOV
[SEAL]

By authorization of the President of the Republic of Hungary:

(Signed) DINNYÉS
[SEAL]

4.1339 Treaty among Belgium, France, Luxembourg, the Netherlands, and the United Kingdom of Great Britain and Northern Ireland

Alliance Members: Belgium, France, Luxembourg, the Netherlands, and the United Kingdom
Signed On: March 17, 1948, in the city of Brussels. In force as of date of publication of this volume.
Alliance Type: Defense Pact (Type I)

Source: *United Nations Treaty,* no. 304.

SUMMARY

This alliance grew out of the bilateral French-British pact signed in 1947. Member states immediately called for the admission of the United States into the alliance in order to counter the growing power and influence of the Soviet Union in Europe. The United States did not join the alliance, opting instead to create the North Atlantic Treaty Organization with six other states. The new institution was headquartered in Brussels. This particular treaty was renegotiated in 1954, and the renewed alliance is still in force.

ALLIANCE TEXT

His Royal Highness the Prince Regent of Belgium, the President of the French Republic, President of the French Union, Her Royal Highness the Grand Duchess of Luxembourg, Her Majesty the Queen of the Netherlands and His Majesty the King of Great Britain, Ireland and the British Dominions beyond the Seas,

Resolved

To reaffirm their faith in fundamental human rights, in the dignity and worth of the human person and in the other ideals proclaimed in the Charter of the United Nations;

To fortify and preserve the principles of democracy, personal freedom and political liberty, the constitutional traditions and the rule of law, which are their common heritage;

To strengthen, with these aims in view, the economic, social and cultural ties by which they are already united;

To cooperate loyally and to coordinate their efforts to create in Western Europe a firm basis for European economic recovery;

To afford assistance to each other, in accordance with the Charter of the United Nations, in maintaining international peace and security and in resisting any policy of aggression;

To take such steps as may be held to be necessary in the event of a renewal by Germany of a policy of aggression;

To associate progressively in the pursuance of these aims other States inspired by the same ideals and animated by the like determination;

Desiring for these purposes to conclude a treaty for collaboration in economic, social and cultural matters and for collective self-defence;

Have appointed as their Plenipotentiaries:

His Royal Highness the Prince Regent of Belgium, His Excellency Mr. Paul-Henri Spaak, Prime Minister, Minister of Foreign Affairs, and His Excellency Mr. Gaston Eyskens, Minister of Finance,

The President of the French Republic, President of the French Union, His Excellency M. Georges Bidault, Minister of Foreign Affairs, and His Excellency Mr. Jean de Hauteclocque, Ambassador Extraordinary and Plenipotentiary of the French Republic in Brussels,

Her Royal Highness the Grand Duchess of Luxemburg, His Excellency M. Joseph Bech, Minister of Foreign Affairs, and His Excellency Mr. Robert Als, Envoy Extraordinary and Minister Plenipotentiary of Luxembourg in Brussels.

Her Majesty the Queen of the Netherlands, His Excellency Baron C. G. W. H. van Boetzelaer van Oosterhout, Minister of Foreign Affairs, and His Excellency Baron Binnert Philip van Harinxma thoe Slooten, Ambassador Extraordinary and Plenipotentiary of the Netherlands in Brussels.

His Majesty the King of Great Britain, Ireland and the British Dominions beyond the Seas, for the United Kingdom of Great Britain and Northern Ireland, The Right Honorable Ernest Bevin, Member of Parliament, Principal Secretary of State for Foreign Affairs, and His Excellency Sir George William Rendel, K.C.M.G. Ambassador Extraordinary and Plenipotentiary of His Britannic Majesty in Brussels, who, having exhibited their full powers found in good and due form, have agreed as follows:

Article I. Convinced of the close community of their interests and of the necessity of uniting in order to promote the economic recovery of Europe, the High Contracting Parties will so organize and coordinate their economic activities as to produce the best possible results, by the elimination of conflict in their economic policies, the coordination of production and the development of commercial exchanges.

The cooperation provided for in the preceding paragraph, which will be effected through the Consultative Council referred to in Article VII as well as through other bodies, shall not involve any duplication of, or prejudice to, the work of other economic organizations in which the High Contracting Parties are or may be represented but shall on the contrary assist the work of those organizations.

Article II. The High Contracting Parties will make every effort in common, both by direct consultation and in specialized agencies, to promote the attainment of a higher standard of living by their peoples and to develop on corresponding lines the social and other related services of their countries.

The High Contracting Parties will consult with the object of achieving the earliest possible application of recommendations of immediate practical interest, relating to social matters, adopted with their approval in the specialized agencies.

They will endeavour to conclude as soon as possible conventions with each other in the sphere of social security.

Article III. The High Contracting Parties will make every effort in common to lead their peoples towards a better understanding of the principles which form the basis of their common civilization and to promote cultural exchanges by conventions between themselves or by other means.

Article IV. If any of the High Contracting Parties should be the object of an armed attack in Europe, the other High Contracting Parties will, in accordance with the provisions of Article 51 of the Charter of the United Nations, afford the Party so attacked all the military and other aid and assistance in their power.

Article V. All measures taken as a result of the preceding Article shall be immediately reported to the Security Council. They shall be terminated as soon as the Security Council has taken the measures necessary to maintain or restore international peace and security.

The present Treaty does not prejudice in any way the obligations of the High Contracting Parties under the provisions of the Charter of the United Nations. It shall not be interpreted as affecting in any way the authority and responsibility of the Security Council under the Charter to take at any time such action as it deems necessary in order to maintain or restore international peace and security.

Article VI. The High Contracting Parties declare, each so far as he is concerned, that none of the international engagements now in force between him and any other of the High Contracting Parties or any third State is in conflict with the provisions of the present Treaty.

None of the High Contracting Parties will conclude any alliance or participate in any coalition directed against any other of the High Contracting Parties.

Article VII. For the purpose of consulting together on all the questions dealt with in the present Treaty, the High Contracting Parties will create a Consultative Council, which shall be so organized as to be able to exercise its functions continuously. The Council shall meet at such times as it shall deem fit.

At the request of any of the High Contracting Parties, the Council shall be immediately convened in order to permit the High Contracting Parties to consult with regard to any situation which may constitute a threat to peace, in whatever area this threat should arise; with regard to the attitude to be adopted and the steps to be taken in case of a renewal by Germany of an aggressive policy; or with regard to any situation constituting a danger to economic stability.

Article VIII. In pursuance of their determination to settle disputes only by peaceful means, the High Contracting Parties will apply to disputes between themselves the following provisions:

The High Contracting Parties will, while the present Treaty remains in force, settle all disputes falling within the scope of Article 36, paragraph 2, of the Statute of the International Court of Justice by referring them to the Court, subject only, in the case of each of them, to any reservation already made by that Party when accepting this clause for compulsory jurisdiction to the extent that that Party may maintain the reservation.

In addition, the High Contracting Parties will submit to conciliation all disputes outside the scope of Article 36, paragraph 2, of the Statute of the International Court of Justice.

In the case of a mixed dispute involving both questions for which conciliation is appropriate and other questions for which judicial settlement is appropriate, any Party to the dispute shall have the right to insist that the judicial settlement of the legal questions shall precede conciliation.

The preceding provisions of this Article in no way affect the application of relevant provisions or agreements prescribing some other method of pacific settlement.

Article IX. The High Contracting Parties may, by agreement, invite any other State to accede to the present Treaty on condition to be agreed between them and the State so invited.

Any State so invited may become a Party to the Treaty by depositing an instrument of accession with the Belgian Government.

The Belgian Government will inform each of the High Contracting Parties of the deposit of each instrument of accession.

Article X. The present Treaty shall be ratified and the instruments of ratification shall be deposited as soon as possible with the Belgian Government.

It shall enter into force on the date of the deposit of the last instrument of ratification and shall thereafter remain in force for fifty years.

After the expiry of the period of fifty years, each of the High Contracting Parties shall have the right to cease to be a party thereto provided that he shall have previously given one year's notice of denunciation to the Belgian Government.

The Belgian Government shall inform the Governments of the other High Contracting Parties of the deposit of each instrument of ratification and of signed the present Treaty and have each notice of denunciation.

In witness whereof, the above mentioned Plenipotentiaries have affixed thereto their seals.

Done at Brussels, this seventeenth day of March 1948, in English and French, each text being equally authentic, in a single copy which shall remain deposited in the archives of the Belgian Government and of which certified copies shall be transmitted by that Government to each of the other signatories.

For Belgium:

(s) P. H. Spaak; G. EYSKENS

For France:

(s) Bidault; J. de Hauteclocque

For Luxembourg:

(s) Jos. Bech; Robert Als

For the Netherlands:

(s) B. v. BOETZELAER; van HARINXMA THOE SLOOTEN

For the United Kingdom of Great Britain and Northern Ireland:

(s) Ernest BEVIN; George RENDEL

4.1340 Treaty of Friendship, Co-operation, and Mutual Assistance between the Union of Soviet Socialist Republics and the People's Republic of Bulgaria

Alliance Members: Union of Soviet Socialist Republics and Bulgaria
Signed On: March 18, 1948, in the city of Moscow. In force until November 10, 1989.
Alliance Type: Defense Pact (Type I)

Source: *United Nations Treaty,* no. 741.

SUMMARY

At the end of World War II, Bulgaria had little choice but to diplomatically engage the Soviet Union, its powerful neighbor. For its part, the Soviet leadership, fearing either a renewed German threat or greater Western influence, sought greater integration with and control of the countries of eastern Europe. Thus, the aims of this pact were to increase political, economic, and military interdependence in order to "ensure . . . peace and security."

This pact and the several treaties initiated by the Soviet Union with the states of eastern Europe formed the foundation for the Warsaw Pact, signed in 1955. Bulgaria effectively ended both these alliances when, on November 10, 1989, the president of Bulgaria, Todor Zhivkov, resigned after thirty-five years of hard-line Communist rule.

ALLIANCE TEXT

The Presidium of the Supreme Soviet of the Union of Soviet Socialist Republics and the Presidium of the National Assembly of the People's Republic of Bulgaria,

With a view to the further development and strengthening of friendly relations between the USSR and Bulgaria,

Being persuaded that the strengthening of the friendship between the Soviet Union and Bulgaria is in accordance with the vital interests of the peoples of both States and will best serve to promote their economic development,

Being anxious to co-operate with one another in the interests of universal peace and security in conformity with the purposes and principles of the United Nations,

Have resolved for this purpose to conclude the present Treaty and have appointed as their plenipotentiaries:

The Presidium of the Supreme Soviet of the Union of Soviet Socialist Republics: Vyacheslav Mihailovich Molotov, Vice-President of the Council of Ministers and Minister of Foreign Affairs of the USSR;

The Presidium of the National Assembly of the People's Republic of Bulgaria: Georgi Dimitrov, President of the Council of Ministers of the People's Republic of Bulgaria,

Who, having exchanged their full powers, found in good and due form, have agreed on the following provisions:

Article 1. The High Contracting Parties agree to take all joint action in their power to obviate any threat of renewed aggression by Germany or any other Power which might be associated with Germany either directly or in any other way.

The High Contracting Parties declare that they intend to participate, in the sincerest fashion, in all international action for ensuring peace and security and will fully contribute to the realization of these lofty aims.

Article 2. Should either of the High Contracting Parties be involved in hostilities with a Germany which might seek to renew its policy of aggression or with any other State which might be associated with Germany in a policy of aggression either directly or in any other way, the other High Contracting Party shall immediately extend to the Contracting Party involved in hostilities military and other assistance with all the means at its disposal.

The present Treaty will be implemented in conformity with the principles of the United Nations Charter.

Article 3. The High Contracting Parties respectively agree not to enter into any alliance or take part in any coalition or in any action or measures directed against the other High Contracting Party.

Article 4. The High Contracting Parties will consult together on all important international questions involving the interests of both countries.

Article 5. The High Contracting Parties declare that they will develop and strengthen the economic and cultural ties between the two States in a spirit of friendship and co-operation, in accordance with the principles of mutual respect for their independence and sovereignty and of non-interference in the internal affairs of the other State.

Article 6. The present Treaty will remain in force for twenty years from the date of signature. If neither of the High Contracting Parties gives notice one year before the expiration of the said twenty-year period that it wishes to denounce the Treaty, it will remain in force for a further five years until such time as either High Contracting Party gives notice in writing one year before the expiration of the current five-year period of its intention to terminate the Treaty.

The present Treaty shall come into force immediately upon signature and shall be subject to ratification in the shortest possible time. The instruments of ratification will be exchanged at Sofia at an early date.

In Faith Whereof the plenipotentiaries have signed the present Treaty and attached their seals thereto.

Done at Moscow on 18 March 1948, in two copies, each in the Russian and Bulgarian languages, both texts being equally authentic.

By authorization of the Presidium of the Supreme Soviet of the USSR:

(Signed) V. MOLOTOV

[SEAL]

By authorization of the Presidium of the National Assembly of the People's Republic of Bulgaria:

(Signed) C. DIMITROV

[SEAL]

4.1341 Treaty of Friendship, Co-operation, and Mutual Assistance between the Union of Soviet Socialist Republics and the Republic of Finland

Alliance Members: Union of Soviet Socialist Republics and Finland
Signed On: April 6, 1948, in the city of Moscow. In force until December 25, 1991.
Alliance Type: Defense Pact (Type I)

Original Source: *United Nations Treaty,* no. 742.

SUMMARY

The Soviet-Finnish alliance was another outgrowth of the Soviet leadership's desire to control its western border. After a brief border war immediately prior to World War II, the Soviet leadership completely dominated the foreign policy of its much weaker neighbor. That is perhaps why this treaty differed from other treaties of mutual assistance signed by the Soviet Union: the obligation to intervene militarily in case of attack fell only to the Soviet Union.

The treaty was initially concluded for a ten-year period. A protocol was signed on September 19, 1955, for the extension of the mutual assistance act for an additional twenty years, after which it was automatically renewed for periods of five years. The fall of the Soviet Union in 1991 ended the treaty obligations.

ALLIANCE TEXT

The Presidium of the Supreme Soviet of the Union of Soviet Socialist Republics and the President of the Republic of Finland,

With a view to the further development of friendly relations between the USSR and Finland,

Being convinced that the strengthening of good-neighbourly relations and co-operation between the Union of Soviet Socialist Republics and the Republic of Finland is in accordance with the vital interests of both countries,

Considering Finland's endeavours not to be involved in clashes between the interests of the great Powers, and

Being inflexibly resolved to co-operate in the interests of maintaining international peace and security in conformity with the purposes and principles of the United Nations,

Have decided for this purpose to conclude the present Treaty and have appointed as their plenipotentiaries:

The Presidium of the Supreme Soviet of the Union of Soviet Socialist Republics: Vyacheslav Mihailovich Molotov, Vice-President of the Council of Ministers and Minister of Foreign Affairs of the USSR;

The President of the Republic of Finland: Mauno Pekkala, Prime Minister of the Republic of Finland,

Who, having exchanged their full powers, found in good and due form, have agreed on the following provisions:

Article 1. Should either Finland, or the Soviet Union through the territory of Finland, become the object of military aggression on the part of Germany or any Power allied with Germany, Finland will carry out its duty as a sovereign State and will fight to repel aggression. In so doing, Finland will direct all the forces at its disposal towards defending the integrity of its territory on land, sea and air, acting within the limits of its boundaries, in accordance with its obligations under the present Treaty, with the help, if necessary, of the Soviet Union or together with the Soviet Union.

In the above-mentioned cases the Soviet Union will extend to Finland any necessary assistance, this to be supplied as mutually agreed between the Parties.

Article 2. The High Contracting Parties will consult together in case there is found to be a threat of the military aggression referred to in Article I.

Article 3. The High Contracting Parties affirm their intention to participate, in the sincerest fashion, in all action for the maintenance of international peace and security in conformity with the purposes and principles of the United Nations.

Article 4. The High Contracting Parties confirm the undertaking contained in article 3 of the Treaty of Peace signed at Paris on 10 February 1947 not to enter into any alliance or take part in any coalition directed against the other High Contracting Party.

Article 5. The High Contracting Parties affirm their resolve to act in a spirit of cooperation and friendship for the further development and strengthening of the economic and cultural ties between the Soviet Union and Finland.

Article 6. The High Contracting Parties agree to act in accordance with the principles of mutual respect for their national sovereignty and independence and of noninterference in the internal affairs of the other State.

Article 7. The present Treaty will be implemented in conformity with the principles of the United Nations.

Article 8. The present Treaty will be subject to ratification and will remain in force for ten years from the date of its coming into force. The Treaty will come into force on the date of the exchange of the instruments of ratification, which will take place at Helsinki as soon as possible.

If neither of the High Contracting Parties gives notice one year before the expiration of the said ten-year period that it wishes to denounce the Treaty, it will remain in force for a further five years, until such time as either High Contracting Party gives notice in writing one year before the expiration of the current five-year period of its intention to terminate the Treaty.

In Faith Whereof the plenipotentiaries have signed the present Treaty and attached their seals thereto.

Done at Moscow on 6 April 1948, in two copies, each in the Russian and Finnish languages, both texts being equally authentic.

By authorization of the Presidium of the Supreme Soviet of the USSR:

(Signed) V. MOLOTOV

[SEAL]

By authorization of the President of the Republic of Finland:

(Signed) Mauno PEKKALA

[SEAL]

4.1342 Treaty of Friendship, Co-operation, and Mutual Assistance between the Polish Republic and the People's Republic of Bulgaria

Alliance Members: Poland and Bulgaria
Signed On: May 29, 1948, in the city of Warsaw. In force until August 7, 1989.
Alliance Type: Defense Pact (Type I)

Source: *United Nations Treaty,* no. 389.

SUMMARY

In the summer of 1948, Poland, Bulgaria, and Hungary signed bilateral defense pacts. The purpose of the treaties was to thwart the possibility of renewed German aggression as well as maintain and strengthen ties among the new communist regimes, and in this sense they echoed similar agreements Poland had already signed with Yugoslavia (1946) and Czechoslovakia (1947). This particular treaty was replaced by a new instrument in 1967, but the overall alliance lasted until 1989, when the Polish government gave way to Lech Walesa and his Solidarity party.

ALLIANCE TEXT

The President of the Polish Republic and the Presidium of the Supreme National Assembly of the People's Republic of Bulgaria,

Desirous of expressing the will of their two peoples to consolidate friendly relations and close co-operation between Poland and Bulgaria,

Fully realizing that the experiences of the Second World War constrain both countries to join in resisting threats to their security and independence,

Being deeply convinced that a lasting rapprochement between these two Slav countries is in conformity with their vital interests and will serve the cause of peace and international security, in accordance with the spirit of the Charter of the United Nations,

Have resolved to conclude a treaty of friendship, co-operation and mutual assistance, and for this purpose have appointed as their plenipotentiaries:

The President of the Polish Republic: Mr. Jozef Cyrankiewicz, President of the Council of Ministers of the Polish Republic, and Mr. Zygmunt Modzelewski, Minister for Foreign Affairs of the Polish Republic;

The Presidium of the Supreme National Assembly of the People's Republic of Bulgaria: Mr. Georgi Dimitrov, President of the Council of Ministers of the People's Republic of Bulgaria, and Mr. Vasil Kolarov, Vice-Premier and Minister for Foreign Affairs of the National People's Republic of Bulgaria,

Who, having exchanged their full powers, found in good and due form, have agreed upon the following provisions:

Article 1. The High Contracting Parties agree to take all action in their power to prevent further aggression by Germany or any other State which might be associated with Germany directly or in any other way.

The High Contracting Parties will, in a spirit of sincerest co-operation, participate in all international action for maintaining international peace and security and will contribute to the realization of these lofty aims.

Article 2. Should either of the High Contracting Parties be subjected to aggression by Germany or any other State which might be associated with Germany directly or indirectly or in any other way, the other High Contracting Party shall immediately afford it military and other assistance and support with all the means at its disposal.

Article 3. The High Contracting Parties agree respectively not to enter into any alliance or take part in any action directed against the other High Contracting Party.

Article 4. The High Contracting Parties will consult together on all the more important international problems affecting the interests of their two countries, more especially their security and territorial integrity or the interests of peace and international co-operation.

Article 5. The High Contracting Parties will develop and strengthen their economic and cultural relations with one another in the interests of the multilateral development of their two countries.

Article 6. The provisions of the present treaty will in no way contravene obligations previously undertaken by either of the High Contracting Parties towards other States and will be implemented in accordance with the Charter of the United Nations.

Article 7. The present treaty shall come into force on the date of the exchange of the instruments of ratification and shall remain in force for a period of twenty years.

The exchange of ratifications shall take place at Sofia. Unless the present Treaty is denounced by one of the High Contracting Parties twelve months before the expiry of the said period of twenty years, it shall remain in force for five years, and for similar periods thereafter, until one of the High Contracting Parties denounces it twelve months before the expiry of the current five-year period.

The present treaty is done in duplicate, in the Bulgarian and Polish languages, both texts being equally authentic.

In Faith Whereof the aforesaid plenipotentiaries have signed the present treaty and have affixed thereto their seals.

Warsaw, 29 May 1948.

For the President of the Polish Republic:

[L.S.] (Signed) J. CYRANKIEWICZ

[L.S.] (Signed) Z. MOCZELEWSKI

For the Presidium of the Supreme National Assembly of the People's Republic of Bulgaria:

[L.S.] (Signed) G. DIMITROV

[L.S.] (Signed) V. KOLAROV

4.1343 Treaty of Friendship, Co-operation, and Mutual Assistance between Poland and the Republic of Hungary

Alliance Members: Poland and Hungary
Signed On: June 18, 1948, in the city of Warsaw. In force until August 7, 1989.
Alliance Type: Defense Pact (Type I)

Source: *United Nations Treaty,* no. 370.

SUMMARY

Another bilateral defense pact among communist governments in eastern Europe, this treaty also targeted any possible German revisionism and sought to strengthen the new communist regimes in both countries. The situation in Hungary was particularly unstable. A coup d'état in 1947 had established the regime, and in less than a decade, popular revolts against the government had to be put down by Soviet forces. The 1956 revolts resulted in 25,000 Hungarian deaths and the flight of more than 100,000 refugees, as well as a considerable loss of public legitimacy for the ruling party. Nevertheless, this treaty lasted through this turbulent period, being replaced by a new instrument in 1968. The alliance ended in 1989 with the dismantling of the communist governments in both countries.

ALLIANCE TEXT

The President of the Republic of Poland and the President of the Republic of Hungary,

Basing themselves upon the age-long tradition of friendship between the two peoples,

Considering that the strengthening and deepening of mutual friendship and co-operation corresponds to the wishes and interests of the Polish and Hungarian peoples and will contribute to the economic development of both countries,

Declaring their firm determination to strengthen universal peace and security in accordance with the purposes and principles of the United Nations,

Have resolved to conclude a treaty of friendship, co-operation and mutual aid and for this purpose have appointed as their plenipotentiaries:

The President of the Republic of Poland: Mr. Jozef Cyrankiewicz, President of the Council of Ministers, and Mr. Zygmunt Modzelewski, Minister of Foreign Affairs;

The President of the Republic of Hungary: Mr. Lajos Dinnyés, President of the Council of Ministers, and Mr. Erik Molnár, Minister for Foreign Affairs;

Who, after having exchanged their full powers, found in good and due form, have agreed on the following provisions:

Article 1. The High Contracting Parties will participate to the fullest extent in all international actions aimed at ensuring international peace and security and will fully contribute to the realization of these lofty aims.

The High Contracting Parties undertake all joint measures within their power to obviate any threat of further aggression by Germany or any other Power associated with her either directly or in any other way.

Article 2. Should either of the High Contracting Parties become involved in hostilities with Germany in consequence of her attempting to renew her policy of aggression, or with any other State associated with Germany in a policy of aggression, the other High Contracting Party shall give him immediate military and all other assistance by every means at his disposal.

Article 3. Each High Contracting Party undertakes not to enter into any alliance or participate in any coalition, action or activity directed against the other High Contracting Party.

Article 4. The High Contracting Parties undertake to consult one another in any important international questions affecting the interests of both countries or those of international peace and co-operation.

Article 5. The High Contracting Parties will continue to develop and strengthen their mutual economic and cultural relations in the spirit of sincere friendship and close co-operation.

Article 6. The High Contracting Parties will carry out the present treaty in conformity with the Charter of the United Nations.

Article 7. The present treaty shall come into force on the date of the exchange of the instruments of ratification and shall remain in force for a period of twenty years.

The exchange of the instruments of ratification shall take place at Budapest.

Should the treaty not be denounced by one of the High Contracting Parties at least one year before the expiry of the twenty-year period agreed upon, it shall remain in force for a further

five years. The same shall apply for subsequent periods until either of the High Contracting Parties gives notice in writing one year before the expiry of the current five-year period of his intention to terminate the treaty.

Done in duplicate, in Polish and Hungarian, both texts being equally authentic.

In Faith Whereof the plenipotentiaries have signed the present treaty and affixed their seals thereto.

Warsaw, the 18th day of June, 1948.

For the President of the Republic of Poland:

[L.S.] (Signed) J. CYRANKIEWICZ

[L.S.] (Signed) Z. MODZELEWSKI

For the President of the Republic of Hungary:

[L.S.] (Signed) L. DINNYÉS

(Signed) E. MOLNÁR

4.1344 Treaty of Friendship, Co-operation, and Mutual Assistance between the Hungarian Republic and the People's Republic of Bulgaria

Alliance Members: Hungary and Bulgaria
Signed On: July 16, 1948, in the city of Sofia (Bulgaria). In force until October 7, 1989.
Alliance Type: Defense Pact (Type I)

Source: *United Nations Treaty,* no. 6921.

SUMMARY

This treaty completed the three-nation set of bilateral treaties among Poland, Hungary, and Bulgaria. As with the other treaties, this alliance concerns the possibility of renewed German revisionism and aims to provide common assistance among the signatories in the case of attack. The treaty was replaced with a new instrument in 1969, but the overall alliance relationship lasted until 1989, when the communist governments in both countries were replaced.

ALLIANCE TEXT

The President of the Hungarian Republic and the Presidium of the Grand National Assembly of the People's Republic of Bulgaria,

Desiring to strengthen the traditional friendship between the people of the Hungarian Republic and the people of the People's Republic of Bulgaria, which is in accordance with their vital interests and serves to promote international peace,

Enlightened by the experience of the last world war, during which Germany trampled under foot the national independence of Hungary and Bulgaria, and firmly resolved to resist jointly any attempt at renewed German aggression,

Have decided to conclude a treaty of friendship, co-operation and mutual assistance and for that purpose have appointed as their plenipotentiaries:

The President of the Hungarian Republic: Lajos Dinnyés, Chairman of the Council of Ministers of the Hungarian Republic, and Erik Molnár, Minister for Foreign Affairs of the Hungarian Republic;

The Presidium of the Grand National Assembly of the People's Republic of Bulgaria: Georgi Dimitrov, Chairman of the Council of Ministers of the People's Republic of Bulgaria, and Vasil Kolarov, Deputy Chairman of the Council of Ministers and Minister for Foreign Affairs of the People's Republic of Bulgaria,

who, having exchanged their full powers, found in good and due form, have agreed as follows:

Article 1. The High Contracting Parties agree, in the interests of the two States and their peoples, to pursue a policy of mutual friendship in relations between them and to strengthen that policy through close co-operation in every sphere.

Article 2. 1. The High Contracting Parties undertake to take all joint action in their power to obviate any threat of renewed aggression by Germany or any other State which might be associated with Germany either directly or in any other way.

2. The High Contracting Parties declare that they intend to participate, in a spirit of the most sincere co-operation, in all international action for ensuring peace and security and will fully contribute to the realization of those lofty aims.

Article 3. 1. Should either of the High Contracting Parties become involved in hostilities with Germany in the event that that country seeks to renew its policy of aggression or with any other State which might be associated with Germany in a policy of aggression either directly or in any other way, the other High Contracting Party shall immediately extend military and other assistance to the Contracting Party involved in hostilities by every means at its disposal.

2. This Treaty shall be implemented in conformity with the principles of the Charter of the United Nations.

Article 4. Each High Contracting Party undertakes not to enter into any alliance or participate in any coalition or in any action or measures directed against the other.

Article 5. The High Contracting Parties shall consult together on all important international questions affecting the interests of the two countries or international security.

Article 6. The High Contracting Parties shall develop and strengthen the economic, cultural and other ties between the two countries in a spirit of friendship and co-operation and in accordance with the treaties and agreements concluded for that purpose.

Article 7. The provisions of this Treaty shall in no way affect engagements entered into by either of the High Contracting Parties with a third State.

Article 8. This Treaty shall enter into force upon the exchange of the instruments of ratification and shall remain in force for a period of twenty years.

The instruments of ratification shall be exchanged at Budapest.

If neither of the High Contracting Parties denounces this Treaty twelve months before the expiry of the said twenty-year period, it shall remain in force for a further period of five years and similarly thereafter until such time as one of the High Contracting Parties denounces it in writing twelve months before

the expiry of the current five-year period.

This Treaty has been drawn up in duplicate, in the Hungarian and Bulgarian languages, both texts being equally authentic.

In Witness Whereof the above-named plenipotentiaries have signed this Treaty and have thereto affixed their seals.

Sofia, 16 July 1948.

For the President of the Hungarian Republic:

DINNYÉS

MOLNÁR Erik

For the Presidium of the Grand National Assembly of the People's Republic of Bulgaria:

G. DIMITROV

V. KOLAROV

4.1345 Treaty of Friendship, Co-operation, and Mutual Assistance between the Czechoslovak Socialist Republic and the Socialist Republic of Romania

Alliance Members: Czechoslovakia and Romania
Signed On: July 21, 1948, in the city of Prague (Czech Republic). In force until December 10, 1989.
Alliance Type: Defense Pact (Type I)

Source: *U.S. State Department 1948, Documents and State Papers,* series 1, vol. 12, p. 683–684.

SUMMARY

This treaty preceded the August 1948 Danube Pact signed by Russia, Ukraine, Bulgaria, Czechoslovakia, Hungary, Yugoslavia, and Romania and also the 1949 six-nation Council for Economic Mutual Assistance (CEMA), which formalized the Molotov Plan created to offset the Marshall Plan. Economic partners in these agreements, Czechoslovakia and Romania confirmed closer military and political ties with this alliance.

The articles of the treaty committed both states to continue measures to obviate any further threat by Germany, and both pledged to offer military assistance if the other were attacked. Neither would take part in any alliance targeting the other signed party, and both would consult with each other on international issues that affected them both.

Tensions between Russia and Romania arose in 1966 when Romania's first secretary, Nicolae Ceausescu, sought greater independence; and in 1968 Romania did not assist in the invasion of Czechoslovakia. Nevertheless, renewal of the agreement in August of 1968 reaffirmed that Czechoslovakia and Romania would continue within the framework established by the Soviet Union and its Warsaw Pact allies.

EXCERPTS OF ALLIANCE TEXT

Article I: The High Contracting Parties undertake to take jointly all measures to render impossible in the future any threat of aggression by Germany or by any other State allying itself directly or in any other manner to Germany.

Article II: In the event that one of the High Contracting Parties becomes involved in an armed conflict with Germany, attempting to resume its aggressive policy, or with other States allying themselves to Germany, directly or in any other manner in its aggressive policy, the other High Contracting Party shall without delay render military assistance or other assistance with all the means at its disposal. . . .

Article IV: The High Contracting Parties bind themselves not to sign any alliance nor to take part in any action directed against either of them.

Article V: The High Contracting Parties will take all necessary measures to develop the closest economic and cultural collaboration.

4.1346 Treaty of Friendship, Co-operation, and Mutual Assistance between the Polish Republic and the People's Republic of Romania

Alliance Members: Poland and Romania
Signed On: January 26, 1949, in the city of Bucharest (Romania). In force until August 7, 1989.
Alliance Type: Defense Pact (Type I)

Source: *United Nations Treaty,* no. 1143.

SUMMARY

This was the last formal alliance signed by representatives of either Poland or Romania until the formalization of the Warsaw Pact in 1955. As with the other bilateral treaties, the text of the alliance was aimed at possible German revisionism, and both countries pledged mutual assistance in the case of attack. The treaty was replaced in 1970. The alliance relationship itself lasted until 1989, when the communist governments at the helms of both countries fell.

Alliance Text

The President of the Polish Republic and the Presidium of the Great National Assembly of the People's Republic of Romania,

Desirous of consolidating friendly relations and close co-operation between the Polish Republic and the People's Republic of Romania,

Bearing in mind the experiences of Hitlerite aggression and the Second World War,

Desirous of maintaining and strengthening universal peace in accordance with the purposes and principles of the United Nations,

Have resolved to conclude a Treaty of friendship, co-operation and mutual assistance, and for this purpose have appointed as their plenipotentiaries:

The President of the Polish Republic: Mr. Jozef Cyrankiewicz, President of the Council of Ministers, and Mr. Zygmunt Modzelewski, Minister of Foreign Affairs;

The Presidium of the Great National Assembly of the People's Republic of Romania: Dr. Petru Groza, President of the Council of Ministers, and Mrs. Ana Pauker, Minister of Foreign Affairs,

Who, having exchanged their full powers, found in good and due fonn, have agreed upon the following provisions:

Article 1. The High Contracting Parties undertake to carry out all joint measures within their power to obviate any threat of further aggression by Germany or any other State associated with Germany either directly or in any other way.

The High Contracting Parties declare that they will participate in any international action aimed at ensuring international peace and security and will contribute fully to the realization of these lofty aims.

Article 2. Should either of the High Contracting Parties become involved in hostilities with Germany in consequence of her renewing her policy of aggression or with any other State associated with Germany in its own policy of aggression either directly or in any other way, the other High Contracting Party shall immediately give the Party involved in hostilities military and all other assistance by every means at its disposal.

The present Treaty will be carried out in conformity with the principles of the United Nations Charter.

Article 3. Each of the High Contracting Parties undertakes not to enter into any alliance or take part in any action directed against the other High Contracting Party.

Article 4. The High Contracting Parties will consult together on all important international questions involving the interests of both countries.

Article 5. The High Contracting Parties shall take, in conformity with the agreements concluded between the Polish Republic and the People's Republic of Romania, all the necessary steps to develop and strengthen the economic and cultural ties between the two States in a spirit of friendship and co-operation.

Article 6. The present Treaty shall come into force on the date of the exchange of the instruments of ratification and shall remain in force for a period of twenty years from the date of entry into force.

The exchange of the instruments of ratification shall take place at Warsaw.

If neither High Contracting Party gives notice in writing one year before the expiry of the aforementioned twenty-year period that it wishes to denounce the Treaty, it shall remain in force for a further period of five years and thus for subsequent five-year periods, until such time as either High Contracting Party gives notice in writing, one year before the expiry of the current five-year period, of its intention to terminate the Treaty.

The present Treaty is done in duplicate, in the Polish and Romanian languages, both texts being equally authentic.

In Faith Whereof the plenipotentiaries have signed the present Treaty and attached their seals thereto.

Done at Bucharest, on 26 January 1949.

By authorization of the President of the Polish Republic:

(Signed) J. CYRANKIEWICZ
(Signed) Z. MODZELEWSKI
[SEAL]

By authorization of the Presidium of the Great National Assembly of the People's Republic of Romania:

(Signed) Petru GROZA
(Signed) A. PAUKER

4.1347 North Atlantic Treaty

Alliance Members: Original members included the United States, Canada, the United Kingdom, the Netherlands, Belgium, Luxembourg, France, Portugal, Italy, Norway, Denmark, and Iceland. The alliance expanded with the membership of Greece and Turkey (October 21, 1951); the German Federal Republic (October 23, 1954); Spain (December 10, 1981); the Czech Republic, Hungary, and Poland (December 16, 1997); and Bulgaria, Estonia, Latvia, Lithuania, Romania, Slovakia, and Slovenia (March 29, 2004). Germany replaced the membership of the German Federal Republic on October 3, 1990.
Signed On: April 4, 1949, in the city of Washington, D.C. In force as of date of publication of this volume.
Alliance Type: Defense Pact (Type I)

Source: North Atlantic Treaty Organization, Online Library, www.nato.int/docu/basictxt/treaty.htm.

SUMMARY

This defense treaty originally targeted the Soviet Union and its satellites. Considering an armed attack on any member an attack against all, the treaty provided for collective self-defense in accordance with Article 51 of the Charter of the United Nations. The treaty was also designed to encourage political, economic, and social co-operation. The organization was reorganized and centralized in 1952. NATO maintains a headquarters in Brussels, Belgium.

In the 1990s, because of the collapse of the Soviet Union and the Warsaw Pact, NATO's role in world affairs changed, and U.S. forces in Europe have been halved. Many East European nations (and to some extent Russia as well) sought NATO membership, but they were offered instead membership in the more limited Partnership for Peace, formed in 1994, although NATO is not required to defend Partnership for Peace nations from attack. Twenty-five countries now belong to Partnership for Peace, which engages in joint military exercises with NATO, and seven partnership countries became full NATO members in 2004. A Joint Permanent Council between NATO and Russia specifies several areas of cooperation between Russia and NATO, most notably the suppression of terrorist activities. That relationship is beginning to change dramatically, however, since the Russian invasion of Georgia in 2008. Several U.S. administration officials, including Vice President Richard Cheney, have called for full Georgian entry into NATO, while most member countries have begun to cut partnership ties with Russia.

NATO air forces were used under UN auspices in punitive attacks on Serb forces in Bosnia in 1994 and 1995, and the alliance's forces were subsequently used for peacekeeping operations in Bosnia. NATO again launched air attacks during March–June 1999, this time on Yugoslavia following the breakdown of negotiations over Kosovo. Article 5, the collective self-defense provision of the alliance, was invoked in defense of the United States following the terrorist attacks on September 11, 2001. NATO forces now work actively in Afghanistan, defending and patrolling allied-controlled territories and also attacking Taliban forces across the country.

ALLIANCE TEXT

The Parties to this Treaty reaffirm their faith in the purposes and principles of the Charter of the United Nations and their desire to live in peace with all peoples and all governments.

They are determined to safeguard the freedom, common heritage and civilisation of their peoples, founded on the principles of democracy, individual liberty and the rule of law. They seek to promote stability and well-being in the North Atlantic area.

They are resolved to unite their efforts for collective defence and for the preservation of peace and security. They therefore agree to this North Atlantic Treaty:

Article 1. The Parties undertake, as set forth in the Charter of the United Nations, to settle any international dispute in which they may be involved by peaceful means in such a manner that international peace and security and justice are not endangered, and to refrain in their international relations from the threat or use of force in any manner inconsistent with the purposes of the United Nations.

Article 2. The Parties will contribute toward the further development of peaceful and friendly international relations by strengthening their free institutions, by bringing about a better understanding of the principles upon which these institutions are founded, and by promoting conditions of stability and well-being. They will seek to eliminate conflict in their international economic policies and will encourage economic collaboration between any or all of them.

Article 3. In order more effectively to achieve the objectives of this Treaty, the Parties, separately and jointly, by means of continuous and effective self-help and mutual aid, will maintain and develop their individual and collective capacity to resist armed attack.

Article 4. The Parties will consult together whenever, in the opinion of any of them, the territorial integrity, political independence or security of any of the Parties is threatened

Article 5. The Parties agree that an armed attack against one or more of them in Europe or North America shall be considered an attack against them all and consequently they agree that, if such an armed attack occurs, each of them, in exercise of the right of individual or collective self-defence recognised by Article 51 of the Charter of the United Nations, will assist the Party or Parties so attacked by taking forthwith, individually and in concert with the other Parties, such action as it deems necessary, including the use of armed force, to restore and maintain the security of the North Atlantic area.

Any such armed attack and all measures taken as a result thereof shall immediately be reported to the Security Council. Such measures shall be terminated when the Security Council has taken the measures necessary to restore and maintain international peace and security .

Article 6. For the purpose of Article 5, an armed attack on one or more of the Parties is deemed to include an armed attack:

- on the territory of any of the Parties in Europe or North America, on the Algerian Departments of France, on the territory of or on the Islands under the jurisdiction of any of the Parties in the North Atlantic area north of the Tropic of Cancer;
- on the forces, vessels, or aircraft of any of the Parties, when in or over these territories or any other area in Europe in which occupation forces of any of the Parties were stationed on the date when the Treaty entered into force or the Mediterranean Sea or the North Atlantic area north of the Tropic of Cancer.

Article 7. This Treaty does not affect, and shall not be interpreted as affecting in any way the rights and obligations under the Charter of the Parties which are members of the United Nations, or the primary responsibility of the Security Council for the maintenance of international peace and security.

Article 8. Each Party declares that none of the international engagements now in force between it and any other of the Parties or any third State is in conflict with the provisions of this Treaty, and undertakes not to enter into any international engagement in conflict with this Treaty.

Article 9. The Parties hereby establish a Council, on which each of them shall be represented, to consider matters concerning the implementation of this Treaty. The Council shall be so organised as to be able to meet promptly at any time. The Council shall set up such subsidiary bodies as may be necessary; in particular it shall establish immediately a defence committee which shall recommend measures for the implementation of Articles 3 and 5.

Article 10. The Parties may, by unanimous agreement, invite any other European State in a position to further the principles of this Treaty and to contribute to the security of the North Atlantic area to accede to this Treaty. Any State so invited may become a Party to the Treaty by depositing its instrument of accession with the Government of the United States of America. The Government of the United States of America will inform each of the Parties of the deposit of each such instrument of accession.

Article 11. This Treaty shall be ratified and its provisions carried out by the Parties in accordance with their respective constitutional processes. The instruments of ratification shall be deposited as soon as possible with the Government of the United States of America, which will notify all the other signatories of each deposit. The Treaty shall enter into force between the States which have ratified it as soon as the ratifications of the majority of the signatories, including the ratifications of Belgium, Canada, France, Luxembourg, the Netherlands, the United Kingdom and the United States, have been deposited and shall come into effect with respect to other States on the date of the deposit of their ratifications.

Article 12. After the Treaty has been in force for ten years, or at any time thereafter, the Parties shall, if any of them so requests, consult together for the purpose of reviewing the Treaty, having regard for the factors then affecting peace and security in the North Atlantic area, including the development of universal as well as regional arrangements under the Charter of the United Nations for the maintenance of international peace and security.

Article 13. After the Treaty has been in force for twenty years, any Party may cease to be a Party one year after its notice of denunciation has been given to the Government of the United States of America, which will inform the Governments of the other Parties of the deposit of each notice of denunciation

Article 14. This Treaty, of which the English and French texts are equally authentic, shall be deposited in the archives of the Government of the United States of America. Duly certified copies will be transmitted by that Government to the Governments of other signatories.

4.1348 Treaty of Friendship, Co-operation, and Mutual Assistance between the Hungarian Republic and the Czechoslovak Republic

Alliance Members: Hungary and Czechoslovakia
Signed On: April 16, 1949, in the city of Budapest (Hungary). In force until October 7, 1989.
Alliance Type: Defense Pact (Type I)

Source: *United Nations Treaty,* no. 6922.

SUMMARY

This was the last formal bilateral alliance between eastern European states following World War II. Germany remained the focus of the defensive obligations for both countries, but the pact also promised close ties and consultation on international events. The treaty was replaced by a new alliance in 1968, which lasted until the fall of the communist regimes in both states in 1989.

ALLIANCE TEXT

The President of the Hungarian Republic and the President of the Czechoslovak Republic,

In the knowledge and conviction that although the peoples of Hungary and Czechoslovakia have lived for centuries as neighbours, they have failed, through the fault of their ruling classes, to understand each other's national and social aspirations and needs,

That the ruling classes have deliberately incited and fomented misunderstanding between the two peoples in order to conceal the fact that their interests are identical,

That this has enabled the ruling classes of the stronger nation to oppress the weaker nation and to stifle the growth of the two peoples' progressive forces,

That the differences thus artificially produced and constantly fostered have been exploited by foreign Powers in order to create enmity between the two nations and compel them to shed their blood in foreign — primarily German — interests,

Have resolved to put an end to this situation, which has long existed and is prejudicial to the ability of the two nations to live together, in the firm conviction

That all the causes of this unfortunate situation have been eliminated and that the assumption of power in both countries by the people has established the conditions necessary for a new and happy development of future relations between the two nations,

That co-operation resting on the foundation of people's democracy is in keeping with the vital interests of the two nations, leads to close and lasting relations between them in every sphere, and will be a significant factor in further strengthening the existing ties between the democratic and peace-loving nations and in the defence of peace and security,

That the bitter experiences of the distant and recent past have shown the need for joint efforts against the threatened revival of German imperialism and for a clear affirmation of the two nations' determination to defend their freedom, independence and territorial integrity;

For this purpose they have decided to conclude a Treaty of friendship, co-operation and mutual assistance and have appointed as their plenipotentiaries:

The President of the Hungarian Republic: István Dobi, Chairman of the Council of Ministers, and Lásló Rajk, Minister for Foreign Affairs;

The President of the Czechoslovak Republic: Anton Zápotocký, Chairman of the Council of Ministers, and Dr. Vladimir Clementis, Minister for Foreign Affairs,

who, having exchanged their full powers, found in good and due form, have agreed as follows:

Article I. The High Contracting Parties agree to join forces in a policy of lasting friendship and to strengthen it by close co-operation in every sphere.

Article II. The High Contracting Parties undertake to take all necessary joint action to obviate any threat of renewed aggression by Germany or any other State which might be associated with Germany either directly or in any other way.

To that end the High Contracting Parties shall participate in all international action for preserving and safeguarding peace and international security and shall effectively contribute to the realization of that aim in conformity with the principles of the Charter of the United Nations.

Article III. Should either of the High Contracting Parties become involved in hostilities with Germany in the event that that country seeks to renew its policy of aggression or with any other State which might be associated with Germany in furtherance of the latter's policy of aggression either directly or in any other way, the other High Contracting Party shall immediately extend military and all other assistance to it by every available means.

Article IV. The High Contracting Parties shall consult together on all important international problems affecting the interests of the two countries or the preservation of peace and international security.

Article V. Each High Contracting Party undertakes not to enter into any alliance or participate in any action directed against the other.

Article VI. The High Contracting Parties shall develop the closest possible economic, cultural and other ties in a spirit of friendship and in accordance with the agreements concluded for that purpose.

Article VII. This Treaty shall enter into force upon signature and shall be ratified at the earliest possible date. The instruments of ratification shall be exchanged at Prague as soon as possible.

This Treaty shall remain in force for a period of twenty years from the date of its signature. If neither of the High Contracting Parties gives notice, twelve months before the expiry of the twenty-year period, of its desire to terminate the Treaty, it shall remain in force for a further period of five years and similarly thereafter until such time as one of the High Contracting Parties gives notice in writing, twelve months before the expiry of the current five-year period, of its intention to terminate the Treaty.

In Witness Whereof the plenipotentiaries have signed this Treaty and have thereto affixed their seals.

This Treaty has been drawn up in duplicate in the Hungarian and Slovak languages, both texts being equally authentic.

Budapest, 16 April 1949.

For the President of the Hungarian Republic:

DOBI ISTVÁN

RAJIC LÁSZLÓ

For the President of the Czechoslovak Republic:

A. ZÁPOTOCKÝ

V. CLEMENTIS

4.1349 Joint Defense and Economic Cooperation Treaty between the States of the Arab League

Alliance Members: Egypt, Lebanon, Saudi Arabia, Syria, Yemen Arab Republic, Iraq (February 2, 1951), Jordan (February 16, 1952), Morocco (June 13, 1961), Kuwait (August 12, 1961), Algeria (September 11, 1964), Libya (September 11, 1964), Sudan (September 11, 1964), Tunisia (September 11, 1964), Bahrain (November 14, 1971), Qatar (November 14, 1971), Yemen People's Republic (November 23, 1971), United Arab Emirates (December 6, 1971), Somalia (May 20, 1974), Oman (September 29, 1974), Djibouti (September 9, 1977), Comoros (November 20, 1993)

Signed On: June 17, 1950, in the city of Cairo. In force as of date of publication of this volume. Egypt's membership was suspended on March 31, 1979, and then reinstated on May 22, 1989. Yemen assumed full membership, replacing the Yemen Arab Republic and Yemen People's Republic, on May 22, 1990.

Alliance Type: Defense Pact (Type I)

Source: *British and Foreign State Papers,* vol. 157, p. 669.
Additional protocol found in *British and Foreign State Papers,* vol. 158, p. 771.

SUMMARY

This pact was based on the draft proposal submitted by Egypt at the 1950 meeting of the Arab League. Signed in the aftermath of the first Arab-Israeli War, this alliance was meant to provide for solidarity among Arab states. The pact has been invoked on at least three occasions—following the three-country (Britain, France, and Israel) invasion of Egypt in 1956, during the 1967 Arab-Israeli War, and during the 1973 war against Israel. Though still in existence, the defense pact has remained dormant. Wars between Iraq and Iran (1980–1988) and the Iraqi invasion of Kuwait (1989) effectively split opinion among Arab states, rendering the collective self-defense provisions moot. However, there have been recent calls to reinvigorate the pact following the U.S. invasion of Iraq in 2003.

ALLIANCE TEXT

The Governments of:—
H.M. The King of Hashemite Kingdom of Jordan.
H.E. The President of the Syrian Republic.
H.E. The King of the Iraqi Kingdom.
H.M. The King of the Saudi Arabian Kingdom.
H.E. The President of the Lebanese Republic.
H.M. The King of the kingdom of Egypt.
H.M. The King of the Kingdom of Yemen.

In view of the desire of the above-mentioned Governments to consolidate relations between the States of the Arab League; to maintain their independence and their mutual heritage, to fulfill the desire of their peoples to rally in support of mutual defence and to maintain security and peace according to the principles of both the Arab League Pact & the United Nations Charter, and in conformity with the aims of the said Pacts and to consolidate stability and security and provide means of welfare and construction in their countries.

The following governments delegate

Having been duly accredited and fully authorised by their respective governments approve the following:

Article 1. In an effort to maintain and stabilize peace and security, the contracting States hereby confirm their desire to settle their international disputes by peaceful means, whether such disputes concern their own relations or those with other Powers.

Article 2. The contracting States consider any act of armed aggression made against any one or more of them or against their forces, to be directed against them all, and therefore in accordance with the right of legal defence, individually and collectively they undertake to hasten to the aid of the State or States against whom such an aggression is made, and to take immediately, individually and collectively, all means available including the use of armed force to repel the aggression and restore security and peace. And, in conformity with Article 6 of the Arab League Pact and Article 51 of the United Nations Charter, the Arab League Council and U.N. Security Council should be notified of such act of aggression and the means and procedure taken to check it.

Article 3. At the invitation of any one of the signatories of this Treaty, the contracting States should hold consultations whenever there are reasonable grounds for the belief that the territorial integrity, the independence or security of any of the parties is threatened. In the event of the risk of war or the existence of an international emergency, the contracting States should immediately proceed to unify their plans and defensive measures as the situation may demand.

Article 4. Desiring to implement the above obligations and to fully and effectively carry them out, the contracting States will cooperate in consolidating and coordinating their armed forces and will participate according to their resources and needs in preparing the individual and collective means of defence to repulse the armed aggression.

Article 5. A Permanent Military Commission composed of representatives of the General Staffs of the forces of the contracting States is to be formed to coordinate the plans of joint defense and their implementation. The powers of the Permanent Military Commission, as set forth in an Annex attached to this Treaty, include the drafting of the necessary reports, covering the method of cooperation and participating mentioned in Article 4. The Permanent Military Commission will submit to the joint Defense Council, provided hereunder in Article 6, reports dealing with questions within its province.

Article 6. Under the control of the Arab League Council shall be formed a Joint Defence Council to deal with all matters concerning the implementation of the provisions of Articles 2, 3, 4 and 5 of this Treaty. It shall be assisted in the performance of its task by the Permanent Military Commission referred to in Article 5. The Joint Defence Council shall consist of the Foreign Ministers and the Defence Ministers of the contracting States, or their representatives. Decision taken by a majority of two thirds shall be binding on all the contracting States.

Article 7. In order to fulfill the aims of this Treaty and to bring about security and prosperity in Arab countries and in an effort to raise the standard of life therein, the contracting States undertake to collaborate for the development of their economic conditions, the exploitation of their natural resources, the exchange of their respective agricultural and industrial products, and generally to organise and coordinate their economic activities and to conclude the necessary inter-Arab agreements to realise such aims.

Article 8. An Economic Council consisting of the Ministers in charge of economic affairs, or their representatives if necessary, is to be formed from the contracting States to submit recommendations for the realisation of all such aims as are set forth in the previous article. The Council can, in the performance of its duties, seek the cooperation of the Committee for Financial and Economic Affairs referred to in Article 4 of the Arab League Pact.

Article 9. The Annex to this Treaty shall be considered as an integral and indivisible part of it.

Article 10. The contracting States undertake not to conclude any international agreements which may be contradictory to the provisions of this Treaty nor to act, in their international relations, in a way which may be contrary to the aims of this Treaty.

Article 11. No provision of this Treaty shall in any way affect nor is intended to affect any of the rights or obligations accruing to the contracting States from the United Nations Charter or the responsibilities borne by the U.N. Security Council for the maintenance of international peace and security.

Article 12. After a lapse of 10 years from the date of the ratification of this Treaty, any one of the contracting States may withdraw from it providing 12 months' notice is previously given to the General Secretariat of the Arab League. The League Secretariat General shall inform the other contracting States of such notice.

Article 13. This Treaty shall be ratified by each contracting State according to the constitutional status of its particular government. The Treaty shall come into force 15 days after the receipt by the Secretariat General of the ratification from at least four States. This Treaty of which one copy is to be deposited in the Secretariat General of the Arab League is written in Arabic in Cairo on April 30, 1950 [*sic.*] Further copies equally authentic shall be transmitted to each of the contracting States.

Military Annex

1. The Permanent Military Commission provided for in Article 5 of the joint Defense and Economic Cooperation Treaty between the States of the Arab League, shall undertake the following:—

(a) In cooperation with the joint Defense Council, the preparation of all military plans to face possible armed aggression

(b) to submit proposals for the organisation of the forces of the contracting States fixing a minimum force for each in accordance with military exigencies and the potentialities of each State.

The preparation of Military Plans to face all anticipated dangers or armed aggression that may be launched against one or more of the contracting States or their forces, such plans to be based on foundations decided by the Joint Defence Council.

(c) To submit proposals for the reorganization of the forces of the contracting States in so far as their equipment, organization and training are concerned so that they may keep pace with modern military methods and developments, and for the unification and coordination of all such forces.

(d) To submit proposals for the exploitation and coordination of the natural agricultural and industrial resources of all contracting States in favour of the inter-Arab military effort and joint defence.

(e) To organise the exchange of missions between the contracting States for the preparation of plans, participation in military exercises and manœuvers and the study of their results, for the recommendation of the

improvement of methods to ensure close collaboration in the field, and for the general improvement of the forces of all contracting States.

(f) The preparation of the necessary data on the resources and military potentialities of each of the contracting States and the part to be played by its forces in the joint military effort.

(g) Study of the facilities and the contributions of each of the contracting States operating in its territory in conformity with the provisions of this Treaty.

2. The Permanent Military Commission may form temporary or permanent sub-committees from among its own members to deal with any of the matters falling within its jurisdiction. It may also seek the advice of any whose views on certain questions may be deemed necessary.

3. The Permanent Military Commission shall submit detailed reports on the results of its activities and studies to the Joint Defence Council provided for in Article 6 of this Treaty, as well as an annual report giving full particulars of its work and studies during the year.

4. The Permanent Military Commission shall establish its headquarters in Cairo but may hold meetings in any other place. The members shall elect a chairman for two years. Candidates for the presidency should hold at least the rank of General. All members of the Commission must hold the original nationality of one of the Contracting States.

5. In the event of war, the general command of the joint forces shall be entrusted to the contracting State possessing the largest military force taking actual part in the field operations unless, by unanimous agreement, the Commander-in-Chief is selected otherwise. The Commander-in-Chief will be supported in the direction of military operations by a Joint Staff.

4.1350 Mutual Defense Treaty between the United States of America and the Republic of the Philippines

Alliance Members: United States and Philippines
Signed On: August 30, 1951, in the city of Washington, D.C. In force as of date of publication of this volume.
Alliance Type: Defense Pact (Type I)

Source: *United Nations Treaty*, no. 2315.

SUMMARY

The goal of this agreement was to extend the ability of the United States to project power into East Asia. Building on the agreements with New Zealand and Australia in the ANZUS Pact, this alliance, together with several ancillary agreements, secured basing rights for the United States and some foreign policy control over a key ally in Asia.

Most of the mutual defense treaties reached by the United States with nations in East Asia are similar in purpose and wording. This particular accord allows for the defense of either nation should an attack occur "on the metropolitan territory of either of the Parties, or on the island territories under its jurisdiction in the Pacific or on its armed forces, public vessels or aircraft in the Pacific." The agreement served as the basis for relations between the two nations and specifically allows the United States to deploy troops in the event of an armed conflict in the Pacific region.

Some of the provisions regarding jurisdiction over and lease length of the U.S. bases in the Philippines were modified by a memorandum signed in 1959, but the main tenets of this treaty are still in effect as of the date of this publication.

ALLIANCE TEXT

The Parties to this Treaty,

Reaffirming their faith in the purposes and principles of the Charter of the United Nations and their desire to live in peace with all peoples and all Governments, and desiring to strengthen the fabric of peace in the Pacific Area,

Recalling with mutual pride the historic relationship which brought their two peoples together in a common bond of sympathy and mutual ideals to fight side-by-side against imperialist aggression during the last war,

Desiring to declare publicly and formally their sense of unity and their common determination to defend themselves against external armed attack, so that no potential aggressor could be under the illusion that either of them stands alone in the Pacific Area,

Desiring further to strengthen their present efforts for collective defense for the preservation of peace and security pending the development of a more comprehensive system of regional security in the Pacific Area,

Agreeing that nothing in this present instrument shall be considered or interpreted as in any way or sense altering or diminishing any existing agreements or understandings between the United States of America and the Republic of the Philippines,

Have agreed as follows:

Article I. The Parties undertake, as set forth in the Charter of the United Nations, to settle any international disputes in which they may be involved by peaceful means in such a manner that international peace and security and justice are not endangered and to refrain in their international relations from the threat or use of force in any manner inconsistent with the purposes of the United Nations.

Article II. In order more effectively to achieve the objective of this Treaty, the Parties separately and jointly by self-help and mutual aid will maintain and develop their individual and collective capacity to resist armed attack.

Article III. The Parties, through their Foreign Ministers or their deputies, will consult together from time to time regarding the implementation of this Treaty and whenever in the opinion of either of them the territorial integrity, political independence or security of either of the Parties is threatened by external armed attack in the Pacific.

Article IV. Each Party recognizes that an armed attack in the Pacific Area on either of the Parties would be dangerous to its own peace and safety and declares that it would act to meet the common dangers in accordance with its constitutional processes.

Any such armed attack and all measures taken as a result thereof shall be immediately reported to the Security Council of the United Nations. Such measures shall be terminated when the Security Council has taken the measures necessary to restore and maintain international peace and security.

Article V. For the purpose of Article IV, an armed attack on either of the Parties is deemed to include an armed attack on the metropolitan territory of either of the Parties, or on the island territories under its jurisdiction in the Pacific or on its armed forces, public vessels or aircraft in the Pacific.

Article VI. This Treaty does not affect and shall not be interpreted as affecting in any way the rights and obligations of the Parties under the Charter of the United Nations or the responsibility of the United Nations for the maintenance of international peace and security.

Article VII. This Treaty shall be ratified by the United States of America and the Republic of the Philippines in accordance with their respective constitutional processes and will come into force when instruments of ratification thereof have been exchanged by them at Manila.

Article VIII. This Treaty shall remain in force indefinitely. Either Party may terminate it one year after notice has been given to the other Party.

In Witness Whereof the undersigned Plenipotentiaries have signed this Treaty.

Done in duplicate at Washington this thirtieth day of August 1951.

For the United States of America:

Dean ACHESON

John FOSTER DULLES

Tom CONNALLY

Alexander WILEY

For the Republic of the Philippines

Carlos P. RÓMULO

J. M. ELIZALDE

Vicente FRANCISCO

Diosdado MACAPAGAL

4.1351 Security Treaty among Australia, New Zealand, and the United States of America (ANZUS)

Alliance Members: Australia, New Zealand, and the United States
Signed On: September 1, 1951, in the city of San Francisco. In force as of date of publication of this volume. New Zealand was effectively expelled from the alliance on August 12, 1986.
Alliance Type: Defense Pact (Type I)

Source: *United Nations Treaty,* no. 1736.

SUMMARY

This treaty, signed during the Korean War when all three countries were then members of the United Nations fighting forces in Korea, formalized the foreign policy cooperation that existed between the three allies during World War II. The alliance members later fought together in the Vietnam War, although at that time the treaty was not invoked. Indeed, while cooperation among the alliance members was consistently high during the cold war, this defense pact was largely unused until the 1980s.

In 1985, Australia balked at the testing of long-range U.S. missiles in the Tasman Sea off the coast of Australia. This was followed by more intense protests in New Zealand because of the docking of nuclear-powered and nuclear-armed ships in its ports. New Zealand's decision to ban these ships led to the suspension by the United States of its alliance commitment to New Zealand.

Australia invoked the self-defense provisions of the treaty for the first time in 2001 as a rationale for sending troops to Afghanistan, but New Zealand provided several units without invoking the treaty. Cooperation remains high among the three countries, but official treaty obligations remain in place for Australia and the United States only.

ALLIANCE TEXT

The Parties to this Treaty,

Reaffirming their faith in the purposes and principles of the Charter of the United Nations and their desire to live in peace with all peoples and all Governments, and desiring to strengthen the fabric of peace in the Pacific Area,

Noting that the United States already has arrangements pursuant to which its armed forces are stationed in the Philippines, and has armed forces and administrative responsibilities in the Ryukyus, and upon the coming into force of the Japanese Peace Treaty may also station armed forces in and about Japan to assist in the preservation of peace and security in the Japan Area,

Recognizing that Australia and New Zealand as members of the British Commonwealth of Nations have military obligations outside as well as within the Pacific Area,

Desiring to declare publicly and formally their sense of unity, so that no potential aggressor could be under the illusion that any of them stand alone in the Pacific Area, and

Desiring further to coordinate their efforts for collective defense for the preservation of peace and security pending the development of a more comprehensive system of regional security in the Pacific Area,

Therefore declare and agree as follows:

Article I. The Parties undertake, as set forth in the Charter of the United Nations, to settle any international disputes in which they may be involved by peaceful means in such a manner that international peace and security and justice are not endangered and to refrain in their international relations from the threat or use of force in any manner inconsistent with the purposes of the United Nations.

Article II. In order more effectively to achieve the objective of this Treaty the Parties separately and jointly by means of continuous and effective self-help and mutual aid will maintain and develop their individual and collective capacity to resist armed attack.

Article III. The Parties will consult together whenever in the opinion of any of them the territorial integrity, political independence or security of any of the Parties is threatened in the Pacific.

Article IV. Each Party recognizes that an armed attack in the Pacific Area on any of the Parties would be dangerous to its own peace and safety and declares that it would act to meet the common danger in accordance with its constitutional processes.

Any such armed attack and all measures taken as a result thereof shall be immediately reported to the Security Council of the United Nations. Such measures shall be terminated when the Security Council has taken the measures necessary to restore and maintain international peace and security.

Article V. For the purpose of Article IV, an armed attack on any of the Parties is deemed to include an armed attack on the metropolitan territory of any of the Parties, or on the island territories under its jurisdiction in the Pacific or on its armed forces, public vessels or aircraft in the Pacific.

Article VI. This Treaty does not affect and shall not be interpreted as affecting in any way the rights and obligations of the Parties under the Charter of the United Nations or the responsibility of the United Nations for the maintenance of international peace and security.

Article VII. The Parties hereby establish a Council, consisting of their Foreign Ministers or their Deputies, to consider matters concerning the implementation of this Treaty. The Council should be so organized as to be able to meet at any time.

Article VIII. Pending the development of a more comprehensive system of regional security in the Pacific Area and the development by the United Nations of more effective means to maintain international peace and security, the Council, established by Article VII, is authorized to maintain a consultative relationship with States, Regional Organizations, Associations of States or other authorities in the Pacific Area in a position to further the purposes of this Treaty and to contribute to the security of that Area.

Article IX. This Treaty shall be ratified by the Parties in accordance with their respective constitutional processes. The instruments of ratification shall be deposited as soon as possible with the Government of Australia, which will notify each of the other signatories of such deposit. The Treaty shall enter into force as soon as the ratifications of the signatories have been deposited.

Article X. This Treaty shall remain in force indefinitely. Any Party may cease to be a member of the Council established by Article VII one year after notice has been given to the Government of Australia, which will inform the Governments of the other Parties of the deposit of such notice.

Article XI. This Treaty in the English language shall be deposited in the archives of the Government of Australia. Duly certified copies thereof will be transmitted by that Government to the Governments of each of the other signatories.

In Witness Whereof the undersigned Plenipotentiaries have signed this Treaty.

Done at the city of San Francisco this first day of September, 1951.

For Australia:

Percy C. SPENDER

For New Zealand:

C.A. BERENDSEN

For the United States of America:

Dean ACHESON

John Foster DULLES

Alexander WILEY

John J. SPARKMAN

4.1352 Security Treaty between the United States of America and Japan

Alliance Members: United States and Japan
Signed On: September 8, 1951, in the city of San Francisco. In force as of date of publication of this volume.
Alliance Type: Defense Pact (Type I)

Source: *United Nations Treaty*, no. 1835.

SUMMARY

After the end of World War II, the United States served as administrator of a defeated Japan, and this security treaty was consistent with several U.S. economic and foreign policy goals for the region, the most important of which was to maintain a forward presence to halt Russian and Chinese expansion. Under this 1951 treaty, the United States had the right to deploy land, air, and sea forces to Japan and to use those forces at the request of the Japanese government, "to put down large-scale internal riots and disturbances in Japan, caused through instigation or intervention by an outside power or powers." The treaty also confirmed that the Japanese government would not grant any bases or the right to station troops in Japan without the prior consent of the United States.

The formal alliance was replaced by a "mutual co-operation and security treaty" in 1960 (signed in Washington on January 19, 1960). Although this treaty reinforced the weakened position of a U.S.-administered Japanese state, the new treaty made Japan an equal partner in a mutual defense pact.

ALLIANCE TEXT

Japan has this day signed a Treaty of Peace with the Allied Powers. On the coming into force of that Treaty, Japan will not have the effective means to exercise its inherent right of self-defense because it has been disarmed.

There is danger to Japan in this situation because irresponsible militarism has not yet been driven from the world. Therefore Japan desires a Security Treaty with the United States of America to come into force simultaneously with the Treaty of Peace between the United States of America and Japan.

The Treaty of Peace recognizes that Japan as a sovereign nation has the right to enter into collective security arrangements, and further, the Charter of the United Nations recognizes that all nations possess an inherent right of individual and collective self-defense.

In exercise of these rights, Japan desires, as a provisional arrangement for its defense, that the United States of America should maintain armed forces of its own in and about Japan so as to deter armed attack upon Japan.

The United States of America, in the interest of peace and security, is presently willing to maintain certain of its armed forces in and about Japan, in the expectation, however, that Japan will itself increasingly assume responsibility for its own defense against direct and indirect aggression, always avoiding any armament which could be an offensive threat or serve other than to promote peace and security in accordance with the purposes and principles of the United Nations Charter.

Accordingly, the two countries have agreed as follows:

Article I. Japan grants, and the United States of American accepts, the right, upon the coming into force of the Treaty of Peace and of this Treaty, to dispose United States land, air and sea forces in and about Japan. Such forces may be utilized to contribute to the maintenance of international peace and security in the Far East and to the security of Japan against armed attack from without, including assistance given at the express request of the Japanese Government to put down large-scale internal riots and disturbances in Japan, caused through instigation or invention by an outside power or powers.

Article II. During the exercise of the right referred to in Article I, Japan will not grant, without the prior consent of the United States of America, any bases or any rights, powers or authority whatsoever, in or relating to bases or the right of garrison or of maneuver, or transit of ground, air or naval forces to any third power.

Article III. The conditions which shall govern the disposition of armed forces of the United States of America in and about Japan shall be determined by administrative agreements between the two Governments,

Article IV. This Treaty shall expire whenever in the opinion of the Governments of the United States of America and Japan there shall have come into force such United Nations arrangements or such alternative individual or collective security dispositions as will satisfactorily provide for the maintenance by the United Nations or otherwise of international peace and security in the Japan Area.

Article V. This Treaty shall be ratified by the United States of America and Japan and will come into force when instruments of ratification thereof have been exchanged by them at Washington.

In Witness Whereof the undersigned Plenipotentiaries have signed this Treaty.

Done in duplicate at the city of San Francisco, in the English and Japanese languages, this eighth day of September, 1951.

For the United States of America:

Dean ACHESON
John Foster DULLES
Alexander WILEY
Styles BRIDGES
For Japan:
Shigeru YOSHIDA

4.1353 Treaty of Friendship and Collaboration among the Federal People's Republic of Yugoslavia, the Kingdom of Greece, and the Turkish Republic

Alliance Members: Yugoslavia, Greece, and Turkey
Signed On: February 28, 1953, in the city of Ankara (Turkey). In force until April 4, 1964.
Alliance Type: Defense Pact (Type I)

Source: *United Nations Treaty*, no. 2199.

SUMMARY

This defense pact was meant to provide a bulwark against the expansion of Soviet influence into the Balkans. Greece and Turkey were members of the North Atlantic Treaty Organization (NATO), but the communist Yugoslavia was unwilling to join the Western defense pact. This treaty thus provided an indirect means of collective defense in southeastern Europe.

Stalin died soon after the signing of this pact. Stalin's death and the warming of relations between the Soviets and Yugoslavia ultimately disinclined Tito toward working with Western powers. This changed somewhat after the Soviet invasion into Hungary in 1956, but Turko-Greek tensions over Cyprus had muted cooperation among the alliance members. By 1964, the rivalry over Cyprus had destroyed all intra-alliance cooperation between Yugoslavia's partners.

ALLIANCE TEXT

The Contracting Parties,

reaffirming their belief in the principles set forth in the Charter of the United Nations,

determined to live in peace with all the peoples and to contribute to the maintenance of international peace,

desirous to consolidate the friendly relations existing between them,

resolved to defend the freedom and independence of their peoples, as well as their territorial integrity against any force exerted from outside,

determined to unite their efforts in order to render more effective the organization of their defence against any aggression from outside and to act in concert collaborate regarding all questions of mutual interest and, particularly, regarding questions concerning their defence,

convinced that the mutual interests of their peoples and all peaceloving peoples require that appropriate measures be taken for the safeguarding of peace and security in this part of the world, pursuant to Article 51 of the United Nations Charter,

Have resolved to conclude this Treaty and the Heads of their States have appointed as their respective Plenipotentiaries:

The President of the Federal People's Republic of Yugoslavia: His Excellency Monsieur Koca Popovic, Secretary of State;

His Majesty the King of the Hellenes: His Excellency Monsieur Stephanos Stephanopoulos,

Minister of Foreign Affairs;

The President of the Turkish Republic: His Excellency Professor Fuad Köprülü

Minister of Foreign Affairs, Deputy of Istanbul;

who, after exhibiting their full powers and finding them in good and proper form, have agreed upon the following provisions:

Article I. In order to ensure their collaboration permanently, the Contracting Parties shall proceed to consultations concerning all problems of mutual interest.

The Ministers of Foreign Affairs of the Contracting Parties shall hold a regular conference once a year and, if necessary, more often, in order to examine the international political situation and make appropriate decisions in accordance with the aims of this Treaty.

Article II. The Contracting Parties intend to pursue their mutual efforts for the safeguarding of peace and security in their region and jointly continue to examine the problems of their security, including the concerted measures of defence, which might become necessary in case of a non-provoked aggression against them.

Article III. The General Staffs of the Contracting Parties shall pursue their collaboration in order to submit to their Governments, by common consent, recommendations concerning questions of defence, with a view to making co-ordinated decisions.

Article IV. The Contracting Parties shall develop their collaboration in the economic, technical and cultural spheres; whenever necessary appropriate agreements shall be concluded and necessary organizations set up for the purpose of solving economic, technical and cultural problems.

Article V. The Contracting Parties undertake to settle any dispute which may arise between them by peaceful means, in accordance with the provisions of the United Nations Charter and in a spirit of understanding and friendship; they also undertake to refrain from interfering with the internal affairs of the other Contracting Parties.

Article VI. The Contracting Parties shall refrain from concluding any alliance, or from taking part in any action, directed against anyone of them, or in any action which may be prejudicial to their interests.

Article VII. The Contracting Parties, each for itself, declare that none of the international obligations now in force between them and one or several other States is in contradiction with the provisions of the present Treaty; on the other hand, they engage themselves not to assume in the future any international obligations conflicting with the present Treaty.

Article VIII. This Treaty does not affect, and cannot be interpreted as affecting in any way, the rights and obligations of Greece and Turkey deriving from the North Atlantic Treaty of April 4, 1949.

Article IX. After the coming of this Treaty into force any other State, whose collaboration for the realization of the aims of this Treaty is deemed useful by all the Contracting Parties, will be able to accede to the Treaty under the same conditions and with the same rights as the three signatory States.

Each State acceding to this Treaty shall become a Contracting Party of the Treaty by depositing an instrument of accession.

Article X. The present Treaty, whose French version shall be authentic, shall be ratified by all the Contracting Parties and the instruments of ratification shall be deposited with the Secretary of State of the Federal People's Republic of Yugoslavia in Beograd; it shall enter into force on the date of deposit of the last instrument of ratification.

At the expiration of five years after the coming into force of the present Treaty, each Contracting Party may cease to be a party to the Treaty by notifying the Governments of the other Contracting Parties one year in advance.

In Witness Whereof the respective Plenipotentiaries have signed this Treaty.

Done in Ankara, this twenty-eight day of February one thousand nine hundred and fifty-three, in three copies, one copy being delivered to each Contracting Party.

Koca POPOVIC, m.p.

Stephanos STEPHANOPOULOS, m.p.

Fuad KÖPRÜLÜ, m.p.

4.1354 Treaty of Friendship and Alliance between Her Majesty in Respect of the United Kingdom of Great Britain and Northern Ireland and His Majesty the King of the United Kingdom of Libya

Alliance Members: United Kingdom and Libya
Signed On: July 29, 1953, in the city of Benghazi (Libya). In force until June 5, 1967.
Alliance Type: Defense Pact (Type I)

Source: *United Nations Treaty,* no. 2491.

SUMMARY

This alliance is quite similar to Britain's alliances with other Commonwealth countries. Both countries sought a stabilized southern Mediterranean, and Britain sought additional influence in northern Africa following the independence of Egypt.

The terms of the alliance provided for the stationing of British armed forces within Libyan borders. Libya's strategic position had become increasingly important for Britain as a quick staging ground to access the Suez Canal, and the alliance terms were exercised by the British during the Suez Crisis of 1956. In exchange for basing rights, the alliance provided for mutual defense in times of war and generous financial assistance from Britain to Libya.

Muammar Gadhafi's coup in the fall of 1969 overthrew the monarchy of King Idris, and Gadhafi's new government proclaimed the formation of a new republic. Following the Arab-Israeli war of 1967, the internal political pressure became too great and, at Libya's request, the treaty was abrogated. The withdrawal of British troops and the liquidation of British bases soon followed.

ALLIANCE TEXT

Her Majesty The Queen of the United Kingdom of Great Britain and Northern Ireland and of Her other Realms and Territories (hereinafter referred to as Her Britannic Majesty) and His Majesty The King of the United Kingdom of Libya (hereinafter referred to as His Majesty The King of Libya);

Considering that on the 24th day of December, 1951, the United Kingdom of Libya became an independent sovereign State in pursuance of resolutions of the General Assembly of the United Nations dated the 21st day of November, 1949 and the 17th day of November, 1950;

And being animated by a sincere desire to consolidate the friendship and good relations which exist between Their Majesties;

And desiring to conclude a Treaty of Friendship and Alliance with this object and with the object of strengthening the contribution which each of them will be able to make to the maintenance of international peace and security in accordance with the provisions and principles of the Charter of the United Nations:

Have accordingly appointed as their Plenipotentiaries:

Her Britannic Majesty: for the United Kingdom of Great Britain and Northern Ireland: Sir Alec Kirkbride, K.C.M.G., O.B.E., M.C., Her Majesty's Envoy Extraordinary and Minister Plenipotentiary.

His Majesty The King of Libya: for the United Kingdom of Libya: Essayed Mahmud Muntasser, Prime Minister and Minister for Foreign Affairs.

Who, having exhibited their full powers found in good and due form, have agreed as follows:—

Article 1. There shall be peace and friendship and a close alliance between the High Contracting Parties in consecration of their cordial understanding and their good relations.

Each of the High Contracting Parties undertakes not to adopt in regard to foreign countries an attitude which is inconsistent with the alliance or which might create difficulties for the other party thereto.

Article 2. Should either High Contracting Party become engaged in war or armed conflict, the other High Contracting Party will, subject always to the provisions of Article 4, immediately come to his aid as a measure of collective defence. In the event of an imminent menace of hostilities involving either of the High Contracting Parties they will immediately concert together the necessary measures of defence.

Article 3. The High Contracting Parties recognise that it is in their common interest to provide for their mutual defence and to ensure that their countries are in a position to play their part in the maintenance of international peace and security. To this end each will furnish to the other all the facilities and assistance in his power on terms to be agreed upon. In return for facilities provided by His Majesty The King of Libya for British armed forces in Libya on conditions to be agreed upon, Her Britannic Majesty will provide financial assistance to His Majesty The King of Libya, on terms to be agreed upon as aforesaid.

Article 4. Nothing in the present Treaty is intended to, or shall in any way, prejudice the rights and obligations which devolve, or may devolve, upon either of the High Contracting Parties under the Charter of the United Nations or under any other existing international agreements, conventions or treaties, including, in the case of Libya, the Covenant of the League of Arab States.

Article 5. This Treaty shall be ratified and shall come into force upon the exchange of instruments of ratification which shall take place as soon as possible.

Article 6. This Treaty shall remain in force for a period of twenty years except in so far as it may be revised or replaced by a new Treaty during that period by agreement of both the High Contracting Parties, and it shall in any case be reviewed at the end of ten years. Each of the High Contracting Parties agrees in this connexion to have in mind the extent to which international peace and security can be ensured through the United Nations. Before the expiry of a period of nineteen years either High Contracting Party may give to the other through the diplomatic channel notice of termination at the end of the said period of twenty years. If the Treaty has not been so terminated, and subject to any revision or replacement thereof, it shall continue in force after the period of twenty years until the expiry of one year after notice of termination has been given by either High Contracting Party to the other through the diplomatic channel.

Article 7. Should any difference arise relative to the application or interpretation of the present Treaty and should the High Contracting Parties fail to settle such difference by direct negotiations, it shall be referred to the International Court of Justice unless the parties agree to another mode of settlement.

In Witness Whereof the above-named Plenipotentiaries have signed the present Treaty and affixed thereto their Seals.

Done in duplicate at Benghazi this twenty-ninth day of July, 1953, in the English and Arabic languages, both texts being equally authentic.

[L.S.]A. KIRKBRIDE
[L.S.]Mahmud MUNTASSER

4.1355 Mutual Defense Treaty between the United States of America and the Republic of Korea

Alliance Members: United States and Republic of Korea (South Korea)
Signed On: October 1, 1953, in the city of Washington, D.C. In force as of date of publication of this volume.
Alliance Type: Entente (Type III)

Source: *United Nations Treaty,* no. 3363.

SUMMARY

This agreement was formed immediately after the cease-fire that ended the Korean War. The alliance gave the United States the right to base and to administer sea, land, and air units under mutual agreement, and the treaty requires consultation between parties "whenever, in the opinion of either of them, the political independence or security of either of the parties is threatened by external armed attack." Note that the language does not include a mutual defense agreement because the United States was unwilling to extend such a commitment immediately after the conflict between North and South Korea. South Korea demanded, however, that the United States station a significant number of troops on Korean soil to reinforce its commitment to a defense of the peninsula, and to this day the United States bases almost 30,000 troops in South Korea.

ALLIANCE TEXT

The Parties to this Treaty,

Reaffirming their desire to live in peace with all peoples and all governments, and desiring to strengthen the fabric of peace in the Pacific area,

Desiring to declare publicly and formally their common determination to defend themselves against external armed attack so that no potential aggressor could be under the illusion that either of them stands alone in the Pacific area,

Desiring further to strengthen their efforts for collective defense for the preservation of peace and security pending the development of a more comprehensive and effective system of regional security in the Pacific area,

Have agreed as follows:

Article I. The Parties undertake to settle any international disputes in which they may be involved by peaceful means in such a manner that international peace and security and justice are not endangered and to refrain in their international relations from the threat or use of force in any manner inconsistent with the Purposes of the United Nations, or obligations assumed by any Party toward the United Nations.

Article II. The Parties will consult together whenever, in the opinion of either of them, the political independence or security of either of the Parties is threatened by external armed attack. Separately and jointly, by self help and mutual aid, the Parties will maintain and develop appropriate means to deter armed attack and will take suitable measures in consultation and agreement to implement this Treaty and to further its purposes.

Article III. Each Party recognizes that an armed attack in the Pacific area on either of the Parties in territories now under their respective administrative control, or hereafter recognized by one of the Parties as lawfully brought under the administrative control of the other, would be dangerous to its own peace and safety and declares that it would act to meet the common danger in accordance with its constitutional processes.

Article IV. The Republic of Korea grants, and the United States of America accepts, the right to dispose United States land, air and sea forces in and about the territory of the Republic of Korea as determined by mutual agreement.

Article V. This Treaty shall be ratified by the United States of America and the Republic of Korea in accordance with their respective constitutional processes and will come into force when instruments of ratification thereof have been exchanged by them at Washington.

Article VI. This Treaty shall remain in force indefinitely. Either Party may terminate it one year after notice has been given to the other Party.

In Witness Whereof the undersigned Plenipotentiaries have signed this Treaty.

Done in duplicate at Washington, in the English and Korean languages, this first day of October 1953.

For the United States of America:

John Foster DULLES

For the Republic of Korea:

Y. T. PYUN

4.1356 Agreement for Friendly Co-operation between Pakistan and Turkey

Alliance Members: Pakistan and Turkey
Signed On: April 2, 1954, in the city of Karachi (Pakistan). In force until September 23, 1955.
Alliance Type: Entente (Type III)

Source: *United Nations Treaty*, no. 2858.

SUMMARY

Pakistan tried to forge better relations with Western powers during the 1950s by pledging to fight communism internally as closer rapprochement with the West would bring Pakistan leverage in its continuing rivalry with India. This agreement was part of that overall policy and attempted to create a long-standing relationship with Turkey, another West-leaning Asian country. The treaty called for mutual consultation in the case of attack.

The alliance members shared good relations for the duration of the treaty. In fact, the cooperation between the alliance partners led in 1955 to a larger agreement (the Baghdad Pact) that included both the United States and Great Britain.

ALLIANCE TEXT

Pakistan and Turkey,

Reaffirming their faith in the Purposes and Principles of the Charter of the United Nations and their determination always to endeavour to apply and give effect to these Purposes and Principles,

Desirous of promoting the benefits of greater mutual cooperation deriving from the sincere friendship happily existing between them,

Recognising the need for consultation and cooperation between them in every field for the purpose of promoting the well-being and security of their peoples,

Being Convinced that such cooperation would be to the interest of all peace-loving nations and in particular also to the interest of nations in the region of the Contracting Parties, and would consequently serve to ensure peace and security which are both indivisible,

Have Therefore Decided to conclude this Agreement for Friendly Co-operation and for this purpose, have appointed as their Plenipotentiaries:

For Pakistan: Muhammad Zafrulla Khan, Minister of Foreign Affairs and Commonwealth Relations;

For Turkey: His Excellency Monsieur Selahattin Refet Arbel, Ambassador of Turkey

who, after presentation of their full powers, found in good and due form, have agreed as follows:

Article 1. The Contracting Parties undertake to refrain from intervening in any way in the internal affairs of each other and from participating in any alliance or activities directed against the other.

Article 2. The Contracting Parties will consult on international matters of mutual interest and, taking into account international requirements and conditions, cooperate between them to the maximum extent.

Article 3. The Contracting Parties will develop the cooperation, already established between them in the cultural field under a separate Agreement, in the economic and technical fields also by concluding, if necessary, other agreements.

Article 4. The consultation and cooperation between the Contracting Parties in the field of defence shall cover the following points:

a. exchange of information for the purpose of deriving benefit jointly from technical experience and progress,

b. endeavours to meet, as far as possible, the requirements of the Parties in the production of arms and ammunition,

c. studies and determination of the ways and extent of cooperation which might be effected between them in accordance with Article 51 of the Charter of the United Nations, should an unprovoked attack occur against them from outside.

Article 5. Each Contracting Party declares that none of the international engagements now in force between it and any third State is in conflict with the provisions of this Agreement and that this Agreement shall not affect, nor can it be interpreted so as to affect, the aforesaid engagements, and undertakes not to enter into any international engagement in conflict with this Agreement.

Article 6. Any State, whose participation is considered by the Contracting Parties useful for achieving the purposes of the present Agreement, may accede to the present Agreement under the same conditions and with the same obligations as the Contracting Parties.

Any accession shall have legal effect, after the instrument of accession is duly deposited with the Government of Turkey from the date of an official notification by the Government of Turkey to the Government of Pakistan.

Article 7. This Agreement, of which the English text is authentic, shall be ratified by the Contracting Parties in accordance with their respective constitutional processes, and shall enter into force on the date of the exchange of the instruments of ratification in Ankara.

In case no formal notice of denunciation is given by one of the Contracting Parties to the other, one year before the termination of a period of five years from the date of its entry into force, the present Agreement shall automatically continue in force for a further period of five years, and the same procedure will apply for subsequent periods thereafter.

In Witness Whereof, the above mentioned Plenipotentiaries have signed the present Agreement.

Done in two copies at Karachi the second day of April one thousand nine hundred and fifty four.

For Pakistan:

(Signed) Zafrulla KHAN

Minister of Foreign Affairs and Commonwealth Relations

For Turkey:

(Signed) S. R. ARBEL

Ambassador of Turkey

4.1357 Southeast Asia Collective Defense Treaty

Alliance Members: United States, United Kingdom, France, Pakistan, Thailand, Philippines, Australia, and New Zealand
Signed On: September 8, 1954, in the city of Manila (Philippines). In force until November 7, 1973.
Alliance Type: Entente (Type III)

Source: *United Nations Treaty,* no. 2819.

SUMMARY

The Southeast Asia Treaty Organization (SEATO) began as a regional pact that linked nuclear deterrence to countries ringing the Soviet bloc, and it existed as an Asian equivalent to NATO (see Alliance no. 4.1347), providing collective defense to all members. U.S. secretary of state John Foster Dulles pushed for the creation of SEATO as part of a greater plan to check communist aggression and expansion. The commitment to stymie "external aggression" and "internal subversion" trumped all other modus vivendi, as economic cooperation made up only a small part of the treaty.

SEATO began to fall apart in the 1960s when France opposed U.S.

intervention in Vietnam. France completely withdrew from military cooperation in 1967, and Great Britain subsequently ran down its bases east of the Suez in 1968. Pakistan officially withdrew from the treaty in 1972 after disputes with the United States during the Indo-Pakistani War. France finally suspended all membership payments in 1974, and the alliance effectively collapsed but was not formally ended until 1977.

ALLIANCE TEXT

The Parties to this Treaty,

Recognizing the sovereign equality of all the Parties,

Reiterating their faith in the purposes and principles set forth in the Charter of the United Nations and their desire to live in peace with all peoples and all governments,

Reaffirming that, in accordance with the Charter of the United Nations, they uphold the principle of equal rights and self-determination of peoples, and declaring that they will earnestly strive by every peaceful means to promote self-government and to secure the independence of all countries whose peoples desire it and are able to undertake its responsibilities,

Desiring to strengthen the fabric of peace and freedom and to uphold the principles of democracy, individual liberty and the rule of law, and to promote the economic well-being and development of all peoples in the treaty area,

Intending to declare publicly and formally their sense of unity, so that any potential aggressor will appreciate that the Parties stand together in the area, and

Desiring further to coordinate their efforts for collective defense for the preservation of peace and security,

Therefore agree as follows:

Article I. The Parties undertake, as set forth in the Charter of the United Nations, to settle any international disputes in which they may be involved by peaceful means in such a manner that international peace and security and justice are not endangered, and to refrain in their international relations from the threat or use of force in any manner inconsistent with the purposes of the United Nations.

Article II. In order more effectively to achieve the objectives of this Treaty, the Parties, separately and jointly, by means of continuous and effective self-help and mutual aid will maintain and develop their individual and collective capacity to resist armed attack and to prevent and counter subversive activities directed from without against their territorial integrity and political stability.

Article III. The Parties undertake to strengthen their free institutions and to cooperate with one another in the further development of economic measures, including technical assistance, designed both to promote economic progress and social well-being and to further the individual and collective efforts of governments toward these ends.

Article IV. I. Each Party recognizes that aggression by means of armed attack in the treaty area against any of the Parties or against any State or territory which the Parties by unanimous agreement may hereafter designate, would endanger its own peace and safety, and agrees that it will in that event act to meet the common danger in accordance with its constitutional processes. Measures taken under this paragraph shall be immediately reported to the Security Council of the United Nations.

2. If, in the opinion of any of the Parties, the inviolability or the integrity of the territory or the sovereignty or political independence of any Party in the treaty area or of any other State or territory to which the provisions of paragraph 1 of this Article from time to time apply is threatened in any way other than by armed attack or is affected or threatened by any fact or situation which might endanger the peace of the area, the Parties shall consult immediately in order to agree on the measures which should be taken for the common defense.

3. It is understood that no action on the territory of any State designated by unanimous agreement under paragraph 1 of this Article or on any territory so designated shall be taken except at the invitation or with the consent of the Government concerned.

Article V. The Parties hereby establish a Council, on which each of them shall be represented, to consider matters concerning the implementation of this Treaty. The Council shall provide for consultation with regard to military and any other planning as the situation obtaining in the treaty area may from time to time require. The Council shall be so organized as to be able to meet at any time.

Article VI. This Treaty does not affect and shall not be interpreted as affecting in any way the rights and obligations of any of the Parties under the Charter of the United Nations or the responsibility of the United Nations for the maintenance of international peace and security. Each Party declares that none of the international engagements now in force between it and any other of the Parties or any third party is in conflict with the provisions of this Treaty, and undertakes not to enter into any international engagement in conflict with this Treaty.

Article VII. Any other State in a position to further the objectives of this Treaty and to contribute to the security of the area may, by unanimous agreement of the Parties, be invited to accede to this Treaty. Any State so invited may become a Party to the Treaty by depositing its instrument of accession with the Government of the Republic of the Philippines. The Government of the Republic of the Philippines shall inform each of the Parties of the deposit of each such instrument of accession.

Article VIII. As used in this Treaty, the "treaty area" is the general area of Southeast Asia, including also the entire territories of the Asian Parties, and the general area of the Southwest Pacific not including the Pacific area north of 21 degrees 30 minutes north latitude. The Parties may, by unanimous agreement, amend this Article to include within the treaty area the territory of any State acceding to this Treaty in accordance with Article VII or otherwise to change the treaty area.

Article IX.   I. This Treaty shall be deposited in the archives of the Government of the Republic of the Philippines. Duly certified copies thereof shall be transmitted by that Government to the other signatories.

2. The Treaty shall be ratified and its provisions carried out by the Parties in accordance with their respective constitutional processes. The instruments of ratification shall be deposited as soon as possible with the Government of the Republic of the Philippines, which shall notify all of the other signatories of such deposit.

3. The Treaty shall enter into force between the States which have ratified it as soon as the instruments of ratification of a majority of the signatories shall have been deposited, and shall come into effect with respect to each other State on the date of the deposit of its instrument of ratification.

Article X. This Treaty shall remain in force indefinitely, but any Party may cease to be a Party one year after its notice of denunciation has been given to the Government of the Republic of the Philippines, which shall inform the Governments of the other Parties of the deposit of each notice of denunciation.

Article XI. The English text of this Treaty is binding on the Parties, but when the Parties have agreed to the French text thereof and have so notified the Government of the Republic of the Philippines, the French text shall be equally authentic and binding on the Parties.

Understanding of the United States of America

The United States of America in executing the present Treaty does so with the understanding that its recognition of the effect of aggression and armed attack and its agreement with reference thereto in Article IV, paragraph 1, apply only to communist aggression but affirms that in the event of other aggression or armed attack it will consult under the provisions of Article IV, paragraph 2.

In Witness Whereof, the undersigned Plenipotentiaries have signed this Treaty.

Done at Manila, this eighth day of September, 1954.

For Australia:

R. G. CASEY

For France:

G. LA CHAMBRE

For New Zealand:

T. Clifton WEBB

For Pakistan:

Signed for transmission to my Government for its consideration and action in accordance with the Constitution of Pakistan

Zafrulla KHAN

For the Republic of the Philippines:

Carlos P. GARCÍA

Francisco A. DELGADO

Tomas A. CABILI

Lorenzo M. TAÑADA

Cornelio T. VILLAREAL

For the Kingdom of Thailand:

WAN WAITHAYAKON KROMMÜN NARADHIP BONGSPRABANDH

For the United Kingdom of Great Britain and Northern Ireland:

READING

For the United States of America:

John Foster DULLES

H. Alexander SMITH

Michael J. MANSFIELD

4.1358 Mutual Defense Treaty between the United States of America and Republic of China (Taiwan)

Alliance Members: United States and Republic of China (Taiwan)
Signed On: December 2, 1954, in the city of Washington, D.C. In force until April 10, 1979.
Alliance Type: Defense Pact (Type I)

Source: *United Nations Treaty,* no. 3496.

SUMMARY

In 1949 the Nationalist Party and its sympathizers fled mainland China to establish the Republic of China on Taiwan. The United States had provided limited political support to Chiang Kai-shek, the Nationalist Party leader, and this provided entry for greater support following the revolution in China that created the People's Republic of China (PRC). The PRC's involvement in the Korean War against the United States–led coalition from the United Nations added to tense relations between the two states, and the United States committed to a firm anti-PRC policy with the agreement to defend Taiwan against any PRC actions.

The following conditions were attached to this pledge: (1) the treaty had no bearing on ultimate legal title to Taiwan, (2) the United States would intervene only in the case of self-defense, and (3) the treaty would not automatically apply to new territories without consent of the Senate. The treaty was to remain in force indefinitely, allowing each party the ability to terminate after a one-year notice.

President Richard Nixon's visit to and recognition of the PRC created a mild crisis in U.S.-Taiwan relations. This was resolved in part by the 1979 Taiwan Relations Act signed by President Jimmy Carter that legalized a new relationship between the two countries. The United States continued to offer support to Taiwan in the form of economic and military assistance, and although the formal security guarantee was lifted, veiled hints continue to be proffered that the United States was willing to support the guarantee even without a treaty.

ALLIANCE TEXT

The Parties to this Treaty,

Reaffirming their faith in the purposes and principles of the Charter of the United Nations and their desire to live in peace with all peoples and all Governments, and desiring to strengthen the fabric of peace in the West Pacific Area,

Recalling with mutual pride the relationship which brought their two peoples together in a common bond of sympathy and mutual ideals to fight side by side against imperialist aggression during the last war,

Desiring to declare publicly and formally their sense of unity and their common determination to defend themselves against external armed attack, so that no potential aggressor could be under the illusion that either of them stands alone in the West Pacific Area, and

Desiring further to strengthen their present efforts for collective defense for the preservation of peace and security pending the development of a more comprehensive system of regional security in the West Pacific Area,

Have agreed as follows:

Article I. The Parties undertake, as set forth in the Charter of the United Nations, to settle any international dispute in which they may be involved by peaceful means in such a manner that international peace, security and justice are not endangered and to refrain in their international relations from the threat or use of force in any manner inconsistent with the purposes of the United Nations.

Article II. In order more effectively to achieve the objective of this Treaty, the Parties separately and jointly by self-help and mutual aid will maintain and develop their individual and collective capacity to resist armed attack and communist subversive activities directed from without against their territorial integrity and political stability.

Article III. The Parties undertake to strengthen their free institutions and to cooperate with each other in the development of economic progress and social well-being and to further their individual and collective efforts toward these ends.

Article IV. The Parties, through their Foreign Ministers or their deputies, will consult together from time to time regarding the implementation of this Treaty.

Article V. Each Party recognizes that an armed attack in the West Pacific Area directed against the territories of either of the Parties would be dangerous to its own peace and safety and declares that it would act to meet the common danger in accordance with its constitutional processes.

Any such armed attack and all measures taken as a result thereof shall be immediately reported to the Security Council of the United Nations. Such measures shall be terminated when the Security Council has taken the measures necessary to restore and maintain international peace and security.

Article VI. For the purposes of Articles II and V, the terms "territorial" and "territories" shall mean in respect of the Republic of China, Taiwan and the Pescadores; and in respect of the United States of America, the island territories in the West Pacific under its jurisdiction. The provisions of Articles II and V will be applicable to such other territories as may be determined by mutual agreement.

Article VII. The Government of the Republic of China grants, and the Government of the United States of America accepts, the right to dispose such United States land, air and sea forces in and about Taiwan and the Pescadores as may be required for their defense, as determined by mutual agreement.

Article VIII. This Treaty does not affect and shall not be interpreted as affecting in any way the rights and obligations of the Parties under the Charter of the United Nations or the responsibility of the United Nations for the maintenance of international peace and security.

Article IX. This Treaty shall be ratified by the United States of America and the Republic of China in accordance with their respective constitutional processes and will come into force when instruments of ratification thereof have been exchanged by them at Taipei.

Article X. This Treaty shall remain in force indefinitely. Either Party may terminate it one year after notice has been given to the other Party.

In witness whereof the undersigned Plenipotentiaries have signed this Treaty.

Done in duplicate, in the English and Chinese languages, at Washington on this second day of December of the Year One Thousand Nine Hundred and Fifty-four, corresponding to the second day of the twelfth month of the Forty-third year of the Republic of China.

For the United States of America:

John Foster DULLES

For the Republic of China:

George K. C. YEH

4.1359 Pact of Mutual Cooperation between Iraq and Turkey (Baghdad Pact)

Alliance Members: Turkey, Iraq, United Kingdom (April 5, 1955); Pakistan (September 23, 1955); Iran (November 3, 1955); and the United States (July 28, 1958)

Signed On: February 24, 1955, in the city of Baghdad (Iraq). In force until March 24, 1959.

Alliance Type: Entente (Type III)

Source: *United Nations Treaty,* no. 3264.

SUMMARY

The Pact of Mutual Cooperation between Iraq and Turkey was one in a series of containment policies promulgated by the United States following World War II. Unwilling to commit to any agreement in the Middle East, Great Britain, after its withdrawal of forces, left the United States little choice but to become involved, according to Secretary of State John Foster Dulles. This early treaty evolved to include Great Britain, Pakistan, and Iran; and it quickly became known as the Baghdad Pact.

The treaty pledged to maintain a regional alliance through security and defense practices, with informal aid expected from the United States. The aid expectations were formalized in 1958 through a series of U.S. executive agreements.

The crisis that eventually ended the treaty began in the spring 1958 when the government of Syria merged with Egypt to form the United Arab Republic. Iraq's pro-Western leader was concurrently ousted in a coup, prompting the Lebanese government to ask the United States for temporary assistance in the face of similar pressures. Iraq formally

withdrew from the alliance in March 1959 and created the Central Treaty Organization.

ALLIANCE TEXT

Whereas the friendly and brotherly relations existing between Iraq and Turkey are in constant progress, and in order to complement the contents of the Treaty of friendship and good neighbourhood concluded between His Majesty The King of Iraq and His Excellency The President of the Turkish Republic signed in Ankara on the 29th of March, 1946, which recognised the fact that peace and security between the two countries is an integral part of the peace and security of all the Nations of the world and in particular the Nations of the Middle East, and that it is the basis for their foreign policies;

Whereas Article 11 of the Treaty of Joint Defence and Economic Co-operation between the Arab League States provides that no provision of that Treaty shall in any way affect, or is designed to affect any of the rights and obligations accruing to the contracting parties from the United Nations Charter;

And having realised the great responsibilities borne by them in their capacity as members of the United Nations concerned with the maintenance of peace and security in the Middle East region which necessitate taking the required measures in accordance with Article 51 of the United Nations Charter;

They have been fully convinced of the necessity of concluding a pact fulfilling these aims and for that purpose have appointed as their Plenipotentiaries:

His Majesty King Faisal II King of Iraq: His Excellency Al Farik Nuri As-Said, Prime Minister; His Excellency Burhanuddin Bash-Ayan, Acting Minister for Foreign Affairs

His Excellency Jalal Bayar President of the Turkish Republic: His Excellency Adnan Menderes, Prime Minister; His Excellency Professor Fuat Köprülü, Minister for Foreign Affairs

who, having communicated their full powers, found to be in good and due form, have agreed as follows:

Article 1. Consistent with Article 51 of the United Nations Charter the High Contracting Parties will co-operate for their security and defence. Such measures as they agree to take to give effect to this co-operation may form the subject of special agreements with each other.

Article 2. In order to ensure the realisation and effect application of the co-operation provided for in Article 1 above, the competent authorities of the High Contracting Parties will determine the measures to be taken as soon as the present Pact enters into force. These measures will become operative as soon as they have been approved by the Governments of the High Contracting Parties.

Article 3. The High Contracting Parties undertake to refrain from any interference whatsoever in each other's internal affairs. They will settle any dispute between themselves in a peaceful way in accordance with the United Nations Charter.

Article 4. The High Contracting Parties declare that the dispositions of the present Pact are not in contradiction with any of the international obligations contracted by either of them with any third state or states. They do not derogate from, and cannot be interpreted as derogating from, the said international obligations. The High Contracting Parties undertake not to enter into any international obligation incompatible with the present Pact.

Article 5. This Pact shall be open for accession to any member state of the Arab League or any other state actively concerned with the security and peace in this region and which is fully recognised by both of the High Contracting Parties. Accession shall come into force from the date of which the instrument of accession of the state concerned is deposited with the Ministry of Foreign Affairs of Iraq.

Any acceding State Party to the present Pact, may conclude special agreements, in accordance with Article 1, with one or more states Parties to the present Pact. The competent authority of any acceding State may determine measures in accordance with Article 2. These measures will become operative as soon as they have been approved by the Governments of the Parties concerned.

Article 6. A Permanent Council at Ministerial level will be set up to function within the frame work of the purposes of this Pact when at least four Powers become parties to the Pact.

The Council will draw up its own rules of procedure.

Article 7. This Pact remains in force for a period of five years renewable for other five year periods. Any Contracting Party may withdraw from the Pact by notifying the other parties in writing of its desire to do so, six months before the expiration of any of the above-mentioned periods, in which case the Pact remains valid for the other Parties.

Article 8. This Pact shall be ratified by the Contracting Parties and ratifications shall be exchanged at Ankara as soon as possible. Thereafter it shall come into force from the date of the exchange of ratifications.

In Witness Whereof, the said Plenipotentiaries have signed the present Pact in Arabic, Turkish and English all three texts being equally authentic except in the case of doubt when the English text shall prevail.

Done in duplicate at Baghdad this second day of Rajab 1374 Hijri corresponding to the twenty-fourth day of February 1955.

For His Majesty the King of Iraq

NURI AS-SAID

BURHANUDDIN BASH-AYAN

For the President of the Turkish Republic

Adnan MENDERES

Fuat KÖPRÜLÜ

4.1360 Warsaw Pact

Alliance Members: Albania, Bulgaria, Czechoslovakia, German Democratic Republic, Hungary, Poland, Romania, and the Union of Soviet Socialist Republics
Signed On: May 14, 1955, in the city of Warsaw. In force until July 1, 1991.
Alliance Type: Defense Pact (Type I)

Source: *United Nations Treaty,* no. 2962.

SUMMARY

In 1954, the North Atlantic Treaty Organization admitted West Germany into its alliance and put Allied commanders in charge of the German army. The Soviets quickly responded by creating the Warsaw Treaty Organization, formalized with the Warsaw Pact. The treaty existed as a regional military alliance under complete control of Soviet high commanders. Every important post was Soviet held, all officers were Soviet born, all equipment was standardized to Soviet specifications, and the alliance headquarters was established in Moscow. The organization also began an economic system among pact members that attempted state specialization and favored an extraction of resources to aid Soviet domestic and foreign policy.

The Warsaw Pact had a brief hiatus in 1956 when Hungary withdrew after a nationalist revolt, but the Soviets quickly restored order, crushed the rebellion, and forced Hungary back into the organization. The alliance officially ended with the demise of the Soviet Union in the early 1990s; it functioned for a brief time as a political entity but lost its raison d'être without the existence of the Soviet Union.

ALLIANCE TEXT

The Contracting Parties,

Reaffirming their desire to create a system of collective security in Europe based on the participation of all European States, irrespective of their social and political structure, whereby the said States may be enabled to combine their efforts in the interests of ensuring peace in Europe;

Taking into consideration, at the same time, the situation that has come about in Europe as a result of the ratification of the Paris Agreements, which provide for the constitution of a new military group in the form of a "West European Union," with the participation of a remilitarized West Germany and its inclusion in the North Atlantic bloc, thereby increasing the danger of a new war and creating a threat to the national security of peace-loving States;

Being convinced that in these circumstances the peace-loving States of Europe must take the necessary steps to safeguard their security and to promote the maintenance of peace in Europe;

Being guided by the purposes and principles of the Charter of the United Nations;

In the interests of the further strengthening and development of friendship, co-operation and mutual assistance in accordance with the principles of respect for the independence and sovereignty of States and of non-intervention in their domestic affairs;

Have resolved to conclude the present Treaty of Friendship, Co-operation and Mutual Assistance and have appointed as their plenipotentiaries:

The Presidium of the National Assembly of the People's Republic of Albania: Mehmet Shehu, President of the Council of Ministers of the People's Republic of Albania;

The Presidium of the National Assembly of the People's Republic of Bulgaria: Vylko Chervenkov, President of the Council of Ministers of the People's Republic of Bulgaria;

The Presidium of the Hungarian People's Republic: András Hegedüs, President of the Council of Ministers of the Hungarian People's Republic;

The President of the German Democratic Republic: Otto Grotewohl, Prime Minister of the German Democratic Republic;

Council of State of the Polish People's Republic: Józef Cyrankiewicz, President of the Council of Ministers of the Polish People's Republic;

The Presidium of the Grand National Assembly of the Romanian People's Republic: Gheorghe Gheorghiu Dej, President of the Council of Ministers of the Romanian People's Republic;

The Presidium of the Supreme Soviet of the Union of Soviet Socialist Republics: Nikolai Aleksandrovich Bulganin, President of the Council of Ministers of the Union of Soviet Socialist Republics;

The President of the Czechoslovak Republic: Viliam Široký, Prime Minister of the Czechoslovak Republic;

who, having exhibited their full powers, found in good and due form, have agreed as follows:

Article 1. The Contracting Parties undertake, in accordance with the Charter of the United Nations, to refrain in their international relations from the threat or use of force and to settle their international disputes by peaceful means in such a manner that international peace and security are not endangered.

Article 2. The Contracting Parties declare that they are prepared to participate, in a spirit of sincere co-operation, in all international action for ensuring international peace and security and will devote their full efforts to the realization of these aims.

In this connexion, the Contracting Parties shall endeavour to secure, in agreement with other States desiring to co-operate in this matter, the adoption of effective measures for the general reduction of armaments and the prohibition of atomic, hydrogen and other weapons of mass destruction.

Article 3. The Contracting Parties shall consult together on all important international questions involving their common interests, with a view to strengthening international peace and security.

Whenever any one of the Contracting Parties considers that a threat of armed attack on one or more of the States Parties to the Treaty has arisen, they shall consult together immediately with a view to providing for their joint defence and maintaining peace and security.

Article 4. In the event of an armed attack in Europe on one or more of the States Parties to the Treaty by any State or group of States, each State Party to the Treaty shall, in the exercise of the right of individual or collective self-defence, in accordance with Article 51 of the United Nations Charter, afford the State or States so attacked immediate assistance, individually and in agreement with the other States Parties to the Treaty, by all the means it considers necessary, including the use of armed force. The States Parties to the Treaty shall consult together immediately concerning the joint measures necessary to restore and maintain international peace and security.

Measures taken under this article shall be reported to the Security Council in accordance with the provisions of the United Nations Charter. These measures shall be discontinued as soon as the Security Council takes the necessary action to restore and maintain international peace and security.

Article 5. The Contracting Parties have agreed to establish a Unified Command, to which certain elements of their armed forces shall be allocated by agreement between the Parties, and which shall act in accordance with jointly established principles. The Parties shall likewise take such other concerted action as may be necessary to reinforce their defensive strength, in order to defend the peaceful labour of their peoples, guarantee the inviolability of their frontiers and territories and afford protection against possible aggression.

Article 6. For the purpose of carrying out the consultations provided for in the present Treaty between the States Parties thereto, and for the consideration of matters arising in connexion with the application of the present Treaty, a Political Consultative Committee shall be established, in which each State Party to the Treaty shall be represented by a member of the Government or by some other specially appointed representative.

The Committee may establish such auxiliary organs as may prove to be necessary.

Article 7. The Contracting Parties undertake not to participate in any coalitions or alliances, and not to conclude any agreements, the purposes of which are incompatible with the purposes of the present Treaty.

The Contracting Parties declare that their obligations under international treaties at present in force are not incompatible with the provisions of the present Treaty.

Article 8. The Contracting Parties declare that they will act in a spirit of friendship and co-operation to promote the further development and strengthening of the economic and cultural ties among them, in accordance with the principles of respect for each other's independence and sovereignty and of non-intervention in each other's domestic affairs.

Article 9. The present Treaty shall be open for accession by other States, irrespective of their social and political structure, which express their readiness, by participating in the present Treaty, to help in combining the efforts of the peace-loving States to ensure the peace and security of the peoples. Such accessions shall come into effect with the consent of the States Parties to the Treaty after the instruments of accession have been deposited with the Government of the Polish People's Republic.

Article 10. The present Treaty shall be subject to ratification, and the instruments of ratification shall be deposited with the Government of the Polish People's Republic.

The Treaty shall come into force on the date of deposit of the last instrument of ratification. The Government of the Polish People's Republic shall inform the other States Parties to the Treaty of the deposit of each instrument of ratification.

Article 11. The present Treaty shall remain in force for twenty years. For Contracting Parties which do not, one year before the expiration of that term, give notice of termination of the Treaty to the Government of the Polish People's Republic, the Treaty shall remain in force for a further ten years.

In the event of the establishment of a system of collective security in Europe and the conclusion for that purpose of a General European Treaty concerning collective security, a goal which the Contracting Parties shall steadfastly strive to achieve, the present Treaty shall cease to have effect as from the date on which the General European Treaty comes into force.

Done at Warsaw, this fourteenth day of May 1955, in one copy, in the Russian, Polish, Czech and German languages, all the texts being equally authentic. Certified copies of the present Treaty shall be transmitted by the Government of the Polish People's Republic to all the other Parties to the Treaty.

In Faith Whereof the Plenipotentiaries have signed the present Treaty and have thereto affixed their seals.

[L. S.]By authorization of the Presidium of the National Assembly of the People's Republic of Albania:

(Signed) M. SHEHU

[L. S.]By authorization of the Presidium of the National Assembly of the People's Republic of Bulgaria:

(Signed) V. CHERVENKOV

[L. S.] By authorization of the Presidium of the Hungarian People's Republic:

(Signed) A. HEGEDÜS

[L. S.] By authorization of the President of the German Democratic Republic:

(Signed) O. GROTEWOHL

[L. S.] By authorization of the Council of State of the Polish People's Republic:

(Signed) J. CYRANKIEWICZ

[L. S.]By authorization of the Presidium of the Grand National Assembly of the Romanian People's Republic

(Signed) G. GHEORGHIU DEJ

[L. S.]By authorization of the Presidium of the Supreme Soviet of the Union of Soviet Socialist Republics

(Signed) N. BULGANIN

[L. S.] By authorization of the President of the Czechoslovak Republic:

(Signed) V. ŠIROKÝ

4.1361 Joint Defence Agreement between Syria and Egypt

Alliance Members: Syria, Egypt, and Jordan (joined on October 24, 1956)
Signed On: October 20, 1955, in the city of Damascus (Syria). In force until March 26, 1979.
Alliance Type: Defense Pact (Type I)

Source: *United Nations Treaty,* no. 3461.

SUMMARY

Baathist influences in both Syria and Egypt fostered close ties between the two countries. The joint defense agreement between the two states was signed in October 1955 to begin a consolidation process, after which the two countries were expected to eventually unite under one leadership. The treaty pledged complete peace between both sides; established that an attack on one country would be considered an attack on both; formed a Joint Command, a War Council, and a Supreme Council; and advocated full consultation on issues of joint interest. By 1958, Syria and Egypt had formed the United Arab Republic (UAR). The unified command lasted only a few years, however, as a coup d'état in Syria installed a government that distanced Syria from the UAR.

ALLIANCE TEXT

The Governments of Syria and Egypt,

With a view to strengthening the principles of the Pact of the League of Arab States and reaffirming the loyalty of the contracting States to those principles,

Desiring to develop and strengthen military co-operation between them with a view to protecting the independence of their two countries and safeguarding their security; firmly believing that the establishment of a security system common to their two countries will constitute a major factor in guaranteeing the security and independence of each; wishing to achieve their desire for their common defence and the maintenance of security and peace in accordance with the principles and purposes of the Pact of the League of Arab States and the Charter of the United Nations,

And pursuant to the provisions of the first paragraph of article 9 of the Pact of the League of Arab States,

Have resolved to conclude an agreement for that purpose and have appointed as their plenipotentiaries:

For the Government of the Syrian Republic: His Excellency Mr. Rashad Barmada, Minister of National Defence,

For the Government of the Republic of Egypt: His Excellency General Mahmoud Riad, Egyptian Ambassador to Syria,

Who, having exchanged their full powers, found in good and due form, have agreed as follows:

Article 1. The two Contracting States affirm their desire for the maintenance of security and peace and their determination and resolve to settle all their international disputes by peaceful means.

Article 2. The two Contracting States consider any armed attack against either State or its forces as an attack against both.

Accordingly, and in exercise of the right of individual or collective self-defence, they undertake to hasten to each other's assistance in case of an attack and to take immediately all appropriate measures and use all the means at their disposal, including armed force, to repel the attack and to restore security and peace.

In accordance with article 6 of the Pact of the League of Arab States and Article 51 of the Charter of the United Nations, the attack, and the measures and procedures adopted to repel it, shall be immediately reported to the Council of the League and to the Security Council.

Each Contracting State undertakes not to conclude a separate peace or to enter into any agreement with the aggressor without the consent of the other.

Article 3. The two Contracting States shall, at the request of either of them, consult together whenever international relations are seriously strained and disrupted in a manner affecting the territorial integrity or independence of either of them.

In the event of an imminent threat of war or of a sudden dangerous emergency, the two Contracting States shall immediately take the preventive and defensive measures required by the situation.

Article 4. In the event of a sudden attack on the frontiers or the forces of either Contracting State, the two States shall immediately determine the necessary measures to put the provisions of this Agreement into effect, in addition to the military measures taken to meet the attack.

Article 5. With a view to accomplishing the purposes of this Agreement, the two Contracting States have agreed to establish the following bodies:

A Supreme Council;

A War Council;

A Joint Command.

Article 6. 1. The Supreme Council shall consist of the Ministers of Foreign Affairs and the Ministers of War (or Defence) of the Contracting States. The Council shall constitute the official authority to which the Commander-in-Chief of the Joint Command shall be subordinate and from which he shall receive all higher directives on military policy. The Council shall have the power to appoint and dismiss the Commander-in-Chief.

2. The Supreme Council shall, on the proposal of the War Council, determine the organization, functions and duties of the Joint Command. It shall be competent to make changes therein on the proposal of the War Council. The Supreme Council shall have the right to set up committees and subsidiary and provisional bodies as required.

3. The Supreme Council shall be competent to examine the recommendations and decisions of the War Council in all matters not within the jurisdiction of the Chiefs of Staff.

4. The Supreme Council shall issue rules of procedure for its meetings and for the work of the War Council.

Article 7. 1. The War Council shall consist of the Chief of Staff of the Egyptian Army and the Chief of the General Staff of the Syrian Army. It shall act as the advisory body to the

Supreme Council. It shall be competent to submit recommendations and directives in matters related to military planning and any of the tasks or functions assigned to the Joint Command.

2. The War Council shall make recommendations concerning war industries and communications facilities required for military purposes, their co-ordination and utilization in the service of the armed forces, and all related matters in the two Contracting States.

3. The War Council shall examine the programmes prepared by the Joint Command for the training, organization, arming and equipment of the forces placed under its command. It shall also study the possibilities of applying those programmes to all the armed forces of the two Contracting States and take appropriate measures to carry them out. It shall submit to the Supreme Council any measure in respect of which it considers the Council's approval necessary.

4. The War Council shall be assisted by a permanent military body to carry out all studies and preparatory work on matters and subjects referred to it. The Council shall prepare rules of procedure to govern the work of this body, and shall draw up its own budget.

Article 8. 1. The Joint Command shall consist of:

(a) The Commander-in-Chief;

(b) The General Staff;

(c) The units assigned to the Joint Command for its security and the conduct of its activities. The Joint Command shall be permanent in character, functioning both in time of peace and in time of war.

2. The Commander-in-Chief shall command the forces placed under his orders. He shall be answerable to the Supreme Council.

3. The Commander-in-Chief shall have the following duties:

(a) To prepare and carry out programmes for the training, organization, arming and equipment of the forces placed under his command by the two Contracting States with a view to making them a unified force; to submit these programmes to the War Council which shall examine them or refer them to the Supreme Council for approval.

(b) To prepare and carry out joint defence plans to meet all eventualities arising out of any armed attack against either of the two States or their armed forces. In preparing these plans, he shall comply with the decisions and directives of the Supreme Council.

(c) To distribute the armed forces which the two Contracting States shall place under his command in time of peace and in time of war, in accordance with joint defense plans.

(d) To prepare the budget of the Joint Command and submit it to the War Council for examination prior to final approval by the Supreme Council.

4. The principal assistants of the Commander-in-Chief shall be appointed and dismissed by the War Council in agreement with the Commander-in-Chief. All other members of the Joint

Command staff shall be appointed by agreement between the Comander-in-Chief and the Chief of Staff of the army concerned.

Article 9.   1. The two Contracting States shall place at the disposal of the Joint Command:

(a) In time of peace: such forces as the War Council, in agreement with the Commander-in-Chief, considers it necessary to place under his command, subject to approval by the Supreme Council;

(b) In time of war: all the forces which the two States have on a war footing;

(c) The forces concentrated on the Palestine frontiers shall be deemed to come automatically under the command of the Commander-in-Chief.

2. The War Council shall, on the proposal of the Commander-in-Chief, determine the installations and bases necessary to carry out the plans, and the priorities for their construction.

Article 10.   1. A joint fund, to which both Contracting States shall contribute, shall be established to defray:

(a) The expenses of the Joint Command, which shall be shared equally by the two States;

(b) The cost of the military installations referred to in article 9, paragraph 2, which shall be borne in the following proportions: 35 per cent by the Syrian Republic; and 65 per cent by the Republic of Egypt.

2. Each Contracting State shall pay the salaries and allowances of the military and civilian staff assigned by it to the Joint Command, the War Council and other committees, in accordance with its own financial regulations.

Article 11. Nothing in this Agreement shall in any way affect or be intended to affect the rights and obligations devolving upon the two Contracting States under the Charter of the United Nations, or the responsibilities of the Security Council for the maintenance of international peace and security.

Article 12. This Agreement is concluded for a period of five years and shall be automatically renewable thereafter for further periods of five years.

Either of the Contracting States may terminate this Agreement by giving notice in writing to the other State one year before the expiry of any of the said five-year periods.

Article 13. The present Agreement shall be ratified in accordance with the constitutional procedure of each of the Contracting States. The instruments of ratification shall be exchanged at the Syrian Ministry of Foreign Affairs at Damascus not later than thirty days from the date of signature of the Agreement, which shall enter into force immediately after the exchange of the instruments of ratification.

Done at Damascus, on 4 Rabi al Awwal of the Hegira year 1375, corresponding to 20 October 1955, in two copies, one for each Party.

For the Syrian Republic:

(Signed) RASHAD BARMADA
Minister of National Defence

For the Republic of Egypt:

(Signed) MAHMOUD RIAD
Ambassador of the Republic of Egypt to the Syrian Republic

4.1362 Agreement between the Government of the United Kingdom of Great Britain and Northern Ireland and the Government of the Federation of Malaya on External Defence and Mutual Security

Alliance Members: United Kingdom and Malaysia
Signed On: October 12, 1957, in the city of Kuala Lumpur (Malaysia). In force until October 15, 1971.
Alliance Type: Defense Pact (Type I)

Source: *United Nations Treaty*, no. 4149.

SUMMARY

This agreement between Malaysia and Great Britain was struck shortly after Malaysian independence and pledged British economic, military, and financial assistance to Malaysia in return for favorable trade policies. The treaty gave Britain a large amount of control over Malaysia's exports, with 70 percent of everything Malaysia produced returning to the United Kingdom. The treaty also granted the British full use of Malaysian military power, including the right to establish military bases on Malaysian soil.

After several confrontations between the two countries in the mid-1960s, Great Britain announced the complete withdrawal of troops from the entire Malayan region by 1971. Malaysia began pursuing other regional security agreements, and Britain disbanded its Far East command. Relations between the two countries remained friendly, and the alliance was replaced by a more equitable trade pact in 1971.

ALLIANCE TEXT

Whereas the Federation of Malaya is fully self-governing and independent within the Commonwealth;

And whereas the Government of the Federation of Malaya and the Government of the United Kingdom of Great Britain and Northern Ireland recognise that it is in their common interest to preserve peace and to provide for their mutual defence;

And whereas the Government of the Federation of Malaya has now assumed responsibility for the external defence of its territory;

Now therefore the Government of the Federation of Malaya and the Government of the United Kingdom of Great Britain and Northern Ireland have agreed as follows:

Article I. The Government of the United Kingdom undertake to afford to the Government of the Federation of Malaya such assistance as the Government of the Federation of Malaya may require for the external defence of its territory.

Article II. The Government of the United Kingdom will furnish the Government of the Federation of Malaya with assistance of the kind referred to in Annex 1 of this Agreement, as may from time to time be agreed between the two Governments for the training and development of the armed forces of the Federation.

Article III. The Government of the Federation of Malaya will afford to the Government of the United Kingdom the right to maintain in the Federation such naval, land and air forces including a Commonwealth Strategic Reserve as are agreed between the two Governments to be necessary for the purposes of Article I of this Agreement and for the fulfilment of Commonwealth and international obligations. It is agreed that the forces referred to in this Article may be accompanied by authorised service organisations, and civilian components (of such size as may be agreed between the two Governments to be necessary) and dependants.

Article IV. The Government of the Federation of Malaya agrees that the Government of the United Kingdom may for the purposes of this Agreement have, maintain and use bases and facilities in the Federation in accordance with the provisions of Annexes 2 and 4 of this Agreement and may establish, maintain and use such additional bases and facilities as may from time to time be agreed between the two Governments. The Government of the United Kingdom shall at the request of the Government of the Federation of Malaya vacate any base or part thereof; in such event the Government of the Federation of Malaya shall provide at its expense agreed alternative accommodation and facilities.

Article V. The conditions contained in Annex 3 of this Agreement shall apply to the forces, the authorised service organisations, the civilian components and the dependants referred to in Article III while in the territory of the Federation of Malaya in pursuance of this Agreement.

Article VI. In the event of a threat of armed attack against any of the territories or forces of the Federation of Malaya or any of the territories or protectorates of the United Kingdom in the Far East or any of the forces of the United Kingdom within those territories or protectorates or within the Federation of Malaya, or other threat to the preservation of peace in the Far East, the Governments of the Federation of Malaya and of the United Kingdom will consult together on the measures to be taken jointly or separately to ensure the fullest co-operation between them for the purpose of meeting the situation effectively.

Article VII. In the event of an armed attack against any of the territories or forces of the Federation of Malaya or any of the territories or protectorates of the United Kingdom in the Far East or any of the forces of the United Kingdom within any of those territories or protectorates or within the Federation of Malaya, the Governments of the Federation of Malaya and of the United Kingdom undertake to co-operate with each other and will take such action as each considers necessary for the purpose of meeting the situation effectively.

Article VIII. In the event of a threat to the preservation of peace or the outbreak of hostilities elsewhere than in the area covered by Articles VI and VII the Government of the United Kingdom shall obtain the prior agreement of the Government of the Federation of Malaya before committing United Kingdom forces to active operations involving the use of bases in the Federation of Malaya; but this shall not affect the right of the Government of the United Kingdom to withdraw forces from the Federation of Malaya.

Article IX. The Government of the United Kingdom will consult the Government of the Federation of Malaya when major changes in the character or deployment of the forces maintained in the Federation of Malaya as provided for in accordance with Article III are contemplated.

Article X. The Government of the Federation of Malaya and the Government of the United Kingdom will afford each other an adequate opportunity for comment upon any major administrative or legislative proposals which may affect the operation of this Agreement.

Article XI. For the purpose of this Agreement, unless the context otherwise requires:

"bases" means areas in the Federation made available by the Government of the Federation of Malaya to the Government of the United Kingdom for the purposes of this Agreement and includes the immovable property and installations situated thereon or constructed therein;

"force" means any body, contingent, or detachment of any naval, land or air forces, or of any such forces, including a Commonwealth Strategic Reserve when in the territory of the Federation pursuant to this Agreement but shall not include any forces of the Federation of Malaya;

"the Federation" means the Federation of Malaya;

"Service authorities" means the authorities of a force who are empowered by the law of the country to which the force belongs to exercise command or jurisdiction over members of a force or civilian component or dependants;

"Federation authorities" means the authority or authorities from time to time authorised or designated by the Government of the Federation of Malaya for the purpose of exercising the powers in relation to which the expression is used;

"civilian component" means the civilian personnel accompanying a force, who are employed in the service of a force or by an authorised service organisation accompanying a force, and who are not stateless persons, nor nationals of, nor ordinarily resident in, the Federation;

"authorised service organisation" means a body organised for the benefit of, or to serve the welfare of, a force or civilian component or dependants;

"dependant" means a person not ordinarily resident in the Federation who is the spouse of a member of a force or civilian component or who is wholly or mainly maintained or employed by any such member, or who is in his custody, charge or care, or who forms part of his family;

"service vehicles" means vehicles, including hired vehicles, which are exclusively in the service of a force or authorised service organisation

the expression "of a force" used in relation to "vessels" or "aircraft" includes vessels and aircraft on charter for the service of a force.

Article XII. This Agreement shall come into force on the date of signature.

In Witness Whereof the undersigned, being duly authorised thereto by their respective Governments, have signed this Agreement.

Done at Kuala Lumpur in duplicate, this 12th day of October, 1957.

For the Government of the United Kingdom of Great Britain and Northern Ireland

(Signed) G. W. TORY

For the Government of the Federation of Malaya:

(Signed) TUNKU ABDUL RAHMAN PUTRA

4.1363 Exchange of Notes Constituting an Agreement between the United States of America and Canada Relating to the North American Air Defence Command

Alliance Members: United States and Canada
Signed On: May 12, 1958, in the city of Washington, D.C. In force as of date of publication of this volume.
Alliance Type: Defense Pact (Type I)

Source: *United Nations Treaty*, no. 4582.

SUMMARY

The North American Air Defence Command (or NORAD) was jointly established by the United States and Canada in 1958 to unify air defenses over North America. NORAD operated under joint U.S. and Canadian chiefs of staff and permitted joint review and approval of all defense plans. NORAD existed primarily as a defensive tool, using interceptor capabilities, a single command structure, and a surveillance system focused on the skies above the United States and Canada. During the 1960s and 1970s, NORAD gradually became obsolete because its early focus on the prevention of aerial bombing attacks became less effective as intercontinental ballistic missiles (ICBMs) rapidly replaced bombers in both Soviet and U.S. nuclear forces. The tactical switch to ICBMs coupled with the 1972 Anti-Ballistic Missile (ABM) Treaty signed by the United States and the Soviet Union rendered NORAD even less meaningful.

NORAD received a boost during the 1980s with President Ronald Reagan's Strategic Defense Initiative and the allowance for ABM technology to be researched under the ABM Treaty. NORAD is still in place as of the date of this publication although its mission has evolved to counter the spread of drugs and terrorism.

EXCHANGE OF NOTES

The Canadian Ambassador to the Secretary of State

Canadian Embassy
Washington, D. C.
12th May, 1958

Sir,

I have the honour to refer to discussions which have taken place between the Canadian and the United States authorities concerning the necessity for integration of operational control of Canadian and United States air defences and, in particular, to the study and recommendations of the Canada-United States Military Study Group. These studies led to the joint announcement of August 1, 1957, by the Minister of National Defence of Canada and the Secretary of Defense of the United States indicating that our two Governments had agreed to the setting up of a system of integrated operational control for the air defences in the continental United States, Canada and Alaska under an integrated command responsible to the Chiefs of Staff of both countries. Pursuant to the announcement of August 1, 1957, an integrated headquarters known as the North American Air Defence Command (NORAD) has been established on an interim basis at Colorado Springs, Colorado.

For some years prior to the establishment of NORAD, it had been recognized that the air defence of Canada and the United States must be considered as a single problem. However, arrangements which existed between Canada and the United States provided only for the co-ordination of separate Canadian and United States air defence plans, but did not provide for the authoritative control of all air defence weapons which must be employed against an attacker.

The advent of nuclear weapons, the great improvements in the means of effecting their delivery, and the requirements of the air defence control systems demand rapid decisions to keep pace with the speed and tempo of technological developments. To counter the threat and to achieve maximum effectiveness of the air defence system, defensive operations must commence as early as possible and enemy forces must be kept constantly engaged. Arrangements for the co-ordination of national plans requiring consultation between national commanders before implementation had become inadequate in the face of a possible sudden attack, with little or no warning. It was essential, therefore, to have in existence in peacetime an organization, including the weapons, facilities and command structure which could operate at the outset of hostilities in accordance with a single air defence plan approved in advance by national authorities.

Studies made by representatives of our two Governments led to the conclusion that the problem of the air defence of our two countries could best be met by delegating to an integrated headquarters the task of exercising operational control over combat units of the national forces made available for the air defence of the two countries. Furthermore, the principle of an integrated headquarters exercising operational control over assigned forces has been well established in various parts of the North Atlantic Treaty area. The Canada-United States region is an integral part of the NATO area. In support of the strategic objectives established in NATO for the Canada-United States region and in accordance with the provisions of the North Atlantic Treaty, our two Governments have, by establishing the North American Air

Defence Command (NORAD), recognized the desirability of integrating headquarters exercising operational control over assigned air defence forces. The agreed integration is intended to assist the two Governments to develop and maintain their individual and collective capacity to resist air attack on their territories in North America in mutual self-defence.

The two Governments consider that the establishment of integrated air defence arrangements of the nature described increases the importance of the fullest possible consultation between the two Governments on all matters affecting the joint defence of North America, and that defence co-operation between them can be worked out on a mutually satisfactory basis only if such consultation is regularly and consistently undertaken.

In view of the foregoing considerations and on the basis of the experience gained in the operation on an interim basis of the North American Air Defence Command, my Government proposes that the following principles should govern the future organization and operations of the North American Air Defence Command.

1) The Commander-in-Chief NORAD (CINCNORAD) will be responsible to the Chiefs of Staff Committee of Canada and the Joint Chiefs of Staff of the United States, who in turn are responsible to their respective Governments. He will operate within a concept of air defence approved by the appropriate authorities of our two Governments, who will bear in mind their objectives in the defence of the Canada-United States region of the NATO area.

2) The North American Air Defence Command will include such combat units and individuals as are specifically allocated to it by the two Governments. The jurisdiction of the Commander-in-Chief, NORAD, over those units and individuals is limited to operational control as hereinafter defined.

3) "Operational Control" is the power to direct, co-ordinate, and control the operational activities of forces assigned, attached or otherwise made available. No permanent changes of station would be made without approval of the higher national authority concerned. Temporary reinforcement from one area to another, including the crossing of the international boundary, to meet operational requirements will be within the authority of commanders having operational control. The basic command organization for the air defence forces of the two countries, including administration, discipline, internal organization and unit training, shall be exercised by national commanders responsible to their national authorities.

4) The appointment of CINCNORAD and his Deputy must be approved by the Canadian and United States Governments. They will not be from the same country, and CINCNORAD staff shall be an integrated joint staff composed of officers of both countries. During the absence of CINCNORAD, command will pass to the Deputy Commander.

5) The North Atlantic Treaty Organization will continue to be kept informed through the Canada-United States Regional Planning Group of arrangements for the air defence of North America.

6) The plans and procedures to be followed by NORAD in wartime shall be formulated and approved in peacetime by appropriate national authorities and shall be capable of rapid implementation in an emergency. Any plans or procedures recommended by NORAD which bear on the responsibilities of civilian departments or agencies of the two Governments shall be referred for decision by the appropriate military authorities to those agencies and departments and may be the subject of intergovernmental co-ordination.

7) Terms of reference for CINCNORAD and his Deputy will be consistent with the foregoing principles. Changes in these terms of reference may be made by agreement between the Canadian Chiefs of Staff Committee and the United States Joint Chiefs of Staff, with approval of higher authority as appropriate provided that these changes are in consonance with the principles set out in this note.

8) The question of the financing of expenditures connected with the operation of the integrated headquarters of the North American Air Defence Command will be settled by mutual agreement between appropriate agencies of the two Governments.

9) The North American Air Defence Command shall be maintained in operation for a period of ten years or such shorter period as shall be agreed by both countries in the light of their mutual defence interests, and their objectives under the terms of the North Atlantic Treaty. The terms of this agreement may be reviewed upon request of either country at any time.

10) The agreement between parties to the North Atlantic Treaty regarding the status of their forces signed in London on June 19, 1951, shall apply.

11) The release to the public of information by CINCNORAD on matters of interest to Canada and the United States will in all cases be the subject of prior consultation and agreement between appropriate agencies of the two Governments.

If the United States Government concurs in the principles set out above, I propose that this note and your reply should constitute an agreement between our two Governments effective from the date of your reply.

Accept, Sir, the renewed assurances of my highest consideration.

N.A. Robertson
The Honourable John Foster Dulles
Secretary of State of the United States
Washington, D.C.

The Secretary of State to the Canadian Ambassador

Department of State
Washington
May 12, 1958
Excellency:

I have the honor to refer to your Excellency's note No. 263 of May 12, 1958 proposing on behalf of the Canadian Government certain principles to govern the future organization and operation of the North American Air Defence Command (NORAD).

I am pleased to inform you that my Government concurs in the principles set forth in your note. My Government further agrees with your proposal that your note and this reply shall constitute an agreement between the two Governments effective today.

Accept, Excellency, the renewed assurances of my highest consideration.

For the Secretary of State:

Christian A. HERTER

His Excellency Norman Robertson
Ambassador of Canada

4.1364 Agreement of Co-operation between the Government of the United States of America and the Imperial Government of Iran

Alliance Members: United States and Iran
Signed On: March 5, 1959, in the city of Ankara (Turkey). In force until February 26, 1979.
Alliance Type: Defense Pact (Type I)

Source: *United Nations Treaty,* no. 4725.

SUMMARY

The United States sought closer ties with Iran following a coup d'état in Iraq and that country's subsequent withdrawal from the Baghdad Pact. Aid to Iran increased as U.S. foreign policy in the Middle East shifted to support for the shah. In this agreement, Iran agreed to avoid the use of force and resist both inward and outward aggression. The treaty acknowledged the right of the United States to use force if necessary to deter possible assaults both in and by Iran, and Iran was pledged military aid by the United States on the condition that it would support U.S. goals and ideas in the region.

The alliance lasted until the shah fell, in early 1979, when Ayatollah Khomeini returned from exile and an anti-U.S. regime was installed, effectively destroying all U.S. influence within the country.

ALLIANCE TEXT

The Government of the United States of America and the Imperial Government of Iran,

Desiring to implement the Declaration in which they associated themselves at London on July 28, 1958;

Considering that under Article I of the Pact of Mutual Cooperation signed at Baghdad on February 24, 1955, the parties signatory thereto agreed to cooperate for their security and defense, and that, similarly, as stated in the above-mentioned Declaration, the Government of the United States of America, in the interest of world peace, agreed to cooperate with the Governments making that Declaration or their security and defense;

Recalling that, in the above-mentioned Declaration, the members of the Pact of Mutual Cooperation making that Declaration affirmed their determination to maintain their collective security and to resist aggression, direct or indirect;

Considering further that the Government of the United States of America is associated with the work of the major committees of the Pact of Mutual Cooperation signed at Baghdad on February 24, 1955;

Desiring to strengthen peace in accordance with the principles of the Charter of the United Nations;

Affirming their right to cooperate for their security and defense in accordance with Article 51 of the Charter of the United Nations;

Considering that the Government of the United States of America regards as vital to its national interest and to world peace the preservation of the independence and integrity of Iran;

Recognizing the authorization to furnish appropriate assistance granted to the President of the United States of America by the Congress of the United States of America in the Mutual Security Act of 1954, as amended, and in the Joint Resolution to Promote Peace and Stability in the Middle East; and

Considering that similar agreements are being entered into by the Government of the United States of America and the Governments of Turkey and Pakistan, respectively,

Have agreed as follows:

Article I. The Imperial Government of Iran is determined to resist aggression. In case of aggression against Iran, the Government of the United States of America, in accordance with the Constitution of {he United States of America, will take such appropriate action, including the use of armed forces, as may be mutually agreed upon and as is envisaged in the Joint Resolution to Promote Peace and Stability in the Middle East, in order to assist the Government of Iran at its request.

Article II. The Government of the United States of America, in accordance with the Mutual Security Act of 1954, as amended, and related laws of the United States of America, and with applicable agreements heretofore or hereafter entered into between the Government of the United States of America and the Government of Iran, reaffirms that it will continue to furnish the Government of Iran such military and economic assistance as may be mutually agreed upon between the Government of the United States of America and the Government of Iran, in order to assist the Government of Iran in the preservation of its national independence and integrity and in the effective promotion of its economic development.

Article III. The Imperial Government of Iran undertakes to utilize such military and economic assistance as may be provided by the Government of the United States of America in a manner consonant with the aims and purposes set forth by the Governments associated in the Declaration signed at London on July 28, 1958, and for the purpose of effectively promoting the economic development of Iran and of preserving its national independence and integrity.

Article IV. The Government of the United States of America and the Government of Iran will cooperate with the other

Governments associated in the Declaration signed at London on July 28, 1958, in order to prepare and participate in such defensive arrangements as may be mutually agreed to be desirable, subject to the other applicable provisions of this agreement.

Article V. The provisions of the present agreement do not affect the cooperation between the two Governments as envisaged in other international agreements or arrangements.

Article VI. This agreement shall enter into force upon the date of its signature and shall continue in force until one year after the receipt by either Government of written notice of the intention of the other Government to terminate the agreement.

Done in duplicate at Ankara, this fifth day of March, 1959.

For the Government of the United States of America:

Fletcher WARREN

[SEAL]

For the Imperial Government of Iran:

Général HASSAN ARFA

[SEAL]

4.1365 Treaty of Friendship and Mutual Non-Aggression between the People's Republic of China and the Union of Burma

Alliance Members: China and Burma
Signed On: January 28, 1960, in the city of Beijing (China). In force until October 6, 1967.
Alliance Type: Non-Aggression Pact (Type II)

Source: *British and Foreign State Papers,* vol. 164, p. 649.

SUMMARY

The Treaty of Friendship and Mutual Non-Aggression between the People's Republic of China and the Union of Burma was signed in 1960 to help prevent border disputes over several small areas along the border between the two countries. According to the terms of the treaty, Burma ceded to China the Hpimaw-Gawlum-Kangfang area and the Panghung-Panglao district (a total of 132 square miles), while China ceded to Burma the Namwan Assigned Tract (85 square miles); both states pledged cooperation, friendship, and neutrality for a period of ten years in order to seal the exchange.

Relations between China and Burma were stable for a number of years because of Burma's extreme isolationism, but in the summer of 1967 relations between China and several other countries deteriorated. Burmese militants attacked small communities in China, troops from the Red Guards attacked foreign embassies abroad, the Chinese government began a propaganda offensive, and China believed a global conspiracy pioneered by the United States was attempting to undermine its power. Burma withdrew from the treaty in October of 1967, and it recalled several technicians and scientists who were working in China at the time. China reciprocated amid a series of anti-Burmese threats and alleged that Burmese troops had murdered a Chinese civilian.

ALLIANCE TEXT

The Government of the People's Republic of China and the Government of the Union of Burma,

Desiring to maintain everlasting peace and cordial friendship between the People's Republic of China and the Union of Burma,

Convinced that the strengthening of good neighbourly relations and friendly co-operation between the People's Republic of China and the Union of Burma is in accordance with the vital interests of both countries,

Have decided for this purpose to conclude the present Treaty in accordance with the Five Principles of peaceful coexistence jointly initiated by the two countries, and have agreed as follows:

Article I. The Contracting Parties recognize and respect the independence, sovereign rights and territorial integrity of each other.

Article II. There shall be everlasting peace and cordial friendship between the Contracting Parties who undertake to settle all disputes between them by means of peaceful negotiation without resorting to force.

Article III. Each Contracting Party undertakes not to carry out acts of aggression against the other and not to take part in any military alliance directed against the other Contracting Party.

Article IV. The Contracting Parties declare that they will develop and strengthen the economic and cultural ties between the two States in a spirit of friendship and co-operation, in accordance with the principles of equality and mutual benefit and of mutual non-interference in each other's internal affairs.

Article V. Any difference or dispute arising out of the interpretation or application of the present Treaty or one or more of its Articles shall be settled by negotiations through the ordinary diplomatic channels.

Article VI. (1) The present Treaty is subject to ratification and the instruments of ratification will be exchanged in Rangoon as soon as possible.

(2) The present Treaty will come into force immediately on the exchange of the instruments of ratification and will remain in force for a period of ten years.

(3) Unless either of the Contracting Parties gives to the other notice in writing to terminate it at least one year before the expiration of this period, it will remain in force without any specified time limit, subject to the right of either of the Contracting Parties to terminate it by giving to the other in writing a year's notice of its intention to do so.

In witness whereof the Premier of the State Council of the People's Republic of China and the Prime Minister of the Union of Burma have signed the present Treaty.

Done in duplicate in Peking on the twenty-eighth day of January 1960, in the Chinese and English languages, both texts being equally authentic.

For the Government of the People's Republic of China:
(Signed) Chou En-lai
For the Government of the Union of Burma:
(Signed) No Win

4.1366 Defence Agreement among the French Republic, the Central African Republic, the Republic of the Congo, and the Republic of Chad

Alliance Members: France, Central African Republic, Congo, and Chad
Signed On: August 15, 1960, in the city of Brazzaville (Congo). In force until December 4, 1976. Republic of the Congo withdrew on January 1, 1974.
Alliance Type: Defense Pact (Type I)

Source: *United Nations Treaty*, no. 11761.

SUMMARY

France signed this agreement to recognize the independence of France's former colonies. The French Union was replaced by the French Community, an organization of African states that practiced mutual defense and cooperation. The alliance also attempted to minimize border disputes among the African signatories so as to encourage development. France recognized self-government but maintained defense, foreign policy, and economic planning for the French Community. In 1961, France finally granted full sovereignty to the African states while continuing informal military aid for a number of years.

ALLIANCE TEXT

The Government of the French Republic, the Government of the Central African Republic, the Government of the Republic of the Congo, and the Government of the Republic of Chad,

Considering that by virtue of the entry into force of the transfer agreements signed by the Community, the Central African Republic, the Republic of the Congo and the Republic of Chad have acceded to independence and that the French Republic has recognized their independence and sovereignty;

Recognizing their responsibilities with regard to the maintenance of peace in accordance with the principles of the Charter of the United Nations;

Considering that it is the wish of the Central African Republic, the Republic of the Congo and the Republic of Chad to co-operate with the French Republic within the Community in which they shall henceforth participate under the terms laid down in the agreements concluded for this purpose;

Desiring to determine the modalities of their co-operation in the field of defence;

Have agreed as follows:

Article 1. The Central African Republic, the Republic of the Congo and the Republic of Chad agree to organize with the French Republic a joint system for the purpose of preparing and ensuring their defence and that of the Community to which they belong.

Article 2. The Contracting Parties shall extend aid and assistance to each other and shall consult each other at all times concerning defence problems.

The general defence problems of the Community shall be dealt with at Conferences of Heads of State and Government.

Regional defence problems at the level of the three States of Equatorial Africa shall be dealt with by the Defence Council for Equatorial Africa.

Local defence problems at the level of each State shall be dealt with by a Defence Committee.

Article 3. The Central African Republic, the Republic of the Congo and the Republic of Chad shall be responsible for their internal and external defence.

To that end, each of these Republics shall have armed forces at its disposal.

Such armed forces shall participate, with the French armed forces, under a single command, in the joint defence system organized under the present agreement.

Article 4. The Contracting Parties shall provide each other with all the facilities and assistance necessary for their defence, and in particular for the establishment, stationing, training and use of defence forces.

On the territory of the Central African Republic, the Republic of the Congo and the Republic of Chad, the defence forces shall have military installations at their disposal and shall enjoy the rights and facilities necessary to their existence, training and security and to the fulfilment of their missions.

In particular, so as to enable the French Republic to discharge its responsibilities with respect to their joint defence and at world level, the Central African Republic, the Republic of the Congo and the Republic of Chad shall grant the French armed forces free use of the bases they require.

Article 5. The defence forces shall in the main be the armed forces of the Central African Republic, the Republic of the Congo and the Republic of Chad and the French armed forces responsible for the defence of the Community.

Article 6. The French Republic shall provide the Central African Republic, the Republic of the Congo and the Republic of Chad with the aid needed to constitute their armed forces.

Article 7. Arrangements for the application of the present Agreement shall be laid down in annexes.

Article 8. Each Contracting Party shall notify the others of the completion of the procedures constitutionally required for the entry into force of the present Agreement and its annexes, which shall take effect on the date of the last notification.

Done at Brazzaville on 15 August 1960.

For the Government of the French Republic:
[Signed]
J. FOYER
For the Government of the Central African Republic:
[Signed]
DAVID DACKO

For the Government of the Republic of the Congo:
[Signed]
Abbé FULBERT YOULOU
For the Government of the Republic of Chad:
[Signed]
FRANÇOIS TOMBALBAYE

ANNEX I

Concerning Mutual Assistance and Facilities in the Field of Defence

In order to provide the defence assistance and aid they have undertaken to extend to each other, the Contracting Parties have agreed on the following provisions:

Article 1. The military authorities of each of the Contracting Parties shall receive from the other Contracting Parties all assistance they may need to carry out their responsibilities. If necessary, special conventions shall be concluded to this end.

Article 2. The armed forces of each of the Contracting Parties shall have the right to unimpeded movement on the territory, in the air space and in the territorial waters of the other Contracting Parties, to organize exercises and manœuvres necessary for their training, and to use port, sea and river, road, railway and air installations.

They shall also have the right to establish and use on the territory and in the territorial waters of the other Contracting Parties air and sea beacons and communications equipment required to ensure the security and accomplishment of their missions.

Article 3. Each Contracting Party shall ensure that the armed forces of the other Contracting Parties benefit from the special entry régimes and tariffs in force on 1 July 1960.

Article 4. The Contracting Parties shall furnish the contingents required for the establishment of the defence forces provided for in article 5 of the Defence Agreement.

The Central African Republic, the Republic of the Congo and the Republic of Chad shall authorize their nationals to serve in the armed forces of each of the other Contracting Parties.

Article 5. Subject to the provisions of article 4 of the bilateral agreement on technical military assistance concluded between the French Republic and each of the other Contracting Parties, the latter shall assign to joint defence the installations, barracks, buildings, aerodromes and land used for defence on the date of signature of the present Agreement.

Special conventions shall, establish new bases, if necessary, in exchange for existing installations.

Article 6. Each of the Contracting Parties shall take, in so far as concerns it, the measures required by the armed forces mission for joint defence and in particular those relating to the requisitioning of persons and goods and to the protection and security of personnel, installations and equipment.

[Signed]
FRANÇOIS TOMBALBAYE
[Signed]
J. FOYER
[Signed]
DAVID DACKO
[Signed]
Abbé FULBERT YOULOU

ANNEX II

Concerning the Defence Council of Equatorial Africa

Article 1. The Defence Council of Equatorial Africa shall be composed of:

- The Heads of State or Government, each assisted by either the Minister of Defence or the Minister of the Interior;
- The Senior Commanding General exercising military command in Equatorial Africa;
- The High Representatives of the President of the French Republic, President of the Community, in each State.

In addition, any prominent person may, by virtue of his competence, be summoned for a hearing by the Council.

Article 2. The Council shall determine its own organisation and work.

Article 3. For all military questions, in particular to prepare the work of the Defence Council, the Senior Commanding General shall be empowered to convene the high military authorities of the Central African Republic, the Republic of the Congo and the Republic of Chad.

Article 4. The permanent secretariat of the Defence Council shall be provided through the good offices of the Senior Commanding General.

[Signed]
FRANÇOIS TOMBALBAYE
[Signed]
J. FOYER
[Signed]
DAVID DACKO
[Signed]
Abbé FULBERT YOULOU

ANNEX III

Concerning Raw Materials and Strategic Materials

Article 1. In the interests of joint defence, the Contracting Parties have decided to follow a concerted strategic raw material policy and to adopt the following measures in this field.

Article 2. The following shall be regarded as raw materials and strategic materials:

- Liquid and gaseous hydrocarbons;
- Uranium, thorium, lithium, beryllium and helium, including their ores and compounds.

This list may be amended by an exchange of letters between the Contracting Parties.

Article 3. The French Republic, the Central African Republic, the Republic of the Congo and the Republic of Chad shall consult each other regularly, particularly at Conferences of Heads of State and Government and meetings of the Defence Council, about the policy they are called upon to adopt in the field of raw materials and strategic materials, particularly in the light of general joint defence requirements, resource development in the States of the Community and the world market situation.

Within the framework of the concerted policy, the Central African Republic, the Republic of the Congo and the Republic of Chad shall keep the French Republic informed of any general or particular measures they intend to take with respect to the prospection, exploitation and external marketing of raw materials and strategic materials. The French Republic shall transmit to the Central African Republic, the Republic of the Congo and the Republic of Chad any background data at its disposal concerning the questions referred to in this paragraph. The Central African Republic, the Republic of the Congo and the Republic of Chad shall keep it informed of decisions taken.

Article 4. The Central African Republic, the Republic of the Congo and the Republic of Chad shall reserve enough of the raw materials and strategic materials produced in their territories to satisfy internal consumption demands. They shall give the French Republic preference as regards the purchase of the surplus and shall procure such materials from it on a priority basis. They shall facilitate their stockpiling for joint defence requirements and, when the interests of that defence so require, shall take the necessary steps to limit or prohibit their export to other countries.

(Signed) FRANÇOIS TOMBALBAYE
(Signed) DAVID DACKO
(Signed)J. FOYER
(Signed) Abbé FULBERT YOULOU

4.1367 Treaty of Alliance among the Republic of Cyprus, Greece, and Turkey

Alliance Members: Cyprus, Greece, and Turkey
Signed On: August 16, 1960, in the city of Nicosia (Cyprus). In force until July 15, 1974.
Alliance Type: Defense Pact (Type I)

Source: *United Nations Treaty,* no. 5712.

SUMMARY

Cyprus was ceded to Britain by the Ottoman Empire in 1878 and became a British Crown Colony in 1925. During the 1950s, a strong movement called for *emosis*, the unification of the entirety of Greece,

which was resisted heavily by Turkey because of the significant number of Turkish Cypriots on the island. In 1959, Britain reached an agreement with Greece and Turkey for Cyprus to become an independent state. Under the conditions of the agreement, *emosis* was formally banned, Britain was allowed to have formal military bases in Cyprus, and Greece and Turkey pledged guarantees for the complete independence and border defense of Cyprus. Greece and Turkey were also allowed to maintain small armies on the island.

The peace did not last long as violence broke out between ethnic populations in Cyprus, and United Nations peacekeeping forces had to be sent to the region in 1964. In July of 1974, after more than a decade of turmoil, a Greek nationalist group supported by the junta in Greece carried out a coup d'état in Cyprus, attempting to implement *emosis*. Shortly thereafter, Turkey invaded Cyprus, and Greece and Turkey were brought to the brink of war. The United Nations negotiated a tense settlement, but this particular alliance had been broken by both the coup and the invasion.

ALLIANCE TEXT

The Kingdom of Greece, the Republic of Turkey and the Republic of Cyprus,

I. In their common desire to uphold peace and to preserve the security of each of them,

II. Considering that their efforts for the preservation of peace and security are in conformity with the purposes and principles of the United Nations Charter,

Have agreed as follows:

Article I. The High Contracting Parties undertake to co-operate for their common defence and to consult together on the problems raised by that defence.

Article II. The High Contracting Parties undertake to resist any attack or aggression, direct or indirect, directed against the independence or the territorial integrity of the Republic of Cyprus.

Article III. For the purpose of this alliance, and in order to achieve the object mentioned above, a Tripartite Headquarters shall be established on the territory of the Republic of Cyprus.

Article IV. Greece and Turkey shall participate in the Tripartite Headquarters so established with the military contingents laid down in Additional Protocol No. I annexed to the present Treaty.

The said contingents shall provide for the training of the army of the Republic of Cyprus.

Article V. The Command of the Tripartite Headquarters shall be assumed in rotation, for a period of one year each, by a Greek, Turkish and Cypriot General Officer, who shall be appointed respectively by the Governments of Greece and Turkey and by the President and the Vice-President of the Republic of Cyprus.

Article VI. The present Treaty shall enter into force on the date of signature.

The High Contracting Parties shall conclude additional agreements if the application of the present Treaty renders them necessary.

The High Contracting Parties shall proceed as soon as possible with the registration of the present Treaty with the

Secretariat of the United Nations, in conformity with Article 102 of the United Nations Charter.

In Witness Whereof the undersigned, being duly authorized thereto, have signed this Treaty.

Done at Nicosia on 16 August 1960 in three copies in the French language, of which one shall be deposited with each of the High Contracting Parties.

For the Kingdom of Greece:

(Signed) G. CHRISTOPOULOS

For the Republic of Turkey:

(Signed) V. TÜREL

For the Republic of Cyprus:

(Signed) MAKARIOS, Archbishop of Cyprus
F. KÜÇÜK

Additional Protocol No. I

I. The Greek and Turkish contingents which are to participate in the Tripartite Headquarters shall comprise respectively 950 Greek officers, non-commissioned officers and men, and 650 Turkish officers, non-commissioned officers and men.

II. The President and Vice-President of the Republic of Cyprus, acting in agreement, may request the Greek and Turkish Governments to increase or reduce the Greek and Turkish contingents.

III. It is agreed that the sites of the cantonments for the Greek and Turkish contingents participating in the Tripartite Headquarters, their juridical status, facilities and exemptions in respect of customs and taxes, as well as other immunities and privileges and any other military and technical questions concerning the organization and operation of the Headquarters mentioned above shall be determined by a Special Convention which shall come into force not later than the Treaty of Alliance.

(Transitional Paragraph)

IV. It is likewise agreed that the Tripartite Headquarters shall be set up not later than three months after the completion of the tasks of the Mixed Commission for the Cyprus Constitution and shall consist, in the initial period, of a limited number of officers charged with the training of the armed forces of the Republic of Cyprus. The Greek and Turkish contingents mentioned above will arrive in Cyprus on the date of signature of the Treaty of Alliance.

In Witness Whereof the undersigned, being duly authorized thereto, have signed this Protocol.

Done at Nicosia on 16 August 1960 in three copies in the French language, of which one shall be deposited with each of the High Contracting Parties.

For the Kingdom of Greece:

G. CHRISTOPOULOS

For the Republic of Turkey:

V. TÜREL

For the Republic of Cyprus:

MAKARIOS, Archbishop of Cyprus
F. KÜÇÜK

Additional Protocol No. II

Article I. A Committee shall be set up consisting of the Ministers for Foreign Affairs of the Republic of Cyprus, Greece and Turkey. It shall constitute the supreme political body of the Tripartite Alliance and may take cognizance of any question concerning the Alliance which the Governments of the three Allied countries shall agree to submit to it.

Article II. The Committee of Ministers shall meet in ordinary session once a year. In a matter of urgency the Committee of Ministers can be convened in special session by its Chairman at the request of one of the members of the Alliance.

Decisions of the Committee of Ministers shall be unanimous.

Article III. The Committee of Ministers shall be presided over in rotation, and for a period of one year, by each of the three Foreign Ministers. It will hold its ordinary sessions, unless it is decided otherwise, in the capital of the Chairman's country. The Chairman shall, during the year in which he holds office, preside over sessions of the Committee of Ministers, both ordinary and special.

The Committee may set up subsidiary bodies whenever it shall judge it to be necessary for the fulfilment of its task.

Article IV. The Tripartite Headquarters established by the Treaty of Alliance shall be responsible to the Committee of Ministers in the performance of its functions. It shall submit to it, during the Committee's ordinary session, an annual report comprising a detailed account of the Headquarter's activities.

In Witness Whereof the undersigned, being duly authorized thereto, have signed this Protocol.

Done at Nicosia on 16 August 1960 in three copies in the French language, of which one shall be deposited with each of the High Contracting Parties.

For the Kingdom of Greece:

G. CHRISTOPOULOS

For the Republic of Turkey:

V. TÜREL

For the Republic of Cyprus:

MAKARIOS, Archbishop of Cyprus
F. KÜÇÜK

4.1368 Defence Agreement between the French Republic and the Gabonese Republic

Alliance Members: France and Gabon
Signed On: August 17, 1960, in the city of Libreville (Gabon). In force as of date of publication of this volume.
Alliance Type: Defense Pact (Type I)

Source: *United Nations Treaty*, no. 11730.

SUMMARY

France recognized complete sovereignty of Gabon with this alliance. As per the terms of the agreement, Gabon guaranteed that it would reinforce French forces for the good of the "African community" should conflict arise, while domestic uprisings were left solely in the hands of the Gabonese. Gabon could request French aid should it feel necessary.

The first president of Gabon stayed in office until a coup d'état in 1967. His successor turned the country into an autocracy. A multi-party system and new constitution were established in the early 1990s, and they helped to open up Gabon's political and economic systems.

ALLIANCE TEXT

The Government of the French Republic on the one hand, and the Government of the Gabonese Republic on the other hand,

Considering that by virtue of the entry into force of the Transfer Agreement, the Gabonese Republic has acceded to independence and that the French Republic has recognized it as an independent and sovereign State;

Recognizing their responsibilities with regard to the maintenance of peace in accordance with the principles of the Charter of the United Nations;

Considering that although both the internal and external defence of Gabon is the responsibility of the Gabonese Republic alone, the latter may, with the agreement of the French Republic, call upon the French armed forces for help in its internal or external defence;

Considering that it is the wish of the Gabonese Republic to co-operate with the French Republic within the Community to which it henceforth belongs under the terms laid down in the Franco-Gabonese agreements of today's date concluded for this purpose;

Desiring to determine the arrangements for their co-operation in the field of defence;

Have agreed as follows:

Article 1. The French Republic and the Gabonese Republic shall jointly prepare and ensure their defence and that of the Community to which they belong.

They shall extend aid and assistance to each other for this purpose and shall co-operate with each other at all times on questions of defence.

The general defence problems of the Community shall be dealt with at Conferences of Heads of State and of Government.

Article 2. A permanent joint Defence Committee shall be established to draw up the plan for defence and co-operation, particularly in the field of external defence, between the French Republic and the Gabonese Republic.

Article 3. The Gabonese Republic shall be responsible for its internal defence. It may request aid from the French Republic in accordance with the terms laid down in special agreements.

Gabonese armed forces shall participate with French armed forces, under a single command, in the external defence of the Community.

Article 4. Each Contracting Party shall provide the other with all facilities and assistance required for its defence and in particular the stationing, training and use of defence forces.

Such defence forces shall be composed in the main of armed forces of the Gabonese Republic and French armed forces responsible for the defence of the Community.

Sites and installations on the territory of the Gabonese Republic determined by mutual agreement shall be placed at the disposal of the latter to enable them to prepare and carry out their joint defence missions at all times and in all circumstances.

The French Republic shall transfer to the Gabonese Republic ownership and enjoyment of the military barracks and buildings required by the Gabonese army.

Article 5. The French Republic shall provide the Gabonese Republic with the aid needed to constitute its national armed forces.

Article 6. The arrangements for the application of this Agreement shall be laid down in annexes.

Article 7. The Contracting Parties shall notify each other of the completion of the procedures required for the entry into force of this Agreement and the annexes thereto, which shall take effect on the date of the last such notification.

Done at Libreville on 17 August 1960.

For the Government of the French Republic:

J.FOYER

For the Government of the Gabonese Republic:

[Signed] LÉON MBA

ANNEX I

Concerning Mutual Assistance and Facilities in the field of Defence

In order to provide the defence assistance and aid they have undertaken to extend to each other, the Contracting Parties have agreed on the following provisions:

Article 1. The military authorities of each of the Contracting Parties shall receive from the other Contracting Parties all the assistance they may need to carry out their responsibilities.

If necessary, special conventions shall be concluded to this end.

Article 2. The French armed forces shall have the right to unimpeded movement between their garrisons and to organize exercises and manoeuvres necessary for their training. The authorities of the Gabonese Republic shall be advised, for their information, of any large movements by land.

The French armed forces shall have the right to use port, sea and river, road, railway and air installations. They shall have unimpeded movement within the air space and the territorial waters of the Gabonese Republic. They shall also have the right to establish and to use whatever beacons may be necessary on the territory and in the territorial waters of the Gabonese Republic.

Article 3. The French armed forces shall have the right to use the post and telecommunications system of the Gabonese Republic.

For strictly military purposes, they shall have the right to establish and operate their own communications on the territory of the Gabonese Republic.

The conditions for the operation of the radioelectric communications systems established on the territory of the Gabonese Republic shall be laid down in technical agreements.

Article 4. If necessary, and in accordance with the terms laid down in the technical agreements on the subject, the Gabonese Republic shall make available to the French armed forces the bases and installations required for carrying out their mission.

Article 5. The materials, equipment and supplies imported for the French armed forces shall come under the special entry régime in force on 1 July 1960.

Article 6. The Contracting Parties shall provide the contingents of troops required to constitute the defence forces mentioned in article 4 of the Defence Agreement.

In accordance with the conditions to be laid down in a subsequent agreement, the Gabonese Republic shall authorize its nationals to serve in the French forces, or to resume service in those forces, in accordance with the regulations applicable to those forces.

For the Government of the French Republic:

J. FOYER

For the Government of the Gabonese Republic:

[Signed] LÉON MBA

ANNEX II

Concerning Technical Military Assistance between the French Republic and the Gabonese Republic

Article 1. In accordance with article 5 of the Defence Agreement, the French Republic shall provide the Gabonese Republic with the aid needed to constitute its *gendarmerie* and national armed forces.

Article 2. Under a plan drawn up by mutual agreement, the French Republic shall furnish without charge the initial military equipment and supplies required for establishing the Gabonese armed forces.

The Gabonese Republic shall, having regard to the assistance given to it by the French Republic and with a view to ensuring the standardization of armaments, apply to the French Republic for the assistance in the maintenance and renewal of the equipment of the Gabonese Army.

The expenses for the maintenance and operation of these forces shall be borne by the Gabonese Republic.

The Gabonese armed forces may seek assistance from the French armed forces in the matter of logistical support.

If items are not supplied free of charge, the financial conditions governing their position shall be laid down by mutual agreement.

Article 3. Gabonese nationals currently serving in the French armed forces shall, at the request of the Government of the Gabonese Republic, be relieved of their obligations towards those armed forces so that they may serve in the Gabonese armed forces.

In particular, Gabonese nationals serving in the French *gendarmerie* shall be transferred at the beginning of 1961.

The personnel transferred shall retain the pension rights and benefits acquired during their service with the French armed forces.

Personnel who have not been transferred shall have the option of requesting no longer to serve in those forces. This provision shall take effect as soon as the transfers have been completed and shall remain applicable for a period of six months. Personnel thus released shall benefit, particularly with regard to retirement, from advantages acquired commensurately with their length of service. Such acquired rights shall remain the responsibility of the French Republic.

The Government of the Gabonese Republic, through the present Agreement, shall agree that the Gabonese nationals currently serving in the French armed forces who have not been transferred under the first paragraph of this article or exercised the option available under the fourth paragraph thereof, should continue to serve in the French armed forces.

Article 4. The French Republic shall be responsible for training and instructing the cadres of the Gabonese Republic's army; in return, the Gabonese Republic shall not call upon any other source than the French Republic for the training of its cadres.

Gabonese nationals shall be admitted to the French *grandes écoles* and military establishments, either by competitive examination under the same conditions as French nationals or under a special quota adjusting those conditions.

For the time being, in order to accelerate the training of cadres, some Gabonese nationals nominated by their Government, by agreement with the French Government, may be accepted as trainees at French *grandes écoles* and military establishments.

The French Republic shall be responsible for the fees of pupils and trainees at French *grandes écoles* and military establishments.

Article 5. The French Republic shall second to the Gabonese Republic, in accordance with the stated requirements of the latter, such French officers and non-commissioned officers as it may need for the organization, training and officering of its armed forces.

The list of posts to be filled shall be drawn up by the Government of the Gabonese Republic, which shall transmit it to the Government of the French Republic. It shall normally be revised every other year.

The aforesaid personnel shall be seconded to the Gabonese armed forces to fill specific posts corresponding to their qualifications.

They shall be paid in full by the French authorities and shall, together with their families, be housed by the Gabonese authorities.

Article 6. Personnel seconded to the Gabonese armed forces shall be appointed by the Government of the French Republic.

The secondment shall be for a fixed period in accordance with French regulations on residence abroad. It may be renewed or interrupted by mutual agreement.

The management and administration of the persons concerned shall be dealt with by a "Mission for Military Assistance to the Gabonese Army" which shall in particular ensure that they receive their pay in accordance with rules laid down by the French authorities.

The "Mission for Military Assistance to the Gabonese Army" shall be placed under the authority of the senior highest-ranking French officer seconded to the Gabonese Republic by the French Republic.

Article 7. French military personnel shall be subject to French military jurisdiction or to Gabonese jurisdiction in accordance with the provisions laid down in annex III to the Defence Agreement.

They shall be subject to the rules of general discipline in force in the Gabonese armed forces.

Any disciplinary action they may incur shall be brought to the notice of the commander of the Mission for Military Assistance.

Military personnel liable to such action may be immediately reassigned to the French armed forces outside the territory of the Gabonese Republic.

French military personnel shall serve at the rank in the hierarchy of the Gabonese armed forces corresponding to their customary rank in the French armed forces.

Article 8. French personnel serving in the Gabonese armed forces shall be seconded to the Gabonese Government in accordance with the rules governing the use of their branch or unit. With the exception of *gendarmerie* personnel, they shall not participate directly in policing operations unless the Defence Committee so decides.

All Gabonese command decisions concerning them shall be brought to the notice of the French military authorities.

Likewise, all French command decisions concerning them shall be brought to the notice of the Gabonese military authorities.

Article 9. French military personnel seconded to the Gabonese Republic shall be taxed by the French Government and shall not be liable to direct taxes levied by the Gabonese Republic and its]ocal authorities.

The Government of the French Republic shall pay to the Government of the Gabonese Republic a counterpart sum which shall be established by mutual agreement account being taken of the size of the French military establishment seconded to the Gabonese Republic and the tax legislation of the Gabonese Republic.

Article 10. Dependants of French military personnel, as determined by French law, shall, for the purposes of application of article 9 of this Agreement, be regarded as such personnel.

However, such persons shall not benefit from the provisions of article 9 if they carry on activities on the territory of the Gabonese Republic which are liable to taxation.

Article 11. The provisions of articles 7 (first paragraph), 9 and 10, concerning French military personnel seconded to the Gabonese Republic, shall also be applicable to members of the French armed forces on the territory of the Gabonese Republic.

For the Government of the French Republic:

J. FOYER

For the Government of the Gabonese Republic:

[Signed] LÉON MBA

Annex III

Concerning the Status of the French Armed Forces in the Territory of the Gabonese Republic

Article 1. French military jurisdiction shall apply in respect of offences ascribed to a member of the French armed forces when they have been committed within those forces' bases and installations.

It shall apply in respect of offences under the general law ascribed to a member of the French annex forces and committed outside those forces' bases and installations only when evidence is produced that the offender was on duty.

In all other cases, the Gabonese courts shall have jurisdiction.

Article 2. Each Government may request from the authorities of the other State a waiver by that State of its right of jurisdiction.

Article 3. The French armed forces may, in liaison with the Gabonese authorities, use military police outside the bases to the extent necessary to maintain order and discipline among the members of the said forces.

Article 4. The French authorities shall make any accused person available to the competent Gabonese judicial authorities for all the proceedings relating to the investigation and for trial.

The Gabonese authorities shall notify the French authorities within 24 hours of the arrest of a member of the French armed forces. The notification shall mention the reasons for the arrest.

Members of the French armed forces brought before a Gabonese court or convicted by it shall be detained in a Gabonese military prison or in the military wing of a Gabonese penal institution. They shall be subject to the military régime.

Article 5. Inquiries within the bases or installations of the French armed forces shall be carried out by the French authorities.

A person or persons committing an offence and accomplices thereto, if they are not members of the French armed forces, shall be handed over to the Gabonese authorities within a period not exceeding 24 hours. In such cases, the Gabonese judicial authorities may be associated with any investigation proceedings undertaken at their request within French military bases and installations.

Article 6. In the case of offences committed in Gabon against the French or Gabonese armed forces or military installations, property and equipment, the French and Gabonese authorities shall take the same steps against persons subject to their respective jurisdictions as would have been taken if those offences had been committed against their own army or their own military installations, property and equipment.

Article 7. The French State shall bear civil liability for acts committed by French military personnel while on duty.

In the same conditions, the Gabonese State shall bear civil liability for acts committed by Gabonese military personnel while on duty.

If the two parties have been unable to reach an amicable settlement within six months, the case shall be subject to the procedure laid down by the agreement on settlement and the Court of Arbitration.

Article 8. Members of the French armed forces shall be furnished with identity or registration cards, specimens of which shall be deposited with the Gabonese Government.

Article 9. The French military command may, for the exclusive use of members of the French armed forces, be provided with logistical support including a military pay office.

For the needs of members of the French armed forces, it may establish and maintain shops, messes, clubs, recreational centres and social services. These establishments shall enjoy the same exemption from licence fees, taxes and sales taxes as similar Gabonese establishments.

The French authorities shall take the necessary steps to ensure first that persons who are not entitled to obtain supplies from such establishments cannot obtain the goods sold there and, secondly, that the members of the French armed forces cannot resell the said goods.

Article 10. Statutory provisions concerning outward tokens of respect applicable in the French armed forces and in the Gabonese armed forces shall be observed by the members of each force towards the members of the other force.

Article 11. The provisions of this Agreement shall apply to members of the French armed forces in Gabon and to the French military personnel seconded to the Gabonese armed forces.

Dependants of members of the French armed forces shall be treated as members of such forces for the purposes of articles 8 and 9 of this Agreement.

For the Government of the French Republic:

J. FOYER

For the Government of the Gabonese Republic:

[Signed] LÉON MBA

4.1369 Sino-Afghan Treaty of Friendship and Mutual Non-Aggression

Alliance Members: China and Afghanistan
Signed On: August 26, 1960, in the city of Kabul (Afghanistan). In force until December 27, 1979.
Alliance Type: Non-Aggression Pact (Type II)

Source: *Peking Review,* December 20, 1960.

SUMMARY

After a series of delegations exchanged visits between Beijing and Kabul in the late 1950s, China's vice premier and foreign minister, Chen Yi, visited Kabul in August of 1960 and signed this treaty of friendship and non-aggression. This reopening of the Silk Road between Asian neighbors began a process by which both countries worked on demarcating their mutual border. By 1964, China had exploded a nuclear bomb in Xinjiang Province, near the Afghan border, prompting the Afghan royal couple to accept a four-year-old standing invitation to visit Beijing. The king of Afghanistan, Mohammed Zahir Shah, returned to Kabul with an agreement that fully demarcated their border. Within a year, the two countries had signed a boundary protocol, a cultural agreement, and a technical and economic co-operation agreement.

On April 27, 1978, a coup d'état in Afghanistan replaced the successor to Zahir Shah with a Soviet-leaning government. The new regime was immediately hostile to China, denounced China's invasion of Vietnam, and accused China of training and supplying anti-Afghan guerrillas in neighboring Pakistan. By December 1979 relations were strained, and the Soviet invasion of Afghanistan on December 27, 1979, led China to condemn the action and halt official relations with the Soviet-backed government.

ALLIANCE TEXT

The Chairman of the People's Republic of China and His Majesty the King of Afghanistan,

Desiring to maintain and further develop lasting peace and profound friendship between the People's Republic of China and the Kingdom of Afghanistan,

Convinced that the strengthening of good-neighbourly relations and friendly cooperation between the People's Republic of China and the Kingdom of Afghanistan conforms to the fundamental interests of the peoples of the two countries and is in the interest of consolidating peace in Asia and the world,

Have decided for this purpose to conclude the present Treaty in accordance with the fundamental principles of the United Nations Charter and the spirit of the Bandung Conference, and have appointed as their respective Plenipotentiaries:

The Chairman of the People's Republic of China: Vice-Premier of the State Council and Minister of Foreign Affairs Chen Yi,

His Majesty the King of Afghanistan: Deputy Prime Minister and Minister of Foreign Affairs Sardar Mohammed Naim.

The above-mentioned Plenipotentiaries, having examined each other's credentials and found them in good and due form, have agreed upon the following:

Article I. The Contracting Parties recognize and respect each other's independence, sovereignty and territorial Integrity.

Article II. The Contracting Parties will maintain and develop peaceful and friendly relations between the two countries. They undertake to settle all disputes between them by means of peaceful negotiation without resorting to force.

Article III. Each Contracting Party undertakes not to commit aggression against the other and not to take part in any military alliance directed against it.

Article IV. The Contracting Parties have agreed to develop and further strengthen the economic and cultural relations between the two countries in a spirit of friendship and cooperation and in accordance with the principles of equality and mutual benefit and of non-interference in each other's internal affairs.

Article V. The present Treaty is subject to ratification and the instruments of ratification will be exchanged in Peking as soon as possible.

The present Treaty will come into force immediately on the exchange of the instruments of ratification and will remain in force for a period of ten years.

Unless either of the Contracting Parties gives to the other notice in writing to terminate it at least one year before the expiration of this period, it will remain in force indefinitely, subject to the right of either Party to terminate it after it has been valid for ten years by giving to the other in writing notice of its intention to do so one year before its termination.

Done in duplicate in Kabul on the twenty-sixth day of August, 1960, in the Chinese, Persian and English languages, all texts being equally authentic.

Plenipotentiary of the People's Republic of China

(Signed) CHEN YI

Plenipotentiary of the Kingdom of Afghanistan

(Signed) SARDAR MOHAMMED NAIM

4.1370 Sino-Cambodian Treaty of Friendship and Mutual Non-Aggression

Alliance Members: China and Cambodia
Signed On: December 19, 1960, in the city of Beijing (China). In effect until May 5, 1970.
Alliance Type: Defense Pact (Type I)

Source: *Treaties of the People's Republic of China 1949–1978*, p. 32–34.

SUMMARY

In 1960, Prince Norodom Sihanouk ascended to the throne in Cambodia and immediately began trying to stabilize foreign policy during a time of regional instability. A Chinese delegation including the premier, Zhou Enlai, and the foreign minister, Marshal Chen Yi, visited Cambodia in May 1960. By statements these representatives made during that visit, the two countries affirmed a pledge to develop better relations. In July, Sihanouk declared that he had guaranteed support to China in the event of a foreign threat and also stated that Chinese delegates had proposed a treaty between the two countries. By December,

after signing peace treaties with the Soviet Union and Czechoslovakia, Sihanouk visited Beijing and signed this treaty of friendship and non-aggression in addition to two agreements regarding economic and technical cooperation.

The treaties committed both countries to support a regional, Asian, and Pacific non-aggression pact and nuclear-free zone. China agreed to spend $6 million on improving the factories that had already been given to Cambodia. China also agreed to build an iron works and machine-tools factory and provide aid for the building of a railway. Upon returning to Cambodia, Sihanouk responded to claims that Cambodia was allying with communism by declaring that any nation, including the United States, could provide aid for Cambodia.

By 1970, the Vietnam War began to spread across the Cambodian border. Prince Sihanouk, with the support of General Lon Nol, met with the Soviets and the Chinese to enlist their help in persuading the Vietnamese Communists to stop fighting on Cambodian soil. In March, protests occurred in Phnom Penh over the Vietnamese border crossings. While Sihanouk was out of the country, local upheaval reached the point where he was voted out of office. Upon returning to the country, Sihanouk protested his removal and declared his intention to organize a liberation army to free Cambodia of its oppressors. That intervention proved unsuccessful, however, and Sihanouk was ousted from power. In Beijing on May 5, 1970, Prince Sihanouk announced a government in exile, the United National Front of Cambodia. The Chinese government immediately granted recognition to the exiled government and severed its ties with the newly formed Cambodian government.

ALLIANCE TEXT

Liu Shao-ch'i, Chairman of the People's Republic of China, and His Royal Highness Prince Norodom Sihanouk, Head of State of Cambodia,

Desiring to maintain a lasting peace and a cordial friendship between the People's Republic of China and the Kingdom of Cambodia.

Convinced that the strengthening of good-neighbourly relations and friendly co-operation between the People's Republic of China and the Kingdom of Cambodia conforms to the vital interests of the two countries.

Have decided to conclude the present Treaty in accordance with the Five Principles of Peaceful Coexistence, the spirit of the Asian-African Conference held in Bandung in 1955 and the principles adopted at it, and

Have for this purpose appointed as their respective plenipotentiaries:

For the People's Republic of China: Chou En-lai, Premier of the State Council of the People's Republic of China.

For the Kingdom of Cambodia: His Excellency Pho Proeung, Prime Minister of the Government of the Kingdom of Cambodia;

Who, having exchanged and examined each other's full powers, found in good and due form, have agreed upon the following:

Article 1. The People's Republic of China and the Kingdom of Cambodia will maintain a lasting peace between them and develop and consolidate their friendly relations.

Article 2. Each Contracting Party undertakes to respect the sovereignty, independence and territorial integrity of the other.

Article 3. The Contracting Parties undertake to settle any disputes that may arise between them by peaceful means.

Article 4. Each Contracting Party undertakes not to commit aggression against the other and not to take part in any military alliance directed against the other.

Article 5. The Contracting Parties will develop and strengthen the economic and cultural ties between the two countries in accordance with the principles of equality and mutual benefit and of non-interference in each other's internal affairs.

Article 6. Any difference of dispute that may arise out of the interpretation or application of the present Treaty or one or several articles of the present Treaty shall be settled by negotiation through normal diplomatic channels.

Article 7. The present Treaty is subject to ratification in accordance with the constitutional procedures of each of the Contracting Parties. It will come into force on the date of exchange of the instruments of ratification which will take place in Phnom-Penh as soon as possible.

It will remain in force so long as neither of the Contracting Parties denounces it with one year's notice.

In faith thereof, the Plenipotentiaries of both sides have signed the present Treaty.

Done in duplicate in Peking on the nineteenth day of December, nineteen sixty, in the Chinese, Cambodian and French languages, all three texts being equally authentic.

Plenipotentiary of the People's Republic of China

(Signed) Chou En-lai

Plenipotentiary of the Kingdom of Cambodia

(Signed) Pho Proeung

4.1371 Charter for the Union of African States

Alliance Members: Mali, Guinea, and Ghana
Signed On: April 29, 1961, in the city of Accra (Ghana). In force until May 25, 1963.
Alliance Type: Defense Pact (Type I)

Source: *Basic Documents of African Regional Organizations (1971)*, vol. I, 49–52.

SUMMARY

Ghana and Guinea had formed a union in 1958 and sought to continue a foreign policy of regionalism by including Mali in a greater alliance. The new Union of African States, signed in April 1961, pledged to strengthen friendship and cooperation between the member states, guarantee full political and territorial sovereignty, and guarantee collective security should one of the nations be attacked. The alliance was short-lived, though, as President Sékou Touré of Guinea declared the dissolution of smaller regional unions after the adoption of the Organization of African Union (OAU) charter.

ALLIANCE TEXT

The President of the Republic of Ghana, the President of the Republic of Guinea, and the President of the Republic of Mali, meeting in Accra on the 27th, 28th and 29th April, 1961,

Having regard to

(a) The Joint Communiqué issued in Accra on the 23rd of November, 1958, which brought into being the Ghana-Guinea Union,

(b) The Joint Communiqué issued in Conakry on the 1st of May, 1959, laying down the practical basis for the achievement of such a Union, and setting out the basic principles for a wider African Community owing no allegiance to any foreign Power,

(c) The Joint Communiqué of the Heads of State of the Republic of Ghana and the Republic of Mali, issued in Bamako in November, 1960, regarding the achievement of African Unity,

(d) The Joint Communiqué by the Head of State of the Republic of Guinea and the Republic of Mali issued at Siguiri on the 5th of December, 1960, recommending a Union of the two States, and deciding that the friendly relations and the ties of co-operation binding them to the Republic of Ghana should be intensified,

(e) The Joint Communiqué that emerged from a meeting between Presidents Kwame Nkrumah, Sékou Touré and Modibo Keita, at Conakry on the 24th December, 1960, reaffirming their joint determination to create a Union between Guinea, Mali and Ghana, giving a mandate to a Special Committee to formulate concrete proposals for implementing such a Union;

Having regard to

The conclusions reached by this Special Committee meeting in Accra from the 13th to the 18th January, 1960, and subject to approval by their respective Parliaments decide that:

Section 1 *GENERAL PROVISIONS*

Article 1. There shall be established between the Republics of Ghana, Guinea and Mali a Union to be known as "The Union of African States (UAS)".

Article 2. The Union of African States (UAS) shall be regarded as the nucleus of the United States of Africa. It is open to every State or Federation of African States which accepts its aims and objectives. It reaffirms the complete adherence of its members to the African Charter and the Casablanca Resolutions.

Article 3. The aims of the Union of African States (UAS) are as follows:

to strengthen and develop ties of friendship and fraternal co-operation between the Member States politically, diplomatically, economically and culturally;

to pool their resources in order to consolidate their independence and safeguard their territorial integrity;

to work jointly to achieve the complete liquidation of

imperialism, colonialism and neo-colonialism in Africa and the building up of African Unity;

to harmonise the domestic and foreign policy of its Members, so that their activities may prove more effective and contribute more worthily to safeguarding the peace of the world.

Article 4. The Union's activities shall be exercised mainly in the following fields:

(a) *Domestic Policy.* The working out of a common orientation for the States.

(b) *Foreign Policy.* The strict observance of a concerted diplomacy, calculated to achieve closer co-operation.

(c) *Defence.* The organisation of a system of Joint Defence, which will make it possible to mobilise all the means of defence at the disposal of the State, in favour of any State of the Union which may become a victim of aggression.

(d) *Economy.* Defining a common set of directives relating to Economic Planning, aiming at the complete decolonisation of the set-ups inherited from the colonial system, and organising the development of the wealth of their countries in the interest of their peoples.

(e) *Culture.* The rehabilitation and development of African culture, and frequent and diversified cultural exchange.

Section 2 POLITICAL

Article 5. The Supreme Executive Organ of the Union of African States shall be the Conference of Heads of State of the Union.

1. *The Union Conference.* This shall meet once a quarter in Accra, Bamako and Conakry respectively. It shall be presided over by the Head of State in the host country, who shall fix the date of the Conference. The Draft Agenda shall be drawn up by him, on the basis of items forwarded by Heads of State. The Union Conference shall pass resolutions, which shall become effective immediately.

2. *Preparatory Committee.* The Union Conference shall always be preceded by a meeting of a Committee entrusted with the task of preparing the ground for it. This Preparatory Committee may be convened at any time by the Head of State of the host country. He shall determine the number of delegates per State having regard to the items on the Draft Agenda. The Preparatory Committee shall make recommendations for the consideration of the Union Conference.

3. *Co-ordinating Committees of the Mass Organisations of the Union.* There shall be established among political organisations, Trade Union Organisations, Women's Movements and Youth Movements of the Union States, a Co-ordinating Committee for organisational purposes, to impart to the said bodies a common ideological orientation which is absolutely necessary for the development of the Union.

These Committees shall be established within three months after the publication of the present Document.

Each of the Co-ordinating Committees here envisaged, at its first Constituent Meeting shall draw up standing rules and shall determine the practical methods to be employed for the attainment of the objectives jointly agreed upon.

4. *National Days.* Before any Union Day is decided upon, the National Days of the Union States shall be marked by celebrations in all the States, in the form of ceremonies and public meetings.

Such occasions may be declared Public Holidays in whole or in part, according to the needs of the countries concerned.

Section 3 DIPLOMACY

Article 6. The principle of harmonisation of the foreign policy of the Union States shall be based upon a concerted diplomacy. To achieve such harmonisation, the following steps should be taken:

(a) at each Union Conference an analysis shall be made by the Heads of State, of the international political situation, and the Union shall decide upon directives to be sent to all the diplomatic Missions of the Member States.

(b) Ambassadors, Chargé d'Affaires, Consuls and other Heads of Missions of the three States, serving abroad shall co-ordinate their activities by way of frequent consultation.

(c) Every latitude shall be given to each State to be represented by the Embassy of another Member State of the Union. Where there is no representation of any of the three States of the Union, the Member State desirous of entrusting its affairs to the Diplomatic Mission of another State which is not a member of the Union, shall consult the Union Conference before proceeding.

(d) At international gatherings, Conferences or Meetings, the delegations of the Union States must as in duty bound consult one another, and arrive at a common stand which no one shall be allowed to ignore, and all are expected to support.

Section 4 JOINT DEFENCE

Article 7. In order to safeguard their sovereignty, the Member States shall oppose any installation of foreign military bases on their soil.

They shall jointly ensure the defence of their territorial integrity. Any aggression against one of the States shall be considered as an act of aggression against other States of the Union.

A common system of defence shall be organised in order to make it possible to secure the permanent defence of the Union States.

Section 5 ECONOMY

Economic Committee of the Union

Article 8. The Economic Committee of the Union shall have the task of co-ordinating and harmonising the Economic and

Financial Policy of the Union States in accordance with directives jointly agreed upon.

Article 9. The Economic Committee shall consist of a delegation of five members per State chosen from among the officials responsible for economy and finance in each State.

Article 10. It shall hold two sessions every year, in the months of March and September. Each State shall serve as the Headquarters of the Economic Committee of the Union for one year, and shall preside over its meetings during that year.

The Economic Committee of the Union shall draw up its standing rules at its first session. The Sessions of the Economic Committee of the Union may not exceed a fortnight.

During its sessions it shall make recommendations to be submitted to the Heads of State.

Section 6 CULTURE

Article 11. The Union States shall relentlessly pursue the rehabilitation of African Culture and the development of African civilisation.

Teaching in two languages, exchange of staff, rediffusion programmes, the establishment of joint Research Institutes shall be intensified in the Union States.

Section 7 MISCELLANEOUS

Article 12. The Institutions shall become effective from the date when this Charter is proclaimed simultaneously in the Union States.

Article 13. Modifications may be made to the present provisions at a meeting of Heads of State, in the event of the admission of a new State or at the request of a Head of State, with the view to giving greater cohesion to the Union.

Modifications shall be passed unanimously by the Conference of Heads of State.

Article 14. Every African State whose Government accepts the aims and objectives of this Charter, shall be eligible for consideration for membership of the Union of African States, from the date following a clear statement by the Head of the State. This statement shall be transmitted to the Heads of Member States of the Union.

Signed:

MODIBO KEITA
President of the Republic of Mali

SÉKOU TOURÉ
President of the Republic of Guinea

KWAME NKRUMAH
President of the Republic of Ghana

4.1372 Treaty of Friendship, Co-operation, and Mutual Assistance between the Union of Soviet Socialist Republics and the Democratic People's Republic of Korea

Alliance Members: Union of Soviet Socialist Republics and North Korea
Signed On: July 6, 1961, in the city of Moscow. In force until September 7, 1995.
Alliance Type: Defense Pact (Type I)

Source: *United Nations Treaty,* no. 6045.

SUMMARY

This pact with the Soviet Union is very similar to the defense agreement signed by North Korea with China just days later. The agreements followed General Park Chung Hee's coup d'état in South Korea in May 1961 and his establishment of a fervently anticommunist regime in Seoul. Soviet premier Nikita Khrushchev proclaimed that the Soviet Union did not believe in military pacts, but the United States, Japan, and South Korea had forced the defensive agreement because they had continually rejected offers to ease tensions on the Korean peninsula.

The agreement effectively ended with the demise of the Soviet Union in December of 1991, and a Russian note to North Korea in September of 1996 confirmed that the treaty would not be renewed.

ALLIANCE TEXT

The Presidium of the Supreme Soviet of the Union of Soviet Socialist Republics and the Presidium of the Supreme National Assembly of the Democratic People's Republic of Korea,

Anxious to develop and strengthen the friendly relations between the Soviet Union and the Democratic People's Republic of Korea based on the principle of socialist internationalism,

Desiring to promote the maintenance and strengthening of peace and security in the Far East and throughout the world in accordance with the purposes and principles of the United Nations,

Resolved to extend assistance and support to one another in the event of military attack upon either of the Contracting Parties by any State or coalition of States,

Convinced that the strengthening of friendship, good-neighbourliness and co-operation between the Soviet Union and the Democratic People's Republic of Korea is in accordance with the vital interests of the people of both States and will best serve to promote their further economic and cultural development,

Have decided for this purpose to conclude the present Treaty and have appointed as their plenipotentiaries:

The Presidium of the Supreme Soviet of the Union of Soviet Socialist Republics: Nikita Sergeevich Khrushchev, Chairman of the Council of Ministers of the USSR;

The Presidium of the Supreme National Assembly of the Democratic People's Republic of Korea: Kim Il Sung, Chairman of the Cabinet of Ministers of the Democratic People's Republic of Korea.

The two plenipotentiary representatives, having exchanged their full powers, found in good and due form, have agreed as follows:

Article 1. The Contracting Parties declare that they will continue to participate in all international action designed to safeguard peace and security in the Far East and throughout the world and will contribute to the realization of these lofty aims.

Should either of the Contracting Parties suffer armed attack by any State or coalition of States and thus find itself in a state of war, the other Contracting Party shall immediately extend military and other assistance with all the means at its disposal.

Article 2. Each Contracting Party undertakes not to enter into any alliance or to participate in any coalition, or in any action or measure, directed against the other Contracting Party.

Article 3. The Contracting Parties shall consult together on all important international questions involving the interests of both States, in an effort to strengthen peace and universal security.

Article 4. The two Contracting Parties undertake, in a spirit of friendship and cooperation in accordance with the principles of equal rights, mutual respect for State sovereignty and territorial integrity, and non-intervention in each other's domestic affairs, to develop and strengthen the economic and cultural ties between the Union of Soviet Socialist Republics and the Democratic People's Republic of Korea, to render each other all possible assistance and to effect the necessary co-operation in the economic and cultural fields.

Article 5. The two Contracting Parties consider that the unification of Korea should be brought about on a peaceful and democratic basis and that such a solution is in keeping both with the national interests of the Korean people and with the cause of maintaining peace in the Far East.

Article 6. This Treaty shall enter into force on the date of the exchange of the instruments of ratification, which shall take place at Pyongyang.

This Treaty shall remain in force for ten years. If neither of the Contracting Parties gives notice one year before the expiration of the said period that it wishes to denounce the Treaty, it shall remain in force for the succeeding five years and shall thereafter continue in force in accordance with this provision.

Done at Moscow, on 6 July 1961, in two copies, each in the Russian and Korean languages, both texts being equally authentic.

By authorization of the Presidium of the Supreme Soviet of the Union of Soviet Socialist Republics:

N. KHRUSHCHEV

By authorization of the Presidium of the Supreme National Assembly of the Democratic People's Republic of Korea:

KIM IL SUNG

4.1373 Treaty of Friendship, Co-operation, and Mutual Assistance between the People's Republic of China and the Democratic People's Republic of Korea

Alliance Members: China and North Korea
Signed On: July 11, 1961, in the city of Beijing (China). In force as of date of publication of this volume.
Alliance Type: Defense Pact (Type I)

Source: *Treaties of the People's Republic of China, 1949–1978*, p. 35–37.

SUMMARY

The second North Korean agreement signed following the coup d'état in South Korea in 1961, this defense pact and non-aggression treaty is still in force today. However, by the 1990s the development of South Korea, combined with the steady economic decline of North Korea, led both China and Russia to seek closer ties to South Korea, North Korea's bitter rival. The potential both countries saw in trade relationships with South Korea rendered close military ties with North Korea counterproductive. Chinese relations with North Korea have focused on North Korea's pursuit of nuclear weapons and the potential for mass migration across the Yalu River if the North Korean government were to collapse. Thus, the alliance remains in force, but China has openly stated that it would not aid North Korea in an attack against South Korea.

ALLIANCE TEXT

The Chairman of the People's Republic of China and the Presidium of the Supreme People's Assembly of the Democratic People's Republic of Korea, determined, in accordance with Marxism-Leninism and the principle of proletarian internationalism and on the basis of mutual respect for state sovereignty and territorial integrity, mutual non-aggression, non-interference in each other's internal affairs, equality and mutual benefit, and mutual assistance and support, to make every effort to further strengthen and develop the fraternal relations of friendship, co-operation and mutual assistance between the People's Republic of China and the Democratic People's Republic of Korea, to jointly guard the security of the two peoples, and to safeguard and consolidate the peace of Asia and the world, and deeply convinced that the development and strengthening of the relations of friendship, co-operation and mutual assistance between the two countries accord not only with the fundamental interests of the two peoples but also with the interests of the peoples all over the world, have decided for this purpose to conclude the present Treaty and appointed as their respective plenipotentiaries:

The Chairman of the People's Republic of China: Chou En-lai, Premier of the State Council of the People's Republic of China.

The Presidium of the Supreme People's Assembly of the Democratic People's Republic of Korea: Kim Il Sung, Premier of the Cabinet of the Democratic People's Republic of Korea,

Who, having examined each other's full powers and found them in good and due form, have agreed upon the following:

Article I. The Contracting Parties will continue to make every effort to safeguard the peace of Asia and the world and the security of all peoples.

Article II. The Contracting Parties undertake jointly to adopt all measures to prevent aggression against either of the Contracting Parties by any state. In the event of one of the Contracting Parties being subjected to the armed attack by any state or several states jointly and thus being involved in a state of war, the other Contracting Party shall immediately render military and other assistance by all means at its disposal.

Article III. Neither Contracting Party shall conclude any alliance directed against the other Contracting Party or take part in any bloc or in any action or measure directed against the other Contracting Party.

Article IV. The Contracting Parties will continue to consult with each other on all important international questions of common interest to the two countries.

Article V. The Contracting Parties, on the principles of mutual respect for sovereignty, non-interference in each other's internal affairs, equality and mutual benefit and in the spirit of friendly co-operation, will continue to render each other every possible economic and technical aid in the cause of socialist construction of the two countries and will continue to consolidate and develop economic, cultural, and scientific and technical co-operation between the two countries.

Article VI. The Contracting Parties hold that the unification of Korea must be realized along peaceful and democratic lines and that such a solution accords exactly with the national interests of the Korean people and the aim of preserving peace in the Far East.

Article VII. The present Treaty is subject to ratification and shall come into force on the day of exchange of instruments of ratification, which will take place in Pyongyang.

The present Treaty will remain in force until the Contracting Parties agree on its amendment or termination.

Done in duplicate in Peking on the eleventh day of July, nineteen sixty-one, in the Chinese and Korean languages, both texts being equally authentic.

(Signed) CHOU EN-LAI
Plenipotentiary of the People's Republic of China
(Signed) KIM IL SUNG
Plenipotentiary of the Democratic People's Republic of Korea

4.1374 Defense Pact of the African and Malagasy Union

Alliance Members: Benin/Dahomey, Burkina Faso/Upper Volta, Cameroon, Central African Republic, Chad, Congo, Gabon, Ivory Coast, Madagascar, Mauritania, Niger, Senegal, Rwanda (March 9, 1963), and Togo (July 9, 1963)
Signed On: September 9, 1961, in the city of Antananarivo (Madagascar). In force until March 10, 1964.

Alliance Type: Defense Pact (Type I)

Source: *Basic Documents of African Regional Organizations*, vol. 2, p. 395–399.

SUMMARY

At a conference in Antananarivo, Madagascar, representatives of twelve countries established a Union Africaine et Malgache (UAM) for political co-ordination and also signed a defense pact creating a joint defense council with staff. This was one of many attempts by the newly independent African states to band together against both internal and external interference.

This defense pact did not last long. Eschewing the political and military nature of a defensive union, the twelve member countries in 1964 replaced the UAM with the Afro-Malagasy Common Organization, which would exclusively be dedicated to economic, technical, and cultural problems among the member states. The political functions of the prior union had already been duplicated by the newly created Organization of African Unity, founded on May 25, 1963.

ALLIANCE TEXT

The States parties to the present pact:

Reaffirm solemnly their attachment to the principles of the Charter of the United Nations and proclaim their desire to live at peace with all Nations,

Recognise the sovereign equality of all States and intend to cement and strengthen the bonds existing between them on the basis of respect for their independence and non-interference in their internal affairs,

Determined to safeguard the freedom of their peoples, their own civilisations, their individual liberties and the rule of law and respect for man,

Conscious of their weakness in isolation and determined to pool their efforts for the maintenance of peace and security in their own State and in the world, as well as for the promotion of African and Malagasy Unity,

They have agreed upon the present pact.

Article 1.–The parties undertake, in accordance with the Charter of the United Nations, to settle by peaceful means all international disputes in which they may be involved in such a manner as not to jeopardise international peace and security, as well as justice, and to refrain in their international relations from resorting to threats and from any form of aggression.

Article 2.–The parties shall contribute to the development of peaceful and friendly international relations by strengthening their free institutions, by ensuring a better understanding of the principles upon which their institutions are based, and by developing the suitable conditions for ensuring security and well-being. They shall strive to eliminate any incompatibility in their policies, particularly in the economic, social, cultural and diplomatic fields, and shall encourage collaboration with each and everyone of them.

Article 3.–In order to ensure more effectively the attainment of the objectives of the present pact, the parties, by individual and joint action, in a sustained and efficient manner, by the development of their own resources and by lending mutual assistance, shall maintain and increase their individual and collective capacity for resisting all aggression.

Article 4.–The parties shall consult each other upon the measures to be taken whenever, in the opinion of one of them, the territorial integrity, political independence or security of one of the parties is threatened.

Article 5.–The parties agree that an aggression, recognised as such under the conditions defined in a protocol annexed thereto and directed against one or several of them, occurring in Africa or Madagascar, shall be deemed to be an aggression directed against all the parties. Consequently, should such aggression occur, each of them, exercising individually or collectively the right of self defence, recognised by article 51 of the Charter of the United Nations, shall come to the assistance of the party or parties thus attacked, by immediately taking measure agreed upon beforehand, then after consultation any other measures deemed necessary, including the use of armed force, to restore and ensure security in Africa and Madagascar.

Article 6.–However, the parties agree that no action shall be undertaken in the territory of a State or any diplomatic action be taken for the benefit of the latter save at its own request or with its consent, except where the extent, violence or rapidity of the aggression have interrupted the free working of its institutions and the exercise of its sovereignty.

Article 7.–Any aggression and all measures taken in consequence thereof shall be notified forthwith to the Security Council of the United Nations.

Article 8.–The parties agree that by "aggression" shall be meant not only armed attacks of a nuclear or conventional type but also such action of a subversive nature, whether armed or not, as may be directed, actively encouraged or sustained from abroad.

Article 9.–The parties agree that none of the undertakings assumed under the present pact shall be construed in such a way as to prejudice any defence conventions or agreements entered into by either of the Contracting Parties with third States.

Article 10.–Each of the parties hereby declares that none of the international undertakings currently existing between itself and any other party or any other State conflicts with the provisions of the present pact, and pledges itself not to assume any international undertaking in conflict with the present pact.

Any new undertaking in defense matters shall be subject to the prior agreement of the parties and the final texts embodying the undertakings assumed shall be deposited with the Government of Madagascar.

Article 11.–The general policy of the Union as well as the orientation of Defence policy shall be settled at Conferences of Heads of State and Government.

Article 12.–The parties agreed to set up a Higher Council of the Pact on which each of them shall be represented by a plenipotentiary delegate.

This Council shall be responsible for studying all matters pertaining to the application of the pact and, within the limits of the powers conferred upon it by the Conference of Heads of State and Government, for taking all measures calculated to guarantee such application, with respect to both the implementation of the pact's provisions and the establishment of the civil and military organs necessary for the proper functioning of the pact, particularly a High Command. Its decisions shall be taken at the majority of two-thirds of the pact's members.

Article 13.–The parties shall establish a Permanent Secretariat of the pact which shall be at the disposal of the Higher Council for ensuring the continuity and rapidity of its proceedings as well as for preparing its sessions.

Article 14.–Special protocols shall define the organization, operation, detailed powers and financing of the Higher Council, the Permanent Secretariat and of such other bodies as may be created in pursuance of the foregoing articles.

Article 15.–The present pact shall be open to other African States which declare their readiness to contribute, by taking part therein, to the Union of the African and Malagasy States with a view to ensuring the peace and security of peoples while respecting the Rights of Man.

The accession to the pact of a new State shall become operative, with the unanimous consent of the signatory States of the pact, after the deposit of the instruments of accession with the Government of Madagascar.

Article 16.–The African and Malagasy Union may, after the unanimous agreement of its members, contract international undertakings promoting the objectives of the present pact with any State or group of States, whether African or not.

Article 17.–This pact shall be ratified by the parties in accordance with their respective constitutional rules. The instruments of ratification shall, within a period of three months after signature, be deposited with the Governments of Madagascar which shall inform all the other parties of the deposit of each instrument of ratification. The pact shall become operative between the States which have ratified it as soon as the instruments of ratification of the simple majority of the signatories have been deposited. It shall come into force with regard to the other signatories on the day of the deposit of their instruments of ratification.

Article 18.–If one of the contracting parties had assumed or were to assume undertakings contrary to the provisions of the present pact or were seriously to disregard the obligations deriving therefrom, it may be excluded from the pact by a decision taken by the other contracting parties at a Conference of the Heads of State and Government and by a two-thirds majority.

However, the exclusion must be preceded by a formal notification affording the party concerned a reasonable delay within which to comply with its obligations.

Article 19.–The parties shall be bound to consult each other every five years with a view to a possible revision of the pact.

However, a revision may be requested at any time by the parties.

Under no circumstances shall any revision take place without the unanimous agreement of the parties.

Article 20.–After the pact has been operative for ten years, any party may withdraw from it. However this measure shall come into effect only one year after the party concerned shall have notified the Government of Madagascar of this denunciation. The latter shall so inform the Governments of the other parties.

Article 21.–In addition to the protocols referred to in the articles, protocols annexed to the present pact shall settle the conditions of its application to the extent necessary.

Article 22.–The original of this pact shall be deposited in the Archives of the Government of Madagascar.

Certified true copies shall be forwarded by the said Government to the Governments of the other signatory States.

In witness whereof the undersigned, Heads of State or duly authorized plenipotentiaries, have signed the present pact.

4.1375 Taif Agreement

Alliance Members: Jordan and Saudi Arabia
Signed On: August 29, 1962, in the city of Taif (Saudi Arabia). In force until May 30, 1967.
Alliance Type: Entente (Type III)

Source: *Keesing's Record of World Events,* August 1962.

SUMMARY

Tensions were high on the Arabian peninsula when a civil war erupted in Yemen in 1962. Egypt aggressively backed a new republican government in Yemen, while the Saudi government continued to support the royalist regime of its neighbor.

Jordan and Saudi Arabia ended a three-day meeting in Taif with the announcement of this treaty. The most important aspect of the treaty was the formation of a joint military command, and the treaty specifically confronted Egypt, making the claim that Cairo was a "reactionary government." The agreement also encouraged a reduction of trade barriers and pledged to work toward Palestinian peace, which was a common refrain in most Arab agreements of the time.

In May 1967, Egypt barred Israel from the shipping route through the Strait of Tiran, and Israel promptly declared Egypt's action an act of war. Feeling strong pressure from Arab fundamentalists, King Hussein of Jordan traveled to Cairo on May 30 and signed a military alliance with Egypt. The agreement placed Jordan's military forces under Egyptian command.

DESCRIPTION OF TERMS

The treaty advocated a policy of "close military, political, and economic collaboration," including the establishment of a joint Saudi-Jordanian military command. Other Arab countries were welcome to join the treaty, which would promote economic unity, trade, and cooperation on frontier problems.

4.1376 Mutual Defence Pact between Kenya and Ethiopia

Alliance Members: Kenya and Ethiopia
Signed On: November 22, 1963, in the city of Addis Ababa (Ethiopia). In force as of date of publication of this volume.
Alliance Type: Defense Pact (Type I)

Source: *Keesing's Record of World Events,* December 1963.

SUMMARY

During the 1960s and 1970s, Kenya faced low-level conflict on its northern border as those of Somali origin wished to secede to Somalia and create a greater Somaliland. This pact, signed in 1963, was an attempt to counter efforts by Somalia to thwart the Soviet-aided buildup of Somali troops and weapons. The Somali buildup eventually led to the launch of the Ogaden War against Ethiopia, during which Kenya fought the Somali irredentist forces along its border. This defense pact is still in force as of publication of this volume.

DESCRIPTION OF TERMS

Both parties pledged to come to the aid of the other in case of attack by a third party. The pact also pledged cultural and economic cooperation between the two countries. The pact was signed in July and announced on November 22. However, it was not ratified until December 27, following Kenyan independence on December 12.

4.1377 Agreement on the Establishment and Operation of the Central-American Defence Council (CONDECA)

Alliance Members: Guatemala, Honduras, Nicaragua, and El Salvador (Costa Rica and Panama were observers only)
Signed On: December 14, 1963, in the city of Guatemala City. In force until July 14, 1969.
Alliance Type: Defense Pact (Type I)

Source: *United Nations Treaty,* no. 7399.

SUMMARY

The Central-American Defense Council (CONDECA) integrated the militaries of several Central American states under one command, providing a structure for shared intelligence and communication among the signatories as well as closer ties to the United States. The effort was directed at internal subversion and attempted to thwart the growing strength of communist groups in Central America. Counterinsurgency forces were linked with several coups d'état and attempted coups in the region.

The alliance was disbanded with the outbreak of the Football War in July of 1969. Rioting during the second qualifying round for the 1970 World Cup exacerbated existing tensions, and the army of El Salvador launched an attack on Honduras. The Organization of American States negotiated a treaty to settle the conflict. An attempt made to revive this alliance in 1983 failed.

ALLIANCE TEXT

The States of El Salvador, Costa Rica, Guatemala, Honduras, Nicaragua and Panama,

Considering that they are a geographical unit for purposes of continental defence, and aware of the obligations which they have assumed in accordance with the Charter of the United Nations, the Charter of the Organization of American States, the Charter of the Organization of Central-American States, the Inter-American Treaty of Reciprocal Assistance and other international instruments for the common defence and the maintenance of the peace and security of the American continent,

Considering:

That the integration of the countries of the Central-American Isthmus as a single unit within the defence system of the American continent is the most effective way of fulfilling their obligations, of assuring peace through adequate means, of providing for effective reciprocal assistance to meet armed attacks, and of dealing with threats of aggression,

Considering:

That the Republics of the Central-American Isthmus base their institutions on the democratic system, in which they find complete satisfaction for the ideals of a better life, and that joint action is required in order to preserve that system in the Isthmus and to defend it against the forces which are attempting to destroy it by violence and the infiltration of totalitarian ideas,

Considering:

That the permanently aggressive character of the international communist movement constitutes today more than ever before, a grave and immediate threat to the peace and security of the Isthmus States, and that the subversive action of that movement, profiting by the principle of non-intervention so deeply rooted in America, is causing unrest among the peoples of the Isthmus and endangering the freedom and democracy on which their institutions are based,

Considering:

That the armed forces or their equivalents in the Central-American Isthmus constitute an important factor in the social, cultural and economic development of its peoples and can, by their structural organization, effectively help to combat the dissemination and effect of alien ideas, and that they should combine their efforts in defence of the democratic interests, freedom and institutions of their peoples, and of human rights,

Now Therefore:

The High Contracting Parties, in accordance with the resolutions adopted at the first meeting of Central-American Defence Ministers held at Antigua in 1956, at the first meeting of the Special Combined Commission held at San Salvador in 1957 and at the first meeting of the Chiefs of Staff of the Central-American Isthmus held at Guatemala City in 1961,

Agree to the establishment of the Central-American Defence Council.

Chapter I The Council

Article 1. The Central-American Defence Council shall serve as the highest organ of consultation on questions of regional defence and shall be responsible for the collective security of the participating States.

Article 2. It shall be the duty of the Council to submit to the Governments of the participating States proposals for closer collaboration between those States for the defence of the Central-American Isthmus.

Article 3. The Central-American Defence Council shall consist of the Ministers of Defence, or of officials of the appropriate department equivalent in rank and functions, of the respective participating States.

Article 4. The Defence Council shall be presided over by the member of the country in which it is meeting. Nevertheless, this prerogative is optional and may be declined, in which case the president of the Council shall be elected, by majority vote or the drawing of lots, from among the other members of the Council.

Article 5. The Council shall meet regularly once a year, at a time mutually agreed upon by the members. Special meetings shall be called at the request of any Government of the Central-American Isthmus.

Article 6. If, for exceptional reasons, any member of the Council is unable to attend any of the meetings provided for in the preceding article, he may be represented by a duly accredited and authorized special delegate, who shall have the legal status of member with full powers at the meetings of the Council.

Chapter II The Permanent Defence Committee

Article 7. The Permanent Defence Committee shall be established as a subsidiary and dependent organ of the Defence Council.

Article 8. The Permanent Committee shall consist of members of the armed forces, or their equivalents, of the signatory countries. Each participating State shall have one representative on the Permanent Committee holding the rank of delegate; nevertheless, each State may at the same time nominate an alternate delegate and such other personnel as it may deem appropriate.

Article 9. The Permanent Defence Committee shall:

(1) Act as a General Staff,

(2) Perform administrative duties.

For the more effective fulfilment of its tasks, the Permanent Defence Committee shall have a General Secretary who shall be appointed by the Committee itself and whose responsibilities shall be defined in the relevant rules of procedure.

Article 10. The Permanent Committee shall be presided over in turn by the delegate of each participating State, in the alphabetical order of the countries, and for a period of one year. During the temporary or permanent absence of the delegate in question, the delegate following him in the order laid down shall take his place. In the case of temporary absence, the titular President's period of office shall not be regarded as interrupted.

Chapter III Collective Security

Article 11. Any armed attack by any State whatsoever against a State of the Central-American Isthmus shall be considered as an attack against all the States of the Isthmus, and each one of the said States accordingly undertakes to assist in meeting the attack in the exercise of the inherent right of individual or collective self-defence.

Article 12. If the inviolability, the territorial integrity, the sovereignty or the independence of any of the States of the Central-American Isthmus should be affected by an aggression which is not an armed attack or by an extra-continental or intra-continental conflict, or by any other fact or situation that might endanger the peace of the Central-American Isthmus, the Defence Council shall meet immediately in order to agree on the measures which should be taken, in case of aggression, to assist the victim of the aggression, or on other measures necessary for the common defence and for the maintenance of the peace and security of the Central-American Isthmus.

Article 13. In the cases referred to in articles 11 and 12 and while the Defence Council is dealing with them, each of the participating States may determine the immediate measures which it may individually take in fulfilment of this Agreement, without prejudice to the other obligations laid down in the Inter-American Treaty of Reciprocal Assistance signed at Rio de Janeiro in 1947.

Article 14. When the defence of the Central-American Isthmus so requires, the Governments of the respective participating States shall determine whether the combined use of their armed forces or public security forces, the formation of a Joint General Staff, or unification of Command, are appropriate or opportune.

Chapter IV General Provisions

Article 15. The resolutions of the Defence Council shall be adopted by unanimous vote and, in order to be binding, shall be approved by the respective Governments.

Article 16. In the Defence Council and in the Permanent Committee, the participating States shall have the right to only one vote.

Article 17. The Defence Council shall normally meet in the different countries of the Central-American Isthmus in turn, in alphabetical order. The seat of the Permanent Committee shall be Guatemala City. Both the Council and the Permanent Committee may be established for a temporary period in any place in the Central-American Isthmus, when special circumstances so require.

Article 18. The Governments of the participating States shall bear the cost of their respective delegations. The necessary cost of the organization and functioning of the Council and the Permanent Committee shall be divided equally between them.

Article 19. The Defence Council shall formulate and approve its own rules of procedure. The Permanent Committee shall formulate its rules of procedure and submit them to the Defence Council for approval. Both sets of rules of procedure shall be approved within sixty days following the date on which this Agreement enters into force.

Article 20. The provisions of this Agreement shall not affect the sovereignty or constitutional procedures of each State; nor shall they be construed as impairing the rights and obligations of the States of the Central-American Isthmus as Members of the United Nations, of the Organization of American States and of the Organization of Central American States, or any particular arrangements made by any one of them as a result of specific reservations to existing treaties or agreements.

Article 21. This Agreement shall be ratified in accordance with the constitutional procedures of each of the participating States and shall enter into force for the first three ratifying States when the third instrument of ratification shall have been deposited, and for the remaining States on the date of deposit of their respective instruments.

Article 22. The instruments of ratification shall be deposited at the Ministry of Foreign Affairs of the Republic of Guatemala, which shall notify the other participating States of each deposit.

Article 23. This Agreement shall remain in force indefinitely. Nevertheless, it may be denounced by any of the High Contracting Parties by written notification to the country in which the ratifications have been deposited; that country shall in its turn communicate such notifications to the other States. One year later the Agreement shall cease to be in force with respect to the denouncing State, but shall remain in full force and effect with respect to the remaining States.

Article 24. In accordance with Article 102 of the Charter of the United Nations, this Agreement shall be registered with the Secretariat of the United Nations.

Chapter V Transitional Provisions

Article 25. The Central-American Defence Council shall form part of the Organization of Central-American States upon entry into force of the new Charter of the Organization signed at Panama City on 12 December 1962.

Article 26. The delegations of Costa Rica and Panama having attended as observers and the delegation of El Salvador having entirely reserved its position, this Agreement shall remain open in order that the Republics of Costa Rica, El Salvador and Panama may accede to it, at whatever time they may deem appropriate, by depositing the relevant instruments of accession and ratification.

In Witness Whereof the undersigned Plenipotentiaries, having communicated to each other their full powers, found in good and due form, sign this Agreement at Guatemala City, capital of the Republic of Guatemala, on the fourteenth day of December nineteen hundred and sixty-three.

For Guatemala:

(Signed) Col. Miguel Angel PONCIANO

For Honduras:
(Signed) Lt. Col. Armando ESCALÓN

For Nicaragua:
(Signed) Col. José Dolores GARCÍA

As Observers:
For Costa Rica:
(Signed) Fernando Goicoechea QUIROS

For Panama:
(Signed) Lt. Col. Julio E. CORDOVEZ

4.1378 Treaty of Friendship, Mutual Assistance, and Co-operation between the Union of Soviet Socialist Republics and the German Democratic Republic

Alliance Members: Union of Soviet Socialist Republics and the German Democratic Republic
Signed On: June 12, 1964, in the city of Moscow. In force until November 7, 1989.
Alliance Type: Defense Pact (Type I)

Source: *United Nations Treaty,* no. 8093.

SUMMARY

Premier Nikita Khrushchev of the Soviet Union responded to the deadlock in the Berlin crisis of 1964 by sending a special emissary, his son-in-law, to Bonn to negotiate a resolution to the impasse. Anti-Khrushchev forces in the Soviet Union, however, undercut the conciliatory move by the premier with this defense pact supporting the Ulbricht regime in East Germany. The East Germans also sought stronger ties and increased economic and military aid from the Soviet Union.

This alliance effectively ended when the communist East German government resigned amid protests in November of 1989. East Germany united with West Germany one year later, on October 3, 1990.

ALLIANCE TEXT

The Union of Soviet Socialist Republics and the German Democratic Republic,

Desiring further to develop and to strengthen brotherly friendship between the Union of Soviet Socialist Republics and the German Democratic Republic, in accordance with the fundamental interests of the peoples of both countries and of the socialist community as a whole,

Taking as their basis the fraternal and all-embracing co-operation which is the cornerstone of the policy governing relations between the two States and which has become still closer and more cordial since the conclusion of the Treaty of 20 September 1955 concerning relations between the Union of Soviet Socialist Republics and the German Democratic Republic,

Being firmly resolved to help to consolidate peace in Europe and throughout the world and consistently to pursue a policy of peaceful coexistence among States with different social systems,

Determined to combine their efforts in order to combat effectively, with the support of the Warsaw Treaty of Friendship, Co-operation and Mutual Assistance of 14 May 1955, the threat to international peace and security presented by revanchist and military forces seeking a revision of the outcome of the Second World War, and to defend the territorial integrity and sovereignty of both States from any attack,

Being at one in the conviction that the first workers' and peasants' State in the history of Germany—the German Democratic Republic, embodying the principles of the Potsdam Agreement—is pursuing a peaceful course and is an important factor in guaranteeing security in Europe and averting the threat of war,

Desiring to facilitate the conclusion of a German peace treaty and to bring about the unification of Germany on a peaceful and democratic basis,

Guided by the Purposes and Principles of the Charter of the United Nations,

Have agreed on the following provisions:

Article 1. The High Contracting Parties shall, on the basis of full equality of rights, mutual respect for State sovereignty, non-intervention in each other's domestic affairs and the lofty principles of socialist internationalism, continue to develop and strengthen their ties of friendship and close co-operation in all fields, realizing the principles of mutual benefit and mutual fraternal assistance.

Article 2. In the interests of peace and of the peaceful future of peoples, including the German people, the High Contracting Parties shall steadfastly strive for the elimination of the remaining vestiges of the Second World War, for the conclusion of a Germany peace treaty and for the establishment of normal conditions in West Berlin on the basis thereof.

The Parties proceed on the assumption that, pending the conclusion of a German peace treaty, the United States of America, the United Kingdom and France will continue to bear their responsibility for the fulfillment in the territory of the Federal Republic of Germany of the requirements and obligations jointly undertaken by the Governments of the four Powers under the Potsdam and other international agreements designed to eradicate German militarism and nazism and to prevent German aggression.

Article 3. The High Contracting Parties shall make a concerted effort to ensure peace and security in Europe and throughout the world in accordance with the Purposes and Principles of the Charter of the United Nations. They shall do all in their power to promote the solution, on the basis of the principles of peaceful coexistence, of such basic international problems as general and complete disarmament, including the adoption of partial measures contributing to the cessation of the armaments race and the relaxation of international tensions, the elimination of colonialism, the settlement of

429

territorial and frontier disputes between States by peaceful means, and other problems.

Article 4. In view of the existing danger of an aggressive war on the part of militaristic and revanchist forces, the High Contracting Parties solemnly declare that the inviolability of the State frontiers of the German Democratic Republic is a basic factor in European security. They reaffirm their determination, in keeping with the Warsaw Treaty of Friendship, Co-operation and Mutual Assistance, jointly to guarantee the inviolability of these frontiers.

The High Contracting Parties shall also take all necessary measures to prevent aggression on the part of the forces of militarism and revanchism, which are seeking a revision of the outcome of the Second World War.

Article 5. In the event of an armed attack in Europe on either of the High Contracting Parties by any State or group of States, the other High Contracting Party shall afford it immediate assistance in accordance with the provisions of the Warsaw Treaty of Friendship, Co-operation and Mutual Assistance.

The measures taken shall be reported to the Security Council, in accordance with the provisions of the United Nations Charter. These measures shall be discontinued as soon as the Security Council takes the necessary action to restore and maintain international peace and security.

Article 6. The High Contracting Parties shall regard West Berlin as an independent political unit.

Article 7. The High Contracting Parties reaffirm their opinion that, in view of the existence of two sovereign German States-the German Democratic Republic and the Federal Republic of Germany-the establishment of a peace-loving, democratic and unified German State can be achieved only by means of negotiations conducted on a footing of equality and by agreement between the two sovereign German States.

Article 8. On the basis of mutual benefit and disinterested fraternal co-operation, in accordance with the principles of the Council for Mutual Economic Assistance, the High Contracting Parties shall develop and strengthen to the utmost, the economic, scientific and technical relations between the two States, promote, in accordance with the principles of the international socialist division of labour, the co-ordination of economic plans and specialization and co-operation in production, and ensure maximum productivity by bringing the national economies of the two States into closer harmony.

The Parties shall continue to develop their relations in the cultural and social fields and also in the fields of sport and tourism.

Article 9. This Treaty shall not affect the rights or obligations of the Parties under bilateral or other international agreements at present in force, including the Potsdam Agreement.

Article 10. This Treaty shall remain in force for a period of twenty years from the date of its entry into force. Unless either of the High Contracting Parties gives notice of termination twelve months before the expiration of that term, the Treaty shall remain in force for a further ten years.

In the event of the establishment of a unified, democratic and peace-loving German State or of the conclusion of a German peace treaty, this Treaty may be reviewed before the expiration of the twenty-year term at the request of either of the High Contracting Parties.

Article 11. This Treaty is subject to ratification and shall enter into force upon the exchange of the instruments of ratification, which shall take place in the near future at Berlin.

Done at Moscow on 12 June 1964, in duplicate, in the Russian and German languages, both texts being equally authentic.

For the Union of Soviet Socialist Republics:

The Chairman of the Council of Ministers of the Union of Soviet Socialist Republics
N. S. KHRUSHCHEV

For the German Democratic Republic:

The Chairman of the State Council of the German Democratic Republic
W. ULBRICHT

4.1379 Mutual Security Agreement among Zaire, Burundi, and Rwanda

Alliance Members: Zaire, Burundi, and Rwanda
Signed On: August 30, 1966, in the city of Kinshasa (Zaire). In force until April 6, 1994.
Alliance Type: Defense Pact (Type I)

Source: *Keesing's Record of World Events,* August 1966.

SUMMARY

Burundi, Rwanda and Zaire signed this mutual security agreement that served as a first step toward the creation of the Economic Community of the Great Lakes Countries (CEPGL). In 1976, the community was officially founded, establishing a developmental bank aimed at increasing financial cooperation. The agreements they signed focused on their goals of African unity, ending colonialism, and increasing sovereignty and human rights. During the late 1980s, the council approved various agreements, including a convention of the free circulation of people and goods as well as the establishment of local and regional institutes to research disease.

On April 6, 1994, tragedy struck the CEPGL when the plane carrying the presidents of Rwanda and Burundi, Juvenal Habyarimana and Cyprien Ntaryamira, was shot down as it approached the airport. The plane crash is associated with the start of the genocide that devastated Rwanda in the mid-1990s. Although the CEPGL remained in force as of time of this writing, the defense pact signed in 1966 ended with the start of the genocide, which devastated the region.

DESCRIPTION OF TERMS

The agreement called for a pact of mutual security against insurgents and those targeting trade among the territories of the allies. The treaty also called for the identical treatment of persons declared undesirable by any allied country and for the settlement of cross-border refugees.

4.1380 Treaty of Friendship, Co-operation, and Mutual Assistance between the Polish People's Republic and the German Democratic Republic

Alliance Members: Poland and the German Democratic Republic
Signed On: March 15, 1967, in the city of Warsaw. In force until August 7, 1989.
Alliance Type: Defense Pact (Type I)

Source: *United Nations Treaty,* no. 8922.

SUMMARY

The growing competition and economic disparity between East and West Germany in the late 1960s and a planned Soviet withdrawal of forces from Eastern Europe led East Germany to seek to strengthen its existing economic and military ties to neighboring communist states. This treaty of friendship was an attempt to further "socialist internationalism" and create an alliance against Western forces because both countries, as they stated in the treaty, were aware that their friendship was an essential factor in thwarting the aggressive intensions of the West German militarist and revanchist forces. As part of the treaty, both countries agreed they would use the Warsaw Pact to maintain stability in the region, come to each other's aid in times of crisis, consult on all issues of joint interest, and work to strengthen economic and cultural ties. The alliance ended with the dissolution of the communist government in Poland in August 1989.

ALLIANCE TEXT

The Polish People's Republic and the German Democratic Republic,

Noting that the two States have established good-neighbourly relations based on lasting friendship, comprehensive co-operation and mutual assistance,

Desiring further to develop and strengthen those relations on the basis of the principles of socialist internationalism,

Convinced that developing their relations in that manner serves the vital interests of both States and helps to strengthen the unity of the socialist community,

Recognizing that their friendship is an essential factor in checking the aggressive schemes of the forces of West German militarism and revanchism and firmly resolved—on the basis of the Warsaw Treaty of Friendship, Co-operation and Mutual Assistance of 14 May 1955—to oppose the threat to peace presented by those forces and to safeguard the inviolability of the frontiers of the two States and their territorial integrity,

Affirming their view that the implementation of the principles of the Potsdam Agreement by the German Democratic Republic and the conclusion of the Agreement of 6 July 1950 concerning the Demarcation of the Established and Existing Polish-German State Frontier have marked an historic turning-point in the relations between the peoples of the two States,

Concurring in the view that the existence of the German Democratic Republic constitutes an important factor in safeguarding peace and that its active peace-loving policy and its participation in international co-operation are of great importance in establishing an enduring system of European security,

Noting that the defeat of militarism and neo-nazism is the prerequisite for a peaceful settlement of the German question and affirming the view that the future creation of a unified, peace-loving and democratic German State will be possible only through the establishment of normal relations between the two German States as a result of agreements concluded between the German Democratic Republic and the Federal Republic of Germany and under conditions which guarantee the security of neighbouring States,

Continuing their efforts to expand relations between States with different social systems on the basis of the principles of peaceful coexistence and to safeguard peace and security in Europe and throughout the world,

Have decided to conclude this Treaty and for that purpose have agreed as follows:

Article 1. The High Contracting Parties shall, in conformity with the principles of socialist internationalism, mutual assistance and mutual benefit and on the basis of equality of rights, respect for each other's sovereignty and non-intervention in each other's domestic affairs, develop and strengthen their friendship and cooperation in all fields.

Article 2. The High Contracting Parties shall pursue in the future, as they have in the past, a policy of peaceful coexistence among States with different social systems, shall continue, in accordance with the purposes and principles of the Charter of the United Nations, their efforts to safeguard peace and security, reduce international tension, halt the arms race and achieve disarmament, and shall oppose all forms of colonialism and neo-colonialism.

Article 3. The High Contracting Parties declare that the territorial integrity of the two States as well as the inviolability of the frontier of the Polish People's Republic on the Oder and the Neisse and of the frontier between the German Democratic Republic and the Federal Republic of Germany are of fundamental importance to European security.

Article 4. The High Contracting Parties shall, in conformity with the Warsaw Treaty of Friendship, Co-operation and Mutual Assistance of 14 May 1955, take all necessary steps to prevent aggression by the forces of West German militarism and revanchism or by any other State or group of States which allies itself with those forces.

Article 5. In the event of an armed attack on either of the High Contracting Parties by any State or group of States referred to in article 4, the other High Contracting Party shall immediately provide it with assistance in conformity with the Warsaw Treaty of Friendship, Co-operation and Mutual Assistance of 14 May 1955. In such cases, the High Contracting Parties shall act in accordance with the provisions of the Charter of the United Nations and shall immediately report to the Security Council the measures which have been taken.

Article 6. The High Contracting Parties regard West Berlin as a separate political unit.

Article 7. The High Contracting Parties take the view that the establishment of normal relations between the two sovereign German States is in line with the requirements of European security.

The High Contracting Parties shall continue their efforts to bring about, on the basis of recognition of the existence of two sovereign German States, a German peace settlement which will help to safeguard peace and security in Europe.

Article 8. The High Contracting Parties shall, on the basis of friendly co-operation and mutual benefit and in accordance with the principles of the Council for Mutual Economic Assistance, develop and strengthen in every way the economic, scientific and technical relations between the two States and shall, in accordance with the principles of the international socialist division of labour, promote the co-ordination of economic plans and co-operation in production and in that way bring the national economies of the two States into closer harmony.

Article 9. The High Contracting Parties shall develop and strengthen their relations in the sphere of culture and science, particularly education, art, the Press, radio, television and cinema, as well as in physical education and tourism.

Article 10. The High Contracting Parties shall consult each other on all important international questions affecting the interests of the two States.

Article 11. This Treaty is concluded for a term of 20 years. It shall remain in force for an additional 10 years unless one of the High Contracting Parties denounces it 12 months before the expiry of the said term.

In the event of the establishment of a unified, peace-loving and democratic German State, this Treaty shall be reviewed.

Article 12. This Treaty is subject to ratification and shall enter into force on the date of the exchange of the instruments of ratification, which shall take place at Berlin as soon as possible.

The Treaty shall, in conformity with Article 102 (1) of the Charter of the United Nations, be registered with the Secretariat of the United Nations.

Done at Warsaw on 15 March 1967, in duplicate in the Polish and German languages, both texts being equally authentic.

For the Polish People's Republic:

W. GOMULKA

E. OCHAB

J. CYRANKIEWICZ

For the German Democratic Republic:

W. ULBRICHT

W. STOPH

4.1381 Treaty of Friendship, Co-operation, and Mutual Assistance between the Czechoslovak Socialist Republic and the German Democratic Republic

Alliance Members: Czechoslovakia and the German Democratic Republic
Signed On: March 17, 1967, in the city of Prague (Czech Republic). In force until November 7, 1989.
Alliance Type: Defense Pact (Type I)

Source: *United Nations Treaty,* no. 8831.

SUMMARY

When the Soviet Union repositioned its forces from Eastern Europe to the border areas near China in early 1967, Soviet troops in Eastern Europe were replaced with increased numbers of Soviets rockets and other weaponry. Although Marshal Andrei Grechko, the Russian commander of the Warsaw Pact, assured member states that the Soviets would continue defending the allied countries, East Germany immediately sought three additional alliances with neighboring countries and reaffirmed several existing alliances in the hopes of countering any moves by West Germany or Western forces to take advantage of the withdrawal. This treaty of friendship, similar in most respects to the other alliances formed in the spring of 1967, assured both states of mutual defense and the inviolability of both states' borders. The alliance ended with the resignation of the communist government in East Germany in November of 1989.

ALLIANCE TEXT

The Czechoslovak Socialist Republic and the German Democratic Republic,

Confirming the purposes and principles set out in the Declaration of 23 June 1950 by the Government of the Czechoslovak Republic and the Provisional Government of the German Democratic Republic,

Noting that since the enmity fomented by German militarism and nazism has been overcome an enduring friendship has developed between the peoples of the two States,

Endeavouring further to consolidate good-neighbourly relations and all-round co-operation between the two States on the basis of the principles of socialist internationalism and to help to strengthen the unity of the socialist community,

Being convinced that the friendship between the Czechoslovak Socialist Republic and the German Democratic Republic, which has put into practice the principles of the Potsdam Agreement, and the policies of both States help to safeguard peace and to create an effective system of collective security in Europe,

Being firmly resolved to combat effectively the threat to peace and international security presented by the forces of West German militarism and revanchism and, on the basis of the Warsaw Treaty of Friendship, Co-operation and Mutual Assistance of 14 May 1955, to guarantee the security of both States and the inviolability of their frontiers against any attack,

Noting that the elimination of militarism and neo-nazism is

the prerequisite for a peaceful settlement of the German question and reaffirming that the creation of a unified, peace-loving and democratic German State is possible only through the establishment of normal relations between the two German States as a result of agreements between the German Democratic Republic and the Federal Republic of Germany and under conditions that will guarantee the security of neighbouring States,

Guided by the purposes and principles of the Charter of the United Nations,

Have decided to conclude this Treaty and for that purpose have agreed as follows:

Article 1. The High Contracting Parties shall, in accordance with the principles of socialist internationalism, strengthen their friendship, develop co-operation in all fields and, on the basis of equal rights, respect for sovereignty and non-interference in the internal affairs of the other Party, provide each other with assistance.

Article 2. The High Contracting Parties shall develop and strengthen their economic, scientific and technical relations on the basis of friendly co-operation and mutual benefit and shall, in accordance with the principles of the Council for Mutual Economic Assistance, implement the co-ordination of economic plans and co-operation in research, development and production, thus ensuring that the national economies of the two States continue to develop and draw closer together.

Article 3. The High Contracting Parties shall develop their relations in the fields of culture, art, science, education, health, the Press, radio, cinema and television, physical culture and tourism.

Article 4. The High Contracting Parties shall promote all-round co-operation between their respective social organizations so that the peoples of the two States may come to know one another better and draw closer together.

Article 5. The High Contracting Parties shall, in accordance with the Charter of the United Nations, continue to contribute to the safeguarding of peace and security in Europe and throughout the world. They shall continue to pursue a policy of peaceful coexistence among States with different social systems and shall arrive for disarmament and the final elimination of colonialism and neo-colonialism in all their manifestations.

Article 6. The High Contracting Parties shall consult with each other on all important international questions affecting the interests of both States.

Article 7. The High Contracting Parties note that the Munich Agreement of 29 September 1938 was brought about by the threat of a war of aggression and by the use of force against Czechoslovakia, that it was part of Nazi Germany's criminal conspiracy against peace and a gross violation of the basic rules of international law which already held good at that time, and that the Agreement was therefore invalid from the start, with all the consequences flowing from that fact.

Article 8. The High Contracting Parties regard West Berlin as a separate political entity.

Article 9. The High Contracting Parties are of the opinion that the attainment of a German peace settlement based on recognition of the existence of two sovereign German States and the establishment of normal relations between then meet the requirements of European security.

Article 10. In accordance with the Warsaw Treaty of Friendship, Co-operation and Mutual Assistance of 14 May 1955, the High Contracting Parties shall effectively defend the inviolability of the State frontiers of both States, including the State frontiers between the two German States, and shall take all necessary measures to prevent aggression on the part of the forces of West German militarism and revanchism, which are seeking a revision of the outcome of the Second World War.

In the event of an armed attack on either of the High Contracting Parties by any State or group of States, the other Contracting Party shall immediately afford it military and other assistance in accordance with the provisions of the Warsaw Treaty of Friendship, Co-operation and Mutual Assistance of 14 May 1955.

In so doing, the High Contracting Parties shall act in accordance with the relevant provisions of the Charter of the United Nations and immediately report the measures taken to the Security Council.

Article 11. This Treaty is concluded for a term of twenty years. Unless it is denounced by one of the High Contracting Parties twelve months before the expiry of that term, the Treaty shall remain in force for a further ten years.

In the event of the establishment of a unified, peace-loving and democratic German State, the further validity of the Treaty shall be reviewed.

Article 12. This Treaty is subject to ratification and shall enter into force upon the exchange of the instruments of ratification, which shall take place as soon as possible at Berlin.

The Treaty shall, in accordance with Article 102 (1) of the Charter of the United Nations, be registered with the Secretariat of the United Nations.

Done at Prague on 17 March 1967, in duplicate in the Czech and German languages, both texts being equally authentic.

For the Czechoslovak Socialist Republic:

Antonin NOVOTNY

Josef LENART

For the German Democratic Republic:

Walter ULBRICHT

Willy STOPH

4.1382 Treaty of Friendship, Co-operation, and Mutual Assistance between the Hungarian People's Republic and the German Democratic Republic

Alliance Members: Hungary and the German Democratic Republic
Signed On: May 18, 1967, in the city of Budapest (Hungary). In force until November 7, 1989.
Alliance Type: Defense Pact (Type I)

Source: *United Nations Treaty,* no. 8905.

SUMMARY

This was an additional alliance formed by East Germany following the Soviet decision to redeploy troops away from Eastern Europe. As in the other agreements, Hungary pledged to accept the status quo East German borders, and both countries pledged mutual aid in case of attack. The alliance was replaced with a new instrument in 1977, and the overall allied relationship ended with the resignation of the communist government in East Germany in November 1989.

ALLIANCE TEXT

The Hungarian People's Republic and the German Democratic Republic,

Desiring, in the common interest of the two States, further to strengthen friendly relations between their peoples on the basis of the principles of socialist internationalism and thus, in conformity with the Warsaw Treaty of Friendship, Co-operation and Mutual Assistance of 14 May 1955 and with the principles and purposes of the Charter of the United Nations, to contribute to the safeguarding of peace in Europe and throughout the world,

Firmly resolved to oppose in an effective manner the threat to peace and international security presented by the forces of West German militarism and revanchism and to guarantee the security of the two Contracting States,

Noting that the defeat of West German militarism and neonazism is the basic prerequisite for a peaceful settlement of the German question,

Desiring to contribute in the future as in the past, in close co-operation with the other socialist countries, to the implementation of the policy of peaceful coexistence among States with different social systems,

Have decided to conclude this Treaty and have for that purpose agreed as follows:

Article I. The High Contracting Parties shall, in conformity with the principles of socialist internationalism, mutual assistance and mutual benefit and on the basis of equality of rights, respect for each other's sovereignty and non-intervention in each other's domestic affairs, develop and strengthen their friendship and co-operation in all fields.

Article 2. The High Contracting Parties shall, in accordance with the purposes and principles of the Charter of the United Nations, contribute in the future, as they have in the past, to the safeguarding of peace and security in Europe and throughout the world. They shall continue to pursue a policy of peaceful coexistence among States with different social systems and shall endeavour to bring about disarmament and the final elimination of colonialism, neo-colonialism and racial discrimination in all their forms.

Article 3. The High Contracting Parties shall, in conformity with the Warsaw Treaty of Friendship, Co-operation and Mutual Assistance of 14 May 1955, effectively defend the inviolability of the frontiers of the two States, including the State frontier between the two German States. They shall take all necessary steps to prevent and repel aggression on the part of West German or any other militarist and revanchist forces which are seeking to alter the results of the Second World War.

Article 4. In the event of an armed attack on either of the High Contracting Parties by any State or group of States, the other Party shall, in exercise of the right of individual and collective self-defense under Article 51 of the Charter of the United Nations, immediately provide the first-mentioned Party with all assistance, including military assistance, and support it by all available means.

The High Contracting Parties shall immediately report to the United Nations Security Council any measures taken pursuant to this article and shall act in accordance with the provisions of the Charter of the United Nations.

Article 5. The High Contracting Parties regard West Berlin as a separate political unit.

Article 6. The High Contracting Parties take the view that the establishment of normal relations between the Government of the German Democratic Republic and the Government of the Federal Republic of Germany is in line with the requirements of European security.

The High Contracting Parties shall continue their efforts to bring about, on the basis of recognition of the existence of two sovereign German States, a German peace settlement which will help to safeguard peace and security in Europe.

Article 7. The High Contracting Parties shall, on the basis of friendly co-operation and mutual benefit and in accordance with the principles of the Council for Mutual Economic Assistance and of the international socialist division of labour, develop and strengthen in every way the economic, scientific and technical relations between the two States, co-ordinate their economic plans, promote co-operation in production and in that way bring the national economies of the two States into closer harmony.

Article 8. The High Contracting Parties shall develop and strengthen their relations in the fields of culture, art, science, education, health, the Press, radio, cinema, television, physical culture and tourism.

Article 9. The High Contracting Parties shall promote comprehensive co-operation between social organizations in order that the peoples of the two States may become better acquainted with each other and draw even closer together.

Article 10. The High Contracting Parties shall consult each other on all important international questions affecting the interests of the two States.

Article 11. This Treaty is concluded for a term of twenty years. It shall remain in force for an additional ten years unless one of the High Contracting Parties denounces it twelve months before the expiry of the said term.

In the event of the establishment of a unified, democratic German State which meets the requirements of international peace and security, the further validity of the Treaty shall be reviewed.

Article 12. This Treaty is subject to ratification and shall enter into force on the date of the exchange of the instruments of ratification, which shall take place at Berlin as soon as possible.

This Treaty shall, in conformity with Article 102 (1) of the Charter of the United Nations, be registered with the Secretariat of the United Nations.

Done at Budapest on 18 May 1967, in duplicate in the Hungarian and German languages, both texts being equally authentic.

For the Hungarian People's Republic:
KÁDÁR JÁNOS LOSONCZI PEL
FOCK J.
For the German Democratic Republic:
W.ULBRICHT
W. STOPE

4.1383 United Arab Republic–Jordan Defense Agreement

Alliance Members: United Arab Republic (Egypt-Syria), Jordan, and Iraq (joined on June 4, 1967)
Signed On: May 30, 1967, in the city of Cairo. In force until March 26, 1979.
Alliance Type: Defense Pact (Type I)

Source: *International Legal Materials,* ser. 6, vol. 3, p. 516–517.

SUMMARY

The United Arab Republic–Jordan Defense Agreement was signed just prior to the Six-Day War. On May 23, 1967, the UAR denied Israeli shipping rights in the Strait of Tiran. Israel immediately declared this an act of war, and many Arab countries rushed to the defense of the UAR. Jordan, the first to do so, allowed Egypt to control its army if war broke out.

During the next several days, Iraq pledged to support the UAR, and Libya declared it would refuse oil to any country that aided Israel in any way. President Nasser stated that any use of the Gulf of Aqaba would be considered as a transgression on the sovereignty of the UAR and would be an act of war. Israel launched a massive preemptive strike and won a short war, forcing a favorable cease-fire that was negotiated on June 10. This alliance continued after the war for more than a decade but finally ended when the Arab League broke relations with Egypt in 1979 in response to Egypt's signature of the Camp David accords, which officially recognized the sovereignty of Israel.

ALLIANCE TEXT

The Governments of the United Arab Republic and the Hashemite Kingdom of Jordan, in response to the wishes of the Arab people in each of the two brotherly countries, inspired by their absolute faith in the common destiny and unity of the Arab nation, and with a view to unifying their efforts to insure and protect their security and national ideals, have agreed to conclude a joint defense agreement to realize those aims in the following manner:

Article 1. The two contracting states shall consider any armed aggression against either as aggression against both countries. Therefore, acting on the basis of the legitimate right of individual and collective self-defense, each is obligated to go to the aid of the state which is the victim of aggression and forthwith take every measure and use all means at its disposal, including the use of armed forces, to repulse the aggression.

Article 2. The contracting states shall consult, at the request of either state, on important international conditions affecting the security or independence of either. In the event of impending war or the sudden occurrence of a menacing situation, the two contracting states shall immediately take the preventive and defensive measures warranted by the situation.

Article 3. In the event of a sudden attack on either of the two contracting states, the two states shall, in addition to the military measures required to deal with the attack, decide immediately upon other measures to be put into force under the plans concluded under this agreement.

Article 4. In pursuit of the aims of this agreement, the two contracting states have decided to establish the following main bodies:

1. A Defense Council
2. A Joint Command which shall consist of:
   A. A Council of the Chiefs of Staff
   B. A Joint General Staff

Article 5. The Defense Council shall consist of the ministers of foreign affairs and defense or war in the two countries. The Council of the Chiefs of Staff shall be responsible to the Defense Council.

The functions of the Defense Council shall include:

A. To prescribe the general principles and bases of the policy of cooperation between the two countries at all levels to repulse aggression against them.
B. To make the necessary recommendations for the direction and coordination of the activities of the two states designed to serve and promote the joint military effort.
C. To ratify the decisions of the Council of the Chiefs of Staff in all matters related to the planning of operations and the preparation of the armed forces of the two states.
D. To establish permanent or provisional special committees when necessary.
E. The Council shall meet periodically once every six months, in Cairo and Amman alternately, or when the need arises at the request of either party.

Article 6. The Council of the Chiefs of Staff consists of the chief of staff of the armed forces in each of the two countries.

The Council of the Chiefs of Staff shall:

A. Implement the principles and bases established by the Defense Council by issuing the necessary directives and instructions.

B. Approve the plans and studies prepared by the Joint General Staff, and submit what should be submitted to the Defense Council for ratification.

C. Issue decisions concerning the formation and organization of the Joint General Staff and its tasks.

The Council shall meet periodically once every three months or when necessary at the request of either of the chiefs of staff.

Article 7. In the event of the beginning of military operations, the staff of the United Arab Republic armed forces shall assume command of the operations in both states.

Article 8. Each of the two states shall bear the cost of the military installations necessary for operations in its territory.

Article 9. This agreement shall be valid for five years, renewable automatically for subsequent periods of five years. Each of the two contracting states shall be entitled to withdraw from it after informing the other state in writing of its desire to do so one year before the expiration of the above mentioned periods.

Article 10. The provisions of this agreement shall in no way infringe upon the rights and commitments of each state which are based or may be based on special agreements, the Arab League Charter, or the Charter of the United Nations.

Article 11. This agreement shall be ratified in accordance with the constitutional procedures in each of the two contracting states. The instruments of ratification shall be exchanged at the United Arab Republic Foreign Ministry. The agreement shall become valid from the date of the exchange of instruments of ratification.

In confirmation of the above, this agreement has been signed and sealed by the seals of the two states.

Done in Cairo on 20 Safar 1387 Hegira, corresponding to 30 May 1967, in two original copies.

Gamal Abdel Nasser
President of the United Arab Republic

Hussein ibn Talal
King of the Hashemite Kingdom of Jordan

4.1384 Treaty of Friendship, Co-operation, and Mutual Assistance between the People's Republic of Bulgaria and the German Democratic Republic

Alliance Members: Bulgaria and the German Democratic Republic
Signed On: September 7, 1967, in the city of Sofia (Bulgaria). In force until November 7, 1989.
Alliance Type: Defense Pact (Type I)

Source: *United Nations Treaty,* no. 8988.

SUMMARY

This is the last of the many East German alliances formed in the wake of the Soviet decision to withdraw forces from Eastern Europe in the spring of 1967. As with each of the other agreements, Bulgaria pledged to accept the borders of East Germany as inviolable, and both countries pledged mutual aid in case of attack. A new alliance instrument replaced this agreement in 1977, and the bilateral alliance held until November 1989, when the East German government fell amid popular anticommunist protests.

ALLIANCE TEXT

The People's Republic of Bulgaria and the German Democratic Republic,

Desiring to develop their ties of fraternal friendship, comprehensive co-operation and mutual assistance on the basis of the principles of socialist internationalism,

Deeply convinced that the further development of these ties serves the vital interests of both States and helps to strengthen the unity of the countries of the socialist community,

Noting the steady expansion of political, economic and cultural co-operation between the People's Republic of Bulgaria and the German Democratic Republic,

Considering that economic co-operation, in particular, between the two States contributes to their development and to a broadening of the international socialist division of labour among the countries members of the Council for Mutual Economic Assistance,

Recalling the experience of the Second World War, which was unleashed by Nazi Germany,

Aware that recognition of the present situation in Europe and the establishment of normal relations on a footing of equality among all European States are necessary in order to guarantee security in Europe,

Noting that the German Democratic Republic has given effect to the principles of the Potsdam Agreement and through its consistent peace-loving foreign policy has become an important factor in guaranteeing peace and security in Europe and that its active peace-loving policy and its participation in the development of international co-operation are of great importance for European security,

Firmly resolved to oppose the threat to peace by the forces of West German militarism and revanchism and their claims to represent the German people, and to guarantee the security of the two Contracting States against any other aggressive designs,

Affirming that the defeat of militarism and neo-nazism is the basic prerequisite for a peaceful settlement of the German question and that the establishment of a unified, peace-loving and democratic German State is possible only through the establishment of normal relations between the two German States as a result of agreements between them,

Determined to combat the threat of imperialism and to safeguard peace and security in Europe in accordance with the Warsaw Treaty of Friendship, Co-operation and Mutual Assistance of 14 May 1955,

Firmly resolved to continue consistently to pursue a policy of peaceful coexistence among States with different social systems and of strengthening peace throughout the world,

Guided by the purposes and principles of the Charter of the United Nations,

Have decided to conclude this Treaty and have agreed as follows:

Article 1. The High Contracting Parties shall, in conformity with the principles of socialist internationalism, mutual assistance and mutual benefit and on the basis of equality of rights, respect for each other's sovereignty and non-intervention in each other's domestic affairs, develop and strengthen their friendship and co-operation in all fields.

Article 2. The High Contracting Parties shall, on the basis of friendly co-operation and mutual benefit, develop and strengthen in every way the economic, scientific and technical relations between the two States, promote the co-ordination of economic plans and specialization and co-operation in production and in that way bring the national economies of the two States into closer harmony. They shall, in accordance with the principles of the international socialist division of labour, promote the further development of co-operation within the framework of the Council for Mutual Economic Assistance.

Article 3. The High Contracting Parties shall develop and strengthen their relations in science, culture, art, education, health, the Press, radio, television, cinema, physical culture, tourism and other fields. They shall promote comprehensive co-operation between the social organizations of the two countries.

Article 4. The High Contracting Parties shall take steps with a view to further increasing the strength and solidarity of the world socialist community and shall continue consistently to pursue a policy of peaceful coexistence among States with different social systems.

In accordance with the purposes and principles of the Charter of the United Nations, they shall continue their efforts to ensure world peace and security, reduce international tension, halt the arms race and achieve general and complete disarmament, establish an effective system of European security and eliminate once and for all colonialism, neo-colonialism and racial discrimination in all its forms.

Article 5. The High Contracting Parties consider that an important condition for European security is effective action against the threat presented by the West German militarist and revanchist forces, which are seeking to alter by force the boundaries established in Europe after the Second World War. They express their firm determination, in accordance with the principles of the Warsaw Treaty of Friendship, Co-operation and Mutual Assistance of 14 May 1955, to guarantee the inviolability of the frontiers of the two States, including the State frontier between the German Democratic Republic and the Federal Republic of Germany.

The two Parties shall take all necessary steps to prevent aggression on the part of any forces of imperialism, militarism and revanchism and decisively to repel the aggressor.

Article 6. In the event of an armed attack on either of the High Contracting Parties by any State or group of States, the other Contracting Party shall regard it as an attack on itself and, in exercise of the right of individual and collective self-defence under Article 51 of the Charter of the United Nations, shall immediately afford all assistance, including military assistance, to the Party subjected to the attack and also support it by all other means available. The High Contracting Parties shall immediately report to the United Nations Security Council any measures taken in accordance with this article. In carrying out such measures, the two Parties shall observe the relevant provisions of the Charter of the United Nations.

Article 7. The High Contracting Parties regard West Berlin as an independent political unit.

Article 8. The High Contracting Parties consider that the achievement of a German peace settlement on the basis of recognition of the existence of two sovereign German States and the establishment of normal relations between those States are in line with the requirements of European security.

Article 9. The High Contracting Parties shall consult each other on all important questions affecting the interests of the two States and shall harmonize their positions on such questions.

Article 10. This Treaty is concluded for a period of twenty years. It shall be extended for successive ten-year terms unless one of the Contracting Parties denounces it twelve months before the expiry of the current term.

In the event of the establishment of a unified, peace-loving and democratic German State. the Treaty may be reviewed at the request of either of the High Contracting Parties.

Article 11. This Treaty is subject to ratification and shall enter into force on the date of the exchange of the instruments of ratification, which shall take place at Berlin as soon as possible.

This Treaty shall, in conformity with Article 102 (1) of the Charter of the United Nations, be registered with the Secretariat of the United Nations.

Done at Sofia on 7 September 1967, in duplicate in the Bulgarian and German languages, both texts being equally authentic.

For the People's Republic of Bulgaria:
T. ZHIVKOV
G. TRAIKOV

For the German Democratic Republic:
W. ULBRICHT
W. STOPH

4.1385 Agreement between the Government of Mauritius and the Government of the United Kingdom of Great Britain and Northern Ireland on Mutual Defence and Assistance

Alliance Members: United Kingdom and Mauritius
Signed On: March 12, 1968, in the city of Port Louis (Mauritius). In force until March 31, 1976.
Alliance Type: Defense Pact (Type I)

Source: *United Nations Treaty,* no. 9267.

SUMMARY

A tiny island located east of Madagascar in the Indian Ocean, Mauritius was controlled by the British for more than 158 years until it gained independence in March 1968. While Mauritius was technically granted full sovereignty, the United Kingdom forced the signing of an eight-year agreement pledging defense of the country's borders, complete consultation on military issues, and, most important, British use of existing facilities (including bases, airports, and naval communication centers). Domestic political strife, including race riots, continued in the country for a number of years after Britain withdrew, but the two nations maintained friendly relations for years following the alliance.

The treaty was formally terminated with an exchange of notes that took place one year before the termination was finalized in 1976. British authorities had never intended the alliance to be permanent and knew an armed presence in Mauritius was not needed.

ALLIANCE TEXT

The Government of Mauritius and the Government of the United Kingdom of Great Britain and Northern Ireland;

Desiring to provide for co-operation in matters of mutual defence and to contribute to the maintenance of peace in accordance with the Charter of the United Nations;

Have agreed as follows:

Article I. The Government of Mauritius and the Government of the United Kingdom each undertake to afford to the other the assistance specified in this Agreement.

Article 2. In the event of armed attack or threat thereof against any of the territories or forces of Mauritius or against any territory of the United Kingdom or under the protection of the United Kingdom or against any of the forces of the United Kingdom or any other threat to the preservation of peace the Governments of Mauritius and of the United Kingdom will consult together for the purpose of deciding what measures should be taken, jointly or separately, in relation to such attack or threat and generally to secure the fullest co-operation between the two Governments.

Article 3. In the event of any threat to the internal security of Mauritius upon any request for assistance made by the Government of Mauritius to the Government of the United Kingdom there shall he consultation between the two Governments.

Article 4. The Government of Mauritius grants to the Government of the United Kingdom the right in peace and war to station armed forces and associated civilian personnel in Mauritius and to use facilities there.

Article 5. The Government of the United Kingdom will if so requested by the Government of Mauritius provide assistance or advice in connection with the staffing, administration, training and equipment of the armed forces and police forces of Mauritius in such manner, to such extent and on such terms including terms as to payment for assistance as may be agreed.

Article 6. Nothing in this Agreement is intended to or shall in any way prejudice the rights and obligations which devolve or may devolve upon either Government under the Charter of the United Nations.

Article 7. The Annex to this Agreement shall have force and effect as an integral part of this Agreement and this Agreement shall be interpreted in accordance with the Annex.

Article 8. All property and equipment constructed, installed, brought into or procured in Mauritius under or prior to this Agreement by the Government of the United Kingdom shall remain the property of the Government of the United Kingdom and may be removed from Mauritius free of restrictions or disposed of in Mauritius by the Government of the United Kingdom prior to or within two years of the date of the termination of this Agreement. Notwithstanding any such termination the Annex to this Agreement shall remain in full force and effect so long as armed forces or associated civilian personnel of the United Kingdom are present in Mauritius.

Article 9. This Agreement shall come into operation on the day of signature and shall continue in force until one year after notice is given by one Government or the other of its desire to terminate this Agreement. Provided that no notice shall be given until the expiration of six years from the date upon which this Agreement comes into operation.

In Witness Whereof the undersigned, being duly authorised thereto by their respective Governments, have signed the present Agreement.

Done at Port Louis on the 12th day of March, 1968.

For the Government of Mauritius:

S. RAMGOOLAM

For the Government of the United Kingdom of Great Britain and Northern Ireland:

A. WOOLLER

4.1386 Charter of the Union of Central African States

Alliance Members: Chad, Democratic Republic of Congo, and Central African Republic
Signed On: April 2, 1968, in the city of Fort-Lamy (Chad). In force until December 9, 1968.
Alliance Type: Defense Pact (Type I)

Source: *Basic Documents of African Regional Organizations (1972),* vol. II, p. 766–779.

SUMMARY

The Union of Central African States (UEAC) was a regional agreement promoted by countries struggling to maintain independence and security in central Africa. In addition to mutual defense and consultation in the event of crises, the alliance members agreed to create a "common market" and harmonize their industrialization policies, their development plans, and their policies in matters of transport and telecommunications.

President Jean-Bedel Bokassa of the Central African Republic, with the backing of several neighboring countries, announced a withdrawal from the alliance later in the year the agreement was created. Bokassa instead supported the Union Douanière des Etats de l'Afrique Centrale (UDEAC), a previous economic agreement among the alliance partners that also included Cameroon, Equatorial Guinea, and Gabon. Bokassa's withdrawal led to increased tensions between the Central African Republic and the Democratic Republic of Congo.

ALLIANCE TEXT

Pursuant to the Protocol of Agreement signed February 2, 1968 at Bangui by the Chiefs of State of the Central African Republic, the Democratic Republic of the Congo, and the Republic of Chad;

Convinced that the peoples have an inalienable right to determine their own destiny;

Knowing that it is their duty to use the natural and human resources of their countries in achieving the general progress of their peoples in all areas of human activity;

Guided by a common, sincere determination to strengthen understanding between their peoples and cooperation between their States in order to satisfy the aspirations of their peoples toward the formation of a brotherhood and solidarity within a broader Union that would transcend ethnic and national differences;

Convinced that in order to apply this firm determination in achieving the progress of their peoples, it is important to create and to maintain a climate of peace and security;

Firmly resolved to safeguard and strengthen the hard-won independence and sovereignty and the territorial integrity of their States and to combat all forms of colonialism and neo-colonialism;

Reaffirming their adherence to the principles of the Universal Declaration of Human Rights, and the Charters of the United Nations and the Organization of African Unity;

Animated by a firm desire to strengthen the age-old bonds of brotherhood existing between their peoples;

Desiring to promote economic, commercial, cultural, and political relations between their States;

Convinced that the geographical location of their States makes it necessary for them to achieve more effective solidarity in a common transportation and telecommunications organization;

Aware of the role that the States of the Union are called upon to play among the nations of Central Africa;

Aware likewise of helping thereby to strengthen African solidarity and with due respect for the international commitments assumed by each of their States;

Resolved to promote the gradual, progressive establishment of a Central African Common Market with a view to regional integration;

Persuaded that the creation of a Common Market through the elimination of the obstacles to interregional trade, the adoption of a procedure for the equitable allocation of industrialization projects, and the coordination of programs for the development of the various sectors of production, will contribute greatly toward improving the standard of living of their peoples;

Desiring to strengthen their economies and to ensure their harmonious development through the adoption of provisions that will take into account the interests of each and every one and that will sufficiently alleviate, through appropriate measures, the special situation of the economically less developed countries;

Resolved to contribute, through the establishment of such a regional economic union and through cooperation on policy and on security matters, toward the attainment of the objectives [of the Organization] of African Unity,

The President of the Central African Republic

The President of the Democratic Republic of the Congo

The President of the Republic of Chad

Hereby decide to establish the Union of Central African States (U.E.A.C.) and

Agree upon the following:

Article 1. By this Charter the High Contracting Parties establish among themselves a Union of Central African States, hereinafter called the Union.

The Union shall be open to any independent and sovereign State that requests admission; new States shall be admitted by a unanimous vote of the members of the Union.

Article 2. The High Contracting Parties hereby decide to establish a Common Market of the Central African States. To that end they hereby agree to coordinate their industrialization policies, their development plans, and their transportation and telecommunications policies in order to promote balanced development and the diversification of the economies of the Member States of the Union within a framework designed to make it possible to expand trade between the States and to improve the living conditions of the people.

They likewise agree upon close cooperation in the cultural field and on security matters.

Article 3. The tasks devolving upon the Union shall be carried out through: the Conference of Chiefs of State, the Council of Ministers, and the Executive Secretariat.

PART ONE — THE INSTITUTIONS

Title I THE CONFERENCE OF CHIEFS OF STATE

Chapter I – Organization

Article 4. The Conference of Chiefs of State shall be constituted by a meeting of the Chiefs of State or their representatives, provided with full powers. The Chiefs of State may be assisted by Ministers and Experts.

Article 5. The Conference shall meet as often as necessary, and at least once a year.

Article 6. The Chairmanship of the meetings shall rotate annually among the Chiefs of State following the alphabetical order of the names of the States, unless the Chiefs of State unanimously decide otherwise. The new Chairman shall be installed at the opening session of the first meeting of each calendar year. If additional States become members of the Union, their Chiefs of State shall act as Chairmen of the Conference after the last State in alphabetical order, of those that sign this Charter.

Article 7. If the Conference lacks a Chairman owing to a change in the regime of a member country, the Chairmanship shall be held by the next Chief of State in alphabetical order of States.

Article 8. The Chairman shall fix the date and place for the meetings and shall summon the members of the Council.

Article 9. In case of emergency, the members of the Conference may be consulted at home if the Chairman so decides.

Chapter II — Powers and Duties

Article 10. The Conference shall be the supreme organ of the Union for purposes of ensuring the attainment of the objectives fixed in this Charter, under the conditions specified by the latter:

1. It shall strengthen the unity and solidarity of the Member States.
2. It shall coordinate and intensify their cooperation and their efforts to ensure better living conditions for their peoples.
3. It shall defend their sovereignty, territorial integrity, and independence.
4. It shall guide and coordinate their general policies, particularly in the following fields:
   (a) Economy, Trade, Customs, Transportation, and Telecommunications;
   (b) Education and Culture;
   (c) Health, Hygiene, and Nutrition;
   (d) Science and Technology;
   (e) Defense and Security.
5. It shall have the following nonrestrictive powers:
   It shall supervise the activities of the Council of Ministers.
   It shall draw up its bylaws and shall approve the bylaws of the Council of Ministers.
   It shall establish the seat of the Union.
   It shall decide regarding the creation of common agencies and services.
   It shall appoint the Executive Secretary and the Deputy Executive Secretary of the Union.
   It shall draw up the Union's Budget and shall fix the amount of the annual contribution of each Member

State upon the recommendation of the Council of Ministers.
   It shall decide regarding tariff negotiations with third countries and the application of a general tariff.
   It shall decide, without appeal, on all questions on which the Council of Ministers is unable to reach a unanimous decision.
   It may, in addition, revise the structures, functions, and activities of all other bodies.
6. It shall arbitrate any differences that arise between the Member States regarding the implementation of this Charter.

Chapter III — Decisions, Notification, Enforcement

Article 11. Decisions of the Conference shall be unanimous. They shall be automatically enforceable in the Member States in accordance with the terms and conditions to be determined by the bylaws of the Conference.

Title II COUNCIL OF MINISTERS

Chapter I – Organization

Article 12. The Council of Ministers shall be composed of the Ministers of Foreign Affairs or any other Ministers designated by the Governments of the Member States. The Delegation from each State, which shall be entitled to speak and vote, must include at least one Minister.

Members of the Council of Ministers may be assisted by experts.

Article 13. The Council may summon any qualified person to act in an advisory capacity at a meeting, but he may not participate in the discussion.

The Council shall meet as often as necessary and at least twice a year.

Article 14. The Chairmanship of the meetings shall rotate annually among the Ministers of the various States following the alphabetical order of the names of the States.

The new Chairman shall be installed at the opening session of the first meeting of each calendar year.

If additional States become members of the Union, their Ministers shall act as Chairmen of the Council after the last State in alphabetical order of those that sign this Charter.

Article 15. If the Council of Ministers lacks a Chairman owing to a change in the régime of a member country, the Chairmanship shall be held by the next Minister in alphabetical order of States.

Article 16. The Chairman shall fix the date and place for the meetings and shall summon the members of the Council.

Article 17. In case of emergency, the members of the Council may be consulted at home. The Council may not hold valid sessions unless each State is represented by at least one Minister.

Chapter II — Powers and Duties

Article 18. The Council shall act by authorization of the Conference of Chiefs of State. Such authorization shall cover the following matters in particular:

Tariff and statistical nomenclature;

Common external customs tariff;

Schedule of import duties, fees, and charges;

Tax on Union products;

Customs code;

Customs legislation and regulations;

Coordination of the internal taxation systems;

Investment code;

Allocation of industrialization projects;

Coordination of development plans and the transportation and telecommunications policy; Consultation with regard to export duties, export prices of goods of common interest, and with regard to wage rates and social benefits;

Educational and cultural exchanges;

Defense and security.

The conditions under which the Council shall exercise these powers and duties are set forth in detail in the title below.

Chapter III — Decisions of the Council (Notification & Enforcement)

Article 19. Decisions of the Council shall be unanimous. They shall automatically be enforceable in the Member States in accordance with the terms and conditions to be determined by the Council's bylaws.

It may likewise formulate recommendations and express its wishes.

Title III THE EXECUTIVE SECRETARIAT

Article 20. The Executive Secretary of the Union, assisted by Deputy Executive Secretaries and an administrative staff, shall constitute the Executive Secretariat.

The Executive Secretary and the Deputy Executive Secretaries shall be appointed for a three-year term, renewable by decision of the Conference of Chiefs of State upon the recommendation of the Council of Ministers. They shall be under the direct authority of the Chairman in office of the Conference.

Article 21. In performing their duties, the Executive Secretary, the Deputy Executive Secretaries, and the staff of the Secretariat may neither request nor receive instructions from any Government, any national entity, or any international entity. They shall not hold any attitude that is incompatible with their capacity as international personnel.

The status of the personnel of the Secretariat shall be fixed by decision of the Conference of Chiefs of State upon the recommendation of the Council of Ministers.

Title IV LEGAL STATUS

Article 22. The Union shall have legal status, particularly the power required:

(a) To contract;

(b) To acquire and to dispose of the personal and real property essential to the attainment of its objectives;

(c) To borrow;

(d) To be a party to legal proceedings;

(e) To accept gifts, legacies, and donations of any sort.

To that end, it shall be represented by the Chairman of the Conference of Chiefs of State, who may delegate his powers.

The power to contract, to acquire, and to transfer real and personal property, and to borrow shall be exercised by the Chairman with the prior consent of the Chiefs of all the Contracting States.

Article 23. The Conference of the Union shall decide regarding the immunities and privileges to be granted to the Union, to the representatives of the Contracting Parties, and to the personnel of the Executive Secretariat in the territories of the Member States.

Title V FINANCIAL PROVISIONS

Article 24. The Budget of the organs of the Union shall be drawn up annually by the Conference of Chiefs of State. It shall be made enforceable by the Chairman of the Conference.

Article 25. The expenses of the organs of the Union shall be met out of contributions by the States, in accordance with terms and conditions to be determined by the Conference.

PART TWO — ECONOMIC AND CUSTOMS PROVISIONS

Title VI ECONOMIC AND CUSTOMS COOPERATION

Article 26. In order to achieve the objectives set forth in Article 2 of this Charter in accordance with the schedules laid down by the Conference of Chiefs of State, the activities of the Union shall comprise:

(a) The adoption of a common customs tariff and schedule of charges in connection with [trade] relations with third countries;

(b) Prohibition of any import and export duties and taxes between the Member States;

(c) Elimination between the Member States of obstacles to the free movement of persons, services, and capital;

(d) The establishment of a common economic policy to ensure Member States of a continuous, well-balanced expansion, greater stability; an accelerated rise in the standard of living, through coordination of the internal taxation system; the adoption of an Investment Code for investments that would favor the areas far from the sea where it is more difficult to operate industries, thereby correcting the natural inequalities within the Union; and the coordination of development plans on the basis of the equitable, well-balanced allocation of industries, with due consideration for available resources and the development level of each of the Member States;

(e) The establishment of a common policy in the field of transportation and telecommunications in order to facilitate trade between the Member States through a reduction in the cost of transportation;

(f) The establishment of a Compensation and Investment Fund;

(g) The institution of an appropriate duty favoring growth in the consumption of the products originating in the

States of the Union;

(h) The establishment of an appropriate procedure to make possible the expansion of trade between the Member States;

(i) The establishment of an Investment Bank to facilitate the economic expansion of the Union through the creation of new resources.

PART THREE

Title VII CULTURAL COOPERATION

Article 27. In order to bring about closer cooperation and to develop cultural exchanges between them, the Member States consider it necessary to expand their cultural relations both in the literary and artistic field and in the scientific and technical field.

Article 28. To that end the Member States shall endeavor, in so far as their means permit:

To encourage the exchange of professors, research workers, or any other persons engaged in the various fields of culture, science, and the arts;

To promote artistic, theatrical, and sports exchanges and to encourage the exchange of students and grantees.

Article 29. To that end, the various academic establishments, institutes, and research centers now existing or to be created in each State shall be open to the nationals of the other States of the Organization.

The Union shall facilitate such exchanges, particularly by granting fellowships and training grants.

PART FOUR — SECURITY

Article 30. In order to ensure the security of their territories and to safeguard their sovereignty, the Member States hereby proclaim their solidarity and their willingness to furnish military assistance to each other in the event of foreign aggression.

Article 31. To that end, each of the Contracting States hereby promises to take all practical measures necessary to ensure the security of the borders of the Member States, particularly through a mutual exchange of information regarding anything that might constitute a threat to the internal and external security of any Member State or to the Union as a whole, through the transmission of reports or data making it possible to extradite persons sought in their countries for crimes or offenses against ordinary law committed in their country of origin or in any other Member State, and all measures intended to stamp out subversion in the territory of any Member State or of the Union as a whole.

PART FIVE — TRANSITORY PROVISIONS

Article 32. Upon the entry into force of this Charter, the Contracting States shall send to the Executive Secretariat of the Union all laws, regulations, and decisions on customs and economic matters, including decisions concerning the granting of preferential treatment. The Executive Secretary shall distribute

them to the Member States.

Article 33. Specialized technical commissions shall meet as soon as possible in order to submit to the Conference of Chiefs of State for decision regulations of execution on the following points:

Customs legislation and regulations;

Guidelines for the allocation of import and export duties;

The coordination of investment codes or the establishment of a common Investment Code;

The coordination of the internal taxation systems;

The procedure for the approval and allocation of industrialization projects and the industrial cooperation policy;

The system for taxation of local products;

The coordination of development plans, and of the transportation and telecommunications policies;

The establishment of a Compensation and Investment Fund;

The system of port, rail, river, highway, and air infrastructure services;

The free movement of persons, services, and capital, and the right of establishment.

Article 34. These regulations of execution shall form an integral part of this Charter.

PART SIX — GENERAL AND FINAL PROVISIONS

Article 35. This Charter shall enter into force upon ratification in accordance with the constitutional formalities of each of the Contracting States.

The instruments of ratification shall be deposited with the Central African Republic, designated the depositary State.

Upon receipt of the instruments of ratification, the depositary Government shall so inform all the Contracting Parties and the Executive Secretariat of the Union.

Article 36. Amendments to this Charter must be ratified by each Member State in the manner specified by its internal legislation.

Article 37. This Charter may be denounced by any Member State. The denunciation shall not enter into force, as regards the State denouncing it, until January 1 following notification of denunciation to the Chairman of the Conference and six months after such notification at the earliest.

Denunciation by one or more Contracting States shall not entail the dissolution of the Union.

The Conference of Chiefs of State alone may decide upon such dissolution and fix the terms and conditions for distribution of the assets and liabilities.

However, the Conference shall establish the principle and the terms and conditions for indemnification if the Contracting State withdraws from the Union.

Article 38. This Charter, duly ratified, shall be registered with the Secretariat of the United Nations by the depositary Government pursuant to Article 102 of the United Nations Charter.

Done at Fort-Lamay, April 2, 1968

General Jean-Bedel Bokassa
President of the Central African Republic

Lieutenant General Joseph-Désiré Mobutu
President of the Democratic Republic of the Congo

Francois Tombalbaye
President of the Republic of Chad

4.1387 Treaty of Friendship, Co-operation, and Mutual Assistance between the Czechoslovak Socialist Republic and the People's Republic of Bulgaria

Alliance Members: Czechoslovakia and Bulgaria
Signed On: April 26, 1968, in the city of Prague (Czech Republic). In force until November 10, 1989.
Alliance Type: Defense Pact (Type I)

Source: *United Nations Treaty,* no. 10344.

SUMMARY

Czechoslovakia and Bulgaria had excellent relations after World War II because of mutual economic, cultural, and political interests. An agreement of friendship signed in 1948 lasted for twenty years. One week after the expiration of the earlier agreement, leaders from both states signed this new treaty of friendship and mutual aid. They pledged complete respect for borders and sovereignty in Europe, mutual defense in case of attack, and the shared goal of advancing international socialism.

The alliance lasted until 1989, when a series of communist governments in Eastern Europe fell during what was later called the "velvet revolutions." Communist power officially ended in Bulgaria in 1989, when President Todor Zhivkov resigned amid internal pressure to liberalize the economy.

ALLIANCE TEXT

The Czechoslovak Socialist Republic and the People's Republic of Bulgaria,

Guided by a constant desire to develop and strengthen the traditional relations of friendship, co-operation and mutual assistance between the two States, which are based on the principles of socialist internationalism,

Firmly convinced that friendship, co-operation and mutual assistance between the two States are in accord with the vital interests of the Czechoslovak and Bulgarian peoples and serve to strengthen the socialist community as a whole,

Noting that economic co-operation between the two States promotes their development and furthers the international socialist division of labour within the framework of the Council for Mutual Economic Assistance,

Mindful of the experience of the Second World War, which was unleashed by Nazi Germany, and firmly resolved to oppose the forces of imperialism, which are threatening peace and security in Europe,

Noting that, while the German Democratic Republic has implemented the principles of the Potsdam Agreement, is pursuing a consistent policy of peace and is an important factor for security in Europe, the forces of West German militarism and revanchism are a threat to peace,

Endeavouring to safeguard peace and security in Europe on the basis of the obligations arising out of the Warsaw Treaty of Friendship, Co-operation and Mutual Assistance of 14 May 1955,

Expressing their determination to pursue a consistent policy of peaceful co-existence among States with different social systems and to continue their efforts to strengthen peace and security in Europe and throughout the world,

Guided by the purposes and principles of the Charter of the United Nations,

Noting that the Treaty of Friendship, Co-operation and Mutual Assistance concluded between the Czechoslovak Republic and the People's Republic of Bulgaria on 23 April 1948 has played a favourable role in the development of friendly relations between the two States,

Bearing in mind the achievements of Czechoslovak-Bulgarian co-operation in past years and the changes which have taken place in Europe and in the world,

Have decided to conclude this Treaty and have agreed as follows:

Article 1. The High Contracting Parties shall, in accordance with the principles of socialist internationalism, continue to strengthen the lasting and unshakable friendship between the peoples of the two States, develop comprehensive co-operation and render each other assistance on the basis of equality of rights, mutual respect for State sovereignty and non-intervention in each other's domestic affairs.

Article 2. The High Contracting Parties shall in every way develop and strengthen their economic, scientific and technical ties on the basis of friendly co-operation and mutual benefit, shall, in accordance with the principles on the international socialist division of labour, carry out the co-ordination of national economic plans as well as specialization and co-operation in production, and shall promote the further development of co-operation within the framework of the Council for Mutual Economic Assistance and thus ensure the development of the national economies of the two States.

Article 3. The High Contracting Parties, desiring to help the peoples of the two States to become better acquainted with each other and to draw closer together, shall develop and strengthen their relations in the fields of culture, art, science, education, health, the press, radio, television, the cinema, physical education and tourism and in other fields. They shall promote comprehensive co-operation between the social organizations of the two States.

Article 4. The High Contracting Parties shall continue to take measures aimed at strengthening the world socialist community and shall, in accordance with the principles of the Charter of the United Nations, continue their efforts to safeguard world peace and the security of peoples, to reduce international tension, to halt the arms race and achieve general and complete disarmament, and to bring about the final elimination of colonialism and neo-colonialism in all their forms and manifestations.

Article 5. The High Contracting Parties note that the Munich Agreement of 29 September 1938 was brought about by the threat of a war of aggression and by the use of force against Czechoslovakia, that it was an integral part of the criminal conspiracy against peace by the Government of Nazi Germany and a gross violation of the basic principles of contemporary international law, and that it was therefore invalid from the outset, with all the consequences which that implies.

Article 6. The High Contracting Parties, consistently pursuing a policy of peaceful co-existence among States with different social systems, shall jointly direct their efforts towards safeguarding peace in Europe and towards the establishment of an effective system of European security, an important factor in which is the inviolability of the existing State frontiers in Europe.

Article 7. The High Contracting Parties express their firm determination, in accordance with the Warsaw Treaty of Friendship, Co-operation and Mutual Assistance of 14 May 1955, to guarantee the inviolability of the frontiers of the two States and to take all necessary measures to prevent aggression by the forces of imperialism and revanchism.

Article 8. In the event of an armed attack by any State or group of States on either of the High Contracting Parties, the other High Contracting Party shall, in accordance with the Warsaw Treaty of Friendship, Co-operation and Mutual Assistance of 14 May 1955, and pursuant to Article 51 of the Charter of the United Nations, immediately afford the first-mentioned Party every kind of assistance and support, including military assistance, with all the means at its disposal.

The High Contracting Parties shall immediately report to the Security Council any measures taken in accordance with this article and shall comply with the relevant provisions of the Charter of the United Nations.

Article 9. The High Contracting Parties shall consult together on all important questions affecting their interests.

Article 10. This Treaty is concluded for a term of twenty years and shall be automatically extend for successive five-years terms if neither of the High Contracting Parties denounces it twelve months before the expiry of the current term.

This Treaty is subject to ratification and shall enter into force on the date of the exchange of the instruments of ratification, which shall take place at Sofia as soon as possible.

Done at Prague on 26 April 1968, in duplicate in the Czech and Bulgarian languages, both texts being equally authentic.

For the Czechoslovak Socialist Republic:
A. DUBČEK
O. ČERNIK
For the People's Republic of Bulgaria:
T. ZHIVKOV

4.1388 Treaty of Brotherhood, Good-Neighbourly Relations, and Co-operation between the Kingdom of Morocco and the Democratic and Popular Republic of Algeria

Alliance Members: Morocco and Algeria
Signed On: January 15, 1969, in the city of Ifrane (Morocco). In force until December 28, 1975.
Alliance Type: Non-Aggression Pact (Type II)

Source: *United Nations Treaty,* no. 10955.

SUMMARY

Algeria had continual border disputes with Morocco following its independence from France in 1962. This agreement pledged to support security and promote stability in the Maghreb. The treaty called for an end to the arms race between the two countries and the abstention from force in all diplomatic disputes. The treaty also sought to encourage economic cooperation and foster a new set of joint responsibilities and burden sharing between the former rivals.

The treaty did not address the border dispute between the two nations, however, and tensions flared again in the mid-1970s. Algeria signed a peace agreement with Libya and began militarizing the territory disputed by Morocco while Morocco forged a new bilateral relationship with Mauritania. Suspicions flared, and both sides withdrew from this agreement in late December 1975. Small-scale fighting erupted one month later.

ALLIANCE TEXT

The Kingdom of Morocco and the Democratic and Popular Republic of Algeria,

Desiring to strengthen the bonds of brotherhood, friendship and good-neighbourly relations which are dictated by the long-standing historical ties existing between their two countries and peoples,

Prompted by their mutual desire to strengthen and reinforce the bonds of brotherhood between them in all fields, and especially in the economic and cultural fields, on the basis of mutual respect for national sovereignty and territorial integrity, non-interference in the internal affairs of the other Party and equality between the two Parties in their common interests,

Desiring to participate, through their mutual relations, in building the greater Arab Maghreb, unifying the Arab nation, strengthening African unity and attaining world justice and peace,

Wishing to establish mutual co-operation and consultation in all matters relating to the attainment of peace and in resistance to all forms of aggression, in accordance with the provisions of the United Nations Charter,

Convinced that the establishment and strengthening of friendly relations and mutual co-operation will benefit both fraternal countries and peoples,

Believing that their mutual relations will contribute to the attainment of the goals and principles of the United Nations Charter, the Charter of the League of Arab States, and the Charter of the Organization of African Unity,

Have resolved for this purpose to conclude the following treaty, and have appointed the following Plenipotentiaries:

His Excellency Dr. Ahmed el-Iraqi, Minister for Foreign Affairs of the Kingdom of Morocco, and

His Excellency Mr. Abdulaziz Boutefliqa, Minister for Foreign Affairs of the Democratic and Popular Republic of Algeria,

who, having exchanged their full powers, found in good and due form, have agreed as follows:

Article 1. The Kingdom of Morocco and the Democratic and Popular Republic of Algeria shall maintain perpetual peace, firm friendship and fruitful good-neighbourly relations, inspired by the spirit of the long-standing brotherhood between the two fraternal peoples, and shall strive to build a prosperous common future.

Article 2. The two Contracting Parties undertake to strengthen their common bonds in all fields, and especially in the economic and cultural fields, as a contribution toward expanding the areas of mutual understanding between the fraternal Moroccan and Algerian peoples and consolidating the friendship and good-neighbourly relations between them.

Article 3. Since mutual economic co-operation provides a firm basis for peaceful and friendly relations and leads to the advancement of both countries, the two Contracting Parties shall promote mutual efforts aimed at the expansion of co-operation in all fields, for the benefit of both countries.

Article 4. In the event of a dispute or conflict of any kind, the two Contracting Parties shall prohibit the use of force against each other and shall strive to settle the dispute by peaceful means, in a spirit of friendship, brotherhood and good-neighbourly relations, in pursuance of the principles and resolutions of the United Nations, the League of Arab States, and the Organization of African Unity.

Article 5. Each Party undertakes not to join any alliance or confederacy directed against the other Party.

Article 6. In order to strengthen the ties of solidarity and brotherhood which bind their two fraternal peoples, in accordance with the spirit of good-neighbourliness and mutual confidence between them, the two Parties resolve to submit all matters pending between them to joint commissions which shall be responsible for finding appropriate solutions thereto within the framework of the relations between the two countries, employing such procedures as they deem appropriate to the attainment of their common wish to overcome all obstacles and to make swift progress toward establishing the co-operation which both Parties desire.

Article 7. This Treaty shall enter into force when it has been signed and the instruments of ratification have been exchanged.

Article 8. This Treaty shall remain in force for twenty years following the date of its entry into force, and shall be automatically renewed for a further period of twenty years unless one of the Contracting Parties informs the other Party in writing, one year before the expiry of the Treaty, of its desire to terminate it.

Done at the royal palace of Ifrane, on 26 Shawwal 1388 (15 January 1969) in two original copies in the Arabic language.

For the Kingdom of Morocco:

Ahmed EL-IRAQI

For the Democratic and Popular Republic of Algeria:

Abdulaziz BOUTEFLIQA

4.1389 Treaty of Brotherhood, Good-Neighbourliness, and Co-operation between Algeria and Tunisia

Alliance Members: Algeria and Tunisia
Signed On: January 6, 1970, in the city of Tunis (Tunisia). In force until March 19, 1983.
Alliance Type: Non-Aggression Pact (Type II)

Source: *Keesing's Record of World Events,* January 1970.

SUMMARY

This agreement represented the successful efforts of both countries to settle several outstanding cross-border differences. The treaty itself pledged non-interference and non-aggression in the domestic affairs of the other party. Additional agreements signed on the same day included new terms for financial and economic cooperation.

The treaty lasted until March 1983, when it was replaced by a new agreement (see Alliance no. 4.1429) that included Mauritania as well.

DESCRIPTION OF TERMS

The parties to the treaty stressed the principles of non-interference in the domestic affairs of their alliance partners and reaffirmed the sovereignty of each state. Both parties also pledged not to enter any pact or join any alliance directed against the other signatory. The treaty also established a joint commission dedicated to advancing mutual security. The treaty was expected to be valid for twenty years with automatic renewals.

4.1390 Treaty of Brotherhood, Good-Neighbourly Relations, and Co-operation between the Kingdom of Morocco and Mauritania

Alliance Members: Morocco and Mauritania
Signed On: June 8, 1970, in the city of Casablanca (Morocco). In force until March 18, 1981.
Alliance Type: Defense Pact (Type I)

Source: *Keesing's Record of World Events,* June 1970.

SUMMARY

Soon after Morocco received its independence in 1956, Moroccan delegates staked claim to Mauritania and parts of Western Sahara. Though its pretenses regarding Senegal and western Africa were never pressed, Morocco continued to lay claim to Mauritania throughout the 1960s.

After engaging in a short war with Algeria over their common borders, Morocco officially dropped its claim to Mauritania. On June 8, 1970, the Mauritanian president, Ould Daddah, and the Moroccan king, Hassan II, signed a treaty of friendship and cooperation in which Morocco officially granted formal diplomatic recognition to the country of Mauritania. Following the non-aggression agreement, Morocco began to push for self-determination in Western Sahara; the belief was that self-determination would eventually cause Mauritania to return to Moroccan governance.

In the late 1970s, Prime Minister Haidalla of Mauritania was facing opposition in the government. After a series of governmental changes, he began experiencing increased opposition from the Alliance for a Democratic Mauritania (AMD), and on March 18, 1981, Haidalla survived a coup d'état led by pro-Moroccan members of the AMD. The coup attempt led Mauritania to break diplomatic relations with Morocco. A few months later, in June, King Hassan II agreed to restore diplomatic relations and cut off the movement of the hostile forces through Morocco. That agreement was never enforced, and Morocco refused to deport any AMD members.

DESCRIPTION OF TERMS

The terms of this treaty were very similar to Morocco's agreement with Algeria (see Alliance no. 4.1388), signed on January 15, 1969. The two countries pledged to prohibit the use of force to settle disputes between them and would not engage in alliances or other actions targeting their allied state.

4.1391 Agreement of Friendship and Cooperation between the United States of America and Spain

Alliance Members: United States and Spain
Signed On: August 6, 1970, in the city of Washington, D.C. In force until December 10, 1981.
Alliance Type: Entente (Type III)

Source: *United Nations Treaty,* no. 10852.

SUMMARY

In the early 1950s the United States began signing agreements with Spain that exchanged economic aid from the United States for leasing rights to U.S. naval and air bases in Spain. This agreement of friendship and cooperation was largely a continuation of earlier agreements with the added stipulation of consultation in case of crisis. The treaty also provided $120 million in Export-Import Bank credits to Spain to be used for the purchase of military aircraft from the United States. The treaty was originally intended to last for five years but was extended. Spain became an official member of the North Atlantic Treaty Organization in May 1982.

ALLIANCE TEXT

The Governments of the United States of America and Spain,

Conscious of the desires of their respective peoples for peace, security and the maintenance of their independence, and

Recognizing that the security and integrity of each of the two countries continues to be a matter of concern to the other, and

Inspired by the purposes and principles of the Charter of the United Nations, and

Desiring to reaffirm and to further the friendship between their peoples, in the spirit of the Treaty of Friendship and General Relations signed at Madrid July 3, 1902, and

Desiring to establish on a more comprehensive basis the cooperation between the two Governments, which has been fostered by such friendship, so that both Governments, through mutual exchanges and support, may promote the well-being and progress of their peoples, enabling them to meet effectively the challenges of the modern world,

Have agreed as follows:

Chapter I General Cooperation

Article 1. The Governments of the United States and Spain will continue their close cooperation and intimate working relationship, including regular mutual consultation by their Foreign Ministers, other members of the Governments, or their representatives, on all matters of common concern or interest, as deemed desirable by the two Governments.

Article 2. Such cooperation and relationship will be developed in those areas in which they have heretofore existed; in new areas deemed by the two Governments to require their urgent mutual attention, as specifically provided hereinafter; and in those other areas which the two Governments may consider appropriate in the future.

Chapter II Educational and Cultural Cooperation

Article 3. In recognition of the importance of the cultural achievements of both countries, and in order to strengthen even more the friendship and understanding that traditionally have existed between their peoples, the Governments of the United States and Spain agree to expand their present exchanges in the educational and cultural fields, in number as well as in scope, subject to the constitutional processes and legislative requirements of the two countries.

Article 4. The expansion of these exchanges will involve teachers, research experts, scientists, scholars and students, and will extend into all branches of learning, especially natural and applied sciences, economics, and the language and culture of the two countries. In the field of arts and letters both Governments will sponsor visits of authors and artists and the reciprocal dissemination of their works.

Article 5. Both Governments recognize the importance of the Fulbright-Hays program to promote educational and cultural exchanges between the two countries, and therefore they consider it desirable to expand the responsibilities of the

Commission for Cultural Exchange between the United States of America and Spain established by the Agreement of October 16, 1958 and renewed by the Agreement of March 18, 1964. The Spanish Government reaffirms its decision to contribute regularly to the financing of the Fulbright-Hays program.

Article 6. In its desire to cooperate with the Spanish Government in the expansion of the Spanish educational system and Spanish scientific and technical development, the Government of the United States, subject to United States legislation and the appropriation of funds by the Congress, will assist Spain in research, development, and advanced training of professors and other teaching personnel, particularly in the scientific disciplines, and training of new professors and other teaching personnel, and will provide documents, equipment, and materials for research laboratories and libraries as appropriate in the new Spanish universities and other centers of higher learning.

Article 7. In order to accomplish the goals of Article 6, the Government of the United States will consider with the greatest interest the specific programs that Spain presents to it in the fields mentioned in Article 6, and will cooperate in such programs, lending such assistance as the United States may provide subject to United States legislation and the appropriation of funds by the Congress. To the extent necessary and appropriate, these matters will be the subject of special agreements between the appropriate authorities of the two Governments.

Article 8. The two Governments consider it a matter of special interest to increase the knowledge of their respective languages in the two countries, by encouraging the activities of institutions and organizations that engage in the teaching of Spanish and the dissemination of Spanish culture in the United States, and at the same time encouraging the activities of institutions and organizations in Spain that carry on similar work with respect to the language and culture of the United States.

Chapter III Scientific and Technical Cooperation

Article 9. Since science and technology are increasingly important for the development of a country, the Governments of the United States and Spain recognize that scientific and technical cooperation will be of great value in advancing the bonds of friendship, the state of the sciences and the resolution of the problems they share in common. Both Governments also recognize the desirability of devoting special attention to cooperation in the exchange of the results of scientific and technical research for their mutual economic and social benefits.

Article 10. Both Governments will undertake a broad program of scientific and technical cooperation for peaceful purposes.

Article 11. The cooperation between the two Governments will be based essentially on the following principles:

(a) Selection of specific scientific and technical sectors of major interest and yield.

(b) Preparation of plans for collaboration between research centers of the two countries.

(c) Programs for sending to Spain American professors and researchers of established reputation to cooperate in the advanced training of scientific and technological researchers.

(d) The establishment of appropriate channels for putting into operation, developing and supervising specific programs of scientific and technical cooperation.

Article 12. For the purposes of this Chapter, the two Governments consider the following areas, among others, to be of special interest:

(a) Civil uses of atomic energy, in accordance with the agreement of August 16, 1957, as amended.

(b) The exploration and use of space, including intercontinental experiments with satellite communications, in accordance with the exchange of notes of September 18, 1964, and January 26, 1965; spaceship tracking stations and operations, in accordance with the exchange of notes of April 14, 1966; and the measurements of winds and temperatures at high altitudes, in accordance with the exchange of notes of April 14, 1966.

(c) Marine sciences, including joint biological, physical and ecological projects to improve and increase the oceanic resources and their use.

(d) Medical and biological sciences, industrial technology, electronics and the social sciences.

Article 13. Any obligations arising pursuant to this Chapter shall be subject to the constitutional processes and legislative requirements of the respective countries.

Chapter IV Cooperation on Environmental and urban Development Problems

Article 14. The Governments of the United States and Spain recognize that among the principal problems with which their peoples are faced are the dangers to which man is exposed by the deterioration of his environment. Both Governments agree on the need to give urgent attention to such problems and they will begin consultations in order to determine how to coordinate their mutual efforts for their solution.

Article 15. Cooperation for the purposes stated in the foregoing Article will be effected through the exchange of information, the development of teaching and research centers, the training of personnel in specialized institutions, the sending of experts, and the supply of material for carrying out projects of common interest.

Article 16. The fields in which cooperation will be developed will be as follows:

(a) The fight against pollution in all its forms, especially in the atmosphere, in waters and in the soil;

(b) Ecology and wildlife conservation;

(c) Urban and regional planning, including urban renewal and improvement, traffic control, reduction of noise, and protection of the landscape.

Chapter V Agricultural Cooperation

Article 17. The Governments of the United States and Spain

recognize that the agricultural sector is of great mutual interest and that it may hold opportunities for exchange of knowledge and assistance; therefore the two Governments agree to study expanding their cooperation in this field.

Article 18. For the purpose of developing the cooperation referred to in the preceding Article, both parties will study the harmonization of standards and common agricultural sanitation provisions; the possibility of carrying out transactions in agricultural surpluses under a system of concessional sales for social or charitable purposes; the preparation of joint plans for teacher training, not only in the classic agricultural disciplines (e.g. agronomy, zootechny, genetics, soil science, horticulture, agricultural engineering) but also in the more modern branches (e.g. food technology, marketing of farm products, rural economics and sociology, forest management); the feasibility of exchange of university professors and agricultural researchers of both countries; scholarships for graduates in agricultural sciences; and the exchange of information on scientific and technical progress in agriculture.

Article 19. In the cooperation between the two Governments, special attention will be given to the Spanish programs of rural management, irrigation, reforestation, and the development of the livestock industry.

Article 20. The two Governments will undertake to exchange their technical knowledge and experience acquired in the sectors named in the preceding Article, whenever possible, including information on the economic aspects of the agricultural market, and to that end they will promote the exchange of technicians and experts in the preparation and execution of such programs.

Chapter VI Economic Cooperation

The Governments of the United States and Spain, desiring to maintain and expand their present cooperation, have examined the situation of their economies in the world context and have reaffirmed their determination to advance and develop their economic relations, and to that end they have agreed as follows:

Article 21. The two Governments reaffirm their determination to expand their trade relations, and consequently they will seek to avoid, insofar as possible and to the extent allowed by their respective economic situations and the development of their balances of payments, measures that effect restrictions on the flow of their reciprocal trade, in accordance with the provisions of the General Agreement on Tariffs and Trade.

Article 22. The two Governments consider it desirable to have a normal flow of United States direct investments in Spain, and to that end they will adopt, provided the United States balance of payments so permits, the necessary measures for encouraging the development of such investments. A similar criterion shall be applied, insofar as circumstances permit, to reducing restrictions imposed by the United States for balance of payments reasons on the purchase of foreign securities, including Spanish securities, by United States citizens in the United States.

Article 23. The two Governments recognize that the loans granted by the Export-Import Bank of the United States have been an important stimulus for the purchase of United States capital goods by Spanish enterprises. Consequently, they will continue in the future to facilitate and give maximum attention to the development of these financial relations.

Article 24. The Government of Spain reiterates its objectives of achieving by progressive steps its full integration in the European Community. The Government of the United States declares its sympathetic understanding of Spain's objectives of full integration. The two Governments agree to consult with each other and to keep in close contact in seeking to arrive at mutually satisfactory solutions for any problems of principle or procedure as may arise for either of them in this connection.

Article 25. The two Governments will exchange information on the negotiations now in progress for the establishment of a generalized system of preferences in favor of developing countries.

Article 26. The two Governments reaffirm their interest in continuing the consultations of the Joint Spanish-United States Economic Committee created in 1968, maintaining the competence and terms of reference vested in it in the exchange of notes of July 15, 1968, for the examination of financial and other economic matters of mutual interest. The Committee will meet alternatively in Washington and Madrid at mutually convenient times, under the chairmanship of representatives of appropriate level designated by their respective Governments.

Chapter VII Cooperation with respect to Public Information

Article 27. The Governments of the United States and Spain recognize the value and significance that have been attained in present times by the information media, and they reaffirm their interest in strengthening their cooperation in this field.

Article 28. In order that public opinion in their respective countries may develop a better mutual understanding, both Governments will encourage by all means at their disposal the exchange of radio and television programs, will mutually assist their respective information media, and will prepare an effective long-range plan for exchange in all fields of information dissemination.

Article 29. The two Governments reaffirm their desire to continue and to expand the exchange of their respective official publications.

Chapter VIII Cooperation for Defense

The Governments of the United States and Spain are in agreement in considering that the threat to peace is the greatest problem faced by the modern world, and that it requires that both Governments remain vigilant and continue to develop their ability to defend themselves against such a threat. Consequently, both Governments, within the framework of their constitutional processes, and to the extent feasible and appropriate, will make compatible their respective defense policies in areas of mutual interest, and will grant each other reciprocal defense, support as follows:

Article 30. Each Government will support the defense system of the other and make such contributions as are deemed necessary and appropriate to achieve the greatest possible effectiveness of those systems to meet possible contingencies, subject to the terms and conditions set forth hereinafter.

Article 31. The Government of the United States agrees to support Spanish defense efforts, as necessary and appropriate, by contributing to the modernization of Spanish defense industries, as well as granting military assistance to Spain, in accordance with applicable agreements. This support will be conditioned by the priorities and limitations created by the international commitments of the United States and the exigencies of the international situation and will be subject to the appropriation of funds by the Congress, whenever the case so requires, and to United States legislation.

Article 32. The Government of Spain, subject to Spanish constitutional provisions and legislation in force, will authorize the Government of the United States to use and maintain for military purposes certain facilities in Spanish military installations agreed upon by the two Governments. Any major construction that may be necessary for the exercise of this use shall be subject to agreement between the two Governments in the Joint Committee created in Article 36 of this Chapter. The United States is further authorized to station and house the civilian and military personnel necessary for such use; to provide for their security, discipline, and welfare; to store and guard provisions, supplies, equipment and materiel; and to maintain the services necessary for such purposes. The exercise of the functions authorized herein shall be subject to such express terms and technical conditions as the two Governments may agree upon.

Article 33.   (a) The Government of Spain assumes the obligation of adopting the security measures necessary for the exercise of the functions authorized in Article 32. The United States may exercise the necessary supervision and protection of its personnel, equipment and materiel.

(b) The above-mentioned use by the Government of the United States of facilities in Spanish military installations will be free of all taxes, charges and encumbrances. The Government of Spain will retain free of all charges the ownership of all permanent works constructed for the purpose of this Agreement.

(c) The Government of the United States may remove at any time nonpermanent constructions installed at its expense, as well as its personnel, property, equipment and materiel. However, any substantial removal prior to the expiration of this Agreement will be the subject of prior consultation of the two Governments in the Joint Committee. In the event that any such removal would bring about adverse security consequences, the two Governments will consult immediately in order to adopt appropriate measures.

(d) Whenever the Government of the United States relinquishes a facility authorized in this Chapter, either prior to or as a result of the expiration of the five or ten year period specified in Article 38, the Government of the United States shall not be obligated to leave such facility in the same state and condition it was in prior to its utilization by the Government of the United States, or to compensate Spain for not having returned it in such state, but shall leave the land and permanent constructions thereon in serviceable condition for use by Spanish authorities, provided that the Government of the United States shall incur no additional expense thereby.

(e) In normal circumstances any substantial increase in the personnel or military equipment of the United States in Spain, or any substantial increase in the use by the United States of facilities in Spanish military installations regulated by this Agreement, will be the subject of prior consultation in the Joint Committee and agreed upon between the two Governments through diplomatic channels.

Article 34. In the case of external threat or attack against the security of the West, the time and manner of the use by the United States of the facilities referred to in this Chapter to meet such threat or attack will be the subject of urgent consultations between the two Governments, and will be resolved by mutual agreement in light of the situation created. Such urgent consultations shall take place in the Joint Committee, but when the imminence of the danger so requires, the two Governments will establish direct contact in order to resolve the matter jointly. Each Government retains, however, the inherent right of self-defense.

Article 35. Both Governments consider it necessary and appropriate that the cooperation for defense regulated by this Chapter form a part of the security arrangements for the Atlantic and Mediterranean areas, and to that end they will endeavor to work out by common accord the liaison deemed advisable with the security arrangements for those areas.

Article 36. In order to establish the necessary coordination between the two Governments and to ensure greater effectiveness of the reciprocal defense support granted by the two Governments to each other, the Governments of the United States and Spain agree to establish a Joint Committee on defense matters. The Joint Committee will be the organ in which the two Governments normally will consult with each other and resolve matters that may arise in connection with the reciprocal defense support referred to in this Chapter. The Joint Committee will be organized and will function as specified in the Annex to this Agreement.

Article 37. The two Governments will determine by common accord, through an exchange of notes on this date, the facilities referred to in Article 32 of this Chapter, as well as the United States force levels in Spain and the assistance programs referred to in Article 31 of this Chapter. Thereafter any change in the number or extent of such facilities will be negotiated in the Joint Committee and agreed upon between the two Governments through an exchange of notes.

Chapter IX Final Provisions

Article 38. This Agreement shall enter into force on September 26, 1970, and will remain in force for five years, whereupon it may be extended, if both Governments agree, for another five years.

Article 39. In order to facilitate the withdrawal of the personnel, property, equipment and material of the Government of the United States located in Spain pursuant to Chapter VIII of this Agreement, a period of one year, during which the withdrawal must be completed, is provided. Such withdrawal shall be commenced immediately upon the expiration of the five year initial period, or, if the Agreement is extended, upon the expiration of the five year extension period. During the withdrawal period above mentioned, not to exceed one year, all of the rights, privileges and obligations deriving from Chapter VIII of this Agreement shall remain in force as long as United States troops remain in Spain.

Article 40. The entry into force of this Agreement will in no way affect the validity or terms of any agreement existing between the Governments of the United States and Spain, with the exception of the Defense Agreement between the United States and Spain, dated September 26, 1953, and its supplementary agreements which shall thereupon be superseded.

Done at Washington in duplicate, in the English and Spanish languages, each of which shall be equally authentic, this sixth day of August, 1970.

For the Government of the United States of America:

[Signed]

WILLIAM P. ROGERS

For the Government of Spain:

[Signed]

GREGORIO LÓPEZ BRAVO

4.1392 Treaty of Friendship, Co-operation, and Mutual Assistance between the People's Republic of Bulgaria and the Socialist Republic of Romania

Alliance Members: Bulgaria and Romania
Signed On: November 19, 1970, in the city of Sofia (Bulgaria). In force until November 10, 1989.
Alliance Type: Defense Pact (Type I)

Source: *United Nations Treaty,* no. 12282.

SUMMARY

This treaty of friendship between Bulgaria and Romania was similar in most respects to the many bilateral alliances among Eastern European states in the Warsaw Pact. The treaty specified the inviolability of borders, called for respect and furtherance of international socialism, and pledged greater bilateral cooperation. The agreement ended in November of 1989 with the resignation of the communist regime in Bulgaria.

ALLIANCE TEXT

The People's Republic of Bulgaria and the Socialist Republic of Romania,

Desiring to strengthen and expand the ties of fraternal friendship, all-round co-operation and good-neighbourly relations between the Bulgarian and Romanian peoples, on the basis of the principles of socialist internationalism, respect for sovereignty and national independence, equality or rights, mutual benefit and comradely mutual assistance, and non-interference in domestic affairs,

Firmly convinced that the development of the ties of fraternal friendship between the Bulgarian and Romanian peoples, forged in the common fight for the aims of national and social liberation and against reaction and fascism, is in accord with the vital interests of the two peoples and the cause of peace and socialism,

Recognizing that fraternal solidarity between the socialist States has its unshakeable foundations in the sharing of a common social system and in the unity of the fundamental aims and aspirations of the peoples of the two countries and of the entire socialist community,

Firmly resolved to consolidate the unity and cohesion of the socialist countries and to respect the obligations laid down in the Warsaw Treaty of Friendship, Co-operation and Mutual Assistance of 14 May 1955 during the period of validity of the Treaty, which was concluded in response to the NATO threat,

Expressing their will to work consistently for the establishment of an atmosphere of understanding and co-operation in the Balkan region and throughout the world, in the interests of common progress, peace and general security, and firmly resolved to oppose the forces of imperialism, militarism and revanchism that threaten peace,

Pursuing a steadfast policy of peaceful co-existence between States with different social systems,

Guided by the purposes and principles of the Charter of the United Nations,

Highly valuing the role played by the Bulgarian-Romanian Treaty of Friendship, Co-operation and Mutual Assistance of 16 January 1948 in the steady development of fraternal friendship and co-operation between the Bulgarian people and the Romanian people,

Having regard to the experience and achievements of the two States in the building of socialism, and the changes that have taken place in Europe and the world,

Have decided to conclude this Treaty and to that end have agreed as follows:

Article 1. The High Contracting Parties shall continue to strengthen the lasting friendship between the Bulgarian and Romanian peoples, and shall develop co-operation between the two States in the political, economic, social, scientific and cultural fields, on the basis of the principles of socialist internationalism, respect for sovereignty and national independence, equality of rights, mutual benefit and comradely mutual assistance, and non-interference in domestic affairs.

Article 2. The High Contracting Parties, proceeding from the principles underlying relations between socialist countries, including the principles of mutual benefit, comradely mutual assistance and the international socialist division of labour, shall continue to develop collaboration and co-operation between the two countries in the economic, scientific and technical fields, and shall contribute to the development and strengthening of economic ties and co-operation both within the framework of the Council for Mutual Economic Assistance and with the other socialist States.

Article 3. The High Contracting Parties shall develop and strengthen their ties in the fields of science, education, art, culture, the press, radio, television, the cinema, health protection, physical culture and tourism and shall support co-operation between public organizations with a view to promoting among the two peoples a better knowledge of each other's material and spiritual values and further strengthening the friendship between them.

Article 4. The High Contracting Parties shall continue to work for the development of ties of friendship and all-round co-operation between the socialist States, and for the strengthening of the unity and cohesion of the world socialist system in the interests of peace and progress in the world.

Article 5. The High Contracting Parties, pursuing a consistent policy of peaceful co-existence, shall strive for the creation of a climate of international détente and of co-operation between all States, regardless of their social system, for the settlement of disputes between States by peaceful means, for the defeat of the aggressive plans of imperialist circles, the cessation of the arms race, the achievement of general and complete disarmament, and the final elimination of colonialism and neo-colonialism. The Contracting Parties shall provide support to the countries that have freed themselves from colonial domination and are pursuing the course of strengthening their sovereignty and national independence.

The two Contracting Parties shall continue to strive for the strengthening of peace and security in Europe and the establishment of an effective system of European security.

The Contracting Parties shall continue actively to support the establishment of good-neighbourly relations and the development of co-operation and mutual understanding between the countries of the Balkan Peninsula with a view to ensuring lasting peace in that region.

Article 6. The High Contracting Parties declare that one of the main prerequisites for the safeguarding of European security is the inviolability of the State frontiers in Europe established after the Second World War.

The Contracting Parties express their firm determination, in accordance with the Warsaw Treaty of Friendship, Co-operation and Mutual Assistance of 14 May 1955, to guarantee, together with the other States Parties, the inviolability of the frontiers of the States Parties to the Treaty, and to take all necessary steps to prevent any aggression on the part of the forces of imperialism, militarism and revanchism.

Article 7. In the event of an armed attack on either of the High Contracting Parties by any State or group of States, the other Party, in exercise of its inalienable right of individual or collective self-defence under article 51 of the Charter of the United Nations, shall immediately provide all-round assistance with all the means at its disposal, including military assistance, necessary to repulse the armed attack.

The Parties shall immediately inform the Security Council of the United Nations of any measures taken on the basis of this article and shall act in accordance with the provisions of the Charter of the United Nations.

Article 8. The High Contracting Parties shall provide each other with information on the building of socialism in the two States, shall exchange views on the development of bilateral relations, and shall consult each other on the major international problems of interest to both countries.

Article 9. The provisions of this Treaty shall not affect the rights and obligations of the High Contracting Parties arising from existing bilateral and multilateral agreements.

Article 10. This Treaty is subject to ratification and shall enter into force on the date of the exchange of the instruments of ratification, which shall take place in Bucharest as soon as possible.

The Treaty is concluded for a term of twenty years from the date of its entry into force. It shall be extended automatically for successive periods of five years unless one of the High Contracting Parties gives written notification, twelve months before the expiry of the current term of the Treaty, of its intention to denounce it.

Done at Sofia on 19 November 1970 in duplicate in the Bulgarian and Romanian languages, both texts being equally authentic.

For the People's Republic of Bulgaria:
[TODOR ZHIVKOV]
[GEORGI TRAIKOV]
For the Socialist Republic of Romania:
[NICOLAE CEAUSESCU]
[ION GHEORGHE MAURER]

4.1393 Treaty of Friendship and Cooperation between the Union of Soviet Socialist Republics and the United Arab Republic

Alliance Members: Union of Soviet Socialist Republics and United Arab Republic (Egypt)
Signed On: May 27, 1971, in the city of Cairo. In force until March 14, 1976.
Alliance Type: Entente (Type III)

Source: *United Nations Treaty,* no. 11379.

SUMMARY

During the mid-1950s and continuing into the 1960s, the Soviet Union supported Egyptian control of the Suez Canal and provided aid in the building of the Aswan High Dam. The Soviets also provided aid and material to Egypt before and during the 1967 Arab-Israeli War. The large amounts of aid for the Egyptian government eventually translated into the signing of this alliance, which called for consultation on issues of security and guaranteed Soviet aid to the Egyptian military. The Soviet leadership believed the treaty would provide them with greater control over Egyptian foreign policy, but Egypt expelled most high-ranking Russian diplomats after just a year, fearing Russia's designs to determine the nature of Egypt's international role.

Egypt lost much of its air force and armor following the 1973–1975 (Yom Kippur) war with Israel and called on the Soviets to resupply its military, but the Soviet refusal to provide spare parts and services to the Egyptian MiG-21 fleet caused a rupture in relations. Seeking repayment for prior aid, the Soviets first halted the supply of spare engines and later stopped shipping all military parts. As the majority of Egypt's inventory was supplied by the Soviets, cooled relations severely strained the Egyptian military.

On March 14, 1976, Egyptian president Anwar Sadat asked the Egyptian People's Assembly to abrogate the Soviet treaty, claiming that the Soviets were trying to make Egypt "kneel before her." The following day, by a 307–2 vote, the assembly accepted Sadat's proposal.

Sadat then began to cooperate with the United States and, in 1978, signed the Camp David accords establishing a separate peace with Israel. Moscow responded by increasing its support for Libya and Syria, both rivals of Sadat's Egypt. Sadat expelled Soviet diplomats and technicians only weeks before his assassination in 1981.

ALLIANCE TEXT

The Union of Soviet Socialist Republics and the United Arab Republic,

Being firmly convinced that the further development of the friendship and all-round co-operation between the Union of Soviet Socialist Republics and the United Arab Republic is in accordance with the interests of the peoples of the two States and serves the cause of strengthening universal peace,

Inspired by the ideals of the struggle against imperialism and colonialism and for the freedom, independence and social progress of peoples,

Determined to struggle steadfastly for the consolidation of international peace and security, in accordance with the unfailing course of their peace-loving foreign policy,

Reaffirming their loyalty to the purposes and principles of the Charter of the United Nations,

Desiring to confirm and strengthen the traditional relations of genuine friendship between the two States and their peoples by means of the conclusion of a Treaty of Friendship and Co-operation, thereby creating a basis for their further development,

Have agreed as follows:

Article 1. The High Contracting Parties solemnly declare that indestructible friendship will always exist between the two countries and their peoples. They shall continue to develop and strengthen the relations of friendship and all-round co-operation existing between them in the political, economic, scientific, technical, cultural and other fields on the basis of the principles of respect for sovereignty, territorial integrity, non-intervention in each other's internal affairs, equal rights and mutual benefit.

Article 2. The Union of Soviet Socialist Republics as a socialist State and the United Arab Republic, which has chosen as its goal the socialist transformation of society, shall co-operate closely and in every way possible to ensure conditions favourable to the maintenance and further development of the social and economic achievements of their peoples.

Article 3. Desiring to contribute in every way possible to the maintenance of international peace and security of peoples, the Union of Soviet Socialist Republics and the United Arab Republic shall continue with all possible determination to make efforts to establish and ensure a lasting and just peace in the Middle East in accordance with the purposes and principles of the Charter of the United Nations.

In pursuance of their peace-loving foreign policy, the High Contracting Parties shall strive for peace, the reduction of international tension, general and complete disarmament and the prohibition of nuclear and other weapons of mass destruction.

Article 4. Guided by the ideals of the freedom and equality of all peoples, the High Contracting Parties condemn imperialism and colonialism in all their forms and manifestations. They shall continue to oppose imperialism and support the complete and final elimination of colonialism pursuant to the United Nations Declaration on the Granting of Independence to Colonial Countries and Peoples, and to wage a steadfast struggle against racism and *apartheid*.

Article 5. The High Contracting Parties shall continue to expand and intensify all-round co-operation and exchange of experience in the economic and scientific and technical fields, in industry, agriculture, water management, irrigation, exploitation of natural resources, the development of power systems and the training of national specialists as well as in other areas of the economy.

The Parties shall expand trade and shipping between the two States on the basis of the principles of mutual advantage and most-favoured-nation treatment.

Article 6. The High Contracting Parties shall promote the further development of co-operation between themselves in science, art, literature, education, health, the press, radio, television, cinematography, tourism and physical culture as well as in other fields.

The Parties shall promote the expansion of co-operation and direct contacts between workers' political and social organizations, enterprises and cultural and scientific institutions so that the peoples of the two countries may become better acquainted with each other's life, work and achievements.

Article 7. Being deeply interested in ensuring the peace and security of peoples and attaching great importance to co-ordinating their activities on the international scene in the struggle for peace, the High Contracting Parties shall for that purpose regularly consult together at various levels regarding all important questions affecting the interests of the two States.

In the event of a situation arising which, in the opinion of the two Parties, constitutes a threat to the peace or a breach of the peace, the Parties shall immediately contact each other for the purpose of co-ordinating their positions in the interests of removing the said threat or of restoring peace.

Article 8. In the interests of strengthening the defence capability of the United Arab Republic, the High Contracting Parties shall continue to develop cooperation in military matters on the basis of appropriate agreements between themselves. Such cooperation shall provide in particular for assistance in the training of the military personnel of the United Arab Republic and instruction in the use of the arms and equipment supplied to the United Arab Republic for the purpose of strengthening its capability to overcome the consequences of aggression and to resist aggression in general.

Article 9. In accordance with the purposes and principles of this Treaty, each of the High Contracting Parties declares that it will not enter into any alliances, join any group of States or participate in any actions or measures directed against the other High Contracting Party.

Article 10. Each of the High Contracting Parties declares that its obligations under international treaties currently in force do not conflict with the provisions of this Treaty and undertakes not to enter into any international agreements which are not consistent therewith.

Article 11. This Treaty shall be valid for a term of 15 years from the date of its entry into force.

If neither of the High Contracting Parties gives notice of its intention to terminate the Treaty one year prior to the expiry of the above-mentioned term, it shall be extended for successive five-year terms until such time as one of the High Contracting Parties gives written notice of its desire to terminate it one year before the expiry of the current five-year term.

Article 12. This Treaty is subject to ratification and shall enter into force on the date of the exchange of the instruments of ratification, which shall take place at Moscow as soon as possible.

This Treaty has been drafted in duplicate in the Russian and Arabic languages, both texts being equally authentic.

Done at Cairo on 27 May 1971, corresponding to 3 Rabi'-al-Akhir 1391 A.H.

For the Union of Soviet Socialist Republics:

[*N. PODGORNY*]

For the United Arab Republic:

[*MOHAMED ANWAR EL-SADAT*]

4.1394 Treaty of Peace, Friendship and Cooperation between India and the Soviet Union

Alliance Members: Union of Soviet Socialist Republics and India
Signed On: August 9, 1971, in the city of New Delhi (India). In force until December 25, 1991.
Alliance Type: Non-Aggression Pact (Type II)

Source: *India Treaty Series 1980,* Ministry of External Affairs, Government of India, http://meaindia.nic.in/treatiesagreement/1971/chap434.htm.

SUMMARY

Relations between the Soviet Union and India deepened during the 1950s as Soviet relations with China soured. The Soviet Union continued its support of India into the early 1960s, providing aid during India's border conflict with China. Indian enmity toward Pakistan and Pakistan's close ties with the United States continued to provide a rationale for cooperation during the 1970s.

On August 9, 1971, Indian prime minister Indira Gandhi signed the Treaty of Peace, Friendship and Cooperation with the Soviet Union, providing for close military cooperation and Soviet military support of India's armed forces. In the six years following the treaty signing, India received roughly $700 million in armaments from its ally as a counter to the aid given to Pakistan by the United States. Although the treaty stipulated the alliance would last for twenty years, the two countries extended the agreement in August 1991, declaring that their strategic partnership was still in both countries' interest. The collapse of the Soviet Union later in 1991 effectively ended the treaty as the transfer of military aid dwindled.

In 1993, President Boris Yeltsin signed a friendship treaty with India, but the new treaty did not include any formal military alliance. In 2000, President Putin visited India, and the two nations signed a declaration announcing a "Russia-India strategic partnership." Since then, relations between the two nations have been stable and friendly.

ALLIANCE TEXT

Desirous of expanding and consolidating the existing relations of sincere friendship between them,

Believing that the further development of friendship and cooperation meets the basic national interests of both States as well as the interests of lasting peace in Asia and the world,

Determined to promote the consolidation of universal peace and security and to make steadfast efforts for the relaxation of international tensions and final elimination of the remnants of colonialism,

Upholding their firm faith in the principles of peaceful coexistence and cooperation between States with different political and social systems,

Convinced that in the world today international problems can only be solved by cooperation and not by conflict,

Reaffirming their determination to abide by the purposes and the principles of the United Nations Charter,

The Republic of India on one side

And

The Union of Soviet Socialist Republic on the other side,

Have decided to conclude the present Treaty, for which purposes the following Plenipotentiaries have been appointed:

On behalf of the Republic of India: SARDAR SWARAN SINGH, Minister of External Affairs.

On behalf of the Union of Soviet Socialist Republic: Mr. A. A. GROMYKO, Minister of Foreign Affairs,

Who, having each presented their Credentials, which are found to be in proper form and due order,

Have agreed as follows:

Article I. The High Contracting Parties solemnly declare that enduring peace and friendship shall prevail between the two countries and their peoples. Each Party shall respect the independence, sovereignty and territorial integrity of the other party and refrain from interfering in the other's internal affairs. The high Contracting Parties shall continue to develop and consolidate relations of sincere friendship, good neighborliness and comprehensive cooperation existing between them on the biasis of the aforesaid principles as well as those of equality and mutual benefit.

Article II. Guided by a desire to contribute in every possible way to ensure an enduring peace and security of their people, the High Contracting Parties declare their determination to continue their efforts to preserve and to strengthen peace in Asia and throughout the world, to hard the arms race and to achieve a general and complete disarmament, including both nuclear and conventional, under effective international control.

Article III. Guided by their loyalty to the lofty ideal of equality of all Peoples and Nations, irrespective of race or creed, the High Contracting Parties condemn colonialism and reclaims in all forms and manifestations, and reaffirm their determination to strive for their final and complete elimination.

The High Contracting Parties shall cooperate with other States to achieve these aims and to support just aspirations of the peoples in their struggle against colonialism and racial domination.

Article IV. The Republic of India respects the peace loving policy of the Union of Soviet Socialist Republics aimed at strengthening friendship and co-operation with all nations.

The Union of Soviet Socialist Republics respects India's policy of non-alignment and reaffirms that this policy constitutes an important factor in the maintenance of universal peace and international security and in lessening of tensions in the world.

Article V. Deeply interested in ensuring universal peace and security attaching great importance to their mutual cooperation in the international field for achieving those aims, the High contracting Parties will maintain regular contacts with each other on major international problems affecting the interests of both States by means of meetings and exchanges of views between their leading statesmen, visits by official delegations and special envoys of the two Governments and through diplomatic channels.

Article VI. Attaching great importance to economic, scientific and technological co-operation between the, the High Contracting Parties will continue to consolidate and expand mutually advantageous and comprehensive co-operation in these fields as well as expand trade, transport and communications between them on the basis of the principles of equality, mutual benefit and most-favoured-nation treatment, subject to the existing agreements and the special arrangements with contiguous countries as specified in the Indo-Soviet Trade Agreement of December 26, 1970.

Article VII. The High Contracting Parties shall promote further development of ties and contacts between them in the fields of science, art, literature, education, public health, press, radio, television, cinema, tourism and sports.

Article VIII. In accordance with the traditional friendship established between the two countries each of the High Contracting Parties solemnly declares that it shall not enter into or participate in any military alliance directed against the other Party.

Each High Contracting Party under-takes to abstain from any aggression against the other Party and to prevent the use of its territory for the commission of any act which might inflict military damage on the other High Contracting Party.

Article IX. Each High Contracting Party undertakes to abstain from providing any assistance to any third party that engages in armed conflict with the other Party. In the event of either Party being subjected to and attach or a threat thereof, the High Contracting Parties shall immediately enter into mutual consultations in order to remover such threat and to take appropriate effective measures to ensure peace and security of their countries.

Article X. Each High Contracting Party solemnly declares that it shall not enter into any obligations, secret or public, with one or more states, which is incompatible with this Treaty. Each high Contracting Party further declares that no obligation exists, nor shall any obligation be entered into, between itself and any other State or States, which might cause military damage to the other Party.

Article XI. This Treaty is concluded for a duration of twenty years and will be automatically extended for each successive period of five years unless either High Contracting Party declares its desire to terminate it by giving notice to the other High Contracting Party twelve months prior to expiration of the Treaty. The Treaty will be subject to ratification and will come into force on the date of exchange of Instruments of Ratification which will take place in Moscow within one month of the signing of this Treaty.

Article XII. Any difference of interpretation of any Article or Articles of this Treaty that may arise between the High Contracting Parties will be settled bilaterally by peaceful means in a spirit of mutual respect and understating.

The said Plenipotentiaries have signed the present Treaty in Hindi, Russian and English, all texts being equally authentic and have affixed thereto their seals.

Done in New Delhi on the ninth day of August in the year one thousand nine hundred and seventy one.

On behalf of the Republic of India

SARDAR SWARAN SINGH
Minister of External Affairs.

On behalf of the Union of Soviet Socialist Republics

A.A. GROMYKO
Minister of Foreign Affairs.

4.1395 Treaty of Peace and Friendship between the Government of India and the Government of the People's Republic of Bangladesh

Alliance Members: Bangladesh and India
Signed On: March 19, 1972, in the city of Dhaka (Bangladesh). In force until March 19, 1997.
Alliance Type: Non-Aggression Pact (Type II)

Source: *India Treaty Series 1980,* Ministry of External Affairs, Government of India, http://meaindia.nic.in/treatiesagreement/1972/chap452.htm.

SUMMARY

In 1971, while Bangladesh was fighting Pakistan in a war for independence, India, suffering from severe refugee flows and manifesting its rivalry with Pakistan, extended military support to Pakistan's rebellious province. India's intervention in December 1971 proved decisive, as the Pakistani army was defeated by joint forces. On March 19, 1972, Bangladeshi prime minister Mujibur Rahman and Indian prime minister Indira Gandhi signed this treaty of peace and friendship. The treaty was signed only three months after the war of independence, and India used the occasion to guarantee Bangladeshi sovereignty and borders as well as Indian support to defend both.

Relations between the two countries quickly became strained. In 1975 India diverted the flow of the River Ganges near the northern border of Bangladesh; India additionally had the ability to control the flow of Bangladesh's second largest river, the Padma. Weak border definition between the two countries created a second problem as large numbers of Bangladeshi refugees fled to India and also instigated insurgency efforts against Indian control of some northern territories. India repeatedly accused Bangladesh of aiding these insurgencies and ignoring the infiltration of Pakistani agents into the rebel movements.

The conflict over water rights eventually led to the assassination of President Mujibur Rahman and his aides in 1981. Although rebels briefly captured the capital of Dhaka and declared their intention of pulling out of the treaty with India, the treaty expired in March of 1997, twenty-five years after it was originally signed. Bangladeshi prime minister Sheikh Hasina announced in 1997 that Bangladesh did not intend to extend the agreement as the Bangladesh government claimed that the treaty had become unnecessary and unworkable since the South Asian Association on Regional Cooperation (SAARC) had been formed. Hostility to the treaty's terms grew in both countries, and the alliance was not renewed.

ALLIANCE TEXT

Inspired by common ideals of peace, secularism, democracy, socialism and nationalism,

Having struggled together for the realisation of these ideals and cemented ties of friendship through blood and sacrifices which led to the triumphant emergence of a free, sovereign and independent Bangladesh,

Determined to maintain fraternal and good-neighbourly relations and transform their border into a border of eternal peace and friendship,

Adhering firmly to the basic tenets of non-alignment, peaceful co-existence, mutual cooperation, non-interference in internal affairs and respect for territorial integrity and sovereignty,

Determined to safeguard peace, stability and security and to promote progress of their respective countries through all possible avenues of mutual cooperation,

Determined further to expand and strengthen the existing relations of friendship between them, convinced that the further development of friendship and cooperation meets the national interests of both States as well as the interests of lasting peace in Asia and the world,

Resolved to contribute to strengthening world peace and security and to make efforts to bring about a relaxation of international tension and the final elimination of vestiges of colonialism, racialism and imperialism,

Convinced that in the present-day world international problems can be solved only through cooperation and not through conflict or confrontation,

Reaffirming their determination to follow the aims and principles of the United Nations Charter, the Republic of India, on the one hand, and the People's Republic of Bangladesh, on the other,

Have decided to conclude the present Treaty.

Article 1. The high Contracting Parties, inspired by the ideals for which their respective peoples struggled and made sacrifices together, solemnly declare that there shall be lasting peace and friendship between their two countries and their peoples, each side shall respect the independence, sovereignty and territorial integrity of the other and refrain from interfering in the internal affairs of the other side.

The high Contracting Parties shall further develop and strengthen the relations of friendship, good-neighbourliness and all-round cooperation existing between them, on the basis of the above-mentioned principles as well as the principles of equality and mutual benefit.

Article 2. Being guided by their devotion to the principles of equality of all peoples and states, irrespective of race or creed, the high Contracting Parties condemn colonialism and racialism in all forms and manifestations and are determined to strive for their final and complete elimination.

The high Contracting Parties shall cooperate with other states in achieving these aims and support the just aspirations of people in their struggle against colonialism and racial discrimination and for their national liberation.

Article 3. The high Contracting Parties reaffirm their faith in the policy of non-alignment and peaceful co-existence as important factors for easing tension in the world, maintaining international peace and security, and strengthening national sovereignty and independence.

Article 4. The high Contracting Parties shall maintain regular contacts with each other on major international problems affecting the interests of both States, through meetings and exchanges of views at all levels.

Article 5. The high Contracting Parties shall continue to strengthen and widen their mutually advantageous and all-round cooperation in the economic, scientific and technical fields. The two countries shall develop mutual cooperation in the fields of trade, transport and communications between them on the basis of the principles of equality, mutual benefit and the most-favoured nation principle.

Article 6. The high Contracting Parties further agree to make joint studies and take point action in the fields of flood control, river basin development and the development of hydro-electric power and irrigation.

Article 7. The high Contracting Parties shall promote relations in the fields of art, literature, education, culture, sports and health.

Article 8. In accordance with the ties of friendship existing between the two countries each of the high Contracting Parties solemnly declares that it shall not enter into or participate in any military alliance directed against the other party.

Each of the high Contracting Parties shall refrain from any aggression against the other party and shall not allow the use of its territory for committing any act that may cause military damage to or constitute a threat to the security of the other high contracting party.

Article 9. Each of the high Contracting Parties shall refrain from giving any assistance to any third party taking part in an armed conflict, against the other party. In case either party is attacked or threatened with attack, the high contracting parties shall immediately enter into mutual consultations in order to take appropriate effective measures to eliminate the threat and thus ensure the peace and security of their countries.

Article 10. Each of the high Contracting Parties solemnly declares that it shall not undertake any commitment secret or open, toward one or more States which may be incompatible with the present Treaty.

Article 11. The present Treaty is signed for a term of twenty five years and shall be subject to renewal by mutual agreement of the high Contracting Parties.

The Treaty shall come into force with immediate effect from the date of its signature.

Article 12. Any differences in interpreting any article or articles of the present Treaty that may arise between the high Contracting Parties shall be settled on a bilateral basis by peaceful means in a spirit of mutual respect and understanding.

Done in Dacca on the nineteenth day of March nineteen hundred and seventy two.

INDIRA GANDHI
Prime Minister
For the Republic of India
SHEIKH MUJIBUR RAHMAN
Prime Minister
For the People's Republic of Bangladesh

4.1396 Soviet-Iraqi Treaty of Friendship and Co-operation

Alliance Members: Union of Soviet Socialist Republics and Iraq
Signed On: April 9, 1972, in the city of Baghdad (Iraq). In force until September 12, 1990.
Alliance Type: Entente (Type III)

Source: *Soviet News,* no. 5633, April 11, 1972, p. 113.

SUMMARY

Cooperation between Russia and Iraq began during the late 1950s when the pro-Western monarchy that ruled Iraq was overthrown. In 1972, the two nations formalized their relationship with this treaty of friendship and co-operation. After the treaty was signed, the Soviets increased arms shipments, including MiG fighters and bombers, ground tactical missiles, T-72 tanks, and several types of anti-tank weapons, to aid Iraq in its conflict with Kurdish rebels. That same year Iraq nationalized its oil industry and began shipping large amounts of oil to the Soviet Union.

Bilateral relations weakened somewhat over the next decade. In December 1979 the Soviet Union invaded Afghanistan, and Saddam Hussein condemned the invasion of another Islamic country. Less than a year later, when Iraq invaded Iran, the Soviet Union cut off arms shipments in protest. Gradually, however, the mutually advantageous relationship of oil for arms overcame diplomatic tensions, and the Soviet Union became Iraq's largest supplier of arms and military technology in the 1980s. The alliance ended in 1990 when President Mikhail Gorbachev and the Russian Parliament broke relations following the Iraqi invasion of Kuwait.

The following description of terms contains excerpts of the official text of the treaty, which is unpublished.

DESCRIPTION OF TERMS

Article I. Iraq and the USSR declared that "inviolable friendship will exist between the two countries and their peoples" and that they would develop all-around co-operation in the political, economic, trade, scientific, technical and other fields "on the basis of respect for State sovereignty, territorial integrity and noninterference in one another's internal affairs."

Article 2. The two countries would "co-operate closely and comprehensively in ensuring conditions for preserving and further developing the social and economic gains of their people and respect for the sovereignty of each of them over all their natural resources."

Article 3 stated that Iraq and the USSR would "continue to come out for peace throughout the world, for the easing of international tensions, and for the attainment of general and complete disarmament, encompassing both nuclear and conventional weapons, under effective international control."

Article 4 said that both countries "condemn imperialism and colonialism in all their forms and manifestations" and would "continue to wage an undeviating struggle against imperialism and Zionism [and] for the complete . . . abolition of colonialism and neo-colonialism, racialism and *apartheid*."

Article 5. Iraq and the USSR would "expand and deepen" their co-operation in the economic, technical and scientific fields; would exchange experience in industry, agriculture, irrigation, water conservation, and the utilization of oil and other natural resources, "as well as in the training of national cadres"; and would expand trade and shipping between the two countries "on the basis of the principles of equality, mutual benefit and most-favoured-nation treatment."

Article 6. The two countries would develop mutual contacts in the fields of science, art, literature, education, public health, the press, radio, cinematography, television, tourism, sport, etc.

Article 7. Iraq and the USSR would consult each other regularly on all important international questions affecting the interests of the two countries, as well as on questions concerning the further development of bilateral relations.

Article 8. "In the event of situations developing which threaten the peace of either of the sides or create a threat to peace or the danger of a violation of peace," Iraq and the USSR would "immediately contact each other with the aim of co-ordinating their positions in the interests of removing the threat or restoring peace."

Article 9. "In the interests of the security of both countries the High Contracting Parties will continue to develop co-operation in the strengthening of their defence capabilities."

Article 10. "Each of the High Contracting Parties declares that it will not enter into alliances or take part in any groupings of States or in actions or undertakings directed against the other High Contracting Party.

"Each of the High Contracting Parties undertakes not to permit the use of its territory for any act capable of doing military harm to the other side."

Article 11. The two countries declared that their commitments under existing international treaties were not in contradiction to the provisions of the present treaty, and undertook not to conclude any international agreements incompatible with it.

Article 12. The treaty was concluded for a period of 15 years and would be automatically prolonged for subsequent periods of five years unless one of the parties expressed its desire to terminate the treaty by notifying the other party 12 months before its expiration.

Article 13. Any differences that might arise between the parties concerning the interpretation of provisions of the treaty would be "resolved bilaterally in the spirit of friendship, mutual respect and understanding."

Article 14. The treaty would enter into force on the exchange of ratification instruments, which would be effected in Moscow "in the shortest possible period of time."

4.1397 Treaty of Friendship, Co-operation, and Mutual Assistance between the Socialist Republic of Romania and the German Democratic Republic

Alliance Members: Romania and the German Democratic Republic
Signed On: May 12, 1972, in the city of Bucharest (Romania). In force until November 7, 1989.
Alliance Type: Defense Pact (Type I)

Source: *United Nations Treaty*, no. 12134.

SUMMARY

In 1972, President Erich Honecker of the German Democratic Republic (East Germany) and President Nicolae Ceausescu of Romania signed a treaty of friendship, cooperation, and mutual assistance. As with most of the bilateral Eastern European treaties of the cold war, the clauses of the agreement reaffirmed ideas set forth in the Warsaw Pact and guaranteed military and economic cooperation. In the years following the signing, East Germany became Romania's second largest trading partner—second only to the Soviet Union.

The treaty ended in 1989 with the resignation of the East German communist government. The Romanian government fell one month later, and President Ceausescu and his wife were executed, having inspired deep antipathy among the Romanian public.

ALLIANCE TEXT

The Socialist Republic of Romania and the German Democratic Republic,

Firmly resolved to develop and strengthen the ties of fraternal friendship, all-round co-operation and mutual assistance between the two States,

Profoundly convinced that the development of those ties is in accord with the vital interests of the peoples of the two countries and contributes to the strengthening of the unity and cohesion of the socialist States,

Recognizing that internationalist solidarity among the socialist States is based on a common social system and common basic aims and aspirations and on the common interests of the struggle against imperialism and reaction,

Expressing the firm desire to contribute to the strengthening of peace and security in Europe and throughout the world, to develop co-operation with European and other States irrespective of their social systems, on the basis of the rules and principles of international law, and to oppose imperialism, revanchism and militarism,

Resolved to act in accordance with the provisions of the Warsaw Treaty of Friendship, Co-operation and Mutual Assistance of 14 May 1955, during the period of validity of that Treaty, which was concluded in response to the threat from the North Atlantic Treaty Organization,

Convinced that the German Democratic Republic, a Socialist and sovereign State, is an important actor for the achievement of European security and that its policy of peace and its participation in international life on a footing of equality is of essential importance to the consolidation of peace and security in Europe,

Guided by the principles and purposes of the Charter of the United Nations,

Having regard to the present state and possibilities of development of all-round co-operation between the Socialist Republic of Romania and the German Democratic Republic and to the changes that have taken place in Europe and throughout the world,

Have decided to conclude this Treaty and have for that purpose agreed as follows:

Article 1. The High Contracting Parties shall develop des of friendship and all-round co-operation between the two States on the basis of the principles of socialist internationalism, mutual advantage and mutual comradely assistance, respect for sovereignty and independence, equal rights and non-interference in internal affairs.

Article 2. The High Contracting Parties, proceeding from the principles underlying relations between the socialist States, and the principles of the international socialist division of labour, shall develop and intensify economic, scientific and technical co-operation, expand co-operation in production and research and contribute to the development of economic relations and co-operation within the framework of the Council for Mutual Economic Assistance as well as with the other socialist States.

Article 3. The High Contracting Parties shall develop and expand cooperation in the fields of science, education, art, culture, the press, radio, television, the cinema, tourism, health protection, physical culture and in other fields. The Parties shall support co-operation between the public organizations of the two countries.

Article 4. The High Contracting Parties, realizing that the unity of the socialist countries is a prerequisite for the achievement of security and peace in the world, shall continually work for the development of ties of friendship and co-operation between the socialist States, and for the strengthening of their unity and cohesion in the interests of the cause of socialism and peace.

Article 5. The High Contracting Parties shall also contribute in the future to the safeguarding of peace and security throughout the world, being guided by the purposes and principles of the Charter of the United Nations. The Parties shall consistently promote a policy of peaceful coexistence among States with different social systems and shall strive for the creation of a climate of *détente* and cooperation among States, for the settlement of international disputes by peaceful means, for the achievement of general and complete disarmament, for the elimination of racial discrimination and the final elimination of colonialism and neocolonialism in accordance with the right of peoples to self-determination.

Article 6. The High Contracting Parties shall continue to strive for the strengthening of peace and the achievement of security in Europe and for the development of good-neighbourly relations between European States.

Article 7. The High Contracting Parties emphasize that the inviolability of the frontiers established after World War II in Europe is a basic prerequisite for the achievement of European security. They shall ensure, in accordance with the Warsaw Treaty of Friendship, Co-operation and Mutual Assistance of 14 May 1955, the inviolability of the frontiers of the two States, including the State frontier between the two German States.

The two Parties shall take the necessary measures, in accordance with the principles of international law, to prevent threats to peace on the part of militarist and revanchist forces seeking a revision of the results of World War II.

Article 8. In the event of an armed attack on one of the High Contracting Parties by a State or group of States, the other Party, in exercise of its inalienable right of individual or collective self-defence under Article 51 of the Charter of the United Nations, shall immediately render the first-mentioned Party all assistance, including military assistance, necessary to repel the armed attack.

The Parties shall immediately report to the United Nations Security Council any measures taken on the basis of this article and shall act in conformity with the provisions of the Charter of the United Nations.

Article 9. The two Contracting Parties regard West Berlin as a special political unit.

Article 10. The High Contracting Parties consider that the establishment of normal relations with equal rights, between the two German States, on the basis of international law, would be an essential contribution to the cause of peace and security in Europe.

Article 11. The High Contracting Parties shall inform and consult one another concerning the development of co-operation between the two States and concerning important international problems affecting their interests.

Article 12. The High Contracting Parties declare that their obligations under international treaties in force do not conflict with the provisions of this Treaty.

Article 13. This Treaty shall be subject to ratification and shall enter into force on the date of the exchange of the instruments of ratification, which shall take place at Berlin as soon as possible.

Article 14. This Treaty is concluded for a period of twenty years, from the date of its entry into force. If neither of the High Contracting Parties denounces it in writing twelve months before the expiry of its validity, the Treaty shall be extended for further periods of five years.

This Treaty shall be registered with the United Nations Secretariat, in accordance with Article 102, paragraph 1, of the Charter of the United Nations.

Done at Bucharest, on 12 May 1972, in two original copies, in the Romanian and German languages, both texts being equally authentic.

For the Socialist Republic of Romania:
[NICOLAE CEAUÇESCU]
[ION GHEORGHE MAURER]

For the German Democratic Republic:
[ERICH HONECKER]
[WILLY STOPH]

4.1398 Mutual Defense Agreement between Sudan and Uganda

Alliance Members: Sudan and Uganda
Signed On: June 28, 1972, in the city of Khartoum (Sudan). In force until April 11, 1979.
Alliance Type: Defense Pact (Type I)

Source: *Keesing's Record of World Events,* June 1972.

SUMMARY

Sudan was embroiled in a civil war of north against south from 1955 to 1972. Ugandan leaders had viewed the Sudanese struggle as Arab against African and favored the southern Sudanese. Even Idi Amin, the Ugandan dictator who took power in a military coup d'état in 1971, had ethnic ties to the region.

After the settlement of the civil war in March of 1972, Sudan and Uganda signed this agreement of mutual defense against external aggression. Relations were relatively quiet until 1976 when Amin claimed that parts of Kenya and southern Sudan were traditional parts of Uganda. Amin was forced to back down after Kenya mobilized troops and armored personnel carriers.

In April of 1979, Amin was overthrown, and Amin's supporters and 200,000 Ugandan refugees fled to southern Sudan. Idi Amin fled to Saudi Arabia.

DESCRIPTION OF TERMS

Each country pledged to give military assistance to the other if either were to suffer "aggression" by any external enemies, including "imperialists" or "Zionists."

4.1399 Defence and Security Treaty between Niger and Libya

Alliance Members: Niger and Libya
Signed On: March 9, 1974, in the cities of Tripoli (Libya) and Niamey (Niger). In force until January 13, 1981.
Alliance Type: Defense Pact (Type I)

Source: *Keesing's Record of World Events,* March 1974.

SUMMARY

During the 1970s Libya engaged in numerous alliances with African nations in an attempt to forge regional co-operation and Libyan influence over that co-operation. Niger was an ideal ally in light of this policy, as it was seeking to increase security and trade within the region, while Libya was trying to increase the number of its trading partners.

Despite the alliance, however, bilateral relations remained troubled. President Hamani Diori of Niger was overthrown in a coup d'état led by Seyni Kountche in the year after this alliance was formed, and

Kountche quickly denied access to a top Libyan official and denounced Libyan interference. Soon after, Kountche survived a coup attempt that was linked to Libya. Nevertheless, the alliance continued for several more years, and Niger even sent uranium to Libya. By 1981, Libyan interference in Chad proved intolerable to the Niger government, which froze its relations with Libya.

DESCRIPTION OF TERMS

Each country pledged to give military assistance to the other if external enemies, "Zionists," or "imperialists" showed any "aggression" toward one of the alliance partners.

4.1400 Agreement between Algeria and Libya

Alliance Members: Algeria and Libya
Signed On: December 28, 1975, in the city of Hassi Messaoud (Algeria). In force until August 13, 1984.
Alliance Type: Defense Pact (Type I)

Source: *Keesing's Record of World Events,* January 1977.

SUMMARY

On December 11, 1975, President Houari Boumediene of Algeria and Colonel Mu'ammar Gadhafi of Libya met and declared their interests to be identical. Seventeen days later, during a second meeting, the two leaders issued a joint statement outlining a defense pact between the countries. Following the meeting, President Boumediene recalled the Algerian ambassador from Rabat, Morocco, and both Morocco and Algeria sent troops to their borders in anticipation of conflict. Tensions abated, but the links between Libya and Algeria proved worrisome for Morocco, which continued to struggle with Algeria over control of Western Sahara. Libya played a key part in the bilateral rivalry with its change in policy, manifested by its signature of the Oujda Union with Morocco (see Alliance no. 4.1431), prompting Algeria to renounce this agreement.

DESCRIPTION OF TERMS

A joint communiqué released by both leaders stated that "any attack carried out against either of the revolutions will be considered by the other as an attack against itself." The two countries also pledged to create institutional links to foster additional cooperation. Future meetings were also agreed to.

4.1401 Sudanese Defense Agreement with Egypt

Alliance Members: Sudan and Egypt
Signed On: July 15, 1976, in the city of Cairo. In force until June 10, 1989.
Alliance Type: Defense Pact (Type I)

Source: *Foreign Broadcast Information Service—Middle East Area,* July 22, 1976, p. D1.

SUMMARY

In 1969, Colonel Jaafar an Nimeiri led a successful military coup d'état in Sudan. His foreign policy relied heavily on close relations with Egypt and active backing by the United States. By 1974, Nimeiri and President Anwar al-Sadat of Egypt had signed an integration pact. This was followed two years later with this joint military defense alliance. Also in 1976, Syria and Egypt established a unified political command for military decision making; and in February 1977, Sudan was added to the unified political command following the ratification of this Egyptian-Sudanese treaty.

Ties between Egypt and Sudan continued to grow. Nimeiri was one of the few Arab leaders to back Sadat's Israeli peace process. Sadat's successor, Hosni Mubarak, advanced bilateral relations when he and Nimeiri established a comprehensive integration charter in 1982. The Egypt-Sudan alliance became so formidable that it partially provoked the formation of a counteralliance comprising Libya, Ethiopia, and South Yemen (see Alliance no. 4.1423).

In 1985, Nimeiri was thrown from office and sought asylum in Egypt. While in Egypt, Nimeiri remained politically active and created controversy for Sudan. The Sudan People's Liberation Army (SPLA) demanded that Sudan abrogate the treaty with Egypt, and Nimeiri's political activism only made the problem worse. Finally, on June 10, 1989, Sudan abrogated the joint defense treaty with Egypt in order to continue negotiations with Sudanese rebels. Sudan stated that the alliance had become suspect since the Nimeiri regime had been ousted from power. The abrogation also occurred as Sudan was working to improve its image among its neighbors.

ALLIANCE TEXT

In response to the viewpoints of the two fraternal peoples: proceeding from their unshakeable belief in their common destiny and interests; in coordination of their efforts to guarantee and safeguard their safety and security; in strengthening their defense capabilities vis-á-vis the challenges which the Arab nation is confronting at the present stage of the joint Arab struggle to liberate the land and regain the usurped right; in deepening the cooperation which was the aim of the joint defense and economic cooperation treaty signed on 17 June 1950 by the members of the Arab League; inspired by the noble objectives of the OAU Charter signed in May 1963; and inspired by the program of political action and economic integration signed on 12 February 1974; the Governments of the Arab Republic of Egypt and the Democratic Republic of the Sudan have agreed to conclude a joint defense pact to bring about these objectives, as follows:

Article 1. The two contracting parties consider any armed aggression against either of them or their armed forces an aggression against both of them. Therefore, in accordance with the legitimate right of single or group defense stipulated in the UN charter and the Arab League Charter, each of them is committed to assist the other state in case of aggression against it. The two states shall immediately take all measures together and will use all the means they possess, including the use of the armed forces, to deter and repulse the aggression.

Article 2. The two states shall exchange information and consult each other at the request of either of them in case of the danger of the outbreak of war, or when a sudden aggression occurs, or in the case of an emergency portending danger. The two states shall immediately unify their plans and movements.

Article 3. To guarantee the effectiveness of the pact, the two sides shall coordinate plans and methods for developing their armed forces in a manner that will insure the mastery of the most sophisticated weapons.

Article 4. The two contracting countries have decided to establish bodies which shall insure the implementation of the pact. The bodies should include: a) a joint defense council, and b) a joint staff command.

Article 5. a) The Defense Council shall consist of the foreign and war ministers of the two countries, and shall be the highest authority of the joint staff command; and b) the responsibilities of the Defense Council shall include the following:

1. To draw up the general bases and principles for a policy of cooperation between the two countries in all fields in order to ward off and prevent any aggression on them.
2. To draw up the necessary recommendations for directing and coordinating the two countries' activities to serve joint war efforts.
3. To endorse the responsibilities of the joint staff command.
4. The council shall meet once every 6 months in Cairo and in Khartoum alternatively, or when either of the two sides feel that circumstances call for a meeting.

Article 6. a) The joint staff command shall be made up of the armed forces chiefs of staff of the two countries and an equal number of staff officers from each of the two countries, the number to be decided by the Defense Council; b) The staff command shall be concerned with drawing up plans and studies that will raise the armed forces' combat competency of both countries, by developing them in the armament and training fields, and by submitting any of these plans and studies which need to be submitted to the Defense council for endorsement; c) The command shall meet every 3 months or when considered necessary, at the request of either of the two countries' chiefs of staff.

Article 7. the duration of the pact shall be 25 years, and it will be automatically renewed every 5 years as long as neither of the contracting countries notifies the other of its wish to withdraw from the pact 1 year before its due date of expiration.

Article 8. The pact shall be endorsed according to the constitutional requirements of each of the two contracting countries. The ratification documents shall be exchanged at the Foreign Ministry of the Democratic Republic of Sudan and shall come into force as of the date the exchange has been effected.

In confirmation of the above, the pact has been signed and sealed with the two countries' seals.

This pact was drafted in Alexandria on 18 Rajab 1396 Hegira, corresponding to 15 July, 1976 in two original copies.

[Signed] Muhammad Anwar as-Sadat, president of the Arab Republic of Egypt; and

Ja'far Muhammad Numayri, president of the Democratic Republic of Sudan.

4.1402 Treaty of Friendship, Co-operation, and Mutual Assistance between the Union of Soviet Socialist Republics and the People's Republic of Angola

Alliance Members: Soviet Union and Angola
Signed On: October 8, 1976, in the city of Moscow. In force until December 25, 1991.
Alliance Type: Entente (Type III)

Source: *United Nations Treaty,* no. 17992.

SUMMARY

Angola won its independence in 1975 from Portugal after fighting a long civil war. Agostinho Neto built upon his Marxist revolutionary victory by forming close ties with both the Soviet Union and Cuba. On October 8, 1976, these closer ties were formally cemented when the Soviet Union and Angola signed a treaty of friendship and cooperation.

During the course of the treaty, the Soviet Union provided Angola with machinery, aircraft, helicopters, equipment, vehicles, medical equipment, and spare parts. The Soviets helped train military officers as well as technicians, mechanics, and even agricultural workers. The allies also established a joint commission for economic, technical, scientific, and commercial cooperation.

In keeping with the treaty, the Soviet Union supported Angola's Marxist government against several different armed rebel groups. Then, in 1981, South Africa sent forces into Angola claiming to pursue Angolan guerrillas fighting for Namibian independence. This led the Soviets to send military advisers and large amounts of equipment to Angola to support the government and fend off attacks from South Africa and UNITA (National Union for the Total Independence of Angola) guerrillas. Cuba, its other ally, also sent 20,000 troops.

The treaty ended with the collapse of the Soviet Union, although Russia and Angola continue to maintain friendly relations.

ALLIANCE TEXT

The Union of Soviet Socialist Republics and the People's Republic of Angola,

Considering that the further development and strengthening of the relations of friendship and all-round co-operation which have evolved between them as a result of the struggle for the freedom and independence of Angola are in accord with the vital national interests of the peoples of the two countries and serve the cause of peace throughout the world,

Inspired by the ideals of the struggle against imperialism, colonialism and racism in all their forms and manifestations and by the unswerving desire to give every manner of support to peoples struggling for freedom, independence and social progress,

Determined to promote the strengthening of international peace and security in the interests of the peoples of all countries,

Reaffirming their loyalty to the purposes and principles of the Charter of the United Nations,

Supporting the unity of all progressive forces in the struggle for peace, freedom, independence and social progress and considering that the development of friendly relations and broad co-operation between the socialist countries and the developing States is in accord with their common interests,

Taking account of the Declaration on the principles of friendly mutual relations and co-operation between the Union of Soviet Socialist Republics and the People's Republic of Angola of 26 May 1976 and desiring to strengthen the existing relations of friendship and mutually advantageous co-operation between the two States and peoples,

Have decided to conclude this Treaty of friendship and co-operation and have agreed as follows:

Article 1. The High Contracting Parties declare that indestructible friendship will exist between the two countries and their peoples and that all-round collaboration will be developed in the political, economic, trade, scientific, technical, cultural and other fields on the basis of respect for sovereignty, territorial integrity, nonintervention in each other's internal affairs and equal rights.

Article 2. The High Contracting Parties declare that they shall co-operate closely and in every way possible to ensure conditions favourable to the maintenance and further development of the social and economic achievements of their peoples and to respect for the sovereignty of each of them over all their natural resources.

Article 3. The Union of Soviet Socialist Republics respects the policy of nonalignment pursued by the People's Republic of Angola, which is an important factor in the maintenance of international peace and security. The People's Republic of Angola respects the peace-loving foreign policy pursued by the Union of Soviet Socialist Republics as a socialist State.

Article 4. The High Contracting Parties shall continue to support peace throughout the world, the furtherance of international détente and its embodiment in specific forms of mutually advantageous collaboration between States, the settlement of international problems by peaceful means, the conclusion of a universal agreement on the non-use of force in international relations and the achievement of general and complete disarmament, including nuclear disarmament, under effective international control.

Article 5. The High Contracting Parties shall continue to wage a steadfast struggle against the forces of imperialism and for the final elimination of colonialism and neo-colonialism, racism and *apartheid* and to promote the full implementation of the United Nations Declaration on the Granting of Independence to Colonial Countries and Peoples.'

The Parties shall co-operate with each other and with other peace-loving States in supporting the just struggle of peoples for their sovereignty, freedom, independence and social progress.

Article 6. The High Contracting Parties, expressing profound concern for the maintenance of universal peace and security and attaching great importance to cooperation between themselves in the international arena to achieve these goals, shall regularly exchange views with each other on important international questions and also on questions concerning bilateral relations.

Such consultations and exchanges of views shall encompass:

- International questions, including situations giving rise to tension in different regions of the world, with a view to promoting détente, the development of cooperation and the strengthening of international security;
- Questions which are the subject of multilateral negotiations, including those being considered in international organizations and at international conferences;
- Questions of a political, economic and cultural nature and other questions concerning the relations between the two countries.

Such consultations and exchange of views shall take place at various levels, *inter alia,* by means of meetings between leading State officials of the Parties, in the course of visits of official delegations and special representatives and through diplomatic channels.

Article 7. In the event of a situation arising which constitutes a threat to the peace or a breach of the peace, the High Contracting Parties shall immediately contact each other for the purpose of co-ordinating their positions in the interests of removing the said threat or of restoring peace.

Article 8. Attaching great importance to economic, technical and scientific co-operation between themselves, the High Contracting Parties shall continue to expand and intensify such co-operation and exchange of experience in industry, transport, agriculture, animal husbandry, fishery, exploitation of natural resources, the development of power systems and communications and the training of national specialists, as well as in other areas of the economy.

The Parties shall expand trade and shipping between themselves on the basis of the principles of equality, mutual advantage and most-favoured-nation treatment.

Article 9. The High Contracting Parties shall promote the further development of contacts and co-operation between themselves in science, art, literature, education, health, the press, radio, cinematography, television, tourism and sport as well as in other fields.

The Parties shall promote the expansion of co-operation and direct contacts between political and social organizations, enterprises and cultural and scientific institutions so that the peoples of the two countries may become better acquainted with each other's lives, work and achievements.

Article 10. In the interests of strengthening their defence capability, the High Contracting Parties shall continue to develop co-operation in military matters on the basis of appropriate agreements concluded between themselves.

Article 11. Each of the High Contracting Parties declares that it will not enter into any alliances, join any group of States or participate in any actions or measures directed against the other High Contracting Party.

Article 12. The High Contracting Parties declare that their obligations under international treaties currently in force do not conflict with the provisions of this Treaty and undertake not to conclude any international agreements which are not consistent therewith.

Article 13. Any questions which might arise between the High Contracting Parties concerning the interpretation or application of any provision of this Treaty shall be resolved bilaterally in a spirit of friendship, mutual respect and understanding.

Article 14. This Treaty shall be valid for a term of 20 years from the date of its entry into force.

If neither of the High Contracting Parties gives notice of its intention to terminate the Treaty one year prior to the expiry of the above-mentioned term, it shall be extended for successive five-year terms until such time as one of the High Contracting Parties gives written notice of its desire to terminate it one year before the expiry of the current five-year term.

Article 15. This Treaty is subject to ratification and shall enter into force on the date of the exchange of the instruments of ratification, which shall take place at Luanda.

This Treaty has been drafted in duplicate in the Russian and Portuguese languages, both texts being equally authentic.

Done at Moscow on 8 October 1976.

For the Union of Soviet Socialist Republics:

[L. I. BREZHNEV]

For the People's Republic of Angola:

[ANTONIO AGOSTINHO NETO]

4.1403 Treaty of Friendship and Co-operation between the Union of Soviet Socialist Republics and the People's Republic of Mozambique

Alliance Members: Union of Soviet Socialist Republics and Mozambique

Signed On: March 31, 1977, in the city of Maputo (Mozambique). In force until December 25, 1991.

Alliance Type: Entente (Type III)

Source: *United Nations Treaty,* no. 18221.

SUMMARY

Mozambique won its independence from Portugal on June 25, 1975, and established a one-party socialist state. The victory had been the result of nearly a decade of fighting led by the Revolutionary Front for the Liberation of Mozambique (FRELIMO). Wanting to export this revolution, the new government began to aid Zimbabwean guerrillas. This led Rhodesia (present-day Zimbabwe), South Africa, and ex-Portuguese settlers to back a resistance group called the Mozambique National Resistance (MNR, but also known as RENAMO). This 1977 treaty with the Soviet Union opened the door for both economic and military aid from the Soviets, which Mozambique used to put down the South African–backed MNR/RENAMO rebels.

This agreement effectively ended with the collapse of the Soviet Union. The conflict between Mozambique and the RENAMO rebels was resolved in 1992 when the two sides signed a cease-fire. Later that year, the United Nations agreed to send troops to Mozambique to disarm the rebels and oversee a democratic election.

ALLIANCE TEXT

The Union of Soviet Socialist Republics and the People's Republic of Mozambique,

Believing that the relations of friendship and co-operation formed between the Soviet and Mozambican peoples during the difficult years of the people's war for the liberation of Mozambique and consolidated following the creation of the People's Republic of Mozambique are in accordance with the vital interests of both Parties and serve the cause of peace throughout the world;

Determined to support one another in creating more favourable conditions for strengthening the revolutionary socio-economic achievements of the two peoples;

Inspired by the ideals of the struggle against imperialism, colonialism and racism;

Prompted by the aspiration to support the struggle for international peace and security in the interests of the peoples of all countries;

Advocating the unity and co-operation of all progressive forces in the struggle for independence, freedom, peace and social progress;

Reaffirming their loyalty to the purposes and principles of the Charter of the United Nations;

Striving to consolidate the existing relations of friendship and mutually advantageous co-operation between the two States and peoples, which are natural allies;

Have decided to conclude this Treaty of friendship and co-operation and have agreed as follows:

Article 1. The High Contracting Parties solemnly declare their determination to strengthen and deepen the indestructible friendship between the two countries and peoples and to develop all-round co-operation. Both Parties shall co-operate in every way, on the basis of respect for sovereignty, territorial integrity, non-intervention in each other's internal affairs and equal rights, to create more favourable conditions for preserving and extending the socioeconomic achievements of the peoples of the Union of Soviet Socialist Republics and the People's Republic of Mozambique.

Article 2. The High Contracting Parties attach great importance to all-round co-operation with one another and to the exchange of experience in the economic, technical and scientific fields. To these ends, they shall expand and deepen co-operation in the fields of industry, transport and communications, agriculture, fisheries, the exploitation of natural resources, the development of the power industry and in other areas of the economy, and also in the training of national specialists.

Both Parties shall expand trade and navigation on the basis of the principles of equality, mutual benefit and most-favoured-nation treatment.

Article 3. The High Contracting Parties shall promote the development of co-operation, mutual assistance and the exchange of experience in science, culture, art, literature, education, health, the press, radio, the cinema, tourism, sport and in other fields.

The Parties shall promote the expansion of co-operation and direct contacts between political and social organizations, enterprises and cultural and scientific institutions so that the peoples of the two countries may become better acquainted with each other's life, work, experience and achievements.

Article 4. In the interest of strengthening their defence capability, the High Contracting Parties shall continue to develop co-operation in military matters on the basis of appropriate agreements concluded with each other.

Article 5. The Union of Soviet Socialist Republics shall respect the policy of non-alignment conducted by the People's Republic of Mozambique, which is an important factor in the maintenance of international peace and security.

The People's Republic of Mozambique shall respect the policy of peace conducted by the Union of Soviet Socialist Republics, which is aimed at strengthening friendship and co-operation with all peoples.

Article 6. The High Contracting Parties shall continue to struggle for peace throughout the world and to make every effort to deepen the process of relaxing international tension. They shall seek to embody détente in specific forms of mutually beneficial co-operation between States. Both Parties shall make every effort to achieve general and complete disarmament, including nuclear disarmament, under effective international control, the settlement of international disputes by peaceful means and the conclusion of a world treaty on the non-use of force in international relations.

Article 7. The High Contracting Parties shall continue their consistent struggle against the forces of imperialism for the final elimination of colonialism, neo-colonialism, racism and *apartheid*. They shall strive for the full implementation of the United Nations Declaration on the granting of independence to colonial countries and peoples.

The Parties shall co-operate with one another and with other peace-loving States in supporting the just struggle of the peoples for freedom, independence, sovereignty and social progress.

Article 8. The High Contracting Parties, expressing their deep interest in ensuring peace and international security and attaching great importance to co-operation with one another in the international arena to achieve those aims, shall regularly exchange views in a spirit of mutual understanding on important international questions. Such consultations and exchanges of views shall also include questions of a political, economic and cultural nature and other questions concerning bilateral relations.

Such consultations and exchanges of views shall take place at various levels, *inter alia* through meetings between leading statesmen of the two Parties, in the course of visits by official delegations and special representatives, and through the diplomatic channel.

Article 9. In the event of situations arising which constitute a threat to peace or a breach of the peace, the High Contracting Parties shall immediately contact each other for the purpose of co-ordinating their positions in the interests of removing the said threat or of restoring peace.

Article 10. Each of the High Contracting Parties solemnly declares that it will not enter into any military or other alliances, join any groups of States or participate in any actions or measures directed against the other High Contracting Party.

Article 11. The High Contracting Parties declare that their obligations under international treaties currently in force do not conflict with the provisions of this Treaty, and undertake not to conclude any international agreements which are inconsistent therewith.

Article 12. Questions which may arise between the High Contracting Parties concerning the interpretation or application of any of the provisions of this Treaty shall be resolved bilaterally in a spirit of friendship, mutual understanding and respect.

Article 13. This Treaty shall be valid for a period of 20 years from the date of its entry into force.

If neither of the High Contracting Parties gives notice of its desire to terminate the Treaty one year before the expiry of the above-mentioned period, it shall remain in force for successive five-year periods until such time as one of the High Contracting Parties gives written notice of its intention to terminate it one year before the expiry of the current five-year period.

Article 14. This Treaty is subject to ratification and shall enter into force on the date of the exchange of the instruments of ratification, which shall take place in Moscow.

This Treaty has been drawn up in duplicate, each in the Russian and Portuguese languages, both texts being equally authentic.

Done at Maputo on 31 March 1977.

For the Union of Soviet Socialist Republics:

[N. V. PODGORNY]

Chairman of the Presidium of the Supreme Soviet of the Union of Socialist Republics

For the People's Republic of Mozambique:

[SAMORA M. MACHEL]

President of the People's Republic of Mozambique

4.1404 Non-Aggression and Defense Assistance Agreement between the States of the West African Economic Community (CEAO) and Togo

Alliance Members: Burkina Faso, Côte d'Ivoire, Mali, Mauritania, Niger, Senegal, and Togo; Benin, Cape Verde, Gambia, Ghana, Guinea, Guinea-Bissau, Liberia, Nigeria, and Sierra Leone joined on April 22, 1978.
Signed On: June 9, 1977, in the city of Abidjan (Côte d'Ivoire). In force until May 29, 1981.
Alliance Type: Non-Aggression Pact (Type II)

Source: *United Nations Treaty,* no. 22866.
Economic Community of West African States (ECOWAS), www.ecowas.int.

SUMMARY

The West African Economic Community (CEAO) was formed in 1974 to create a free-trade zone that encouraged trade among its members. In June of 1977, the West African nation of Togo met with the member states of the CEAO—Côte d'Ivoire, Mali, Mauritania, Niger, Senegal, and Upper Volta—to sign a pact of non-aggression and mutual assistance.

In 1981, this pact was finalized when member states met to discuss the terms of their agreement for the third and final time. The final meeting included an agreement on the specific legal and financial aspects to the protocol and also a defense pact, which effectively replaced this treaty.

ALLIANCE TEXT

Preamble

The Governments of the States members of CEAO and Togo:

Considering the ties of friendship and co-operation existing between their countries;

Conscious of their responsibilities for maintaining peace in accordance with the principles of the Charter of the United Nations and the Charter of OAU;

Considering the fact that they belong to the same geographical region;

Aware of the serious threats of aggression that increasingly menace the African continent in general and their countries in particular as a result of foreign intervention;

Considering the fact that while the external defence of their States is the sovereign responsibility of each of them, that defence would nevertheless be made more effective by pooling their respective resources;

Desiring to establish the methods of their co-operation in matters of defence on the basis of equality, respect and mutual interest;

Have agreed as follows:

Article 1. The Governments of the countries that are signatories to this Agreement undertake not to use force to settle differences between them. They also undertake to provide mutual aid and assistance for their defence against any aggression.

General defence problems shall be dealt with at the level of Chiefs of State and Heads of Government, who shall meet at least once a year, in each member country in turn.

A ministerial council shall be responsible for drawing up defence measures, which shall be submitted to the Conference of Chiefs of State and Heads of Government for approval, and implementing them.

Article 2. A permanent Secretariat shall be established with headquarters in Abidjan.

It shall be responsible for the administration and follow-up of decisions as well as for the preparation and management of the Secretariat budget.

The Secretary-General, who shall be appointed by the Conference for a three-year term, shall have no power of decision and take no initiative on questions outside his competence.

Article 3. In the event of a threat or of aggression, the Chiefs of State and Heads of Government shall decide to meet in conference.

The meeting shall be preceded by the convening of a ministerial council to consider the situation, express an opinion as to the advisability of military action and, if necessary, to prepare a study on the strategy to be adopted and the means of intervention to be employed.

Article 4. The Ministerial Council shall include the chiefs of staff of the armies of the member countries or their representatives.

It shall determine the manner in which each State shall participate in any joint action.

Upon completion of each mission, the Council shall meet and draw up a report for submission to the Chiefs of State and Heads of Government.

It shall submit the Permanent Secretariat's budget to the Conference.

Article 5. The only official appointed by the Conference of the Chiefs of State and Heads of Government, on the proposal of the Council of Ministers, shall be responsible for implementing the measures decided upon. He shall dispose of all the resources decided by the Conference.

He shall report to the Ministerial Council on the progress of his mission.

Once an action is under way, any further requests for resources shall be submitted to the Ministerial Council for approval.

Article 6. Commitments under this Agreement may not be interpreted as affecting defence conventions or agreements concluded by either party with third States.

Article 7. Non-member States wishing to become party to the Agreement must submit a request to that effect to the Permanent Secretariat, which shall inform all member States.

The request shall be approved by the Conference of Chiefs of State and Heads of Government and the accession shall become effective from the date on which the Secretariat amends the list of States parties.

Article 8. This Agreement shall enter into force as soon as it is ratified by the seven signatory States.

Any one of the Contracting Parties may denounce the Agreement at any time by giving one year's notice of its intention to do so.

Abidjan, 9 June 1977
For the Republic of the Ivory Coast:
[Signed]
FÉLIX HOUPHOËT-BOIGNY
President of the Republic
For the Republic of the Upper Volta:
[Signed]
EL HADJ ABOUBACAR SANGOULÉ LAMIZANA
President of the Republic
For the Republic of Mali:
[Signed]
H. E. MOUSSA TRAORÉ
President of the Military Committee for National Liberation
Head of State
For the Islamic Republic of Mauritania:
[Signed]
MOKTAR OULD DADDAH
President of the Republic
For the Republic of the Niger:
[Signed]
SEYNI KOUNTCHE
President of the Supreme Military Council
Head of State
For the Republic of Senegal:
[Signed]
LÉOPOLD SÉDAR SENGHOR
President of the Republic
For the Republic of Togo:
[Signed]
GNASSINGBÉ EYADEMA
President of the Republic

4.1405 Treaty of Friendship and Co-operation between the Union of Soviet Socialist Republics and the Socialist Republic of Viet Nam

Alliance Members: Union of Soviet Socialist Republics and Vietnam
Signed On: November 3, 1978, in the city of Moscow. In force until December 25, 1991.
Alliance Type: Entente (Type III)

Source: *United Nations Treaty*, no. 17968.

SUMMARY

Relations between the USSR and the Democratic Republic of Vietnam began in 1950, and within five years, Ho Chi Minh visited Moscow. During the 1960s, the Soviet Union provided small amounts of military assistance to Vietnam. After South Vietnam fell to the North, the government of Vietnam attempted to maintain normal relations with both China and Russia. In 1978, however, increasing border tensions led China to cut its aid, prompting Vietnam to turn to Russia for continued assistance.

With this alliance the Vietnamese offered to the Soviets the use of their naval and air bases—including bases at Cam Ranh Bay, Haiphong Port, and Da Nang. In exchange for use of the military bases, the Soviets supported Vietnam with aid and military equipment that Vietnam then used in its invasion of Cambodia, despite the warnings of the Chinese. China responded to the invasion with its own punishing offensive against the Vietnamese, and a tense truce followed.

This alliance was essential for the Vietnamese military and economy. By 1979, Soviet military aid to Vietnam was over $1 billion annually, increasing to $1.7 billion annually between 1982 and 1985. The Soviets also supplied 70 percent of Vietnam's grain imports and 90 percent of its iron, steel, cotton, and petroleum imports during the 1980s.

ALLIANCE TEXT

The Union of Soviet Socialist Republics and the Socialist Republic of Viet Nam,

Considering their existing close fraternal relations of all-round collaboration, unshakeable friendship and solidarity based on the principles of Marxism-Leninism and socialist internationalism,

Being firmly convinced that the strengthening of the solidarity and friendship between the Union of Soviet Socialist Republics and the Socialist Republic of Viet Nam by every possible means is in accord with the vital interests of the peoples of the two States and serves the cause of the further strengthening of the fraternal solidarity and unity of the countries of the socialist community,

Guided by the principles and purposes of socialist foreign policy and by the desire to establish the most propitious international conditions for building socialism and communism,

Reaffirming that the two Parties consider it their international duty to assist each other in strengthening and defending the socialist achievements won at the cost of heroic efforts and the selfless toil of their peoples,

Resolutely advocating the solidarity of all forces struggling for peace, national independence, democracy and social progress,

Declaring their firm resolve to promote the strengthening of peace in Asia and throughout the world and to make their contribution to the development of good relations and mutually advantageous co-operation between States having different social systems,

Desiring to continue the development and improvement of all-round collaboration between the two countries,

Attaching great importance to the further development and strengthening of the basis in treaty law of their mutual relations,

Acting in accordance with the purposes and principles of the Charter of the United Nations,

Have decided to conclude this Treaty of friendship and co-operation and have agreed as follows:

Article 1. The High Contracting Parties shall, in accordance with the principles of socialist internationalism, continue to strengthen their relations of unshakeable friendship, solidarity and fraternal mutual assistance. They shall steadily develop their political relations, intensify their all-round collaboration and support each other in every way possible on the basis of mutual respect for State sovereignty and independence, equal rights and non-intervention in each other's internal affairs.

Article 2. The High Contracting Parties shall make joint efforts to strengthen and broaden mutually advantageous economic, scientific and technical collaboration with a view to hastening the building of socialism and communism and achieving a steady increase in the material and cultural level of living of the peoples of the two countries. The Parties shall pursue the long-term co-ordination of their national economic plans, adopt co-ordinated long-term measures to develop the most important sectors of the economy as well as science and technology, and exchange knowledge and experience acquired in building socialism and communism.

Article 3. The High Contracting Parties shall promote co-operation between organs of State power and social organizations and develop broad contacts in science and culture, education, literature and art, the press, radio and television, health, environmental protection, tourism, physical culture and sport as well as in other fields. They shall stimulate the development of contacts between the workers of the two countries.

Article 4. The High Contracting Parties shall strive consistently and in every way possible for the further strengthening of fraternal relations, unity and solidarity between the socialist countries on the basis of Marxism-Leninism and socialist internationalism.

They shall do everything in their power to strengthen the world socialist system and shall actively contribute to the development and safeguarding of socialist achievements.

Article 5. The High Contracting Parties shall continue to make every effort to defend international peace and the security of peoples, shall actively oppose all the stratagems and intrigues of imperialism and the forces of reaction, shall support the just struggle for the final eradication of colonialism and racism in all their forms and manifestations, shall give support to the struggle of the non-aligned countries, the struggle of the peoples of Asia, Africa and Latin America against imperialism, colonialism and neo-colonialism and for the strengthening of independence, in defence of sovereignty, for the right to dispose freely of their own natural resources and for the establishment of new international economic relations free of inequality, diktat and exploitation, and shall support the aspiration of the peoples of South-East Asia for peace, independence and collaboration among themselves.

They shall steadfastly promote the development of relations between countries having different social systems on the basis of the principle of peaceful co-existence, the broadening and intensification of the process of détente in international relations and the final elimination of aggression and expansionist wars from the life of peoples, in the name of peace, national independence, democracy and socialism.

Article 6. The High Contracting Parties shall consult each other on all important international questions affecting the interests of the two countries. In the event of an attack or the threat of an attack against one of the Parties, the High Contracting Parties shall immediately hold mutual consultations with a view to eliminating that threat and taking appropriate effective measures for the maintenance of peace and the security of their countries.

Article 7. This Treaty shall not affect the rights and obligations of the Parties in accordance with existing bilateral and multilateral agreements concluded with their participation and is not directed against any third country.

Article 8. This Treaty is subject to ratification and shall enter into force on the date of the exchange of the instruments of ratification, which shall take place at Hanoi as soon as possible.

Article 9. This Treaty is concluded for a term of 25 years and shall be automatically extended for successive 10-year terms if neither of the High Contracting Parties states its desire to terminate it by giving notice to that effect 12 months before the expiry of the current term.

Done at Moscow on 3 November 1978 in duplicate in the Russian and the Vietnamese languages, both texts being equally authentic.

For the Union of Soviet Socialist Republics:

[L. I. BREZHNEV]

[A. N. KOSYGIN]

For the Socialist Republic of Viet Nam:

[LE DUAN]

[PHAM VAN DONG]

4.1406 Treaty of Friendship and Co-operation between the Union of Soviet Socialist Republics and Socialist Ethiopia

Alliance Members: Union of Soviet Socialist Republics and Ethiopia
Signed On: November 20, 1978, in the city of Moscow. In force until December 25, 1991.
Alliance Type: Entente (Type III)

Source: *United Nations Treaty*, no. 17975.

SUMMARY

In 1974, Ethiopian leader Haile Selassie was overthrown, and Lt. Col. Mengistu Haile Mariam who replaced him installed what he called "Ethiopian Socialism." With Ethiopia struggling domestically, the Soviets moved to provide aid and establish ties as a way of increasing their influence within Africa. Although the USSR had strong relations with Ethiopia's enemy, Somalia, the Soviets tried to court both nations with promises of aid and support, and by 1977, Ethiopia signed a treaty with the Soviets outlining the "foundation for relationships and cooperation."

The Soviets immediately began sending small amounts of arms to Ethiopia and providing limited military training. This added to the uncertainty in Somalia, which launched an attack on Ethiopia in the hopes of capturing territory before the Soviet Union had effectively armed Ethiopia. Ethiopian forces beat back the Somali attack, however, and Somalia's leader, Siad Barre, expelled all Soviet advisers and diplomats. Barre's reaction prompted the Soviets to send Ethiopia an additional $1 billion in weapons.

On November 20, 1978, Ethiopian leader Mengistu Haile Mariam signed a twenty-year treaty of friendship with President Leonid Brezhnev of the Soviet Union. The treaty outlined military cooperation between the two nations and mirrored the USSR's other friendship treaties with African nations. With this treaty, the Soviets had effectively switched their alliance with Somalia for a stronger partnership with Ethiopia, and following ratification, the Soviets increased again their level of military aid to Ethiopia, which continued to fight Somali guerrillas in the Ogaden desert and secessionist forces in Eritrea.

By 1990, Ethiopia and President Mariam were still struggling with famine as well as war with both the Tigray People's Liberation Front (TPLF) and the Eritrean People's Liberation Front (EPLF). The Soviet Union was still willing to continue the alliance but also wanted a diplomatic solution instead of simply continuing aid. In 1991, political instability forced Mariam to resign. The Soviet Union collapsed later that year, effectively ending the treaty.

ALLIANCE TEXT

The Union of Soviet Socialist Republics and Socialist Ethiopia,

Believing that the further development and strengthening of the relations of friendship and all-round co-operation which have come into being between them meet the basic national interests of the peoples of the two countries and serve the cause of strengthening peace and security throughout the world;

Desirous of making their corresponding contribution to the development of peaceful relations between States and fruitful international co-operation;

Determined to advance social and economic achievements of the Soviet and Ethiopian peoples;

Inspired by the ideals of consistent struggle against imperialism and expansionism as well as against colonialism, racism, *apartheid* in all their forms and manifestations and being guided by the desire to render support to the peoples fighting for their freedom, independence and social progress;

Reaffirming their adherence to the principles and purposes of the United Nations Charter, including the principles of respect for sovereignty, territorial integrity and non-interference in the internal affairs of each other;

Bearing in mind the Declaration on Basic Principles of Friendly Relations and Co-operation between the Union of Soviet Socialist Republics and Socialist Ethiopia of May 6, 1977, and motivated by the desire to consolidate still further these relations of friendship and mutually beneficial co-operation between the two States and peoples;

Have agreed as follows:

Article 1. The High Contracting Parties shall develop and deepen the relations of unbreakable friendship and comprehensive co-operation in the political, economic, trade, scientific and technical, cultural and other fields on the basis of equality, non-interference in internal affairs, respect for sovereignty, territorial integrity and inviolability of borders.

Article 2. The High Contracting Parties declare that they shall closely cooperate in every way in ensuring the conditions for preserving and further developing socio-economic achievements of their peoples and respect for the sovereignty of each of them over all their natural resources.

Article 3. The Union of Soviet Socialist Republics respects the policy pursued by Socialist Ethiopia based on the purposes and principles of the Charter of the Organization of African Unity and the nonaligned movement which constitutes an important factor in the development of international co-operation and peaceful coexistence.

Socialist Ethiopia respects the peace-loving foreign policy pursued by the Union of Soviet Socialist Republics, which is aimed at strengthening friendship and cooperation with all countries and peoples.

Article 4. The High Contracting Parties shall continue to make every effort to safeguard international peace and the security of peoples, deepen the process of international détente, extend it to all areas of the world, lend it concrete forms of mutually beneficial co-operation between States, and settle international controversial issues by peaceful means without prejudice to the legitimate rights of States to defend themselves, individually or collectively, against aggression, in accordance with the Charter of the United Nations. They shall actively contribute to the cause of general and complete disarmament, including nuclear disarmament, under effective international control.

Article 5. The High Contracting Parties shall continue actively to work for the complete elimination of colonialism and neo-colonialism, racism and *apartheid,* and the full implementation of the United Nations Declaration on the Granting of Independence to Colonial Countries and Peoples.

Article 6. The High Contracting Parties shall consult each other on important international questions directly involving the interests of the two countries.

Article 7. In the event of situations which constitute a threat to or a breach of international peace, the High Contracting Parties shall endeavour to immediately contact each other with a view to co-ordinating their positions in the interests of removing the threat that has arisen or restoring peace.

Article 8. The High Contracting Parties shall, attaching great importance to economic, trade and scientific co-operation between them, expand and deepen cooperation and the exchange of experiences in these fields. The Parties shall expand all-round co-operation between them on the basis of the

principles of equality, mutual benefit and most-favoured-nation treatment.

Article 9. The High Contracting Parties shall promote the further development of ties and co-operation between them in the fields of science, culture, art, literature, education, health, press, radio, cinema, television, tourism, sports and in other fields for the purpose of a more profound mutual acquaintance with the life, work, experience and achievements of the peoples of the two countries.

Article 10. In the interests of ensuring the defense capability of the High Contracting Parties, they shall continue to co-operate in the military field.

Article 11. Each of the High Contracting Parties declares that it shall not enter into any alliance or participate in any alignment of States or in actions or measures directed against the other High Contracting Party.

Article 12. The High Contracting Parties declare that the provisions of the present Treaty are not inconsistent with their commitments under international treaties in force and undertake not to enter into any international agreements incompatible with this Treaty.

Article 13. Any questions that may arise between the High Contracting Parties with regard to the interpretation or application of any provision of this Treaty shall be resolved on a bilateral basis in the spirit of friendship, mutual respect and understanding.

Article 14. This Treaty shall remain in force for twenty years after its entry into force.

Unless either High Contracting Party declares, one year prior to the expiration of the said period, its desire to terminate the Treaty, it shall remain in force for the successive periods of five years until one of the High Contracting Parties gives, one year prior to the expiration of the current five-year period, a written notice of its intention to terminate it.

Article 15. This Treaty shall be subject to ratification and shall enter into force on the date of the exchange of instruments of ratification, which shall take place in Addis Ababa as early as possible.

This Treaty is made in two copies, each in the Russian, Amharic and English languages, all the texts being equally authentic.

Done in Moscow on November 20, 1978.

For the Union of Soviet Socialist Republics:

[Signed] L. I. Brezhnev

For Socialist Ethiopia:

[Signed] Mengistu Haile Mariam

4.1407 Defense and Non-Aggression Pact between Guinea and Liberia

Alliance Members: Guinea and Liberia
Signed On: January 23, 1979, in the city of Monrovia (Liberia). In force until September 22, 2000.

Alliance Type: Defense Pact (Type I)

Source: *Keesing's Record of World Events,* January 1979.

SUMMARY

On January 23, 1979, Guinea and Liberia signed this treaty dedicated to mutual security against internal aggression. The alliance would immediately prove useful for the Liberian government because soon after the alliance was signed a group calling itself the Progressive Alliance of Liberia (PAL) organized and attempted a coup d'état in response to the abysmally poor economic conditions in Liberia. Guinea responded to the internal strife by sending one hundred troops to help secure the capital city during fierce riots.

As members of the Economic Community of West African States (ECOWAS), the two nations continued to cooperate during the 1980s on both economic and security issues. For example, in 1986, Liberia, Sierra Leone, and Guinea signed a treaty of non-aggression and cooperation on security called the Mano River Union (MRU).

This alliance and the Mano River Union were dissolved during the early 1990s in response to cross-border strife. By September 2000, Guinea began raiding Liberian border villages in an attempt to crack down on rebels who had been launching attacks into Guinea. The government in Guinea declared that Liberia was supporting the rebels, while Liberia declared Guinea's attacks were an act of war.

DESCRIPTION OF TERMS

This bilateral non-aggression and mutual defense treaty sought to promote principles of non-interference, respect for territorial integrity, and peaceful settlements to disputes within both countries. The two nations also expressed their desire to promote regional cooperation and economic security within West Africa.

4.1408 Treaty of Friendship and Co-operation between the German Democratic Republic and Angola

Alliance Members: German Democratic Republic and Angola
Signed On: February 19, 1979, in the city of Luanda (Angola). In force until November 7, 1989.
Alliance Type: Non-Aggression Pact (Type II)

Source: *Keesing's Record of World Events,* February 1979.

SUMMARY

This non-aggression agreement was part of a larger effort by the East German government to establish ties with sympathetic countries in Africa. The treaty called for non-aggression, but the larger relationship established with the alliance included East German military and economic aid as well as the stationing of advisers in Angola to conduct military training.

The alliance effectively ended with the dissolution of the East German government, one year before German unification.

DESCRIPTION OF TERMS

The allied parties pledged close friendship and co-operation. Both countries also agreed to a policy of non-aggression.

Neither country would sign an alliance that undermined the other party nor to take any step or action that would be directed against the other party.

4.1409 Treaty of Friendship and Co-Operation between the German Democratic Republic and Mozambique

Alliance Members: German Democratic Republic and Mozambique
Signed On: February 24, 1979, in the city of Maputo (Mozambique). In force until November 7, 1989.
Alliance Type: Defense Pact (Type I)

Source: *United Nations Treaty,* no. 18474.

SUMMARY

On September 7, 1974, the Mozambique resistance movement (Frelimo) and the Portuguese government signed an official independence agreement. This settlement brought an end to the civil war that had lasted for more than ten years. The Marxist group Frelimo took control of the government and gave power to Samora Machel.

The new government quickly established ties with the Soviet Union and its allies, formalizing this agreement with East Germany in 1979. Following the treaty, in October of 1980, a high-level military delegation traveled to East Germany to establish cooperation on internal and external security measures. However, over the course of their alliance, East Germany provided little military aid or weaponry for Mozambique and instead concentrated on providing Frelimo with technical training and support, especially for the secret police.

ALLIANCE TEXT

The German Democratic Republic and the People's Republic of Mozambique,

Acknowledging their parties' and their peoples' fraternal friendship and cooperation established already during the armed national liberation struggle of the people of Mozambique and based on Marxism-Leninism and proletarian internationalism,

Firmly determined to contribute towards the creation of favourable conditions for continuing the revolutionary process in the world,

Desiring to further promote the fraternal friendship and cooperation between the German Democratic Republic and the People's Republic of Mozambique and thus to contribute towards strengthening the natural anti-imperialist alliance between the socialist States and the national liberation movements and towards further uniting all forces fighting for peace, democracy and social progress,

Inspired by the ideals of the struggle against imperialism, colonialism, neocolonialism, racism and *apartheid,*

Determined to contribute towards strengthening the peace and security of all peoples,

Resolved to further develop the social and economic achievements of the two States and to assist each other in this endeavour,

469

Reaffirming their loyalty to the purposes and principles of the Charter of the United Nations,

Have resolved to sign this Treaty of Friendship and Co-operation, and have agreed as follows:

Article 1. The High Contracting Parties solemnly manifest their resolve to strengthen and broaden the friendship between the two States and peoples and to co-operate in the interest of the further development of the socio-economic achievements of their peoples. They will further develop their political, economic, scientific-technical and cultural relations and, in doing so, be guided by the principles of respect for sovereignty, territorial integrity, non-interference in internal affairs and equality.

They will enhance co-operation and direct contacts between the political and social organizations of the two States.

Article 2. The High Contracting Parties will make every effort to expand mutually advantageous economic co-operation and to intensify exchanges of experience in the fields of industry, agriculture, fishery, transport and telecommunications, in the training of personnel and in other areas.

Both States will further develop their co-operation in trade on the basis of the principles of equality, mutual advantage and most-favoured nation treatment.

Article 3. The High Contracting Parties will develop their co-operation in science and technology, art, literature, education, public health, the press, radio broadcasting, the cinema, sports and other fields with a view to promoting mutual acquaintance with the life and the achievements of the two peoples.

Article 4. The German Democratic Republic and the People's Republic of Mozambique pursue a policy of peace, aimed at strengthening friendship and cooperation among all peoples.

The German Democratic Republic appreciates the peace policy of the People's Republic of Mozambique as an essential factor for the maintenance of world peace and for détente and international security and pays tribute to the policy of non-alignment of the People's Republic of Mozambique. The People's Republic of Mozambique appreciates the peace policy of the German Democratic Republic as an essential factor for the maintenance of world peace and for détente and international security.

Article 5. In the interest of strengthening their defence capabilities, the High Contracting Parties will fix the modalities of their co-operation in the military field by bilateral agreements.

Article 6. The High Contracting Parties will continue their struggle for peace in the world and for the strengthening of international security. They undertake efforts to deepen international détente with a view to extending it to all regions and making it irreversible. In order to banish war forever from the life of the peoples, they work towards achieving general and complete disarmament, including nuclear disarmament, under effective international control.

Article 7. The High Contracting Parties advocate the establishment of a new international economic order on an equal and democratic basis and free from imperialist exploitation. They subscribe to the sovereign right of peoples to exercise control over their natural resources.

Article 8. The High Contracting Parties will continue, as before, to fight consistently against the forces of imperialism and for the final elimination of fascism, colonialism, neo-colonialism, racism and *apartheid*. They work for the full implementation of the United Nations Declaration on the Granting of Independence to Colonial Countries and Peoples. They subscribe to the right of peoples to freely choose their road of development.

Both States support the just struggle of the peoples for freedom, national independence and social progress and will undertake joint efforts and co-operate with all other peace-loving States to attain these ends.

Article 9. With a view to enhancing the intensity and extending the scope of their co-operation, harmonizing foreign policy actions and discussing international issues of mutual interest, the High Contracting Parties will exchange information and views and conduct consultations at various levels.

Article 10. Should there arise a situation threatening or violating the peace, the High Contracting Parties will contact each other without delay in order to harmonize their positions regarding the removal of such dangerous situation or the restoration of peace.

Article 11. Each of the High Contracting Parties solemnly declares that it will not enter into any alliance, or participate in any action, directed against the other High Contracting Party.

Article 12. The High Contracting Parties declare that their obligations under this Treaty are not contradictory to previous international agreements to which either of them is a party, and they undertake not to enter into any international accord inconsistent with this Treaty.

Article 13. Any question that may arise between the High Contracting Parties concerning the interpretation or application of any provision of this Treaty shall be resolved by direct bilateral negotiation in a spirit of friendship, mutual respect and mutual understanding.

Article 14. This Treaty is subject to ratification. It shall enter into force on the date of exchange of the instruments of ratification which shall take place in Berlin, capital of the German Democratic Republic.

Article 15. This Treaty is concluded for a period of twenty years and shall thereafter be automatically extended by further periods of five years unless one of the High Contracting Parties expresses the desire in writing, twelve months before the validity expires, to terminate it.

Done in Maputo on 24 February 1979 in two copies in the German and Portuguese languages, both texts being equally authentic.

For the German Democratic Republic:

[Signed]

ERICH HONECKER

General Secretary of the Central Committee of the Socialist Unity Party of Germany and Chairman of the Council of State of the German Democratic Republic

For the People's Republic of Mozambique:
[Signed]
SAMORA MOISÉS MACHEL
President of the FRELIMO Party and President of the People's Republic of Mozambique

4.1410 Defense Pact between Angola and Zambia

Alliance Members: Angola and Zambia
Signed On: May 10, 1979, in the city of Ndola (Zambia). In force until March 15, 1999.
Alliance Type: Defense Pact (Type I)

Source: *Keesing's Record of World Events,* May 1979.

SUMMARY

As Angola was becoming an independent nation, three competing movements formed, each aiming to determine the direction of the country. The first was the People's Movement for the Liberation of Angola (MPLA). The other two groups, the National Front for the Liberation of Angola (FNLA) and the National Union for the Total Independence of Angola (UNITA), formed later—the FNLA had evolved from an earlier group by the late 1950s and UNITA formed in 1966. Following independence from Portugal in 1975, the MPLA fought against the FNLA and UNITA. After years of fighting, the MPLA finally took power in 1975 under the socialist leadership of Agostinho Neto. In response, the FNLA and UNITA proclaimed their own nation of the Democratic Republic of Angola based in Huambo. For many years UNITA mounted a civil war against Angola with the aid and support of South Africa.

Zambia, another former Portuguese colony, also had trouble with insurgents who were backed principally by South Africa. As a result of their converging security interests, Zambia and Angola formed this alliance to fight the cross-border insurgency movements.

On March 15, 1999, relations between Angola and Zambia soured as Angola declared itself in possession of evidence that Zambia was supporting UNITA rebels. Zambia responded by accusing Angola of engaging UNITA rebels on Zambian soil. The alliance ended, and their conflict became the flash point for an increasing number of border outbursts. In recent years, the two nations have managed to slowly improve relations to the point of stability.

DESCRIPTION OF TERMS

The agreement signed by President Kenneth Kaunda of Zambia and President Agostinho Neto of Angola proclaimed that the two nations would treat an act of aggression against the other country as an act of aggression against themselves. They also agreed to set up a joint security force to respond to any threats from South Africa or Rhodesia.

4.1411 Non-Aggression Pact among Angola, Zaire, and Zambia

Alliance Members: Angola, Zaire, and Zambia
Signed On: October 12, 1979, in the city of Ndola (Zambia). In force until December 1, 1996.
Alliance Type: Non-Aggression Pact (Type II)

Source: *Keesing's Record of World Events,* October 1979.

SUMMARY

This treaty was an attempt by the fledgling African governments to put an end to the many insurgencies targeting their regimes. These groups included the African rebel organizations of the FNLA (National Front for the Liberation of Angola), UNITA (National Union for the Total Independence of Angola), and the FNLC (Front for the National Liberation of the Congo), and also the Cuban troops that had invaded Zaire from Angola during 1978 and 1979.

The agreement held together, for the most part, until Angola began actively aiding groups targeting the Democratic Republic of the Congo (formerly Zaire). The invasion of the DRC by most of southern Africa in the First Congo War soon followed.

DESCRIPTION OF TERMS

The allies agreed that their territories would not be used as staging grounds for subversive activities or any attack directed against the other parties to the agreement. Also signed on the same day was a commitment to strengthen economic cooperation between the signatories, especially in the areas of transportation and communication.

4.1412 Treaty of Friendship and Co-operation between the Union of Soviet Socialist Republics and the People's Democratic Republic of Yemen

Alliance Members: Union of Soviet Socialist Republics and the People's Democratic Republic of Yemen
Signed On: October 25, 1979, in the city of Moscow. In force until December 25, 1991.
Alliance Type: Entente (Type III)

Source: *United Nations Treaty,* no. 18907.

SUMMARY

In 1979 South Yemen signed a twenty-year treaty of friendship and cooperation with the USSR that allowed the Soviets to station troops within the country, specifically in Aden and nearby Socotra Island. This agreement was coupled with Soviet attempts to woo North Yemen (the Yemen Arab Republic) with military aid shipments that began arriving during the same month as the signing of this treaty. North Yemen demonstrated its gratitude to the Soviets by refusing to join other Arab states in a United Nations vote condemning the Soviet invasion of Afghanistan.

Soviet interest in both North and South Yemen made sense given Yemen's proximity to the oil-rich territories on the Saudi peninsula and its potentially controlling position on the Gulf of Aden and the entrance to the Red Sea. But these actions were met with stiff resistance and ultimatums by the Saudis, who threatened to cut aid to North Yemen unless it reversed course and repudiated its closer ties to the Soviet Union. North Yemen eventually relented, but the strategic pull between East and West continued to roil Yemeni territory, keeping North and South Yemen divided. The South's alliance with the Soviet Union ended with the unification of Yemen in 1990.

ALLIANCE TEXT

The Union of Soviet Socialist Republics and the People's Democratic Republic of Yemen,

Considering that the further development and consolidation of the relations of friendship and all-round co-operation existing between them are in accordance with the fundamental national interests of the peoples of the two States and serve the cause of strengthening peace and security throughout the world,

Desiring to contribute in every possible way to the development of peaceful relations among States and of fruitful international co-operation,

Determined to develop the social and economic achievements of the peoples of the USSR and the People's Democratic Republic of Yemen, and to support the unity and co-operation of all forces struggling for peace and national independence, democracy and social progress,

Inspired by the ideals of the struggle against imperialism, colonialism and racism in all their forms and manifestations,

Attaching particular importance to co-operation between the two countries in the struggle for a just and durable peace in the Middle East,

Reaffirming their loyalty to the purposes and principles of the Charter of the United Nations, including the principles of respect for sovereignty, territorial integrity and non-intervention in internal affairs,

Desiring to develop and strengthen the existing relations of friendship and cooperation between the two countries,

Have agreed as follows:

Article 1. The High Contracting Parties solemnly declare their determination to strengthen the indestructible friendship between the two countries, and steadily to develop political relations and all-round co-operation on the basis of equal rights, respect for national sovereignty, territorial integrity and non-intervention in each other's internal affairs.

Article 2. The High Contracting Parties shall co-operate closely and in every way possible to ensure conditions favourable to the maintenance and further development of the socio-economic achievements of their peoples and to respect for the sovereignty of each of them over all their natural resources.

Article 3. The High Contracting Parties shall strive to consolidate and expand the mutually advantageous economic, scientific and technical co-operation between them. To this end, the Parties shall develop and extend co-operation in industry, agri-culture, fishing, utilization of natural resources, economic development planning and other areas of the economy, as well as in the training of national specialists. The Parties shall expand trade and shipping on the basis of the principles of equality, mutual advantage and most-favoured-nation treatment.

Article 4. The High Contracting Parties shall promote the development of cooperation and exchange of experience in science, culture, art, literature, education, health, the press, radio, television, the cinema, tourism, sport and other fields.

The Parties shall promote the development of contacts and co-operation between State bodies, trade unions and other social organizations, as well as the expansion of direct links between enterprises and cultural and scientific institutions, so that the peoples of the two countries may become better acquainted with each other's life, work, experience and achievements. The Parties shall encourage the development of contacts between workers of the two countries.

Article 5. The High Contracting Parties shall continue to develop cooperation in military matters on the basis of appropriate agreements concluded between them for the purpose of strengthening their defence capability.

Article 6. The Union of Soviet Socialist Republics respects the non-aligned policy of the People's Democratic Republic of Yemen, which is an important factor in the development of international co-operation and peaceful coexistence.

The People's Democratic Republic of Yemen respects the peace-loving foreign policy of the Union of Soviet Socialist Republics, which is designed to strengthen friendship and co-operation with all countries and peoples.

Article 7. The High Contracting Parties shall, now and in the future, make all efforts to safeguard international peace and the security of peoples, to further the reduction of international tension, extend that reduction to all regions of the world and embody it in specific forms of mutually advantageous co-operation among States, to settle international disputes by peaceful means, to transform the principle of non-use of force into an effective law of international conduct, and to eliminate any manifestations of a policy of hegemonism and aggression from the practice of international relations. The Parties shall actively further the cause of general and complete disarmament, including nuclear disarmament, under effective international control.

Article 8. The High Contracting Parties shall continue their active struggle against the intrigues of imperialism and in support of the final elimination of colonialism and racism in all their forms and manifestations.

The Parties shall co-operate with each other and with other peace-loving States in support of the just struggle of peoples for their freedom, independence, sovereignty and social progress.

Article 9. The High Contracting Parties shall do everything within their power to ensure a lasting and just peace in the Middle East and to achieve, with that end in view, a comprehensive settlement of the Middle East question.

Article 10. The High Contracting Parties shall further the development of cooperation among Asian States, the establishment among them of relations based on peace, good-neighbourliness and mutual trust, and the creation of an effective system of security in Asia based on the joint efforts of all States of that continent.

Article 11. The High Contracting Parties shall consult together regarding important international questions which directly affect the interests of the two States.

In the event of situations arising which constitute a threat to the peace or a breach of international peace, the Parties shall seek urgent and immediate contact with each other for the purpose of co-ordinating their positions in the interests of removing the said threat or of restoring peace.

Article 12. Each of the High Contracting Parties solemnly declares that it will not enter into any military or other alliances, join any group of States or participate in any actions or measures directed against the other High Contracting Party.

Article 13. The High Contracting Parties declare that the provisions of this Treaty do not conflict with their obligations under international treaties currently in force, and undertake not to conclude any international agreements which are not consistent with this Treaty.

Article 14. Any differences that may emerge between the High Contracting Parties regarding the interpretation or application of any provision of this Treaty shall be settled bilaterally, in a spirit of friendship, mutual respect and mutual understanding.

Article 15. This Treaty shall be valid for a term of 20 years from the date of its entry into force.

If neither of the High Contracting Parties gives notice, six months before the expiry of the above-mentioned term, of its desire to terminate the Treaty, it shall be extended for successive five-year terms until such time as one of the High Contracting Parties gives written notice, six months before the expiry of the current five-year term, of its intention to terminate it.

Article 16. This Treaty is subject to ratification and shall enter into force on the date of the exchange of the instruments of ratification, which shall take place at Aden.

This Treaty has been drawn up in two copies, each in the Russian and Arabic languages, both texts being equally authentic.

Done at Moscow on 25 October 1979.

For the Union of Soviet Socialist Republics:

[Signed] L. BREZHNEV

General Secretary of the Central Committee of the Communist Party of the Soviet Union, Chairman of the Presidium of the Supreme Soviet of the Union of Soviet Socialist Republics

For the People's Democratic Republic of Yemen:

[Signed] A. F. ISMAIL

General Secretary of the Central Committee of the Yemen Socialist Party, Chairman of the Presidium of the

Supreme People's Council of the People's Democratic Republic of Yemen

4.1413 Treaty of Friendship and Co-operation between the German Democratic Republic and Socialist Ethiopia

Alliance Members: German Democratic Republic and Ethiopia
Signed On: November 15, 1979, in the city of Addis Ababa (Ethiopia). In force until November 7, 1989.
Alliance Type: Non-Aggression (Type II)

Source: *United Nations Treaty,* no. 19506.

SUMMARY

Cooperation with East Germany began quickly for Mengistu's Socialist regime that came to power in 1977. East Germany provided training to Ethiopian officers and cooperated with Soviet engineers to help build roads. East Germany also tried to broker a peaceful solution to the ongoing insurgency in Ethiopia, but when talks broke down, the Germans committed to a policy of military aid for the Socialist government.

Following this 1979 agreement, East Germany proved itself an important source of military assistance, providing rifles, ammunition, artillery, and vehicles for the Ethiopian government while also continuing its policy of training Ethiopian military officers and secret police. Joint efforts between the allies were so integrated that East Germany had taken control of the Red Star operation against Eritrean separatists by 1982. The closeness of this military aid relationship was revealed with the collapse of the East German government in 1989, which greatly weakened Ethiopia and led to a greater sense of urgency in the peace negotiations with the rebels.

ALLIANCE TEXT

The German Democratic Republic and Socialist Ethiopia,

Proceeding from the traditional close relations of friendship, co-operation and anti-imperialist solidarity that exist between the two States and peoples,

Convinced that the further strengthening and enhancement of the relations of friendship and all-round co-operation which have come into being between them meet the fundamental national interests of the peoples of the two countries,

Conscious of their responsibility to contribute to the strengthening of international peace and security in the interest of the peoples of all countries,

Inspired by the ideals of the struggle for national independence and social progress and against imperialism, colonialism, neo-colonialism, hegemonism, expansionism, racism and *apartheid,*

Desiring to promote unity of action and co-operation among all progressive forces in the struggle for peace, freedom, independence, and social progress,

Reaffirming their commitment to the purposes and principles of the United Nations Charter,

Mindful of the Declaration on the principles of friendship and co-operation between the German Democratic Republic and Socialist Ethiopia of 29 November 1978,

Reaffirming their desire to further strengthen and develop the existing relations of friendship and the mutually advantageous co-operation between the two States and peoples, and

Determined to assist each other in the creation and shaping of the conditions for strengthening and developing the revolutionary social and economic gains achieved by the two peoples,

Have resolved to conclude this Treaty and have agreed as follows:

Article 1. The High Contracting Parties declare their resolve to strengthen the relations of friendship between their States and peoples and, to this end, to shape and further expand their co-operation in the political, economic, trade, scientific, cultural, technical and other fields on the basis of the principles of sovereign equality of States, territorial integrity, inviolability of frontiers, equal rights, and non-interference in internal affairs.

Article 2. The High Contracting Parties shall promote their all-round co-operation in the fields of science, culture, education, literature, art, press, radio, television, cinema, health, sports, the training of personnel, exchange of experience and in all other fields for the purpose of a more profound understanding of the life, work and achievements of the peoples of the two countries.

Article 3. The High Contracting Parties, giving great importance to economic co-operation and trade between them, shall expand and deepen co-operation and the exchange of experiences in these fields. These relations shall be on the basis of equal rights, mutual benefit and most-favoured-nation treatment.

Article 4. The High Contracting Parties shall pursue a policy of peace to strengthen friendship and co-operation among all peoples.

The German Democratic Republic shall respect the peaceful foreign policy of Socialist Ethiopia which is based on the purposes and principles of the Charter of the Organization of African Unity and the Non-Aligned Movement and which constitutes an important factor in the development of international co-operation and peaceful co-existence.

Socialist Ethiopia shall respect the peaceful foreign policy of the German Democratic Republic which is in the nature of a socialist State and is aimed at strengthening friendship and co-operation among all peoples.

Article 5. The High Contracting Parties shall continue to make active contributions to the struggle for peace and international security and shall make every effort to deepen and extend the process of détente, to achieve general and complete disarmament, including nuclear disarmament, and shall advocate settlement of all international disputes by peaceful means, without prejudice to the legitimate right of States, under the Charter of the United Nations, to individual or collective self-defence against aggression.

Article 6. The High Contracting Parties shall also in future closely co-operate in the struggle against the forces of imperialism, neo-colonialism, hegemonism, expansionism and for the liquidation of all the remnants of colonialism and of racism and apartheid in all their forms and manifestations.

They shall support all measures taken for the full implementation of the United Nations Declaration on the Granting of Independence to Colonial Countries and Peoples, shall always render active solidarity and support to all peoples fighting for their freedom, independence, sovereignty and social progress, and, to this end, shall co-operate with other democratic and peace-loving States.

Article 7. The High Contracting Parties shall work for the establishment of a new international economic order on an equal and democratic basis, free from imperialist exploitation.

They reaffirm and further support the sovereign right of peoples to exercise permanent control over, and use of, their natural resources.

Article 8, The High Contracting Parties shall consult each other on important international questions affecting the interests of the two countries.

Article 9. The High Contracting Parties solemnly declare that neither will enter into any alliance or participate in any step or action directed against the other High Contracting Party.

Article 10. The High Contracting Parties declare that nothing in the present Treaty shall affect their obligations under existing international treaties or obligations arising from regional and international organizations of which they are members, and undertake not to enter into any international agreements inconsistent with the provisions of the present Treaty.

Article 11. All questions arising between the High Contracting Parties with regard to the interpretation or application of this Treaty shall be settled by bilateral negotiation in a spirit of friendship, understanding and mutual respect.

Article 12. This Treaty is subject to ratification and shall enter into force with the exchange of the instruments of ratification, which shall take place in Berlin, Capital of the German Democratic Republic.

Article 13. This Treaty shall be valid for a period of 20 years after its entry into force. It shall automatically be extended for successive periods of five years, unless one of the High Contracting Parties gives notice, in writing, of its desire to terminate it twelve months prior to the expiry of the said period.

This Treaty is made in two copies each in the German, Arabic and English languages, all the texts being equally authentic.

Done at Addis Ababa on 15 November 1979.

[Signed] Erich Honecker
For the German Democratic Republic

[Signed] Mengistu Haile Mariam
For Socialist Ethiopia

4.1414 Treaty of Friendship and Co-operation between the German Democratic Republic and the Democratic Republic of Yemen

Alliance Members: German Democratic Republic and the Democratic Republic of Yemen (South Yemen)
Signed On: November 17, 1979, in the city of Aden (Yemen). In force until November 7, 1989.
Alliance Type: Non-Aggression Pact (Type II)

Source: *United Nations Treaty,* no. 19788.

SUMMARY

Two days after signing a non-aggression treaty with Ethiopia, East German leader Erich Honecker signed this very similar agreement with South Yemen. The treaty called for cooperation in agriculture, education, television, radio, and cinema. The treaty also pledged non-aggression between the parties and consultation should any international issues of importance arise that affected both allies. The agreement mirrored a similar agreement between the Soviet Union and South Yemen, signed one month earlier, but Yemeni ties with East Germany never matched the closeness of Yemen's relations with the Soviets.

The agreement ended with the fall of the communist East German government in November 1989. Yemen was unified seven months later, on May 22, 1990.

ALLIANCE TEXT

The German Democratic Republic and the People's Democratic Republic of Yemen,

Proceeding from the existing relations of solid friendship, trustful cooperation and anti-imperialist solidarity between the two states and peoples, in conformity with the national interests of the peoples of the two states and with a view to strengthening peace and security in the world,

Reaffirming their desire to contribute with all means to the development of peaceful relations among states and to fruitful cooperation among them,

Determined to safeguard and develop the economic and social gains of the peoples of the two states and to work for the unity and cohesion of all forces fighting for peace, national independence, democracy and social progress,

Inspired by the noble ideals of the struggle for national independence and social progress and against imperialism, colonialism, neo-colonialism and racism in all its manifestations,

Reaffirming their loyalty to the purposes and principles of the Charter of the United Nations, including the principles of respect for sovereignty, territorial integrity and non-interference in internal affairs,

Willing to develop, strengthen and consolidate the relations of friendship and fruitful cooperation between the two peoples and states,

Have resolved to conclude this Treaty and have agreed as follows:

Article 1. The High Contracting Parties shall strengthen the close and lasting friendship between the two states and peoples and develop further their mutual political relations and all-round cooperation on the basis of equality and respect for the principles of sovereignty and non-interference in internal affairs.

Article 2. The High Contracting Parties shall closely and extensively work together in the creation of conditions necessary to secure and promote the development of the social and economic achievements of both peoples, and they shall mutually respect their sovereignty over all their natural resources.

Article 3. The High Contracting Parties shall undertake efforts to deepen and expand economic and scientific-technological cooperation for their mutual benefit. For this purpose, they shall develop and broaden cooperation in industry, agriculture, in the utilization of natural resources, planning the national economy and in other economic sectors as well as in the training of national personnel.

They shall widen cooperation in the areas of trade and shipping on the basis of the principles of equality, mutual advantage and most-favoured nation treatment.

Article 4. The High Contracting Parties shall continue their cooperation in the fields of science, culture, art, literature, education, health, the press, radio, television, film and sports and exchange experience in other areas. They shall encourage contacts and cooperation between government authorities and between mass organizations and shall expand direct contacts between cultural and scientific institutions for the purpose of a more profound understanding of the life, work, experience and achievements of the peoples of the two states.

Article 5. The German Democratic Republic and the People's Democratic Republic of Yemen shall pursue a policy of peace aimed at strengthening friendship and cooperation.

The German Democratic Republic shall respect the policy of non-alignment of the People's Democratic Republic of Yemen, which constitutes an important factor in the development of international cooperation and peaceful coexistence.

The People's Democratic Republic of Yemen shall respect the peaceful foreign policy of the German Democratic Republic, which is in the nature of a socialist state and is aimed at strengthening friendship and cooperation among peoples.

Article 6. The High Contracting Parties shall continue to make active contributions to the struggle for peace and international security. They shall undertake every effort to strengthen international détente, to achieve general and complete disarmament, including nuclear disarmament, to eliminate all manifestations of hegemonism and expansionism in international relations and to solve international disputes by peaceful means, without prejudice to the legitimate rights of peoples in their struggle for national independence and to self-defence under the Charter of the United Nations.

Article 7. The High Contracting Parties shall continue to work for the achievement by the peoples of equal rights and their right to self-determination, and they shall oppose all forms of oppression of peoples and any violation of their basic rights.

They shall also in future stand closely and resolutely together in the struggle against imperialism and its machinations, against colonialism and neo-colonialism, and for the elimination of racism in all its manifestations.

They shall support all efforts aimed at the full implementation of the United Nations Declaration on the Granting of Independence to Colonial Countries and Peoples, shall always practise active solidarity with all peoples fighting for their freedom, independence, sovereignty and social progress, and to this end shall cooperate with other peace-loving states.

Article 8. The High Contracting Parties shall support the attainment of a just and durable peace in the Middle East and a comprehensive settlement for this purpose.

Article 9. The High Contracting Parties shall consult each other on important international issues directly affecting the interests of their states.

For the purpose of strengthening and broadening their cooperation, coordinating foreign policy activities and discussing international questions of interest to both sides, they shall exchange information and views and hold consultations at various levels.

Article 10. Each High Contracting Party solemnly declares that it will not enter into any military alliance or participate in any step or action directed against the other High Contracting Party.

Article 11. The High Contracting Parties shall support the establishment of a new international economic order on an equal and democratic basis, free from imperialist exploitation and dependence. They shall support the sovereign right of peoples to exercise control over their natural resources.

Article 12. The High Contracting Parties declare that nothing in the present Treaty is in contradiction to their obligations under existing international treaties. They undertake not to enter into any international agreement inconsistent with the provisions of the present Treaty.

Article 13. All questions arising between the High Contracting Parties with regard to the interpretation or application of the provisions of this Treaty shall be settled by bilateral negotiation in a spirit of friendship, understanding and mutual respect.

Article 14. This Treaty shall be valid for a period of twenty years after its entry into force.

It shall automatically be extended for successive periods of five years, unless one of the High Contracting Parties gives notice, in writing, of its desire to terminate it six months prior to the expiry of the said period.

Article 15. This Treaty is subject to ratification. It shall enter into force on the date of the exchange of the instruments of ratification, which shall take place in Berlin, capital of the German Democratic Republic.

This Treaty is made in two copies, each in the German and Arabic languages, both texts being equally authentic.

Done at Aden on 17 November 1979.

For the German Democratic Republic:

[ERICH HONECKER]

For the People's Democratic Republic of Yemen:

[ABDUL FATTAH ISMAIL]

4.1415 Treaty of Friendship and Co-operation between the People's Democratic Republic of Yemen and Ethiopia

Alliance Members: People's Democratic Republic of Yemen (South Yemen) and Ethiopia
Signed On: December 2, 1979, in the city of Aden (Yemen). In force until February 1, 1986.
Alliance Type: Non-Aggression Pact (Type II)

Source: *Middle East Contemporary Survey,* vol. 4, p. 676–678.

SUMMARY

Following the Ogaden War (1977–1978) between Ethiopia and Somalia, both rivals began actively courting superpower interests in the Horn of Africa. Ethiopia signed agreements with the Soviet Union (see Alliance no. 4.1406) in 1978 and East Germany (see Alliance no. 4.1413) in 1979 that traded military assistance for access to military bases. The United States then countered the alliance by forging a similar arrangement with Somalia in 1979 and continuing to aid friendly governments such as Kenya and Saudi Arabia. These treaties of aid and friendship were becoming relatively common in the region as South Yemen had also signed similar agreements with the Soviets (see Alliance no. 4.1412) and the East Germans (see Alliance no. 4.1414).

This agreement completed the triangle of leftist-leaning nations in the region as the Soviet allies, South Yemen, and Ethiopia pledged fifteen years of friendship and non-aggression. These commitments were most likely symbolic, given that both parties to this treaty were embroiled in border conflicts and did not have the economic or military capacity to aid or attack their treaty partners.

This agreement did lead to additional treaties, however, as Libya joined South Yemen and Ethiopia in a larger, trilateral defense pact (see Alliance no. 4.1423) in 1981. The three nations pledged to set up a political committee to facilitate meetings of their heads of state and agreed to aid each other in the event of attack. The conclusion of the Yemeni civil war effectively ended both treaties.

ALLIANCE TEXT

In view of the warm and close relations and historic ties between their two peoples and countries; their common experience and destiny; their faith in the need to constantly strengthen friendship and co-operation between the PDRY and socialist Ethiopia in the interests of the two countries; the need to serve the development of peaceful relations among states and to strengthen international peace and co-operation; their determination to maintain and develop the economic and social gains of the peoples of their two countries; their determination to promote the incessant struggle against imperialism, colonialism, neocolonialism, expansionism, apartheid and racism in all their forms and manifestations and to support the peoples struggling for freedom, independence and social progress; their determination to preserve the Indian Ocean and the Red Sea as zones of peace; their desire for a just and durable peace in the ME and their (?adherence) to the principles and objectives of the UN Charter, including respect for sovereignty, national independence, territorial integrity and noninterference I the internal affairs of other countries, the PDRY and socialist Ethiopia have decided to conclude a friendship and co-operation treaty.

Article 1. The two sovereign contracting parties undertake to develop the close friendship and co-operation between the PDRY and socialist Ethiopia on the basis of the principles of equality, mutual benefit, mutual respect for sovereignty, national independence and territorial integrity and noninterference in the internal affairs of the other.

Article 2. The two sovereign contracting parties will co-operate closely and comprehensively to protect the economic and social gains of their two peoples and sovereignty over natural resources.

Article 3. The two sovereign contracting parties will work to entrench and expand mutual economic, scientific, technical and trade co-operation in the interests of the two peoples and countries. They will develop and deepen mutual co-operation in the fields of industry, agriculture, communications, the training of cadres and in other economic fields.

Article 4. The two sovereign contracting parties will work to develop and consolidate mutual co-operation and exchange of experience in the fields of science, culture, the arts, literature, education, health, journalism, broadcasting, television, cinema, tourism and sports with the aid of deepening their people's common understanding of their life, work and experience and achievements.

Article 5. The two sovereign contracting parties agree to enter into trade agreements on a most favoured nation basis.

Article 6. The two sovereign contracting parties will mutually cooperate in the military field, each to assure the defensive capability of the other.

Article 7. The two sovereign contracting parties will continue their efforts to strengthen the unity of the nonaligned movement and to apply its principles to promote international détente and world peace, and friendship and co-operation among peoples and to back the struggle against imperialism, colonialism, neocolonialism, expansionism, apartheid and racism in all their forms and manifestations.

Socialist Ethiopia respect the peace-loving foreign policy pursued by the PDRY based on the principles of internationalist solidarity and peaceful coexistence, aimed at strengthening Arab solidarity and opposed to imperialism, colonialism, neocolonialism, expansionism and racism in all their forms and manifestations.

The PDRY respects the peace-loving foreign policy pursued by socialist Ethiopia, which accords with the goals and principles of the Organization of African Unity Charter and constitutes and important factor in the development of international co-operation and peaceful coexistence.

Article 8. The two sovereign contracting parties will continue their active and peaceful efforts to preserve the Red Sea and the Indian Ocean as a zone of peace and to maintain the freedom of shipping in the Red Sea.

Article 9. The two sovereign contracting parties will continue their efforts to develop and strengthen the relations of peace and co-operation among all the Red Sea littoral countries.

Article 10. The two sovereign contracting parties will consult on important international issues directly relevant to the interests of their countries.

Article 11. The two sovereign contracting parties will continue their active efforts to find a just and durable peace in the ME.

Article 12. The two sovereign contracting parties will continue their efforts to maintain international peace and security and to deepen international détente. They will contribute positively to the solidarity and growth of the nonaligned movement. They will contribute energetically to the issue of general and comprehensive disarmament, including nuclear disarmament under effective international surveillance.

Article 13. [Passage indistinct] and for the sake of complete destruction of colonialism, neocolonialism, apartheid and racism in all their forms and manifestations and for the sake of full application of the UN declaration to grant independence to the colonized countries and peoples.

Article 14. The two sovereign contracting parties will continue their efforts to bring about the establishment of a new international economic order founded on the principles of equality, justice, democracy and sovereignty over natural resources.

Article 15. Each of the two sovereign contracting parties declares officially that it will not enter into military alliances or other alliances: it will not join any blocs of states or engage in any actions or measures directed against the other sovereign contracting side.

Article 16. The two sovereign contracting parties declare that the provisions of this treaty do not contradict their undertakings under the international agreements in force. They undertake not to conclude any international agreements contradicting this treaty.

Article 17. Any issue which may arise between the two sovereign contracting parties as to the interpretation or application of any provisions of this treaty shall be solved bilaterally in the spirit of friendship, understanding and mutual respect.

Article 18. This treaty shall remain in force for a period of 15 years from the date it comes into effect and unless either of the sovereign contracting parties express its desire to end the treaty six months before its expiration the treaty shall remain in force for successive periods, each of which will not be longer than five years or until either of the sovereign contracting parties declares its intention to end it six months before the expiration of the five-year period.

Article 19. This treaty requires ratification in conformity with constitutional measures in operation in the countries of the two sovereign contracting parties. This treaty becomes effective when the instruments of ratification are exchanged, which will take place in Addis Ababa.

This treaty has been prepared in two [as heard] copies, each in Arabic, Amharic and English, each of equal applicability.

Signed on behalf of the PDRY by Ahd al-Faffah Ismail, Secretary-General of the YSP Central Committee and Chairman of the Presidium of the Supreme People's Council of the PDRY.

Signed on behalf of socialist Ethiopia by Mengistu Haile Mariam, Chairman of the Provisional Military Administrative Council, Chairman of the Council of Ministers and Commander-in-Chief of the Revolutionary Army of socialist Ethiopia.

4.1416 Treaties of Friendship, Non-Aggression and Mutual Defense between Guinea and Guinea-Bissau

Alliance Members: Guinea and Guinea-Bissau
Signed On: January 25, 1980, in the city of Conakry (Guinea). In force until May 7, 1999.
Alliance Type: Defense Pact (Type I)

Source: *Keesing's Record of World Events,* January 1980.

SUMMARY

In the late 1970s and early 1980s, West African nations began to take more proactive steps toward increasing regional economic and cultural cooperation, especially after the formation of the Economic Community of West African States (ECOWAS) in 1975. ECOWAS also encouraged member states to increase their own bilateral ties, which Guinea and Guinea-Bissau did with a set of agreements signed in January of 1980.

In November 1980, a bloodless coup d'état in Guinea-Bissau brought to power a government led by Joao Bernardo Vieira. After ruling at the helm of an oppressive government for more than ten years, Vieira won the country's free first elections in 1994. In 1998, however, a military coup threatened his government, and Guinea and Senegal were forced to intervene in defense of Vieira. A successful coup then occurred in May 1999, and Vieira was replaced by Malam Bacai Sanha, which effectively ended this alliance. During the next five years Guinea-Bissau underwent a series of military coups and leadership changes, but Vieira was able to return to power through presidential elections in October 2005.

DESCRIPTION OF TERMS

Guinea and Guinea-Bissau signed six documents in Conakry, including a treaty of friendship and cooperation, a treaty of non-aggression, and a mutual defense agreement. Both countries pledged to set up a joint committee to discuss and solve a dispute of the demarcation of territorial waters. The other agreements encouraged the free exchange of goods and the free movement of people.

4.1417 Treaty of Friendship and Alliance between the Socialist People's Libyan Arab Jamahiriya and the Republic of Chad

Alliance Members: Libya and Chad
Signed On: June 15, 1980, in the city of Tripoli (Libya). In force until June 19, 1982.
Alliance Type: Defense Pact (Type I)

Source: *United Nations Treaty,* no. 19185.

SUMMARY

In the middle of the 1960s, civil war broke out between the Chad government and the National Liberation Front (Frolinat). Libya began giving military supplies to the Frolinat in hopes of annexing the northern parts of Chad or the entire country. In 1978, the Frolinat captured nearly half of the Chadian army and assumed control of the government, and Hissene Habre was named prime minister. In 1979, Frolinat split into two factions, and Libya aided Goukouni Oueddei's army, contributing to Hissene Habre's defeat by 1980. On June 15, 1980, Chad agreed to this treaty of mutual defense and non-aggression with Libya. Crucially, the treaty allowed for intervention by Libya if Chad had a political crisis, and it also established the early framework for a merger between the two countries.

Goukouni's tenure in power lasted from March 1979 until November 1979, when Habre returned with French and U.S. aid, driving Goukouni out of the country. Upon his return to government, Habre severed ties with the Libyan regime that had been supporting his opponent and thereby renounced the treaty that Goukouni had signed in 1980. Libya and Chad continued fighting until a United Nations panel ruled in 1994 that the Aozou Strip belonged to Chad.

ALLIANCE TEXT

The Socialist People's Libyan Arab Jamahiriya and the Republic of Chad, Having faith in the deep-rooted spiritual, economic, human and cultural ties created between the two fraternal peoples by geographic proximity and centuries of common history;

Convinced that these vital ties are reflected in a common destiny and common objectives and aspirations, transcending all barriers;

Have agreed as follows:

Article 1. The two Parties shall defend each other if either Party or both Parties are exposed to direct or indirect foreign aggression.

The two Parties shall deem any aggression against one Party to constitute aggression against the other, which shall be bound to take such action as may be necessary to check the said aggression.

Article 2. The Parties undertake to exchange information on military matters and on matters pertaining to internal and external security and to assist each other if either Party or both Parties are exposed to direct or indirect danger.

Article 3. Within the framework of the alliance between the great revolution of 1 September and the Chadian revolution under the leadership of FROLINAT (Front de Liberation Nationale du Tchad), the Parties shall endeavour to:

(a) Strengthen economic, political, cultural and military co-operation between the two countries with a view to the realization of the aspirations of the two fraternal peoples;

(b) Combat all forms of colonialism, neo-colonialism and imperialism throughout the African continent;

(c) Resist any foreign invasion of the African continent;

(d) Oppose the exploitation and oppression of the peoples, support the struggle of the African masses for freedom from all forms of domination and uphold the right of the peoples to self-determination.

Article 4. The two Parties undertake not to be bound by any treaty, agreement or alliance with any country or countries that is inconsistent with the provisions of this Treaty.

Article 5. The two Parties shall ensure personal freedom of movement between the two countries, without any impediments or restrictions.

Article 6. The Socialist People's Libyan Arab Jamahiriya shall make its economic, material and cultural resources available for the economic and military reconstruction of Chad. The Libyan Arab Jamahiriya shall also provide the people of Chad with educational and cultural opportunities.

Article 7. The Republic of Chad undertakes not to permit the presence of any foreign base or colonialist, imperialist troops in its national territory and reserves the right to call upon the Socialist People's Libyan Arab Jamahiriya for assistance in the event of a threat to its independence, territorial integrity or internal security, in accordance with the provisions of article 1.

Article 8. The provisions of this Treaty shall enter into force on the date of signature. A Joint Libyan-Chadian-High Commission shall be established to ensure the practical implementation of the provisions of this Treaty. The records of the Commission shall constitute an integral part of the Treaty.

Done at Tripoli on 2 Sha'ban 1389 from the death of the Prophet, corresponding to 15 June 1980, in duplicate in the Arabic and French languages, both texts being equally authentic.

For the Republic of Chad:
[Signed] IBRAHIM Youssouf
For the Socialist People's Libyan Arab Jamahiriya:
[Signed] ALI TREKI

4.1418 Exchange of Notes Constituting an Agreement between the Government of the Republic of Italy and the Government of Malta on the Neutrality of Malta

Alliance Members: Italy and Malta
Signed On: September 15, 1980, in the city of Rome. In force until December 5, 1984.
Alliance Type: Entente (Type III)

Source: *United Nations Treaty,* no. 19962.

SUMMARY

Malta rests in a historically important geostrategic location, in the middle of the Mediterranean, within easy reach of North Africa and half of Europe by most modern aircraft. Malta has attempted to use this position to seek aid in exchange for neutrality, trying to secure guarantees from Western nations such as the United States. Malta ousted a NATO (see Alliance no. 4.1347) base and signaled Washington that it would seek guarantees from the Soviet Union should the United States not offer a guarantee first.

Italy took the initiative and provided a grant of $80 million plus $15 million in soft loans ending in 1983. On September 15, 1980, the governments of Malta and Italy met to verbally exchange the official security notes. During the exchange, Malta affirmed its stance of neutrality and committed to not use its military offensively or to allow the use of its bases, except in self-defense. Italy agreed not to engage in actions that threatened Malta, to consult with Malta regarding security concerns, to provide aid, and to support any efforts by Malta in the United Nations if its security were threatened. Italy provided one exclusionary note, stating that if Malta were to change its stance of neutrality, then Italy could withdraw from the agreement.

On December 5, 1984, the Maltese prime minister, Dom Mintoff, told Parliament that the agreement with Italy would not be renewed as economic assistance had ended. Mintoff also announced a military agreement with Libya, including a Libyan pledge to intervene on Malta's behalf (see Alliance no. 4.1432).

ALLIANCE TEXT

Exchange of Notes Constituting an Agreement Between the Government of the Republic of Italy and the Government of the Republic of Malta on the Neutrality of Malta

I

Ministry of Foreign Affairs
Malta

The Government of the Republic of Malta presents its compliments to the Embassy of Italy in Valletta and in relation to the conversations which have taken place between the Representatives of the two Governments, has the honour to confirm that it will make a Declaration of neutrality of the territory over which it exercises its sovereignty, in the terms of the text annexed to this Note, and to request the Government of the Republic of Italy to make a Declaration recognizing such neutrality in the terms of the text also annexed to this Note.

The Government of the Republic of Malta confirms its agreement that, in connection with the said Declarations, there shall simultaneously enter into force the Protocol, agreed between the Representatives of both Governments in the terms of the text annexed to the present Note, concerning the financial, economic and technical assistance which the Republic of Malta will receive from the Republic of Italy.

This Note Verbale and the Note Verbale in reply thereto of the Italian Government to the Embassy of the Republic of Malta in Rome will constitute an agreement between the two Countries, which will be submitted to the respective constitutional authorities competent to authorize its ratification.

Upon the exchange of the instruments of ratification, the aforesaid Declaration will be made by the two Governments and the Protocol connected therewith will enter into force.

The texts constituting the agreement between the two countries will be registered with the Secretariat of the United Nations, in accordance with the requirements imposed on members of the United Nations Organization by Article 102 of the Charter of the Organization.

To the text of this Note, which is drawn up in the English language, there is annexed an official translation in the Italian language, both texts being equally authentic.

The Government of the Republic of Malta avails itself of this opportunity to renew to the Embassy of Italy in Valletta the expressions of its highest consideration.

[Initialed] Initialed by Dom Mintoff, Prime Minister for the Republic of Malta.
15 September 1980
Embassy of Italy
Valletta

Declaration by the Government of the Republic of Malta Concerning the Neutrality of Malta

The Government of the Republic of Malta,

Faithful to the decision of the People of the Republic of Malta to eliminate all foreign military bases after March 31, 1979 and to contribute to peace and stability in the Mediterranean region by changing their country's unnatural role of a fortress into a centre of peace and a bridge of friendship between the Peoples of Europe and of North Africa;

Conscious of the special contribution the Republic of Malta can make towards that end by assuming a status of neutrality strictly founded on the principles of non-alignment;

Aware of the support which neighbouring European and Arab Mediterranean States will give to Malta's new role and to such a status of neutrality;

1. Solemnly declares that the Republic of Malta is a neutral state actively pursuing peace, security and social progress among all nations by adhering to a policy of non-alignment and refusing to participate in any military alliance;

2. Affirms that such a status will, in particular, imply that:

(a) No foreign military base will be permitted on Maltese territory;

(b) No military facilities in Malta will be allowed to be used by any foreign forces except at the request of the Government of Malta, and only in the following cases:

(i) In the exercise of the inherent right of self-defence in the event of any armed violation of the area over which the Republic of Malta has sovereignty, or in pursuance of measures or actions decided by the Security Council of the United Nations; or

(ii) Whenever there exists a threat to the sovereignty, independence, neutrality, unity or territorial integrity of the Republic of Malta;

but the Government of Malta will immediately inform the neighbouring Mediterranean States which have made like Declarations welcoming the present Declaration and giving appropriate undertakings, of the steps taken under this paragraph;

(c) Except as aforesaid, no other facilities in Malta will be allowed to be used in such manner or extent as will amount to the presence in Malta of a concentration of foreign forces;

(d) Except as aforesaid, no foreign military personnel will be allowed on Maltese territory, other than military personnel performing, or assisting in the performance of, civil works or activities, and other than a reasonable number of military technical personnel assisting in the defence of the Republic of Malta;

(e) The shipyards of the Republic of Malta will be used for civil commercial purposes, but may also be used, within reasonable limits of time and quantity, for the repair of military vessels which have been put in a state of non-combat or for the construction of vessels; and in accordance with the principles of nonalignment the said shipyards will be denied to the military vessels of the two superpowers;

3. Expresses its hope that, with the concurrence of the Government of the Republic of Malta, neighbouring Mediterranean States will make like Declarations welcoming the present Declaration and giving such undertakings as may be appropriate. The Government of the Republic of Malta will inform each of such States of the Declarations made by other States.

Protocol Relating to the Financial, Economic and Technical Assistance between the Republic of Italy and the Republic of Malta

The Government of the Republic of Italy,
The Government of the Republic of Malta,

Desirous of intensifying their friendly relations and of cooperating for their reciprocal development and the security of their region, have agreed as follows:

Article I. The Government of the Republic of Italy undertakes to make to the Government of the Republic of Malta for a period of five years commencing from 1979, a financial contribution in the sum of twelve million United States dollars each year.

Article II. With the object of favouring and promoting the economic and social progress of Malta, the Government of the Republic of Italy shall make available to the Government of the Republic of Malta, according to the procedures set out in Law No. 38 of 9 February, 1979, a concessionary financial credit of fifteen million United States dollars, to be utilised in development projects to be identified by agreement between the parties.

Article III. Within the framework of the collaboration between the two countries, the Government of the Republic of Italy will contribute to the economic and social and to the technical and cultural development of Malta through the implementation of projects of cooperation, envisaged by the law of the Italian Republic No. 38 of 9 February, 1979, in an amount of not less than four million United States dollars per annum, to be utilized before the end of 1983.

While the status of the Italian cooperating personnel in Malta and of the Maltese personnel on scholarship in Italy will be guaranteed by agreements made specifically for that purpose, the Government of the Republic of Malta will ensure that the necessary cooperation will be afforded to the competent Italian institutions, in order that they may fulfil the requirements of the law mentioned in the first paragraph of this Article.

Article IV. The Government of the Republic of Malta will, in respect of each payment of the financial contribution envisaged under Article I of the present Protocol, forward to the Government of the Republic of Italy the most appropriate indications concerning the public works and the socio-economic development programmes financed during the year out of the said contribution. The Government of the Republic of Malta will furthermore, in relation to the utilization of the finances provided under the preceding Article II, supply the documentation concerning the individual projects or programmes intended to favour or promote the economic and social progress of Malta.

Article V. In order to facilitate the realization of the objectives of the present Protocol, there shall be set up a Mixed Commission, whose members shall be designated by the respective Ministers of Foreign Affairs.

The Commission shall meet alternately in Malta and in Italy at least once a year and whenever it shall be deemed necessary.

Article VI. The manner in which this Protocol shall be implemented shall be regulated on the basis of specific agreements concluded by the technical authorities of the two countries.

II

The Ministry of Foreign Affairs presents its compliments to the Embassy of the Republic of Malta in Rome and, with reference to the Note Verbale dated 15 September, 1980 forwarded by its Government to the Embassy of Italy in Valletta in relation to the conversations which have taken place between the Representatives of the two Governments, has the honour to confirm that the Government of the Republic of Italy will make a Declaration recognising the neutrality of the territory over which the Government of the Republic of Malta exercises its sovereignty, in the terms of the text annexed to the aforesaid Note, in relation to the Declaration of neutrality made by that Government, in the terms of the text also annexed to the said Note.

At the same time the Government of the Republic of Italy confirms its agreement to the text of the Protocol, connected with the said Declarations, concerning the financial, economic and technical assistance which the Italian Republic will provide to the Republic of Malta, in the terms of the text annexed to the Note aforesaid.

That Note Verbale and the present Note Verbale will constitute an agreement between the two countries, which will be submitted to the respective constitutional authorities competent to authorize its ratification.

Upon the exchange of the instruments of ratification, the aforesaid Declarations will be made by the two Governments and the Protocol connected therewith will enter into force.

The texts constituting the agreement between the two countries will be registered with the Secretariat of the United Nations in accordance with the requirement imposed on members of the United Nations Organization by Article 102 of the Charter of the Organization.

To the text of this Note, which is drawn up in the Italian language, there is annexed an official translation in the English language, both texts being equally authentic.

The Ministry of Foreign Affairs avails itself of this opportunity to renew to the Embassy of the Republic of Malta in Rome the expressions of its highest consideration.

[Initialed] Initialed by Emilio Colombo, Foreign Minister for the Republic of Italy.

15 September 1980
Embassy of Malta
Rome

Declaration by the Government of the Republic of Italy with Respect to the Neutrality of Malta

The Government of the Republic of Italy

Welcoming with satisfaction the Declaration whereby the Republic of Malta has made known that, in the exercise of its sovereignty, it has assumed a status of neutrality;

Taking note of that Declaration which, with the concurrence of the Government of the Republic of Malta, is incorporated in the present Declaration as an integral part thereof, and the text of which is as follows:

[See Declaration by the Government of the Republic of Malta]

1. Solemnly declares that it recognises and will respect the sovereignty, independence, neutrality, unity and territorial integrity of the Republic of Malta, and will act in conformity therewith in all respects;

2. Undertakes, in particular:

(a) Not to take any action whatsoever which could in any way, directly or indirectly, endanger the sovereignty, independence, neutrality, unity or territorial integrity of the Republic of Malta;

(b) Not to take any action whatsoever which could in any

way, directly or indirectly, endanger peace and security in the Republic of Malta;

(c) Not to take any part in any act of such nature;

(d) Not to induce the Republic of Malta to enter into a military alliance, or to sign an agreement of this kind, or to accept the protection of a military alliance;

3. Invites all other States to recognize and respect the sovereignty, independence, neutrality, unity and territorial integrity of the Republic of Malta, to act in conformity therewith in all respects, and to refrain from taking any action which is incompatible with those principles;

4. Undertakes to consult, at the request of the Government of the Republic of Malta or of the Government of a neighbouring Mediterranean State making a like Declaration as the present one, with the Government of the Republic of Malta and of the other States aforesaid whenever one of them declares that there exists a threat of violation or a violation of the sovereignty, independence, neutrality, unity and territorial integrity of the Republic of Malta;

5.1. Without prejudice to the application of Article 35 of the Charter of the United Nations, undertakes that, on the happening of any of the events mentioned in paragraph 2(b) of the Maltese Declaration, the situation will be brought to the attention of, or referred to, the Security Council;

5.2. It further undertakes that, at the request of the Republic of Malta and after consulting the aforementioned States, it will, in any of the events and under the conditions of the preceding paragraph 4 of the Italian Declaration, or should the need arise for the exercise of the right of self-defence in the circumstances set out in Article 51 of the Charter of the United Nations, adopt any other measure, not excluding military assistance, it will consider necessary to meet the situation;

6. Reserves the right, if it considers that changes have taken place which alter substantially the neutrality of the Republic of Malta as envisaged in the Declaration of the Government of the Republic of Malta reproduced above, to request that consultations take place between it and the Governments of the Republic of Malta and of other neighbouring Mediterranean States making a like declaration as the present, and if, following such consultations, it considers that the maintenance of the neutrality of Malta is not ensured, it may decide to cease to be bound by the present Declaration. Any such decision will be communicated to the Republic of Malta and other interested States.

4.1419 Treaty of Friendship and Co-operation between the Syrian Arab Republic and the Union of Soviet Socialist Republics

Alliance Members: Syria and the Union of Soviet Socialist Republics
Signed On: October 8, 1980, in the city of Moscow. In force as of date of publication of this volume.
Alliance Type: Entente (Type III)

Source: *United Nations Treaty,* no. 19728.

SUMMARY

Syrian co-operation with the Soviet Union and Russia in the military and technology sectors began as early as 1956, and in 1974 General Secretary Leonid Brezhnev of the Soviet Union made a commitment to President Hafez al-Assad of Syria to defend Syria against foreign aggression. The two sides formalized their alliance in October 1980 with the signing of this treaty of friendship and cooperation. The treaty calls for joint consultation and actions in response to regional security threats.

The Soviets became a major source of military aid to Syria. Between 1980 and 1991 the Soviet Union delivered more than $26 billion worth of military equipment to Syria, and by 1998, nearly 90 percent of Syrian military equipment was Soviet made.

The collapse of the Soviet Union did not fundamentally alter the relationship between Syria and Russia, the largest successor state to the USSR. Starting in 1996, President Boris Yeltsin of Russia expressed a willingness to cooperate militarily, and Russia began supplying Syria with training and consulting services from Russian military experts again. In exchange, the Syrians allowed Russia to use Tartus harbor as a base in the Mediterranean.

ALLIANCE TEXT

The Syrian Arab Republic and the Union of Soviet Socialist Republics,

Inspired by the desire to strengthen and develop the relations of friendship and all-round co-operation existing between them in the interests of the peoples of the two States, the cause of peace and security throughout the world, the consolidation of international détente and the development of peaceful cooperation among States,

Determined to deal a strong rebuff to the policy of aggression pursued by imperialism and its accomplices, to continue the struggle against colonialism, neo-colonialism and racism in all their forms and manifestations, including zionism, and to support national independence and social progress,

Attaching particular importance to the continuation of co-operation between the two countries aimed at establishing a just and durable peace in the Middle East,

Reaffirming their loyalty to the purposes and principles of the Charter of the United Nations, including the principles of respect for sovereignty, national independence, territorial integrity and non-intervention in internal affairs,

Have decided to conclude this Treaty and have agreed as follows:

Article 1. The High Contracting Parties declare their determination steadily to develop and strengthen friendship and co-operation between the two States and peoples in the political, economic, military, scientific, technical, cultural and other fields on the basis of the principles of equal rights, mutual benefit, respect for sovereignty, national independence, territorial integrity and non-intervention in each other's internal affairs.

Article 2. The High Contracting Parties shall contribute in every way possible to the strengthening of international peace and the security of peoples, the reduction of international tension and its embodiment in specific forms of co-operation among States, the settlement of disputes by peaceful means, and the elimination of any manifestations of a policy of hegemonism and aggression from the practice of international relations.

The Parties shall actively co-operate with each other in tackling the problems of putting an end to the arms race and achieving general and complete disarmament, including nuclear disarmament, under effective international control.

Article 3. The High Contracting Parties, guided by their faith in the equality of all peoples and States, independent of race and religion, condemn colonialism, racism and zionism, which is one of the forms and manifestations of racism, and reaffirm their determination to wage a steadfast struggle against them. The Parties shall co-operate with other States in providing support for the just striving of peoples to combat imperialism, eliminate colonialism and racial domination once and for all, and achieve freedom and social progress.

Article 4. The Syrian Arab Republic respects the peace-loving foreign policy pursued by the Union of Soviet Socialist Republics, which is designed to strengthen friendship and co-operation with all countries and peoples.

The Union of Soviet Socialist Republics respects the non-aligned policy pursued by the Syrian Arab Republic, which is an important factor in the maintenance and consolidation of international peace and security and the reduction of international tension.

Article 5. The High Contracting Parties shall develop and expand the practice of mutual exchanges of views and regular consultations on matters concerning bilateral relations and on international problems of interest to both Parties, foremost among them being the problems of the Middle East. The consultations and exchanges of views shall continue at various levels, primarily by means of meetings between leading State officials of both Parties.

Article 6. In the event of situations arising which threaten the peace or security of one of the Parties or constitute a threat to the peace or a breach of international peace and security, the High Contracting Parties shall immediately contact each other for the purpose of co-ordinating their positions and co-operating in order to remove the said threat and to restore peace.

Article 7. The High Contracting Parties shall co-operate closely and in every way possible to ensure conditions favourable to the maintenance and development of the social and economic achievements of their peoples and to the respect for the sovereignty of each of them over their natural resources.

Article 8. The High Contracting Parties shall promote the steady consolidation and expansion of mutually advantageous economic, scientific and technical co-operation and the exchange of experience between them in industry, agriculture, irrigation and water resources, as well as in communications, utilization of oil and other natural resources, transport and other areas of the economy, and in the training of national specialists. The Parties shall expand trade and shipping between them on the basis of the principles of equality, mutual advantage and most-favoured-nation treatment.

Article 9. The High Contracting Parties shall continue to develop cooperation and the exchange of experience in science, art, literature, education, health, information, the cinema, tourism, sport and other fields.

The Parties shall promote the expansion of contacts and cooperation between State bodies, mass organizations, including trade unions and other social organizations, enterprises and cultural and scientific institutions, so that the peoples of the two countries may become better acquainted with each other's life, work, experience and achievements.

Article 10. The High Contracting Parties shall continue to develop co-operation in military matters on the basis of appropriate agreements concluded between them for the purpose of strengthening their defence capability.

Article 11. Each of the High Contracting Parties declares that it will not enter into any alliances, join any group of States or participate in any actions or measures directed against the other High Contracting Party.

Article 12. Each of the High Contracting Parties declares that its obligations under international treaties currently in force do not conflict with the provisions of this Treaty, and undertakes not to conclude any international agreements which are not consistent therewith.

Article 13. Any differences that may emerge between the High Contracting Parties regarding the interpretation or application of any provision of this Treaty shall be settled bilaterally, in a spirit of friendship, mutual understanding and respect.

Article 14. This Treaty shall be valid for a term of 20 years from the date of its entry into force.

If neither of the High Contracting Parties gives notice, six months before the expiry of the above-mentioned term, of its desire to terminate the Treaty, it shall be extended for successive five-year terms until such time as one of the High Contracting Parties gives written notice, six months before the expiry of the current five-year term, of its intention to terminate it.

Article 15. This Treaty is subject to ratification and shall enter into force on the date of the exchange of the instruments of ratification, which shall take place at Damascus.

Done at Moscow on 8 October 1980, in two copies, each in the Arabic and Russian languages, both texts being equally authentic.

For the Union of Soviet Socialist Republics:

[L. I. BREZHNEV]

For the Syrian Arab Republic:

[HAFEZ AL-ASSAD]

4.1420 Treaty of Friendship and Co-operation between the Union of Soviet Socialist Republics and the People's Republic of the Congo

Alliance Members: Union of Soviet Socialist Republics and the People's Republic of the Congo
Signed On: May 13, 1981, in the city of Moscow. In force until January 1, 1991.
Alliance Type: Entente (Type III)

Source: *United Nations Treaty,* no. 21937.

SUMMARY

Congo won its independence from French colonial rule in 1960, and three years later its leadership declared the country to be Africa's first Marxist nation. Despite the overt commitment to Marxism, foreign trade remained high and Marxist doctrine did not permeate society as it had in other countries. In 1979, however, the government of Colonel Sassou-Nguesso came to power and established a stricter, one-party Communist regime. Congo then became the first African nation to sign an alliance with the Soviet Union.

Although this treaty affirmed each nation's willingness to cooperate in all fields, the Soviets and the Congolese never had close ties. The Soviets refused to aid Congo's development plan and continued to offer extremely low prices for Congolese exports. The Congolese similarly failed to cooperate with the Soviet Union, refusing a request to let the Soviet Union build a deepwater port while also seeking friendlier relations with France.

Democratic resistance overthrew the Sassou-Nguesso regime in 1990, and the government of Congo abandoned Marxism and liberalized party competition. The shift in leadership also effectively ended the treaty with the Soviets. By 1992, a new president was elected, but only five years later conflict erupted with the political resurrection of the former president.

ALLIANCE TEXT

The Union of the Soviet Socialist Republics and the People's Republic of the Congo, hereinafter referred to as the "High Contracting Parties",

Considering that the further development and strengthening of the relations of friendship and harmonious co-operation between them are in accord with the vital national interests of the people of the two countries and serve the cause of peace throughout the world,

Inspired by the ideals of the struggle against imperialism, colonialism and racism in all their forms and manifestations and by the unswerving desire to give maximum support to peoples struggling for freedom, independence and social progress,

Determined to promote the strengthening of international peace and security in the interests of the peoples of all countries,

Supporting the unity of all progressive forces in the struggle for peace, freedom, independence and social progress and considering that the development of friendly relations and co-operation between the socialist and the developing countries is in accord with their common interests,

Inspired by the desire to strengthen and consolidate the relations of friendship and mutually advantageous co-operation between the two Governments and peoples and to create a basis for the continued development of these relations,

Reaffirming their loyalty to the purposes and principles of the United Nations Charter,

Have agreed as follows:

Article 1. The High Contracting Parties shall develop and deepen the relations of unbreakable friendship and harmonious co-operation in the political, economic, commercial, scientific and technical and cultural fields on the basis of equality of rights, non-interference in internal affairs, respect for sovereignty, territorial integrity and inviolability of frontiers.

Article 2. The High Contracting Parties shall co-operate closely to ensure conditions favourable to the maintenance and development of the socio-economic achievements of their peoples and respect for the sovereignty of each of them over all their natural resources.

Article 3. The Union of Soviet Socialist Republics respects the policy of nonalignment pursued by the People's Republic of the Congo, which is an important factor in the development of international co-operation and peaceful co-existence.

The People's Republic of the Congo respects the policy of the defence of peace pursued by the Union of Soviet Socialist Republics with a view to the strengthening of friendship and co-operation with all countries and peoples.

Article 4. The High Contracting Parties shall continue to make every effort to safeguard international peace and the security of peoples, to further the process of international détente, extend it to all regions of the world and embody it in specific forms of mutually advantageous co-operation among States, and to settle international disputes by peaceful means. They shall promote actively the cause of general and complete disarmament, including nuclear disarmament, under effective international control.

Article 5. The High Contracting Parties shall continue to wage a steadfast struggle against the forces of imperialism and for the final elimination of colonialism and neo-colonialism, racism and *apartheid* and to promote the full implementation of the United Nations Declaration on the Granting of Independence to Colonial Countries and Peoples.

The High Contracting Parties shall co-operate with each other and with other peace-loving States in supporting the just struggle of peoples for their sovereignty, freedom, independence and social progress.

Article 6. The High Contracting Parties shall consult each other regarding all important international questions affecting the interests of the two States.

Article 7. In the event of situations arising which constitute a threat to the peace or a breach of peace, the High Contracting Parties shall seek immediate contact with each other for the purpose of co-ordinating their positions in the interest of removing the said threat or of restoring peace.

Article 8. The High Contracting Parties shall make every effort to consolidate and expand the mutually advantageous political, economic, social, cultural and scientific and technical co-operation between them. To this end, they shall extend and deepen their co-operation in the fields which are the subjects of special agreements.

The High Contracting Parties shall develop their commercial exchanges and the merchant shipping between them on the basis of the principles of equality of rights, mutual advantage and most-favoured-nation treatment.

Article 9. The High Contracting Parties shall promote the development of friendly and co-operative relations between the socio-political and cultural organizations of their countries in order to foster a deeper mutual acquaintance with the life, work, experience and achievements of their peoples.

Article 10. Each of the High Contracting Parties declares that it will not participate in any actions or measures directed against the other High Contracting Party.

Article 11. The High Contracting Parties declare that this Treaty does not affect their rights and obligations under existing international treaties concluded with their participation and they undertake not to conclude international agreements incompatible with this Treaty.

Article 12. Any questions which may arise between the High Contracting Parties concerning the interpretation or application of any provision of this Treaty shall be resolved bilaterally in a spirit of friendship, mutual respect and understanding.

Article 13. This Treaty shall be valid for a term of 20 years.

If neither of the High Contracting Parties gives notice, six months before the expiry of the above-mentioned term, of its desire to terminate the Treaty, it shall be extended for successive five-year terms until such time as one of the High Contracting Parties gives written notice, six months before the expiry of the current five-year term, of its intention to terminate it.

Article 14. This Treaty is subject to ratification and shall enter into force on the date of the exchange of the instruments of ratification, which shall take place at Brazzaville.

Article 15. The High Contracting Parties shall transmit a copy of this Treaty to the United Nations Secretariat for registration.

Article 16. This Treaty has been drafted in duplicate in the Russian and French languages, both texts being equally authentic.

Done at Moscow on 13 May 1981.

For the Union of Soviet Socialist Republics:

[L. BREZHNEV]

For the People's Republic of the Congo:

[DENIS SASSOU-NGUESSO]

4.1421 Non-Aggression and Defense Assistance Agreement between the States of the West African Economic Community (CEAO) and Togo

Alliance Members: Benin, Burkina Faso, Cape Verde, Côte d'Ivoire, Gambia, Ghana, Guinea, Guinea-Bissau, Liberia, Mali, Mauritania, Niger, Nigeria, Senegal, Sierra Leone, and Togo
Signed On: May 29, 1981, in the city of Freetown (Sierra Leone). In force as of date of publication of this volume, except for Mauritania, which withdrew on December 26, 2000.
Alliance Type: Defense Pact (Type I)

Source: *United Nations Treaty,* no. 29137.

SUMMARY

In 1975, the Economic Community of West African States (ECOWAS) was established by treaty. The goal of the agreement was to foster better relations and economic growth across the region of West Africa. As the states of ECOWAS realized that economic growth could occur only with stability and peace, the ECOWAS members signed the Protocol of Non-Aggression in 1978, followed by this non-aggression and defense assistance agreement on May 29, 1981.

The non-aggression and defense assistance agreement united the member states in an agreement to confront any external threat to an alliance member's security and respond to any foreign-backed resistance movements within member nations. Following this agreement, ECOWAS intervened to stop conflicts in Liberia, Sierra Leone, and Guinea-Bissau with ad hoc coalitions formed among ECOWAS members specifically for these actions.

In an effort to move beyond reliance on ad hoc assortments of forces, the member states revised their treaty in 1999 to aid member states in pursuing effective joint peacekeeping operations. That revision followed a strengthening of the economic union that was formed in 1993.

ALLIANCE TEXT

Preamble

The Governments of the Member States of the Economic Community of West African States;

Recalling Article 2 of the United Nations Charter which calls upon all Member States to refrain in their international relations from resorting to the use of threats or force either against the territorial integrity or the independence of all States in any manner that is incompatible with the aims of the United Nations or from interfering in the internal affairs of other States;

Recalling Article 3 of the Charter of the Organisation of African Unity which calls upon Member States to respect the sovereignty and territorial integrity of each State and its inalienable right to an independent existence;

Mindful of the Treaty setting up the Economic Community of West African States;

Recalling the Protocol on Non-Aggression signed in Lagos on 22nd April 19782 in accordance with which Member States resolved not to use force as a means of settling their disputes;

Convinced that economic progress cannot be achieved unless the conditions for the necessary security are ensured in all Member States of the Community;

Considering that Member States belong to the same geographical area;

Conscious of the serious continuous threats of aggression on the African continent in general and their own countries in particular;

Conscious of the serious risks that the presence of foreign military bases on the African continent may constitute as support forces to external aggression;

Firmly Resolve to safeguard and consolidate the independence and the sovereignty of Member States against foreign intervention.

Conscious of the fact that external defence of their states depends entirely on each sovereign state, and that such a defence will be more effective with the coordination and pooling together of the means of mutual assistance provided by respective Member States within the framework of this Protocol;

Desirous of maintaining the ties of friendship existing amongst Member States and of strengthening their cooperation in all fields on the basis of equality, mutual interests and respects;

Have Agreed as follows:

Chapter I Definitions

Article 1. Within the context of this Protocol,

"Treaty" means the Treaty of the Economic Community of West African States;

"Community" means the Economic Community of West African States;

"Authority" means the Authority of Heads of State and Government as defined in Article 5 of the Treaty;

"Member State" or 'Member States" means a Member State or Member States of the Community;

"Executive Secretary" means Executive Secretary of the Community as defined in Article 8 of the Treaty:

"Aggression" means the use of armed force by any State against the sovereignty and territorial integrity or political independence of mother State or by any other manner incompatible with the Charter of the United Nations and OAU;

"Assistance on Defence" means all military aid (material, technical and personnel).

Chapter II Objectives

Article 2. Member States declare and accept that any armed threat or aggression directed against any Member State shall constitute a threat or aggression against the entire Community.

Article 3. Member States resolve to give mutual aid and assistance for defence against any armed threat or aggression.

Article 4. Member States shall also take appropriate measures such as specified in Articles 17 and 18 of the present Protocol in the following circumstances:

(a) In case of armed conflict between two or several Member States if the settlement procedure by peaceful means as indicated in Article 5 of the Non-Aggression Protocol mentioned in the Preamble proves ineffective;

(b) In case of internal armed conflict within any Member State engineered and supported actively from outside likely to endanger the security and peace in the entire Community. In this case the Authority shall appreciate and decide on this situation in full collaboration with the Authority of the Member State or States concerned.

Chapter III Institutions

Article 5. The institutions for the implementation of this Protocol shall be:

The Authority
The Defence Council
The Defence Commission

Section I- The Authority

Article 6.   1. The Authority on the occasion of the annual ordinary meeting of ECOWAS shall examine general problems concerning peace and security of the Community;

2. The Authority nay also hold extraordinary sessions on defence matters where circumstances so require;

3. The Authority shall decide on the expediency of military action and entrust its execution to the Force Commander of the Allied Forces of the Community (AAPC);

4. Decisions taken by the Authority shall be immediately enforceable on Member States.

Section II – The Defence Council

Article 7.   1. A Defence Council of the Community shall be established by the Authority.

2. It shall consist of Ministers of Defence and Foreign Affairs of Member States. However, in cases of crisis, the Defence Council shall be chaired by the current Chairman of the Authority and it shall be enlarged to include any other Minister from Member States according to the circumstances. The Executive Secretary and the Deputy Executive Secretary in charge of military matters shall be in attendance at meetings of the Council.

Article 8.   1. The Defence Council shall meet on the convocation by its Chairman to prepare the items of the Agenda of Sessions of the Authority dealing with defence matters.

2. In an emergency, the Defence Council shall examine the situation, the strategy to be adopted and the means of intervention to be used.

Article 9. In case of armed intervention, the Defence Council assisted by the Defence Commission shall supervise with the authority of the State or States concerned, all measures to be taken by the Force Commander and ensure that all necessary means for the intervention are made available to him. The actions of the Force Commander shall be subject to competent political authority of the Member State or States concerned.

Article 10. At the end of the operation, the Defence Council shall write a factual report to be addressed to the Authority.

Section III – The Defence Commission

Article 11   1. A Defence Commission shall be established by the Authority and shall consist of a Chief of Staff from each Member State.

2. The Defence Commission shall be responsible for examining the technical aspect of defence matters.

3. The Defence Commission shall establish its Rules of Procedure especially in respect of the convening of its meetings, the conduct of the business and the implementation of duties as assigned to it by the Defence Council.

Chapter IV Administration

Article 12.   1. The Defence Council shall appoint a Deputy Executive Secretary (Military) at the Executive Secretariat for a period of four years renewable only once,

2. The Deputy Executive Secretary (Military) shall be a senior serving military officer.

3. He shall be in charge of the administration and Pillow-up of the decisions taken by the Authority and in accordance with the present Protocol and under the authority of the Executive Secretary.

4. He shall update plans for the movement of troops and logistics and initiate joint exercises as provided for in paragraph 3 of Article 13 below.

5. He shall be assisted in the discharge of his functions by the necessary staff members and personnel as determined by the Defence Council.

6. He shall prepare and manage the military budget of the Secretariat.

7. He shall study and make proposals to the Executive Secretariat in respect of all matters relating to personnel and equipment within his jurisdiction.

Chapter V Modalities of Intervention and Assistance

Article 13.   1. All Member States agree to place at the disposal of the Community, earmarked units from the existing National Armed Forces in case of any armed intervention.

2. These Units shall be referred to as the Allied Armed Forces of the Community (AAFC).

3. In order to better realise the objectives set forth in this Protocol, the Member States may organise, from time to time, as nay be approved by the Authority, joint military exercises among two or more earmarked Units of the AAFC.

Article 14. The Allied Armed Forces of the Community shall be under the command of the Forces Commander appointed by the Authority on the proposal of the defence Council. He shall be entrusted with powers that are conferred upon him by the Authority.

He together with the Chief of Defence staff of the assisted country, shall be the joint Chief of Defence Staff of the Allied Armed Forces and shall be responsible for the implementation of armed intervention and assistance as decided by the Authority. He shall have at his disposal all necessary means of defence.

Article 15.   1. Intervention by A.A.F.C. shall in all cases be justified by the legitimate defence of the territories of the Community.

2. It shall therefore be carried out in accordance with the mechanism described in Articles 16, 17 and 18 below.

Article 16. When an external armed threat or aggression is directed against a Member State of the Community, the Head of State of that country shall send a written request for assistance to the current Chairman of the Authority of ECOWAS, with copies to other Members. This request shall mean that the Authority is duly notified and that the A.A.F.C. are placed under a state of emergency. The Authority shall decide in accordance with the emergency procedure as stipulated in Article 6 above.

Article 17.   1. When there is a conflict between two Member States of the Community, the Authority shall meet urgently and take appropriate action for mediation. If need be, the Authority shall decide only to interpose the A.A.F.C. between the troops engaged in the conflict.

Article 18.   1. In the case where an internal conflict in a Member State of the Community is actively maintained and sustained free outside, the provisions of Articles 6, 9 and 16 of this Protocol shall apply.

2. Community forces shall not intervene if the conflict remains purely internal.

Chapter VI Special Provisions

Article 19. The implementation of this Protocol shall be supplemented by additional Protocols.

Article 20.   1. Undertakings devolving from the provisions of this Protocol shall not be interpreted as being against the spirit of Conventions or Agreements binding one Member State to another third State or States; provided such Conventions and Agreements are not in conflict with the spirit of this Defence Assistance.

2. Nonetheless, a Defence Agreement concluded with some other State shall be denounced by the Member State concerned as soon as such other State shall have been identified by the Authority as an aggressor against a Member State.

3. Member States shall undertake to end the presence of foreign military bases within their national territories as soon as the Community is in the position to meet their requirements in matters relating to defence.

Chapter VII General and Final Provisions

Article 21.   1. Any Member State which accedes to the Treaty automatically accedes to this Protocol and to the Protocol of Non-Aggression signed in Lagos on the 22nd April, 1978.

2. On the other hand, any Member State signatory to this present Protocol and having ratified it, or having acceded to it, becomes party to the above-mentioned Non-Aggression Pact.

Article 22.   1. Any Member State may submit proposals for the amendment or revision of this Protocol.

2. Any such proposals shall be submitted to the Executive Secretary who shall communicate them to other Member States not later than thirty days after the receipt of such proposals. Amendments or revisions shall be considered by the Authority after Member States have been given one month's notice thereof.

Article 23. 1. Any Member State wishing to withdraw from the Protocol shall give to the Executive Secretary one year's written notice. At the end of this period of one year, if such notice is not withdrawn, such a State shall cease to be a party to the Protocol.

2. During the period of one year referred to in the preceding paragraph, such a Member State shall nevertheless observe the provisions of this Protocol and shall remain liable for the discharge of its obligations under this Protocol.

Article 24. 1. This Protocol shall enter into force provisionally at the signing by the Heads of State and Government, and definitively after ratification by not less than seven (7) signatories, in accordance with the Constitutional Laws of each Member State.

2. This Protocol, as well as all instruments of ratification shall be deposited with the Executive Secretariat which shall transmit certified true copies to all Member States and notify them of the dates of deposits of the instruments of ratification and shall register it with the Organisation of African Unity (OAU) , as well as the United Nations (UN) and any other Organisation as the Authority shall decide.

3. The Present Protocol shall be annexed to and shall form an integral part of the Treaty.

In faith whereof, We, the Heads of State and Government of the Economic Community of West African States, have signed the Present Protocol.

Done at Freetown, this 29th day of May, 1981, in [one] single original in the English and French languages, both texts being equally authentic.

[Signed]

H. E. Colonel MATHIEU KEREKOU
President of the People's Republic of Benin
[Signed]
H. E. ABDOULAYE KONE
Minister of Economy and Finance for and on behalf of the President of the Republic of Ivory Coast
[Signed]
H. E. Dr HILLA LIMANN
President of the Republic of Ghana
[Signed]
H. E. Commandant Joao BERNADO VIERA
President of the Republic of Guinea Bissau
[Signed]
H. E. Master Sergeant SAMUEL K. DOE
Chairman, People's Redemption Council and Head of State of the Republic of Liberia

[Signed]
H.E. PEDRO PERES
Prime Minister, for and on behalf of the President of the Republic of Cape Verde
[Signed]
H.E. Dr MoMoDou S. K. MANNEH
Minister of Economic Planning and Industrial Development, for and on behalf of the President of the Republic of Gambia
[Signed]
H. E. AHMED SEKOU TOURE
President of the People's Revolutionary Republic of Guinea
[Signed]
H. E. Lt Colonel FELIX TIEMTARUBOUM
Minister of Foreign Affairs and Cooperation for and on behalf of the Head of State of the Republic of Upper Volta
[Signed]
H. E. M. DRISSA KEITA
Minister of Finance and Commerce, for and on behalf of the President of the Republic of Mali
[Signed]
H. E. M. MOHAMED KHOUNA OULD HAIDALLA
Chairman of the Military Council for National Redemption, Head of State of the Islamic Republic of Mauritania
[Signed]
H. E. Alhaji SHEHU SHAGARI
President of the Federal Republic of Nigeria
[Signed]
H. E. Dr SIAKA STEVENS
President of the Republic of Sierra Leone
[Signed]
H. E. HAMID ALGABID
Minister of Commerce, for and on behalf of the Supreme Military Council of the Republic of Niger
[Signed]
H.E. ABDOU DIOUF
President of the Republic of Senegal
[Signed]
H.E. General GNASSINGBE EYADEMA
President of the Republic of Togo

4.1422 Treaty Establishing the Organization of Eastern Caribbean States (Treaty of Basseterre)

Alliance Members: Antigua and Barbuda, Dominica, Grenada, Montserrat, St. Kitts and Nevis, St. Lucia, and St. Vincent and the Grenadines.
Signed On: June 18, 1981, in the city of Basseterre (St. Kitts and Nevis). In force as of date of publication of this volume.
Alliance Type: Defense Pact (Type I)

Source: *United Nations Treaty*, no. 22435.

SUMMARY

Following the eastern Caribbean islands' independence from Britain, the newly sovereign states recognized the need for a more structured framework for economic development. The Organisation of Eastern Caribbean States was created on June 18, 1981, when seven Caribbean nations signed what became known as the Treaty of Basseterre.

The OECS was to foster cooperation among the member states, and the treaty stressed economic integration, international law, and cooperation in defending the sovereignty of the member states. On October 25, 1983, President Reagan used the latter clause, in conjunction with the pledge for collective security, as justification for intervention in Grenada.

The organization exists today primarily within the region to coordinate economic activities and externally with organizations such as the Caribbean Development Bank.

ALLIANCE TEXT

Preamble

The Governments of the Contracting States,

Convinced that the West Indies (Associated States) Council of Ministers since its establishment in 1966 has done much to further regional co-operation in many fields and has rendered valuable services to its member countries;

Recognising that since the establishment of the said Council of Ministers significant constitutional and other changes have taken place in the region;

Affirming their determination to achieve economic and social development for their peoples as enunciated in the Agreement of the 11th day of June 1968 establishing the East Caribbean Common Market;

Inspired by a common determination to strengthen the links between themselves by uniting their efforts and resources and establishing and strengthening common institutions which could serve to increase their bargaining power as regards third countries or groupings of countries;

Having in mind the strong views expressed by the said Council of Ministers regarding the desirability of retaining and formalising the arrangements for joint action by its member countries;

Determined to satisfy the legitimate aspirations of their peoples for development and progress;

Have agreed as follows:

Article 1. Establishment of the Organisation of Eastern Caribbean States

By this Treaty the Contracting Parties establish among themselves the Organisation of Eastern Caribbean States (hereinafter called "the Organisation") having the membership, powers and functions hereinafter specified.

Article 2. Membership

1. Full membership of the Organisation shall be open to those countries which immediately prior to the establishment of the Organisation have been members of the West Indies (Associated States) Council of Ministers, namely:

   (a) Antigua;
   (b) Dominica;
   (c) Grenada;
   (d) Montserrat;
   (e) St. Kitts/Nevis;
   (f) Saint Lucia;
   (g) Saint Vincent and the Grenadines.

2. The independent States listed in the preceding paragraph the Governments of which sign and ratify this Treaty in accordance with Article 20 thereof shall immediately become full members (hereinafter referred to as "the Member States") of the Organisation.

3. Notwithstanding that a territory or group of territories listed in paragraph 1 of this Article is not a sovereign independent State, the Heads of Government of the Member States of the Organisation (hereinafter referred to as "the Authority") may by a unanimous decision admit such territory or group of territories as a full member of the Organisation and such territory or group of territories shall thereby qualify as a Member State under this Treaty.

4. Any other States or territories in the Caribbean region may apply to become Full or Associate Members and shall be admitted as such by a unanimous decision of the Authority. The nature and extent of the rights and obligations of Associate Members shall be determined by the Authority.

Article 3. Purposes and Functions of the Organisation

1. The major purposes of the Organisation shall be:

   (a) To promote co-operation among the Member States and at the regional and international levels having due regard to the Treaty establishing the Caribbean Community and the Charter of the United Nations;
   (b) To promote unity and solidarity among the Member States and to defend their sovereignty, territorial integrity and independence;
   (c) To assist the Member States in the realisation of their obligations and responsibilities to the international community with due regard to the role of international law as a standard of conduct in their relationship;
   (d) To seek to achieve the fullest possible harmonisation of foreign policy among the Member States; to seek to adopt, as far as possible, common positions on

international issues and to establish and maintain wherever possible, arrangements for joint overseas representation and/or common services;

(e) To promote economic integration among the Member States through the provisions of the Agreement Establishing the East Caribbean Common Market; and

(f) To pursue the said purposes through its respective institutions by discussion of questions of common concern and by agreement and common action.

2. To this end the Member States will endeavour to co-ordinate, harmonise and pursue joint policies particularly in the fields of:

(a) External relations including overseas representation;

(b) International trade agreements and other external economic relations;

(c) Financial and technical assistance from external sources;

(d) International marketing of goods and services including tourism;

(e) External transportation and communications including civil aviation;

(f) Economic integration among the Member States through the provisions of the Agreement Establishing the East Caribbean Common Market;

(g) Matters relating to the sea and its resources;

(h) The judiciary;

(i) Currency and central banking;

(j) Audit;

(k) Statistics;

(1) Income tax administration;

(m) Customs and excise administration;

(n) Tertiary education including university;

(o) Training in public administration and management;

(p) Scientific, technical and cultural co-operation;

(q) Mutual defence and security; and

(r) Such other activities calculated to further the purposes of the Organisation as the Member States may from time to time decide.

Article 4. General Undertaking as to Implementation

Member States shall take all appropriate measures, whether general or particular, to ensure the carrying out of obligations arising out of this Treaty or resulting from decisions taken by the institutions of the Organisation. They shall facilitate the achievement of the purposes of the Organisation; in particular, each Member State shall take all steps to secure the enactment of such legislation as is necessary to give effect to this Treaty and decisions taken thereunder.

Article 5. Institutions of the Organisation

1. There are hereby established the following principal institutions through which the Organisation shall accomplish the functions entrusted to it under this Treaty:

(a) The Authority of Heads of Government of the Member States of the Organisation (referred to in this Treaty as "the Authority");

(b) The Foreign Affairs Committee;

(c) The Defence and Security Committee;

(d) The Economic Affairs Committee; and

(e) The Central Secretariat.

2. The institutions of the Organisation shall perform the functions and act within the limits of the powers conferred upon them by or under this Treaty and by the Protocols thereto. They may establish such subsidiary institutions as they deem necessary for the performance of their functions.

Article 6. Composition and Functions of the Authority

1. The Authority shall be composed of Heads of Government of the Member States.

2. Any member of the Authority may, as appropriate, designate a Minister to represent such member at any meeting of the Authority.

3. Only Member States possessing the necessary competence in respect of matters under consideration from time to time shall take part in the deliberations of the Authority.

4. The Authority shall be the supreme policy-making institution of the Organisation. It shall be responsible for, and have the general direction and control of the performance of the functions of the Organisation, for the progressive development of the Organisation and the achievement of its purposes.

5. The Authority shall have power to make decisions on all matters within its competence. All such decisions shall require the affirmative vote of all Member States present and voting at the meeting of the Authority at which such decisions were taken provided that such decisions shall have no force and effect until ratified by those Member States, if any, which were not present at that meeting, or until such Member States have notified the Authority of their decision to abstain. Such decisions by the Authority shall be binding on all Member States and on all institutions of the Organisation and effect shall be given to any such decisions provided that it is within the sovereign competence of Member States to implement them.

6. The Authority may make such recommendations and give such directives as it deems necessary for the achievement of the purposes of the Organisation and for ensuring the smooth functioning of the institutions of the Organisation.

7. The Authority may establish, and designate as such, institutions of the Organisation in addition to those specified in sub-paragraphs (b), (c), (d) and (e) of paragraph 1 of Article 5 of this Treaty, as it deems necessary for the achievement of the purposes of the Organisation.

8. Subject to the relevant provisions of this Treaty, the Authority shall be the final authority for the conclusion of treaties or other international agreements on behalf of the Organisation and for entering into relationships between the Organisation and other International Organisations and third countries.

9. Subject to the relevant provisions of this Treaty, the Authority shall take decisions for the purpose of establishing the financial arrangements necessary for meeting the expenses of the Organisation and shall be the final authority on questions arising in relation to the financial affairs of the Organisation.

10. The Authority shall meet at least twice a year. It shall determine its own procedure including that for convening meetings, for the conduct of business thereat and at other times, and for the annual rotation of the office of Chairman among its members in accordance with the principle of alphabetical order of the Member States.

11. The Authority shall in addition meet in extraordinary session whenever it deems necessary in accordance with the regulations laid down in its rules of procedure.

Article 7. Composition and Functions of the Foreign Affairs Committee

1. The Foreign Affairs Committee shall consist of the Ministers responsible for Foreign Affairs in the Governments of the Member States or such other Ministers as may be designated by the Heads of Government of the Member States.

2. Only Member States possessing the necessary competence in respect of matters under consideration from time to time shall take part in the deliberations of the Foreign Affairs Committee.

3. The Foreign Affairs Committee shall be responsible to the Authority. It shall take appropriate action on any matters referred to it by the Authority and shall have the power to make recommendations to the Authority.

4. The Foreign Affairs Committee shall have responsibility for the progressive development of the foreign policy of the Organisation and for the general direction and control of the performance of the executive functions of the Organisation in relation to its foreign affairs.

5. The decisions and directives of the Foreign Affairs Committee shall be unanimous and shall be binding on all subordinate institutions of the Organisation unless otherwise determined by the Authority.

6. Subject to any directives that the Authority may give, the Foreign Affairs Committee shall meet as and when necessary. It shall determine its own procedure, including that for convening meetings, for the conduct of business thereat, and at other times and for the annual rotation of the office of Chairman among its members in accordance with the principle of alphabetical order of the Member States.

Article 8. Composition and Functions of the Defence and Security Committee

1. The Defence and Security Committee shall consist of the Ministers responsible for Defence and Security or other Ministers or Plenipotentiaries designated by Heads of Government of the Member States.

2. Only Member States possessing the necessary competence in respect of matters under consideration from time to time shall take part in the deliberations of the Defence and Security Committee.

3. The Defence and Security Committee shall be responsible to the Authority. It shall take appropriate action on any matters referred to it by the Authority and shall have the power to make recommendations to the Authority. It shall advise the Authority on matters relating to external defence and on arrangements for collective security against external aggression, including mercenary aggression, with or without the support of internal or national elements.

4. The Defence and Security Committee shall have responsibility for coordinating the efforts of Member States for collective defence and the preservation of peace and security against external aggression and for the development of close ties among the Member States of the Organisation in matters or external defence and security, including measures to combat the activities of mercenaries, operating with or without the support of internal or national elements, in the exercise of the inherent right of individual or collective self-defence recognised by Article 51 of the Charter of the United Nations.

5. The decisions and directives of the Defence and Security Committee shall be unanimous and shall be binding on all subordinate institutions of the Organisation unless otherwise determined by the Authority.

6. Subject to any directives that the Authority may give, the Defence and Security Committee shall meet as and when necessary. It shall determine its own procedure, including that for convening meetings, for the conduct of business thereat and at other times, and for the annual rotation of the Office of Chairman among its members in accordance with the principle of alphabetical order of the Member States.

Article 9. Composition and Functions of the Economic Affairs Committee

1. The Economic Affairs Committee (hereinafter referred to in this Article as "the Committee") shall consist of such Ministers in the Governments of the Member States as may from time to time be appointed to the Committee by Heads of Government of the Member States.

2. Only Member States possessing the necessary competence in respect of matters under consideration from time to time shall take part in the deliberations of the Committee.

3. The Committee shall have as its functions those functions entrusted to the Council of Ministers under the Agreement of 11th June 1968 establishing the East Caribbean Common Market.

4. The provisions of the said Agreement, to the extent that they are not incompatible with the provisions of this Treaty, shall be deemed to be incorporated in and to form an integral part of this Treaty. The provisions of the said Agreement are set out in Annex 11 to this Treaty.

Article 10. The Central Secretariat

1. The Central Secretariat (hereinafter referred to as "the Secretariat") shall be the principal institution responsible for the general administration of the Organisation.

2. The Secretariat shall comprise a Director-General and such other staff as the Organisation may require.

3. The Director-General shall be the Chief Executive Officer of the Organisation and shall have responsibility for the general direction and control of the Organisation. He shall be appointed by the Authority to serve in that capacity for a term of four (4) years and shall be eligible for re-appointment.

4. In the performance of his functions, the Director-General shall be responsible to the Authority, the Foreign Affairs Committee, the Defence and Security Committee and the Economic Affairs Committee. He shall be responsible for the general efficiency of the administrative service, for co-ordination of the activities of the Organisation and for the operation of the administrative apparatus in general. He shall similarly be responsible to any institution established by the Authority pursuant to paragraph 7 of Article 6 of this Treaty.

In particular, his duties shall include the following:

(a) To service meetings of institutions of the Organisation;

(b) To take appropriate follow-up action on decisions, recommendations or directives taken at such meetings;

(c) To keep the functioning of the Organisation under continuous review and to report his findings to the appropriate Chairman;

(d) To make reports of activities and an annual report to the Authority on the work of the Organisation; and

(e) To undertake such work and studies and perform such services relating to the functions of the Organisation as may be assigned to him from time to time and also make such proposals relating thereto as may assist in the efficient and harmonious functioning and development of the Organisation.

5. The terms and conditions of service of the Director-General and other staff of the Secretariat shall be governed by such rules and regulations as are approved by the Authority.

6. In appointing officers to posts in the Secretariat, due regard shall be paid, subject to the paramount consideration of securing the highest standards of efficiency, competence and integrity, to the desirability of maintaining an equitable distribution of appointments to such posts among citizens of the Member States. Subject to the provisions of this paragraph, the Director-General shall have the discretion to appoint all staff to the Secretariat provided that Directors are appointed with the prior approval of the Authority.

7. The Director-General shall have the responsibility to ensure that all persons found suitable for employment are duly cleared before engagement in respect of security.

8. In the performance of their duties the Director-General and other members of the staff of the Secretariat shall neither seek nor accept instructions from any Government or from any other authority external to the Organisation. They shall refrain from any action which might reflect on their position as international officials responsible only to the Organisation.

9. Each Member State undertakes to respect the exclusive international character of the responsibilities of the Director-General and other members of the staff of the Organisation and not to seek to influence them in the discharge of their responsibilities.

Article 11. Co-ordination and Harmonisation of Foreign Policy

1. Unless objection is offered by the receiving States or international organisations and conferences concerned, Member States of the Organisation may establish and maintain arrangements for joint overseas diplomatic or other representation, including, where appropriate, the accreditation of one representative to one or more States, international organisations or conferences.

2. Where such objection, referred to in the preceding paragraph, is made by an international organisation or conference by virtue of its constitution or rules of procedure or for any other reason and where the Member States are members of such organisation or conference, the Director-General shall take all appropriate steps, consistent with the constitution or rules of procedure of such organisation or conference, as to ensure the optimum realisation of the benefits of their membership of such organisation or conference.

3. The Director-General shall have the authority and responsibility for transmitting directives of the Authority on joint foreign policy matters to heads of overseas diplomatic and other missions established by the Organisation. He shall take precedence in matters of protocol over the heads of such missions.

4. Heads of diplomatic or other missions of the Organisation shall be recommended for appointment by the Authority after consultation with the Foreign Affairs Committee. Provided that they may at any time resign their offices by written notice to the Director-General, who shall promptly transmit such notice to the Member States of the Organisation.

5. Subject to the preceding paragraph, the staff of such missions shall be appointed by the Director-General. In appointing such staff he shall have due regard to the provisions of paragraphs 6 and 7 of Article 10 of this Treaty. The terms and conditions of service of such staff shall be governed by such rules and regulations as govern the staff at the headquarters of the Organisation.

6. The expenses for diplomatic or other representatives referred to in paragraph 1 of this Article shall be apportioned among the Member States participating in such arrangements.

Article 12. External Auditor

1. There shall be an External Auditor of the Organisation who shall be appointed and removed by the Authority.

2. Subject to the provisions of the preceding paragraph the regulations governing the terms and conditions of service and powers of the External Auditor shall be approved by the Authority.

Article 13. The Budget of the Organisation

1. There shall be established a budget of the Organisation.

2. All expenses of the Organisation shall be approved in respect of each financial year by the Authority and shall be chargeable to the budget.

3. Revenues of the budget shall be derived from annual contributions by the Member States and from such other sources as may be determined by the Authority.

4. The budget shall be in balance as to revenues and expenditures.

5. A draft budget for each financial year shall be prepared by the Director-General for the approval of the Authority.

6. There shall be special budgets to meet extraordinary expenditures of the Organisation.

7. Each Member State undertakes to pay regularly its annual contribution to the budget of the Organisation.

Article 14. *Procedure for the Settlement of Disputes*

1. Any dispute that may arise between two or more of the Member States regarding the interpretation and application of this Treaty shall, upon the request of any of them, be amicably resolved by direct agreement.

2. If the dispute is not resolved within three months of the date on which the request referred to in the preceding paragraph has been made, any party to the dispute may submit it to the conciliation procedure provided for in Annex A to this Treaty by submitting a request to that effect to the Director-General of the Organisation and informing the other party or parties to the dispute of the request.

3. Member States undertake to accept the conciliation procedure referred to in the preceding paragraph as compulsory. Any decisions or recommendations of the Conciliation Commission in resolution of the dispute shall be final and binding on the Member States.

Article 15. *Participation in Other Arrangements*

1. Nothing in this Treaty shall preclude any Member State from participating in other arrangements either with other Member States or non-Member States provided that its participation in such arrangements does not derogate from the provisions of this Treaty.

2. The rights and obligations arising from agreements concluded before the entry into force of this Treaty between Member States, or between Member States and other countries or organisations shall not be affected by the provisions of this Treaty.

3. To the extent that such agreements are not compatible with this Treaty, the Member State or States concerned shall take all appropriate steps to eliminate the incompatibilities established. Member States shall, where necessary, assist each other to this end and shall, where appropriate, adopt a common attitude.

Article 16. *Relations with Other International Organisations and Other Countries*

1. The Organisation shall seek to establish such relations with other international organisations and other countries as may facilitate the attainment of its purposes. To this end, the Organisation may conclude formal agreements or establish effective working relationships with such Organisations and Governments of other countries.

2. The Organisation may decide, in accordance with its rules of procedure, to admit as observers at its deliberations representatives of non-Member States or other entities.

Article 17. *Privileges and Immunities*

1. The Organisation as an international organisation shall enjoy legal personality.

2. The Organisation shall have in the territory of each Member State:

(a) The legal capacity required for the performance of its functions under this Treaty; and

(b) Power to acquire, hold or dispose of movable or immovable property.

3. In the exercise of its legal personality under this Article, the Organisation shall be represented by the Director-General.

4. The privileges and immunities to be granted to the senior officials of the Organisation at its headquarters and in the Member States shall be the same as accorded to members of a diplomatic mission accredited at the headquarters of the Organisation and in the Member States under the provisions of the Vienna Convention on Diplomatic Relations of 18 April 1961. Similarly the privileges and immunities granted to the Secretariat at the headquarters of the Organisation shall be the same as granted to diplomatic missions at the headquarters of the Organisation and in the Member States under the said Convention. Other privileges and immunities to be recognised and granted by the Member States in connection with the Organisation shall be determined by the Authority.

Article 18. *Headquarters of the Organisation*

The location of the headquarters of the Organisation shall be determined by the Authority.

Article 19. *Setting-up of the Institutions*

1. At its first meeting after the entry into force of this Treaty the Authority shall, *inter alia*:

(a) Admit to membership in the Organisation the non-independent territories included in paragraph 1 of Article 2 of this Treaty, before consideration of any other matter;

(b) Appoint the Director-General;

(c) Determine the headquarters of the Organisation;

(d) Make decisions for the establishment of financial arrangements for meeting the expenses of the Organisation; and

(e) Give such directions to the institutions of the Organisation as are necessary for the expeditious and effective implementation of the provisions of this Treaty.

Article 20. Signature and Ratifications

1. This Treaty and any Protocols thereto which shall form an integral part of the Treaty, shall be open for signature to all countries specified in paragraph 1 of Article 2 of this Treaty.

2. This Treaty is subject to ratification by the signatories in accordance with their respective constitutional processes.

3. The original text of this Treaty shall be deposited with the Government of Saint Lucia which shall transmit certified copies thereof to all the signatories.

4. Instruments of ratification or accession shall be deposited with the Government of Saint Lucia, which shall notify all signatories of each such deposit.

Article 21. Entry into Force

This Treaty shall enter into force immediately upon receipt by the Government of Saint Lucia of the second instrument of ratification from the countries specified in paragraph 1 of Article 2 of this Treaty which have the status of Independent States.

Article 22. Admission to Membership; Accession and Adherence

1. After this Treaty has entered into force in accordance with the provisions of Article 21 thereof, any independent State or Territory specified in Article 2 of this Treaty may apply to the Authority to become a Full Member or Associate Member of the Organisation and may, if the Authority so decides, be admitted as such in accordance with paragraphs 3 and 4 of Article 2 of this Treaty respectively.

2. Unless otherwise desired by the Authority, admission to full membership of the Organisation shall take effect immediately upon a decision to that effect by the Authority.

3. Each Territory admitted to full membership of the Organisation shall accede to this Treaty in accordance with the provisions of paragraph 4 of Article 20 thereof upon its attainment of independent statehood.

4. Any independent State or Territory in the Caribbean region may at any time notify the Director-General of its intention to adhere to this Treaty.

5. The Director-General shall, on receipt of such notification, transmit a copy of it to all signatories and to the Government of Saint Lucia.

6. The terms and conditions of adherence in any particular case shall be determined by the Authority.

Article 23. Declaration of non-Participation

Any Member State may, either on becoming a member of the Organisation or within a period not exceeding twelve (12) months thereafter, declare in writing to the Director-General its intention to withhold its participation in respect of Foreign Affairs and/or Defence and Security matters of the Organisation. The Director-General shall on receipt of such declaration promptly transmit a copy of it to all the other Member States of the Organisation. Such declaration shall take effect on the date of its receipt by the Director-General.

Article 24. Withdrawal

1. This Treaty shall be of unlimited duration.

2. Any Member State, whether a Full Member or an Associate Member, may withdraw from the Organisation if it decides that extraordinary events, related to the subject matter of this Treaty, have seriously endangered its supreme national interests. It shall give written notice of such withdrawal to the Director-General who shall promptly notify the other Member States and the Government of Saint Lucia. Such withdrawal shall take effect twelve (12) months after the notice is received by the Director-General.

3. Any Member State which withdraws from the Organisation shall discharge its financial obligations to the Organisation and shall respect any commitments undertaken before the effective date of withdrawal.

4. Any Member State which withdraws from the Organisation during the period of its operation has no claim to any part of the proceeds until the liquidation of the assets of the Organisation on the termination of this Treaty at which time it shall be entitled to the value of its assets as at the date of withdrawal.

Article 25. Amendments

1. Any Member State may make written proposals for the amendment of this Treaty and any Protocols thereto.

2. Amendments shall be effected by a unanimous decision of the Authority. They shall come into force on the thirtieth day following the date of their receipt by the Government of Saint Lucia. The text of any amendment shall be promptly communicated by the Director-General to the said Government which shall transmit certified copies thereof to all the signatories to this Treaty and shall also inform them of the date of entry into force of any such amendment.

Article 26. Registration

This Treaty and all its Protocols shall be registered by the Government of Saint Lucia with the Secretariat of the United Nations pursuant to Article 102 of the Charter of the United Nations and shall also be registered with the Secretariat of the Caribbean Community.

Article 27. Transitional Arrangements

Until such time as the Director-General is appointed the powers and functions of the said officer shall be exercised by the Executive Secretary of the Council of Ministers of the West Indies Associated States.

In Witness Whereof, the undersigned plenipotentiaries, being duly authorised thereto by their respective Governments, have signed the present Treaty.

Done at Basseterre this eighteenth day of June, one thousand nine hundred and eighty-one.

For the Government of
Antigua:
LESTER BIRD

Dominica:

M. EUGENIA CHARLES

Grenada:

MAURICE BISHOP

Montserrat:

F. A. L. MARGETSON

St. Kitts/Nevis:

KENNEDY A. SIMMONDS

Saint Lucia:

WINSTON F. CENAC

Saint Vincent and the Grenadines:

HUDSON TANNIS

4.1423 Trilateral Treaty of Friendship and Co-operation among Ethiopia, Libya, and the People's Democratic Republic of Yemen

Alliance Members: Ethiopia, Libya, and the People's Democratic Republic of Yemen (South Yemen)
Signed On: August 19, 1981, in the city of Aden (Yemen). In force until February 1, 1986.
Alliance Type: Defense Pact (Type I)

Source: *Keesing's Record of World Events,* January 1982, p. 31280.

SUMMARY

This treaty of friendship and cooperation supported better political and military ties among three nations closely allied with the Soviet Union. The signatories, Ali Nasser Mohammed (South Yemen), Col. Mu'ammar Gadhafi (Libya), and Lt. Col. Mengistu Haile Mariam (Ethiopia), sought, in their words, to counter the growing influence of the U.S. military in surrounding areas, including the Indian Ocean, Red Sea, Persian Gulf, and Mediterranean Sea.

The treaty was immediately denounced by Oman and Egypt, which argued that the alliance was instigated by the Soviets for the political purpose of spreading Soviet influence in the Arab region. The alliance ended when Mohammed-led forces backed by Libya and Ethiopia attempted to recapture South Yemen following a coup d'état on January 19, 1986.

The following description of terms contains excerpts of the official text of the treaty, which is unpublished.

DESCRIPTION OF TERMS

The three signatory parties agreed to co-operate to "guarantee the common struggle of the three revolutionary countries" (Art. 2) and to "resist" and "foil" the "conspiracies of imperialism, Zionism and reactionary forces which aim to strangulate progressive forces and countries by strengthening their military forces as well as establishing and expanding military bases in countries located in the Indian Ocean, the Mediterranean Sea, the Red Sea and countries of the region" (Art. 3). The three parties rejected the 1978 Camp David agreements (which led to the Egyptian-Israeli peace treaty) (Art. 4) and reaffirmed their "solidarity with Arab, African and other national liberation movements, and in particular the Palestine Revolution [and those of] Namibia and South Africa. . ." (Art. 5). They also agreed to "exchange ideas to enable them to co-ordinate their stand on international and continental issues" (Art. 6) and to "make every possible effort to strengthen and deepen their relations with the region's progressive countries and forces, as well as with socialist countries" (Art.7).

Under Arts. 8 and 9 a political committee was set up consisting of the foreign ministers of each of the three countries, the duties of this committee being inter alia to "monitor the implementation of laid down political lines" and to assist a Supreme Council. With a view to developing economic co-operation an economic committee was established (Art. 14), its members being the economic ministers of each country. Both the political and economic committees would, in accordance with Art. 20, meet once every six months in the capitals of the signatory countries in rotation; an emergency meeting could be held at any time at the request of any one country.

A Supreme Council was also set up (Art. 18) consisting of the leaders of the three signatory countries as well as the chairmen of the political, economic (and other) committees, and was to meet once a year in the three capital cities in rotation, with emergency meetings being convened at any time if requested by one of the member states. The Supreme Council would "analyse the work of the political, economic and other committees" and "take measures for the full implementation of this work" and "establish other ministerial committees or secretariats as necessary."

The three countries furthermore agreed that "in the case of an aggression committed against any one of them" they would "assist the victim of aggression in all necessary ways individually or collectively, since an aggression on one shall be considered an aggression directed against all the signatory parties" (Art. 16), and that "in accordance with the agreements to be signed between them," they would "make efforts to strengthen their defensive capabilities and promote their own freedom and territorial integrity" (Art. 17). (It was subsequently reported that in the course of the summit, agreement had also been reached on the formation of a defense committee, made up of the competent ministers of each country, which would co-ordinate defense policy between the three countries. Details of such a committee were not, however, given in the text of the treaty.)

The three countries affirmed that the treaty was not "contrary to the international treaties and obligations entered into by the three countries" and that they themselves would not undertake or enter into "any kind of international agreement which runs contrary to the articles of this treaty" (Art. 23). Having "reaffirmed" their adherence to the charter and principles of the United Nations and to the principles of the non-aligned movement, the three parties offered membership of their treaty to other states which "follow the objectives and goals of this treaty as well as the provision of the UN Charter and the guidelines of the non-aligned movement" (Art. 26).

4.1424 Treaty of Friendship and Co-operation between the Hungarian People's Republic and the People's Republic of Angola

Alliance Members: Hungary and Angola
Signed On: October 9, 1981, in the city of Budapest (Hungary). In force until October 7, 1989.
Alliance Type: Neutrality Pact (Type II)

Source: *United Nations Treaty,* no. 22339.

SUMMARY

Hungary first established diplomatic relations with Angola in 1975 after a Marxist revolution replaced the existing regime. Just one year later, Angola signed a treaty of cooperation with the Soviet Union. In 1981, Hungary and Angola formalized their relations when Hungarian president Pal Losonczi and Angolan president Jose Eduardo dos Santos signed a treaty of friendship and cooperation.

In the four years following the treaty, the two nations approved eight separate bilateral agreements. Trade between the two countries became substantial as Hungary bought coffee and diamonds and Angola purchased mechanical goods and medicines. The alliance effectively ended with the collapse of the Hungarian government in 1989.

ALLIANCE TEXT

The Hungarian People's Republic and the People's Republic of Angola,

Recognizing that the relations of friendship and fraternal co-operation between the Hungarian and Angolan peoples, which were shaped during the struggle for the national liberation of Angola and strengthened after the proclamation of the People's Republic of Angola, serve the interests of both peoples,

Proceeding from the relations between the Hungarian Socialist Workers' Party and the MPLA—Labour Party, based on the principles of Marxism-Leninism and proletarian internationalism,

Guided by the desire to protect and to develop further the revolutionary achievements of the two peoples in every sphere,

Favouring unity of action and co-operation between all progressive forces in the struggle for peace, freedom, independence and social progress,

Endeavouring to contribute to international peace and security,

Inspired by the common ideals of the struggle against all forms of imperialism, colonialism, neo-colonialism and racism,

Convinced of the need to intensify efforts for the elimination of underdevelopment and for the establishment of a new international economic order,

Reaffirming their full support for the purposes and principles of the Charter of the United Nations,

Have decided to sign this Treaty of friendship and co-operation, in the context of which they have agreed as follows:

Article 1. The Contracting Parties solemnly declare their decision to develop, broaden and deepen the relations of friendship and co-operation between the two countries on the basis of the principles of respect for sovereignty, independence, territorial integrity, equality of rights and non-interference in internal affairs.

Article 2. The Contracting Parties shall expand the political, military, economic, technical, scientific and cultural co-operation between them, as well as the direct contacts between their political and social organizations and between their scientific and cultural institutions, with a view to giving the peoples of the two countries a better understanding of each other's life, work, experiences and achievements.

Article 3. The Contracting Parties shall make every effort to expand co-operation in the fields of industry, agriculture, transport and communications, the exploitation of natural resources, the training of specialists and commercial relations, on the basis of the principles of equality and mutual benefit.

Article 4. The Contracting Parties shall develop co-operation between them in the fields of science and technology, the arts, literature, education, public health, the press, radio, television, the cinema and sports.

Article 5. The Contracting Parties shall continue to make their contribution to the struggle for the safeguarding of peace and international security and shall make every effort to deepen the process of international détente, make it irreversible and extend it to all the regions of the world.

Article 6. The Contracting Parties favour general and complete disarmament, including nuclear disarmament, under effective international control, and they support the elimination of the use of force in international relations and the settlement of disputes between States by peaceful means.

Article 7. The Hungarian People's Republic respects the policy of nonalignment of the People's Republic of Angola as an important factor in the struggle against imperialism, for the total liberation of the world's peoples and for peace and co-operation between all the countries in the world.

The People's Republic of Angola respects the principled socialist foreign policy of the Hungarian People's Republic as an important contribution to the cause of safeguarding peace in Europe and in the world, consolidating international security and strengthening the process of détente.

Article 8. The Contracting Parties shall wage a consistent struggle against the forces of imperialism and for the final elimination of colonialism, neocolonialism and racism.

The Contracting Parties shall continue to act for the full implementation of the United Nations Declaration on the Granting of Independence to Colonial Countries and Peoples' and recognize the right of every people to self-determination and to the free choice of its political, economic and social system.

Article 9. The Contracting Parties shall endeavour to bring about the democratic restructuring of international economic relations and declare their solidarity with the struggle for the establishment of a just and equitable new international economic order.

Article 10. In order to implement the provisions of this Treaty, the Contracting Parties shall hold periodic consultations at various levels for the exchange of views concerning the development of relations between the two States and concerning international questions of mutual interest.

In the event of situations which disturb or threaten peace, the Contracting Parties shall immediately contact each other and consult with a view to coordinating their efforts in the interest of ending the threatening situation or restoring peace.

Article 11. Each Contracting Party solemnly undertakes not to participate in any alliance, action or activity directed against the other Party.

Article 12. The Contracting Parties declare that their obligations arising out of other international agreements concluded by them are not contrary to the provisions of this Treaty, and they undertake not to enter into any international agreement inconsistent with this Treaty.

Article 13. Any questions that may arise between the Contracting Parties with regard to the interpretation or application of any provision of this Treaty shall be settled in the spirit of friendship, understanding and mutual respect through direct bilateral negotiations.

Article 14. This Treaty shall be subject to ratification and shall enter into force on the date of the exchange of the instruments of ratification, which shall take place at Luanda, the capital of the People's Republic of Angola.

Article 15. This Treaty shall remain in force for a period of 20 years after the date of its entry into force and shall be automatically extended for further periods of five years unless one of the Parties declares in writing, at least one year before the date of expiry, its intention to denounce the Treaty.

Done at Budapest on 9 October 1981, in duplicate in the Hungarian and Portuguese languages, both texts being equally authentic.

For the Hungarian People's Republic:

[PÁL LOSONCZI]

President of the Presidential Council of the Hungarian People's Republic

For the People's Republic of Angola:

[JOSÉ EDUARDO DOS SANTOS]

Chairman of the MPLA—Labour Party and President of the People's Republic of Angola

---

4.1425 Agreement between the Republic of The Gambia and the Republic of Senegal Concerning the Establishment of a Senegambia Confederation

Alliance Members: Gambia and Senegal
Signed On: December 17, 1981, in the city of Dakar (Senegal). In force until September 21, 1989.
Alliance Type: Defense Pact (Type I)

Source: *United Nations Treaty*, no. 20735.

SUMMARY

In September 1981, President Dawda Jawara of Gambia was overthrown by a left-wing political uprising. At the request of President Jawara, Senegalese forces then moved into the Gambian capital city of Banjul and put down the coup d'état. This important act of cooperation gave way to an alliance, and four months later, on December 17, President Abdou Diouf of Senegal agreed to a treaty of unification.

The treaty of unification between Gambia and Senegal established a Senegambia confederation that included principally the integration of the armed forces in order to defend the sovereignty, territory, and security of the new state, and a monetary union to foster economic growth. In addition to economic and military integration, the two states agreed to coordinate their foreign policies, telecommunications, and road construction.

During the course of the alliance, the two countries formed a confederation army and parliament and jointly coordinated numerous policies. The alliance began to suffer, however, as the Gambian public feared a push for greater unification that might cost Gambia its independence. Similar problems festered over control of the economy: while Gambia adopted a British-style, liberal trade policy, Senegal maintained strong protectionist policies, including a high tariff rate. These policy differences eventually proved too great, and the alliance eventually collapsed. On September 21, 1989, President Jawara formally dissolved the Senegambia Confederation.

ALLIANCE TEXT

The Republic of the Gambia and the Republic of Senegal,

Aware that they constitute a single people divided into two States by the vicissitudes of History;

Taking due account of the geographical fact of their ties;

Conscious of the historical, moral and material imperatives which unite the two countries;

Considering the many past and present experiments made with a view to rapprochement, solidarity and sub-regional and regional cooperation;

Respectful of the Charter of the United Nations, the Charter of the Organisation of African Unity and the Treaty of the Economic Community of West African States;

Affirming their devotion to the rights of their peoples declared in the Universal Declaration of Human Rights of 1948; in the United Nations Covenants on Human Rights; and in the African Charter of Human and Peoples Rights of 1981;

Intending to strengthen the unity of their defence and their economies and co-ordination of their policies in other fields;

Resolved to establish an institutional framework, consistent with national sovereignty and democratic principles, within which these intentions may be gradually realized,

Have decided to create a Confederation and have agreed as follows:

[Section I]. Principles

Clause 1. By this Agreement a Confederation of the Republic of the Gambia and the Republic of Senegal [is] constituted with the name of the Senegambia Confederation.

Clause 2. The Republic of the Gambia and the Republic of Senegal shall constitute the Confederation know as Senegambia. Each State maintaining its independence and sovereignty.

The Confederation shall be based on:

- The integration of the armed forces and of the security forces of the Gambia and the Republic of Senegal, to defend their sovereignty, territorial integrity and independence;
- Development of an economic and monetary union;
- Co-ordination of policy in the field of external relations;
- Co-ordination of policy in the field of communications and in all other fields where the Confederated States may agree to exercise their jurisdiction jointly;
- Joint institutions.

Clause 3. The institutions of the Confederation shall be as follows:

- The President and Vice-President of the Confederation;
- The Council of Ministers of the Confederation;
- The Confederal Parliament.

Clause 4. The official languages of the Confederation shall be

- Such African languages as are specified by the President and Vice-President of the Confederation;
- English and French.

Clause 5. Within the framework of this Agreement the Confederated States shall enter into protocols of implementation for the realization of the purposes set out in Clause 2.

Section II. The President and Vice-President of the Confederation

Clause 6. The President of the Republic of Senegal shall be the President of the Confederation.

The President of the Republic of the Gambia shall be the Vice-President of the Confederation.

Clause 7. In agreement with the Vice-President, the President shall decide on the policy of the Confederation on matters of Defence and Security.

He shall co-ordinate the policies of the Confederated States on matters within the responsibilities of the Confederation.

In agreement with the Vice-President, the President of the Confederation shall make appointments to all confederal posts.

Clause 8. The President of the Confederation shall command the Armed Forces and the Security Forces of the Confederation. He shall be responsible for the Defence and Security of the Confederation.

A protocol shall establish the modalities of implementation of this provision in accordance with the constitutional requirements of each State.

The President of the Republic of the Gambia shall continue to be Commander in chief of the Armed Forces of the Republic of the Gambia in accordance with its constitutional requirements.

Clause 9. The President of the Confederation shall preside over the Defence and Security Council of the Confederation.

The Defence Council shall comprise the President and Vice-President of the Confederation and such other persons as the President in agreement with the Vice-President of the Confederation may determine.

Section III. The Council of Ministers

Clause 10. There shall be a Council of Ministers of the Confederation whose members shall be appointed by the President of the Confederation in agreement with the Vice-President.

The President and the Vice-President of the Confederation shall be the President and the Vice-President of the Council of Ministers respectively.

The Council of Ministers shall deal with matters submitted to their consideration by the President of the Confederation.

Section IV. The Confederal Parliament

Clause 11. The Representative Parliament of the Confederation shall be known as "the Confederal Parliament".

Its members shall have the title "Member of the Confederal Parliament".

One third of the members of the Confederal Parliament shall be selected by the House of Representative[s] of the Gambia from among its members, and the other two thirds shall be selected by the National Parliament of Senegal, from among its members.

The Confederal Parliament shall select its President.

The Confederal Parliament shall establish its rules of procedure.

Clause 12. The Confederal Parliament shall deliberate on matters of common interest.

Furthermore, the President of the Confederation or the Vice-President of the Confederation, may consult the Confederal Parliament by submitting to its vote any other matter of social, economic or financial interest to the Confederation.

Clause 13. Only the President of the Confederation, the Vice-President of the Confederation and the members of the Confederal Parliament can initiate matters or proposals.

The Confederal Parliament shall convene when matters are submitted to it by the President or Vice-President or at the request of one third of the members of the Confederal Parliament.

Clause 14. The rules governing submission of matters to the Confederal Parliament by the President or the Vice-President of the Confederation, voting matters or propositions and promulgation of such rules by the President shall be drawn up in a protocol of implementation.

Section V. Settlement of Differences

Clause 15. Any difference arising out [of] the interpretation and the implementation of this Agreement shall be submitted to the President of the Confederation for settlement, in agreement with the Vice-President.

In the event that the President of the Confederation and the Vice-President are unable to agree upon the settlement of a difference submitted to them either of them may refer the matter to arbitration.

A protocol of implementation shall lay down rules for constituting an arbitration tribunal for the settlement of a difference and for regulating its procedure.

Section VI. International treaties and Agreements

Clause 16. Where authority is granted to the Confederation pursuant to this Agreement and its protocols for the conclusion of an International Agreement, the Agreement shall be negotiated by the President of the Confederation in agreement with the Vice-President. Subsequent to authorization by the Confederal Parliament and enactment by the Confederated States of any legislation necessary for its implementation the President of the Confederation may ratify the Agreement.

Clause 17. Each Confederated State may conclude International Agreements in accordance with its constitutional requirements. Without prejudice to article 103 of the United Nations Organisations Charter, if any disagreement arises between this Agreement and any other international obligation, the provisions of this Agreement shall prevail.

[Section VII. Final Clauses]

Clause 18. **Ratification.** This Agreement shall be ratified by the Parties in accordance with their constitutional requirements.

Clause 19. **Entry into Force.** This Agreement shall come into force on the first day of the month following that in which instruments of ratification are exchanged.

Clause 20. **Amendment.** Each Confederated State may submit proposals for the amendment of the Agreement to the depositories of the Agreement. The depositories of the Agreement shall submit the proposals to the Confederal Parliament for its opinion.

When the Confederal Parliament has delivered an opinion on the proposals the Confederated States shall enter into negotiations for the purpose of determining by common accord the amendments to be made to the Agreement.

Any amendments agreed shall enter into force after being ratified by the Confederated States in accordance with their respective constitutional requirements.

The foregoing procedure shall not apply to protocols of implementation which may be amended from time to time by agreement between the Confederated States.

Clause 21. **Review.** The Confederal Parliament shall convene every two years and shall prepare a Report on the functioning of the Confederation for submission to the President and the Vice-President of the Confederation and the Confederated States. If requested by a Confederated State following the submission of a Report a Conference of representatives of the Government of both Confederated States shall be summoned to review the Agreement.

Clause 22. [**Status of the protocols of Implementation**]. Status of the Protocols of Implementation shall be an integral part of the Agreement, and, unless otherwise specified, any reference to the Agreement shall also constitute a reference to these protocols.

Clause 23. **Depositories.** The President and the Vice-President of the Confederation shall be the depositories of this Agreement, and of the protocols and the amendments relating thereto.

Clause 24. **Authentic Texts.** The Agreement, done in the English and French languages, both texts being equally authentic, shall be communicated to the Secretary General of the United Nations for the purpose of registration.

In Witness Whereof, the President of the Republic of the Gambia and the President of the Republic of Senegal have signed the present Agreement.

At Dakar, on 17 December 1981.

For the Republic of the Gambia:

Sir DAWDA KAIRABA JAWARA
President of the Republic

For the Republic of Senegal:

ABDOU DIOUF
President of the Republic

4.1426 Non-Aggression Pact between South Africa and Swaziland

Alliance Members: South Africa and Swaziland
Signed On: February 12, 1982, in the city of Mbabane (Swaziland). In force until May 10, 1994.
Alliance Type: Non-Aggression Pact (Type II)

Source: *International Legal Materials,* vol. 23, p. 286–287.

SUMMARY

South Africa completely surrounds the kingdom of Swaziland, and the two countries had several seemingly intractable border disputes during the 1970s and 1980s concerning South Africa's Lowveld and KwaZulu-Natal regions, which were home to populations wishing to join Swaziland. South Africa was also battling rebel groups that were seeking to oust the exclusively white, apartheid government.

On February 13, 1982, Swaziland signed a secret non-aggression treaty with South Africa. The treaty outlined South Africa's willingness to alter borders in exchange for Swaziland's cooperation in fighting the insurgents. Following this secret security agreement, Swaziland began clamping down on African National Congress (ANC) members who were carrying out guerrilla attacks against the South African government.

The treaty ended in on April 27, 1994, when the apartheid government in South Africa fell and Nelson Mandela became president.

ALLIANCE TEXT

His Majesty
King Sobhuza II of Swaziland
Mbabane
Swaziland
Your Majesty

I have the honour to refer to various discussions and correspondence between the Foreign Ministers of the Kingdom of

Swaziland and the Republic of South Africa which resulted in mutual agreement between our respective Governments to the effect that both Governments are aware of the fact that international terrorism, in all its manifestations, poses a real threat to international peace and security and that our respective Governments should take steps to protect our respective states and nationals against this threat.

Therefore, I now have the honour to inform you that the Government of the Republic of South Africa proposes the following Agreement between our respective Governments:

Article 1. The Contracting Parties undertake to combat terrorism, insurgency and subversion individually and collectively and shall call upon each other wherever possible for such assistance and steps as may be deemed necessary or expedient to eliminate this evil.

Article 2. In the conduct of their mutual relations the Contracting Parties shall furthermore respect each other's independence, sovereignty and territorial integrity and shall refrain from the unlawful threat or use of force and from any other act which is inconsistent with the purposes and principles of good neighbourliness.

Article 3. The Contracting Parties shall live in peace and further develop and maintain friendly relations with each other and shall therefore not allow any activities within their respective territories directed towards the commission of any act which involves a threat or use of force against each other's territorial integrity.

Article 4. The Contracting Parties shall not allow within their respective territories the installation or maintenance of foreign military bases or the presence of foreign military units except in accordance with their right of self-defence in the event of armed attacks as provided for in the charter of the United Nations and only after due notification to the other.

Should the Government of the Kingdom of Swaziland agree with the abovementioned provisions, this letter and your affirmative reply thereto shall constitute an Agreement between our two Governments.

Please accept, Your Majesty, the renewed assurance of my highest consideration.

P. W. BOTHA
PRIME MINISTER OF THE REPUBLIC OF SOUTH AFRICA

4.1427 Treaty of Friendship and Cooperation between the Czechoslovak Socialist Republic and the Socialist People's Libyan Arab Jamahiriya

Alliance Members: Czechoslovakia and Libya
Signed On: September 9, 1982, in the city of Prague (Czech Republic). In force until December 10, 1989.
Alliance Type: Non-Aggression Pact (Type II)

Source: *United Nations Treaty,* no. 22736.

SUMMARY

Czechoslovakian ties to Libya date to the Libyan socialist revolution of the 1960s. Following the Soviets' lead, many communist nations established treaties of cooperation with budding socialist republics around the world. During the next twenty years, Czechoslovak-Libyan relations grew strong enough to warrant formalization with this treaty of friendship and alliance. In addition to military cooperation, the treaty strengthened economic and commercial ties between the two nations, which buoyed the Libyan economy.

The alliance effectively ended with regime change in Czechoslovakia. Trade ties suffered further when Czechoslovakia's new government joined the prevailing international consensus and denounced Libyan involvement in terrorist activities and levied sanctions against Colonel Gadhafi's government.

ALLIANCE TEXT

The Czechoslovak Socialist Republic and the Socialist People's Libyan Arab Jamahiriya,

Believing that the further strengthening of friendship and the intensification of comprehensive co-operation between them is in the interest of the peoples of the two friendly countries and in the interest of consolidating international peace and security,

Resolved to continue contributing, in the spirit of anti-imperialistic solidarity, to the strengthening of unity and co-operation between all progressive and peace-loving forces struggling against imperialism, for peace and the freedom of peoples, and for independence, democracy and social progress,

Declaring their desire to continue taking an active part in the struggle against imperialism, colonialism, neo-colonialism, zionism and racism in all their forms and manifestations,

Reaffirming their loyalty to the purposes and principles of the Charter of the United Nations, especially the principles of sovereign equality and non-interference in internal affairs,

Emphasizing the importance of further developing and strengthening the relations between them,

Have decided to conclude this Treaty and have agreed as follows:

Article 1. The High Contracting Parties solemnly declare their determination to strengthen the firm friendship between the two countries and to develop constantly their reciprocal relations and the comprehensive co-operation between them on the basis of equality, respect for sovereignty, political independence, territorial integrity and non-interference in internal affairs.

Article 2. The Czechoslovak Socialist Republic appreciates the Socialist People's Libyan Arab Jamahiriya's policy based on the principles and purposes of nonalignment, guided by the struggle against imperialism, for national liberation and for the strengthening of peace and co-operation between States.

The Socialist People's Libyan Arab Jamahiriya appreciates the foreign policy of the Czechoslovak Socialist Republic as an important contribution to the safeguarding of peace, the consolidation of international security and the relaxation of international tension.

Article 3. The High Contracting Parties shall, through co-operation between them, continue striving to bring about the conditions for the consolidation and further deepening of the two countries' social and economic achievements.

To that end, they shall develop mutually beneficial co-operation in individual areas of the national economy, scientific and technical co-operation and co-operation in the expansion of trade between them on the basis of respect for the principles of equality and mutual benefit. The specific areas and conditions of such cooperation shall be regulated in implementation documents.

Article 4. The High Contracting Parties shall actively support the reciprocal development of contacts and the exchange of experience in the field of science and culture, education, health, the press, radio, television, cinematography, sports and tourism and in other fields.

They shall also support the expansion of contacts between social organizations and the expansion of direct contacts between cultural and scientific institutions for the purpose of promoting a knowledge of the life, work, experience and achievements of the peoples of the two countries.

Article 5. The High Contracting Parties shall make every effort for the preservation of international peace and security and for the consolidation and development of the process of détente, the ending of the arms race and the achievement of general and complete disarmament, including nuclear disarmament, under effective international control. They shall strive for the consistent implementation of the principles of peaceful coexistence in relations between States with different social systems.

Article 6. The High Contracting Parties shall continue to provide active support to the struggle against the aggressive policies of world imperialism and for the final elimination of colonialism, zionism and racism in all their forms and manifestations.

In the spirit of the unity of anti-imperialistic and progressive forces, they shall support the legitimate struggle of peoples for freedom, independence, sovereignty and social progress and their struggle to ensure full respect for the sovereignty of those States over their natural resources.

Article 7. The High Contracting Parties shall consult each other concerning all important international questions directly affecting the interests of the two countries.

Article 8. The High Contracting Parties declare that they will not enter into any military or other alliances and will not participate in any grouping of States or any military acts or measures directed against the other High Contracting Party.

Article 9. The High Contracting Parties declare that this Treaty shall not affect their international obligations and is not directed against any third country. At the same time, the two Parties undertake not to conclude in the future any international treaty which would be contrary to this Treaty.

Article 10. All questions that may arise in connection with the interpretation or application of any provision of this Treaty shall be settled in a spirit of friendship, mutual respect and understanding through direct negotiations between the two High Contracting Parties.

Article 11. This Treaty is subject to ratification in accordance with the legal provisions of each Contracting Party and shall enter into force on the date of the exchange of the instruments of ratification, which shall take place at Tripoli.

Article 12. This Treaty is concluded for a term of 10 years, and its validity shall be automatically extended for further terms of 10 years unless it is denounced by either of the High Contracting Parties 12 months before the expiry of the current term.

Done at Prague on 9 September 1982 in duplicate in the Czech and Arabic languages, both texts being equally authentic.

For the Czechoslovak Socialist Republic:

[GUSTÁV HUSÁK]

For the Socialist People's Libyan Arab Jamahiriya:

[MUAMMAR QADDAFI]

4.1428 Treaty of Friendship and Co-operation between the People's Republic of Bulgaria and the Socialist People's Libyan Arab Jamahiriya

Alliance Members: Bulgaria and Libya
Signed On: January 21, 1983, in the city of Sofia (Bulgaria). In force until November 10, 1989.
Alliance Type: Non-Aggression Pact (Type II)

Source: *United Nations Treaty,* no. 23662.

SUMMARY

Much like the agreement with Czechoslovakia signed during the previous year, this Libyan agreement with Bulgaria was meant to establish trade ties and closer relations with an Eastern Bloc country. As mandated in the treaty, both parties agreed to condemn the U.S.-backed Israeli policy and demand a full military withdrawal from Lebanon. This mutual political interest formed the basis for the overall framework, which aimed at eventually establishing close economic ties.

After the collapse of Bulgarian communist rule in 1989, the treaty ended. Bilateral relations continued to deteriorate, and trade between the two nations ceased when Bulgaria joined those countries imposing sanctions on Libya in 1992.

ALLIANCE TEXT

The People's Republic of Bulgaria and the Socialist People's Libyan Arab Jamahiriya, convinced that the further development and strengthening of the relations of friendship and co-operation existing between the two friendly countries is in the interests of their peoples and serves the cause of international peace and security,

Expressing their readiness to continue to work for the strengthening of anti-imperialist solidarity and the unity and cohesion of the forces struggling to promote peace, freedom, independence, democracy and social progress for all peoples,

Determined to resist the aggressive policy of imperialism and to struggle against all forms and manifestations of colonialism, neo-colonialism, zionism, racism and reaction,

Affirming their adherence to the purposes and principles of the Charter of the United Nations,

Bearing in mind the Declaration on the development of friendship and cooperation between the People's Republic of Bulgaria and the Socialist People's Libyan Arab Jamahiriya, signed on 25 December 1976,

And desiring to develop their mutual relations, have decided to conclude this Treaty and have agreed as follows:

Article 1. The High Contracting Parties declare their resolve to strengthen the firm bonds of friendship between the two countries and to strive for continued development of their political relations and all-round co-operation, on the basis of the principles of equality, respect for sovereignty, national independence and territorial integrity and non-interference in internal affairs.

Article 2. The People's Republic of Bulgaria respects the policy of the Socialist People's Libyan Arab Jamahiriya, based on the purposes and principles of the Movement of Non-Aligned Countries and dedicated to the struggle against imperialism and for the liberation of peoples and the promotion of peace and co-operation among nations.

The Socialist People's Libyan Arab Jamahiriya respects the foreign policy of the People's Republic of Bulgaria, based on the principles and goals of the socialist community, which is making an effective contribution to the safeguarding of peace and the strengthening of security and détente in international relations.

Article 3. The High Contracting Parties shall continue their close and comprehensive co-operation with a view to creating the conditions necessary for the maintenance and further intensification of economic and social exchanges between the two countries.

For that purpose, the Parties shall develop co-operation for their mutual benefit in the various sectors of the national economy, and also scientific and technical cooperation and co-operation in the expansion of trade between the two countries on the basis of respect for the principles of equality and mutual advantage.

The specific areas of and conditions for such co-operation shall be established in additional instruments of execution.

Article 4. The High Contracting Parties shall help to strengthen and develop contacts and co-operation in the fields of science, culture, education, health, the press, radio and television broadcasting, the cinema, sport, tourism, and other fields, with a view to promoting a deeper mutual knowledge of the life, work, experience and achievements of the peoples of the two countries.

Article 5. The High Contracting Parties shall continue to make every effort to preserve international peace and security, to promote and develop the process of international détente, to end the arms race and to achieve general and complete disarmament, including nuclear disarmament, under effective international control. They shall also strive for the consistent application of the principles of peaceful coexistence in relations between States, with different social systems.

Article 6. The High Contracting Parties shall continue to cooperate with each other in the struggle against the aggressive policy of world imperialism, with a view to resisting all forms and manifestations of colonialism, neo-colonialism, zionism and racism.

In a spirit of unity between progressive anti-imperialist forces they shall support the just struggle of the peoples for freedom, independence, sovereignty and social progress and for full respect for the right of those peoples to dispose of their natural resources. They shall also promote efforts to restructure international economic relations on a just and democratic basis.

Article 7. The High Contracting Parties shall provide each other with information and hold consultations for the purpose of exchanging views on important international problems and issues affecting the interests of the two countries.

Article 8. Each of the High Contracting Parties declares that it will not enter into any military alliance, join any grouping or take part in any military action or measure directed against the other High Contracting Party.

Article 9. The High Contracting Parties declare that this Treaty does not affect their existing international obligations and that the Treaty is not directed against any third country. They undertake not to enter into any international agreement which is incompatible with the provisions of this Treaty.

Article 10. Any questions that may arise concerning the interpretation or implementation of this Treaty shall be settled by the two High Contracting Parties in a spirit of friendship, understanding and mutual respect.

Article 11. This Treaty shall be ratified in accordance with the procedure established in each of the two countries and shall enter into force on the date of the exchange of the instruments of ratification, which shall take place at Tripoli.

Article 12. This Treaty is concluded for a term of 10 years reckoned from the date of its entry into force and shall be renewed automatically for successive 10-year periods unless one of the High Contracting Parties gives written notice, 12 months before the expiry of the current term, of its intention to terminate it.

Done at Sofia on 21 January 1983 (7 Rabi' 4 1392 MWR) in two original copies in the Bulgarian and Arabic languages, both texts being equally authentic.

For the People's Republic of Bulgaria:

[Signed]

TODOR ZHIVKOV

For the Socialist People's Libyan Arab Jamahiriya:

[Signed]

MUAMMAR QADDAFI

4.1429 Treaty of Friendship and Concord among Algeria, Tunisia, and Mauritania

Alliance Members: Algeria, Tunisia, and Mauritania (December 13, 1983)
Signed On: March 20, 1983, in the city of Tunis (Tunisia). In force until February 17, 1989.
Alliance Type: Non-Aggression Pact (Type II)

Source: *Christian Science Monitor,* March 21, 1983.
Additional Citations: *BBC Summary of World Broadcasts,* March 21, 1983; *Xinhua General Overseas News Service,* December 14, 1983; *Keesing's Record of World Events,* June 1984.

SUMMARY

Signed by the Tunisian prime minister and the Algerian interior minister after an exchange of visits during the preceding two months, this treaty began the process toward a regional union of cooperation for the Maghreb states. The agreement also resolved a dispute over the delineation of the allies' shared border.

The treaty proved provocative as Libya and Morocco quickly inked a similar non-aggression agreement in August of 1983 (see Alliance no. 4.1431) and began holding regular joint defense meetings. This did not prevent cooperation among the allies, however, who eventually established the Maghreb Union (see Alliance no. 4.1434) on February 17, 1989.

DESCRIPTION OF TERMS

Both countries pledged that they would abstain from the threat or use of force against the other. Further, both parties committed to not support or allow on their territory any group whose aim was the overthrow of the other ally. The allies also agreed on a resolution of their dispute over border demarcation.

Other parties from the Maghreb would be allowed to join the alliance. The agreement was set to last for twenty years.

4.1430 Agreement on Non-Aggression and Good Neighbourliness (Accord of Nkomati)

Alliance Members: Mozambique and South Africa
Signed On: March 16, 1984, in the city of Komatipoort (South Africa). In force until July 4, 1992.
Alliance Type: Non-Aggression Pact (Type II)

Source: *United Nations Treaty,* no. 22802.

SUMMARY

The signing of the Accord of Nkomati followed a prolonged border war between South Africa and Mozambique. Months before the agreement, South Africa agreed to a treaty ending the fighting with guerrillas in Angola. At the behest of mediation sanctioned by the United States, Samora Machel, the Marxist president of Mozambique, and Prime Minister Pieter W. Botha of South Africa committed to a written accord.

The accord sought to stop both Mozambique and South Africa from supporting or allowing rebel groups to infiltrate the other country.

South Africa had been supporting the Mozambican National Resistance (RENAMO) against the black-ruled country, and Mozambique had responded with support for antiapartheid insurgents. The treaty included the elimination of bases and posts that incited aggression, and it forbade the stationing or support of irregular or guerrilla forces. With international support for RENAMO curtailed, a major obstacle to peace was removed.

Throughout the 1980s, RENAMO continued to pose a grave threat to Mozambique. Although it never achieved overwhelming political support within or beyond Mozambique, the group did prove destabilizing to the country as a whole. Finally, in 1990, RENAMO and Mozambique signed a peace treaty to end a conflict that had at that point been frozen for several years. President Chissano of Mozambique and the RENAMO leader Alfonso Dhlakama signed a final agreement in October of 1992. The treaty pledged a cease-fire, democratic elections, and the entry of United Nations peacekeeping forces.

ALLIANCE TEXT

The Government of the People's Republic of Mozambique and the Government of the Republic of South Africa, hereinafter referred to as the High Contracting Parties,

Recognising the principles of strict respect for sovereignty and territorial integrity, sovereign equality, political independence and the inviolability of the borders of all states;

Reaffirming the principle of non-interference in the internal affairs of other states;

Considering the internationally recognized principle of the right of peoples to self-determination and independence and the principle of equal rights of all peoples;

Considering the obligation of all states to refrain, in their international relations, from the threat or use of force against the territorial integrity or political independence of any state;

Considering the obligation of states to settle conflicts by peaceful means, and thus safeguard international peace and security and justice;

Recognising the responsibility of states not to allow their territory to be used for acts of war, aggression or violence against other states;

Conscious of the need to promote relations of good neighbourliness based on the principles of equality of rights and mutual advantage;

Convinced that relations of good neighbourliness between the High Contracting Parties will contribute to peace, security, stability and progress in Southern Africa, the Continent and the World;

Have solemnly agreed to the following:

Article One. The High Contracting Parties undertake to respect each other's sovereignty and independence and, in fulfilment of this fundamental obligation, to refrain from interfering in the internal affairs of the other.

Article Two. (1) The High Contracting Parties shall resolve differences and disputes that may arise between them and that may or are likely to endanger mutual peace and security or peace and security in the region, by means of negotiation, enquiry, mediation, conciliation, arbitration or other peaceful means, and undertake not to resort, individually or collectively, to the threat or use of force against each other's sovereignty, territorial integrity or political independence.

(2) For the purposes of this article, the use of force shall include *inter alia*:

(a) Attacks by land, air or sea forces;

(b) Sabotage;

(c) Unwarranted concentration of such forces at or near the international boundaries of the High Contracting Parties;

(d) Violation of the international land, air or sea boundaries of either of the High Contracting Parties.

(3) The High Contracting Parties shall not in any way assist the armed forces of any state or group of states deployed against the territorial sovereignty or political independence of the other.

Article Three. (1) The High Contracting Parties shall not allow their respective territories, territorial waters or air space to be used as a base, thoroughfare, or in any other way by another state, government, foreign military forces, organisations or individuals which plan or prepare to commit acts of violence, terrorism or aggression against the territorial integrity or political independence of the other or may threaten the security of its inhabitants.

(2) The High Contracting Parties, in order to prevent or eliminate the acts or the preparation of acts mentioned in paragraph (1) of this article, undertake in particular to:

(a) Forbid and prevent in their respective territories the organisation of irregular forces or armed bands, including mercenaries, whose objective is to carry out the acts contemplated in paragraph (1) of this article;

(b) Eliminate from their respective territories bases, training centres, places of shelter, accommodation and transit for elements who intend to carry out the acts contemplated in paragraph (1) of this article;

(c) Eliminate from their respective territories centres or depots containing armaments of whatever nature, destined to be used by the elements contemplated in paragraph (1) of this article;

(d) Eliminate from their respective territories command posts or other places for the command, direction and co-ordination of the elements contemplated in paragraph (1) of this article;

(e) Eliminate from their respective territories communication and telecommunication facilities between the command and the elements contemplated in paragraph (1) of this article;

(f) Eliminate and prohibit the installation in their respective territories of radio broadcasting stations, including unofficial or clandestine broadcasts, for the elements that carry out the acts contemplated in paragraph (1) of this article;

(g) Exercise strict control, in their respective territories, over elements which intend to carry out or plan the acts contemplated in paragraph (1) of this article;

(h) Prevent the transit of elements who intend or plan to commit the acts contemplated in paragraph (1) of this article, from a place in the territory of either to a place in the territory of the other or to a place in the territory of any third state which has a common boundary with the High Contracting Party against which such elements intend or plan to commit the said acts;

(i) Take appropriate steps in their respective territories to prevent the recruitment of elements of whatever nationality for the purpose of carrying out the acts contemplated in paragraph (1) of this article;

(j) Prevent the elements contemplated in paragraph (1) of this article from carrying out from their respective territories by any means acts of abduction or other acts, aimed at taking citizens of any nationality hostage in the territory of the other High Contracting Party; and

(k) Prohibit the provision on their respective territories of any logistic facilities for carrying out the acts contemplated in paragraph (1) of this article.

(3) The High Contracting Parties will not use the territory of third states to carry out or support the acts contemplated in paragraphs (1) and (2) of this article.

Article Four. The High Contracting Parties shall take steps, individually and collectively, to ensure that the international boundary between their respective territories is effectively patrolled and that the border posts are efficiently administered to prevent illegal crossings from the territory of a High Contracting Party to the territory of the other, and in particular, by elements contemplated in Article Three of this Agreement.

Article Five. The High Contracting Parties shall prohibit within their territory acts of propaganda that incite a war of aggression against the other High Contracting Party and shall also prohibit acts of propaganda aimed at inciting acts of terrorism and civil war in the territory of the other High Contracting Party.

Article Six. The High Contracting Parties declare that there is no conflict between their commitments in treaties and international obligations and the commitments undertaken in this Agreement.

Article Seven. The High Contracting Parties are committed to interpreting this Agreement in good faith and will maintain periodic contact to ensure the effective application of what has been agreed.

Article Eight. Nothing in this Agreement shall be construed as detracting from the High Contracting Parties' right of self-defence in the event of armed attacks, as provided for in the Charter of the United Nations.

Article Nine. (1) Each of the High Contracting Parties shall appoint high-ranking representatives to serve on a Joint Security Commission with the aim of supervising and monitoring the application of this Agreement.

(2) The Commission shall determine its own working procedure.

(3) The Commission shall meet on a regular basis and may

be specially convened whenever circumstances so require.

(4) The Commission shall:

(a) Consider all allegations of infringements of the provisions of this Agreement;

(b) Advise the High Contracting Parties of its conclusions; and

(c) Make recommendations to the High Contracting Parties concerning measures for the effective application of this Agreement and the settlement of disputes over infringements or alleged infringements.

(5) The High Contracting Parties shall determine the mandate of their respective representatives in order to enable interim measures to be taken in cases of duly recognized emergency.

(6) The High Contracting Parties shall make available all the facilities necessary for the effective functioning of the Commission and will jointly consider its conclusions and recommendations.

Article Ten. This Agreement will also be known as "The Accord of Nkomati".

Article Eleven. (1) This Agreement shall enter into force on the date of the signature thereof.

(2) Any amendment to this Agreement agreed to by the High Contracting Parties shall be effected by the Exchange of Notes between them.

In Witness Whereof, the signatories, in the name of their respective governments, have signed and sealed this Agreement, in quadruplicate in the Portuguese and English languages, both texts being equally authentic.

Thus done and signed at the common border on the banks of the Nkomati River, on this the sixteenth day of March 1984.

[Signed]

SAMORA MOISÉS MACHEL
Marshal of the Republic
President of the People's Republic of Mozambique
President of the Council of Ministers
For the Government of the People's Republic of Mozambique

[Signed]

PIETER WILLEM BOTHA
Prime Minister of the Republic of South Africa
For the Government of the Republic of South Africa

4.1431 "Union of States" between the Kingdom of Morocco and Libya

Alliance Members: Morocco and Libya
Signed On: August 13, 1984, in the city of Oujda (Morocco). In force until August 29, 1986.
Alliance Type: Entente (Type III)

Source: *International Legal Materials,* vol. 23, p. 1022.

SUMMARY

This defense treaty reflected a striking change in regional relations. Interaction between the two countries had been hostile, with Libya supporting the Polisario insurgency for the independence of Moroccan Western Sahara and Morocco considering sending troops to support the French in the Libyan-influenced country of Chad. King Hassan of Morocco claimed to have thought of the idea of a loose union in which the two states agreed to neutralize conflict and exchange Libyan oil and money for Moroccan food and labor. As a pan-Arabist, the Libyan leader Mu'ammar Gadhafi was receptive to the idea, as he had promoted Arab solidarity through a regional union (see the Maghreb Union, Alliance no. 4.1434).

The Oujda Union followed the rapprochement of Algeria, Tunisia, and Mauritania that was signed on March 20, 1983 (see Alliance no. 4.1429). Relations between Libya and Algeria had been deteriorating for some time, and the 1983 treaty signed by Libya's neighbors greatly angered Gadhafi. Algeria was also the principal backer of the Polisario movement fighting Morocco, so the alliance was in part a response to Algeria's actions in the region.

This "Union of States" sent an aftershock through the diplomatic world, surprising both France and the United States. President Francois Mitterrand of France, who made two visits to Morocco in the month following the treaty, tried to assuage tensions in the region. The Reagan administration, concerned because U.S. and Libyan aircraft had exchanged fire several times over the Mediterranean prior to the agreement, questioned Morocco's intentions in case the United States became involved in a conflict with Libya. When the United States attacked Libya on August 29, 1986, in retaliation for the Libya-backed bombing of a Berlin discotheque, Morocco did not aid Libya as per the terms of their treaty, a breach of promise that signaled the death of the alliance.

ALLIANCE TEXT

Joint Communique

His Excellency Muammar Qadhafi, Chief of the Revolution of September First, conducted a working visit to the Kingdom of Morocco Monday, August 13, 1984, and was welcomed by His Majesty King Hassan II upon his arrival in Oujda.

This visit followed an exchange of correspondences and visits of emissaries which have taken place in recent days between His Majesty King Hassan II and His Excellency Colonel Muammar Qadhafi, Chief of the Revolution of September First, relating to the search for means to reinforce the ties of brotherhood between the two nations and expand the scope of their cooperation.

These negotiations, undertaken directly between His Majesty King Hassan II and His Excellency Muammar Qadhafi during the visit conducted by the Libyan leader to the Kingdom of Morocco, resulted in the conclusion of a treaty instituting a Union of States between the Kingdom of Morocco and the Socialist People's Libyan Arab Jamahiriya.

Through the institution of this Union of States, His Majesty the King and His Excellency Muammar Qadhafi seek to further reinforce the solid ties which exist between their two nations in order to bring about the consolidation of the Arab Maghreb, and take a historic step forward towards the realization of the unity of the Arab nation which will allow the avoidance of the dangers which confront the Arab nation, the Islamic world, and principally Palestine and Jerusalem.

The treaty instituting the Union of States between the two nations has been signed, but will not enter into force until after receiving the approval of the two peoples, in conformity with the existing procedures in each of the two countries.

Done in Oujda, Monday August 13, 1984

Treaty of Union of States

Following is an unofficial translation of the Treaty of the Union of States concluded between the Kingdom of Morocco and the Socialist People's Libyan Arab Jamahiriya.

The Kingdom of Morocco and the Socialist People's Libyan Arab Jamahiriya , aware of the dangers confronting the Arab nation and the Moslem world in general and Palestine and Jerusalem in particular, as a result of the policy of violence and aggressions carried out by Zionists who, stirred by pride and blinded by arrogance, continue to threaten the sacred values of Islam and to violate the rights of Moslems and Arabs, rejecting the principles and ideals an which the international community is founded and disregarding the resolutions emanating from international organizations of all levels;

Considering that, in order to avert the dangers threatening the Arab nation and the Moslem world, and in particular Palestine and Jerusalem, it is necessary to achieve an identity of views, and mobilize efforts with a view to driving back aggression and assuring the triumph of justice, the safeguarding of Arab and Moslem interests and the defense of their right to existence and dignity;

Convinced that the adoption of such conduct will constitute a positive factor enabling the Arab nation and the Moslem world to regain their glory of yore, to occupy in the world a place worthy of their prestigious past and to devote their efforts to work for the promotion of their peoples and to prepare them to enter the twenty-first century, armed with everything that can provide them with a high rank among developed peoples: in scientific and technical areas as well as in other areas of human progress and civilization;

Taking into account the obstacles facing the materialization of Arab unity as was proven by the failures of previous experiences, and considering that wisdom requires drawing lessons from setbacks, as a result of having under-estimated the difficulties of such an undertaking, and that the best conduct to adopt in this area consists of persevering an untiring action to progressively attain the expected aim, without hurrying its conception or improvising its implementation;

Aware, more particularly, of the solid ties existing among the peoples of the Arab Maghreb, united by their common origin, geography, history, religion, language and similar way of life and civilization, and taking into account the old aspiration of these peoples and their leaders to establish among them a union that will strengthen their relationship founded on neighborliness and common destiny, that will enable them to proceed on the way to creating an integrated set that will have considerable weight in political and economic areas among the peoples of the developed world, and notably among those of the Mediterranean Basin;

Wishing to meet these aspirations and to contribute to their materialization, in a realistic way, so that they become a reality;

Considering that the best means to attain this goal is to institute between them a union likely to become a starting point f or the establishment of larger structures whose aim will be to serve the unity of Arab and Moslem peoples and to meet their aspirations;

Considering that this union constitutes an essential contribution to the unity of the Arab Maghreb, and, consequently, a historical step on the way to the achievement of the unity of the Arab nation;

The two leaders agreed upon the following:

Article First. Under the name of an Arab-African Union, a Union of States between the Kingdom of Morocco and the Socialist People's Libyan Arab Jamahiriya is established.

Article 2. The supreme body of the Union is the Chairmanship, jointly exercised by His Majesty the King of Morocco and His Excellency the Leader of the September First Revolution.

Only the Chairmanship of the Union has the decision-making powers.

Article 3. Under the authority of the Chairmanship, a Permanent secretariat is established.

The Permanent Secretariat's Headquarters is alternately based in each of the two countries.

It is comprised of a permanent delegation in each of the countries.

The Secretary General is of the nationality of the state on whose territory the Permanent

Secretariat is not based.

The Assistant Secretary General is of the other nationality.

The alternation of Secretary General and headquarters occurs every two years.

Article 4. The Union is comprised of the following Councils:
- A Political Council
- A Defense Council
- An Economic Council
- A Council of Cultural and Technical Action

These Councils are, by decision of the Chairmanship, composed by equal parts, of delegates of each of the two states.

These Councils, being consultative in nature, are charged, each its area of competence, with:
- Studying issues submitted to it by the Chairmanship
- Proposing solutions
- Preparing any useful projects at the request of the Chairmanship.

Article 5. The Union is provided with an Assembly of Union composed of members of the House of Representatives of the

Kingdom of Morocco and of the members of the General Congress of the Libyan Jamahiriya People.

The mission of this Assembly is to submit to the Chairmanship recommendations with a view to strengthening the Union and attaining its goals.

Article 6. The Union comprises an Executive Commission formed of the Council of Ministers of the Kingdom of Morocco and the General Popular Commission of the Libyan Jamahiriya.

The Executive Commission whose task is to follow-up the decisions of the chairmanship and to ensure their implementation, convenes at regular intervals, alternately in each of the two countries.

Article 7. The Union is provided with a Court of Justice whose composition is fixed by decision of the Chairmanship.

If a dispute arises between the two contracting parties concerning the execution and the interpretation of the present treaty, each of them has the right to take the matter before the Court of the Union.

The decisions and judgments of the Court are definitive and binding.

Article 8. The Union's goal is:

- To strengthen the links of brotherhood between the two states and the two peoples
- To promote progress in the Arab Community and to defend its rights
- To participate in the safeguarding of peace each time it is founded on justice and equity and marked by stability and permanence
- To implement joint policies
- To contribute to the unification of the Arab Maghreb and, consequently, to the achievement of the unity of the Arab Nation.

Article 9. The joint policies mentioned in the preceding article concern:

- In the international arena, the fraternal understanding between the two Countries and their close diplomatic cooperation
- In the area of defense, the safeguarding of the independence of each of the two countries
- In the field of economics, industrial, agricultural, commercial and Social development, through the creation of joint ventures and the elaboration of specific or general economic programs
- In the cultural area, cooperation aimed at the development of Instruction St all levels, the preservation of moral and spiritual values founded on the teachings of Islam and the safeguarding of the Arab national identity, notable through the exchange of students and teachers, and the creation of cultural mid joint research institutions and universities.

Article 10. The Union is provided with a functioning budget and a developmental budget.

Article 11. With unreserved respect for their respective sovereignty, each of the two states commits itself not to interfere with the other country's internal affairs.

Article 12. Any aggression towards one of the two states would constitute an aggression towards the other.

Article 13. The Union does not exclude for any of the two contracting parties the conclusion of analogous or similar agreements that each of them might conclude with third states.

With the agreement of the two contracting parties, third states belonging to the Arab Nation or to the African Community can adhere to the present treaty and become members of the Union.

Article 14. An Ad Hoc Commission whose members will be appointed by the Chairmanship will present complementary draft agreements aimed at specifying or developing the provisions mentioned above.

These draft agreements will be submitted to the Chairmanship for decision.

Article 15. The interests of each of the two states will be represented in the other by a Minister or a Resident Secretary.

Article 16. The present Treaty will become effective after approval, through a referendum, of the people of the Kingdom of Morocco and the people of the Libyan Jamahiriya in conformity with the procedures applicable in each of two states.

Done in Oujda, Monday August 13, 1984

4.1432 Treaty of Friendship and Cooperation between the Government of the Republic of Malta and the Socialist People's Libyan Arab Jamahiriya

Alliance Members: Malta and Libya
Signed On: November 29, 1984, in the city of Tripoli (Libya). In force until November 26, 1989.
Alliance Type: Defense Pact (Type I)

Source: Government of Malta, Ministry of Justice and Home Affairs, docs.justice.gov.mt/lom/legislation/english/leg/vol_7/chapt311.pdf.

SUMMARY

Following the election of Dom Mintoff as prime minister in 1971, Malta, a former British colony, began to pursue stronger relations with Libya. Closer relations were formalized ten years later with this five-year treaty of friendship and cooperation that outlined a military and security alliance between the two nations. According to the agreement, Malta pledged "not to allow its territory to be used militarily against the security, territorial integrity of Libya." In turn, Libya pledged to assist and defend Malta against aggression from hostile threats. Libya also agreed to train Maltese military members and supply Malta with arms. At the signing of this alliance, Mintoff announced that Malta would not renew an agreement with Italy in which Italy was to provide Malta with $12 million annually in exchange for neutrality. Soon after these actions were announced, Mintoff visited the Soviet Union to confirm his nation's ties to Moscow. During the course of the treaty, Malta warned the Libyan leader, Mu'ammar Gadhafi, of an impending attack from the United Sates.

In the mid-1980s, however, the ruling Labor Party was defeated in elections and a new government headed by the Nationalist Party came to power. Led by Prime Minister Edward Fenech Adami, this new government sought to alter the former government's Marxist leanings and increase cooperation with Western nations such as the United States. In November of 1989, the original treaty of cooperation and friendship expired. The two nations negotiated a new treaty that ended all military cooperation but still allowed for economic ties.

ALLIANCE TEXT

The Government of the Republic of Malta,
and
The Socialist People's Libyan Arab Jamahiriya

1. On the basis of their desire to preserve the bonds of friendship and the strategical relationship which exists between them, and their willingness for the consolidation and development of the relation of co-operation on the basis of mutual benefit and welfare of the Maltese people and the Libyan Arab people,

2. Desirous of turning the Mediterranean into a lake of peace and of cooperating to achieve this end,

3. Taking into consideration the decision of the People of the Republic of Malta to shed forever the harmful and humiliating role of a foreign military base and to become instead a bridge of friendship between Europe and North Africa,

4. Resolve by this Treaty to strengthen mutual security, friendship and cooperation between the two countries, in conformity with the principles of non-alignment and the Charter of the United Nations and therefore agree as follows:

Article 1. The Socialist People's Libyan Arab Jamahiriya and the Republic of Malta undertake not to participate in any Military Alliance which may affect the security interests of the other side.

Article 2. Malta undertakes not to allow foreign military bases to be established on its territory and undertakes not to allow its territory to be used militarily against the security, territorial integrity of the Socialist People's Libyan Arab Jamahiriya.

Article 3. The Socialist People's Libyan Arab Jamahiriya undertakes to respect and support Malta's neutrality and will assist Malta whenever the Government of the Republic of Malta explicitly requests so in case of threats or acts of aggression against Malta's territorial integrity and sovereignty.

Article 4. In view of the importance of Malta's economic viability it is agreed that economic cooperation will be prompted in the fields of joint ventures, balanced commercial exchanges, and the utilisation of Maltese labour. For this purpose, agreements in the fields of defence, information and economy will form an integral part of this Treaty.

Article 5. The two sides will work toward the development of co-operation between them in the information and cultural fields with the aim of achieving stronger bonds between the two peoples.

Article 6. The two sides will hold consultations aiming at harmonising their viewpoints on political, economic, security and international issues which affect their interests whether directly or indirectly, and will endeavour to support one another's viewpoints whenever this mutual support is required.

Article 7. The two sides will do their utmost to coordinate their efforts in the preservation of international peace and security, especially in the Mediterranean region, and emphasise their faithful adherence to the principles and goals of the United Nations and Non-Alignment.

Article 8. The two sides agree to set up a Mixed Commission which shall meet at Ministerial level alternately in Valletta and Tripoli, at least once every six months, to review progress in the above fields of cooperation and to plan and see to the implementation of co-operation in new sectors.

Article 9. Any differences between the two sides which may arise from the interpretation of these provisions will be settled in a brotherly manner.

Article 10. The duration of this "Treaty" shall be five years renewable automatically for further five-year periods so long as none of the two sides express a desire in writing to adjust it or abrogate it six months at least before its expiration date.

Article 11. This Treaty will come into force with immediate effect on the date of the exchange of the instruments of ratification but not later than January 1985.

Done in Valletta on the nineteenth day of November, One Thousand Nine Hundred and Eighty Four corresponding to the 25 Safar 1394 in two originals in the English and Arabic Languages both texts being equally authentic.

Colonel Muammar El Gaddafi
Leader of the First of September Revolution
For the Socialist People's Libyan Arab Jamahiriya

Dom Mintoff
Prime Minister
For the Republic of Malta

4.1433 Treaty of Peace and Friendship between Chile and Argentina

Alliance Members: Chile and Argentina
Signed On: November 29, 1984, in Vatican City. In force as of date of publication of this volume.
Alliance Type: Neutrality Pact (Type II)

Source: *United Nations Treaty,* no. 23392.

SUMMARY

During the 1970s border disputes between Argentina and Chile became increasingly tense, and in 1978 the two nations began negotiations and appealed to Pope John Paul II to settle the boundary dispute.

The purpose of this agreement was to put an end to the six-year-old border conflict in the Beagle Channel. The agreement stipulated that Chile would have authority over the channel while Argentina would have control over the banks and the areas in which the channel met the sea.

The treaty resolved the Beagle dispute, but by 1990 a dispute was intensifying over the Laguna del Desierto, or Desert Lake. The 1984 treaty set a framework for cooperation, and the former rivals soon began cooperating on issues such as the regional economy. Cooperation continued to increase over time, and by 1999 Chile and Argentina were conducting joint naval exercises around the Beagle Channel.

ALLIANCE TEXT

In the Name of God the All-Powerful

The Government of the Republic of Chile and the Government of the Argentine Republic,

Recalling that on 8 January 1979 they requested the Holy See to act as a Mediator in the dispute which has arisen in the southern zone, with the aim of guiding them in the negotiations and assisting them in the search for a solution; and that they sought his valuable aid in fixing a boundary line, which would determine the respective areas of jurisdiction to the east and to the west of this line, from the end of the existing boundary;

Convinced that it is the inescapable duty of both Governments to give expression to the aspirations of peace of their peoples;

Bearing in mind the Boundary Treaty of 1881, the unshakeable foundation of relations between the Argentine Republic and the Republic of Chile, and its supplementary and declaratory instruments;

Reiterating the obligation always to solve all its disputes by peaceful means and never to resort to the threat or use of force in their mutual relations;

Desiring to intensify the economic co-operation and physical integration of their respective countries;

Taking especially into account the "Proposal of the Mediator, Suggestions and Advice", of 12 December 1980;

Conveying, on behalf of their peoples, their thanks to His Holiness Pope John Paul II for his enlightened efforts to reach a solution of the dispute and to strengthen friendship and understanding between both nations;

Have resolved to conclude the following Treaty, which constitutes a compromise, for which purpose they have designated as their representatives:

His Excellency the President of the Republic of Chile Mr. Jaime del Valle Allende, Minister for Foreign Affairs,

His Excellency the President of the Argentine Republic Mr. Dante Mario Caputo, Minister for Foreign Affairs and Worship, who have agreed as follows:

Peace and Friendship

Article 1. The High Contracting Parties, responding to the fundamental interests of their peoples, reiterate solemnly their commitment to preserve, strengthen and develop their unchanging ties of perpetual friendship.

The Parties shall hold periodic meetings of consultation in which they shall consider especially any occurrence or situation which is likely to alter the harmony between them, they shall try to ensure that any difference in their viewpoints does not cause controversy and they shall suggest or adopt specific measures to maintain and strengthen good relations between both countries.

Article 2. The Parties confirm their obligation to refrain from resorting directly or indirectly to any form of threat or use of force and from adopting any other measures which may disturb the peace in any sector of their mutual relations.

They also confirm their obligation to solve, always and exclusively by peaceful means, all controversies, of whatever nature, which for any cause have arisen or may arise between them, in conformity with the following provisions.

Article 3. If a dispute arises, the Parties shall adopt appropriate measures to maintain the best general conditions of coexistence in all aspects of their relations and to prevent the dispute from becoming worse or prolonged.

Article 4. The Parties shall strive to reach a solution of any dispute between them through direct negotiations, carried out in good faith and in a spirit of cooperation.

If, in the judgement of both Parties or one of them, direct negotiations do not achieve a satisfactory result, either of the Parties may invite the other to seek a solution to the dispute by means of peaceful settlement chosen by mutual agreement.

Article 5. In the event that the Parties, within a period of four months from the invitation referred to in the preceding article, do not reach agreement on another means of settlement and on the time-limit and other procedures for its application, or in the event that, such agreement having been obtained, a solution is not reached for any reason, the conciliation procedure stipulated in annex 1, chapter I, shall be applied.

Article 6. If both Parties or any one of them has not accepted the settlement terms proposed by the Conciliation Commission within the time-limit fixed by its Chairman, or if the conciliation procedure should break down for any reason, both Parties or any one of them may submit the dispute to the arbitral procedure established in annex 1, chapter II.

The same procedure shall apply when the Parties, in conformity with article 4, choose arbitration as a means of settlement of the dispute, unless they agree on other rules.

Questions which have been finally settled may not be brought up again under this article. In such cases, arbitration shall be limited exclusively to questions raised about the validity, interpretation and implementation of such agreements.

Maritime Boundary

Article 7. The boundary between the respective sovereignties over the sea, seabed and subsoil of the Argentine Republic and the Republic of Chile in the sea of the southern zone from the end of the existing boundary in the Beagle Channel, i.e., the point fixed by the co-ordinates 55°07.3' South latitude and 66°25.0' West longitude shall be the line joining the following points:

From the point fixed by the co-ordinates 55°07.3' South latitude and 66°25.0' West longitude (point A), the boundary shall follow a course towards the south-east along a loxodromic line until a point situated between the coasts of the Isla Nueva and the Isla Grande de Tierre del Fuego whose co-ordinates are South latitude 55°11.0' and West longitude 66°04.7' (point B);

from there it shall continue in a south-easterly direction at an angle of 45° measured at point B and shall extend to the point whose co-ordinates are 55°22.9' South latitude and 65°43.6' West longitude (point C); it shall continue directly south along that meridian until the parallel 56°22.8' of South latitude (point D); from there it shall continue west along that parallel, 24 miles to the south of the most southerly point of Isla Hornos, until it intersects the meridian running south from the most southerly point of Isla Hornos at co-ordinates 56°22.8' South latitude and 67°16.0' West longitude (point E); from there the boundary shall continue south to a point whose co-ordinates are 58°21.1' South latitude and 67°16.0' West longitude (point F). . . .

The exclusive economic zones of the Argentine Republic and the Republic of Chile shall extend respectively to the east and west of the boundary thus described.

To the south of the end of the boundary (point F), the exclusive economic zone of the Republic of Chile shall extend, up to the distance permitted by international law, to the west of the meridian 67°16.0' West longitude, ending on the east at the high sea.

Article 8. The Parties agree that in the area included between Cape Horn and the easternmost point of Isla de los Estados, the legal effects of the territorial sea shall be limited, in their mutual relations, to a strip of three marine miles measured from their respective base lines.

In the area indicated in the preceding paragraph, each Party may invoke with regard to third States the maximum width of the territorial sea permitted by international law.

Article 9. The Parties agree to call the maritime area delimited in the two preceding articles "Mar de la Zona Austral" (Sea of the Southern Zone).

Article 10. The Argentine Republic and the Republic of Chile agree that at the eastern end of the Strait of Magellan (Estrecho de Magallanes) defined by Punta Dungeness in the north and Cabo del Espíritu Santo in the south, the boundary between their respective sovereignties shall be the straight line joining the "Dungeness Marker (Former Beacon)", located at the very tip of the said geographical feature, and "Marker I on Cabo del Espíritu Santo" in Tierra del Fuego. . . .

The sovereignty of the Argentine Republic and the sovereignty of the Republic of Chile over the sea, seabed and subsoil shall extend, respectively, to the east and west of this boundary.

The boundary agreed on here in no way alters the provisions of the 1881 Boundary Treaty, whereby the Strait of Magellan is neutralized forever with free navigation assured for the flags of all nations under the terms laid down in article V.

The Argentine Republic undertakes to maintain, at any time and in whatever circumstances, the right of ships of all flags to navigate expeditiously and without obstacles through its jurisdictional waters to and from the Strait of Magellan.

Article 11. The Parties give mutual recognition to the base lines which they have traced in their respective territories.

Economic Co-operation and Physical Integration

Article 12. The Parties agree to establish a permanent Bi-National Commission with the aim of strengthening economic co-operation and physical integration. The Bi-National Commission shall be responsible for promoting and developing initiatives, *inter alia,* on the following subjects: global system of terrestrial links, mutual development of free ports and zones, land transport, air navigation, electrical interconnections and telecommunications, exploitation of natural resources, protection of the environment and tourist complementarity.

Within six months following the entry into force of this Treaty, the Parties shall establish the Bi-National Commission and shall draw up its rules of procedure.

Article 13. The Republic of Chile, in exercise of its sovereign rights, shall grant to the Argentine Republic the navigation facilities specified in articles 1 to 9 of annex 2.

The Republic of Chile declares that ships flying the flag of third countries may navigate without obstacles over the routes indicated in articles 1 and 8 of annex 2, subject to the pertinent Chilean regulations.

Both Parties shall allow in the Beagle Channel the navigation and pilotage system specified in annex 2, articles 11 to 16.

The stipulations in this Treaty regarding navigation in the southern zone shall replace those in any previous agreement on the subject between the Parties.

Final Clauses

Article 14. The Parties solemnly declare that this Treaty constitutes the complete and final settlement of the questions with which it deals.

The boundaries indicated in this Treaty shall constitute a final and irrevocable confine between the sovereignties of the Argentine Republic and the Republic of Chile.

The Parties undertake not to present claims or interpretations which are incompatible with the provisions of this Treaty.

Article 15. Articles 1 to 6 of this Treaty shall be applicable in the territory of Antarctica. The other provisions shall not affect in any way, nor may they be interpreted in any way, that they can affect, directly or indirectly, the sovereignty, rights, juridical positions of the Parties, or the boundaries in Antarctica or in its adjacent maritime areas, including the seabed and subsoil.

Article 16. Welcoming the generous offer of the Holy Father, the High Contracting Parties place this Treaty under the moral protection of the Holy See.

Article 17. The following form an integral part of this Treaty:

(a) Annex 1 on conciliation and arbitration procedure, consisting of 41 articles;

(b) Annex 2 on navigation, consisting of 16 articles; and

(c) The maps referred to in articles 7 and 10 of the Treaty and articles 1, 8 and 11 of annex 2.

References to this Treaty shall be understood as references also to its respective annexes and maps.

Article 18. This Treaty is subject to ratification and shall enter into force on the date of the exchange of the instruments of ratification.

Article 19. This Treaty shall be registered in conformity with Article 102 of the Charter of the United Nations.

In witness whereof, they sign and affix their seals to this Treaty in six identical copies of which two shall remain in the possession of the Holy See and the others in the possession of each of the Parties.

Done in Vatican City on 29 November 1984.

[DANTE MARIO CAPUTO]
[JAIME DEL VALLE ALLIENDE]

Before me:
[AGOSTINO Cardinal CASAROLI]

ANNEX 1

Chapter I. Conciliation Procedure Provided for in Article 5 of the treaty of Peace and Friendship

Article I. Within six months following the entry into force of this Treaty, the Parties shall establish an Argentino-Chilean Permanent Conciliation Commission, hereinafter called "the Commission".

The Commission shall be composed of three members. Each one of the Parties shall appoint a member, who may be chosen from among its nationals. The third member, who shall act as Chairman of the Commission, shall be chosen by both Parties from among the nationals of third States who do not have their habitual residence in the territory of the Parties and are not employed in their service.

Members shall be appointed for a period of three years and may be reappointed. Each of the Parties may proceed at any time with the replacement of the member appointed by it. The third member may be replaced during his term of office by agreement between the Parties.

Vacancies caused by death or any other reason shall be filled in the same manner as initial appointments, within a period not longer than three months.

If the appointment of the third member of the Commission cannot be made within a period of six months from the entry into force of this Treaty or within a period of three months from the beginning of the vacancy, as the case may be, any one of the Parties may request the Holy See to make the appointment.

Article 2. In the situation provided for in article 5 of the Treaty of Peace and Friendship, the dispute shall be brought before the Commission in the form of a written request, either jointly by the two Parties or separately, addressed to the Chairman of the Commission. The subject of the dispute shall be briefly indicated in the request.

If the request is not submitted jointly, the Party making it shall immediately notify the other Party.

Article 3. The written request or requests whereby the dispute is brought before the Commission shall contain, as far as possible, the designation of the delegate or delegates by whom the Party or Parties originating the request will be represented on the Commission.

It shall be the responsibility of the Chairman of the Commission to invite the Party or Parties who have not appointed a delegate to proceed promptly with such an appointment.

Article 4. Once a dispute has been brought before the Commission, and solely for this purpose, the Parties may designate, by common agreement, two more members to form part of it. The third member already appointed shall continue to serve as the Chairman of the Commission.

Article 5. If, when a dispute is brought before the Commission, any of the members appointed by a Party is unable to participate fully in the conciliation procedure, that Party must replace him as soon as possible for the sole purpose of the conciliation.

At the request of any one of the Parties, or on his own initiative, the Chairman may require the other Party to proceed with such a replacement.

If the Chairman of the Commission is unable to participate fully in the conciliation procedure, the Parties must replace him by common agreement as soon as possible for the sole purpose of the conciliation. If there is no such agreement, any of the Parties may request the Holy See to make the appointment.

Article 6. Having received a request, the Chairman shall fix the place and the date of the first meeting and shall invite to it the members of the Commission and the delegates of the Parties.

At the first meeting the Commission shall appoint its Secretary, who shall not be a national of any of the Parties, shall not have a permanent residence in their territory and shall not be employed in their service. The Secretary shall remain in office as long as the conciliation lasts.

At the same meeting, the Commission shall determine the procedure which is to govern the conciliation. Except if the Parties agree otherwise, the procedure shall be adversarial.

Article 7. The Parties shall be represented in the Commission by their delegates; they may also be accompanied by advisers and experts appointed by them for these purposes and they may request any testimony they consider appropriate.

The Commission shall have the power to request explanations from the delegates, advisers and experts of the Parties and from other persons they consider useful.

Article 8. The Commission shall meet in a place the Parties agree on and, failing such an agreement, in the place designated by its Chairman.

Article 9. The Commission may recommend that the Parties adopt measures to prevent the dispute from becoming worse or the conciliation from becoming more difficult.

Article 10. The Commission may not meet without the presence of all its members.

Unless the Parties agree otherwise, all the Commission's decisions shall be taken by a majority vote of its members. In the Commission's records no mention shall be made of whether decisions were made unanimously or by a majority.

Article 11. The Parties shall facilitate the work of the Commission and shall, as far as possible, provide it with all useful documents and information. Similarly, they shall allow it to proceed in their respective territories with the summoning and hearing of witnesses and experts and with the carrying out of on-the-spot inspections.

Article 12. In finalizing its consideration of the dispute, the Commission shall strive to define the terms of a settlement likely to be accepted by both Parties. The Commission may, for this purpose, proceed to exchange views with the delegates of the Parties, whom they may hear jointly or separately.

The terms proposed by the Commission shall be only in the nature of recommendations submitted for the consideration of the Parties to facilitate a mutually acceptable settlement.

The terms of the settlement shall be communicated in writing by the Chairman to the delegates of the Parties, whom he shall invite to inform him, within the time-limit fixed by him, whether the respective Governments accept the proposed settlement or not.

In making this communication, the Chairman shall explain personally the reasons why, in the Commission's opinion, they advise the Parties to accept the settlement.

If the dispute is only about questions of fact, the Commission shall confine itself to investigating these facts and shall draw up its conclusions in a report.

Article 13. Once the settlement proposed by the Commission is accepted by both Parties, a document embodying the settlement shall be drawn up; it shall be signed by the Chairman, the Secretary of the Commission and the delegates. A copy of the document, signed by the Chairman and the Secretary, shall be sent to each Party.

Article 14. If both Parties or one of them does not accept the settlement proposed and if the Commission deems it useless to try to obtain agreement on different settlement terms, a document shall be drawn up, signed by the Chairman and Secretary, which, without reproducing the settlement terms, shall state that the Parties could not be reconciled.

Article 15. The work of the Commission shall be concluded within six months from the day on which the dispute was brought to its attention, unless the Parties agree otherwise.

Article 16. No statement or communication of the delegates or members of the Commission on the substance of the dispute shall be included in the records of the meetings, unless the delegate or member responsible for the statement or communication consents. On the other hand, the written or oral reports of experts, the records of on-the-spot inspections and the statements of witnesses shall be annexed to the records, unless the Commission decides otherwise.

Article 17. Authentic copies of the records of meetings and their annexes shall be sent to the delegates of the Parties through the Secretary of the Commission, unless the Commission decides otherwise.

Article 18. The Commission's discussions shall be made public only by virtue of a Decision taken by the Commission with the assent of both Parties.

Article 19. No admission or proposal made during the conciliation proceedings, whether by one of the Parties or by the Commission, may prejudge or affect, in any way, the rights or claims of either Party in the event that the conciliation procedure is not successful. Similarly, the acceptance by either Party of a draft settlement formulated by the Commission shall in no way imply acceptance of considerations of fact or law on which such a settlement may be based.

Article 20. Once the Commission's work is completed, the Parties shall consider whether they will authorize the total or partial publication of the relevant documentation. The Commission may address to them a recommendation for this purpose.

Article 21. During the work of the Commission, each of its members shall receive financial remuneration the amount of which shall be fixed by common agreement between the Parties. The Parties shall each pay half of this remuneration.

Each of the Parties shall pay its own expenses and half of the Commission's joint expenses.

Article 22. At the end of the conciliation, the Chairman of the Commission shall deposit all the relevant documentation in the archives of the Holy See, thus maintaining the reserved nature of this documentation, within the limits indicated in articles 18 and 20 of this annex.

Chapter II. Arbitral Procedure Provided for in Article 6 of the Treaty of Peace and Friendship

Article 23. The Party intending to have recourse to arbitration shall so inform the other in writing. In the same communication, it shall request the constitution of the arbitral tribunal, hereinafter called "the Tribunal", shall indicate briefly the nature of the dispute, shall name the arbitrator it has chosen as a member of the Tribunal and shall invite the other Party to reach an arbitral settlement.

The other Party shall co-operate in the constitution of the Tribunal and in the elaboration of the settlement.

Article 24. Except as otherwise agreed by the Parties, the Tribunal shall consist of five members designated in their personal capacity. Each of the Parties shall appoint a member, who may be one of their nationals. The other three members, one of whom shall be Chairman of the Tribunal, shall be elected by common agreement from among the nationals of third States. These three arbitrators must be of different nationality, must not have their habitual residence in the territory of the Parties and must not be employed in their service.

Article 25. If all the members of the Tribunal have not been appointed within a time-limit of three months from the reception of the communication provided for in article 23, the appointment of the members in question shall be made by the

Government of the Swiss Confederation at the request of either Party.

The Chairman of the Tribunal shall be designated by common agreement between the Parties within the time-limit specified in the preceding paragraph. If there is no such agreement, the designation shall be made by the Government of the Swiss Confederation at the request of either Party.

When all the members have been designated, the Chairman shall convene them to a meeting in order to declare the Tribunal constituted and to adopt the other agreements necessary for its operation. The meeting shall be held at the place, day and time indicated by the Chairman and the provisions of article 34 of this annex shall be applicable to it.

Article 26. Vacancies which may occur as a result of death, resignation or any other cause shall be filled in the following manner:

- If the vacancy is that of a member of the Tribunal appointed by a single one of the Parties, that Party shall fill it as soon as possible and, in any case, within a period of 30 days from the time the other Party invites it in writing to do so;
- If the vacancy is that of one of the members of the Tribunal appointed by common agreement, the vacancy shall be filled within a period of 60 days from the time one of the Parties invites the other in writing to do so;
- If, within the periods indicated in the foregoing paragraphs, the vacancies in question have not been filled, any of the Parties may request the Government of the Swiss Confederation to fill them.

Article 27. In the event that there is no agreement to bring the dispute before the Tribunal within a period of three months from the time of its constitution, either Party may bring the dispute before it following a written request.

Article 28. The Tribunal shall adopt its own rules of procedure, without prejudice to those which the Parties may have agreed upon.

Article 29. The Tribunal shall have the powers to interpret the settlement and decide on its own competence.

Article 30. The Parties shall co-operate in the work of the Tribunal and shall provide it with all useful documents, facilities and information. Similarly, they shall allow the Tribunal to conduct hearings in their respective territories, to summon and bear witnesses or experts and to practise on-the-spot inspections.

Article 31. The Tribunal shall have the power to order provisional measures designed to safeguard the rights of the Parties.

Article 32. When one of the Parties in the dispute does not appear before the Tribunal or refrains from defending its case, the other Party may request the Tribunal to continue the hearing and announce a decision. The fact that one of the Parties is absent or fails to appear shall not be an obstacle to the progress of the hearing or the announcement of a decision.

Article 33. The Tribunal shall base its decisions on international law, unless the Parties have agreed otherwise.

Article 34. The Tribunal's decisions shall be adopted by a majority of its members. The absence or abstention of one or two of its members shall not prevent the Tribunal from meeting or reaching a decision. In the case of a tie, the Chairman shall cast the deciding vote.

Article 35. The Tribunal's decision shall be accompanied by a statement of reasons. It shall mention the number of the members who have taken part in its adoption and the date on which it was rendered. Each member of the Tribunal shall have the right to have his separate or dissenting opinion added to the decision.

Article 36. The decision shall be binding on the Parties, final and unappealable. Its implementation shall be entrusted to the honour of the nations signing the Treaty of Peace and Friendship.

Article 37. The decision shall be executed without delay in the form and within the time-limits specified by the Tribunal.

Article 38. The Tribunal shall not terminate its functions until it has declared that, in its opinion, the decision has been carried out materially and completely.

Article 39. Unless the Parties have agreed otherwise, the disagreements which may arise between the Parties about the interpretation or the manner of execution of the arbitral decision may be brought by any Party before the Tribunal which rendered the decision. For this purpose, any vacancy occurring in the Tribunal shall be filled in the manner established in article 26 of this annex.

Article 40. Any Party may request the revision of the decision before the Tribunal which rendered it provided that the request is made before the time-limit for its execution has expired, and in the following cases:

1. If the decision has been rendered on the basis of a false or adulterated document;
2. If the decision is wholly or partly the result of an error of fact resulting from the hearings or documentation in the case.

For this purpose, any vacancy occurring in the Tribunal shall be filled in the manner established in article 26 of this annex.

Article 41. Each of the members of the Tribunal shall receive remuneration the amount of which shall be fixed by common agreement between the Parties, who shall each pay half of such remuneration.

Each Party shall pay its own expenses and half the joint expenses of the Tribunal.

[JAIME DEL VALLE ALLIENDE]
[DANTE MARIO CAPUTO]

ANNEX 2 NAVIGATION

Navigation between the Strait of Magellan and Argentine ports in the Beagle Channel and vice versa

Article 1. For maritime traffic between the Strait of Magellan and Argentine ports in the Beagle Channel and vice versa, through Chilean internal waters, Argentine vessels shall enjoy navigation facilities exclusively along the following route:

Canal Magdalena, Canal Cockburn, Paso Brecknock or Canal Ocasión, Canal Ballenero, Canal O'Brien, Paso Timbales, north-west arm of the Beagle Channel and the Beagle Channel as far as the meridian 68°36'38.5" West longitude and vice versa. . . .

Article 2. The passage shall be navigated with a Chilean pilot, who shall act as technical adviser to the commandant or captain of the vessel.

For the proper designation and embarkation of the pilot, the Argentine authority shall inform the Commander-in-Chief of the Third Chilean Naval Zone, at least 48 hours in advance, of the date on which the vessel will begin the navigation.

The pilot shall perform his functions between the point whose geographical co-ordinates are: 54°02.8' South latitude and 70°57.9' West longitude and the meridian 68°36'38.5' West longitude in the Beagle Channel.

In the passage from or to the eastern mouth of the Strait of Magellan, the pilot shall embark and disembark at the pilot station of Bahía Posesión in the Strait of Magellan. In the passage from or to the western mouth of the Strait of Magellan, the pilot shall embark and disembark at the corresponding point indicated in the previous paragraph. He shall be conveyed to and from the previously designated points by Chilean means of transport.

In the passage from or to Argentine ports in the Beagle Channel, the pilot shall embark and disembark in Ushunia and shall be conveyed from Puerto Williams to Ushuaia or from Ushuaia to Puerto Williams by Argentine means of transport.

Merchant vessels must pay the pilot fees laid down in the Tariff Regulations of the General Department of Maritime Territory and Merchant Navy of Chile.

Article 3. The passage of Argentine vessels shall be continuous and uninterrupted. In case of stoppage or anchorage as a result of *force majeure* along the route indicated in article 1, the commander or captain of the Argentine vessel shall inform the nearest Chilean naval authority.

Article 4. In cases not provided for in this Treaty, Argentine vessels shall be subject to the norms of international law. During the passage, such vessels shall abstain from any activity not directly related to the passage, such as exercises or practices with arms of any nature; launching, landing or reception of aircraft or military devices on board; embarkation or disembarkation of persons; fishing activities; investigations; hydrographical surveys; and activities which may disturb the security and communication systems of the Republic of Chile.

Article 5. Submarines and any other submersible vessels must navigate on the surface. All vessels shall navigate with their lights on and flying their flags.

Article 6. The Republic of Chile may suspend temporarily the passage of vessels in case of any impediment to navigation as a result of *force majeure* for the duration of such an impediment. The suspension shall take effect as soon as notice is given to the Argentine authority.

Article 7. The number of Argentine warships which may navigate simultaneously along the route described in article 1 may not exceed three. The vessels may not carry embarkation units on board.

Navigation between Argentine ports in the Beagle Channel and Antarctica and vice versa; or between Argentine ports in the Beagle Channel and the Argentine Exclusive Economic Zone adjacent to the maritime boundary between the Republic of Chile and the Argentine Republic and vice versa

Article 8. For maritime traffic between Argentine ports in the Beagle Channel and Antarctica and vice versa; or between Argentine ports in the Beagle Channel and the Argentine Exclusive Economic Zone adjacent to the maritime boundary between the Republic of Chile and the Argentine Republic and vice versa, Argentine vessels shall enjoy navigation facilities for the passage through Chilean internal waters exclusively via the following route:

Paso Picton and Paso Richmond, then following from a point fixed by the co-ordinates 55°21.0' South latitude and 66°41.0" West longitude, the general direction of the arc between true 090° and 180°, emerging in the Chilean territorial sea; or crossing the Chilean territorial sea in the general direction of the arc between true 270° and 000°, and continuing through Paso Richmond and Paso Picton.

The passage may be effected without a Chilean pilot and without notice. . . .

Article 9. The provisions contained in articles 3, 4 and 5 of this annex shall apply to passage via the route indicated in the preceding article.

Navigation to and from the north through the Estrecho de Le Maire

Article 10. For maritime traffic to and from the north through the Estrecho de Le Maire, Chilean vessels shall enjoy navigation facilities for the passage of that strait, without an Argentine pilot and without notice.

The provisions contained in articles 3, 4 and 5 of this annex shall apply to passage via this route *mutatis mutandis.*

System of navigation and pilotage in the Beagle Channel

Article 11. The system of navigation and pilotage defined in the following articles shall be established in the Beagle Channel on both sides of the existing boundary between the meridian 68°36'38.5" West longitude and the meridian 66°25.0' West longitude. . . .

Article 12. The Parties shall grant freedom of navigation for Chilean and Argentine vessels along the route indicated in the preceding article.

Along the route indicated merchant vessels flying the flags of third countries shall enjoy the right of passage subject to the rules laid down in this annex.

Article 13. Warships flying the flags of third countries heading for a port of one of the Parties situated along the route indicated in article 11 of this annex must have the prior authorization of that Party. The latter shall inform the other Party of the arrival or departure of a foreign warship.

Article 14. Along the route indicated in article 11 of this annex, in the zones which are under their respective jurisdictions, the Parties undertake reciprocally to develop aids to navigation and to co-ordinate them in order to facilitate navigation and guarantee its security.

The usual navigation routes shall be permanently cleared of all obstacles or activities which may affect navigation.

The Parties shall agree on traffic control systems for the security of navigation in geographical areas where passage is difficult.

Article 15. Chilean and Argentine vessels are not required to take on pilots on the route indicated in article 11 of this annex.

Vessels flying the flags of third countries which navigate from or to a port situated along that route must obey the Pilotage Regulations of the country of the port of departure or destination.

When such vessels navigate between ports of either Party, they shall obey the Pilotage Regulations of the Party of the port of departure and the Pilotage Regulations of the Party of the port of arrival.

Article 16. The Parties shall apply their own regulations in the matter of pilotage in the ports situated within their respective jurisdictions.

Vessels using pilots shall hoist the flag of the country whose regulations they are applying.

Any vessel which uses pilotage services must pay the appropriate fees for these services and any other charge that exists in this respect in the regulations of the Party responsible for the pilotage.

The Parties shall provide pilots with maximum facilities in the performance of their task. Pilots may disembark freely in the ports of either Party.

The Parties shall strive to establish concordant and uniform rules for pilotage.

[JAIME DEL VALLE ALLIENDE]
[DANTE MARIO CAPUTO]

4.1434 Treaty Instituting the Arab Maghreb Union

Alliance Members: Algeria, Mauritania, Morocco, Libya, and Tunisia
Signed On: February 17, 1989, in the city of Marrakesh (Morocco). In force as of date of publication of this volume.
Alliance Type: Defense Pact (Type I)

Source: *United Nations Treaty,* no. 26844.

SUMMARY

Originally devised by Libya's Mu'ammar Gadhafi, this agreement had as its main goal to encourage the integration of all North African Arab states. The treaty mandated that members respond to any activities that jeopardize the security of the other members. The treaty also aimed to increase trade within the region by allowing free movement across state borders. Also established were numerous organizational structures, including a supreme council headed by the five nation-state leaders, a Maghreb commission, a court, and a consultative chamber. The nations also agreed to meet twice each year to discuss important economic and social issues.

Aside from the mandates of the treaty, the treaty had two important regional effects. First, it promised a clear framework for cooperation between Morocco and Algeria, whose relations remained tense after the Western Sahara war. Second, it provided an opportunity for Libya to remain active in regional affairs in spite of the U.S. attempt to isolate Gadhafi.

The alliance proved ineffective in 1994 when the dispute between Algeria and Morocco regarding Western Sahara resurfaced. Although the organization still exists and meets, many of the nations involved in the pact have turned their focus to other economic alliances, including the European Union's Euro-Mediterranean Partnership and the community of Sahel-Saharan States.

ALLIANCE TEXT

In the name of God, the Clement, the Merciful
His Majesty Hassan II, King of the Kingdom of Morocco,
His Excellency Zein El Abidin Ben Ali, President of the Republic of Tunisia,
His Excellency Shadli Ben Jedid, President of the People's Democratic Republic of Algeria,
The leader of the Great first of September Revolution,
Colonel Muammar Kaddafi, the Great Arab People's Socialist Libyan Jamahiriya,
And His Excellency Colonel Muawiya Uld Sidi Ahmed Tayea, Chairman of the Military Committee for National Salvation and Head of State of the Islamic Republic of Mauritania,

Having faith in the strong ties based on common history, religion and language that unite the peoples of the Arab Maghreb,

In response to the deep and firm aspirations of these peoples and their leaders to establish a Union that would reinforce the existing relations and provide them with the appropriate ways and means to gradually proceed toward achieving a more comprehensive integration among themselves,

Conscious that this integration will have effects that will enable the Arab Maghreb Union to acquire a specific weight allowing it to make an effective contribution to world balance, to the consolidation of peaceful relations within the international community and to the establishment of security and stability in the world,

Aware that the institution of the Arab Maghreb Union requires tangible achievements and the setting up of common rules embodying the effective solidarity among its components and ensuring their economic and social development,

Expressing their sincere determination to make the Arab Maghreb Union a means for the construction of total Arab unity and a staffing point for a wider union comprising other Arab and African countries,

Have agreed on the following:

Article One. By virtue of this Treaty, a Union, to be called the "Arab Maghreb Union", is hereby instituted.

Article Two. The Union aims at:

- trengthening the ties of brotherhood which link the member States and their peoples to one another;
- Achieving progress and prosperity of their societies and defending their rights;
- Contributing to the preservation of peace based on justice and equity;
- Pursuing a common policy in different domains; and
- Working gradually towards achieving free movement of persons and transfer of services, goods and capital among them.

Article Three. The common policy referred to in the previous Article aims at reaching the following goals:

- In the international field: to achieve concord among the member States and establish between them a close diplomatic cooperation based on dialogue;
- In the field of defence: to preserve the independence of each of the member States;
- In the economic field: to achieve industrial, agricultural, commercial and social development of member States and take the necessary measures for this purpose particularly by setting up joint ventures and working out general and specific programmes in this respect;
- In the cultural field: to establish a cooperation aimed at promoting education on its various levels, at safeguarding the spiritual and moral values emanating from the tolerant teachings of Islam, and at preserving the Arab national identity, and to take the necessary measures to attain these goals, particularly by exchanging teachers and students and creating joint university and cultural institutions as well as joint institutions specialized in research.

Article Four. The Union shall have a Presidential Council composed of the Heads of State of the member States and constituting the supreme authority of the Union.

The chairmanship of the Council shall be for a period of six months in rotation among the Heads of State of the member States.

Article Five. The Presidential Council of the Union shall hold its ordinary sessions every six months; it may hold extraordinary sessions whenever deemed necessary.

Article Six. Only the Presidential Council shall have the authority to take decisions, and its decisions shall be taken unanimously.

Article Seven. The Prime Ministers of the member States, or their homologues. may meet whenever deemed necessary.

Article Eight. The Union shall have a Council of Foreign Ministers which shall prepare the sessions of the Presidential Council and look into the points submitted by the follow-up Committee and the specialized ministerial Committees.

Article Nine. Each State shall appoint a member of its ministerial Council, or General Popular Committee, to be in charge of Union Affairs; these appointees shall form a Committee for the follow-up of the affairs of the Union and shall submit the results of their proceedings to the Council of Foreign Ministers.

Article Ten. The Union shall have Specialized Ministerial Committees set up by the Presidential Council which shall determine their tasks.

Article Eleven. The Union shall have a General Secretariat composed of one representative for each member State; the General Secretariat shall exercise its functions in the country presiding over the session of the Presidential Council under the supervision of the Chairman of the session whose country shall cover the expenses involved.

Article Twelve. The Union shall have a Consultative Council comprising ten members for each State, to be chosen by the legislative bodies of the member States or according to the internal system of each State.

The Consultative Council shall hold an ordinary session every year as well as extraordinary sessions at the request of the Presidential Council.

The Consultative Council shall advise on all draft decisions handed over to it by the Presidential Council, as it may submit to the Presidential Council any recommendations it might consider likely to strengthen the action of the Union and achieve its goals.

The Consultative Council shall elaborate its rules of procedure and submit them to the Presidential Council for approval.

Article Thirteen. The Union shall have a Judicial Organ, composed of two judges for each State to be appointed by the State concerned for a six-year period, and renewed by half every three years. The Judicial Organ shall elect a chairman from its members for a one-year period.

The Judicial Organ shall specialize in examining conflicts related to the interpretation and implementation of the Treaty and the agreements concluded within the framework of the Union and submitted by the Presidential Council or any of the States parties to the conflict or as provided for by the Statutes of the Judicial Organ, the verdicts of which shall be binding and final.

Likewise, the Judicial Organ shall give advisory opinions on legal questions laid before it by the Presidential Council.

The Judicial Organ shall elaborate its Statutes and submit them to the Presidential Council for ratification. The Statutes shall constitute an integral part of the Treaty.

The Presidential Council shall determine the seat of the Judicial Organ and its budget.

Article Fourteen. Any aggression directed against one of the member States shall be considered as an aggression against the other member States.

Article Fifteen. Member States pledge not to permit on their territory any activity or organization liable to threaten the security, the territorial integrity or the political system of any of them.

They also pledge to abstain from joining any alliance or military or political bloc directed against the political independence or territorial integrity of the other member States.

Article Sixteen. Member States are free to conclude any agreements between them or with other States or groups provided these agreements do not run counter to the provisions of this Treaty.

Article Seventeen. Other States belonging to the Arab Nation or the African community may join this Treaty if member States give their approval.

Article Eighteen. Provisions of this Treaty may be amended upon the proposal of one of the member States, and such amendment becomes effective after its ratification by all member States.

Article Nineteen. This Treaty goes into effect after its ratification by the member States according to procedures in force in each member State.

Member States are committed to take the necessary measures to this end within a maximum period of six months from the date of signature of this Treaty.

Done in the city of Marrakesh on the blessed day of Friday the tenth of Rajab 1409 of the Hegira (1398 of the Death of the Prophet), corresponding to 17 February (Nuar) 1989.

For the Kingdom of Morocco:
HASSAN II

For the People's Democratic Republic of Algeria:
SHADLI BEN JEDID

For the Republic of Tunisia:
ZEIN EL ABIDIN BEN ALI

For the Great Arab People's Socialist Libyan Jamahiriya:
MUAMMAR KADDAFI

The President of the Islamic Republic of Mauritania:
MUAWIYA ULD SIDI AHMED TAYEA

4.1435 Pact of Non-Aggression between Iraq and Saudi Arabia

Alliance Members: Iraq and Saudi Arabia
Signed On: March 27, 1989, in the city of Baghdad (Iraq). In force until August 2, 1990.
Alliance Type: Defense Pact (Type I)

Source: *BBC Summary of World Broadcasts,* March 29, 1989.
Additional Citations: *Financial Times,* London, March 28, 1989.

SUMMARY

On March 28, 1989, following the end of the Iran-Iraq War, Saudi Arabia and Iraq signed this non-aggression pact. The two sides agreed to not interfere in each other's internal affairs and to not use force against one another. One of the primary motives behind the treaty was to ease concerns over Iraqi aggression and ambitions in the region, specifically with regard to the border dispute with Kuwait. The agreement was also a signal to Israel because additional accords signed with this agreement pledged financing for the construction of a nuclear facility to replace the one that Israel had destroyed in a preventive attack.

The agreement between Iraq and Saudi Arabia did not last long. On August 2, 1990, Iraq invaded Kuwait and was poised to continue its march southward. Saudi Arabia requested help from the United States. During the war to liberate Kuwait, the United States and other international coalition forces used Saudi Arabia as a base for military action. Saudi armed forces participated in bombing campaigns and ground attacks, and Iraq fired missiles into Saudi Arabian territory.

DESCRIPTION OF TERMS

The two states pledged noninterference in each other's internal affairs and to resolve their disputes using peaceful means.

4.1436 Soviet-French Cooperation Treaty

Alliance Members: France and the Union of Soviet Socialist Republics
Signed On: October 29, 1990, in the city of Rambouillet (France). In force until December 25, 1991.
Alliance Type: Entente (Type III)

Source: *BBC Summary of World Broadcasts,* October 31, 1990, Part 1.

SUMMARY

This agreement between France and the Soviet Union provided important political and economic gains for the Soviets during the waning years of the Soviet regime. President Mikhail Gorbachev was set to sign a historic treaty of friendship with a united Germany in November of 1990. This agreement with the French would ensure that Soviet partnerships in Western Europe were not solely focused on Germany.

The economic incentives for the Soviets were also large. France promised assistance for the Soviet Union as it developed a market-based economy, possibly leading to the eventual incorporation of the Soviets into the European Community. These pledges were accompanied by a $1 billion French aid package of loans and credits for the purchase of French grain and other items.

The treaty did not last long as the Soviet Union collapsed slightly more than one year later. However, by February of 1992, France and Russia renewed ties with a similar agreement (Alliance no. 4.1441).

ALLIANCE TEXT

Basing themselves on long traditions of friendship and co-operation and also on the relations of a preferential nature which have become firmly established between them;

convinced of the need for rapprochement between states on the basis of common human values, freedom, democracy, justice and solidarity;

striving, through interaction and co-operation with other states, to ensure humanity a period of peace and prosperity;

aware of their special responsibility as permanent members of the Security Council for maintaining international peace and security;

loyal to the UN Charter and confirming the obligations undertaken by them within the framework of the Conference on Security and Co-operation in Europe;

and taking into consideration the powers of the European Communities and the prospects for the transformation of these communities into a political alliance, and equally the transformations taking place in the Soviet Union;

The Union of Soviet Socialist Republics and the French Republic have resolved to impart a new quality to the policy of accord pursued by them and for this purpose, have agreed on the following

Article One. The Union of Soviet Socialist Republics and the French Republic look upon one another as friendly states and base their relations on trust, solidarity and co-operation.

Europe

Article Two. The sides are pooling their efforts to overcome the division of the European continent into antagonistic blocs and transform it into a peaceful Europe of solidarity endowed with permanent mechanisms of security and co-operation. They stress the role that the CSCE process should play in this.

The sides are to facilitate the transformation of Europe into a community of law and democracy. They are to co-operate to strengthen the bonds of solidarity, resulting in turning Europe into a common home and creating a European confederation, of themselves and all European states.

Article Three. The creation of a single community for the whole of Europe presupposes that each of the European states shall base their systems and policies on the following principles

- the right of all peoples freely to determine their destiny without external interference and carry out their economic, social and cultural development as they see fit;
- respect for the dignity and rights of man, protection of basic freedoms, the creation of a law- governed state and the safeguarding of democracy;
- respect for social justice, collective freedoms and individual initiative;
- protection of the natural assets and cultures of all nations.

The creation of such a Europe also presupposes that relations between European states shall be determined by the following principles

- respect for sovereign equality, territorial integrity and political independence;
- inviolability of frontiers;
- renunciation of the threat or use of force, apart from those cases envisaged by the UN Charter;
- the right of every state to decide for itself on the defensive measures and alliances that it needs, whilst observing

international undertakings;

- an undertaking to resolve disputes by peaceful means in accordance with international law;
- acceptance of general juridical principles as a means of harmonising the legal systems of European countries.

The Soviet Union and France undertake to promote all of these principles.

Article Four. France pledges to promote the development of deeper relations and the conclusion of agreements between the Soviet Union and the European Communities. French obligations under the bilateral Soviet-French agreement are in accordance with the competence that belongs to the European Communities and the judicial norms adopted by the institution of these communities.

Article Five. The sides are to facilitate the development of co-operation in Europe, accompanied by simplification of the bonds of solidarity between Europe and other regions and continents.

International Security and Co-operation

Article Six. The Soviet Union and France have agreed to expand and deepen the consultations being held between their governments.

The subject of these consultations will be the key problem of today, the strengthening of security and co-operation in Europe and the world, the development of bilateral relations and any other issues which are of mutual interest.

The sides will strive to bring their positions as close as possible with the aim of carrying out joint or co-ordinated actions.

They are to co-operate in the area of analysing and forecasting the basic trends of world developments by means of holding special consultations and carrying out joint research.

In the event of situations arising which, in the opinion of either side, create a threat to the world or violate peace or which give rise to international tension, the governments of the Soviet Union and France shall immediately contact each other in order to reach accords on all aspects of these situations, harmonise their positions as much as possible and reach agreement on measures that may make it possible to improve the position or handle the situation and act jointly.

If either side takes the view that a situation arising concerns its highest security interests it may ask the other side for consultations on this issue to take place between them immediately.

Article Seven. In their international activity the USSR and France are proceeding from the fact that concord and co-operation between them represent an important constant factor in world politics. They shall step up interaction in the spheres of ensuring international security, developing co-operation in the world and effectively fulfilling the provisions in the UN Charter. They shall assist the prevention of international conflicts.

The sides recognise the primacy of the international law in international relations.

Proceeding from the inadmissibility of the threat of force and its use in international relations they shall take advantage of all the opportunities they have to settle controversial international problems by peaceful means. They shall act in this way in order to exploit any opportunity to settle conflicts envisaged in the UN Charter, in particular, by setting in motion the appropriate mechanisms of the organisation.

The USSR and France shall increasingly devote more attention to global problems which humanity is facing, especially in its fight against famine and epidemics.

The sides shall come out in favour of industrially developed countries extending their aid to developing countries, taking into account their economic possibilities and at the same time guided by international experience.

They shall co-operate, especially in various international economic organisations of which they are members, in arranging effective mechanisms for stabilising prices on raw material commodities.

Article Eight. The sides undertake to develop co-operation within the framework of the international economic system. In the event that one of the sides wishes to establish relations of co-operation with an international organisation of which it is not a member, the other side shall lend it its assistance.

The sides shall co-operate closely within the framework of the European Bank of Reconstruction and Development.

Disarmament

Article Nine. The sides agree that carrying out a defensive military policy and the practice of the implementation by all states of the principle of sufficiency represent a decisive contribution to the matter of European and international security.

The sides are convinced of the need to implement in stages universal and complete disarmament under strict and effective international control. To this end, they shall interact at all international talks in which both take part.

Article 10. The sides shall act jointly within the framework of the Conference for Security and Co-operation in Europe in order to facilitate an increase in stability on the European continent and progress in the process of a balanced reduction in conventional weapons and a strengthening of trust. They shall co-operate in the matter of implementing appropriate measures for setting up institutes within the framework of the CSCE, in particular, in setting up a centre to prevent conflicts and in its activities.

They commit themselves to obeying rigorously the agreed measures of trust and also aid in the elaboration, on a multilateral and bilateral basis, of new measures of trust.

The sides acknowledge the contribution which other European states may make in guaranteeing security and stability in Europe and shall strive to co-operate with them, with these aims, taking into account their own corresponding obligations.

Bilateral Co-operation

Article 11. Proceeding from the decisive significance of contacts between the presidents of the Union of Soviet Socialist Republics and the French Republic for the definition of the main trends in their co-operation, the sides agreed that summit meetings would be held at least once a year and also each time when the necessity for this might arise, in particular by means of realising unofficial working contacts.

Meetings between members of the governments of both states shall be held on issues representing mutual interest.

The foreign ministers shall hold consultations as necessary and not less than twice a year.

Meetings between defence ministers shall be held regularly.

The sides shall implement periodical consultations on the level of experts.

Article 12. The Soviet Union and France shall ensure the diversification of their bilateral relations, taking account of the decentralised structures that exist in their two countries.

Article 13. The sides shall develop their mutually advantageous co-operation in the fields of the economy, industry, science and technology with the objectives of raising the standard of living of the people in both countries and making efficient use of their human and material resources.

To these ends they shall seek the accelerated implementation of such accords as exist between them. New agreements or programmes shall be drawn up as and when necessary.

An inter-governmental commission on economic, commercial, scientific and technical co-operation shall aid the strengthening of co-operation within the spheres of its competence.

Article 14. The sides shall develop close co-operation in spheres which have special significance for their future and the prospective creation of a European space, in particular in the following spheres

- the development of agriculture;
- the use of nuclear energy for peaceful purposes, in particular the safety of nuclear power engineering;
- transport and infrastructure;
- high precision television;
- space;
- industrial reconversion;
- the distribution network.

With these aims they shall facilitate the conclusion of appropriate agreements.

They shall encourage the establishment of relations of co-operation between state enterprises of both countries.

Article 15. The sides attach paramount significance to the protection of the environment. They are committed to extending bilateral co-operation and facilitating an increase in concerted actions in this sphere, on a European and an international scale.

Article 16. Striving towards the creation of favourable conditions for joint initiatives and projects, the sides shall encourage new forms of co-operation, including direct links between partners from the two countries.

They shall strive towards an improvement in the operating conditions of enterprises from the partner countries, in particular in spheres of direct investment and the protection of invested capital.

They shall aid the widest possible exchange of economic information and access to information for business people and scholars from both countries.

Article 17. Wishing to assist the transition of the USSR to a market economy, the sides shall pay special attention to the development of co-operation in this direction, including in particular the training of qualified specialists for working in the economic and social spheres. If necessary they shall conclude agreements to this effect.

Article 18. The sides shall hold consultations and implement co-operation programmes on problems of the economy, law, the organisation of structures and state administration.

Article 19. Striving fully to exploit the technological achievements of the modern world, the USSR and France shall develop co-operation in the spheres of fundamental and applied research, while taking into account the economic and industrial feasibility of implementing its results. They shall assist the promotion of joint projects which may fit in with European and international programmes.

In the sphere of the latest technology the sides shall encourage the creation of associations and joint projects, while respecting appropriate national rules and especially having in mind the enhancement of the level of competence and efficiency of managers' activities.

They shall promote an exchange of young highly qualified research staff and scientists.

Article 20. The Soviet Union and France, relying on the longstanding traditions of close cultural links between the peoples of both countries and wishing to make a more active contribution to the creation of a cultural space open to all European peoples, shall develop their own exchanges in the spheres of culture, education and information.

The sides shall facilitate the conclusion of agreements between higher educational establishments and research centres and co-operation between universities in Europe taking into account appropriate European programmes. They shall also encourage the study of the languages of the peoples of the Soviet Union in France and the French language in the Soviet Union. The standing committee for education issues is empowered, acting within the framework of the Soviet-French commission for cultural co-operation, to aid the advancement of a whole set of these issues.

Devoting special attention to projects which are part of the European perspective, the Soviet Union and France shall encourage joint initiatives in the sphere of the audio-visual media, cinematography, book publishing, theatre, music and the fine arts.

Article 21. With the aims of more extensive acquaintance and mutual understanding between Soviet and French youth, the sides shall encourage the development of exchanges between the two countries on various levels.

Other Spheres of Co-operation

Article 22. The Soviet Union and France shall develop humanitarian co-operation, aiding in particular the activities of charitable organisations from both countries.

Article 23. Competent bodies of the Soviet Union and France shall co-operate in the struggle against organised crime and the illegal traffic in drugs and contraband, including the illegal transport of works of art across borders.

They shall strive to establish appropriate co-operation in the struggle against international terrorism.

Article 24. The sides shall develop and deepen contacts and exchanges on military lines. They shall regularly, on a bilateral and multilateral basis, exchange opinions on military doctrines.

Meetings at the level of the general staff of the USSR armed forces and the staff of the French armed forces as well as the headquarters of the different branches of the armed forces shall be held regularly.

Bilateral exchange programmes between the armed forces of the USSR and France, directed towards strengthening mutual understanding and trust, shall be elaborated.

Article 25. The Soviet Union and France commit themselves, within the shortest possible time-limits, to reaching agreement on the settlement of mutual financial and property claims, concerning the interests of actual and legal persons of both countries.

Article 26. The sides commit themselves to taking the necessary measures aimed at simplifying on the basis of reciprocity the procedure for issuing and extending visas.

They shall render, on a reciprocal basis, the utmost assistance in the activities on their territories of the diplomatic and consular representations of the other side.

They shall conclude between them an agreement on mutual legal aid in civic affairs.

Article 27. The statutes of this treaty do not affect in any way the sides' obligations to the third states and are not directed against any of them.

Article 28. This treaty is concluded for a period of ten years. Its validity shall be automatically renewed for further five-year periods if neither of the contracting parties notifies the other about its decision to renounce the treaty in writing one year in advance of the given period.

This treaty is subject to ratification in accordance with the constitutional procedures of each side party and shall take effect after 30 days upon the exchange of the ratification documents.

Executed in Rambouillet on 29th October 1990, in two copies, each in French and Russian and both having equal force.

For the Union of Soviet Socialist Republics USSR President M. Gorbachev; Minister of Foreign Affairs E. Shevardnadze;
For the Republic of France President of the French Republic F. Mitterrand; Premier M. Rocard; Minister of Foreign Affairs R. Dumas

4.1437 Treaty on Friendship and Cooperation between the Union of Soviet Socialist Republics and the Italian Republic

Alliance Members: Union of Soviet Socialist Republics and Italy
Signed On: November 18, 1990, in the city of Rome. In force until December 25, 1991.
Alliance Type: Entente (Type III)

Source: *BBC Summary of World Broadcasts,* November 22, 1990.

SUMMARY

This treaty was signed in Italy one day prior to the historic non-aggression pact between NATO and Warsaw Pact members (see Alliance no. 4.1438). The text of the treaty stipulates that both countries will "co-ordinate necessary initiatives aimed at relieving tension if a situation arises which in the opinion of one of the sides threatens peace and undermines international stability." This entente is one of many agreements signed in the waning days of the Soviet Union that tried to foster a new international atmosphere of cooperation with Western countries.

The alliance was short-lived. On December 25, 1991, Gorbachev resigned as Soviet president and transferred control of the Soviet nuclear arsenal to the new president, Boris Yeltsin, as the United States recognized six independent republics: Armenia, Belarus, Kazakhstan, Kyrgyzstan, Russia, and Ukraine. Although the friendly relationship between Russia and Italy remained, the alliance was considered obsolete with the dissolution of the Soviet Union.

ALLIANCE TEXT

The Union of Soviet Socialist Republics and the Italian Republic;

recognising that the changes which are taking place in the world provide mankind with a unique chance to build a peaceful international order based on the pre-eminence of law; relying on age-old traditions of friendship, spiritual closeness and the reciprocal cultural enrichment of their peoples as well as on the fact that their basic interests do not contradict each other;

aspiring to assert their pioneering role in many undertakings to overcome the split of Europe;

convinced of the need to build relations between states on the common human values of democracy, liberty, pluralism, solidarity and respect for human rights;

confirming their adherence to the provisions of the Helsinki Final Act and subsequent CSCE documents and confident that the results of the all-European summit conference in Paris will strengthen the irreversible nature of the process of peaceful development in Europe; desiring to strengthen relations between the EC and the USSR;

showing resolve to consolidate the prestige of the UN;

convinced that the biggest problems of the modern world can be resolved on the basis of the new political philosophy and new systems exclusively within the framework of broad-based international co-operation;

deriving inspiration from the ideals and principles laid down in the joint Soviet-Italian Declaration of 30th November 1989,

have decided to add a new quality to their bilateral relations and have agreed on the following

Article 1. The Union of Soviet Socialist Republics and the Italian Republic will develop their relations as friendly states on the principles of sovereignty, territorial integrity, equal rights, mutual respect and solidarity.

Article 2. Convinced that in accordance with the UN Charter and with the stipulation envisaged in Article 51 of the Charter war, whether nuclear or conventional, as well as the threat of force or the use of force must be ruled out as a means of resolving international disputes, the sides pledge to resolve their disputes exclusively by peaceful means.

The USSR and Italy will increase their efforts to enhance the role of the UN. They will also make efforts to ensure complete respect by all member states for the principles of the UN Charter and to ensure that the UN, using the necessary means, can fully carry out the functions of the supreme guarantor of peace throughout the world.

Article 3. The sides will continue their efforts to overcome splits and disagreements in order to turn Europe into a continent of peace where relations of trust, openness and solidarity between states are dominant and where permanent security and co-operation machinery is created.

In this context the sides intend to protect the CSCE process, developing and enriching it, and also to act in such a way as to guarantee stability on the continent of Europe in all its dimensions.

Article 4. The USSR and Italy firmly intend primarily through the CSCE to promote the strengthening of democracy, the law-governed state, friendly relations between all states, security, protection of human rights and also the development of economic, scientific and technical, cultural and ecological co-operation.

The Soviet Union and Italy consider that the elaboration of principles and rules based on the example of the CSCE can promote stability, security and the well-being of other regions, particularly the Mediterranean and Near East.

Article 5. The USSR and Italy are convinced that along with the emergence of the new Europe an increasing stability which envisages a radical reduction of the arms levels, including a reduction of nuclear weapons, must be ensured. They will facilitate the attainment of corresponding agreements on the basis of the principle of strict verification.

The sides will co-operate to ensure that the security is based not on confrontation but on interaction by means of strengthening trust and security measures on a pan-European scale, creating security structures and revising military doctrines aiming at attaching a strictly defensive character to them.

Article 6. The USSR and Italy will inform each other and immediately contact each other in order to co- ordinate necessary initiatives aimed at relieving tension if a situation arises which in the opinion of one of the sides threatens peace and undermines international stability. If one of the sides considers that a situation arises which affects its highest security interests, it can contact the other side so that bilateral consultations are held between them urgently.

Article 7. The USSR and Italy confirm the principles of non-aggression as a first principle of the relations between them and all other states.

In the case of one of the sides becoming the object of unprovoked aggression, the other side without prejudice to its obligations, which somehow or other result from its participation in existing treaties of alliance and from the relations which follow on from these, will not give the aggressor any military or other assistance. Both sides also state that they will resort to the mechanism of the UN or to other security structures for the settling of conflicts.

Article 8. The USSR and Italy, on the basis of the bilateral protocol of 1972, will give a broader and more regular character to their consultations.

Meetings at the highest level will take place at least once a year, and also, every time that both sides consider it necessary. The Ministers of Foreign Affairs will meet no less than twice a year. Periodic meetings of the Ministers of Defence will take place. There will be consultations between other members of government on issues of mutual interest in accordance with the necessity for them.

With the aim of easing direct contacts a communications line will be set up between the departments of the USSR President and the chairman of the Italian Council of Ministers ("Kremlin - Palazzo Chigi")

Working groups which will meet on a regular basis will be set up for the examination of international problems or specific issues of bilateral relations.

Article 9. The sides pledge to maintain and develop a broad dialogue between the Soviet and Italian peoples, taking into account the historical and contemporary development of the two countries, the distinctive features of their cultures and also public opinion. This dialogue will be held in a spirit of mutual understanding and friendship, respect for the national character, customs, diverse religious and other special features and also the originality of the Soviet and Italian peoples.

Special attention will be paid to developing inter-parliamentary ties and contacts between other elected bodies of power in the two countries.

Article 10. The sides consider it important to develop contacts and exchanges on military policy. In this context they envisage visits by military delegations, including high-level delegations, and a periodical exchange of opinions and information on their military doctrines.

Article 11. The sides pledge to expand and deepen economic, industrial, financial, scientific and technical and ecological co-operation. They are agreed that the conditions exist to achieve a qualitatively new level of economic co-operation.

They acknowledge the importance of this co-operation both from the point of view of implementing the programme of economic reforms in the Soviet Union and from that of the contribution which the USSR and Italy will be able to make to

establishing a new international economic order. They note the fundamental role of the European Community in creating a single economic zone on the scale of the continent of Europe and also the great significance of international economic and financial organisations for the balanced development of the world economy.

Article 12. The sides will promote the development and deepening of relations between the Soviet Union and the European Community.

Article 13. The sides pledge to intensify the implementation of agreements which they have concluded in the spheres listed in Article 11 of this treaty, especially that of the long term programme for developing economic, industrial and technical co-operation up to the year 2000, the programme for deepening co-operation in the field of science and technology and also all other current economic agreements.

The intergovernmental joint commissions for economic, scientific and technical co-operation between the USSR and Italy and their working bodies are called upon to further the strengthening of this co- operation within the framework of their competence. Other permanent or ad hoc bodies may be set up where necessary with the sides' mutual agreement.

Article 14. The sides will actively co-operate in the sphere of the conversion of the defence industry, on the basis of the joint intergovernmental statement of 30th November 1989. Taking into account the positive changes in the situation in Europe, they will strive towards the conclusion of separate agreements on conversion, in particular, in the sphere of power-engineering and the production of industrial and consumer goods and foodstuffs.

Article 15. The sides undertake to mutually provide for commercial, industrial and financial activities a regime which is no less favourable than that provided for third countries. Within this framework encouragement will be given to the establishment of industrial-economic free enterprise zones, and similarly, an even wider economic integration within Europe.

They will promote the setting up of joint enterprises, including those in which partners from third countries will participate, in the harmonisation of legal standards in the economic sphere, and in the joint training of cadres, including managers.

Article 16. The sides are giving priority to the co-operation in the areas of energy, transport and telecommunications. They shall speed up the joint development of the technical aspects of the industrial activity in these areas, primarily bearing in mind the energy saving and modernisation of the infrastructure. The sides will make efforts to establish the organic co-operation in these areas at the European level and will encourage co-operation between organisations and enterprises of the two countries.

Article 17. The sides will give new impulse to their co-operation in the area of science and advanced technology, including space research, on the basis of the already agreed programmes and will also determine the new directions of priority in the area of scientific research and technological modernisation.

Realising the growing role of science and technology in the society of the future the sides have agreed to make the appropriate efforts towards a more active involvement of the competent Soviet and Italian organisations in the multilateral programmes of scientific and technological co-operation, creation of the science and technology parks.

The USSR and Italy intend to continue increasing the close interaction within the framework of the "universal laboratory".

Article 18. On the premise of the global importance of the problems of the environment, the sides intend to promote their co-operation in this sphere in the programme-setting areas indicated in the corresponding bilateral agreement. They will devote particular attention to protection of the environment in the Mediterranean and Black Seas.

Utilising the positive experience gathered in this field, the sides will step up co-operation in combating natural disasters.

Article 19. The Soviet Union and Italy will facilitate the expansion of contacts between citizens of their countries along the lines of parties, trade unions, foundations, educational establishments, women's organisations, sports organisations, churches, and religious, ecological and other associations. They will promote youth exchanges in every way. The sides will encourage the development of exchanges on the level of towns, oblasts and other territorial-administrative formations.

Article 20. The sides have it in mind, on a mutual basis, to simplify visa entry procedures, as far as is possible, concerning citizens of the other side, for visits for business, cultural, tourist and personal purposes.

They will ensure conditions for the normal work of diplomatic, consular and other official representatives of the other side.

Article 21. The USSR and Italy intend to increase their co-operation in the humanitarian sphere, including the means of activating contacts between the competent organisations in the two countries. With this in view the sides will co-operate in the matter of resolving issues connected with Soviet citizens who died in Italy and Italian citizens who died in the USSR during the Second World War.

Article 22. The USSR and Italy confirm their obligation to effectively co-operate in combating organised crime and the illegal trafficking of drugs. They will, in particular, constantly develop the exchange of operational information and experience between the competent organisations regarding the reasons for and the means of combatting the aforementioned phenomena, and also, they will co-operate in the relevant multilateral organisations.

The sides in equal measure confirm their obligation to co-operate in combatting terrorism and hijacking, by expanding their consultations on this issue, and also their co-operation within the framework of the UN and other relevant international organisations.

Article 23. The USSR and Italy, relying upon their people's century long history of mutual cultural enrichment and their invaluable contribution to European civilisation, will spare no effort to further the development of bilateral cultural co-operation.

Special attention will be paid to acquainting their people with the great wealth of heritage in music, architecture and arts

- with achievements in modern culture, art and literature and film-making;
- with everyday and cultural life in provincial parts, towns and various ethnic communities.
- The sides confirm the pledge taken in accordance with their agreements to set up cultural centres and will promote activity there by all means possible. They confirm their readiness to facilitate access to the language and the culture of the other side by way of using state, public and private channels for exchanging apprentices, students, school children, among others, and by supporting appropriate initiatives.

The sides will encourage direct co-operation between university, cultural and artistic establishments of the two countries, and also between associations operating in this sphere.

The USSR and Italy pledge to ensure opportunities to teach the language of the other side in schools and higher educational establishments. For these purposes they will provide the other side with the opportunities to prepare and enhance teachers' qualifications, and also school manuals, including the use of television, radio, audio, visual and computer technology. They will support the initiative for creating bilingual schools.

Article 24. The Soviet Union and Italy undertake on a reciprocal basis to extend assistance in the preservation and use of the cultural and artistic property of the other side.

They also agree that stolen or illegally exported works of art present in their territory will be returned to the other contracting side.

Article 25. The provisions of the present treaty in no way affect the commitments of the sides under bilateral and multilateral treaties and agreements previously concluded by them.

The present treaty is not directed against any third states.

Article 26. The present treaty is subject to ratification and will come into force on the day that instruments of ratification are exchanged.

Article 27. The present treaty is concluded for a term of 20 years and will automatically be extended for subsequent five-year periods unless one of the contracting sides gives written notification to the other side of its wish to dissolve the treaty a year prior to the expiry of the relevant period.

Concluded in Rome on 18th November 1990 in two copies, each in the Russian and Italian languages, with both texts having the same force.

The treaty was signed by Mikhail Gorbachev for the Union of Soviet Socialist Republics and Giulio Andreotti for the Italian Republic.

4.1438 Non-Aggression Declaration Signed by the Sixteen NATO Nations and Six Warsaw Pact Countries

Alliance Members: Belgium, Bulgaria, Canada, the Czech and Slovak Federal Republic, Denmark, France, Germany, Greece, Hungary, Iceland, Italy, Luxembourg, the Netherlands, Norway, Poland, Portugal, Romania, Spain, Turkey, the Union of Soviet Socialist Republics, the United Kingdom, and the United States of America
Signed On: November 19, 1990, in the city of Paris. In force until July 1, 1991.
Alliance Type II: Non-Aggression Pact (Type II)

Source: North Atlantic Treaty Organization, www.NATO.int.

SUMMARY

This was a non-aggression pact signed between member states of NATO (Alliance no. 4.1347) and the Warsaw Pact (Alliance no. 4.1360). The members of both alliances also signed, on the same day, the Treaty on Conventional Armed Forces in Europe (CFE) that provided for equal ceilings for major weapons and equipment systems in Europe. The growing willingness of the Soviet Union and United States to cooperate over European security led to a flurry of similar agreements before the dissolution of the Warsaw Pact. This treaty is probably unique in the sense that two alliances pledged non-aggression in foreign affairs.

The Soviet Union announced that the military structure of the Warsaw Pact would be ended by March 31, 1991, and a meeting of member countries convened for this purpose in February 1991. The Warsaw Pact was formally dissolved at a meeting held in Prague on July 1, 1991, and the termination date of this alliance corresponds with that date.

ALLIANCE TEXT

The Heads of State or Government of Belgium, Bulgaria, Canada, the Czech and Slovak Federal Republic, Denmark, France, Germany, Greece, Hungary, Iceland, Italy, Luxembourg, the Netherlands, Norway, Poland, Portugal, Romania, Spain, Turkey, the Union of Soviet Socialist Republics, the United Kingdom and the United States of America:

Greatly welcoming the historic changes in Europe,

gratified by the growing implementation throughout Europe of a common commitment to pluralist democracy, the rule of law and human rights, which are essential to lasting security on the continent,

affirming the end of the era of division and confrontation which has lasted for more than four decades, the improvement in relation among their countries and the contribution this makes to the security of all,

confident that the signature of the Treaty on Conventional Armed Forces in Europe represents a major contribution to the common objective of increased security and stability in Europe, and

convinced that these developments must form part of a continuing process of cooperation in building the structures of a more united continent,

Issue the following declaration:

1. The signatories solemnly declare that, in the new era of European relations which is beginning, they are no longer adversaries, will build new partnerships and extend to each other the hand of friendship.

2. They recall their obligations under the Charter of the United Nations and reaffirm all of their commitments under the Helsinki Final Act. They stress that all of the ten Helsinki Principles are of primary significance and that, accordingly, they will be equally and unreservedly applied, each of them being interpreted taking into account the others. In that context, they affirm their obligations and commitment to refrain from the threat or use of force against the territorial integrity or the political independence of any State, from seeking to change existing borders by threat or use of force, and from acting in any other manner inconsistent with the principles and purposes of those documents. None of their weapons will ever be used except in self-defense or otherwise in accordance with the Charter of the United Nations.

3. They recognize that security is indivisible and that the security of each of their countries is inextricably linked to the security of all the States participating in the Conference on Security and Cooperation in Europe.

4. They undertake to maintain only such military capabilities as are necessary to prevent war and provide for effective defense. They will bear in mind the relationship between military capabilities and doctrines.

5. They reaffirm that every state has the right to be or not to be a party to a treaty of alliance.

6. They note with approval the intensification of political and military contacts among them to promote mutual understanding and confidence. They welcome in this context the positive responses made to recent proposals for new regular diplomatic liaison.

7. They declare their determination to contribute actively to conventional, nuclear and chemical arms control and disarmament agreements which enhance security and stability for all. In particular, they call for the early entry into force of the Treaty on Conventional Armed Forces in Europe and commit themselves to continue the process of strengthening peace in Europe through conventional arms control within the framework of the CSCE. They welcome the prospect of new negotiations between the United States and the Soviet Union on the reduction of their short-range nuclear forces.

8. They welcome the contribution that confidence and security-building measures have made to lessening tensions and fully support the further development of such measures. They reaffirm the importance of the "Open Skies" initiative and their determination to bring the negotiations to a successful conclusion as soon as possible.

9. They pledge to work together with the other CSCE participating States to strengthen the CSCE process so that it can make an even greater contribution to security and stability in Europe. They recognize in particular the need to enhance political consultations among CSCE participants and to develop

other CSCE mechanisms. They are convinced that the Treaty on Conventional Armed Forces in Europe and agreement on a substantial new set of CSBM's [confidence and security building measures], together with new patterns of cooperation in the framework of the CSCE, will lead to increased security and thus to enduring peace and stability in Europe.

10. They believe that the preceding points reflect the deep longing of their peoples for close cooperation and mutual understanding and declare that they will work steadily for the further development of their relations in accordance with the present Declaration as well as with the principles set forth in the Helsinki Final Act.

4.1439 Agreement on the Prohibition of Attack against Nuclear Installations

Alliance Members: India and Pakistan
Signed On: January 27, 1991, in the city of Islamabad (Pakistan). In force as of date of publication of this volume.
Alliance Type: Non-Aggression Pact (Type II)

Source: *Keesing's Record of World Events,* January 1991.

SUMMARY

This treaty, first proposed in 1985, was signed in December 1988 by Prime Ministers Rajiv Gandhi of India and Benazir Bhutto of Pakistan. However, cross-border tensions kept the agreement from being ratified until January 1991.

Once ratified, the Agreement on the Prohibition of Attack against Nuclear Installations committed both nations to not attack the other party's nuclear installations so as to avoid dangerous radioactive fallout. According to the agreement, both nations committed to exchanging lists of nuclear installations (primarily including power plants) annually on the first day of the year. The first exchange occurred on January 1, 1992.

DESCRIPTION OF TERMS

The treaty pledged that neither India nor Pakistan would attack each other's nuclear facilities.

4.1440 Agreement on Reconciliation, Non-Aggression, and Exchanges and Co-operation between the South and the North

Alliance Members: Democratic People's Republic of Korea (North Korea) and Republic of Korea (South Korea)
Signed On: December 13, 1991, in the city of Seoul. In force as of date of publication of this volume.
Alliance Type: Non-Aggression Pact (Type II)

Source: The People's Korea, Resource Material, www1.korea-np.co.jp/pk/011th_issue/97100101.htm.
Additional Citations: U.S. Department of State, Under Secretary for Arms Control and International Security, www.state.gov/t/ac/rls/or/2004/31012.htm; also printed in *Peace and Cooperation, White Paper on Korean Unification,* Ministry of National Unification, Republic of Korea, 1996, p. 200.

SUMMARY

In 1972, North Korea and South Korea signed a joint accord pledging to work toward reunification. The agreement ended a year later over a scandal involving the arrest of opposition leaders in South Korea. By September 1990, peace talks were renewed, and these eventually led to the December 13, 1991, agreement included here. This non-aggression agreement stated that both nations "shall not interfere in the internal affairs of the other" and "shall refrain from all acts aimed at destroying and overthrowing the other side." The treaty also stated that both countries would "discontinue confrontations and competition" and would cooperate in "joint development of resources." Although relations on the peninsula remain tense, the agreement is still in force.

ALLIANCE TEXT

The South and the North,

In keeping with the yearning of the entire Korean people for the peaceful unification of the divided land;

Reaffirming the three principles of unification set forth in the July 4 {1972} South-North Joint Communiqué;

Determined to remove the state of political and military confrontation and achieve national reconciliation;

Also determined to avoid armed aggression and hostilities, reduce tension and ensure peace;

Expressing the desire to realize multi-faceted exchanges and cooperation to advance common national interests and prosperity;

Recognizing that their relations, not being a relationship between states, constitute a special interim relationship stemming from the process towards unification;

Pledging to exert joint efforts to achieve peaceful unification;

Hereby have agreed as follows:

CHAPTER 1 SOUTH-NORTH RECONCILIATION

Article 1. The South and the North shall recognize and respect each other's system.

Article 2. The two sides shall not interfere in each other's internal affairs.

Article 3. The two sides shall not slander or vilify each other.

Article 4. The two sides shall not attempt any actions of sabotage or overthrow against each other.

Article 5. The two sides shall endeavor together to transform the present state of armistice into a solid state of peace between the South and the North and shall abide by the present Military Armistice Agreement {July 27, 1953} until such a state of peace has been realized.

Article 6. The two sides shall cease to compete or confront each other and shall cooperate and endeavor together to promote national prestige and interests in the international arena.

Article 7. To ensure close consultations and liaison between the two sides, South-North Liaison Officers shall be established at Panmunjom within three (3) months after the coming into force of this Agreement.

Article 8. A South-North Political Committee shall be established within the framework of the South-North High-Level Talks within (1) month of the coming into force of this Agreement with a view to discussing concrete measures to ensure the implementation and observance of the accords on South-North reconciliation.

CHAPTER II SOUTH-NORTH NONAGGRESSION

Article 9. The two sides shall not use force against each other and shall not undertake armed aggression against each other.

Article 10. Differences of views and disputes arising between the two sides shall be resolved peacefully through dialogue and negotiation.

Article 11. The South-North demarcation line and areas for non-aggression shall be identical with the Military Demarcation Line specified in the Military Armistice Agreement of July 27, 1953 and the areas that have been under the jurisdiction of each side until the present time.

Article 12. To implement and guarantee non-aggression, the two sides shall set up a South-North Joint Military Commission within three (3) months of the coming into force of this Agreement. In the said Commission, the two sides shall discuss and carry out steps to build military confidence and control of major movements of military units and major military exercises, the peaceful utilization of the Demilitarized Zone, exchanges of military personnel and information, phased reductions in armaments including the elimination of weapons of mass destruction and attack capabilities, and verifications thereof.

Article 13. A telephone hotline shall be installed between the military authorities of the two sides to prevent accidental armed clashes and their escalation.

Article 14. A South-North Military Committee shall be established within the framework of the South-North High-Level Talks within one (1) month of the coming into force of this agreement in order to discuss concrete measures to ensure the implementation and observance of the accords on non-aggression and to remove military confrontation.

CHAPTER III SOUTH-NORTH EXCHANGES AND COOPERATION

Article 15. To promote an integrated and balanced development of the national economy and the welfare of the entire people, the two sides shall engage in economic exchanges and cooperation, including the joint development of resources, the trade of goods as domestic commerce and joint ventures.

Article 16. The two sides shall carry out exchanges and cooperation in various fields such as science and technology, education, literature and the arts, health, sports, environment, and publishing and journalism including newspapers, radio and television broadcasts and publications.

Article 17. The two sides shall promote free intra-Korea travel and contacts for the residents of their respective areas.

Article 18. The two sides shall permit free correspondence, meetings and visits between dispersed family members and other relatives and shall promote the voluntary reunion of divided families and shall take measures to resolve other humanitarian issues.

Article 19. The two sides shall reconnect railroads and roads that have been cut off and shall open South-North sea and air transport routes.

Article 20. The two sides shall establish and link facilities needed for South-North postal and telecommunications services and shall guarantee the confidentiality of intra-Korean mail and telecommunications.

Article 21. The two sides shall cooperate in the economic, cultural and various other fields in the international arena and carry out jointly undertakings abroad.

Article 22. To implement accords on exchanges and cooperation in the economic, cultural and various other fields, the two sides shall establish joint commissions for specific sectors, including a Joint South-North Economic Exchanges and Cooperation Commission, within three (3) months of the coming into force of this Agreement.

Article 23. A South-North Exchanges and Cooperation Committee shall be established within the framework of the South-North High-Level Talks within one (1) month of the coming into force of this Agreement with a view to discussing concrete measures to ensure the implementation and observance of the accords on South-North exchanges and cooperation.

CHAPTER IV AMENDMENTS AND EFFECTUATION

Article 24. This Agreement may be amended or supplemented by concurrence between the two sides.

Article 25. This Agreement shall enter into force as of the day the two sides exchange appropriate instruments following the completion of their respective procedures for bringing it into effect.

Signed on December 13, 1991

Chung Won-shik
Prime Minister of the Republic of Korea
Chief delegate of the South delegation to the South-North High-Level Talks

Yon Hyong-muk
Premier of the Administration Council of the Democratic People's Republic of Korea
Head of the North delegation to the South-North High-Level Talks

4.1441 Treaty of Friendship and Co-operation between France and Russia

Alliance Members: France and Russia
Signed On: February 7, 1992, in the city of Paris. In force as of date of publication of this volume.
Alliance Type: Entente (Type III)

Source: *United Nations Treaty,* no. 30175.

SUMMARY

In February 1992, President Francois Mitterrand of France and President Boris Yeltsin of Russia signed this agreement declaring a willingness to cooperate on numerous issues including energy, nonproliferation, and trade. In the more substantial parts of the treaty, both nations agreed to consult each other regarding mutual security concerns and important foreign policy decisions. France also agreed to support Russian accession into any trade or economic organization to which it was party and for which Russia was eligible. During the meeting, France also pledged to grant Russia most favored nation status as well as provide it with a large loan.

The Russo-French treaty declared that it would stay in force for ten years and would automatically be extended every five years unless one of the two nations objected. Since its inception, France and Russia have maintained good relations.

Alliance Text

The French Republic and the Russian Federation,

On the basis of long-standing traditions of understanding, friendship and cooperation;

Noting that the Russian Federation is the successor State to the Union of Soviet Socialist Republics;

Wishing to give a new dimension to their relationship;

Convinced of the need to base their improved relations on partnership, mutual trust and a commitment to the values of freedom, democracy, justice and solidarity which they hold in common;

Having resolved to put definitively behind them the consequences of the division of the world and of Europe into opposing blocs;

Faithful to their obligations arising from international law, in particular the Charter of the United Nations, and confirming the commitments they have entered into within the framework of the Conference on Security and Cooperation in Europe;

Aware of their special responsibility for the maintenance of peace and international security by reason of their capacity as permanent members of the Security Council of the United Nations;

Taking account of the decision of the States members of the European Community to create a European Union;

Taking into consideration the creation of the Commonwealth of Independent States;

Have agreed as follows:

Article 1. The French Republic and the Russian Federation, faithful to the traditional friendship and sympathetic feeling between their peoples, shall develop their new understanding on the basis of trust, solidarity and cooperation.

Article 2. The French Republic and the Russian Federation shall combine their efforts to contribute to the maintenance of international security and the prevention of conflicts, and also to the effective implementation of the provisions of the Charter of the United Nations and the upholding of the primacy of international law.

The two Parties shall act jointly in defence of human rights and the promotion of democratic values, in particular within the competent international organizations.

Article 3. The French Republic and the Russian Federation agree to expand and develop the consultations between their two Governments.

Such consultations shall cover the strengthening of security and cooperation in Europe and throughout the world, the search for solutions to the major international problems, the development of bilateral relations and any other issue of common interest.

The Parties shall endeavour as far as possible to harmonize their positions in those areas with a view to reaching agreement, wherever they deem it necessary, on joint or concerted action.

Should a situation arise which, in the opinion of one of the Parties, would create a threat to peace or a breach of the peace, or give rise to international tension, the French and Russian Governments shall enter into contact without delay in order to consult on all aspects of such situations and, as far as possible, to harmonize their positions with a view to reaching agreement on measures which would improve the situation or bring it under control, and to take joint action.

If one of the Parties considers that a situation threatens its major security interests, it may contact the other Party with a request that consultations should be held between them on that matter without delay.

Article 4. The French Republic and the Russian Federation shall combine their efforts with a view to establishing security relations of a new kind between all European States and building a peaceful and interdependent Europe equipped with permanent machinery for security and cooperation.

The two Parties emphasize the role to be played in that connection by the Conference on Security and Cooperation in Europe. They shall act jointly to strengthen its institutions and to provide it with appropriate means, in particular at the legal level, to guarantee stability and security throughout the continent.

The French Republic and the Russian Federation acknowledge the respective contributions made to European security by the various international institutions, in particular the Conference on Security and Cooperation in Europe, the Western European Union and the North Atlantic Alliance.

The two Parties shall cooperate with each other and with other States concerned with a view to the conclusion of a treaty on European security.

The French Republic emphasizes the importance of the formation of the European Union which, in particular through the implementation of a common foreign and security policy, will lead to the strengthening of cooperation between European States and will make an essential contribution to the stability of the continent and of the whole world. The Russian Federation takes note thereof.

France shall promote the establishment of cooperative relations between Russia and the Western European Union, and with other international organizations that contribute to European security.

Article 5. The French Republic and the Russian Federation are convinced of the decisive importance of the agreements on disarmament to European and international security. They agree on the need to ensure that weapons, in particular nuclear weapons, are established at a minimum level of sufficiency.

The two Parties shall continue to participate, within the framework of the Conference on Security and Cooperation in Europe, in the process of the balanced reduction in conventional weapons and shall contribute to the development of new measures to build confidence among all its member States.

The two Parties shall contribute to the conclusion of similar agreements in other regions of the world.

They attach particular importance to measures designed to avoid the proliferation of weapons of mass destruction and, to that end, they shall act in a concerted manner in international forums.

Article 6. The French Republic and the Russian Federation shall promote the development of Europe into a common area of law and democracy. They shall contribute to the prevention of new divisions in the European continent and to the strengthening—both between themselves and among all European States—of a network of solidarity within the framework of a confederal approach.

Noting the commitment of the Russian Federation to respect the standards established by the Council of Europe in the field of democracy and human rights, the French Republic shall support the application of the Russian Federation for membership in that organization.

France undertakes to promote, in particular through the conclusion of agreements, a rapprochement between the European Communities and Russia in order to facilitate the latter's integration into the European economy. The commitments undertaken by the French Republic in Franco-Russian bilateral agreements shall respect the competence of the European Communities and the provisions adopted by their institutions.

Article 7. The French Republic and the Russian Federation undertake to develop their cooperation within the framework of the international economic system.

The two Parties shall cooperate, in particular within the various international economic organizations and financial institutions of which they are members, to bring about the establishment of effective machinery for the stabilization of the prices of raw materials.

France shall support the participation or membership of Russia in the international financial institutions and economic organizations of which the latter is not a member.

The two Parties shall cooperate closely within the framework of the European Bank for Reconstruction and Development.

Article 8. The French Republic and the Russian Federation are agreed that meetings at the highest level shall take place at least once a year, and whenever the need arises, *inter alia* in the form of informal working meetings.

The Ministers for Foreign Affairs shall hold consultations as often as necessary, and at least twice a year. Close cooperation shall be established between their ministerial departments.

The other members of the Governments of the two States shall meet regularly to address issues of common interest.

Article 9. The French Republic and the Russian Federation shall develop and expand their contacts in the military field. To that end, the Parties shall establish bilateral exchange programmes. They shall, on both a bilateral and a multilateral basis, regularly engage in exchanges of views on their concepts of defence and on the organization of their armed forces.

Article 10. The French Republic and the Russian Federation shall develop cooperation in the field of democratic institutions and the status of law. Such cooperation shall be established, *inter alia*, in the following areas:

- Constitutional, legislative and regulatory standards;
- The monitoring of constitutionality and legality;
- The rights of the citizen vis-à-vis the administration;
- Public freedoms; human rights, the rights of national minorities;
- Electoral systems.

Article 11. The French Republic and the Russian Federation shall develop their cooperation in the fields of the economy, industry, science and technology.

Close cooperation shall take place in the sectors of particular importance to the future of the two States and in the context of the creation of a European community, in particular in the following fields:

- The agri-foodstuffs sector;
- Energy;
- The utilization of nuclear energy for peaceful purposes, particularly with respect to nuclear security;
- Transport, infrastructure and related equipment;
- Telecommunications and high-definition television;
- Outer space;
- Industrial reconversion;
- Distribution networks.

The Parties shall encourage the establishment of direct cooperative links between participants in economic activities in the two countries.

Article 12. Wishing to promote the transition of the Russian Federation to a market economy based on the principles of free enterprise, social justice and solidarity, and being convinced that there is a close relationship between the material progress of societies and their democratization, the French Republic and the Russian Federation agree to develop cooperation and training programmes.

To that end, they attach particular importance to support for the modernization of public administrations, enterprises and trade union and social organizations. The two Parties shall promote training programmes suitable for incorporation in the framework of action undertaken at the European and international levels.

The Parties shall also develop their cooperation in the fields of social affairs and health.

Article 13. The French Republic and the Russian Federation shall endeavour to create conditions favourable to the activities of the enterprises of the partner country; each Party shall encourage and protect, within its own territory, the investments of the other Party.

They shall organize the broadest possible exchange of economic information and ensure that the business people and scientists of the two countries have access to such information.

Article 14. The French Republic and the Russian Federation attach the utmost importance to the protection of the environment. In that field, they commit themselves to strengthening their bilateral cooperation and promoting the development of joint action at the European and international levels.

Article 15. The French Republic and the Russian Federation shall develop their cooperation in the fields of fundamental and applied research, bearing in mind, *inter alia,* their economic and industrial implications. The two Parties shall endeavour to promote joint projects suitable for incorporation into European or international programmes.

In the field of advanced technologies, the Parties, while respecting their national regulations, shall encourage partnerships and joint ventures, in particular with a view to enhancing the competence and efficiency of their participants in industrial activity.

Article 16. The French Republic and the Russian Federation shall organize close cooperation between research institutions, *inter alia* through the form of exchanges of research workers.

Article 17. The French Republic and the Russian Federation shall develop their exchanges in the fields of culture, art, education and communication, in particular audio-visual communication.

The two Parties shall place particular emphasis on projects which could contribute to the creation of a common European cultural area.

They shall support, by all appropriate means, the teaching and dissemination of the French language in Russia and of the Russian language in France.

Direct relations between higher educational establishments, research centres, organizations and individuals participating in cultural life shall be encouraged.

New cooperative initiatives shall also be encouraged, in particular those involving training in the fields of culture and the national heritage, translation, publishing and co-publishing, as well as cooperation between universities.

The Parties shall facilitate the establishment and operation of cultural centres in their territories.

Article 18. The French Republic and the Russian Federation shall encourage contacts between their peoples, in particular exchanges between French and Russian youth.

Article 19. The French Republic and the Russian Federation shall promote contacts and cooperation between the Parliaments and parliamentarians of the two States.

Article 20. The French Republic and the Russian Federation shall encourage decentralized cooperation between local communities, in particular twinning arrangements, in accordance with the objectives specified in this Treaty.

They shall develop humanitarian cooperation, in particular by facilitating the activities of the charitable organizations of the two countries.

Article 21. The French Republic and the Russian Federation shall promote cooperation between judicial institutions in the two States, in particular with respect to mutual assistance in civil judicial matters.

The Parties shall organize cooperation between the competent bodies responsible for public safety, *inter alia* to combat organized crime, illicit trafficking in narcotic drugs, and smuggling, including the illegal trade in *objets d'art.* The Parties shall endeavour to establish appropriate cooperation in combating international terrorism.

Article 22. The French Republic and the Russian Federation undertake to reach agreement, with the least possible delay, on the settlement of claims brought up by either Party in connection with the financial and material aspects of the property and interests of individuals and bodies corporate in the two countries.

Article 23. The French Republic and the Russian Federation undertake to take the necessary measures to simplify, on a reciprocal basis, the procedures for the granting and extension of visas.

Each Party shall, on a reciprocal basis, give all necessary assistance to the activities within its territory of the diplomatic missions and consulates of the other Party.

Article 24. The French Republic and the Russian Federation shall conclude such special agreements and arrangements as may be necessary to give effect to the provisions of this Treaty.

They shall continue to apply the existing bilateral agreements and shall review them as necessary.

Article 25. The provisions of this Treaty shall in no way affect the commitments of the Parties vis-à-vis third States and are not directed against any of them.

Article 26. This Treaty, which shall be subject to ratification in accordance with the constitutional procedures of each Party, shall enter into force 30 days after the exchange of the instruments of ratification.

This Treaty is concluded for a period of 10 years. It shall be automatically renewed for successive five-year periods, unless one of the Parties gives the other Party written notice of its decision to denounce the Treaty one year prior to the expiry of the current period of validity.

Done at Paris, on 7 February 1992, in duplicate in the French and Russian languages, both texts being equally authentic.

For the French Republic:
[FRANÇOIS MITTERRAND]
President of the French Republic
[EDITH CRESSON]
Prime Minister
[ROLAND DUMAS]
Minister of State
Minister for Foreign Affairs

For the Russian Federation:
[BORIS YELTSIN]
President of the Russian Federation
[A. KOSSYGIN]
Minister for Foreign Affairs

4.1442 Treaty on Collective Security

Alliance Members: Armenia, Azerbaijan, Kazakhstan, Kyrgyz Republic, Moldova, Russia, Tajikistan, Turkmenistan, Ukraine, Uzbekistan (September 24, 1993), Georgia (December 9, 1993), and Belarus (December 31, 1993).
Signed On: May 15, 1992, in the city of Tashkent (Uzbekistan). In force as of date of publication of this volume, except for Azerbaijan, Georgia, and Uzbekistan (three countries that left the alliance on April 20, 1999).
Alliance Type: Defense Pact (Type I)

Source: *United Nations Treaty,* no. 32307.

SUMMARY

This agreement on collective security provided a mutual defense network for the Commonwealth of Independent States (CIS). Meant to reduce instability in the region after the collapse of the Soviet Union and the introduction of so many independent states into the international system, the alliance pledged to abstain from the use of force and committed all members to refrain from aggression against member states and other military alliances.

ALLIANCE TEXT

The States Parties to the present Treaty, hereinafter referred to as "States Parties",

Guided by the declarations on sovereignty of the Independent States,

Taking into account the formation by the States Parties of their own Armed Forces,

Taking concerted action in order to ensure collective security,

Recognizing the necessity to strictly implement the concluded treaties, concerning arms reduction, Armed Forces and to build confidence measures, have agreed as follows:

Article 1. The States Parties reconfirm the obligation to abstain from the use or threat of force in interstate relations. They shall resolve all the differences among them and other states only by peaceful means.

The States Parties shall not join military alliances or take part in any groupings of states as well as in actions directed against any other State Party.

In case a collective security system is created in Europe and Asia and treaties on collective security to that effect are concluded, this being the aim the contracting parties are striving for, the States Parties shall immediately proceed to consultations with each other to bring about necessary modifications into the present Treaty.

Article 2. The States Parties shall conduct consultations with each other on all major international security matters that affect their interests and coordinate their positions on these matters.

In case of any threat to security, territorial integrity and sovereignty to one or several States Parties, or in case of a threat to international peace and security, the States Parties shall immediately put into action the mechanism of joint consultations in order to coordinate their positions and take measures to eliminate the arisen threat.

Article 3. The States Parties shall create a Collective Security Council consisting of the Heads of the States Parties and the Commander-in-Chief of the Allied Armed Forces of the Commonwealth of Independent States.

Article 4. In case one of States Parties is subjected to an aggression by any state or a group of states, this shall be considered as an aggression against all the States Parties of the present Treaty.

In case an act of aggression is directed against any of the States Parties, all other States Parties shall provide it necessary assistance, including military assistance, and shall also support it by all means available in exercise of the right of collective defense under Article 51 of the Charter of the United Nations.

The States Parties shall immediately report to the Security Council of the United Nations Organization about the measures taken in conformity with the present Article. While implementing these measures the States Parties shall abide by the relevant provisions of the United Nations Charter.

Article 5. Coordination and joint actions of the States Parties under the present Treaty shall be taken by the Collective Security Council of the States Parties and the bodies it may establish. Before the above-mentioned bodies are established, coordination of the Armed Forces activities of the States Parties shall be carried out by the Major Command of the Allied Armed Forces of the Commonwealth.

Article 6. The decision on the use of the Armed Forces to rebuff aggression under Article 4 of the present Treaty shall be taken by the Heads of the States Parties.

The use of the Armed Forces outside the territories of the States Parties shall be made exclusively in the interests of international security in strict conformity with the United Nations Charter and national legislation of the States Parties to the present Treaty.

Article 7. Deployment and operation of the objects of the collective security system on the territory of the States Parties shall be subject to special agreements.

Article 8. This Treaty does not affect the rights and obligations stemming from other valid bilateral and multilateral treaties and agreements concluded by the States Parties with other states, and is not aimed against any third countries,

This Treaty does not affect the right of the States Parties to individual and collective defense against aggression in conformity with the United Nations Charter.

The States Parties undertake not to conclude international agreements incompatible with this Treaty.

Article 9. Any questions which may arise among the States Parties regarding either interpretation or implementation of any provision of this Treaty shall be settled jointly in the spirit of friendship, mutual respect and mutual understanding.

Amendments to this Treaty may be initiated by one or more States Parties and shall be adopted on the basis of mutual consent.

Article 10. This Treaty is open for accession to all interested states, sharing its purposes and principles.

Article 11 . This Treaty is concluded for five years with further prolongation.

Any State Party shall have the right to withdraw from this Treaty if it informs other parties about its intention no less than six months prior to that and if it has fulfilled all obligations coming out of this Treaty in connection with the withdrawal.

This Treaty is subject to ratification by each State signatory in accordance with its constitutional procedure. The instruments of ratification shall be deposited with the Government of the Republic of Belarus which is hereby appointed as a depository.

This Treaty shall enter into force immediately following the deposit of the instruments of ratification of the signatories.

Done at Tashkent on 15 May 1992 in the single original copy in Russian. The original copy shall be kept in the Archives of the Government of the Republic of Belarus which shall convey certified copies to the States signatories of this Treaty.

For the Azerbaijan Republic:

——

For the Republic of Armenia
LEVON TERPETROSSIAN

For the Republic of Belarus:

——

For the Republic of Kazakhstan:
NURSULTAN A. NAZARBAEV

For the Kyrgyz Republic:
FELIKS KULOV

For the Republic of Moldova:

——

For the Russian Federation:
BORIS N. YELTSIN

For the Republic of Tajikistan:
E. RAKHMONOV

For Turkmenistan:

——

For the Republic of Uzbekistan:
ISLAM KARIMOV

For Ukraine:

——

4.1443 Treaty of Friendship and Cooperation between Russia and Mongolia

Alliance Members: Russia and Mongolia
Signed On: January 20, 1993, in the city of Moscow. In force as of date of publication of this volume.
Alliance Type: Non-Aggression Pact (Type II)

Source: *United Nations Treaty,* no. 32861.

SUMMARY

The collapse of the Soviet Union was especially difficult on Mongolia because it had to negotiate separate treaties with the former Soviet republics to reestablish the aid and ties on which it was dependent. In addition, Mongolia for the first time established direct ties with several Russian Federation regions along its border. Given this flurry of cooperation agreements to ensure continued trade and travel, this treaty of friendship and cooperation was signed to provide a legal framework for the broader bilateral relationship. The treaty assured a landlocked Mongolia that Russian economic and political cooperation would continue, and it granted Mongolia most-favored-nation trading status.

ALLIANCE TEXT

Mongolia and the Russian Federation,

On the basis of the traditions of friendship, mutual trust and many-sided cooperation between the peoples of the two countries,

Desiring to expand and deepen equitable and mutually beneficial cooperation between Mongolia and the Russian Federation and, for that purpose, to strengthen its legal basis in accordance with the current realities and trends of international life,

Emphasizing their commitment to the purposes and principles of the Charter of the United Nations,

Wishing to promote the maintenance and strengthening of peace and the security of peoples, and the establishment of an atmosphere of mutual understanding and cooperation in the Asia-Pacific region,

Noting that the Agreement between the People's Government of Mongolia and the Government of the Russian Soviet Federative Socialist Republic of 5 November 1921 played a significant part in the development of good-neighbourly relations and cooperation between the two countries,

Guided by the provisions of the Declaration of Friendship and Good-Neighbourly Cooperation between the People's Republic of Mongolia and the Russian Soviet Federative Socialist Republic of 12 February 1991,

Have agreed as follows:

Article 1. The Parties shall regard each other as friendly States and shall be guided in their relations by the principles of respect for sovereignty and independence, sovereign equality, the non-use of force or threat of force, the inviolability of borders, territorial integrity, non-interference in internal affairs, respect for human rights and fundamental freedoms, the equality of peoples and their right to be the arbiters of their own destiny, the performance of obligations in good faith, good-neighbourliness, partnership and cooperation.

Article 2. The Parties shall, on a stable and long-term basis, develop equitable and mutually beneficial cooperation in the fields of politics, economics, culture, art, education, science and technology, public health, defence, security, the environment, transport and communications, information and human relations and in other fields.

Article 3. The Parties shall regularly exchange opinions at various levels on questions relating to the development and broadening of bilateral relations and cooperation, and on questions relating to international relations of mutual concern.

The Parties shall promote the development of links and contacts between the Parliaments and other elective organs of power of the two countries.

Article 4. The Parties shall not participate in any military-political unions directed against each other and undertake not to conclude with third countries any treaties or agreements which are incompatible with the interests of the sovereignty and independence of the other Party.

Neither Party shall allow its territory to be used by a third State for the purposes of aggression or any other act of force against the other Party.

The Russian Federation shall respect the policy of Mongolia directed towards the prohibition of the deployment in and transit through its territory of foreign troops, or of nuclear or other weapons of mass destruction.

Article 5. Should any new situation arise which, in the opinion of one of the Parties, poses a threat to international peace and security and may give rise to international complications, the Parties shall inform each other of possible means of resolving it.

At the request of one of the Parties that considers that its interests and security may be at risk, immediate consultations shall be held.

Article 6. The Parties shall develop cooperation between their two States within the framework of the United Nations and other international organizations in the interests of resolving current international problems relating to peace and security, stable economic development, the protection of the environment and other problems at the global and regional levels.

Article 7. The Parties shall use every means to promote the strengthening of stability and the establishment of an atmosphere of trust and a spirit of collaboration in the Asia-Pacific region and shall cooperate on a bilateral and multilateral basis in the interests of promoting the development of links in the economic, cultural, humanitarian and other fields between the States of the region.

Article 8. The Parties shall conduct an open economic policy in relation to each other and shall develop equitable and mutually beneficial cooperation. To that end, they undertake to grant most-favoured-nation treatment to participants in the commercial, industrial and financial activities of State and non-State enterprises, individuals and other entities. The Parties shall encourage cooperation in investment, *inter alia,* with the participation of partners from third countries.

The Parties shall use every means to promote the development of trade and cooperation in frontier areas.

Article 9. The Parties shall encourage the development of cooperation in the field of communications by rail, air, road and other forms of transport. They shall take measures to increase the transport capacity of their roads and to improve the organization of through carriage across their territory. Mindful of the fact that Mongolia has no outlet to the sea, the Russian Federation shall promote the realization of its right to access to the sea, in accordance with the rules of international law.

Article 10. The Parties shall develop cooperation in the field of environmental protection and environmental safety and in the joint prevention of environmental crises and the elimination of their effects. To that end, they shall periodically exchange information and shall consult on matters of direct interest to one or both of the Parties.

Article 11. The Parties shall develop cooperation in the humanitarian field on the basis of respect for the distinctive history, cultures and customs of their two countries.

They shall take all measures to promote the broadening of contacts between nationals of the two Parties. For that purpose they shall take measures to regulate administrative procedures and practices for reciprocal travel by their nationals.

Article 12. The Parties shall cooperate on a bilateral and multilateral basis in combating organized crime, terrorism, unlawful acts directed against the safety of civil aviation, illicit trafficking in drugs and weapons and smuggling, including the illicit crossborder transfer of works of art and objects of cultural or historical value.

The necessary conditions shall also be established for the rendering of mutual judicial assistance in civil, family and criminal cases.

Article 13. The Parties shall devote particular attention to the reciprocal establishment of conditions for the conduct of joint programmes and projects with a view to the utilization of modern technological achievements, cooperation in the field of fundamental and applied research and the incorporation of the outcome of such research in the economy and in industry.

Article 14. The Parties shall expand and deepen their links in the fields of culture, art, science, the historical heritage, education and information. They shall promote the establishment of direct links between higher educational establishments and scientific research centres and between cultural institutions, the expansion of the exchange of books, periodicals, cinematographic films, theatrical productions and television and radio programmes, and shall encourage the study of the languages of the Parties.

Article 15. The Parties shall support the establishment and development of direct links between the *aimags* of Mongolia, the constituent republics of the Russian Federation and other administrative and territorial entities at all levels, and also between State, mixed and private enterprises, establishments and organizations for the development of cooperation in the spirit of this Treaty and in implementation thereof.

Article 16. In accordance with the principles set forth in this Treaty, the Governments of both Parties and other competent organs shall conclude separate agreements with each other on matters contained therein and on other matters.

Article 17. The Parties shall resolve any disputed issues that may arise in relations between them through negotiation in a spirit of good will.

Should it prove impossible to resolve any dispute by such means, the Parties may choose other means for the peaceful settlement of disputes in accordance with the Charter of the United Nations.

Article 18. This Treaty shall not affect the obligations arising under any bilateral or multilateral agreement concluded by the Parties with other States.

Article 19. This Treaty is concluded for a period of twenty years and shall be automatically renewed for successive periods of five years, unless one of the Parties notifies the other Party in writing twelve months prior to the expiration of the current period of validity of its decision to denounce it.

Article 20. This Treaty is subject to ratification and shall enter into force on the date of the exchange of the instruments of ratification.

Done at Moscow, on 20 January 1993, in two copies, in the Mongolian and Russian languages, both texts being equally authentic.

For Mongolia:

PUNSALMAAGIIN OCHIRBAT

For the Russian Federation:

BORIS NIKOLAEVICH YELTSIN

4.1444 Agreement between the Government of Australia and the Government of the Republic of Indonesia on Maintaining Security

Alliance Members: Australia and Indonesia
Signed On: December 18, 1995, in the city of Jakarta (Indonesia). In force until September 16, 1999.
Alliance Type: Entente (III)

Source: *Australian Treaty Series,* 1996, no. 13.

SUMMARY

During the 1960s, Indonesia fought a small, undeclared war with Malaysia in an effort to thwart British control in the region, and Indonesian and Australian troops engaged in hostilities against each other. Over the course of the next twenty-five years, Australia committed to a foreign policy goal of friendly relations with its neighbor to the northwest, and these efforts culminated with the Agreement between the Government of Australia and the Government of the Republic of Indonesia on Maintaining Security. The main provisions of the agreement upheld the sovereignty of both states and guaranteed consultation over important mutual security issues, including United Nations involvement to resolve any territorial disputes.

The spirit of cooperation that fostered the treaty did not last long. Regional competitiveness combined with nationalist and ethnic issues in Indonesia split relations between Australia and Indonesia, and the situation boiled over in the crisis over East Timor. In spite of formal recognition of East Timor by the Australian government, the large number of Timorese refugees and a sympathetic Australian public pressed to keep the treatment of the Timorese and East Timor a dividing issue. In 1998, the Australian government pushed for the Indonesian government to allow a referendum in East Timor for independence. When Indonesia's leader. B. J. Habibie, announced such a referendum and the United Nations tried to ensure a fair vote, many prointegrationist militias in Indonesia blamed Australia. During the following year and after a vote for independence, violence and looting erupted in East Timor, but the Indonesian government failed to intervene. The public outcry against Timorese integrationists in Australia was strong and resulted in Australia taking a leading role in the international peacekeeping mission. Australia followed by cutting off all military assistance to Indonesia, and on September 16, 1999, Indonesia canceled the security treaty with Australia, blaming Australia's reaction to East Timor.

ALLIANCE TEXT

THE GOVERNMENT OF AUSTRALIA AND THE GOVERNMENT OF THE REPUBLIC OF INDONESIA (hereafter referred to as the "Parties"),

DESIRING to strengthen the existing friendship between them;

RECOGNISING their common interest in the peace and stability of the region;

DESIRING to contribute to regional security and stability in order to ensure circumstances in which their aspirations can be best realised for the economic development and prosperity of their own countries and the region;

REAFFIRMING their respect for the sovereignty, political independence and territorial integrity of all countries;

REAFFIRMING their commitment to the settlement of all international disputes by peaceful means in accordance with the Charter of the United Nations and international law;

RECOGNISING that each Party has primary responsibility for its own security;

MINDFUL of the contribution that would be made to their own security and that of the region by cooperating in the development of effective national capabilities in the defence field and hence their national resilience and self-reliance;

NOTING that nothing in this Agreement affects in any way the existing international commitments of either Party;

THEREFORE AGREE as follows:

Article 1. The Parties undertake to consult at ministerial level on a regular basis about matters affecting their common security and to develop such cooperation as would benefit their own security and that of the region.

Article 2. The Parties undertake to consult each other in the case of adverse challenges to either party or to their common security interests and, if appropriate, consider measures which might be taken either individually or jointly and in accordance with the processes of each Party.

Article 3. The Parties agree to promote—in accordance with the policies and priorities of each—mutually beneficial cooperative activities in the security field in areas to be identified by the two Parties.

Article 4. This Agreement shall enter into force on the date of the later notification by either Government of the fulfilment of its requirements for entry into force of this Agreement.

IN WITNESS WHEREOF, the undersigned, being duly authorised by their respective Governments, have signed this Agreement.

DONE at Jakarta on the eighteenth day of December, one thousand nine hundred and ninety-five in the English and Indonesian languages, both texts being equally authentic.

FOR THE GOVERNMENT OF AUSTRALIA:

GARETH EVANS
Minister for Foreign Affairs

FOR THE GOVERNMENT OF THE REPUBLIC OF INDONESIA:

ALI ALATAS
Minister for Foreign Affairs

4.1445 Treaty on Deepening Military Trust in Border Regions

Alliance Members: China, Kazakhstan, Kyrgyzstan, Russia, Tajikistan, and Uzbekistan (Uzbekistan rejoined on June 15, 2001, when the Shanghai Cooperation Organization was established)
Signed On: April 27, 1996, in the city of Shanghai (China). In force as of date of publication of this volume.
Alliance Type: Non-Aggression Pact (Type II)

Source: International Telecommunications Union, http://missions.itu.int/~kazaks/eng/sco/sco02.htm

SUMMARY

Relations between the Soviet Union and China have often been tense. During the cold war, the Soviet Union and China disagreed ideologically and competed for spheres of influence. The two countries also share the world's longest border, which has provided a consistent source of conflict. Since the late 1980s, however, both sides began to gradually reduce border tensions, and in 1989, President Mikhail Gorbachev of Russia called for demilitarization along the border.

Cross-border cooperation was formalized by China, Russia, Kazakhstan, Kyrgyzstan, Tajikistan, and Uzbekistan when their representatives met in April 1996 in Shanghai and signed an agreement concerning their border areas. On April 24, 1997, the Shanghai Five (the members of the April 27, 1996, alliance minus Uzbekistan) once again met and agreed to reduce the number of forces stationed along the former Sino-Soviet border.

Since the original 1996 meeting, the Shanghai Five have continued to cooperate on various issues and have signed an increasing number of confidence-building measures. Each year the five nations have also held annual summits to discuss regional security issues. Both China and Russia agreed to withdraw offensive weaponry from within 200 kilometers of the border. There have also been agreements to decrease the likelihood of military accidents as well as declarations detargeting their nuclear weapons.

On June 15, 2001, cooperation led to the creation of the Shanghai Cooperation Organization (SCO). The charter of the SCO declared that the goal of the organization was to increase mutual trust and relations as well as foster cooperation in economics, trade, security, and other issues of regional interest.

DESCRIPTION OF TERMS

The allies pledged that none of the parties would station troops on the border for attacks against one of the parties. The parties also agreed not to threaten the use of force or any type of aggression that would destabilize the security of the border regions.

All parties also agreed to exchange information regarding their military forces along the border, pledged not to conduct military exercises targeting other allies, and would inform all parties regarding troops and munitions that temporarily entered the 100-kilometer zone along the border.

4.1446 Defense Pact between the Democratic Republic of the Congo and the Central African Republic

Alliance Members: Congo and the Central African Republic
Signed On: May 11, 1998, in the city of Kinshasa (Congo). In force as of date of publication of this volume.
Alliance Type: Defense Pact (Type I)

Source: *BBC Summary of World Broadcasts,* May 14, 1998.

SUMMARY

In 1997, the Alliance of the Democratic Forces for the Liberation of the Congo (ADFL) ousted the leader of the Democratic Republic of the Congo (Zaire), Mobutu Sese Seko, and replaced him with Laurent Kabila. In 1998, conflict was renewed as ethnic Tutsis who had fought with the ADFL turned against Kabila. The rebellion was backed by Rwanda and Uganda.

As more African nations became involved in the war in the Congo, regional leaders began to take sides in the conflict. The Central African Republic (CAR) backed Kabila and signed this joint defense agreement on May 11, 1998. The agreement declared that both nations would provide "mutual assistance" to each other as well as give support to the other's "internal defence and security." The two nations also agreed to permanently consult regarding issues of security and defense.

In 1999, the rebellion in the Congo was put down with aid from Zimbabwe, Angola, and Namibia, but violence continued as Kabila was assassinated and replaced by his son. Finally, in 2003, a peace accord was reached between the government and the rebels. The government of the CAR remained stable until 2003 when President Ange-Felix Patasse was deposed and a new government was established.

Although the leaders have changed over time and this alliance has probably remained dormant awaiting new leadership in the CAR, the alliance has remained continuously in force since its signing.

ALLIANCE TEXT

Conscious of their responsibility in connection with peacekeeping and nonaggression, in line with the principles of the UN Charter; taking into consideration that the Central African Republic and the Democratic Republic of Congo firmly desire to cooperate in matters of defence; and in view of their desire to determine the nature of this cooperation, they have agreed on the following:

Article 1: The Central African Republic and the Democratic Republic of Congo have agreed to establish a bilateral defence agreement.

Article 2: The Central African Republic and the Democratic Republic of Congo are responsible for internal and external defence.

Article 3: To this end, the contracting parties will give one another mutual assistance, and will permanently consult one another on issues of defence and security.

Article 4: Each of the contracting parties undertakes to give to the other party all the necessary facilities and any assistance for internal defence and security, as well as for the security of the borders of its territory.

Article 5: The defence forces are essentially the armed forces of the two countries.

Article 6: This agreement will be completed later by one or several memorandums.

Article 7: The present agreement will go into force after its ratification.

4.1447 Luanda Defense Protocol

Alliance Members: Angola, Democratic Republic of the Congo, Namibia, and Zimbabwe
Signed On: April 9, 1999, in the city of Luanda (Angola). In force until August 14, 2001.
Alliance Type: Defense Pact (Type I)

Source: Institute for Security Studies, www.iss.co.za/Pubs/Monographs/No43/BilateralTreaties.html.

SUMMARY

The Luanda protocol was the attempt by the president of the Democratic Republic of the Congo, Laurent Kabila, to quell concerted action by Rwanda and Uganda to back rebel groups within the Congo. The Angolan president, José Eduardo dos Santos, responded by hosting a one-day regional summit for the leaders, during which they signed this defense alliance that committed all parties to come to the aid of any ally if attacked. Angola, Namibia, and Zimbabwe were actually already assisting Kabila with troops and munitions.

The leaders also expressed concern over the continued fighting of UNITA forces in Angola and pledged aid to dos Santos, who had been labeled a war criminal by Southern African leaders. The summit ended with a call to all African nations to comply with the United Nations Security Council sanctions against UNITA.

The alliance lasted only two years; it was replaced by an amended Southern African Development Community (SADC) that included terms for socioeconomic cooperation and integration as well as political and security cooperation among the southern African nations. The SADC serves as a regional complement to the African Union.

EXCERPTS OF ALLIANCE TEXT

Article 4: "That an armed attack against one of them shall be considered an attack against the other and that in the event of such an attack, each of them will assist the Party so attacked by taking forthwith individually or in collaboration with other parties, such action as it deems necessary, including the use of armed force, to repel such attack and restore peace and security in the territory of the Party so attacked. Any such armed attack and measures taken as a result thereof shall immediately be reported to the Security Council of the United Nations."

Article 7 determines that no action in terms of the protocol may be undertaken within the territory of a signatory save at the request of that country ". . . except where the extent, violence or rapidity of the aggression has disrupted the free and effective functioning of its institutions and rendered the exercise of its sovereignty impracticable."

Article 9 demands co-operation in all defence matters, particularly regarding training, the exchange of military intelligence, and military industrial co-operation.

Article 11 establishes ". . . a Joint Committee to be called the 'Angola-DRC-Namibia-Zimbabwe Co-operation Committee' whose function shall be to ensure the smooth implementation of this Protocol."

4.1448 Treaty of Friendship, Good-Neighborly Relations, and Cooperation between Russia and North Korea

Alliance Members: Russia and North Korea
Signed On: February 9, 2000, in the city of Pyongyang (North Korea). In force as of date of publication of this volume.
Alliance Type: Entente (Type III)

Source: *The Current Digest of the Post-Soviet Press,* September 5, 2001.

SUMMARY

Following the 1999 election of President Vladimir Putin in Russia, North Korean and Russian leaders met to settle lingering tensions, forge greater cooperation, and sign this treaty of friendship, good-neighborliness, and cooperation in February 2000. Meeting in Moscow, the two nations outlined specific areas of partnership, including science, technology, and economic interests. Specific cooperation included an agreement to work toward building a railway tying the Korean peninsula with Russia and Europe.

Russia and North Korea also agreed to support the peaceful resolution of the issue of Korean reunification. By committing to this, Russia secured a place in any negotiations regarding the half-century dispute on the peninsula, and North Korea gained another relatively powerful negotiating partner.

Russia has been proven an important ally of North Korea, providing both aid and support. However, that support has not been unconditional. Putin balked following North Korea's withdrawal from the Nuclear Non-Proliferation Treaty in 2003 and North Korea's suspension of six-party talks in 2005. Though the entente remains, Putin signed an order forbidding Russian state and government agencies and private companies from aiding North Korea's nuclear efforts in any way.

DESCRIPTION OF TERMS

Both parties agreed that if either state became the target of outside aggression, or if there was a threat to peace and security, the two countries would consult and cooperate immediately. Both parties also agreed that neither would sign any treaties or involve itself in any arrangements that targeted the sovereignty or territorial integrity of the other party.

4.1449 Defense Pact among the Gulf Cooperation Council

Alliance Members: Bahrain, Kuwait, Oman, Qatar, Saudi Arabia, and the United Arab Emirates
Signed On: December 31, 2000, in the city of Manama (Bahrain). In force as of date of publication of this volume.
Alliance Type: Defense Pact (Type I)

Source: *Agence France-Presse,* December 31, 2000.
Additional Citations: *Keesing's Record of World Events,* January 2001; *Washington Institute for Near East Policy,* Policy Watch no. 511, January 16, 2001.

SUMMARY

The Gulf Cooperation Council (GCC) was established in 1981, after the beginning of the Iran-Iraq War, by Arab states seeking closer cooperation over political, economic, and military issues. The agreement itself had no declarations of mutual defense, but the agreement was nevertheless based largely on security concerns. Thus, while the GCC included a joint military force called the Peninsula Shield, which consisted of roughly 5,000 troops, the treaty had no military obligations. During the 1990 invasion of Kuwait by Iraq, it took several months for the council to officially concede military action was needed.

This changed on December 31, 2000, as the six member states met and signed this defense agreement, which pledged that all GCC members would come to the aide of an ally in case of attack. The agreement also increased the number of joint military defense troops assigned to the GCC and established a system of early warnings and communication links between the military headquarters of respective GCC members. Nevertheless, despite the closer ties, the GCC continues to suffer from small rifts among its membership, and member states remain cautious in their political and military maneuvers.

DESCRIPTION OF TERMS

The treaty committed member states to come to the aid of any alliance member targeted by an external attack. A supreme defense council would be established to oversee the implementation of the defense pact, and the rapid deployment force of the GCC was enlarged to 22,000 troops.

CHAPTER FIVE: 21st Century

Map 8. 2005

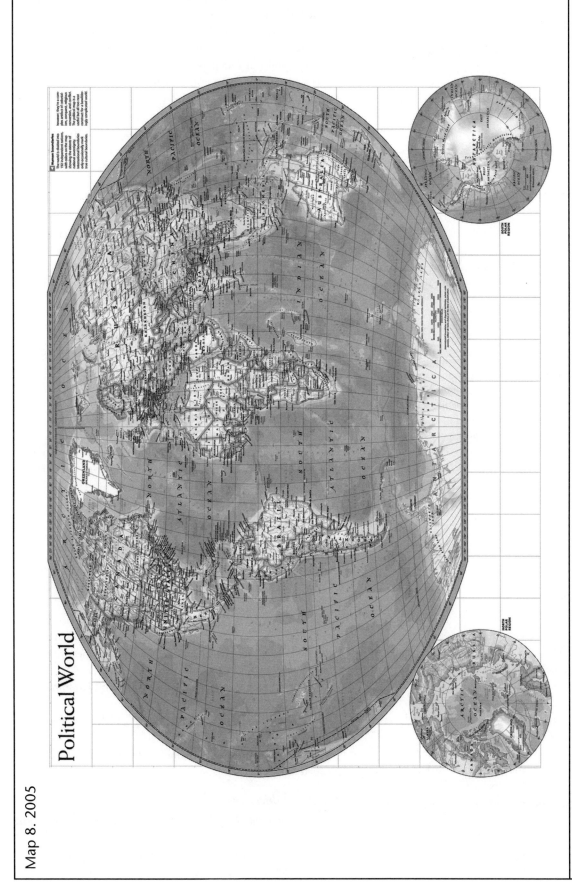

Political World

Many new issues confront the current international system, but chief among these issues continues to be the global response to terrorism. New alliance ties among the major states have focused on military cooperation against insurgencies and terrorist groups (Alliance nos. 5.1450 and 5.1455), while states like Syria and Iran (Alliance no. 5.1454) have allied in the hopes of thwarting direct attacks. Still dominant, however, is the overarching role played by regional organizations such as the Organization of American States (Alliance nos. 4.1289 and 4.1333), the European Union (supported by Alliance no. 4.1339), and the African Union (Alliance no. 4.1371). These organizations provide a forum for regional dialogue in times of crisis while they also support the institutions necessary for facilitating active cooperation and coordination on key regional issues. These large, regional pacts and their constancy through major changes in the international system remain the real story of alliance making at the beginning of the twenty-first century.

5.1450 Protocol on Politics, Defence, and Security Cooperation by the Southern African Development Community

Alliance Members: Angola, Botswana, Democratic Republic of Congo, Lesotho, Malawi, Mauritius, Mozambique, Namibia, Seychelles, South Africa, Swaziland, Tanzania, Zambia, Zimbabwe
Signed On: August 14, 2001, in the city of Blantyre (Malawi). In force as of date of publication of this volume, although the Seychelles gave notice of its withdrawal on July 1, 2003, and a new treaty was implemented on August 26, 2003.
Alliance Type: Non-Aggression Pact (Type II)

Source: Southern African Development Community, Declaration and Treaty, Annex A, www.sadc.int/index/browse/page/157.

SUMMARY

Beginning in the 1970s, the black-majority countries of southern Africa started to band together in the hopes of providing mutual aid against all threats to their development. These frontline states were loosely organized, but by 1980 leaders from nine southern African states met at the Sothern African Development Coordination Conference (SADCC) and established rudimentary rules for economic and political cooperation.

The SADCC evolved into the Southern African Development Community (SADC) in 1992, with the Windhoek declaration and treaty. This treaty was amended on August 14, 2001, and included the following provisions for military cooperation and mutual pledges of nonaggression. Although the treaty remains in force as of publication, the institutions of the SADC remain relatively weak and underfunded.

ALLIANCE TEXT

Preamble

We, the Heads of State and Government of:

> The Republic of Angola
> The Republic of Botswana
> The Democratic Republic of Congo
> The Kingdom of Lesotho
> The Republic of Malawi
> The Republic of Mauritius
> The Republic of Mozambique
> The Republic of Namibia
> The Republic of Seychelles
> The Republic of South Africa
> The Kingdom of Swaziland
> The United Republic of Tanzania
> The Republic of Zambia
> The Republic of Zimbabwe

TAKING COGNISANCE of the decision of SADC to create the

ORGAN on Politics, Defence and Security Co-operation which appears in the Gaborone Communiquée of 28th June 1996;

NOTING Article 9 of the Treaty which establishes the Organ;
BEARING IN MIND that Chapter VIII of the UN Charter

recognizes the role of regional arrangements in dealing with such matters relating to the maintenance of international peace and security as are appropriate for regional action;

RECOGNISING AND RE-AFFIRMING the principles of strict respect for sovereignty, sovereign equality, territorial integrity, political independence, good neighbourliness, interdependence, non-aggression and non-interference in internal affairs of other States;

RECALLING the 1964 resolution of the Assembly of Heads of State and Government of the Organisation of African Unity, declaring that all Member States pledge to respect the borders existing on their achievement of national independence;

FURTHER REAFFIRMING the primary responsibility of the United Nations Security Council in the maintenance of international peace and security, and the role of the Central Organ of the Organisation of African Unity Mechanism for Conflict Prevention, Management and Resolution;

CONVINCED that peace, security and strong political relations are critical factors in creating a conducive environment for regional cooperation and integration;

CONVINCED FURTHER that the Organ constitutes an appropriate institutional framework by which Member States could co-ordinate policies and activities in the area of politics, defence and security;

DETERMINED to achieve solidarity, peace and security in the Region through close cooperation on matters of politics, defence and security;

DESIROUS TO ENSURE that close cooperation on matters of politics, defence and security shall at all times promote the peaceful settlement of disputes by negotiation, conciliation, mediation or arbitration;

ACTING in pursuance of Article 10A of the Treaty;
HEREBY AGREE AS FOLLOWS:

Article 1: Definitions

1. In this Protocol terms and expressions defined in Article 1 of the Treaty shall bear the same meaning unless the context otherwise requires.

2. In this Protocol, unless the context otherwise requires:

"Chairperson" means the Chairperson of the Organ;
"ISDSC" means the Inter-State Defence and Security Committee;
"ISPDC" means the Inter-State Politics and Diplomacy Committee.
"Signatory" means a Member State which signs this Protocol;
"State Party" means a Member State that has ratified or acceded to this Protocol.

Article 2: Objectives

1. The general objective of the Organ shall be to promote peace and security in the Region.

2. The specific objectives of the Organ shall be to:

a) protect the people and safeguard the development of the

Region against instability arising from the breakdown of law and order, intra-state conflict, inter-state conflict and aggression;

b) promote political co-operation among State Parties and the evolution of common political values and institutions;

c) develop common foreign policy approaches on issues of mutual concern and advance such policy is collectively in international fora;

d) promote regional co-ordination and co-operation on matters related to security and defence and establish appropriate mechanisms to this end;

e) prevent, contain and resolve inter- and intra-state conflict by peaceful means;

f) consider enforcement action in accordance with international law and as a matter of last resort where peaceful means have failed;

g) promote the development of democratic institutions and practices within the territories of State Parties and encourage the observance of universal human rights as provided for in the Charters and Conventions of the Organisation of African Unity and United Nations respectively;

h) consider the development of a collective security capacity and conclude a Mutual Defence Pact to respond to external military threats;

i) develop close co-operation between the police and state security services of State Parties in order to address:
   (i) cross border crime; and
   (ii) promote a community based approach to domestic security;

j) observe, and encourage State Parties to implement, United Nations, African Union and other international conventions and treaties on arms control, disarmament and peaceful relations between states;

k) develop peacekeeping capacity of national defence forces and co-ordinate the participation of State Parties in international and regional peacekeeping operations; and

l) enhance regional capacity in respect of disaster management and co-ordination of international humanitarian assistance.

Article 3: Structures

1. The Organ shall be an institution of SADC and shall report to the Summit.

2. The Organ shall have the following structures:

a) the Chairperson of the Organ;

b) the Troika;

c) a Ministerial Committee;

d) an Inter-State Politics and Diplomacy Committee (ISPDC);

e) an Inter-State Defence and Security Committee (ISDSC); and

f) such other sub-structures as may be established by any of the ministerial committees.

3. The Troika shall consist of;

(a) the Chairperson of the Organ;

(b) the Incoming Chairperson who shall be the Deputy Chairperson of the Organ; and

(c) the Outgoing Chairperson.

Article 4: Chairperson of the organ

1. The Summit shall elect a Chairperson and a Deputy Chairperson of the Organ on the basis of rotation from among the members of the Summit except that the Chairperson and the Deputy Chairperson of the Summit shall not simultaneously be the Chairperson of the Organ.

2. The term of office of the Chairperson and Deputy Chairperson of the Organ shall be one year respectively.

3. The Chairperson of the Organ shall consult with the Troika of SADC and report to the Summit.

4. The Chairperson, in consultation with the Troika of SADC, shall be responsible for the overall policy direction and the achievement of the objectives of the Organ.

5. The Chairperson may request reports from any ministerial committee of the Organ on any matter which is within the competence of the committee

6. The Chairperson may request any ministerial committee of the Organ to consider any matter, which is within the competence of the committee.

7. The Chairperson may request the Chairperson of SADC to table for discussion any matter that requires consideration by the Summit.

Article 5: Ministerial committee

1. The Ministerial Committee shall comprise the ministers responsible for foreign affairs, defence, public security and state security from each of the State Parties.

2. The Committee shall be responsible for the co-ordination of the work of the Organ and its structures.

3. The Committee shall report to the Chairperson.

4. The Committee shall be chaired by a Minister from the same country as the Chairperson for a period of one year on a rotation basis.

5. The Chairperson of the Committee shall convene at least one meeting on an annual basis.

6. The Chairperson of the Committee may when necessary convene other meetings of the Ministerial Committee at a request of either ISPDC or ISDSC.

7. The Committee may refer any relevant matter to, and may request reports from, ISPDC and ISDSC.

Article 6: Inter-state politics and diplomacy committee

1. ISPDC shall comprise the ministers responsible for foreign affairs from each of the State Parties.

2. ISPDC shall perform such functions as may be necessary to achieve the objectives of the Organ relating to politics and diplomacy.

3. ISPDC shall report to the Ministerial Committee without

prejudice to its obligation to report regularly to the Chairperson.

4. ISPDC shall be chaired by a Minister from the same country as the Chairperson for a period of one year and on a rotation basis.

5. The Chairperson of ISPDC shall convene at least one meeting on an annual basis.

6. The Chairperson of ISPDC may convene such other meetings as he or she deems necessary or as requested by another Minister serving on ISPDC.

7. ISPDC may establish such sub-structures as it deems necessary to perform its functions.

Article 7: Inter-state defence and security committee

1. ISDSC shall comprise the ministers responsible for defence, ministers responsible for public security and ministers responsible for state security from each of the State Parties.

2. ISDSC shall perform such functions as may be necessary to achieve the objectives of the Organ relating to defence and security, and shall assume the objectives and functions of the existing Inter—State Defence and Security Committee.

3. ISDSC shall report to the Ministerial Committee without prejudice to its obligation to report regularly to the Chairperson.

4. ISDSC shall be chaired by a Minister from the same country as the Chairperson for a period of one year and on a rotating basis.

5. The Chairperson of ISDSC shall convene at least one meeting on an annual basis.

6. The Chairperson of ISDSC may convene such other meetings as he or she deems necessary or as requested by another minister serving on ISDSC.

7. ISDSC shall retain the Defence, State Security and Public Security Sub-Committees and other subordinate structures of the existing Inter-State Defence and Security Committee.

8. ISDSC may establish such other structures as it deems necessary to perform its functions.

Article 8: Committee procedures

The following provisions shall apply to the ministerial committees of the Organ:

a) the quorum for all meetings shall be two-thirds of the State Parties;

b) the ministerial committees shall determine their own rules of procedure; and

c) decisions shall be taken by consensus.

Article 9: Secretariat

The SADC Secretariat shall provide secretariat services to the Organ.

Article 10: Co-operation with non-state parties and international organisations

1. In recognition of the fact that political, defence and security matters transcend national and regional boundaries,

co-operation agreement on these matters between State Parties and non-State Parties, and between State Parties and organisations, other than SADC, shall be accepted provided that such agreements shall not:

a) be inconsistent with the objectives and other provisions of the Treaty and this Protocol;

b) impose obligations upon a State Party that is not a party to such cooperation agreement, and

c) impede a State Party from fulfilling its obligations under the Treaty and this Protocol.

2. Any agreement between the Organ and a non-State Party, or between the Organ and an international organisation, shall be subject to approval by the Summit.

Article 11: Conflict prevention, management and resolution

1. Obligation of the Organ under International Law

a) In accordance with the Charter of the United Nations, State Parties shall refrain from the threat or use of force against the territorial integrity or political independence of any state, other than for the legitimate purpose of individual or collective self-defence against an armed attack.

b) State Parties shall manage and seek to resolve any dispute between two or more of them by peaceful means.

c) The Organ shall seek to manage and resolve inter- and intra-state conflict by peaceful means.

d) The Organ shall seek to ensure that the State Parties adhere to and enforce all sanctions and arms embargoes imposed on any party by the United Nations Security Council.

2. Jurisdiction of the Organ

a) The Organ may seek to resolve any significant inter-state conflict between State Parties or between a State Party and non- State Party and a "significant inter-state conflict" shall include:

(i) a conflict over territorial boundaries or natural resources;

(ii) a conflict in which an act of aggression or other form of military force has occurred or been threatened; and

(iii) a conflict which threatens peace and security in the Region or in the territory of a State Party which is not a party to the conflict.

b) The Organ may seek to resolve any significant intra-state conflict within the territory of a State Party and a "significant intra-state conflict" shall include:

(i) large-scale violence between sections of the population or between the state and sections of the population, including genocide, ethnic cleansing and gross violation of human rights;

(ii) a military coup or other threat to the legitimate authority of a State;

(iii) a condition of civil war or insurgency; and

(iv) a conflict which threatens peace and security in the

Region or in the territory of another State Party.

(c) In consultation with the United Nations Security Council and the Central Organ of the Organisation of African Unity Mechanism for Conflict Prevention, Management and Resolution, the Organ may offer to mediate in a significant inter- or intra-state conflict that occurs outside the Region.

3. Methods

a) The methods employed by the Organ to prevent, manage and resolve conflict by peaceful means shall include preventive diplomacy, negotiations, conciliation, mediation, good offices, arbitration and adjudication by an international tribunal.

b) The Organ shall establish an early warning system in order to facilitate timeous action to prevent the outbreak and escalation of conflict.

c) Where peaceful means of resolving a conflict are unsuccessful, the Chairperson acting on the advice of the Ministerial Committee may recommend to the Summit that enforcement action be taken against one or more of the disputant parties.

d) The Summit shall resort to enforcement action only as a matter of last resort and, in accordance with Article 53 of the United Nations Charter, only with the authorization of the United Nations Security Council.

e) External military threats to the Region shall be addressed through collective security arrangements to be agreed upon in a Mutual Defence Pact among the State Parties.

4. Procedures

a) In respect of both inter- and intra-state conflict, the Organ shall seek to obtain the consent of the disputant parties to its peacemaking efforts.

b) The Chairperson, in consultation with the other members of the Troika, may table any significant conflict for discussion in the Organ.

c) Any State Party may request the Chairperson to table any significant conflict for discussion in the Organ and in consultation with the other members of the Troika of the Organ, the Chairperson shall meet such request expeditiously.

d) The Organ shall respond to a request by a State Party to mediate in a conflict within the territory of that State and the Organ shall endeavour by diplomatic means to obtain such request where it is not forthcoming.

e) The exercise of the right of individual or collective self-defence shall be immediately reported to the United Nations Security Council and to the Central Organ of the Organisation of African Unity Mechanism for Conflict Prevention, Management and Resolution.

Article 12: Confidentiality of information

1. The State Parties undertake not to disclose any classified information, obtained under this Protocol or as a result of their participation in the Organ, other than to members of their own staff to whom such disclosure is essential for purposes of giving effect to this Protocol or any decision taken by the Organ.

2. State Parties shall ensure that the staff referred to in paragraph 1 of this Article shall at all times maintain strict secrecy.

3. State Parties further undertake not to use any classified information obtained during any multilateral co-operation between them to the detriment of any Member State.

4. A State Party shall remain bound by the requirement of confidentiality under this Article even after it withdraws from the Organ.

Article 13: Settlement of disputes

Any dispute arising between two or more State Parties from the interpretation or application of this Protocol which cannot be settled amicably shall be referred to the Tribunal.

Article 14: Withdrawal

A signatory may withdraw from this Protocol upon the expiration of twelve (12) months from the date of giving written notice to that effect to the Chairperson of the Organ. Such Signatory shall cease to enjoy all rights and benefits under this Protocol upon the withdrawal becoming effective.

Article 15: Relationship with other international agreements

1. This Protocol in no way detracts from the rights and obligations of State Parties under the Charters of the United Nations and the Organisation of African Unity.

2. This Protocol in no way detracts from the responsibility of the United Nations Security Council to maintain international peace and security.

3. This Protocol shall not derogate from existing agreements between a State Party and another State Party or a non-State Party and an international organisation, other than SADC, provided that such agreements are consistent with the principles and objectives of this Protocol.

4. Where an existing agreement is inconsistent with the principles and objectives of this Protocol, the Member State shall take steps to amend the agreement accordingly.

Article 16: Signature

This Protocol shall be signed by duly authorized representatives of the Member States.

Article 17: Ratification

This Protocol shall be subject to ratification by the Signatories in accordance with their respective constitutional procedures.

Article 18: Accession

This Protocol shall remain open for accession by any Member State.

Article 19: Amendments

1. Any State Party may propose an amendment to this Protocol.

2. Proposals for amendments to this Protocol shall be made to the Chairperson who shall duly notify all State Parties of the proposed amendments at least three (3) months in advance of the amendments being considered by the Ministerial Committee and the Chairperson shall advise the Chairperson of Summit of the recommendation of the Committee.

3. An amendment to this Protocol shall be adopted by a decision of three-quarters of the State Parties.

Article 20: Entry into force

This Protocol shall enter into force thirty (30) days after the deposit of the instruments of ratification by two-thirds of the State Parties.

Article 21: Depositary

1. The original texts of this Protocol shall be deposited with the Executive Secretary who shall transmit certified copies to all Member States.

2. The Executive Secretary shall register this Protocol with the Secretariat of the United Nations and the Organisation of African Unity.

IN WITNESS WHEREOF, WE, the Heads of State or Government, or duly authorised representatives, of SADC Member States, have signed this Protocol.

Done at Blantyre, on the 14th day of August 2001 in three (3) languages English, French and Portuguese, all texts being equally authentic.

Republic of Angola
Republic of Botswana
Democratic Republic of Congo
Kingdom of Lesotho
Republic of Malawi
Republic of Mauritius
Republic of Mozambique
Republic of Namibia
Republic of Seychelles
Republic of South Africa
Kingdom of Swaziland
United Republic of Tanzania
Republic of Zambia
Republic of Zimbabwe

5.1451 Treaty of Friendship and Cooperation between the Kingdom of Spain and the Republic of Albania

Alliance Members: Spain and Albania
Signed On: November 22, 2001, in the city of Tirana (Albania). In force as of date of publication of this volume.
Alliance Type: Non-Aggression Pact (Type II)

Source: *United Nations Treaty Series,* no. 39284.

SUMMARY

This friendship treaty was one of the first treaties establishing formal ties between Spain and Albania. Signed during a visit to Albania by the Spanish state secretary, Ramon de Miguel, the treaty was expected to lay the foundation for greater economic and political cooperation. The treaty also pledged noninterference and restraint from the use of force (Article II) and consultation in the event of crisis (Article VII).

The treaty was important for Albania because, in addition to promised Spanish investment, the visiting state secretary also pledged Spanish support for the European Union (EU)-Albanian Stabilization Association Agreement. Spain ascended to the rotating presidency of the EU in the following year.

ALLIANCE TEXT

The Kingdom of Spain and the Republic of Albania, hereinafter referred to as "the
Contracting Parties",

Guided by deep feelings of friendship and mutual respect between their peoples,

Firmly committed to contributing to the establishment of a more just, humane, peaceful and democratic international order,

Conscious of their responsibility for the maintenance of peace in Europe and the world and resolved to promote the purposes and principles of the Charter of the United Nations, and reaffirming their attachment to the commitments derived from international law,

Recognizing the importance of the commitments undertaken in the Helsinki Final Act and the Paris Charter for a New Europe and in subsequent documents of the Organization for Security and Cooperation in Europe,

Reaffirming the importance of the development of cooperation between the Republic of Albania and the European Union,

Have agreed as follows:

Article I. The Contracting Parties shall collaborate actively in all areas, on the basis of mutual respect and trust, in accordance with the democratic principles and values which they share and shall work actively to bring their peoples closer within the framework of a united Europe.

Article II. Pursuant to the purposes and principles of the Charter of the United Nations, the Helsinki Final Act and the Paris Charter for a New Europe, the Contracting Parties shall develop their bilateral relations as friendly States, guided by the principles of sovereign equality, of territorial integrity, of the inviolability of borders, of the political independence of States, of refraining from the use or threat of force, of the settlement of international disputes by peaceful means, of equality of rights and self-determination of peoples, of respect for human rights and fundamental freedoms, of cooperation between States and of compliance in good faith with their obligations assumed under international law.

Article III. Within the framework of the Organization for Security and Cooperation in Europe, the Kingdom of Spain and the Republic of Albania shall contribute to the overall strengthening of democracy, political pluralism, the rule of law and the protection of human rights.

The two Parties shall establish close cooperation in the areas of special importance from the viewpoint of the European integration processes.

In addition, the Kingdom of Spain shall support the efforts of the Republic of Albania to promote closer cooperation with the European Union.

Article IV. Within the framework of the Organization for Security and Cooperation in Europe, the Contracting Parties shall work towards increasing stability on the European continent, bearing in mind the interests of each of them in the area of security. Likewise, they shall work towards the implementation of a balanced process of conventional disarmament and of greater trust and transparency, based on the effective application by all States of the principle of sufficiency for their defence and bearing in mind all the security conditions as a whole in Europe.

The Parties shall contribute to the establishment and enhanced operation of appropriate institutional structures and mechanisms for strengthening the effectiveness of the process of the Organization for Security and Cooperation in Europe.

Article V. The Contracting Parties shall hold regular consultations at different levels for the purpose of facilitating the development of their bilateral relations and harmonizing insofar as possible their position on international issues that are of common interest.

Meetings at the highest political level shall take place whenever they may be deemed necessary.

The Ministers for Foreign Affairs shall meet at least once a year.

Meetings between other members of the two Governments shall take place whenever they may be deemed necessary.

Periodic consultations at the level of experts shall be held regularly.

Article VI. The Contracting Parties shall develop and strengthen their cooperation in the field of defence.

Article VII. In the event that situations arise which, in the judgement of one of the Parties, represent a threat to peace and security, thus heightening international tension, the Governments of the Kingdom of Spain and the Republic of Albania shall urgently contact each other through the most appropriate channels, with a view to exchanging views regarding the action that can be taken to alleviate the tension and resolve the situation.

If one of the Contracting Parties considers that its security interests are affected, it may propose to the other Party that bilateral consultations be held immediately.

Article VIII. The Contracting Parties shall develop bilateral economic cooperation and shall create favourable conditions for such cooperation, underscoring its importance for the success of economic reforms in the Republic of Albania, as well as for its gradual assimilation of European structures.

Within the framework of their respective national legislation and respective bilateral agreements, each of the Parties undertakes to create conditions favourable to stimulating investments in its territory by the other Party and guaranteeing their protection, with a view to improving conditions for the activity of companies of the other Party in its territory.

With a view to creating conditions favourable to the implementation of joint initiatives and projects, the Parties shall foster direct relations between Spanish and Albanian companies and new arrangements of financial cooperation, especially in the areas of investments and joint companies.

The Contracting Parties shall promote the exchange of financial information and access to it by experts from both countries, as well as the development of cooperation among business organizations and associations of the two countries.

With a view to facilitating the transition to a market economy in the Republic of Albania, the Kingdom of Spain shall cooperate through technical assistance and the training of specialists and top managers in this field.

Article IX. The Contracting Parties undertake to promote their cooperation in the areas of agriculture, industry, infrastructure and construction, transport and telecommunications, services and tourism.

Article X. Bearing in mind the importance of protection of the environment, the Contracting Parties shall strive to broaden their cooperation in this sphere, both bilaterally and multilaterally, especially on a European scale.

Article XI. The Contracting Parties, motivated by a desire to work together towards a fuller exchange of artistic values in the creation of a European cultural area, shall develop insofar as possible their cooperation in the fields of culture, science and education.

The Parties recognize the special importance of language teaching as a precondition for lasting cooperation and mutual knowledge of the cultures of their peoples. They shall each foster the teaching of the languages and literature of the other Party in their territory.

The two Parties shall support direct cooperation and exchanges between public institutions, universities and other higher education establishments, scientific research centres, private organizations and individuals, in the sphere of culture, science and education and shall collaborate on the implementation of joint scientific projects.

The Contracting Parties attach great importance to the creation and development of activity of cultural centres where the languages and cultures of their respective countries may be taught and disseminated.

Particular assistance shall be given to teacher training and the facilities required for access to teaching materials and specialized literature and for the use of audio-visual and computer technology.

Each of the Parties shall foster cooperation in the area of the media and dissemination of the printed works of the other Party.

Article XII. The Contracting Parties shall develop and facilitate their cooperation in the areas of public health, social assistance, physical education, sport and tourism, as well as the development of youth exchanges.

Article XIII. The Contracting Parties shall pay special attention to enhancing relations between the Parliaments of Spain and Albania.

Taking into consideration the constitutional systems of the two States, the Parties shall support direct contacts and cooperation between regional and local authorities.

In the same spirit, the Parties shall facilitate cooperation between the political, social and trade-union organizations of the two countries.

Article XIV. The Contracting Parties shall develop cooperation in the international legal sphere pursuant to the existing international conventions.

Article XV. The Parties shall cooperate in combating organized crime and illegal drug trafficking through the exchange of experience and practical information between their competent agencies.

The Parties also undertake to cooperate in combating terrorism, hijacking of means of maritime and air transport and smuggling, including the import, export and illegal transfer of ownership of cultural assets.

Article XVI. The provisions of this Treaty shall not affect the rights and obligations arising from international bilateral or multilateral treaties concluded by the Kingdom of Spain and the Republic of Albania with third States.

Article XVII. This Treaty shall be ratified by each of the Parties and shall enter into force thirty days after the exchange of the respective instruments of ratification.

This Treaty shall be valid for ten years, being tacitly renewable for five-year periods. When one of the Parties wishes to denounce the Treaty, it must notify the other Party in writing through the diplomatic channel one year before the end of each period of validity.

DONE at Tirana on 22 November 2001 in two copies in Spanish and Albanian, both texts being equally authentic.

For the Kingdom of Spain:
RAMÓN DE MIGUEL Y EGEA
Secretary of State for European Affairs

For the Republic of Albania:
ARTA BADE
Minister for Foreign Affairs

5.1452 Joint Statement between the Government of the People's Republic of China and the Government of the Republic of the Fiji Islands on Consolidating and Promoting Friendly Relations and Cooperation

Alliance Members: China and Fiji
Signed On: May 27, 2002, in the city of Beijing (China). In force as of date of publication of this volume.
Alliance Type: Non-Aggression Pact (Type II)

Source: Ministry of Foreign Affairs of the People's Republic of China, www.fmprc.gov.cn/eng/wjb/zzjg/tyfls/tyfl/2631/t15520.htm.

SUMMARY

This treaty, signed before a meeting between the Fijian prime minister and President Jiang Zemin of China, included recognition by Fiji of the one-China policy, in which Taiwan is considered a wayward territory of a greater China. As part of the agreement, the two countries pledged economic and political cooperation. Additional treaties signed during the visit included frameworks for greater trade and economic cooperation.

The treaty represents an effort by China to reach out to various countries in the Pacific Ocean area and establish stronger ties. In the case of Fiji, China's foreign policy also extended to closer military ties; in December 2002, the Chinese government donated military equipment and training to the Fijian army. The treaty remains in force as cooperation between the two countries continues to improve.

ALLIANCE TEXT

Prime Minister Laisenia Qarase of the Republic of the Fiji Islands paid an official visit to the People's Republic of China from 27 May to 1 June 2002 at the invitation of Premier Zhu Rongji of the State Council of the People's Republic of China. Premier Zhu Rongji and Prime Minister Laisenia Qarase had an in-depth exchange of views on the bilateral relations, regional situation and international issues of shared interest in a warm and friendly atmosphere, and they reached broad consensus.

1. The two sides cherish their profound friendship and mutually beneficial relations and cooperation in all fields.

They are of the view that it is in the fundamental and long-term interest of both countries to push forward the long-term, steady and overall development of their relations on the basis of the principles of mutual respect for sovereignty and territorial integrity, mutual non-aggression, non-interference in each other's internal affairs, equality and mutual benefit, and peaceful coexistence. They reiterate their strict observance of the Joint Communique of the Government of the People's Republic of China and the Government of Fiji on the Establishment of Diplomatic Relations Between China and Fiji.

2. The two sides are ready to strengthen political dialogue at all levels, and encourage and support exchanges and cooperation between the Governments, parliaments, other official institutions, local governments and social organizations of the two countries so as to enhance mutual understanding and trust.

3. The two sides believe that bilateral economic cooperation and trade should be strengthened. They stand ready to encourage and support, under conditions of the market economy, enterprises of the two countries in their efforts to step up contact, deepen mutual understanding and conduct multi-form and mutually beneficial cooperation so as to facilitate continued development of the bilateral economic and trade ties. They will provide facilities for the participation of each other's enterprises and personnel in their respective economic development.

The Chinese side is ready to continue to give what assistance it can to Fiji for its economic development, for which the Fijian side expresses its gratitude.

The two sides will continue to take positive measures to further the cooperation and exchanges between them in the scientific, technological, cultural, education, health and other fields.

4. The Fijian side reiterates its support for the position of the Government of the People's Republic of China that there is but one China in the world, that the Government of the People's Republic of China is the sole legal government representing the whole of China and that Taiwan is an inalienable part of Chinese territory.

The Fijian side further agrees that the question of Taiwan is entirely China's internal affairs and that it respects and supports the efforts of China in safeguarding its national unity and hopes to see its early reunification.

Accordingly the Fijian side reassures the Government of the People's Republic of China that its relationship with Taiwan is strictly for the purpose of promoting economic and commercial ties and it will not engage in any form of contact with Taiwan that is not consistent to the one China position of the People's Republic of China.

The Chinese side highly appreciates the clear position of the Fijian side on the Taiwan question.

5. The Chinese side reiterates that it supports the independence, sovereignty and territorial integrity of the Republic of the Fiji Islands, and supports Fiji in its vigorous efforts to safeguard national independence, sovereignty and territorial integrity. The Chinese side hopes to see Fiji enjoy social stability, ethnic harmony and economic growth and actively contributing to safeguarding and promoting stability and prosperity in the South Pacific region.

The Fijian side values the important role played by China in international affairs and speaks highly of the positive contribution made by China as a permanent member of the U.N. Security Council in safeguarding world peace and expects China's continued role in this regard.

6. The two sides believe that democratization of the international relations meets and reflects the requirements and desires of the vast majority of countries in the international community. All countries, big or small, rich or poor, strong or weak, are equal members of the international community and have the equal rights to take part in international affairs. Every country has the right to choose, in light of its national conditions, its social system and road to development independently. The two

sides stand ready to boost cooperation in the UN and other international organizations and work with the rest of the international community for the establishment of a fair, rational and equitable new international political and economic order.

7. The two sides hold that terrorism is a serious challenge to human civilization and that it poses a threat to international peace and security. They support the fight against all forms of terrorism and call for the prevention and suppression of terrorist acts in all forms. They stress that there should be no double standard on the question of counter-terrorism and that the root causes for terrorism should be eradicated once and for all. They maintain that international cooperation and solidarity should be reinforced on combating international terrorism and that the leading role of the United Nations and its Security Council should be brought into full play.

Zhu Rongji
Premier of the State Council of the People's Republic of China

Laisenia Qarase
Prime Minister of the Republic of the Fiji Islands

Done in Beijing on 27 May 2002.

5.1453 Treaty on Allied Relations between Russia and Uzbekistan

Alliance Members: Russia and Uzbekistan
Signed On: November 14, 2005, in the city of Moscow. In force as of date of publication of this volume.
Alliance Type: Defense Pact (Type I)

Source: *Moscow News*, November 16, 2005.

SUMMARY

The Uzbek government had been a staunch ally of the United States during the U.S. "war on terror" after September 11, 2001. Because Uzbekistan shares a border with Afghanistan, the U.S. military used the Karshi-Khanabad installation for air operations in the region, while President Islom Karimov's government received $500 million annually in economic and military aid from the U.S. government. This close relationship began to change following the Andijon massacre on May 13, 2005.

The so-called color revolutions had been progressing across the Eurasian region during the two years before the massacre; they included protests leading to the ouster of authoritarian governments in Georgia's 2003 Rose Revolution, Ukraine's 2004 Orange Revolution, and Kyrgyzstan's 2005 Tulip Revolution. Fearing the effects of similar protests in their own country, Uzbek troops fired into protesting crowds in the eastern Uzbek city of Andijon and killed approximately 200 people, according to Uzbek government estimates, or as many as 5,000 people, according to some outside evaluations of the massacre. The United States joined the European Union (EU) in calling for investigations into the incident. President Karimov responded by severing military ties with the United States, closing Uzbek air bases to the U.S. military on July 29, 2005.

This mutual defense pact was signed with Russia less than six months after the U.S.-Uzbek row. The treaty gave Karimov's government a great deal of protection against EU and U.S. moves to weaken the regime. The treaty also provided Russia increased influence in the "near abroad" region of Central Asia that had been drifting toward friendlier relations with the United States.

DESCRIPTION OF TERMS

The treaty, signed by President Vladimir Putin of Russia and President Islom Karimov of Uzbekistan, pledged that "in case of aggression against one of the parties by a third state, it will be viewed as an act of aggression against both countries." The mutual defense pact also gave each ally "the right to use military installations" on each other's territory "on the basis of separate agreements." No expiry date was included in the treaty, though either country could withdraw from the alliance with twelve months notice.

5.1454 Memorandum of Understanding between Iran and Syria

Alliance Members: Iran and Syria
Signed On: June 15, 2006, in the city of Tehran (Iran). In force as of date of publication of this volume.
Alliance Type: Entente (Type III)

Source: *BBC Monitoring International Reports,* July 4, 2006.

SUMMARY

Although Iran and Syria have been aligned since the 1970s, ties have only recently increased to a level that would include close military cooperation. Syria, with a strong majority Sunni population, had never fully embraced the predominantly Shiite Iran. However, the presence of U.S. military forces in Iraq beginning in 2003 strengthened this marriage of convenience and ultimately led to a much more tangible collaborative relationship. In a flurry of activity from 2004 through 2007, leaders of the two countries sought and agreed on various understandings related to economic and political issues affecting their region of the Middle East.

These agreements were of course dominated by the war in Iraq, particularly U.S. efforts to quell the violence. Most analysts assumed an ascendant Iran was seeking political legitimacy with this alliance as the Iranian government faced international pressure to cull its nuclear ambitions. Syria, for its part, shared Iran's enmity for the United States but also sought new Iranian investment, which probably totaled more than $3 billion at the time of writing.

The United States consistently charged that Iran played the role of spoiler in Iraq and greatly contributed to its increasingly violent internal conflict by funding and supplying insurgent groups across its border. Syria's porous border has similarly aided the transmigration of foreign fighters, but it is less clear whether President Bashar al-Assad's government is actively providing aid to anti-U.S. forces in the region.

DESCRIPTION OF TERMS

Though contemporary reports billed the agreement as a mutual defense pact, most experts believe the memorandum included only close cooperation on military affairs. No mutual self-defense pact was agreed upon. Instead, both parties pledged the creation of joint supreme defense commission that would meet on a permanent and regular basis.

5.1455 Dakar Agreement between Chad and Sudan

Alliance Members: Chad and Sudan
Signed On: March 13, 2008, in the city of Dakar (Senegal). In force until March 31, 2008.
Alliance Type: Non-Aggression Pact (Type II)

Source: *Sudan Tribune,* "Dakar Agreement between Chad and Sudan," March 18, 2008.

SUMMARY

At a summit of the fifty-seven-nation Organization of the Islamic Conference held in Senegal, the president of Senegal, Maitre Abdoulaye Wade, negotiated a cease-fire and non-aggression pact between the neighboring countries of Chad and Sudan. Both countries had been accusing each other of funding and harboring armed insurgents for cross-border attacks in the area that includes the war-torn Darfur region of Sudan. The two countries agreed (in paragraph number 3 below) to establish a "contact group" that would provide assurances that the non-aggression pact was being observed.

This agreement was actually the fourth peace accord signed between the two nations in two years. Cross-border conflict quickly destroyed the first three agreements, but this pact was supposedly unique in that the agreement included the contact-group monitoring mechanism in addition to the formal pledge of non-aggression. Unfortunately, it took less than one week after the agreement for each side to accuse the other of incursions upon its territory. By the end of March 2008, Sudanese-backed rebels from Chad, based in Darfur, attacked Chadian forces in the border town of Adré and killed several people and wounded almost fifty more. This attack rendered the agreement meaningless although observers to the agreement continue to press both countries to remain committed to its terms.

ALLIANCE TEXT

We,

Idriss Déby Itno, President of the Republic of Chad
Omar Hassan al-Bashir, President of the Republic of Sudan

To put a definitive end to disputes between our two countries, restore peace and security in the sub-region, we agree as follows:

1. Resolve before our peers and the representatives of the international community to make peace and normalize relations between our two countries;

2. Reiterate respect our previous commitments, including the Tripoli Agreement of 8 February 2006, the framework agreement in Khartoum and its additional protocols of the

August 28, 2006, declaration of Cannes from February 15, 2007 and the agreement of Riyadh May 3, 2007.

In order to implement effectively these agreements, we call upon the international community in general and in particular on Libya, Congo, Senegal, Gabon, Chad, the CEN-SAD, the ECCAS and the African Union to take all necessary steps towards the establishment of the force of peace and security to ensure and observe the joint operations security of the common border;

3. Agree in this regard to set up a contact group which meets once a month in one of the capitals of member countries of the group. It is composed of the Foreign Ministers of the countries listed in paragraph 2 or any designated representative for this purpose. The contact group is charged with the follow-up, the implementation in good faith of this agreement and the monitoring of possible violations. It is co-chaired by Libya and the Congo;

4. We solemnly pledge to ban all activities of armed groups and to prevent the use of our respective territories for the destabilization of any of our States;

5. Express our sincere thanks and deep appreciation to His Excellency Maitre Abdoulaye Wade, President of the Republic of Senegal, Chairman of the 11th Islamic Summit Session, for the efforts he has deployed so that reign Peace, security, stability and cooperation between the two countries in the sub region and the entire African continent;

6. Also express our deep appreciation to His Excellency, the President El Hadj Omar Bongo Ondimba for his tireless efforts for harmony and peace in the sub-region;

7. Finally, thanks to their presence and contribution, the group of observers, in particular the United Nations Secretary General.

Was signed and initialed in Dakar (Senegal) on March 13, 2008:

PARTIES AND FACILITATORS

His Excellency Idriss Déby Itno President of the Republic of Chad
His Excellency Omar Hassan al-Bashir President of the Republic of Sudan
His Excellency Abdoulaye Wade President of the Republic of Senegal
His Excellency El Hadj Omar Bongo Ondimba President of the Gabonese Republic
For the current Chairman of African Union HE Jakaya Kikwete
His Excellency Alpha Oumar Konare, Chairperson of the African Union Commission

In the presence of:
- The European Union
- The United States of America
- The France
- The United Nations Secretary General
- The Secretary General of OIC

CHAPTER SIX: The Changing Nature of Military Alliances

Contained in this two-volume collection are descriptions of more than 450 alliances, spanning more than 350 years. Even the most casual reader will realize that alliances have changed greatly over time. Initially, most alliances were simple tools for coordination. Two kings promised aid to each other in case of attack, and the treaty text provided details of coordination, stipulating the number of troops and how they would be fed, sheltered, and equipped. These rather basic coordination agreements slowly gave way to the more provocative use of alliances as tools for influencing the policies of other nonallied states. Although the structure of coordination between alliance partners remained well-defined in these treaties, leaders also began incorporating into the agreements the ideas of mutual interests and aggressive bargaining with other states.

By the beginning of the nineteenth century, aggressive signaling had become the norm for alliance agreements. Different types of alliances were slowly emerging as tools for managing conflict. These agreements focused on internal rebellions or pledged neutrality in case of attack. Other alliance types served to recognize new leaders and states, and probably the most common of the conflict management alliances were the agreements to settle the terms of control over disputed territories.

The evolution of alliance making took another turn after World War II, as both the United States and the Soviet Union began defining their spheres of influence around the globe. With these mostly bilateral alliances, the superpowers pledged defense of their partners in exchange for basing rights, access to ports and resources, and other similar goods. Large regional organizations such as the Organization of American States (OAS), the North Atlantic Treaty Organization (NATO), and the Western European Union (WEU) were also formed, at least in part, to influence and protect Western alliance partners. These large regional organizations also inspired the creation of other regional groupings such as the African Union and the League of Arab States, which were dedicated to internal security and trade. Gradually, the original anticommunist alliances also evolved to primarily manage intra-alliance conflict, trade, and other issues. In fact, the evolution of NATO, the OAS, and like

institutions had become so complete that there was no call to disband these alliances after the Soviet Union dissolved. These institutions were instead repurposed as tools for managing the so-called new world order.

This conclusion to the two volumes describing alliances since 1648 presents two significant trends in the evolution of alliance making. The first trend concerns the globalization of alliances. Having begun mostly in Europe, alliances are now common tools for leaders around the globe. The second trend, presented in the second section below, discusses how the purposes of alliances can change with time: first, how alliance goals have changed, and then how institutions such as NATO and the OAS have been transformed.

Globalization of Alliances

Perhaps the best way of describing just how pervasive in the international system alliances have become is to point to the number of states that are actually in an alliance in any given year. Figure 1 charts the number of dyads (or pairs of states) in the international system for each year since 1816. The concept of a dyad is useful when describing alliance relationships because it takes at least two states to form an alliance. In 1816, for example, there were 23 states in the international system according to the Correlates of War project; these 23 states could combine in 226 different dyads. By 1900 there were 42 states and 666 dyads, by 1945 there were 66 states and 840 dyads, and by 2000 there were 191 states and 3,132 different dyads in the international system.

The other two lines in Figure 1 show the percentage of dyads that were in at least one alliance in any given year. In 1816, more than half (55 percent) of the mostly European international system was allied. The number of alliances remained steady through the nineteenth century, but the number of dyads in the international system began to increase as states in the Western Hemisphere, Asia, and the Middle East became independent. Thus, the percentage of allied dyads slowly decreased throughout the century.

FIGURE 1 Number of Dyads Allied in the International System, 1816–2000

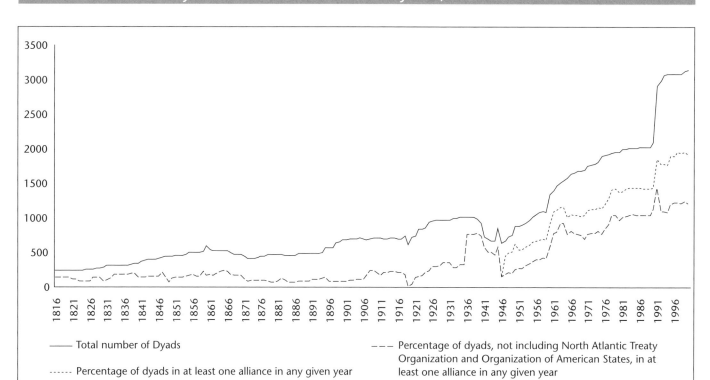

—— Total number of Dyads

------ Percentage of dyads in at least one alliance in any given year

– – – Percentage of dyads, not including North Atlantic Treaty Organization and Organization of American States, in at least one alliance in any given year

Sources: Author's data; Correlates of War (www.correlatesofwar.org) system membership data were used for total number of states in the system for each year.

Only six dyads remained allied after the end of World War I, but the percentage allied increased gradually during the interwar period. Then, between 1935 and 1939, the percentage of dyads that were allied jumped from 30 percent to 80 percent. The wartime alliances ended following World War II, but the number of alliances began to increase gradually as the cold war intensified. By 1960, the percentage of the states of the world that was allied (67.78 percent) was greater than the percentage allied in 1945 (63.38 percent). While the number of alliances continued to increase throughout the cold war years, the third line on Figure 1 indicates the magnitude of the effect that NATO and the OAS have had on the system. In many years, more than half of the allied dyads in the international system could be found in just these two alliances.

With or without NATO and the OAS, however, almost all states in the international system have been allied with other states for at least some period of time. Although initially concentrated in Europe, alliance behavior has become a global norm. Figure 2 examines these data by region. Dividing the world into five separate regions (Europe, Middle East, sub-Saharan Africa, Asia, and the Western Hemisphere), Figure 2 charts how many states in each particular region have had experience with alliances. Thus, for example, Figure 2 shows that Europe by 1720 had fifteen states that had previously been involved in an alliance; this number grew to more than thirty by 1990.

There are some interesting trends in the regional data for alliance experience. First, alliances are clearly a European invention, beginning with the Anglo-Portuguese alliance (Alliance no. 1.1000) and with a trend that gradually increased during the eighteenth and nineteenth centuries. The various dips in the trend line are caused by states that existed in the system at various times; these data show that alliance formation does not always guarantee state survival.

Alliance-making practices spread from Europe to the New World, as states of the Western Hemisphere began to form alliances in the mid-nineteenth century. Fifteen states had alliance-making experience before World War I, and by World War II, this number had increased to more than twenty. After the signing of the OAS alliance, there were more than twenty-five states with alliance experience by the final stages of the cold war.

Asia and the Middle East developed similarly in terms of alliance practice, as both regions began moving toward independence and statehood at the start of the twentieth century. In Africa, the large regional alliances that were formed after most of the states in the region gained independence account for the dramatic increase in the African trend line after 1960. By the early 1980s, almost thirty African states had taken part in at least one alliance.

Alliance practices began in Europe and will probably always be associated with the diplomatic history of that continent,

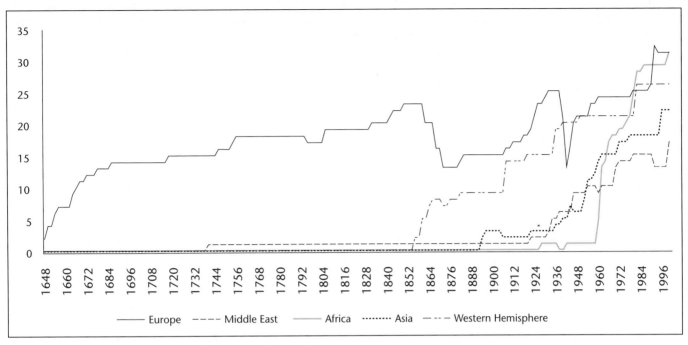

FIGURE 2 State Experience in Alliances, by Region of the World, 1648–2000

Sources: Author's data; Correlates of War (www.correlatesofwar.org) system membership data were used for total number of states in the system for each year.

from the early days of the Westphalian system to the Concert of Europe and Bismarck's system. But these regional trends demonstrate clearly that alliance practices, including bilateral alliance treaties and large multilateral alliance organizations, have spread around the globe. As alliance treaties are now a commonly used tool on all the continents, the percentage of the system in an alliance (Figure 1) has continued to increase.

Changing Purposes of Alliances

One reason alliances have become ubiquitous in the international system is their ability to adapt to different situations. Traditionally used as tools for balancing the capabilities of rival states, alliances have evolved into tools for conflict management that serve far-ranging purposes, from controlling insurgencies to confirming state recognition.

This section focuses on a type of alliance treaty that is common within the alliance data but is often missed by traditional theories that focus on power: the territorial settlement treaty. These treaties have existed for centuries and have had strong pacific effects on alliance members and their surrounding states but have been largely ignored by alliance scholars. Many alliances, however, have evolved to mirror the purposes of the territorial settlement treaty. Large, regional alliances have repurposed their institutional structures so that interstate cooperation can continue, and this cooperation often involves resolution of border disputes and other territorial issues.

Evolution of Alliance Goals

Alliances have often been used as tools for balancing power, but alliances have served other purposes as well. As close readers of the treaties contained in this volume realize, alliances have been formed to recognize the independence of states, to clear passage or territory for trade, to put down insurgencies on both land and sea, to create regional organizations, and even to exchange or secure territories among alliance members. As the introduction to these volumes pointed out, all of these purposes are at odds with traditional alliance theory, but it is this last purpose that is perhaps most unconventional in terms of theories that emphasize balance of power.

Territorial settlement treaties often attempted to avoid war by removing the most contentious of issues from the system. Instead of trying to establish peace through realist prescriptions of balancing, these alliances resolved disputes by removing the issue of territory from the agendas of states. The territorial settlement treaty is an alliance that also contains provisions for the maintenance of the status quo by states in a given region, or it contains an agreement between the alliance partners to exchange territories. The alliance signed after the territorial settlement formalizes the states' commitments to the agreement.

The Quadruple Alliance that established the Congress of Vienna and the Concert of Europe in 1815 is one of the best examples of a territorial settlement treaty. In the period immediately following the Napoleonic Wars, the major states had the choice of creating a traditional balance of power system or of devising a new international status quo based on universalism and the resolution of conflict. The major states chose the latter and established a system that not only created the structure of the congress system but also included detailed provisions for the division of territory following the war. Even defeated France was admitted to the alliance within four years—once it had reestablished the monarchy and had agreed to its new borders.

Alliances that resolve territorial issues can generally be identified by whether signatories have either (1) exchanged territory by treaty or (2) agreed by treaty to a de facto settlement of territory as it existed at the time of the alliance. Exchange settlements must contain explicit terms for the transfer of territory from one alliance member to another; exchanges that occur outside the treaty text are not considered. De facto settlements represent the formal acceptance by treaty members of the current distribution of territorial control in a treaty-specified region.

Many of the territorial settlements involved an actual exchange of territory, as in the 1925 transfer of Fiume from Yugoslavia to Italy. However, a significant number involved de facto settlements; the post–Napoleonic Wars alliance making is a good example of this type. A more recent example would be the agreement reached by India and Bangladesh in 1972. Not included as alliances settling territorial divisions are those alliances that guarantee a future distribution of territory. Obviously, these alliances are provocative in nature because they redraw the regional map surrounding the states in the alliance.

Territorial settlement treaties are surprisingly peaceful. The summaries in this volume often describe the conflicts that led to alliance formation and the conflicts that alliances created. Territorial settlements, however, almost always describe cooperation among allied members for the settlement of dangerous issues. Beyond anecdotal data are empirical studies that confirm the relationship between territorial settlement treaties and peace. One recent study (Gibler 1996) showed that only one of twenty-seven territorial settlement treaties in the past two centuries was followed by war within five years (compared with a likelihood of war of more than 30 percent for members of alliances in general).

Unlike other types of alliances—alliances that focus on manipulations of power—the anticipated reactions to the territorial settlement treaties include decreased armament levels, decreased membership in other alliances, and decreased involvement in crises. The territorial settlements send a signal that the member states are attempting to resolve their conflicts through peaceful measures. Thus, there is no need for aggressive bargaining and military adventuring. Instead, peace in the region becomes much more likely.

Even those alliances that do not begin as territorial settlement treaties can evolve into territorial management alliances over time. Leaders must pay a range of transaction costs in order to form an alliance. These costs may include such simple items as the transportation costs and the amount of time expended in order to negotiate a treaty. For leaders 200 years ago, these costs were sometimes substantial. In the modern era,

however, the real transaction costs of alliance formation often involve changes in public opinion in democracies and the expenditure of domestic political power to get an agreement negotiated and signed. If leaders want to signal their commitment to the new agreement, they often must move troops, begin building organizational offices, and otherwise make known to other leaders that the new alliance represents a credible commitment to aid the other alliance partner. Thus, alliance making can sometimes become a costly endeavor.

Fortunately for leaders, most of these transaction costs are spent only once, when an alliance treaty is newly signed. The nature of these costs creates incentives for leaders in an alliance to use the existing structure of cooperation to perform new tasks. Because the transaction costs had already been paid to form an alliance, it would make little sense to recreate an alliance in order to serve a different need. These incentives make it likely that some of the longest-lasting alliances are really treaties of alliance cooperation that have evolved over time.

Today's Defensive Alliances Finding New Goals

Consider the changes that have taken place within the OAS, NATO, and the WEU. All three alliances trace their beginnings to the start of the cold war between the United States and the Soviet Union, which is why each treaty carried specific provisions for collective self-defense.

For the OAS, Article 28 of the Charter states:

> Every act of aggression by a State against the territorial integrity or the inviolability of the territory or against the sovereignty or political independence of an American State shall be considered an act of aggression against the other American States.

Article 5 of the NATO Charter:

> The Parties agree that an armed attack against one or more of them in Europe or North America shall be considered an attack against them all.

And, finally, Article 4 of the WEU:

> If any of the High Contracting Parties should be the object of an armed attack in Europe, the other High Contracting Parties will, in accordance with the provisions of Article 51 of the Charter of the United Nations, afford the Party so attacked all the military and other aid and assistance in their power.

These strong collective self-defense provisions embodied the core goals of those who signed the original alliances. Western leaders were concerned about the Soviet threat and wanted to provide some type of collective defense against the spread of communism in Western Europe and Latin America.

Each of the three treaties also encouraged cooperation in other issue areas. Returning again to the theme of borders and territorial issues, each alliance treaty included specific provisions for the maintenance of the territorial status quo and for judicial settlements of any disputes involving territorial issues.

TABLE 1 Jointly Democratic Dyad Years in Selected Regional Organizations, 1900–2000

Year signed	Name of alliance	Jointly democratic signatories		Allied jointly democratic dyad years		Percentage of total allied democratic dyad years
		No.	Percent	No.	Percent	
1947	Organization of American States	3 of 171	1.8	1,696 of 9,506	17.8	28.82
1948	Western European Union	9 of 9	100.0	405 of 449	90.2	6.88
1949	North Atlantic Treaty Organization	45 of 55	81.8	3,259 of 4,117	79.2	55.38
Totals		57 of 235	24.3	5,360 of 14,072	38.1	91.08

Source: Douglas M. Gibler, "Alliances That Never Balance: The Territorial Settlement Treaty," *Conflict Management and Peace Science* 16, no. 1 (1996): 75–97.
Note: Organization of American States is Alliance no. 4.1333; Western European Union is Alliance no. 4.1339; and North Atlantic Treaty Organization is Alliance no. 4.1347.

Article 21 of the OAS:

> The territory of a State is inviolable; it may not be the object, even temporarily, of military occupation or of other measures of force taken by another State, directly or indirectly, on any grounds whatever. No territorial acquisitions or special advantages obtained either by force or by other means of coercion shall be recognized.

Article 1 of NATO:

> . . . to settle any international dispute in which they may be involved by peaceful means in such a manner that international peace and security and justice are not endangered, and to refrain in their international relations from the threat or use of force.

Similarly, Article 8 of the WEU included specific procedures for International Court of Justice jurisdiction over disputes as well as additional measures for mediation among alliance members.

The emphasis placed on various clauses within the alliance treaties changed with time. As the cold war rivalry locked into a virtual stalemate, the alliance organizations began to emphasize the resolution of disputes, especially territorial disputes, among their members. After the Soviet Union imploded and the original rationale for these alliances ended, most observers expected these cold war alliances to disband. Instead, NATO and the OAS repurposed their organizational structures so that each alliance was responsible for continued maintenance of peace among their allied states, including the resolution of internal territorial issues. The defense pact among the WEU states was somewhat different because it had already provided the underlying basis of

collective defense necessary for the integration of Europe through what would eventually become the European Union.

The changing nature of alliance goals can sometimes have dramatic effects. In addition to resolving territorial issues, alliances also began encouraging the formation of democratic governments among their members. The organizations, especially the OAS, provided aid and support to new regimes and discouraged interference among their democratic governments. The collective nature of self-defense and the judicial settlement of territorial issues also discouraged the creation of large armies and increased militarization among alliance members. Virtually free of external threats and also free of possible threats from large land armies, democratic governments were provided a favorable environment in which they could flourish. In many ways the territorial settlement goals of the alliances proved to be better tools for meeting the original needs of the alliance members.

Table 1 presents changes that were made over time by the member states of the three large regional alliances. Recall from Figure 1 that a large percentage of alliance dyads can be found in these alliances. As the final column of Table 1 shows, approximately 91 percent of all dyads with two democracies are contained in these three alliances. Democratic dyads were not dominant among the original signatories of the alliances, and those governments that were democracies were also relatively new, possibly unstable democracies. Of the OAS states, in only three dyads were both states democratic, but by 2000, a large majority of states were democratic. For NATO and the WEU, the fledgling democracies were encouraged, and nondemocratic states that joined the alliances in later years also evolved into democracies. That these alliances, which were dedicated to cold war deterrence, would reorganize themselves as conflict management tools is not surprising. That these alliances would have such a strong unanticipated effect on their member states is astounding.

Alliances as Tools of Cooperation

The alliance treaties in this volume should make it apparent that not all alliances are alike. Alliances are rarely formed only to balance power or avoid threat. Instead, alliances are created for a multitude of reasons, and their purposes can change dramatically over time. That is why theories of alliances that focus solely on the capabilities of states, or even on changes in these capabilities, often perform so poorly in explaining simple alliance relationships. There is a tendency to overemphasize the strategic nature of power and statecraft at the expense of understanding alliances as useful tools of cooperation.

This discussion has focused on the territorial settlement treaties and their effects. Similar descriptions can be written regarding treaties that involve trade, regional cooperation, and several other alliance types. Readers of these volumes who understand the multifaceted nature of alliance making are taking a crucial step forward in their thinking about alliances.

Reference

Gibler, Douglas M. 1996. "Alliances That Never Balance: The Territorial Settlement Treaty." *Conflict Management and Peace Science* 16(1): 75–97.

Map Credits

Map 1 1648
"Europe in 1648: The Peace of Westphalia." Reproduced from Robert H. Labberton, *An Historical Atlas Containing a Chronological Series of One Hundred and Four Maps, at Successive Periods, from the Dawn of History to the Present Day,* 6th ed. 1884. Courtesy of the University of Texas Libraries, The University of Texas at Austin.

Map 2 1721
"Historical Map of Europe in 1721 after the Treaties of Utrecht & Nystad." Reproduced from *The Cambridge Modern History Atlas,* edited by A. W. Ward et al. (London: Cambridge University Press, 1912). Courtesy of the University of Texas Libraries, The University of Texas at Austin.

Map 3 1808
"English Double Hemisphere Map, 1808, by Laurie and Whittle." Courtesty of The Granger Collection, New York.

Map 4 1815
"Europe, 1815–1905." Reproduced from *The Public Schools Historical Atlas,* edited by C. Colbeck (Longmans, Green, and Co., 1905). Courtesy of the University of Texas Libraries, The University of Texas at Austin.

Map 5 1911
"Europe at the Present Time." Reproduced from William R. Shepherd, *The Historical Atlas* (New York: Henry Holt and Company, 1911). Courtesy of the University of Texas Libraries, The University of Texas at Austin.

Map 6 1949
"Europe and the Near East." Reproduced from *National Geographic Magazine*, June 1949. Courtesy of the National Geographic Society.

Map 7 1993
"Russia and the Newly Independent Nations of the Former Soviet Union." Reproduced from *National Geographic Magazine*, March 1993. Courtesy of the National Geographic Society.

Map 8 2005
"The Political World." From *The National Geographic Atlas of the World,* 8th ed. (Washington, D.C.: The National Geographic Society, 2005). Reproduced by permission.

Bibliography

Official Sources

Australian Treaty Series

Belgian State Diplomatic Documents

British and Foreign State Papers

British State Papers

Bulgarian State Papers

Dokumente zur Aussenpolitik der Deutschen Demokratischen Republik [Documents on the foreign policy of the German Democratic Republic]

French State Papers

India State Papers

ITAR-TASS (official news agency of Russia), www.itar-tass.com/eng/

Keesing's Record of World Events. Cambridge, 1931–2008

League of Arab States, www.arableagueonline.org

League of Nations Treaty Series

North Atlantic Treaty Organization, www.nato.int/structur/library/natodocs-e.html

Organization of American States, www.oas.org/DIL/treaties_and_agreements.htm

Parliamentary Papers (Accounts). London. 1816, vol. 17, p. 429

Peking Review (official publication of Communist Party of China; current title is *Beijing Review*)

Recueil des traités de la France [Digest of the treaties of France]. Edited by A. de Clercq. Paris: Amyot, Pedone, 1864–1907.

Soviet Documents on Foreign Policy. Jane Tabrisky Degras. Oxford: Oxford University Press, 1951.

Tratados Publicos y Acuerdos Internacionales de Venezuela [Public treaties and international agreements of Venezuela]

United Nations Treaty Series

U.S. State Department Documents

U.S. State Department Bulletins

Nongovernment and Unofficial Sources

Consolidated Treaty Series. Edited by Clive Parry. Dobbs Ferry, N.Y.: Oceana Publishing, 1979.

Danmark-Norges traktater, 1523–1750: med dertil hørende aktstykker [Denmark-Norway treaties, 1523–1750: with related records]. 11 volumes. Copenhagen: G. E. C. Gad, 1907–1949.

Documents on German Foreign Policy, 1918–1945. Arlington, Va.: Open-Door Press, 1976.

Documents on International Affairs. Edited by D. C. Watt and John Major et al. London, New York: Oxford University Press for the Royal Institute of International Affairs, 1965.

European Diplomatic History: Documents and Interpretations, 1815–1914. Edited by Herman N. Weill. New York: Exposition Press, 1972.

European Treaties Bearing on the History of the United States. Edited by Frances G. Davenport. Washington, D.C.: Carnegie Institution, 1917–1937.

Founding of the German Empire by William I. Edited by Heinrich von Sybel; translated by Marshall Livingston Perrin and Gamaliel Bradford Jr. New York: T. Y. Crowell & Co., 1890–1891.

Hertslet's Commercial Treaties. London: Butterworth (vol. 1–19) and H. M. Stationery Office (vol. 20–31), 1840–1925.

Imperial Russia: A Source Book, 1700–1917. Edited by Basil Dmytryshyn. Gulf Breeze, Fla.: Academic International Press, 1971.

International Legal Materials. Washington, D.C.: American Society of International Law, 1962–2008.

Key Treaties for the Great Powers, 1814–1914. Edited by Michael Hurst. New York: St. Martin's Press, 1972.

Le Relazioni Diplomatiche Fra L'Austria E Il Regno Di Sardegna [Diplomatic relations between Austria and the Kingdom of Sardinia]. Series 2: 1830–1848. Volume 1. Edited by Narciso Nada. Rome: Instituto Storico Italiano Per L'eta Moderna E Contemporanea, 1972.

Major International Treaties, 1914–1973: History and Guide with Texts. Edited by John Grenville. London: Metheun, 1974.

Middle East and North Africa in World Politics, A Documentary Record. Edited by Jacob Hurewitz. New Haven: Yale, 1979.

Nouveau Recueil General De Traites, Conventions Et Autres Transactions Remarquables, Servant A La Connaissance Des Relations Estrangeres Des Puissances Et Etats Dans Leurs Rapports Mutuels: Redige Sur Copies, Collections Et Publications Authentiques [New general digest of treaties, conventions and other important transactions, with foreign powers and states in their mutual relations: written copies, collections and authentic publications]. Series 1. Volume 14, 1843–1852. Edited by G. F. de Martens. Gottingue: Librairie De Dieterich, 1856.

Österreichische Staatsverträge [Austrian state treaties]. 2 volumes. Edited by Alfred Franzis Pribram. Innsbruck: Wagner'sche Universitäts-Buchhandlung; Vienna: Adolf Holzhausen, 1907–1913.

Pan-Africanism: A Short Political Guide. Edited by Colin Legum. New York: F. A. Praeger, 1965.

Readings in European International Relations since 1879. Edited by W. Henry Cooke and Edith P. Stickney. New York: Harper & Bros., 1931.

Recueil des Traites et Conventions conclus par la Russie avec les Puissances etrangeres [Collection of treaties and conventions concluded by Russia with foreign powers]. 15 volumes. Edited by Fedor F. Martens. St. Petersburg: Ministry of Communications, 1874–1909.

Recueil des principaux traités d'alliance, de paix, de trêve, etc., conclus par les puissances de l'Europe, tant entre elles qu'avec les puissances et états dans d'autres parties du monde depuis 1761 jusqu'à présent (1801) [Reports of major treaties of alliance, peace, truce, etc., concluded by the powers of Europe, both among themselves and with powers and states in other parts of the world since 1761 until now (1801)]. 7 volumes. Edited by G. F. de Martens. Göttingen: J. C. Dieterich, 1791–1801.

Survey of International Affairs: The Far East, 1942–1946. Edited by F. C. Jones, Hugh Borton, and B. R. Pearn. London, New York: Oxford University Press, 1955.

Alphabetical Treaty Index